VOIP TECHNOLOGIES

Edited by **Shigeru Kashihara**

VoIP Technologies
Edited by Shigeru Kashihara

Published by InTech
Janeza Trdine 9, 51000 Rijeka, Croatia

Publishing Process Manager Jelena Marusic

Technical Editor Teodora Smiljanic

Cover Designer InTech Design Team

Additional hard copies can be obtained from orders@intechopen.com

VoIP Technologies, Edited by Shigeru Kashihara
p. cm.
ISBN 978-953-307-549-5

For EU product safety concerns:
IN TECH d.o.o., Prolaz Marije Krucifikse Kozulić 3, 51000 Rijeka, Croatia,
info@intechopen.com or visit our website at intechopen.com.

Meet the editor

Shigeru Kashihara, PhD is an assistant professor in the Graduate School of Information Science, Nara Institute of Science and Technology (NAIST), Japan. His research interests include quality of service in mobile and wireless networks, mobility management, mobile ad-hoc networks, and delay/disruption-tolerant networks. He has recently been developing an end-to-end handover method to maintain voice over IP quality, as contributed in Chapter 14. He received his bachelor of management science and his master of business information science from Kobe University of Commerce, Japan in 1999 and 2001, respectively, and his PhD in information science from NAIST in 2003. From January 2004 to February 2005, he was a postdoctoral researcher at Kyushu Institute of Technology, Japan. Since then, he has been a faculty member at NAIST. From February 2010, he has also been a visiting researcher in the Network Research Laboratory of the Computer Science Department, University of California, Los Angeles.

Contents

Preface

Voice over IP (VoIP) is undoubtedly a powerful and innovative communication tool. Compared with the public switched telephone network (PSTN), VoIP offers the benefit of reducing communication and infrastructure cost. This makes it possible for everyone to easily keep in touch with family, friends, and clients around the world. Furthermore, VoIP has the potential to create new and attractive communication tools by integrating with various applications, such as Web systems, presentation software, and photo viewers. In the near future, we expect VoIP to provide a rich multimedia communication service.

However, voice communication over the Internet is inherently less reliable than PSTN. Since the Internet essentially works as a best-effort network without a Quality of Service (QoS) guarantee, and since voice data cannot be retransmitted, voice quality may suffer from packet loss, delay, and jitter due to interference from other data packets. In wireless networks, such problems may be compounded by various characteristics of wireless media, including reduction of signal strength and radio interference. Additionally, we need to pay closer attention to security issues related to VoIP communications. Thus, VoIP technologies are challenging research issues.

This book comprises 15 chapters and encompasses a wide range of VoIP research, from VoIP quality assessment to security issues. Much of the content is focused on the key areas of VoIP performance investigation and enhancement. Each chapter includes various approaches that illustrate how VoIP aspires to be a powerful and reliable communication tool. We hope that you will enjoy reading these diverse studies, and will find a lot of useful information about VoIP technologies. Finally, I would like to thank all authors of the chapters for their great contributions.

Shigeru Kashihara
Nara Institute of Science and Technology
Japan

1

VoIP Quality Assessment Technologies

Mousa AL-Akhras and Iman AL Momani
The University of Jordan
Jordan

1. Introduction

Circuit Switching technology has been in use for long time by traditional Public Switched Telephone Network (PSTN) carriers for carrying voice traffic. Before users may communicate in circuit switching network, a dedicated channel or circuit is established from the sender to the receiver and that path is selected over the most efficient route using intelligent switches. Accordingly, it is not necessary for a phone call from the same sender to the same receiver to take the same route every time a phone call is made.

During call setup once the route is determined, that path or circuit stays fixed throughout the call and the necessary resources across the path are allocated to the phone call from the beginning to the end of the call. The established circuit cannot be used by other callers until the circuit is released, it remains unavailable to other users even when no actual communication is taking place, therefore, circuit switching is carrying voice with high fidelity from source to destination (Collins, 2003). Circuit switching is like having a dedicated railroad track with only one train, the call, is permitted on the track at one time.

Today's commercial telephone networks that based on circuit switching technology have a number of attractive features, including: Availability, Capacity, Fast Response and High Quality (Collins, 2003). The quality is the main focus of this chapter.

One alternative technology to circuit switching telephone networks for carrying voice traffic is to use data-centric packet switching networks such as Internet Protocol (IP) networks. In packet switching technology, no circuit is built from the sender to the receiver and packets are sent over the most effective route at time of sending that packet, consequently different packets may take different routes from the same sender to the same receiver within the same session.

Transmitting Voice over IP (VoIP) networks is an important application in the world of telecommunication and is an active area of research. Networks of the future will use IP as the core transport network as IP is seen as the long-term carrier for all types of traffic including voice and video. VoIP will become the main standard for third generation wireless networks (Bos & Leroy, 2001; Heiman, 1998).

Transmission of voice as well as data over IP networks seems an attractive solution as voice and data services can be integrated which makes creation of new and innovative services possible. This provides promises of greater flexibility and advanced services than the traditional telephony with greater possibility for cost reduction in phone calls. VoIP also has other advantages, including: number portability, lower equipment cost, lower bandwidth requirements, lower operating and management expenses, widespread availability of IP, and other advantages (Collins, 2003; Heiman, 1998; Low, 1996; Moon et al., 2000; Rosenberg et al.,

1999). VoIP can be used in many applications, including: call centre integration, directory services over telephones, IP video conferencing, fax over IP, and Radio/ TV Broadcasting (Collins, 2003; Miloslavski et al., 2001; Ortiz, 2004; Schulzrinne & Rosenberg, 1999).
VoIP technology was adopted by many operators as an alternative to circuit switching technology. This adoption was motivated by the above advantages and to share some of the high revenue achieved by telecommunication companies. However, to be able to compete with the highly reputable PSTN networks, VoIP networks should be able to achieve comparable quality to that achieved by PSTN networks. Although VoIP services often offer much cheaper solutions than what PSTN does, but regardless of how low the cost of the service is, it is the user perception of the quality what matters. If the quality of the voice is poor, the user of the traditional telephony will not be attracted to the VoIP service regardless of how cheap the service is. This comes from the fact that customers who are used to the high-quality telephony networks, expect to receive a comparable quality from any potential competitor.
IP networks were originally designed to carry non real-time traffic such as email or file transfer and they are doing this task very well, however, as IP networks are characterised by being best-effort networks with no guarantee of delivery as no circuit is established between the sender and the receiver, therefore they are not particularly appropriate to support real-time applications such as voice traffic in addition to data traffic. The best-effort nature of IP networks causes several degradations to the speech signal before it reaches its destination. These degradations arise because of the time-varying characteristics (e.g. packet loss, delay, delay variation (jitter), sharing of resources) of IP networks.
These characteristics which are normal to data traffic, cause serious deterioration to the real-time traffic and prevent IP networks from providing the high quality speech often provided by traditional PSTN networks for voice services. Sharing of resources in IP networks causes no resources to be dedicated to the voice call in contrast to what is happening in traditional circuit switching telephony such as PSTN where the required resources are allocated to the phone call from the start to the end. With the absence of resource dedication, many problems are inevitable in IP networks.
Among the problems is packet loss which occurs due to the overflow in intermediate routers or due to the long time taken by packets to reach their destinations (Collins, 2003). Real-time applications are also sensitive to delay since they require voice packets to arrive at the receiving end within a certain upper bound to allow interactivity of the voice call (ITU-T, 2003a;b). Also, due to their best-effort nature, packets could take different routes from the same source to the same destination within the same session which causes packets interarrival time to vary, a phenomenon known as jitter. Due to the problem of jitter, it is not easy to play packets in a steady fashion to the listener (Narbutt & Murphy, 2004; Tseng & Lin, 2003; Tseng et al., 2004). The above challenges cause degradation to the quality of the received speech signal before it reaches its destination. Many solutions have been proposed to alleviate these problems and the quality of the received speech signal as perceived by the end user is greatly affected by the effectiveness of these solutions.
Another approach is to reserve resources across the path from the sender to the receiver. A mechanism called Call Admission Control (CAC) is needed to determine whether to accept a call request if it is possible to allocate the required bandwidth and maintain the given QoS target for all existing calls, or otherwise to reject the call (Mase, 2004). Among the solutions that have been proposed to implement CAC and to manage the available bandwidth efficiently are: Resource Reservation Protocol (RSVP), Differentiated Service (DiffServ),

MultiProtocol Label Switching (MPLS), and End-to-end Measurement Based Admission Control (EMBAC). Reserving resources is difficult and very expensive proposal as it requires changes to all routers across the network which is inapplicable in non-managed networks such as the Internet.

Therefore, it is important to measure the quality of VoIP applications in live networks and take appropriate actions when necessary. This importance comes from legal, commercial and technical reasons. Measurement of the quality would be a necessity as customers and companies are bound by a service level agreement usually requiring the company to provide a certain level of quality, otherwise, customers may sue the companies for poor quality. Also, measuring the quality gives the chance to network administrators to overcome temporal problems that could affect the quality of ongoing voice calls. Measurement of the quality also allows service providers to evaluate their own and their competitors' service using a standard scale. It is also a strong indicator of users' satisfaction of the service provided (Takahashi et al., 2004; Zurek et al., 2002).

To this end, a specialised mechanism is required for measuring the speech quality accurately. One of driving forces in the world of telecommunication is the International Telecommunication Union (ITU). ITU is the leading United Nations (UN) agency for information and communication technology. As the global focal point for governments and the private sector in developing telecommunication networks and services, ITU's role is to help the world communicate. ITU - Telecommunication Standardisation Sector (ITU-T, http://www.itu.int/ITU-T/) is a permanent organ of the ITU that plays a driving force role toward standardising and regulating international telecommunications worldwide. Toward this goal, ITU-T study technical, operating and tariff questions and produce standards under the name of Recommendations for the purpose of standardising telecommunications worldwide. ITU-T's Recommendations are divided into categories that are identified by a single letter, referred to as the series, and Recommendations are numbered within each series, for example P.800 (ITU-T, 1996b). ITU-T has a formal recognition as it is part of ITU which is a UN Organisation (UNO).

Many ITU-T Recommendations are concerned with standardising the measurement of speech quality for voice services, many of these standards are considered in this chapter. Speech quality in ITU-T standards is expressed as Mean Opinion Score (MOS) which ranges between 1 and 5, with 1 corresponds to poor quality and 5 to excellent quality.

Some standards measure the speech quality or the MOS **subjectively** by setting lab conditions and asking subjects to listen to the speech signal and give their estimation of the quality in terms of MOS. This method is standardised in ITU-T Recommendation P.800 (ITU-T, 1996b). Other methods are **objective** that depend on comparison of the received signal with the original signal to measure the perceived quality in terms of MOS, these methods are known as **intrusive** methods as they require the injection of the original signal to analyse the distortion of the received signal. The most recent method for measuring the speech quality intrusively is known as Perceptual Evaluation of Speech Quality (PESQ). PESQ is standardised as ITU-T Recommendation P.862 (ITU-T, 2001). Yet another **objective** category depends on either the received signal or the networking parameters to estimate the quality **non-intrusively** without the need for the original signal. The two main methods in this category are Recommendation P.563 (ITU-T, 2004) and the E-model as defined in ITU-T Recommendation G.107 (ITU-T, 2009). Many other standards and methods have been proposed by other organisations, other researchers, and the authors of this chapter independent of the ITU-T, these attempts will be discussed in detail later in the chapter.

The selection of a method for VoIP quality assessment should take the characteristics of IP networks and voice calls into consideration. Such characteristics that affect the selection include the requirement to measure the quality of live-traffic while the network is running in a real environment during a voice call. To able to do this, an objective solution that measures the quality without human interference and depending on the received signal at the receiver side without the need for the original speech signal at the sender side; i.e. a non-intrusive measurement is needed.

This chapter aims to serve as a reference and survey for readers interested in the area of speech quality assessment in VoIP networks. The rest of this chapter is organised as follows: Section 2 categorises speech quality assessment techniques and discusses the main requirements of an applicable technique in VoIP environment. Sections 3 and 4 discusses subjective and objective quality assessment technologies, respectively. To avoid ambiguity, different qualifiers are used to distinguish between different quality measurement methods and presented in section 5. Conclusions and possibilites for future work are given in section 6.

2. Categories of VoIP quality assessment technologies

VoIP quality assessment methods can be categorised into either subjective methods or objective methods. Objective methods can be either intrusive or non-intrusive. Non-intrusive methods can be either signal-based or parametric-based. Figure 1 depicts different classifications.

The primary criterion for voice and video communication is subjective quality, the user's perceptions of service quality. A subjective quality assessment method is used to measure the quality. Subjective quality factors affect the quality of service of VoIP, among those factors are: packet loss, delay, jitter, loudness, echo, and codec distortion. To measure the subjective quality, a subjective quality assessment method is used, the most widely accepted metric is the Mean Opinion Score (MOS) as defined by ITU-T Recommendation P.800 (ITU-T, 1996b).

However, although subjective quality assessment is the most reliable method, it is also time-consuming and expensive as any other subjective test. Thus other methods to automatically estimate quality objectively should be considered. This can be done intrusively by comparing the reference signal with the degraded signal or non-intrusively utilising physical quality parameters or the received signal without using the reference signal.

The applicability of any solution for measuring the speech quality in VoIP networks should take into consideration the nature of IP networks and the characteristics of voice traffic. Among the desired features for a VoIP speech quality assessment solution are:

1. Automatic: It should provide measurement of speech quality online while the network is running.
2. Non-intrusive: It should be able to provide measurement of the speech quality depending on the received speech signal or network parameters without the need for the original signal.
3. Accurate: It should provide accurate measurement of speech quality to reflect how the quality is perceived by the end-user.
4. With the changing world, it should be applicable to new and emerging applications and networking conditions. As such it should avoid the subjectivity in estimating parameters. The E-model (section 4.2) for example depends on subjective tests to estimate packet loss parameters which hinders its applicability for new networking conditions.

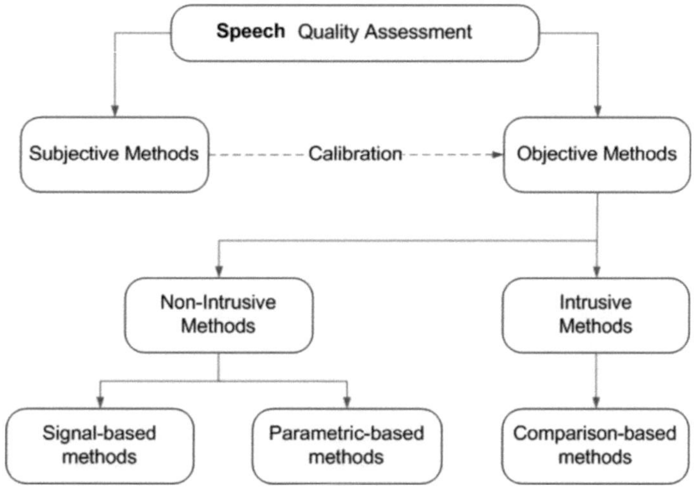

Fig. 1. Overview of VoIP measurement methods (Sun, 2004)

Based on the above requirements and from the previous discussion, the subjective and intrusive solutions that will be discussed in sections 3 and 4.1 respectively cannot be used for such task as they are manual and intrusive, respectively. The non-intrusive objective solutions that will be discussed in section 4.2 are candidates for such task. The most famous and widely used non-intrusive subjective solutions for measuring the speech quality are P.563 (ITU-T, 2004) and the E-model (ITU-T, 2009).

3. Subjective assessment of quality

The most widely used subjective quality assessment methodology is opinion rating defined in ITU-T Recommendation P.800 in which a panel of users (test subjects) perform the subjective tests of voice quality and give their opinions on the quality (ITU-T, 1996b). Subjective tests could be conversational or listening-only tests. In conversational test, two subject share a conversation via the transmission system under test, where they are placed in separated and isolated rooms to report their opinion on the opinion scale recommended by ITU-T and the arithmetic mean of these opinions is calculated. In listening tests, one subject is listening to pre-recorded sentences (ITU-T, 1996b).

To conduct a subjective experiment according to the ITU-T Recommendation P.800, strict lab conditions should be in place. Such conditions concerns the room size, noise level, and the use of sound-proof cabinet in a room with a volume not less than 20 m^3. In case of recording the test room must be a volume of 30 m^3 up to 120 m^3, with an echo duration lower than 500 ms (200-300 ms is preferred) and a background noise lower than 30 decibel (dB). The recording system must be of high quality and recorded voice signals must consist of simple, meaningful, short phrases, taken from newspapers or non-technical lectures, randomly ordered (phrases of 3-6 seconds of length or conversations of 2-5 minutes of length), all the used material must be recorded with a microphone at a distance of 140-200 mm from the speakers mouth. Also, the sound pressure level should be measured from a vertical position above the subjects seat while the furniture in place (ITU-T, 1996b).

Recommendation P.800 also specifies other conditions regarding the subjects who participate in the test such as they have not been directly involved in work connected with assessment of the performance of telephone circuits, or related work such as speech coding, also they have not participated in any subjective test whatever for at least the previous six months, and not in a conversational/listening test for at least one year. In case of listening-test they have never heard the same sentence lists before (ITU-T, 1996b).

In opinion rating methodology the performance of the system is rated either directly (Absolute Category Rating, ACR) or relative to the subjective quality of a reference system as in (Degradation Category Rating, DCR), or Comparison Category Rating (CCR) (ITU-T, 1996b; Takahashi, 2004; Takahashi et al., 2004).

The most common metric in opinion rating is Mean Opinion Score (MOS) which is an ACR metric with five-point scale: (5) Excellent, (4) Good, (3) Fair, (2) Poor, (1) Bad (ITU-T, 1996b). MOS is internationally accepted metric as it provides direct link to the quality as perceived by the user. A MOS value is obtained as an arithmetic mean for a collection of MOS scores (opinions) for a set of subjects. When the subjective test is listening-only, the results are in terms of listening subjective quality; i.e. MOS - Listening Quality Subjective or MOS_{LQS}. When the subjective test is conversational, the results are in terms of conversational subjective quality; i.e. MOS - Conversational Quality Subjective or MOS_{CQS} (ITU-T, 1996b; 2006). Although the overall quality of VoIP must be discussed in term of conversational quality, listening quality assessment is also quite helpful in analysing the effect of individual quality factors such as distortion due to speech coding and packet loss.

In DCR test two samples (A and B) are present: A represents the reference sample with the reference quality, while B represents the degraded sample. The subjects are instructed to acoustically compare the two samples and rate the degradation of the B sample in relation to the A sample according to the following five-point degradation category scale: degradation is (5) inaudible, (4) audible but not annoying, (3) slightly annoying, (2) annoying, and (1) very annoying. The samples must be composed of two periods, separated by silence (for example 0.5 seconds), firstly sample A then sample B.

The results (opinions) are averaged as Degraded MOS (DMOS). Each configuration is evaluated by means of judgements on speech samples from at least four talkers. DCR test affords higher sensitivity and used with high-quality voice samples, this is especially useful when the impairment is small and a sensitive measure of the impairment is required as ACR is inappropriate to discover quality variations as it tends to lead to low sensitivity in distinguishing among good quality circuits (ITU-T, 1996b; Takahashi et al., 2004).

The CCR method is similar to the DCR method as subjects are presented with a pair of speech samples (A and B) on each trial. In the DCR procedure, a reference sample is presented first sample (A) followed by the degraded sample (B). In the DCR method, listeners always rate the amount by which sample B is degraded relative to sample A. In the CCR procedure, the order of the processed and unprocessed samples is chosen at random for each trial. On half of the trials, the unprocessed sample is followed by the processed sample. On the remaining trials, the order is reversed. Listeners use the following scale: (3) Much Better, (2) Better, (1) Slightly Better, (0) About the Same, (-1) Slightly Worse, (-2) Worse, and (-3) Much Worse (ITU-T, 1996b). In this technique listeners provide two judgements with one response where the advantage of the CCR method over the DCR procedure is the possibility to assess speech processing that either degrades or improves the quality of the speech. The quantity evaluated from the scores is represented as Comparison MOS (CMOS).

Results of MOS scores should be dealt with care as results may vary depending on the speaker, hardware platform, listening groups and test data and slight variation between different subjective tests should be expected although the above rigid conditions should guarantee

minimisation of such cases.
Although opinion rating methods are the most famous subjective quality assessment methodology, but other methods have also been proposed. Diagnostic Rhyme Test (DRT) is an intelligibility measure where the subject task is to recognise one of two possible words in a set of rhyming pairs (e.g. meat-beat). Diagnostic Acceptability Measure (DAM) scores are based on results of test methods evaluating the quality of a communication system based on the acceptability of speech as perceived by a trained normative listener (Spanias, 1994). Li (2004) proposed the use of intelligibility index as an additional parameter that can be used along with the commonly used MOS score. Opinion rating methods are still the most famous and widely used method.
Although subjective quality measurement is the most accurate and reliable assessment method to measure the quality as it reflects the user's perceptions of service quality, but there are few problems associated with subjective tests. It is apparent from the strict conditions associated with opinion rating methods as mentioned above that the inherent problems in subjective MOS measurement are that it is: time-consuming, expensive, lacks repeatability , and inapplicable for monitoring live voice traffic as commonly needed for VoIP applications. This has made objective methods very attractive to estimate the subjective quality for meeting the demand for voice quality measurement in communication networks to avoid the limitations of the subjective tests.

4. Objective assessment of quality

Objective speech quality assessment simulates the opinions of human testers algorithmically or using computational models to automatically evaluate the transmitted speech quality over IP networks to replace the human subjects, where the aim is to predict MOS values that are as close as possible to the rating obtained from subjective test and to avoid the limitations of subjective assessment methods. However, as subjective methods are the most accurate and reliable methods for measuring speech quality, they are used to calibrate objective methods. Therefore the accuracy, effectiveness and performance evaluation of objective methods are determined by their correlation with the subjective MOS scores.
Objective assessment of speech quality is based on objective metrics of speech signal or properties of the carrier network. Objective quality assessment methodologies can be categorised into two groups: Intrusive speech-layer models and Non-Intrusive models (Signal-based and parametric-based). Figure 2 shows the three main types of objective measurement.

4.1 Intrusive objective assessment of quality

Intrusive measures, often referred to as input-to-output measures or comparison-based methods, base their quality measurement on comparing the original (clean or input) speech signal with the degraded (distorted or output) speech signal as reconstructed by the decoder at the receiver side, this is shown in Figure 2 (a). Intrusive objective assessment of speech quality or speech-layer objective models are full-reference methods for measuring the quality. They provide an accurate method for measuring speech quality as they require the original or reference speech signal as input and produce measurement of listening MOS by comparing the post-transmitted signal with the original one (double-ended) using a distance measure, based on this comparison the quality of the degraded signal is measured in comparison with the quality of the original signal. However, such methods are inapplicable in monitoring live traffic because it is difficult or impossible to obtain actual speech samples as the

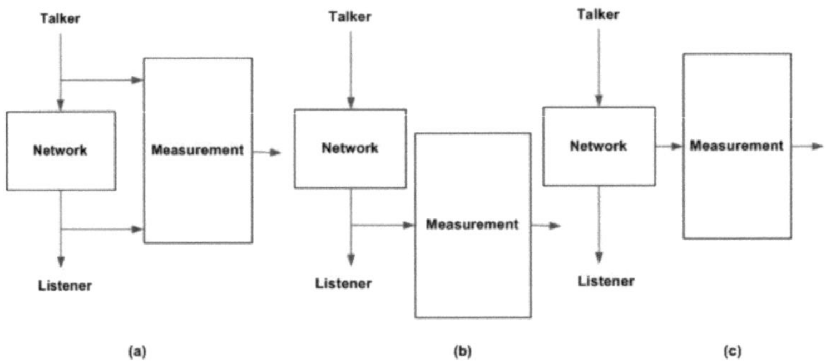

Fig. 2. Three main categories of objective quality measurement: (a) Comparison-based intrusive method, (b) Signal-based non-intrusive method, (c) Parametric-based non-intrusive method (Sun, 2004)

reference signal is not available at the receiver side. Some intrusive algorithms are used in time-domain, other objective quality assessment methods make use of spectral distortion (frequency-domain) to evaluate the performance of LBR codecs. None of these standards were accurate enough to be adopted by ITU-T. Later, perceptual domain measures were introduced and standardised.

Perceptual domain measures are based on models of human auditory perception. These measures transform the speech signal into a perceptually relevant domain such as bark spectrum or loudness domain, and incorporate human auditory models (Sun, 2004). In perceptual measure the original and the degraded signal are both transformed into a psychophysical representation that approximates human perception or simulate the psychophysics of hearing such as the critical-band spectral resolution, frequency selectivity, the equal-loudness curve and the intensity-loudness power law to derive an estimate of the auditory spectrum. Then the perceptual difference between the original and the degraded signal is mapped into estimation of perceptual quality difference as perceived by the listener. Perceptual domain measures have shown to be highly accurate objective performance measures because many modern codecs are nonlinear and non-stationary making the shortcomings of the previous objective measures even more evident. Perceptual domain measures include: Measuring Normalising Block (MNB), Perceptual Analysis Measurement System (PAMS), Perceptual Speech Quality Measure (PSQM), and Perceptual Evaluation of Speech Quality (PESQ) which is the latest ITU-T intrusive standard for assessing speech quality for communication systems and networks (ITU-T, 1998; 2001; Sun, 2004; Voran, 1999a;b).

4.1.1 Signal to noise ratio (SNR) and segmental signal-to-noise-ratio (SegSNR)

Time domain measures are the simplest intrusive measures that consist of an analogue or waveform-comparison algorithms in which the target is to reproduce a copy of input waveform such that the original and distorted signals can be time-aligned and noise can be accurately calculated, SNR and SegSNR are the most important method of this category. Signal refers to useful information conveyed by some communications medium, and noise refers to anything else on that medium. SNR gives a measure of the signal power improvement related to the noise power calculated for the original signal and the degraded signal. In SNR sample-by-sample comparison is performed. SEGmental SNR (SegSNR) can also be utilised where SNR is computed for each N point segment of speech to detect temporal variations. As time-domain measures, SNR and SegSNR can be used for evaluation of non-speech signals (Quackenbush et al., 1988; Mahdi and Picoviciv, 2009). SNR is defined as the ratio of a signal power to the noise power corrupting the signal:

$$SNR = 10\log_{10}\frac{\sum_n x^2(n)}{\sum_n (x(n) - d(n))^2}, \tag{1}$$

where x(n) represents the original (undistorted) speech signal, d(n) represents the distorted speech reproduced by a speech processing system and n is the sample index (determined points on time domains). SegSNR calculates the SNR for each N-points segment of speech. The result is an average of SNR values of segments, and can be computed as follows:

$$SSNR = \frac{10}{M}\sum_{m=0}^{M-1}\log_{10}\left(\frac{\sum_{n=Nm}^{Nm+N-1} x^2(n)}{\sum_{n=Nm}^{Nm+N-1}[d(n) - x(n)]^2}\right), \tag{2}$$

Where x(n) represents the original speech signal, d(n) represents the distorted speech signal, n is the sample index, N is the segment length, and M is the number of segments in the speech signal. Classical windowing techniques are used to segment the speech signal into appropriate speech segments.

SNR and SegSNR algorithms are easy to implement, have low computational complexity, can provide good performance measure of voice quality of waveform codecs.

Although SNR is the most common method, its main problem is that it cannot be used with Low-Bit-Rate (LBR) codecs as these codecs do not preserve the shape of the signal. As such SNR cannot compare the pre-encoded signal with the post-decoded signal as they show little correlation to perceived speech quality when applied to LBR codecs such as vocoders as in these codecs the shape of the signal is not preserved and they become meaningless (Kondoz, 2004). These measures are also sensitive to a time shift, and therefore require precise signal alignment such that to achieve the correct time alignment it may be necessary to correct phase errors in the distorted signal or to interpolate between samples in a sampled data system.

4.1.2 Spectral domain measures

Spectral domain measures or frequency-domain measures are known to be significantly better correlated with human perception, but still relatively simple to implement. One of their critical advantages is that they are less sensitive to signal misalignment and phase shift between the original and the distorted signals than time domain measures. Most spectral domain measures are related to speech codecs design and use the parameters of speech production models. Their capability to effectively describe the listeners auditory response is limited by the constraints of the speech production models. Some of the most popular frequency domain techniques are the Log-Likelihood (LL) (Itakura, 1975), the ItakuraSaito (IS) (Itakura & Saito, 1978), and the Cepstral Distance (CD) (Kitawaki et al., 1988).

4.1.3 Measuring normalising blocks (MNB)

In this algorithm, both the input and the output speech signals are perceptually transformed and a distance measure that consists of a hierarchy of Measuring Normalising Blocks (MNB) is then calculated. Each MNB integrates two perceptually transformed signals over some time or frequency interval to determine the average difference across the interval. This difference is then normalised out of one signal to provide one or more measurements.

MNB algorithm starts by estimating the delay between the input speech signal and the output speech signal due to the device or system (possibly IP network) under test. This is done using cross-correlation of speech envelops because LBR codecs do not preserve the speech waveform, therefore waveform cross correlation gives misleading estimation for the delay. Once the delay is estimated and compensated for, MNB proceed to the next step which is perceptual transformation.

In perceptual transformation, the representation of the audio signal is modified in such a way it is approximately equivalent to the human hearing process and only perceptual information is retained. The following steps are performed by Voran in (Voran, 1999a;b) on the speech signal sampled at a rate of 8000 samples/s before perceptual transformation. The speech signal is divided into frames of size 128 samples with 50% frame overlap. Each frame is multiplied by a Hamming window and transformed using FFT transform and only the squared magnitudes of the FFT coefficients are preserved. As Voran pointed out, the nonuniform ear's frequency resolution on the Hertz scale and nonlinear relation between loudness perception and signal intensity are the most important perceptual properties to model (Voran, 1999a).

For modelling the nonuniform frequency resolution, the Hertz frequency scale is replaced by a psychoacoustic frequency scale such as the bark frequency scale using the relation:

$$b = 6.\sinh^{-1}\left(\frac{f}{600}\right) \tag{3}$$

where b is the Bark frequency scale variable. f is Hertz frequency scale variable.

Figure 3 shows the transformation from Hertz to Bark scale. In bark scale, roughly equal frequency intervals are of equal importance. From the figure it can be seen that on the band 0-1 kHz in Hertz scale (corresponding to 0-7.703 Bark) is given equal importance by Bark scale as the band 1-4 kHz. It is worth noting that bark scale is used recently for measuring speech quality for wideband speech coding (Haojun et al., 2004). To model the nonlinear relation between loudness perception and signal intensity, the logarithmic function is used to convert signal intensity to perceived loudness.

The distance between the two signals is calculated using a hierarchy of Time MNB (TMNB) and Frequency MNB (FMNB). The hierarchy structure works from larger time and frequency scales down to smaller time and frequency scales. Each block integrates the perceptually transformed signals over time or frequency to determine the average difference between the two signals. Once all the measurements of the hierarchy are calculated on different levels, these measurement are linearly combined to calculate the Auditory Distance (AD) between the two signals. Finally the AD can be mapped using a logistic function into a finite set of values from 0 to 1 to increase correlation with subjective tests (Voran, 1999a;b).

4.1.4 Perceptual analysis measurement system (PAMS)

Developed by Psytechnics, a UK-based company associated with British telecommunications (BT). The PAMS process uses an auditory model that combines a mathematical description of the psychophysical properties of human hearing with a technique that performs a perceptually relevant analysis taking into account the subjectivity of the errors in the received signal. PAMS extracts and selects parameters describing speech degradation addressed by damaging factors such as time clipping, packets loss, delay and distortion due to the codec usage and constrained mapping to subjective quality. PAMS compares the original and the received signals and produces two scores, listening quality score (Ylq) and listening effort

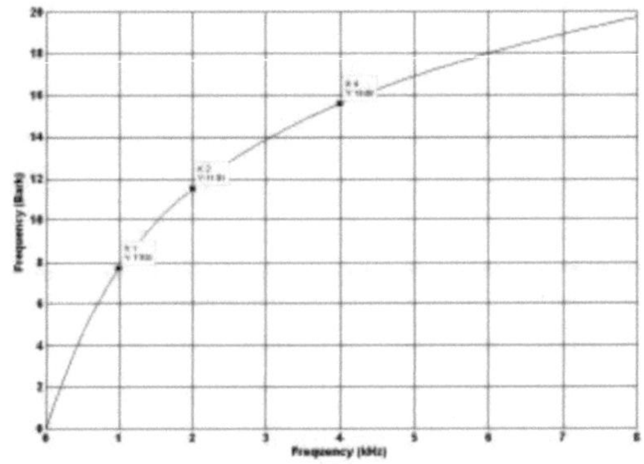

Fig. 3. Transformation from Hertz scale to Bark scale

score (Yle). Both scores are in the range 1 to 5 and MOS score can be estimated using a linear combination of both scores (Duysburgh et al., 2001; Zurek et al., 2002).

4.1.5 Perceptual speech quality measure (PSQM)

PSQM originally developed by KPN, Netherlands and then standardised by ITU-T as Recommendation P.861. PSQM transforms the speech signal into the loudness domain, applies a nonlinear scaling factor to the loudness vector of distorted speech. The scaling factor is obtained by calculating the loudness ratio of the reference and the distorted speech. The difference between the scaled loudness of the distorted speech and loudness of the reference speech is called Noise Disturbance (ND). The final estimated distortion is an average ND over all the frames processed where a small weight is given to silence portions during calculations. PSQM computes the distortion frame by frame, with the frame length of 256 samples with 50% overlap. The result is shown in ND as a function of time and frequency. The average ND is directly related to the quality of coded speech. There are two meaningful scores in the PSQM measure: one is a distortion measure and the other is a mapped number such as MOS. PSQM measurements are in the range 0 to 6.5 with lower values means lower distortion which indicates better quality. PSQM scores can be mapped into MOS scores using a nonlinear mapping (ITU-T, 1998; Sun, 2004; Zurek et al., 2002).
PSQM was designed to work under error-free coding conditions, therefore it is inapplicable for VoIP environment which suffers from packet loss especially in mobile communications that suffer from bit errors. PSQM+ was proposed by KPN to improve the performance of PSQM for loud distortions and temporal clipping. PSQM+ uses the same perceptual transformation module as PSQM. Comparing to PSQM, an additional scaling factor is introduced when the overall distortion is calculated. This scaling factor makes the overall distortion proportional to the amount of temporal clipping distortion. Otherwise, the cognition module is the same as PSQM.

4.1.6 Perceptual evaluation of speech quality (PESQ)

PESQ is the latest ITU-T standard for objective evaluation of speech quality in narrowband telephony network and codecs. It was a result of a collaboration project between KPN and BT by combining the two speech quality measures PSQM+ and PAMS. Later it was standardised by ITU-T as Recommendation P.862 (ITU-T, 2001; Rix et al., 2001). Upon its standardisation, PSQM in Recommendation P.861 was withdrawn by ITU-T (ITU-T, 2001; 2005b; Rohani & Zepernick, 2005; Zurek et al., 2002).

Real systems may include filtering and variable delay, as well as distortions due to channel errors and LBR codes. PSQM was designed to assess speech codec and is not able to take proper account of filtering, variable delay, and short localised distortions. PESQ was specifically developed to be applicable to end-to-end voice quality testing under real network conditions, such as VoIP, ISDN etc. The results obtained by PESQ was found to be highly correlated with subjective tests with correlation factor of 0.935 on 22 ITU benchmark experiments, which cover 9 languages (American English, British English, Dutch, Finnish, French, German, Italian, Swedish and Japanese).

In PESQ the original and the degraded signals are time-aligned, then both signals are transformed to an internal representation that is analogous to the psychophysical representation of audio signals in the human auditory system, taking account of perceptual frequency (Bark) and loudness (Sone). After this transformation to the internal representation, the original signal is compared with the degraded signal using a perceptual model. This is achieved in several stages: level alignment to a calibrated listening level, compressive loudness scaling, and averaging distortions over time as illustrated in Figure 4 (ITU-T, 2001; Rix et al., 2001).

PESQ score lies in the range -0.5 to 4.5, to make such score comparable with ACR MOS score, a function is provided in Recommendation P.862.1 to map these values to the range 1 to 5. The function in equation (4) do the conversion from a PESQ score to a MOS - Listening Quality Objective or MOS_{LQO} which makes the comparison with other MOS results very convenient independent of the implementation of ITU-T Recommendation P.862 (ITU-T, 2005b).

$$MOS_{LQO} = 0.999 + \frac{4.999 - 0.999}{1 - e^{(-1.4945*PESQ+4.6607)}} \tag{4}$$

ITU-T Recommendation P.862.1 (ITU-T, 2005b) also provides a formula to move back to PESQ score from an available MOS_{LQO} score. The equation is:

$$PESQ = \frac{4.6607 - \ln\left(\frac{4.999 - MOS_{LQO}}{MOS_{LQO} - 0.999}\right)}{1.4945} \tag{5}$$

In 2005, the ITU-T issued Recommendation P.862.2 ITU-T (2005c). P.862.2 extends the application of P.862 PESQ to wideband audio systems (50-7000 Hz). The definition of a new output mapping function, which is a modification to that recommended in P.862.1, to be used with wideband applications is as follows:

$$MOS_{LQO} = 0.999 + \frac{4.999 - 0.999}{1 + e^{-1.3669PESQ+3.8224}} \tag{6}$$

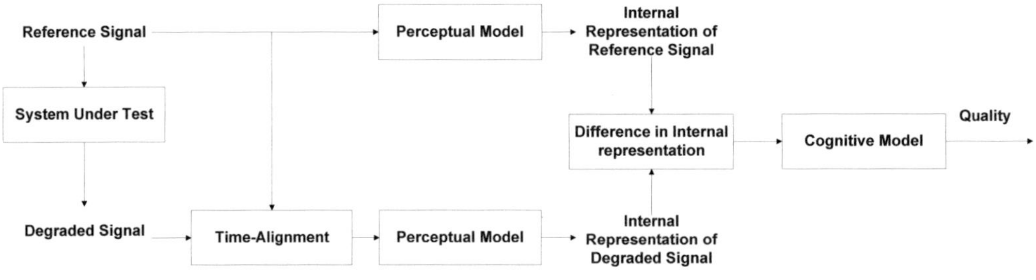

Fig. 4. Conceptual diagram of PESQ philosophy (ITU-T, 2001)

4.1.7 Other methods

Many other intrusive objective methods have been proposed by other researchers. Fu et al. proposed using an ANN model where the feature vector of the input vector and output vector corresponding to the original and degraded signal respectively are fed to the ANN model in addition with MOS subjective score as calculated using set of subjects as a target for the ANN. Utilising the proposed method and using the error between the original input signal and the output signal as input to the ANN model, MOS score can be estimated directly using one-step rather than the usual approach of estimating the distortion and then mapping the quality (Fu et al., 2000).

4.2 Non-intrusive objective assessment of quality

The intrusive methods described in section 4.1 need the input signal as a reference for comparison with the output signal which is a problem in live network as it is difficult to obtain the original speech signal at the receiver side. Additionally, in some situations the input speech may be distorted by background noise, and hence, measuring the distortion between the input and the output speech does not provide an accurate indication of the speech quality of the communication system.

On the other hand, non-intrusive measures (also known as output-based or passive measures) use only the degraded signal without access to the original signal. Non-intrusive methods provide a convenient measure for monitoring of live networks. Real-time quality assessment is important for instance if the application is to perform some form of dynamic quality control, e.g. by changing encoding or redundancy parameters to optimise quality when network conditions worsen.

Different methods have been proposed for objectively estimating the speech quality non-intrusively. These methods vary in complexity and accuracy from very simple techniques to very complex ones. It is identified that the non-intrusive objective assessment of quality is the most appropriate method for monitoring the speech quality in VoIP networks. This section discusses different non-intrusive methods for measuring the speech quality objectively. Non-intrusive methods are also divides into to subcategories, signal-based and parametric-based methods.

Signal-based methods are based on digital signal processing techniques that estimate the speech quality when the envelope of the speech signal may have suffered from degradation overtime due to LBR coding or transmission over noisy wireless links, in other words signal-based methods process the audio stream that is decoded after buffer playout to extract relevant information for estimating the voice quality. ITU-T Recommendation P.563 or 3SQM (Single-Sided Speech Quality Measurement) that achieves a correlation coefficient with subjective tests of around 0.8 defined to be a standard for this type of measure (ITU-T, 2004).

On the other hand, parametric-based methods based their results on various properties relevant to telecommunication network parameters for example packet loss, delay and jitter. This makes parametric model to be more specific for a particular type of communications network by depending their prediction on the parameters of that network, which makes parametric-based methods to be more accurate than signal-based methods for that network which are more suitable for general prediction for a wider variety of networks and conditions. The E-model which is one of the most widely used parametric-based methods defined according to ITU-T Recommendation G.107 (ITU-T, 2009). The details of the ITU-T Recommendation P.563 or 3SQM and the E-Model are discussed in the next sections.

4.2.1 ITU-T recommendation P.563 or 3SQM

In 2004 ITU-T standardised its P.563 Recommendation (ITU-T, 2004) for single-ended objective speech quality assessment in narrow-band telephony applications. Recommendation P.563 approach is the first ITU-T Recommendation for single-ended signal-based non-intrusive measurement application that takes into account perceptual distortions to predict the speech quality on a perception-based scale to produce MOS - Conversational Quality Objective or MOS_{CQO}. This Recommendation is not restricted to end-to-end measurements; it can be used at any arbitrary location in the transmission Path. The basic block diagram of P.563 is shown in Figure 5.

This visualisation explains also the main application and allows the user to rate the scores gained by P.563. The quality score predicted by P.563 is related to the perceived quality by linking a conventional handset at the measuring point. Hence, the listening device has to be part of the P.563 approach. To achieve this, the algorithm combines 4 processing stages as illustrated in Figure 6: preprocessing; basic distortion classes and speech parameters extraction; detection of dominant distortion; and mapping to final quality estimate. Brief overview of the main steps is given here:

- **Preprocessing**: The first preprocessing step in the Intermediate Reference System (IRS) filtering, where the speech signal to be assessed is filtered to simulate a standard receiving telephone handset. This is followed by a Voice Activity Detector (VAD) to separate speech from silence. The speech level is then calculated and adjusted to -26 dBov.
- **Extraction of basic distortion classes and speech parameters**: The preprocessed speech signal is analysed to detect a set of characterising signal parameters. In total there are 51 distortion parameters that are divided up into 3 independent functional blocks, namely: vocal tract analysis and unnaturalness of speech; analysis of strong additional noise; and speech interruptions, mutes and time clipping. All of these distortion classes are based on very general principles that make no assumptions about the underlying network or distortion types occurring under certain conditions. Additionally, a set of basic speech descriptors like active speech level, speech activity and level variations are used, mainly for adjusting the pre-processing and the VAD. Some of the signal parameters calculated within the pre-processing stage are used in these 3 functional blocks.
- **Detection of dominant distortion**: This analysis is applied at first to the signal. Based on a restricted set of key parameters, an assignment to a main distortion class will be made. The key parameters and the assigned distortion class are used for the adjustment of the speech

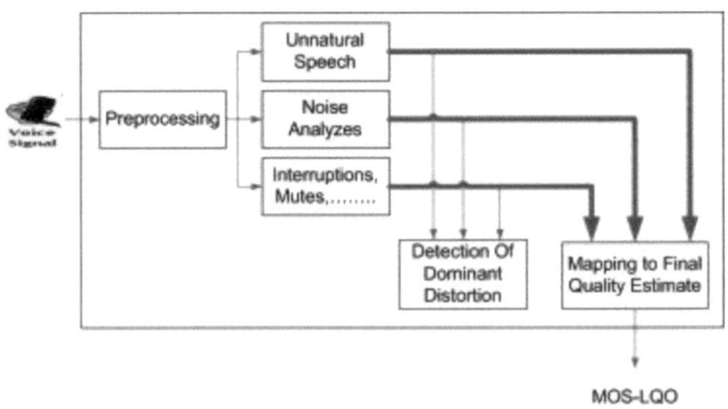

Fig. 5. Basic block diagram of P.563 overall structure (ITU-T, 2004)

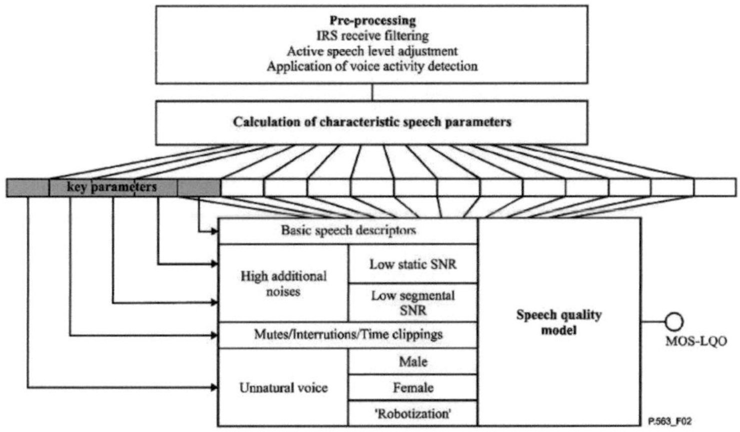

Fig. 6. Block diagram of P.563 algorithm detailing the various distortion classes used (ITU-T, 2004)

quality model. This provides a perceptual based weighting where several distortions occur in the signal but one distortion class is more prominent than the others. The process models the phenomenon that any human listener focuses on the foreground of the signal stream; i.e. the listener would not judge the quality of the transmitted voice by a simple sum of all occurred distortions but because of a single dominant noise artifact in the signal.
In the case of several distortions occurring to the signal, a prioritisation is applied on the distortion classes according to the distortions relevance with respect to the average listeners opinions. This is followed by estimation of an intermediate speech quality score for each class distortion. Each class distortion uses a linear combination of parameters to generate the intermediate speech quality. The final speech quality estimate is calculated by combining the intermediate quality results with some additional signal features.

- **Final quality estimate**: In this stage, a speech quality model is used to map the estimated distortion values into a final quality estimate equivalent to MOS_{CQO}. The speech quality model is composed of 3 main blocks:
  - decision on a distortion class.
  - speech quality evaluation for the corresponding distortion class.
  - overall calculation of speech quality.

4.2.2 The E-model

One of the most widely used methods for objectively evaluating the speech quality non-intrusively is opinion modelling. In opinion models subjective quality factors are mapped into manageable network and terminal quality parameters to automatically produce an estimate of subjective quality. The most famous standard for opinion modelling is the E-model which is defined according to ITU-T Recommendation G.107 (ITU-T, 2009; Takahashi et al., 2004).
The E-model, abbreviated from the European Telecommunications Standards Institute (ETSI), was developed by a working group within ETSI during the work on ETSI Technical Report ETR 250 (ETSI, 1996). It is a computational tool originally developed as a network planning tool, but it is now being used for objectively estimating voice quality for VoIP applications

using network and terminal quality parameters. In the E-model, the original or reference signal is not used to estimate the quality as the estimation is based purely on the terminal and network parameters. Network parameters such as packet loss rate can be estimated from information contained in the headers of Real-time Transport Protocol (RTP) and Real-time Transport Control Protocol (RTCP). The E-model is a non-intrusive method of measuring the quality as it does not require the injection of the reference signal (ITU-T, 2009; Sun, 2004; Takahashi et al., 2004).

In the E-model, the subjective quality factors are mapped into manageable network and terminal quality parameters. Among the network quality parameters are: network delay and packet loss. Among the terminal quality parameters are: jitter buffer overflow, coding distortion, jitter buffer delay, and echo cancellation. Example of mapping is the mapping of delay subjective quality parameter into network delay and jitter buffer delay.

The fundamental principle of the E-model is based on a concept established by J. Allnatt around 35 years ago (Allnatt, 1975):

Psychological factors on the psychological scale are additive

It is used for describing the perceptual effects of diverse impairments occurring simultaneously on a telephone connection. Because the perceived integral quality is a multidimensional attribute, the dimensionality is reduced into one-dimension so-called transmission rating factor, *R*-Rating Factor. Based on Allnatt's psychological scale all the impairments are - by definition - additive and thus independent of one another.

In the E-model all factors responsible for quality degradation are summed on the psychological scale. Due to its additive principle, the E-model is able to describe the effect of several impairments occurring simultaneously.

The E-model is a function of 20 input parameters that represent the terminal, network, and environmental quality factors (quality degradation introduced by speech coding, bit error, and packet loss is treated collectively as an equipment impairment factor).

The E-model starts by calculating the degree of quality degradation due to individual quality factors on the same psychological scale. Then the sum of these values is subtracted from a reference value to produce the output of the E-model which is the *R*-Rating Factor. The *R*-Rating Factor lies in the range of 0 and 100 to indicate the level of estimated quality where R=0 represents an extremely bad quality and R=100 represents a very high quality. The *R*-Rating Factor can be mapped into a MOS score based on the G.107 ITU-T's Recommendation (ITU-T, 2009) as explained later in this section. The reference model that represents the E-model is depicted in Figure 7 (ITU-T, 2009). The input parameters to the E-model, beside their default values and permitted range are listed in Table 1.

By following the additive principle, the E-model is able to describe the effect of several impairments occurring simultaneously, the *R*-Rating Factor combines the effects of various transmission parameters such as (packet loss, jitter, delay, echo, noise). The *R*-Rating Factor is calculated according to the following formula which follows the previous summation principle:

$$R = R_0 - Is - Id - Ie\text{-}eff + A \tag{7}$$

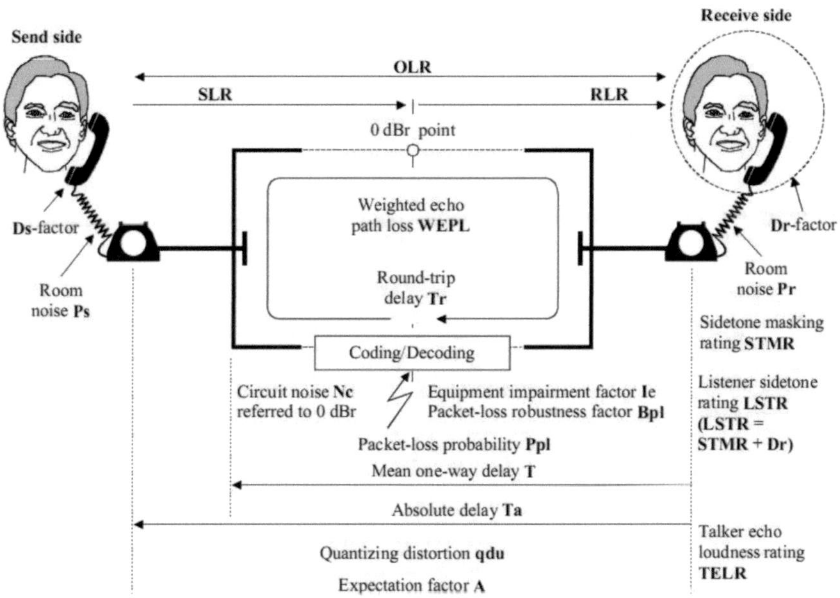

Fig. 7. Reference connection of the E-model (ITU-T, 2009)

Parameter	Default value	Permitted range
Send Loudness Rating	8	0...+18
Receive Loudness Rating	2	-5...+14
Sidetone Masking Rating	15	10...20
Listener Sidetone Rating	18	13...23
D-Value of Telephone, Send Side	3	3...+3
D-Value of Telephone, Receive Side	3	-3...+3
Talker Echo Loudness Rating	65	5...65
Weighted Echo Path Loss	110	5...110
Mean one-way Delay of the Echo Path	0	0...500
Round-Trip Delay in a 4-wire Loop	0	0...1000
Absolute Delay in echo-free Connections	0	0...500
Number of Quantisation Distortion Units	1	1...14
Equipment Impairment Factor	0	0...40
Packet-loss Robustness Factor	1	1...40
Random Packet-loss Probability	0	0...20
Burst Ratio	1	1 2
Circuit Noise referred to 0 dBr-point	-70	-80...-40
Noise Floor at the Receive Side	-64	
Room Noise at the Send Side	35	35...85
Room Noise at the Receive Side	35	35...85
Advantage Factor	0	0...20

Table 1. Default values and permitted ranges for the E-model's parameters (ITU-T, 2009)

where

R_0	Basic signal-to-noise ratio (groups the effects of noise)
Is	Impairments which occur more or less simultaneously with the voice signal e.g. (quantisation noise, sidetone level)
Id	Impairments due to delay, echo
Ie-eff	Impairments due to codec distortion, packet loss and jitter
A	Advantage factor or expectation factor (e.g. 10 for GSM)

The advantage factor captures the fact that users might be willing to accept some degradation in quality in return for the ease of access, e.g. users may find the speech quality is acceptable in cellular networks because of its access advantages. The same quality would be considered poor in the public circuit-switched telephone network. In the former case A could be assigned the value 10, while in the later case A would take the value 0 (Estepa et al., 2002; Markopoulou et al., 2003).
Each of the parameters in equation (7) except the Advantage factor (A) is further decomposed into a series of equations as defined in ITU-T Recommendation G.107 (ITU-T, 2009). When all parameters set to their default values (Table 1), *R*-Rating Factor as defined in equation (7) has the value of 93.2 which is mapped to an MOS value of 4.41.
When the effect of delay is considered, the estimated quality according to the E-model is conversational; i.e. MOS - Conversational Quality Estimated MOS_{CQE}. When the effect of delay is ignored and *Id* is set to its default value the estimation is listening only; i.e. MOS - Listening Quality Estimated MOS_{LQE}.
Packet loss as defined in equation (7) is characterised by packet loss dependent Effective Equipment Impairment Factor (*Ie-eff*), *Ie-eff* is calculated according to the following formula (ITU-T, 2009):

$$Ie\text{-}eff = Ie + (95 - Ie).\frac{Ppl}{\frac{Ppl}{BurstR} + Bpl} \tag{8}$$

where

Ie	Codec-specific Equipment Impairment Factor
Bpl	Codec-specific Packet-loss Robustness Factor
Ppl	Packet loss Probability
$BurstR$	Burst Ratio (BurstR-to count for burstiness in packet loss)

Ie-eff -as defined in equation (8) - is derived using codec-specific values for Ie and Bpl at zero packet-loss. The values for Ie and Bpl for several codecs are listed in ITU-T Recommendation G.113 Appendix I (ITU-T, 2002) and they are derived using subjective MOS test results. For example for the speech coder defined according to the ITU-T Recommendation G.729 (ITU-T, 1996a), the corresponding Ie and Bpl values are 11 and 19 respectively. On the other hand Ppl and $BurstR$ depend on the packet loss presented in the system. BurstR is defined by the latest version of the E-model as (ITU-T, 2009):

$$BurstR = \frac{\text{Average length of observed bursts in an arrival sequence}}{\text{Average length of bursts expected for the network under random loss}} \tag{9}$$

When packet loss is random; i.e., independent, $BurstR = 1$ and when packet loss is bursty; i.e., dependent, $BurstR > 1$.
The impact of packet loss in older versions of the E-model (prior to the 2005 version) was characterised by Equipment Impairment (*Ie*) factor. Specific impairment factor values for

codec operating under random packet loss have been previously tabulated to be packet-loss dependent. In the new versions of the E-model (after 2005), Bpl is defined as codec-specific value and Ie is replaced by the *Ie-eff*.

R-Rating Factor from equation (7) can be mapped into an MOS value. Equation (10) (ITU-T, 2009) gives the mapping function between the computed R-Rating Factor and the MOS value.

$$MOS = \left\{ \begin{array}{cc} 1 & R < 0 \\ 1 + 0.035R + R(R-60)(100-R).7.10^{-6} & 0 < R < 100 \\ 4.5 & R > 100 \end{array} \right\} \quad (10)$$

ITU-T Recommendation G.107 (ITU-T, 2009) also provides a formula to move back to R-Rating Factor from an available MOS score. The equation is:

$$R = \frac{20}{3}\left(8 - \sqrt{226}\left(h + \frac{\pi}{3}\right)\right) \quad (11)$$

with

$$h = \frac{1}{3}atan2\left(18566 - 6750MOS, 15\sqrt{-903522 + 1113960MOS - 202500MOS^2}\right) \quad (12)$$

where

$$atan2(x,y) = \left\{ \begin{array}{cc} atan\left(\frac{x}{y}\right) & for\ x \geq 0 \\ \pi - atan\left(\frac{y}{-x}\right) & for\ x < 0 \end{array} \right\} \quad (13)$$

The calculated R-Rating Factor and the mapped MOS value can be translated into a user satisfaction as defined by ITU-T Recommendation G.109 (ITU-T, 1999) and listed in Table 2. Connections with R values below 50 are not recommended. Understanding the degree of user's needs and expectations and having a direct measurement of user's satisfaction is important for commercial reasons as a network that does not satisfy user's expectations is not expected to be a commercial success. If the quality of the network is continuously low, more percentage of users are expected to look for a an alternative network with a consistent quality.

The E-model is a good choice for non-intrusive estimation of voice quality non-intrusively, but it has some drawbacks. It depends on the time-consuming, expensive and hard to conduct subjective tests to calibrate its parameters (Ie and Bpl), consequently, it is applicable to a limited number of codecs and network conditions (because subjective tests are required to derive model parameters) and this hinders its use in new and emerging applications. Also, it is less accurate than the intrusive methods such as PESQ because it does not consider the contents of the received signal in its calculations which rises questions about

R-Rating factor	MOS	Quality	User Satisfaction
$90 \leq R < 100$	$4.34 \leq MOS < 4.50$	Best	Very Satisfied
$80 \leq R < 90$	$4.02 \leq MOS < 4.34$	High	Satisfied
$70 \leq R < 80$	$3.60 < MOS < 4.02$	Medium	Some users dissatisfied
$60 \leq R < 70$	$3.10 \leq MOS < 3.60$	Low	Many users dissatisfied
$50 \leq R < 60$	$2.58 \leq MOS < 3.10$	Poor	Nearly all users dissatisfied

Table 2. User satisfaction as defined by ITU-T Recommendation G.109

its accuracy. Consequently, the E-model as standardised by the ITU-T satisfies only the first two requirements but does not satisfy the other two requirements from the list of desired requirements of speech quality assessment solutions.

Several efforts have been going on to extend the E-model based on the intrusive-based *PESQ* speech quality prediction methodology (Ding & Goubran, 2003a;b; Sun, 2004; Sun & Ifeachor, 2003; 2004; 2006). These studies, despite their importance, but they focused on a previous version of the E-Model (ITU-T, 2000) where burstiness in packet loss was not considered although Internet statistics according to several studies have shown that there is a dependency in packet loss; i.e. when packet loss occurs, it occurs in bursts (Borella et al., 1998; Liang et al., 2001). These and similar studies illustrate the importance of taking burstiness into account. In the current version of the E-model (ITU-T, 2009) burstiness is taken into account.

The authors of this book chapter has avoided these limitations by taking burstiness into consideration in their previous publications as newer versions of the E-model (ITU-T, 2005a; 2009) are used in the extension. Utilising the intrusive-based PESQ solution as a base criterion to avoid the subjectivity in estimating the E-model's parameters, the E-model was extended to new network conditions and applied to new speech codecs without the need for the subjective tests. The extension is realised using several methods, including: linear and nonlinear regression (AL-Akhras, 2007; ALMomani & AL-Akhras, 2008), Genetic Algorithms (AL-Akhras, 2008), Artificial Neural Network (ANN) (AL-Akhras, 2007; AL-Akhras et al., 2009), and Regression and Model Trees (AL-Akhras & el Hindi, 2009). In these implementations the modified E-model calibrated using PESQ is compared with the E-model calibrated using subjective tests to prove their effectiveness.

Another extension implemented by the authors to improve the accuracy of the E-model in comparison with the PESQ, analyses the content of the received degraded signal and classifies packet loss into either Voiced or Unvoiced based on the received surrounding packets. An emphasis on perceptual effect of different types of loss on the perceived speech quality is drawn. The accuracy of the proposed method is evaluated by comparing the estimation of the new method that takes packet class into consideration with the measurement provided by PESQ as a more accurate, intrusive method for measuring the speech quality (AL-Akhras, 2007).

The above two extensions for quality estimation of the E-model were combined to offer a complete solution for estimating the quality of VoIP applications objectively, non-intrusively, and accurately without the need for the time-consuming, expensive, and hard to conduct subjective tests (AL-Akhras, 2007). In other words a solution that satisfies all the requirements for a good VoIP speech quality assessment solution. Complete details about these extensions can be found and downloaded (AL-Akhras, 2007).

4.2.3 Other methods

Wide range of non-intrusive methods for non-intrusive VoIP quality assessment have been proposed, next reference to some attempts are mentioned, including: (Kim & Tarraf, 2006; Raja et al., 2006; Raja & Flanagan, 2008; Sun, 2004; Sun & Ifeachor, 2002; AL-Khawaldeh, 2010; Picovici & Mahdi, 2004; Mohamed et al., 2004; Da Silva et al., 2008). Many other attempts can be found in (AL-Akhras, 2007; AL-Khawaldeh, 2010).

5. Relationship among different subjective and objective assessment techniques

To avoid ambiguity, different qualifiers used to distinguish among different quality measurement methods are presented. Careful selection of terminology is used and differentiation among different terms used to describe the quality is clearly stated. A qualifier is added to the terms used to make sure of no vagueness in the meaning of the term. ITU-T Recommendation P.800.1 (ITU-T, 2006) gives a clear terminology distinction among different MOS terms whether the test is listening or conversational and whether it a result of subjective or objective test by adding an appropriate qualifier. This section shows how different quantifiers are obtained and how they are related to each other. In the recommendation it is stated that the identifiers in the following Table are to be used:

LQ	Listening Quality
CQ	Conversational Quality
S	Subjective
O	Objective
E	Estimated

Table 3. MOS Qualifiers

It is recommended to use these identifiers together with the MOS to avoid confusion and distinguish the area of application. The result of such qualification is (ITU-T, 1996b; 2001; 2004; 2006; 2009):

- **Subjective Tests**
  - **Listening Quality:** For the score collected by calculating the arithmetic mean of listening subjective tests conducted according to Recommendation P.800, the results are qualified as MOS - Listening Quality Subjective or MOS_{LQS}.
  - **Conversational Quality:** For the score collected by calculating the arithmetic mean of conversational subjective tests conducted according to Recommendation P.800, the results are qualified as MOS - Conversational Quality Subjective or MOS_{CQS}.
- **Network Planning Estimation Tests**
  - **Listening Quality:** For the score calculated by a network planning tool to estimate the listening quality according to Recommendation G.107 and then transformed into MOS, the results are qualified as MOS - Listening Quality Estimated or MOS_{LQE}.
  - **Conversational Quality:** For the score calculated by a network planning tool to estimate the conversational quality according to Recommendation G.107 and then transformed into MOS, the results are qualified as MOS - Conversational Quality Estimated or MOS_{CQE}.
- **Objective Tests**
  - **Listening Quality:** For the score calculated by an objective model to predict the listening quality according to Recommendation P.862 and then transformed into MOS, the results are qualified as MOS - Listening Quality Objective or MOS_{LQO}.
  - **Conversational Quality:** For the score calculated by an objective model to predict the conversational quality according to Recommendation P.563 and then transformed into MOS, the results are qualified as MOS - Conversational Quality Objective or MOS_{CQO}.

The relation between different listening MOS qualifiers is depicted in Figure 8 where the related speech signal and the MOS from the subjective tests, PESQ and the E-model are related together.

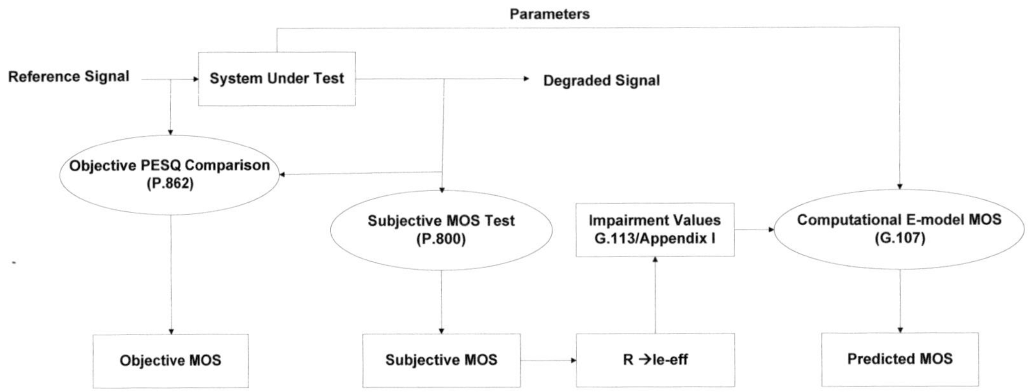

Fig. 8. Relationship between MOS qualifiers (ITU-T, 2006)

6. Conclusions and future work

Measuring the quality of VoIP is important for legal, commercial and technical reasons. This chapter presented the requirements for a successful VoIP quality assessment technology. The chapter also critically reviewed different VoIP quality assessment technologies. Sections 3 and 4 discussed subjective and objective speech quality measurement methods, respectively. In objective measurement methods both intrusive (section 4.1) and non-intrusive (section 4.2) methods were discussed.

Based on the requirements of measuring the speech quality non-intrusively and objectively, it can be concluded that objective and non-intrusive methods such as P.563 and the E-Model are the best methods for VoIP quality assessment. Still the accuracy of these methods can be improved to make their estimation of the quality as accurate as possible.

7. References

AL-Akhras, M. (2007). *Quality of Media Traffic over Lossy Internet Protocol Networks: Measurement and Improvement*, PhD thesis, Software Technology Research Laboratory (STRL), School of Computing, Faculty of Computing Sciences and Engineering, De Montfort University, U.K.
URL: *http://www.tech.dmu.ac.uk/STRL/research/theses/thesis/40-thesis-mousa-secure.pdf*

AL-Akhras, M. (2008). A genetic algorithm approach for voice quality prediction, *The 5th IEEE International Multi-Conference on Systems, Signals & Devices, 2008. IEEE SSD' 08, Amman, Jordan* pp. 1–6.

AL-Akhras, M. & el Hindi, K. (2009). Function approximation models for non-intrusive prediction of voip quality, *IADIS International Conference Informatics 2009, Algarve, Portugal* .

AL-Akhras, M., Zedan, H., John, R. & ALMomani, I. (2009). Non-intrusive speech quality prediction in voip networks using a neural network approach, *Neurocomputing* 72(10-12): 2595 – 2608. Lattice Computing and Natural Computing (JCIS 2007) / Neural Networks in Intelligent Systems Designn (ISDA 2007).

AL-Khawaldeh, R. (2010). *Ant colony optimization for voip quality optimization*, Master's thesis, Computer Information Systems Department, King Abdullah II School for Information Technology (KASIT), The University of Jordan, Jordan.

Allnatt, J. (1975). Subjective Rating and Apparent Magnitude, *International Journal Man -Machine Studies* 7: 801–816.

ALMomani, I. & AL-Akhras, M. (2008). Statistical speech quality prediction in voip networks, *The 2008 International Conference on Communications in Computing (CIC'8), Las Vigas* .

Borella, M., Swider, D., Uludag, S. & Brewster, G. (1998). Internet Packet Loss: Measurement and Implications for End-to-End QoS, *Architectural and OS Support for Multimedia Applications/Flexible Communication Systems/Wireless Networks and Mobile Computing: Proceedings of the 1998 ICPP Workshops on*, pp. 3–12.

Bos, L. & Leroy, S. (2001). Toward an All-IP-Based UMTS System Architecture, *IEEE Network* 15(1): 36–45.

Collins, D. (2003). *Carrier Grade Voice over IP*, 2nd edn, McGraw-Hill Companies.

Da Silva, A., Varela, M., de Souza e Silva, E., Rosa, L. & G.Rubino, G. (2008). Quality assessment of interaction voice applications, ***Computer Networks*** 52(6): 1179–1192.

Ding, L. & Goubran, R. (2003a). Assessment of Effects of Packet Loss on Speech Quality in VoIP, *Proceedings. of the 2nd IEEE Internatioal Workshop on Haptic, Audio and Visual Environments and their Applications, 2003. HAVE 2003*, pp. 49–54.

Ding, L. & Goubran, R. (2003b). Speech Quality Prediction in VoIP Using the Extended E-Model, *IEEE Global Telecommunications Conference, 2003. GLOBECOM '03.*, Vol. 7, pp. 3974–3978.

Duysburgh, B., Vanhastel, S., De Vreese, B., Petrisor, C. & Demeester, P. (2001). On the Influence of Best-Effort Network Conditions on the Perceived Speech Quality of VoIP Connections, *Proceedings. Tenth International Conference on Computer Communications and Networks, 2001.*, pp. 334–339.

Estepa, A., Estepa, R. & Vozmediano, J. (2002). On the Suitability of the E-Model to VoIP Networks, *Proceedings of Seventh International Symposium on Computers and Communications,2002. ISCC 2002.*, pp. 511–516.

ETSI (1996). ETSI Tech. Report (ETR) 250 - Speech Communication Quality from Mouth to Ear of 3.1 kHz Handset Telephony Across Networks, *Technical report*, European Telecommunications Standards Institute.

Fu, Q., Yi, K. & Sun, M. (2000). Speech Quality Objective Assessment Using Neural Network, *Proceedings of IEEE International Conference on Acoustics, Speech, and Signal Processing, 2000. ICASSP '00.*, Vol. 3, pp. 1511–1514.

Haojun, A., Xinchen, Z., Ruimin, H. & Weiping, T. (2004). A Wideband Speech Codecs Quality Measure Based on Bark Spectrum Distance, *Proceedings of 2004 International Symposium on Intelligent Signal Processing and Communication Systems, 2004. ISPACS 2004.*, pp. 155–158.

Heiman, F. (1998). A Wireless LAN Voice over IP Telephone System, *Northcon/98 Conference Proceedings*, pp. 52–54.

Itakura, F. (1975). Minimum prediction residual principle applied to speech recognition, *IEEE Transactions on Acoustics, Speech and Signal Processing* 23(1): 67 – 72.

Itakura, F. & Saito, S. (1978). Analysis synthesis telephony based on the maximum likelihood method, *Acoustics, Speech and Signal Processing* pp. C17–C20.

ITU-T (1996a). *Recommendation G.729 - Coding of Speech at 8 kbit/s Using Conjugate-Structure Algebraic-Code-Excited Linear-Prediction (CS-ACELP)*, International Telecommunication Union-Telecommunication Standardization Sector (ITU-T).

ITU-T (1996b). *Recommendation P.800 - Methods for Subjective Determination of*

Transmission Quality, International Telecommunication Union-Telecommunication Standardization Sector (ITU-T).

ITU-T (1998). *Recommendation P.861 - Objective Quality Measurement of Telephoneband (300-3400 Hz) Speech Codecs*, International Telecommunication Union-Telecommunication Standardization Sector (ITU-T).

ITU-T (1999). *Recommendation G.109 - Definition of Categories of Speech Transmission Quality*, International Telecommunication Union-Telecommunication Standardization Sector (ITU-T).

ITU-T (2000). *Recommendation G.107 - The E-model, a Computational Model for use in Transmission Planning*, International Telecommunication Union-Telecommunication Standardization Sector (ITU-T).

ITU-T (2001). *Recommendation P.862 - Perceptual Evaluation of Speech Quality (PESQ): An Objective Method for End-to-End Speech Quality Assessment of Narrow-Band Telephone Networks and Speech Codecs*, International Telecommunication Union-Telecommunication Standardization Sector (ITU-T).

ITU-T (2002). *Recommendation G.113 Appendix I - Provisional Planning Values for the Equipment Impairment Factor Ie and Packet-Loss Robustness Factor Bpl*, International Telecommunication Union-Telecommunication Standardization Sector (ITU-T).

ITU-T (2003a). *Recommendation G.114 - One-Way Transmission Time*, International Telecommunication Union-Telecommunication Standardization Sector (ITU-T).

ITU-T (2003b). *Recommendation G.114 Appendix II - Guidance on One-Way Delay for Voice over IP*, International Telecommunication Union-Telecommunication Standardization Sector (ITU-T).

ITU-T (2004). *Recommendation P.563 - Single-ended method for objective speech quality assessment in narrow-band telephony applications*, International Telecommunication Union-Telecommunication Standardization Sector (ITU-T).

ITU-T (2005a). *Recommendation G.107 - The E-model, a Computational Model for use in Transmission Planning*, International Telecommunication Union-Telecommunication Standardization Sector (ITU-T).

ITU-T (2005b). *Recommendation P.862.1-Mapping Function for Transforming P.862 Raw Result Scores to MOS-LQO*, International Telecommunication Union-Telecommunication Standardization Sector (ITU-T).

ITU-T (2005c). *Recommendation P.862.2-Wideband extension to recommendation P.862 for the assessment of wideband telephone networks and speech codecs*, International Telecommunication Union-Telecommunication Standardization Sector (ITU-T).

ITU-T (2006). *Recommendation P.800.1 - Mean Opinion Score (MOS) Terminology*, International Telecommunication Union-Telecommunication Standardization Sector (ITU-T).

ITU-T (2009). *Recommendation G.107 - The E-model, a Computational Model for use in Transmission Planning*, International Telecommunication Union-Telecommunication Standardization Sector (ITU-T).

Kim, D.-S. & Tarraf, A. (2006). Enhanced Perceptual Model for Non-Intrusive Speech Quality Assessment, *IEEE International Conference on Acoustics, Speech and Signal Processing, 2006. ICASSP 2006*, Vol. 1, pp. I–I.

Kitawaki, N., Nagabuchi, H. & Itoh, K. (1988). Objective quality evaluation for low-bit-rate speech coding systems, *IEEE Journal on Selected Areas in Communications* 6(2): 242–248.

Kondoz, A. M. (2004). *Digital Speech Coding for Low Bit Rate Communication Systems*, 2nd edn, John Wiley and Sons Ltd, New York, NY, USA.

Li, F. (2004). Speech Intelligibility of VoIP to PSTN Interworking - A Key Index for the QoS, *IEE Telecommunications Quality of Services: The Business of Success, 2004. QoS 2004.*, pp. 104–108.

Liang, Y., Steinbach, E. & Girod, B. (2001). Multi-stream Voice over IP Using Packet Path Diversity, *IEEE Fourth Workshop on Multimedia Signal Processing, 2001*, pp. 555–560.

Low, C. (1996). The Internet Telephony Red Herring, *IEEE Global Telecommunications Conference, 1996. GLOBECOM '96.*, pp. 72–80.

Mahdi and Picoviciv (2009). Advances in voice quality measurement in modern telecommunications, *Digital Signal Processing* 19: 79–103.

Markopoulou, A., Tobagi, F. & Karam, M. (2003). Assessing the Quality of Voice Communications over Internet Backbones, *IEEE/ACM Transactions on Networking* 11(5): 747–760.

Mase, K. (2004). Toward Scalable Admission Control for VoIP Networks, *IEEE Communications Magazine* 42(7): 42–47.

Miloslavski, A., Antonov, V., Yegoshin, L., Shkrabov, S., Boyle, J., Pogosyants, G. & Anisimov, N. (2001). Third-party Call Control in VoIP Networks for Call Center Applications, *2001 IEEE Intelligent Network Workshop*, pp. 161–167.

Mohamed, S., Rubino, G. & Varela, M. (2004). Performance Evaluation of Real-Time Speech Through a Packet Network: A Random Neural Networks-Based Approach, *Performance Evaluation* 57(2): 141–161.

Moon, Y., Leung, C., Yuen, K., Ho, H. & Yu, X. (2000). A CRM Model Based on Voice over IP, *2000 Canadian Conference on Electrical and Computer Engineering*, Vol. 1, pp. 464–468.

Narbutt, M. & Murphy, L. (2004). Improving Voice over IP Subjective Call Quality, *IEEE Communications Letters* 8(5): 308–310.

Ortiz, S., J. (2004). Internet Telephony Jumps off the Wires, *Computer* 37(12): 16–19.

Picovici, D. & Mahdi, A. (2004). New Output-based Perceptual Measure for Predicting Subjective Quality of Speech, *Proceedings IEEE International Conference on Acoustics, Speech, and Signal Processing, 2004. (ICASSP '04)*, Vol. 5, pp. V–633–6.

Quackenbush, S., Barnawell, T. & Clements, M. (1988). *Objective Measures of Speech Quality*, Prentice Hall, Englewood Cliffs, NJ.

Raja, A., Azad, R. M. A., Flanagan, C., Picovici, D. & Ryan, C. (2006). Non-Intrusive Quality Evaluation of VoIP Using Genetic Programming, *1st Bio-Inspired Models of Network, Information and Computing Systems, 2006.*, pp. 1–8.

Raja, A. & Flanagan, C. (2008). *Genetic Programming*, chapter Real-Time, Non-intrusive Speech Quality Estimation: A Signal-Based Model, pp. 37–48.

Rix, A., Beerends, J., Hollier, M. & Hekstra, A. (2001). Perceptual Evaluation of Speech Quality (PESQ)-A New Method for Speech Quality Assessment of Telephone Networks and Codecs, *Proceedings. IEEE International Conference on Acoustics, Speech, and Signal Processing, 2001. (ICASSP '01)*, Vol. 2, pp. 749–752.

Rohani, B. & Zepernick, H.-J. (2005). An Efficient Method for Perceptual Evaluation of Speech Quality in UMTS, *Proceedings Systems Communications, 2005.*, pp. 185–190.

Rosenberg, J., Lennox, J. & Schulzrinne, H. (1999). Programming Internet Telephony Services, *IEEE Network* 13(3): 42–49.

Schulzrinne, H. & Rosenberg, J. (1999). The IETF Internet Telephony Architecture and Protocols, *IEEE Network* 13(3): 18–23.

Spanias, A. (1994). Speech Coding: A Tutorial Review, *Proceedings of the IEEE* 82(10): 1541–1582.

Sun, L. (2004). *Speech Quality Prediction for Voice over Internet Protocol Networks*, PhD thesis, School of Computing, Communications and Electronics, University of Plymouth, U.K.

Sun, L. & Ifeachor, E. (2002). Perceived Speech Quality Prediction for Voice over IP-Based Networks, *IEEE International Conference on Communications, 2002. ICC 2002.*, Vol. 4, pp. 2573–2577.

Sun, L. & Ifeachor, E. (2003). Prediction of Perceived Conversational Speech Quality and Effects of Playout Buffer Algorithms, *IEEE International Conference on Communications, 2003. ICC '03.*, Vol. 1, pp. 1–6.

Sun, L. & Ifeachor, E. (2004). New Models for Perceived Voice Quality Prediction and their Applications in Playout Buffer Optimization for VoIP Networks, *IEEE International Conference on Communications, 2004*, Vol. 3, pp. 1478–1483.

Sun, L. & Ifeachor, E. (2006). Voice Quality Prediction Models and their Application in VoIP Networks, *IEEE Transactions on Multimedia* 8(4): 809–820.

Takahashi, A. (2004). Opinion Model for Estimating Conversational Quality of VoIP, *IEEE International Conference on Acoustics, Speech, and Signal Processing, 2004. Proceedings. (ICASSP '04).*, Vol. 3, pp. iii–1072–5.

Takahashi, A., Yoshino, H. & Kitawaki, N. (2004). Perceptual QoS Assessment Technologies for VoIP, *IEEE Communications Magazine* 42(7): 28–34.

Tseng, K.-K., Lai, Y.-C. & Lin, Y.-D. (2004). Perceptual Codec and Interaction Aware Playout Algorithms and Quality Measurement for VoIP Systems, *IEEE Transactions on Consumer Electronics* 50(1): 297–305.

Tseng, K.-K. & Lin, Y.-D. (2003). User Perceived Codec and Duplex Aware Playout Algorithms and LMOS-DMOS Measurement for Real Time Streams, *International Conference on Communication Technology Proceedings, 2003. ICCT 2003.*, Vol. 2, pp. 1666–1669.

Voran, S. (1999a). Objective Estimation of Perceived Speech Quality-Part I: Development of the Measuring Normalizing Block Technique, *IEEE Transactions on Speech and Audio Processing* 7(4): 371–382.

Voran, S. (1999b). Objective Estimation of Perceived Speech Quality-Part II: Evaluation of the Measuring Normalizing Block Technique, *IEEE Transactions on Speech and Audio Processing* 7(4): 383–390.

Zurek, E., Leffew, J. & Moreno, W. (2002). Objective Evaluation of Voice Clarity Measurements for VoIP Compression Algorithms, *Proceedings of the Fourth IEEE International Caracas Conference on Devices, Circuits and Systems, 2002.*, pp. T033–1–T033–6.

2

Assessment of Speech Quality in VoIP

Zdenek Becvar, Lukas Novak and Michal Vondra
Czech Technical University in Prague, Faculty of Electrical Engineering
Czech Republic

1. Introduction

In VoIP (Voice over Internet Protocol), the voice is transmitted over the IP networks in the form of packets. This way of voice transmission is highly cost effective since the communication circuit need not to be permanently dedicated for one connection; however, the communication band is shared by several connections. On the other hand, the utilization of IP networks causes some drawbacks that can result to the drop of the Quality of Service (QoS). The QoS is defined by ITU-T E.800 recommendation (ITU-T E.800, 1994) as a group of characteristics of a telecommunication service which are related to the ability to satisfy assumed requirements of end users. The overall QoS of the telecommunication chain (denoted as end-to-end QoS) depends on contributions of all individual parts of the telecommunication chain including users, end devices, access networks, and core network. Each part of the chain can introduce some effects which lead to the degradation of overall speech quality. Lower speech quality causes user's dissatisfaction and consequently shorter duration of calls (Holub et al., 2004) which reduces profit of telecommunication operators. Therefore, both sides (users as well as operators or providers) are discontented.

The end device decreases speech quality by coding and/or compression of the speech signal. The speech quality can be also influenced by a distortion of the speech by its processing in the end device e.g. in the manner of filtering. It can lead to the saturation of the speech, insertion of a noise, etc. The processed speech is carried in packets via routers in the networks. Individual packets are routed to the destination as conventional data packets. Therefore, the packets can be delayed or lost. According to ITU-T G.114 recommendation (ITU-T G.114, 2003), the delay of speech should be lower than 150 ms to ensure high quality of the speech. Each packet is routed independently; therefore the delay of packets can vary in time. The variation of packet delay is usually denoted jitter.

The impact of all above mentioned effects on the speech quality can be evaluated either by subjective or objective tests. The first group, subjective tests, uses real assessments of the speeches by users. Therefore it cannot be performed in real-time. The second set of tests, objective tests, tries to estimate the speech quality by speech processing and evaluation.

The rest of chapter is organized as follows. The next section gives an overview on the related work in the field of VoIP speech quality. The third one describes basic principles of the speech quality assessment. The speech processing for all performed tests are described in section four. Section five presents the results of realized assessments of the speech quality. Last section sums up the chapter and provides major conclusions.

2. Related works

Voice packets transmitted over the IP network may be lost or delayed. In non-real-time applications, packet loss is solved by appropriate control protocol, e.g., Transfer Control Protocol (TCP) by retransmission. This solution is not suitable for voice transmission since it increase the delay of voice packets (Linden, 2004).

Clear advantage of VoIP is the ability to use wideband codecs. However, higher transmission bandwidth results in high sampling frequency and escalates requirements on hardware components. Bandwidth of roughly 10 kHz is sufficient for sampling a speech signal. Nevertheless, 8 kHz bandwidth (16 kHz sampling frequency) is the best trade-off between bit rate and speech quality (Benesty et al., 2008). The extension of the bandwidth improves the intelligibility of fricative sounds such as *'s'* and *'f'* which are very difficult to distinguishing in conventional narrowband telephony applications (Benesty et al., 2008).

The impact of random packet losses for different packet sizes on the speech quality is evaluated in (Ding & Goubran, 2003). The results show that MOS (Mean Opinion Score) decreases more rapidly if larger packet size is used. These results are confirmed also in (Oouchi et al., 2002). The paper (Oouchi et al., 2002) presents the negative dependence between packet loss ratio and the speech quality. Moreover, the authors performed speech quality tests to show that the tolerance to packet losses is getting lower with higher duration of packets. In this chapter, we compare not only the speech quality over the length of lost packet as in previous paper, but also, the impact of losses in narrowband speeches is compared with wideband.

In real networks, bursts of packets are lost more frequently than single packets, due to effects such as network overload or router queuing (Ulseth & Stafsnes, 2006). The paper (Clark, 2002) presents a review of the effect of burst packet loss compared with random packet loss. The results are similar for small packet loss ratio (approximately up to 3 %). However, the quality of the burst packet loss is decreasing more significantly than in case of the random packet loss for higher packet loss ratio. In this chapter, we additionally consider two different bandwidths of speech, i.e., 3.1 kHz and 7 kHz.

Packet losses can be eliminated by using Packet Loss Concealment (PLC) algorithms. These algorithms can replace missing part of the speech signal and make a smooth transition between the previous decoded speech and lost segments. Several PLC algorithms is described, e.g., in (Kondo & Nakagawa, 2006); (Tosun & Kabal, 2005). The PLC algorithms are based on various methods, each of them more or less suitable for specific use. All PLC algorithms work with the frequency characteristic of speech. Therefore, one of the criterions for the right choice of the proper PLC algorithm can be its frequency characteristic since each frequency band is perceived individually by human ear (Fastl & Zwicker, 1999); (Robinson & Hawksford, 2000). In this chapter, influence of the harmonic distortion on the speech quality is analyzed. Harmonic distortion cause unequal transfer of all frequency components. With the knowledge of this influence, the suitable frequency characteristic of PLC method can be chosen. The harmonic distortion analysis is based on the Mel-cepstrum (Molau et al., 2001) as it follows the psychoacoustic model of human sound perception.

In general speech quality assessment, the random placement of packet losses is assumed (Ulseth & Stafsnes, 2006). Nevertheless, the placement of the packet loss can significantly influence the final speech quality evaluation since each phonetic element can have different significance for the voice intelligibility. For example, speech sound carrying high energy (e.g., voiced sound) is more important than the low energy one (e.g., unvoiced sound) (Sing &

Chang, 2009); (Bachu et al., 2010). The knowledge of an impact of losses of individual phonetic elements can be exploited in design of codecs or for speech synthesis. In the paper (Sun et al., 2001), the authors proofs the more noticeable impact of losses placed in the voiced sounds than unvoiced sounds on the speech quality. All phonetic elements are classified into voiced and unvoiced without any further division. In this chapter, we consider further classification on smaller groups of phonetic elements. Moreover, the subjective listening tests are performed.

3. Speech quality assessment in VoIP

Speech quality can be measured and rated either by using by R-factor or by MOS scale (ITU-T P.800.1, 2003). The R-factor is based on E-model (ITU-T G.107, 2005). Its range is from 0 to 100. The R-factor represents level of user's satisfaction with the speech. The expression of user's satisfaction related to the R-factor is presented in Table 1.

R-factor	Quality	Users' satisfaction
90 - 100	Best	Very satisfied
80 - 89	High	Satisfied
70 - 79	Medium	Some users dissatisfied
60 - 69	Low	Many users dissatisfied
50 - 59	Poor	Nearly all users dissatisfied

Table 1. Users' satisfaction with the speech quality according to R-factor.

The parameter MOS is an average value from given range, which is used for assessment of the speech quality by subjects (persons). It is in the range from 1 to 5 (see Table 2). Both subjective and objective methods give their outputs in specific MOS scale; nevertheless it is possible to convert them. The scales for objective and subjective listening tests are denoted MOS-LQO (MOS-Listening Quality Objective) and MOS-LQS (MOS-Listening Quality Subjective) respectively. Another type of MOS, MOS-LQE (MOS-Listening Quality Estimated) is derived from R-factor.

MOS	Quality
5	Excellent
4	Good
3	Fair
2	Poor
1	Bad

Table 2. Speech quality expressed by MOS scale.

In this chapter, the MOS scale is considered since it is largely used in praxis.
The speech quality can be assessed either by a subjective or by an objective test. The practical utilization of both types is related to their principle.

3.1 Subjective tests

The first group of test is subjective speech quality assessment. This test uses statistical evaluation of assessments of the several speeches by real persons. To obtain valid and precise results, several requirements and parameters must be fulfilled. These requirements for subjective tests are defined by ITU-T recommendations P.800 (ITU-T P.800, 1996) and P.830 (ITU-T P.830, 1996). The documents define procedures of selecting speakers for recording of source speeches, methods for recording and preparing of input samples, required quantities and formats of speeches, parameters of testing environment and methods for selection and guidance of test attendants. The content of individual phases of the experiment and the content of the speeches are not defined.

Two types of subjective tests can be performed: conversational and listening. The conversational tests are executed in laboratory environment. Two tested objects (persons) are placed in the separated sound proof rooms with suppressed noise. Both persons are performing phone call and assessing its quality.

The requirements on the listening tests are not too high as on conversational test. The process of listening speech quality assessment is as follows. First, the speeches are transmitted over telecommunication chain. Then, the tested objects listening several speeches and assess it according to MOS-LQS. The final value of MOS is calculated as an average over all tested objects and all speeches obtained under the same conditions.

In all of our subjective and objective tests, every individual speech is modified in MATLAB software to obtain specific degradation of the speech. The speech processing is applied to be inline with conventional degradation of the speech in the common telecommunication equipments. More details on the speech processing are described in section four of this chapter.

3.2 Objective tests

The realization of the subjective test is very time consuming. Therefore, the objective tests are defined for speech quality measurement. These tests are based on substitution of the subjective tests by appropriate mathematical models or algorithms. The objective tests can be divided on intrusive and non-intrusive. The intrusive one uses two speeches for determination of final speech quality. The first speech is original non-degraded speech and the second one is the same speech degraded by transmission over the telecommunication chain. It enables to obtain more precise results, however this method cannot be used for real-time speech quality measurement. On the other hand, non-intrusive methods do not require the original source speech, since the evaluation of speech quality is based only on the degraded speech signal processing. Hence, the non-intrusive methods are suitable for real-time monitoring of speech quality. The non-intrusive methods are standardized by series of recommendations ITU-T P.56x such as ITU-T P.561 recommendation known as INMD (In-service Non-intrusive Measurement Device), its enhancement ITU-T P.562, or ITU-T P.563 denoted as 3SQM (Single Sided Speech Quality Measurement) which contains all procedures defined by ITU-T P.561 and ITU-T P.562 and additionally, it considers several new aspects such as additional noise, distortion, or time alignment.

One of the first largely expanded intrusive methods was PSQM (Perceptual Speech Quality Measurement) defined by recommendation ITU-T P.861. This recommendation was replaced by another one, labeled ITU-T P.862, in 2001 since the former one cannot evaluate some effects such as jitter, short losses, signal distortion, or impact of low speed codecs in compliance with human perception. The latter recommendation is generally denoted PESQ (Perceptual Evaluation of Speech Quality) (ITU-T P.862, 2001). The PESQ is one of the most widely used objective methods developed for end-to-end speech quality assessment in a conversational voice communication.

The principle of PESQ is depicted in Fig. 1. The PESQ method is based on the comparison of original (non-degraded) signal *X(t)* with degraded signal *Y(t)*. The signal *Y(t)* is result of a transmission of the signal *X(t)* through a communication system. The PESQ method generates a prediction of the quality which would be given to the signal *Y(t)* in subjective listening test.

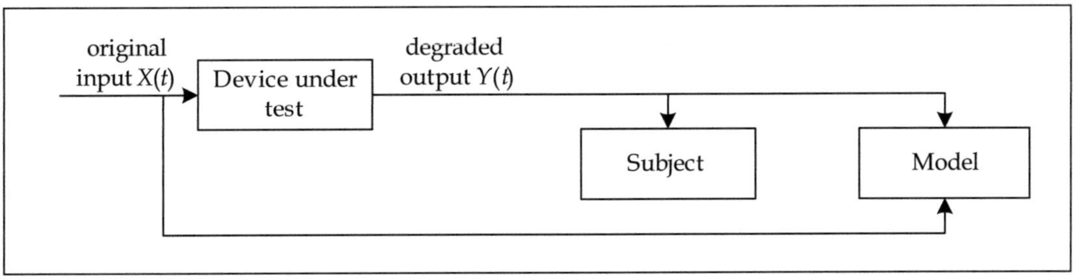

Fig. 1. Principle of PESQ method for speech quality assessment.

The range of the PESQ MOS score (according to ITU-T P.862) is between -0.5 and 4.5. Since this range does not match to a scale used for the subjective test, the ITU-T P.862.1 recommendation (ITU-T P.862.1, 2003) enables to recalculate the PESQ MOS to better comport the results of subjective listening test. The range of converted value is from 1 to 4.55. The recalculation is defined by the next formula:

$$y = 0.999 + \frac{4.999 - 0.999}{1 + e^{-1.4945 \times x + 4.6607}} \tag{1}$$

where x is an objective PESQ MOS score and y is a matching ITU-T P.862.1 MOS score.
The ITU-T P.862 recommendation describes all requirements on the tested speeches (e.g. character of speech signals, duration of speech, etc.). Frequency characteristics of the speech signal and signal level alignment must be in accordance with recommendation ITU-T P.830.

4. Speech processing for speech quality assessment

The speeches used for subjective and objective tests are original digital studio recordings, obtained by separation from dialogs of two people. Their content does not imply any emotional response at the listeners. All recordings are in Czech language spoken by natural born Czech speakers without speech aberrations.
The length of utterances is selected to fulfil the requirements of both types of tests. Therefore it is between 8 an 12 s. Tested signals is coded by 16-bit linear PCM (Pulse Code Modulation) sampled with 8 kHz or 16 kHz sample rate (down sampled from the original studio quality recordings sampled with 48 kHz).
Speeches are modified in MATLAB in line with speech processing in conventional telecommunication chain. Furthermore, the analysed phenomenons, such as distortion or packet losses are also incorporated in MATLAB.
Three individual cases are analysed: i) comparison of the impact of individual and consecutive packet losses of conventional telecommunication frequency bandwidth (3.1 kHz) with wideband systems (7 kHz); ii) analysis on the impact of harmonic distortion; iii) impact of the losses of individual phonetic elements on the speech quality.

4.1 Speech processing for losses of packets for narrow and wideband channels

Forty speeches are used for the analysis of the impact of bandwidth and packets length on speech quality. Each of the speeches is encoded using PCM. The speeches sampled with 8 kHz frequency are filtered according to recommendation ITU-T G.711 with bandwidth of 3.1 kHz (from 300 Hz to 3400 Hz) (ITU-T G.711, 1988). The speeches sampled with frequency 16 kHz (ITU-T G.711.1, 2008) are filtered according to recommendation ITU-T G.711.1 with bandwidth of 7 kHz.

At the beginning, the analyzed speech is split into sections with the same length. The individual sections can be understood in terms of packet that will be transmitted through a network. The length of all packets is chosen, in each round of analysis, to be equal to the following values: 10, 20, 30, or 40 ms. These lengths are the most frequently used in practice for the transmission and the evaluation (Hassan & Alekseevich, 2006). The lengths of packets correspond to 80, 160, 240, or 320 samples per packet for the speeches sampled with 8 kHz and 160, 320, 480, or 640 samples for the speeches sampled with 16 kHz.

After the division of certain analyzed speech to packets, random vector $V_L=\{v_{L1}, v_{L2}, ..., v_{LR}\}$ is generated. The number of elements in the vector (R) corresponds to the number of packets, to which the speech is divided. The random vector V_L contains random numbers in the range from 0 to 1 generated with uniform distribution. The number of vector elements does not depend only on the length of the speech, but depends also on the length of individual packets.

The packet losses are randomly determined and the number of lost packets is calculated according to the Packet Loss Ratio (PLR) and the total number of packets in the speech. The original random vector V_L is consequently recalculated to vector of packet losses ($V_{PL}=\{v_{PL1}, v_{PL2}, ..., v_{PLR}\}$) according to subsequent formula:

$$\begin{aligned} v_{PLr} &= 1 \qquad \forall v_{Lr} \geq T_0,\ \ 0 < r < R \\ v_{PLr} &= 0 \qquad \forall v_{Lr} < T_0,\ \ 0 < r < R \end{aligned} \tag{2}$$

where T_0 is the threshold for setting up the element to zero. The threshold is determined according to the required PLR. The vector V_{PL} contains only numbers "one" and "zero", where zeros represent the losses.

The final speech is a product of multiplication of the modified vector V_{PL} and the relevant speech split into R packets. Packets, which are multiplied by zero corresponds to the lost parts, and packets multiplied by the number one remained unchanged.

The total duration of lost packets is the same for all speeches with the same PLR, regardless of the amount of packets contained in a speech (R). For example, if the speech is divided into packets with 10 ms length, the number of these packets is twice the number of packets created in case of the packets with 20 ms length.

Random vector v_L is generated twenty times for each value of PLR, each sections length, and for each of the speeches. Repetition of generation of the random vector limits negative effects of random drop of losses, which could affect results.

The random losses of packets, described above, are characterized by random appearance in time. Beside this, the consecutive losses frequently occur in real networks. For example, during the short outage in communication e.g. during overload of a node, the loss of only one packet is not very likely to happen. More probable is the loss of several packets. Therefore, the consecutive packet loss can be expressed as a loss of sequence of subsequent packets.

Speech processing of consecutive packet losses is similar to the generation of the individual losses, with slight modification to follow the effect of losing packets in groups. Randomly generated vector V_L is thus shortened to the length r. The length r of the new reduced vector $V_R = \{v_{R1}, v_{R2}, ..., v_{Rr}\}$ is calculated according to the next formula:

$$r = R - \left(P \cdot \left(n_{CP} - 1\right)\right) \tag{3}$$

where R is the number of packets in the whole speech; n_{CP} is the amount of packets in the consecutive loss; and P represents the number of elements in the reduced vector that will be set to zero. The P can be determined by the following equation:

$$P = \frac{PLR \cdot r}{n_{CP}} \tag{4}$$

In all cases, the speech quality assessments are performed for up to twenty consecutive lost packets due to the limitation by the length of speeches according to the ITU-T P.862 recommendation. The considered PLR for this test is 10 %. The shortest of the analyzed speeches has length of 8 s. For the packets with duration of 40 ms in groups of twenty packets, it gives the overall duration of the 800 ms. It is 10 % of the speech with duration of 8 s. Hence, the higher length of consecutively lost packet cannot be accommodated into these speeches.

To eliminate the random factor of position of consecutive packet loss, twenty repetitions for each of the speeches and for each of the length of group of consecutive packet loss are performed, as in the case of the random individual packet losses to suppress the affection of results by effect of placement of losses into different parts of speeches.

4.2 Speech processing for investigation of harmonic distortion

Individual frequency bands of speech are suppressed for the analysis of harmonic distortion influence i.e. all speech components with frequencies of that band. For our analysis, the narrowband telecommunication channel (300 – 3400 Hz) is separated to four sub-bands. Lower count of frequency bands would give less information on individual frequency influence and higher count would distort the speech too little as it would be undistinguishable from the original non-distorted speech. Another parameter which has to be set is the choice of corner frequencies of these bands. One possibility is to take them linearly according to the telecommunication channel band and the other one is to choose corner frequencies nonlinearly with unequal bandwidth of each band. An ear perceives each frequency differently, which means that if the frequency of perceiving tone will increase linearly, the listener will subjectively sense only logarithmic increase. Relating to this fact, the corner frequencies are chosen with geometrical interval. Mel-frequency (*mel*) band for the calculation of corner frequencies is defined by the subsequent equation:

$$mel = 2595 \cdot \log\left(1 + \frac{f}{700}\right) \tag{5}$$

The communication band is divided into four Mel-frequency bands with equal wide. The resulting Mel-frequencies are presented in Table 3. Note that the lowest band (band 1) is extended to 50 Hz.

Band	1	2	3	4	
Mel [mel]	402	800	1197	1595	1992
Frequency f [Hz]	300	723	1325	2181	3400
Designed f_c [Hz]	50	723	1325	2181	3400

Table 3. Frequency bands used for harmonic distortion.

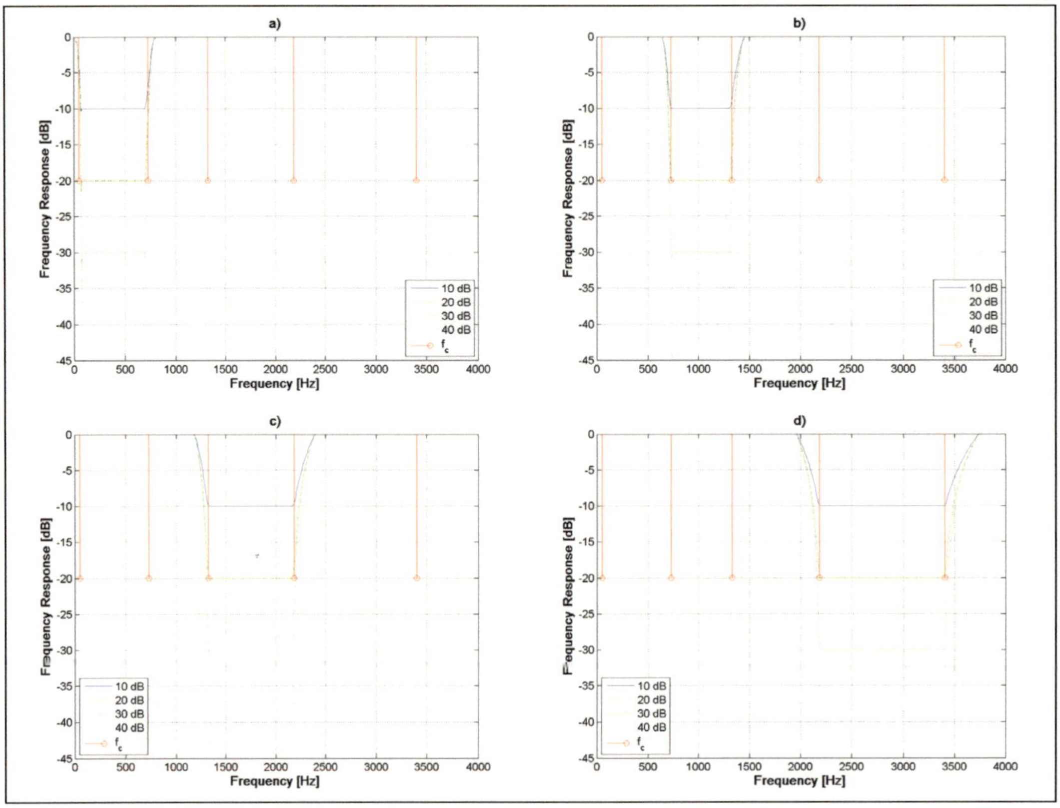

Fig. 2. Frequency responses of band stop filter for all four levels of suppression and four Mel-bands a) band 1; b) band 2; c) band 3; d) band 4.

Band stop filters designed in MATLAB by Yulewalk method (Friedlander & Porat, 1984) is used for filtering of speeches. The Yulewalk method designs recursive IIR (Infinite Impulse Response) digital filters by fitting a specified frequency response. Each band is suppressed in four levels: 10, 20, 30, and 40 dB. Frequency responses of band stop filters for all four bands and suppression levels are shown in Fig. 2.

4.3 Speech processing for losses of individual phonetic elements

Following approach is considered for the analysis of the relevance of individual group of phonetic elements on the speech quality. The algorithm for generation of packet losses with exact ratio is modified to place the lost packet only to the specific location of the particular phonetic elements. It requires the phonetic transcription of the speech and subsequent exact definition of the first and the last samples of each phonetic element. Since no reliable automatic algorithm is available, it was done manually. The speech is transcript to CTU IPA (Hanzl & Pollak, 2002) which is well transparent and optimized for processing by computer. All individual speech sounds of the speech are considered as analyzed phonetic elements. All phonetic elements are classified according its lexical meaning into four groups: i) vowels & diphthongs; ii) nasal & liquids; iii) plosives & affricates; iv) fricatives. The vowels and diphthongs are always voiced sounds, therefore they carry higher energy. Also the nasals and liquids are predominantly voiced with higher energy level. The plosives and affricates as well as fricatives contain either voiced or unvoiced consonants, which have the same mechanism of its origination in voice organs. The classification of the speech sounds into groups is presented in Table 4.

Group	Speech sounds
Vowels & diphthongs	‘a‘,‘á‘,‘e‘,‘é‘,‘i‘,‘í‘,‘y‘,‘ý‘,‘o‘,‘ó‘,‘u‘,‘ú‘,‘au‘,‘eu‘,‘ou‘
Nasal & liquids	‘m‘,‘n‘,‘ň‘,‘r‘,‘l‘
Plosives & affricates	‘p‘,‘b‘,‘t‘,‘ť‘,‘d‘,‘ď‘,‘k‘,‘g‘,‘c‘,‘č‘,‘dž‘,‘dz‘
Fricatives	‘f‘,‘v‘,‘s‘,‘z‘,‘ř‘,‘Ř‘,‘š‘,‘ž‘,‘j‘,‘ch‘,‘h‘

Table 4. Classification of the speech sounds into groups for speech quality assessment purposes.

For the speech processing in MATLAB, we assume 10 ms packet length; it corresponds to 80 samples per packet. The speech is furthermore processed in the following way.
First, the amount of packets contained only in speech sounds of investigated group of phonetic elements is determined (denoted R). Then, the coefficient K, which expresses the ratio of all packets in the speech (denoted T) to the amount on packets in the specific phonetic elements, is derived as follows: $K=T/R$. Subsequently, the coefficient K is recalculated to the new one (denoted H), which corresponds to the loss ratio only among selected group of phonetic elements; $H=K*PLR$, where PLR is a packet loss ratio related to the overall speech. The coefficient H expresses the probability of loss of each packet in investigated group of phonetic elements. Next, the vector of losses $V_g=\{v_{g1}, v_{g2}, ..., v_{gR}\}$ is randomly generated according to the coefficient H. The length of V_g is equal to R and each element of V_g represent whether the packet belonging to an element of a selected group will be lost or not. Furthermore, the new vector $V_s=\{v_{s1}, v_{s2},...,v_{sT}\}$ is created from vector V_g by filling up vector V_g to the length of complete speech T by insertion of "no loss" labels to the position of phonetics elements not belonging to the group of investigated phonetic elements. At the end, the packets labeled as "lost" are replaced by zeros (silence).

5. Results of speech quality assessment

As mentioned in previous section, three types of speech modification are investigated. This section provides the results of all performed tests.

5.1 Impact of losses of packets for narrow and wideband channels

Since the PESQ is not designed to evaluate the wideband speeches, the recalculation of output of conventional ITU-T P.862 PESQ according to the subsequent equation is required (Barriac et al., 2004):

$$y = 1 + \frac{4}{1 + e^{-2x+6}} \tag{6}$$

The results of objective tests for five packet lengths and two bandwidths are presented in Fig. 3. While maintaining all speech packets (no packets are lost), the speech quality reach the maximum. Of course this maximum is independent on the packet length. By increasing the *PLR* the significant speech quality degradation can be observed from Fig. 3.
The comparison of speeches with 3.1 kHz bandwidth and speeches with 7 kHz bandwidth show a higher rating of speech with lower frequency bandwidth (3.1 kHz) for $PLR \geq 4$ %. On the other hand, the speeches with bandwidth of 7 kHz achieve higher score than speeches with 3.1 kHz bandwidth (by approximately 0.3 MOS) for $PLR < 4$ %. For PLR > 4%, the difference between both frequency bandwidths grows with *PLR* up to $PLR = 12$ % (for packet length 10 ms), where speech quality for both bandwidths differs the most. The maximum gap between results for both bandwidths is approximately up to 0.8 MOS. With further increase of the PLR, both bandwidths perform in closer way. The impact of bandwidth is also decreasing with higher duration of packets. For packet duration of 40 ms, the maximum difference between both bandwidths is up to 0.6 MOS. Only the results of objective test are presented in this section since the results of subjective one are included in (Becvar et al., 2008).
Based on the results of objective as well as subjective tests, the consideration of wideband codecs is profitable only for systems with very low PLR (up to 4%).
Fig. 3 also shows that the same *PLR* imply lower degradation of speech divided in shorter sections although the total ratio of lost part of the speech is always the same. Thus the separation of the speech into packets with 40 ms length results in a higher impairment than splitting the speech into 10, 20, or 30 ms segments. The largest divergence (comparing 10 and 40 ms packet lengths) in the speech quality rating over the packet length is at $PLR = 4$ % for speeches with bandwidth 7 kHz. This discrepancy is roughly 1.4 MOS. The largest difference for speeches with bandwidth 3.1 kHz is at $PLR = 8$ %, it is approximately 1.2 MOS). This analysis clearly shows that it is profitable to utilize shorter speech packets.
The evaluation of the quality of speech influenced by consecutive packet losses is performed under the same conditions as the tests of individual packet losses.

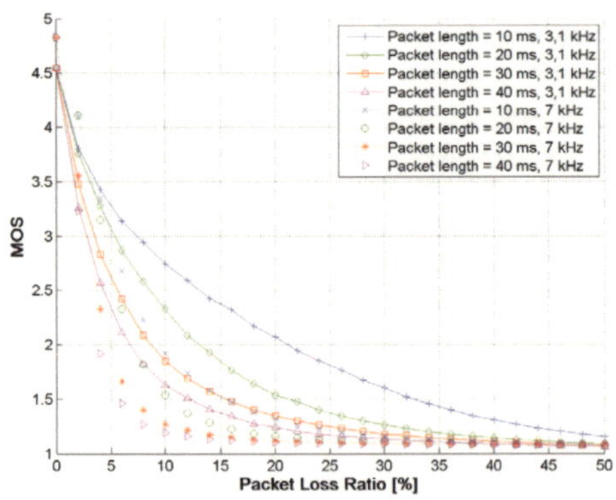

Fig. 3. Objective assessment of the different frequency bandwidth and lengths of packets over packet loss ratio.

The results plotted in Fig. 4 show the impact of the length of consecutive packet losses on the speech quality for objective assessment by PESQ method for 10 % *PLR*. Several lengths of packets are considered for analysis.

The longer duration of consecutive losses firstly lower the speech quality from approximately 2.7 MOS for 10 ms packet length and 3.1 kHz bandwidth. Then, the speech quality gradually increases with length of consecutive packet losses to 600 ms, where the MOS rating is again approximately 2.7 MOS. Further increase of the consecutive packet loss leads to only insignificant speech quality improvement. This effect is not noticeable for packet length over 40 ms, where the MOS score is continuously rising over the length of consecutive loss. From Fig. 4 can be determined the minimum amount of consecutive packet losses to obtain higher speech quality than in case of individual losses. This limit is sixty, ten and, three losses for packets with length of 10, 20, and 30 ms respectively for 3.1 kHz channel. The situation for 7 kHz channel is the same, however the final speech quality is lower (between 0.2 and 0.8 MOS) than the quality of 3.1 kHz.

Note that the PLR is equal to 10 %for all lengths of packets.

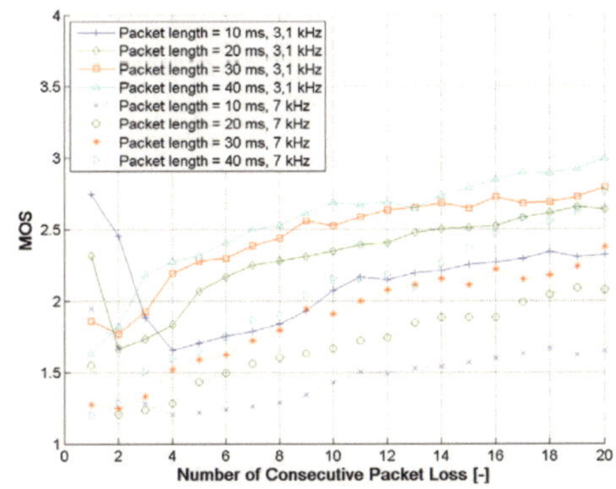

Fig. 4. Objective assessment of the impact of consecutive packet losses.

From Fig. 4 can be further seen that the lowest value of the objective speech quality is achieved for the overall duration of consecutive losses of 40 ms duration. This is achieved at four, two, or one consecutively lost packets with length of 10, 20, and 40 ms respectively.

The results also show that the same summarized duration of lost parts of speech are almost identical and independent on the length of individual packets. For example, MOS score for the loss of sections with 40 ms length is the same like for consecutive loss of bursts of two packets with 20 ms length or loss of bursts of four packets of 10 ms length. This fact is more noticeable in Fig. 5. This figure presents the impact of individual packet lengths over the overall length of consecutive losses. The results presented in Fig. 4 are converted into Fig. 5 with the new scale on x-axis by recalculation of x-axis according to the subsequent formula:

$$D_{total} = n_{CP} \cdot d \tag{7}$$

where d represents the length of packets.

The results presented in Fig. 5 depict that the worst rating is achieved for packet losses (either consecutive or individual) with overall duration of 40 ms. Hence, the division of packets to 40 ms length is not appropriate from the point of view of the individual losses.

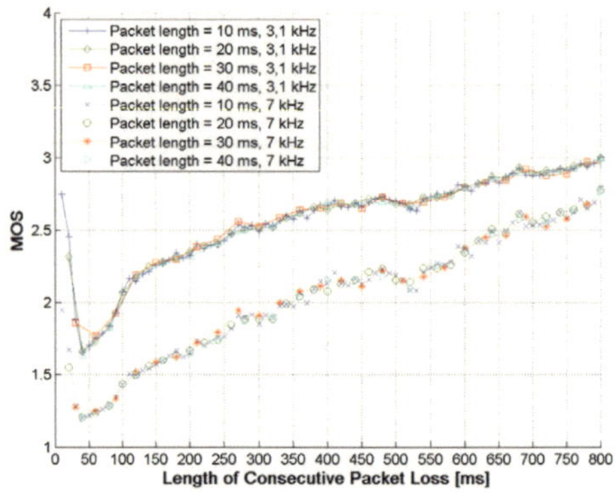

Fig. 5. The converted results of the objective tests of consecutive packet losses.

5.2 Impact of harmonic distortion

The subjective as well as the objective tests are considered for the evaluation of the impact of harmonic distortion. The subjective tests are prepared in accordance with ITU-T P.800 and ITU-T P.830 recommendations. Five different speeches for four bands and four suppression levels are processed for each distortion. It leads to 80 speeches (5 speeches * 4 bands * 4 levels) in total. Therefore, the overall duration of the subjective listening test is approximately 20 minutes per a listener.

Overall, 26 listeners participates on the subjective listening test. Software Tester (Brada, 2006) developed at Czech technical University in Prague is used for the listening test. The listeners participated on the subjective testing have been selected from students and employees of the university with respect to above mentioned recommendations.

The results are presented in Fig. 6 for the subjective tests and Fig. 7 for objective tests over four suppression levels (10, 20, 30 and 40 dB) in four bands.

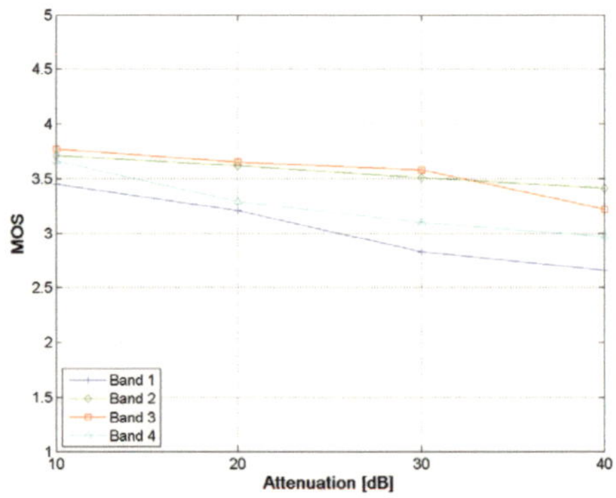

Fig. 6. Subjective assessment of the harmonic distortion.

The results show that the biggest influence at the reception quality of speech is obtained by the components contained in the first band (50 - 723 Hz). This phenomenon is caused by higher energy carried by lower frequency components in comparison with lower energy of higher frequency components. Therefore, the suppression of low frequencies causes

significant decrease in the speech quality. Only slightly lower impact is caused by the frequency components contained in the fourth frequency band (2181 - 3800 Hz). The lowest degradation of the speech quality is noticeable in the second and in the third bands (723 - 1325 Hz and 1325 - 2181 Hz). In all cases, the higher attenuation of the signal in individual bands leads to the decrease of the speech quality.
While the objective method PESQ is used for the speech quality assessment (see Fig. 7), only minor differences in the quality can be noticed for all four bands. The suppression of all bands has the similar impact on the speech quality according to PESQ. Also the impact of the level of attenuation is negligible since the drop of the speech quality is only between 0.25 and 0.5 MOS for all bands while attenuation varies between 10 to 40 dB.

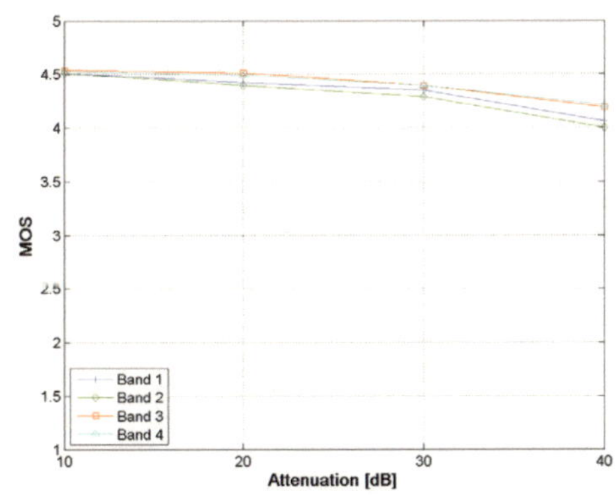

Fig. 7. Objective assessment of the harmonic distortion by PESQ method.

The average MOS score of subjective listening test and objective speech quality assessment by PESQ for individual bands is summarized in Table 5. The average subjective score is always lower than objective one. The difference between results of both tests is very significant for all bands (between 0.74 and 1.31 MOS).

Group	Subjective score (MOS)	Objective PESQ score (MOS)
Band 1	3.03	4.34
Band 2	3.56	4.30
Band 3	3.56	4.40
Band 4	3.26	4.41

Table 5. Average MOS score of each bands over levels of suppression.

5.3 Impact of losses in individual phonetic elements

The impact of individual phonetic elements is investigated by subjective listening tests and by PESQ objective method. The subjective listening test, executed in accordance with ITU-T P.800 a ITU T P.830 recommendations, performs 25 listeners. The software Tester is also used for the subjective speech quality assessment. As well the listeners participated on the subjective testing have been selected from students and employees of the Czech Technical University in Prague.

We have considered following parameters: four groups of phonetic elements and five ratios of packet losses (2, 4, 6, 8, and 10 %). Four speeches are generated for each pair of parameters (group and packet loss ratio) to eliminate effect of random drop of losses. Above mentioned assumptions results into 80 speeches utilized for speech quality testing (4 groups * 5 ratios * 4 speech). The overall duration of the subjective listening test is approximately 20 minutes per a listener.

The results of subjective test are presented in Fig. 8. From this figure can be observed that the most significant group of phonetic elements from the speech quality point of view are groups containing vowels and diphthongs. This fact is caused by two reasons. The first one, based on lexical aspect, says that the vowels are basement of nearly all syllables and words; hence its modification or unintelligibility can cause the change of the meaning of the whole word. The second aspect is the signal processing. From this side, the vowels as well as sound voices contains high amount of energy. Therefore, its loss leads to the loss of major part of information.

The second most important group consists of nasals and liquids since all speech sounds included in this group are voiced and thus they carry high energy. The difference between this group and group with vowels and diphthongs is marginal; it is roughly 0.15 MOS in average in subjective tests.

The next most perceptible impact is caused by fricatives. This group contains voiced as well as unvoiced consonants. Therefore the speech quality in comparison to the first and second group is higher (roughly from 0.4 to 0.55 MOS).

The lowest important group consists of plosives and affricates. This group contains also voiced and unvoiced consonants; however its energy is the lowest of all groups. Its impact on the speech quality is less perceptible by users. The average MOS score is by roughly 0.5 MOS higher than the score of speech with losses in fricatives.

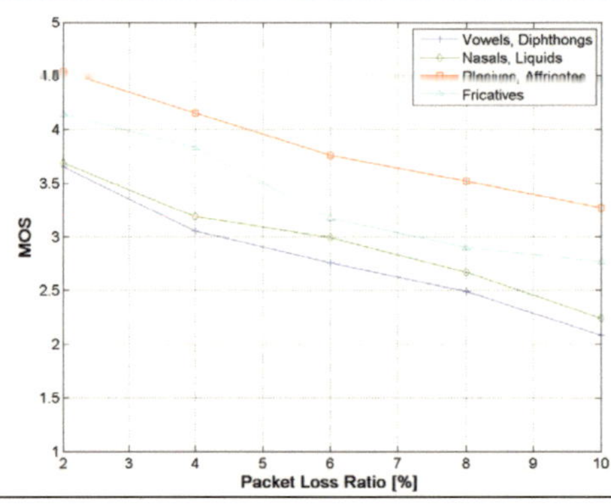

Fig. 8. Subjective assessment of an impact of phonetic elements.

The results of objective speech quality measurement are depicted in Fig. 9. These results show slightly lower speech quality than subjective test. Contrary to the subjective tests, the second group (nasals & liquids) seems marginally more important (but by only 0.18 MOS in average) than the first group (vowels & diphthongs) at higher packet loss. Nevertheless, the impact of both groups is more perceptible than another two groups (fricatives, plosives & affricates) since fricative, plosives and affricates carry less energy in general. The significance of the losses in fricatives is very close to the impact of plosives & affricates. The slightly higher negative impact (less than 0.1 MOS) is achieved by losses in fricatives.

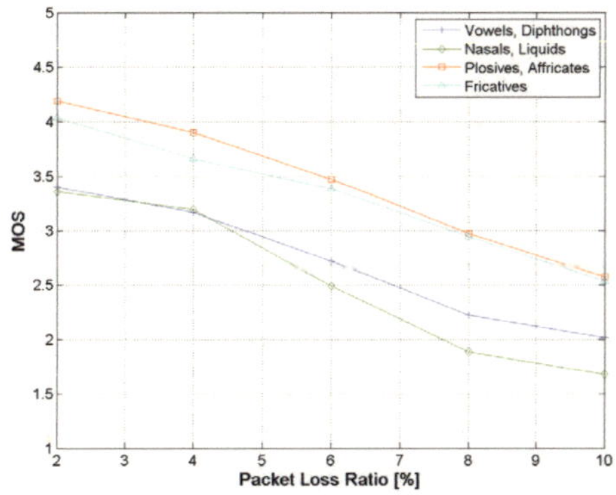

Fig. 9. Objective assessment of an impact of phonetic elements by PESQ method.

The average MOS score of subjective listening test and objective speech quality assessment by PESQ is summarized in Table 6. The average subjective score is always higher than the results of objective evaluation. The difference is negligible for vowels & diphthongs; however it is more significant in case of nasals & liquids and plosives & affricates.

Group	Subjective score (MOS)	Objective PESQ score (MOS)
Vowels& diphthongs	2.81	2.70
Nasal & liquids	2.96	2.52
Plosives & affricates	3.85	3.42
Fricatives	3.36	3.31

Table 6. Average MOS score of each group of phonetic elements.

The difference in speech quality of groups containing only voice sounds and groups containing also unvoiced sound is considerable in results of both subjective as well as objective tests. For example, the speech quality is roughly by 1 MOS higher if the packet losses hit only plosives and affricates than if the losses are in vowels and diphthongs. This fact should influence the design of packet loss concealment mechanisms to put more focus on elimination of losses of vowels, diphthongs, nasals or liquids.

6. Conclusions

This chapter provides an overview on the speech quality assessment in VoIP networks. Several effects that can influence the speech quality are investigated by objective PESQ and/or subjective tests.
The results of objective tests show advantage of wideband communication channel only for high quality networks (with PLR up to 4%). On the other hand, while the speech is affected by consecutive packet losses or by individual losses with higher packet loss ratio, the narrowband channel reaches better score. The most significant difference between wide and narrow band speeches is at 12 % of lost packets.
The consecutive packet losses can leads to the higher speech quality while the duration of losses is long enough comparing to the individual losses. The exact duration of loss that reaches higher score than individual one depends on the length of packets.

The tests of harmonic distortion performed in the means of a suppression of a part of bandwidth, leads to the conclusion that the most important parts of the frequency band are the lowest and the highest bands. The objective method PESQ is not able to handle with the harmonic distortion and its results do not match the subjective one.
The evaluation of the importance of the groups of phonetic elements shows that the most considerable elements are vowels and diphthongs. On the other hand, the speech quality is affected only slightly by losses of plosives or affricates.

7. References

Bachu, R. G.; Kopparthi, S.; Adapa, B. & Barkana B. D. (2010). Voiced/Unvoiced Decision for Speech Signals Based on Zero-Crossing Rate and Energy, In: *Advanced Techniques in Computing Sciences and Software Engineering*, Khaled Elleithy, 279-282, Springer, ISBN 978-90-481-3659-9.

Barriac, V.; Saout, J.-Y. L. & Lockwood, C. (2004). Discussion on unified objective methodologies for the comparison of voice quality of narrowband and wideband scenarios. *Proceedings of Workshop on Wideband Speech Quality in Terminals and Networks: Assessment and Prediction*, June 2004.

Becvar, Z.; Pravda, I. & Vodrazka, J. (2008). Quality Evaluation of Narrowband and Wideband IP Telephony. *Proceeding of Digital Technologies 2008*, pp. 1-4, ISBN 978-80-8070-953-2, November 2008, Žilina, Slovakia.

Benesty, J; Sondhi, M. M. & Huang Y. (2008). *Springer handbook of speech processing*, Springer-Verlag, pp. 308, ISBN: 978-3-540-49125-5, Berlin Heidelberg, Germany.

Brada, M. (2006). Tools Facilitating Realization of Subjective Listening Tests. *Proceedings of Research in Telecommunication Technology 2006*, pp. 414-417, ISBN 80-214-3243-8, September 2006, Brno, Czech Republic.

Clark, A. D. (2002). Modeling the Effects of Burst Packet Loss and Recency on Subjective Voice Quality. *The 3rd IP Telephony Workshop 2002*, New York, 2002.

Ding, L. & Goubran, R. A. (2003). Assessment of Effects of Packet Loss on Speech Quality in VoIP. *Proceedings of The 2nd IEEE International Workshop on Haptic, Audio and Visual Environments and Their Applications, 2003*, pp. 49–54, ISBN 0-7803-8108-4, September 2003.

Fastl, H. & Zwicker, E. (1999). *Psychoacoustics. Facts and Models, Second edition*, Springer, ISBN 3-540-65063-6, Berlin.

Friedlander, B. & Porat, B. (1984). The Modified Yule-Walker Method of ARMA Spectral Estimation, *IEEE Transactions on Aerospace Electronic Systems*, Vol. 20, No. 2, March 1984, pp. 158-173, ISSN 0018-9251.

Hanzl, V. & Pollak, P. (2002). Tool for Czech Pronunciation Generation Combining Fixed Rules with Pronunciation Lexicon and Lexicon Management Tool. *In Proceedings of 3rd International Conferance on Language Resources and Evaluation*, pp. 1264-1269, ISBN 2-9517408-0-8, Las Palmas de Gran Canaria, Spain, May 2002.

Hassan, M. & Alekseevich, D. F. (2006). Variable Packet Size of IP Packets for VoIP Transmission. *Proceedings of the 24th IASTED international conference on Internet and multimedia systems and applications*, pp. 136-141, Innsbruck, Austria, February 2006.

Holub, J.; Beerend, J. G. & Smid, R. (2004). A Dependence between Average Call Duration and Voice Transmission Quality: Measurement and Applications. *In Proceedings of Wireless Telecommunications Symposium*, pp. 75-81, May 2004.

ITU-T Rec. E.800 (1994). Terms and definitions related to quality of service and network performance including dependability. August 1994.

ITU-T Rec. G.107 (2005). The E-model, a computational model for use in transmission planning. March 2005.

ITU-T Rec. G.114 (2003). One-way transmission time. May 2003.

ITU-T Rec. G.711 (1988). Pulse Code Modulation of Voice Frequencies. 1988.

ITU-T Rec. G.711.1 (2008). Wideband embedded extension for ITU-T G.711 pulse code modulation. March 2008.

ITU-T Rec. P.800 (1996). Methods for Subjective Determination of Transmission Quality. August 1996.

ITU-T Rec. P.800.1 (2003). Mean Opinion Score (MOS) terminology. March 2003.

ITU-T Rec. P.830 (1996). Subjective Performance Assessment of Telephone-Band Wideband Digital Codecs . February 1996.

ITU-T Rec. P.862 (2001). Perceptual evaluation of speech quality (PESQ): An objective method for end-to-end speech quality assessment of narrow-band telephone networks and speech codecs. February 2001.

ITU-T Rec. P.862.1 (2003). Mapping function for transforming P.862 raw result scores to MOS-LQO. November 2003.

Kondo, K. & Nakagawa, K. (2006). A Speech Packet Loss Concealment Method Using Linear Prediction. *IEICE Transactions on Information and Systems*, Vol. E89-D, No. 2, February 2006, pp. 806-813, ISSN 0916-8532.

Linden, J. (2004). Achieving the Highest Voice Quality for VoIP Solutions, *Proceedings of GSPx The International Embedded Solutions Event*, Santa Clara, September 2004.

Molau, S.; Pitz, M.; Schluter, R. & Ney, H. (2001). Computing Mel-frequency cepstral coefficients on the power spectrum, *Proceedings of IEEE International Conference on Acoustics, Speech, and Signal Processing*, pp. 73-76, ISBN 0-7803-7041-4, Salt Lake City, USA, August 2001.

Oouchi, H.; Takenaga, T.; Sugawara, H. & Masugi M. (2002). Study on Appropriate Voice Data Length of IP Packets for VoIP Network Adjustment. *Proceedings of IEEE Global Telecommunications Conference*, pp. 1618-1622, ISBN 0-7803-7632 3, November 2002.

Robinson, D. J. M. & Hawksford, M. O. J. (2000). Psychoacoustic models and non-linear human hearing, In: *Audio Engineering Society Convention 109*, September 2000.

Sing, J. H. & Chang, J. H. (2009). Efficient Implementation of Voiced/Unvoiced Sounds Classification Based on GMM for SMV Codec. *IEICE Transactions on Fundamentals of Electronics, Communications and Computer Sciences*, Vol. E92–A, No.8, August 2009, pp. 2120-2123, ISSN 1745-1337.

Sun, L. F.; Wade, G.; Lines, B. M. & Ifeachor, E. C. (2001). Impact of Packet Loss Location on Perceived Speech Quality. *Proceedings of 2nd IP-Telephony Workshop*, pp. 114-122, Columbia University, New York, April 2001.

Tosun, L. & Kabal, P. (2005). Dynamically Adding Redundancy for Improved Error Concealment in Packet Voice Coding. *In Proceedings of European Signal Processing Conference (EUSIPCO)*, Antalya, Turkey, September 2005.

Ulseth, T. & Stafsnes, F. (2006). VoIP speech quality - Better than PSTN?. *Telektronikk*, Vol. 1, pp. 119-129, ISSN 0085-7130.

3

Enhanced VoIP by Signal Reconstruction and Voice Quality Assessment

Filipe Neves[1,2], Salviano Soares[3,4], Pedro Assunção[1,2] and Filipe Tavares[5]
[1]*Instituto Politécnico de Leiria*
[2]*Instituto de Telecomunicações*
[3]*Universidade de Trás-os-Montes e Alto Douro*
[4]*Instituto de Engenharia Electrónica e Telemática de Aveiro*
[5]*Portugal Telecom Inovação*
Portugal

1. Introduction

The Internet and its packet based architecture is becoming an increasingly ubiquitous communications resource, providing the necessary underlying support for many services and applications. The classic voice call service over fixed circuit switched networks suffered a steep evolution with mobile networks and more recently another significant move is being witnessed towards packet based communications using the omnipresent Internet Protocol (IP) (Zourzouvillys & Rescorla, 2010). It is known that, due to real time requirements, voice over IP (VoIP) needs tighter delivery guarantees from the networking infrastructure than data transmission. While such requirements put strong bounds on maximum end to end delay, there is some tolerance to errors and packet losses in VoIP services providing that a minimum quality level is experienced by the users. Therefore, voice signals delivered over IP based networks are likely to be affected by transmission errors and packet losses, leading to perceptually annoying communication impairments. Although it is not possible to fully recover the original voice signals from those received with errors and/or missing data, it is still possible to improve the quality delivered to users by using appropriate error concealment methods and controlling the Quality of Service (QoS) (Becvar et al., 2007).

This chapter is concerned with voice signal reconstruction methods and quality evaluation in VoIP communications. An overview of suitable solutions to conceal the impairment effects in order to improve the QoS and consequently the Quality of Experience (QoE) is presented in section 2. Among these, simple techniques based on either silence or waveform substitution and others that embed voice parameters of a packet in its predecessor are addressed. In addition, more sophisticated techniques which use diverse interleaving procedures at the packetization stage and/or perform voice synthesis at the receiver are also addressed. Section 3 provides a brief review of relevant algebra concepts in order to build an adequate basis to understand the fundamentals of the signal reconstruction techniques addressed in the remaining sections. Since signal reconstruction leads to linear interpolation problems defined as system of equations, the characterization of the corresponding system matrix is necessary because it provides relevant insight about the problem solution. In such characterisation, it will be shown that eigenvalues, and particularly the spectral radius, have a fundamental role on problem conditioning. This is analysed in detail because existence of a solution for the interpolation problem and its accuracy both depend on the characterisation of the problem conditioning. Section 4 of this chapter describes in detail effective signal reconstruction techniques capable to cope with missing data in voice communication systems. Two linear interpolation signal reconstruction algorithms, suitable to be used in VoIP technology, are presented along with comparison between their main features and performance. The difference between maximum and minimum dimension problems, as well as the difference between iterative and direct computation for finding the problem solution are also addressed. One of the interpolation algorithms is the discrete version of the Papoulis-Gerchberg algorithm, which is a maximum dimension iterative algorithm based on two linear operations: sampling and band limiting. A particular emphasis will be given to the iterative algorithms used to obtain a target accuracy subject to appropriate convergence conditions. The importance of the system matrix spectral radius is also explained including its dependence from the error pattern geometry. Evidence is provided to show why interleaved errors are less harmful than random or burst errors. The other interpolation algorithm presented in section 4 is a minimum dimension one which leads to a system matrix whose dimension depends on the number of sample errors. Therefore the system matrix dimension is lower than that of the Papoulis-Gerchberg algorithm. Besides an iterative computational variant, this type of problem allows direct matrix computation when it is well-conditioned. As a consequence, it demands less computational effort and thus reconstruction time is also smaller. In regard to the interleaved error geometry, it is shown that a judicious choice of conjugated interleaving and redundancy factors permits to place the reconstruction problem into a well conditioned operational point. By combining these issues with the possibility of having fixed pre-computed system matrices, real-time voice reconstruction is possible for a great deal of error patterns. Simulation results are also presented and discussed showing that the minimum dimension algorithm is faster than its maximum dimension counterpart, while achieving the same reconstruction quality. Finally section 6 presents a case study including experimental results from field testing with voice quality evaluation, recently carried out at the Research Labs of Portugal Telecom Inovação (PT Inovação). Based on these results, a Mean Opinion Score (MOS)-based quality model is derived from the parametric E-Model and validated using the algorithm defined by ITU-T Perceptual Evaluation of Speech Quality (ITU-T, 2001).

2. Voice signal reconstruction and quality evaluation

2.1 Voice signal reconstruction

Transmission errors in voice communications and particularly in voice over IP networks are known to have several different causes but the single effect of delivering poor quality of service to users of such services and applications. In general this is due to missing/lost samples in the signal delivered to the receiver.

Channel coding can be used to protect transmitted signals from packet loss but it introduces extra redundancy and still does not guarantee error-free delivery. In order to achieve higher quality in VoIP services with low delay, effective error concealment techniques must be used at the receiver. Typically such techniques extract features from the received signal and use them to recover the lost data.

The different approaches to deal with voice concealment can be classified in either source-coder independent or source-coder dependent (Wah et al., 2000). The former schemes implement loss concealment methods only at the receiver end. In such receiver-based reconstruction schemes, lost packets may be approximately recovered by using signal reconstruction algorithms. The latter schemes might be more effective but also more complex and in general higher transmission bandwidth is necessary. In such schemes, the sender first processes the input signals, extract the features of speech, and transmit them to the receiver along with the voice signal itself. For instance, in (Tosun & Kabal, 2005) the authors propose to use additional redundant information to ease concealment of lost packets.

Source-coder independent techniques are mostly based on signal reconstruction algorithms which use interpolation techniques combined with packetization schemes that help to recover the missing samples of the signal (Bhute & Shrawankar, 2008), (Jayant & Christensen, 1981).

Among several possible solutions, it is worth to mention those algorithms that try to reconstruct the missing segment of the signal from correctly received samples. For instance, waveform substitution is a method which replaces the missing part of the signal with samples of the same value as its past or future neighbours, while the pattern matching method builds a pattern from the last M known samples and searches over a window of size N the set of M samples which best matches the pattern (Goodman et al., 1986), (Tang, 1991). In (Aoki, 2004) the proposed reconstruction technique takes account of pitch variation between the previous and the next known signal frames.

In (Erdol et al., 1993) two reconstruction techniques are proposed based on slow-varying parameters of a voice signal: short-time energy and zero-crossing rate (or zerocrossing locations). The aim is to ensure amplitude and frequency continuity between the concealment waveform and the lost one. This can be implemented by storing parameters of packet k in packet k-1. Splitting the even and odd samples into different packets is another method which eases interpolation of the missing samples in case of packet loss. Particularly interesting to this work is an iterative reconstruction method proposed in (Ferreira, 1994a), which is the discrete version of the Papoulis Gerchberg interpolation algorithm.

A different approach, proposed in (Cheetham, 2006), is to provide mechanisms to ease signal error concealment by acting at packet level selective retransmissions to reduce the dependency on concealment techniques. Another packet level error concealment method base on time-scale modification capable of providing adaptive delay concealment is proposed in (Liu et al., 2001).

In practical receivers, the performance of voice reconstruction algorithms includes not only the signal quality obtained from reconstruction but also other parameters such as computational complexity which in turn has implications in the processing speed. Furthermore in handheld devices power consumption is also a critical factor to take into account in the implementation of these type of algorithms.

2.2 Voice quality evaluation methods

The Standardization Sector of International Telecommunication Union (ITU-T) has released a set of recommendations in regard to evaluation of telephony voice quality. These methods take into account the most significant human voice and audition characteristics along with possible impairments introduced by current voice communication systems, such as noise, delay, distortion due to low bitrate codecs, transmission errors and packet losses. Quality evaluation methods for voice can be classified into subjective, objective and parametric methods. In the first case there must be people involved in the evaluation process to listen to a set of voice samples and provide their opinion, according to some predefined scale which corresponds to a numerical score. The Mean Opinion Score (MOS) collected from all listeners is then used as the quality metric of the subjective evaluation. The evaluation methods are further classified as reference and non-reference methods, depending on whether a reference signal is used for comparison with the one under evaluation. When the MOS scores refer to the listening quality, this is usually referred to as MOS_{LQS}[1] (ITU-T, 2006). If the MOS scores are obtained in a conversational environment, where delays play an important role in the achieved intelligibility, then this is referred to as MOS_{CQS}[2]. Even though a significant number of participants should be used in subjective tests (ITU-T, 1996), every time a particular set of tests is repeated does not necessarily lead to exactly the same results. Subjective testing is expensive, time-consuming and obviously not adequate to real-time quality monitoring. Therefore, objective tests without human intervention, are the best solutions to overcome the constraints of the subjective ones (Falk & Chan, 2009). Nowadays, the Perceptual Evaluation of Speech Quality (PESQ), defined in Rec. ITU-T P.862 (ITU-T, 2001), is widely accepted as a reference objective method to compute approximate MOS scores with good accuracy. Among the voice codecs of interest to VoIP, there are the ITU-T G.711, G.729 and G.723.1. Since the reference methods interfere with the normal operation of the communication system, they are usually known as intrusive methods.

The PESQ method transforms both the original and the degraded signal into an intermediate representation which is analogous to the psychophysical representation of audio signals in the human auditory system. Such representation takes into account the perceptual frequency (Bark) and loudness (Sone). Then, in the Bark domain, some perceptive operations are performed taking into account loudness densities, from which the disturbances are calculated. Based on these disturbances, the PESQ MOS is derived. This is commonly called the raw MOS since the respective values range from -1 to 4.5. It is often necessary to map raw MOS into another scale in order to compare the results with MOS obtained from subjective methods. The ITU-T Rec. P.862.1 (ITU-T, 2003) provides such a mapping function, from which the so-called MOS_{LQO}[3] is obtained.

Another standards, such as the Single-ended Method for Objective Speech Quality Assessment in Narrow-band Telephony Applications described in Rec. ITU-T P.563 (ITU-T, 2004), do not require a reference signal to compare with the one under evaluation. They are also called single-ended or non-intrusive methods.

The E-Model, described in the Rec. ITU-T G.107, (ITU-T, 2005) is a parametric model. While signal based methods use perceptual features extracted from the speech signal to estimate quality, the parametric E-Model uses a set of parameters that characterize the communication chain such as codecs, packet loss pattern, loss rate, delay and loudness. Then the impairment factors are computed to estimate speech quality. This model assumes that the transmission voice impairments can be transformed into psychological impairment factors in an additive psychological scale. The evaluation score of such process is defined by a rating factor R given by

---

1 "Listening Quality Subjective"

2 "Conversational Quality Subjective"

3 "Listen Quality Objective"

$$R = R_0 - I_s - I_d - I_{e-eff} + A \qquad (1)$$

where R_0 is a base factor representative of the signal-to-noise ratio, including noise sources such as circuit noise and room noise, I_s is a combination of all impairments which occur more or less simultaneously with the signal transmission, I_d includes the impairments due to delay, $I_{e\text{-}eff}$ represents impairments caused by equipment (e.g., codec impairments at different packet loss scenarios) and A is an advantage factor that allows for compensation of impairment factors. Based on the value of R, which is comprised between 0 and 100, Rec. ITU-T G.109 (ITU-T, 1999) defines five categories of speech transmission quality, in which 0 corresponds to the worst quality and 100 corresponds to the best quality. Annex B of Rec. ITU-T G.107 includes the expressions to map R ratings to MOS scores which provide an estimation of the conversational quality usually referred to as MOS_{CQE}[4]. If delay impairments are not considered, the I_d factor is not taken into account, and by means of ITU-T G.107 Annex B expressions, MOS_{CQE} is referred to as MOS_{LQE}[5].

3. Algebraic fundamentals

This section presents the most relevant concepts of linear algebra in regard to the voice reconstruction methods described in detail in the next sections. The most important mathematical definitions and relationships are explained with particular emphasis on those with applications in signal reconstruction problems.

Let us define $\mathbb{C}$, $\mathbb{R}$ and $\mathbb{Z}$ as the sets of complex, real and integer numbers respectively, and $\mathbb{C}^N$, $\mathbb{R}^N$ and $\mathbb{Z}^N$ as complex, real and integer $\mathbf{N}$ dimensional spaces. An element of any of these sets is called a vector. Let us consider f a continuous function. An indexed sequence $\mathbf{x}[\mathbf{n}]$ given by

$$x[n] = f(nT), \qquad n \in Z, \qquad T \in R \qquad (2)$$

is defined as a sampled version of f.

A complex sequence of length $\mathbf{N}$ is represented by the column vector $x \in \mathbb{C}^N$ with components $[x_0, x_1, \ldots, x_{N-1}]^T$, where x^T is the transpose of x. In digital signal processing, such vector components are known as signal samples.

The solution of many signal processing problems is often found by solving a set of linear equations, i.e., a system of n equations and n variables $x_1, x_2, \ldots x_n$ defined as,

$$\begin{cases} a_{11}x_1 + a_{12}x_2 + \cdots + a_{1n}x_n = b_1 \\ a_{21}x_1 + a_{22}x_2 + \cdots + a_{2n}x_n = b_2 \\ \vdots \\ a_{n1}x_1 + a_{n2}x_2 + \cdots + a_{nn}x_n = b_n \end{cases} \qquad (3)$$

where elements $a_{ij}, b_i \in \mathbb{R}$. The above equation can be written in either matricial form,

[4] "Conversational Quality Estimated"

[5] "Listenen Quality Estimated"

$$\begin{bmatrix} a_{11} & a_{12} & \cdots & a_{n4} \\ a_{21} & a_{22} & \cdots & a_{2n} \\ \cdots & \cdots & \ddots & \cdots \\ a_{n1} & a_{n2} & \cdots & a_{nn} \end{bmatrix} \begin{bmatrix} x_1 \\ x_2 \\ \vdots \\ x_n \end{bmatrix} = \begin{bmatrix} b_1 \\ b_2 \\ \vdots \\ b_n \end{bmatrix} \quad (4)$$

or in compact algebraic form

$$Ax = b \quad (5)$$

A is known as the system matrix and if $A=A^T$, then it is called a symmetric matrix. Let the complex number $\overline{z} = a - bi$ be the conjugate of $z = a + bi$, where i is the imaginary unit. The conjugate transpose of the mxn matrix A is the nxm matrix A^H obtained from A by taking the transpose and the complex conjugate of each element a_{ij}. For real matrices $A^H=A^T$ and A is normal if $A^TA=AA^T$. Any matrix A, either real or complex, is said to be hermitian if $A^H=A$. Denoting by I_n an nxn identity matrix, any nxn square matrix A is invertible or non-singular when there is a matrix B that satisfies the condition $AB=BA=I_n$. Matrix B is called the inverse of A, and it is denoted by A^{-1}. If A is invertible, then $A^{-1}Ax=A^{-1}b$ and the system equation $Ax=b$ has an unique solution given by

$$x = A^{-1}b \quad (6)$$

An nxn complex matrix A that satisfies the condition $A^HA=AA^H=I_n$, (or $A^{-1}=A^H$) is called an unitary matrix.
Considering an nxm matrix A and the index sets $\alpha=\{i_1, i_2, \ldots i_p\}$ and $\beta=\{j_1,j_2, \ldots, j_q\}$, with $p<n$ and $q<m$, a submatrix of A, denoted by $A(\alpha,\beta)$, is obtained by taking those rows and columns of A that are indexed by α and β, respectively. For example

$$\begin{bmatrix} 1 & 2 & 3 \\ 4 & 5 & 6 \\ 7 & 8 & 9 \end{bmatrix}(\{1,3\},\{1,2,3\}) = \begin{bmatrix} 1 & 2 & 3 \\ 7 & 8 & 9 \end{bmatrix} \quad (7)$$

If $\alpha=\beta$, the resulting submatrix is called a principal submatrix of A.
An eigenvector v of a square matrix A is a non-zero column vector that satisfies the following condition:

$$Av=\lambda v \quad (8)$$

for a scalar λ, which is said to be an eigenvalue of A corresponding to the eigenvector v. In other words, when A is multiplied by v, the result is the same as a scalar λ multiplied by v. Note that it is much easier to multiply a scalar by a vector than a matrix by a vector.
The spectrum of A is defined as the set of its eigenvalues, while the spectral radius of A, denoted by $\rho(A)$, is the supremum[6] among the absolute values of its spectrum elements. Since the number of eigenvalues is finite, the supremum can be replaced with the maximum. That is

$$\rho(A) = \max_i |\lambda_i| \quad (9)$$

---

[6] The supremum of a set S, $\sup\{S\}$, is v if and only if: i) v is an upper bound for S and ii) no real number smaller than v is an upper bound for S (Kincaid & Cheney, 2002).

If $\rho(A)<1$, then the inverse of $I-A$ exists and the system of (5) has a possible solution. This solution can be obtained by a direct calculation method as given in (6) or by an iterative method.
A vector norm can be thought of as the length or magnitude of vector x. Several types of norms are defined (Kincaid & Cheney, 2002). The most familiar norm is the Euclidian l_2-norm, defined as

$$\|x\|_2 = \left(\sum_{i=1}^{N} x_i^2 \right)^{1/2}$$

Other norms, such as the l_∞- and l_1-norms are also relevant,

$$\|x\|_\infty = \max_{1 \le i \le N} |x_i| , \quad \|x\|_1 = \sum_{i=1}^{N} |x_i|$$

The matrix norm subordinate to a vector norm is defined as

$$\|A\| = \sup\left\{ \|Au\| : u \in \Re^N , \|u\| = 1 \right\}$$

Conditioning of a problem is another important concept, informally used to indicate how sensitive the solution of a problem is to small changes in the input data. A problem is said to be ill-conditioned if small changes in the input data produce large variations in the solution, whereas the solution of a well conditioned problem is less sensitive to variations in the input data.
For certain types of problems, a condition number can be defined as follows. Concerning the problem defined in (5), a perturbation on b will produce a corresponding perturbation on x, thus (5) can be written as

$$A\tilde{x} = \tilde{b} \tag{10}$$

where $\tilde{x}$ stands for the perturbation on x caused by the perturbation $\tilde{b}$ on b. The relation between relative perturbations is given by

$$\frac{\|x - \tilde{x}\|}{x} \le \|A\| . \left\|A^{-1}\right\| \frac{\left\|b - \tilde{b}\right\|}{b} \tag{11}$$

which permits to define the condition number as expression (Kincaid & Cheney, 2002)

$$k(A) = \|A\| . \left\|A^{-1}\right\| \tag{12}$$

Thus, if the condition number is large, even a small error in b may cause a large error in x. If the condition number is small, then the error in x will not be much higher than the error in b. The condition number is a property of the problem obtained from matrix A, which leads to well-conditioned problems whenever its value is close to unity. In the case where A is a normal matrix, the condition number assumes the form

$$k(A) = \left| \frac{\lambda_{\max}(A)}{\lambda_{\min}(A)} \right| \tag{13}$$

The eigenvalues of the system matrix and the relation between them play an important role in the problem conditioning. In this context, special attention should be paid to the spectral radius. As it will be explained in section 5, a spectral radius near or greater than 1 leads to a ill-conditioned problem whereas a smaller spectral radius between 0 and 1 leads to a well-conditioned problem.

Another important property is idempotence by which an operation can be repeated over the same data without changing the result. In algebra context, an nxn matrix $\boldsymbol{A}$ is said to be idempotent if $\boldsymbol{A}^2=\boldsymbol{A}$.

In a Toeplitz matrix $\boldsymbol{A}$, each of its elements satisfies $a_{ij}=a_{i-j}$, which is equivalent to $a_{ij}=a_{i-1,j-1}$, thus, each descending diagonal from left to right is constant, as shown below.

$$A=\begin{bmatrix} a_0 & a_{-1} & a_{-2} & \cdots & a_{-(N-1)} \\ a_1 & a_0 & a_{-1} & \cdots & a_{-(N-2)} \\ a_2 & a_1 & a_0 & \ddots & \\ \vdots & \vdots & \ddots & \ddots & a_{-1} \\ a_{(N-1)} & a_{(N-2)} & \cdots & a_1 & a_0 \end{bmatrix}.$$

In the case of a complex matrix where a_{-k} is the conjugate of a_k, then it is called an hermitian Toeplitz whereas if the matrix is real, then it is a symmetric Toeplitz. In the system equation (5), if A is a mxn Toeplitz matrix, then the system has only $m+n$-1 degrees of freedom, rather than mxn.

A matrix A is positive definite if the associated quadratic form is positive, i.e., if $x^HAx>0$, $\forall x\neq 0$. If A is positive definite and symmetric, then all of its eigenvalues λ_i are real and positive (Kincaid & Cheney, 2002). Every positive definite matrix is invertible and its inverse is also positive definite (Horn & Johnson, 1985). A matrix A is non-negative definite if the associated quadratic form is non-negative, that is, if $x^HAx\geq 0$, $\forall x\neq 0$.

There are several possible methods to find the solution of (5), which may be classified in either direct or iterative methods. Concerning the direct methods, the solution can theoretically be found by left-multiplying by A^{-1}, if it is known, resulting in the equation (6). There are several approaches, from Gauss-Jordan elimination to factorization methods such as LU decomposition. Some special structures of A can lead to simple solutions. As an example, equation (5) has a trivial solution when matrix A is diagonal. In this case, the solution is

$$x=\begin{bmatrix} b_1 / a_{11} \\ b_2 / a_{22} \\ \vdots \\ b_n / a_{nn} \end{bmatrix} \tag{14}$$

If $a_{ii}=0$ and $b_i=0$, for any i, then x_i may be any real number. If $a_{ii}=0$ and $b_i\neq 0$ there is no solution for the system. If the entries below or above the main diagonal of a mxn matrix A are zero, then A is either a lower (L) or upper (U) triangular matrix, respectively, as follows.

$$L=\begin{bmatrix} l_{11} & 0 & \cdots & 0 \\ l_{21} & l_{22} & \cdots & 0 \\ \cdots & \cdots & \ddots & \cdots \\ l_{n1} & l_{n2} & \cdots & l_{nn} \end{bmatrix} \qquad U=\begin{bmatrix} u_{11} & u_{12} & \cdots & u_{1n} \\ 0 & u_{22} & \cdots & u_{2n} \\ \cdots & \cdots & \ddots & \cdots \\ 0 & 0 & \cdots & u_{nn} \end{bmatrix}$$

If all entries of the main diagonal of a triangular matrix are zero, then such matrix is called either strictly upper or strictly lower triangular. Assuming a lower triangular matrix A and $a_{ii}\neq 0$, $\forall i$, equations from (5) become

$$\begin{bmatrix} a_{11} & 0 & \cdots & 0 \\ a_{21} & a_{22} & \cdots & 0 \\ \cdots & \cdots & \ddots & \cdots \\ a_{n1} & a_{n2} & \cdots & a_{nn} \end{bmatrix} \begin{bmatrix} x_1 \\ x_1 \\ \vdots \\ x_n \end{bmatrix} = \begin{bmatrix} b_1 \\ b_2 \\ \vdots \\ b_n \end{bmatrix}$$

and then obtaining x_1 from the first equation becomes trivial.

LU decomposition is a simplified method to solve a system of equations where matrix A can be defined as the product between a lower triangular matrix and an upper triangular matrix, i.e., $A=LU$. Thus, the linear set of equations to solve becomes $Ax=(LU)x=L(Ux)=b$ and the solution can be found by first solving it for vector y such that $Ly=b$ and then solving for x, using $Ux=y$. The advantage of breaking up one linear set of equations into two successive ones is that the solution of a triangular set of equations is quite trivial (Press et al., 2007).

A particular case of LU decomposition is the Cholesky decomposition where decomposition of matrix A is given by the product of a lower triangular matrix with its conjugate transpose, i.e., $A=LL^T$ and L is a lower triangular matrix with all diagonal elements positive. When applicable, the Cholesky decomposition is about twice as fast as other methods used for solving systems of linear equations (Press et al., 1994). Note that this method requires that A is real, symmetric and positive-definite.

Direct methods to resolve the type of equations such as (6) ideally produce a solution correct to machine accuracy. However, when the system order is high, with thousands of equations, the computational effort may be critical either in terms of execution time or other resources like memory. In this case, iterative methods might be the answer to overcome such constraints. In their *modus operandi*, iterative methods produce a sequence of vectors that converge to the final solution as the computational process evolves. The process halts when either some pre-defined number of iterations is reached or an acceptable level of accuracy is obtained at any possible iteration. In high dimensional systems, if precision is not a strong requirement, it is possible to approximate the solution with just a few iterations. Particularly, in sparse systems, where the number of zero entries in the iteration matrix is high, iterative methods prove to be very efficient in the sense that only a small number of computations are necessary.

There are several specific iterative methods particularly suited to solve systems of the form of (5). Among them, Jacobi and Gauss-Seidel methods are paradigmatic. The Jacobi method follows from the individual analysis of each of the n system equations as defined in (5). If the following expression holds for the ith equation,

$$\sum_{j=1}^{n} a_{ij}x_j = b_i \tag{15}$$

then x_i can be solved assuming that other entries do not vary, i.e.,

$$x_i = (b_i - \sum_{j=1}^{n} a_{ij}x_j) \Big/ a_{ii}, \qquad j \neq i \tag{16}$$

which suggests an iterative resolution for the ith equation, as given by

$$x_i^{(k)} = (b_i - \sum_{j=1}^{n} a_{ij} x_j^{(k-1)}) \Big/ a_{ii}, \qquad j \neq i \tag{17}$$

The Gauss-Seidel method can be seen as an enhancement of Jacobi method in which updated values of x_i on the right-hand side of (17) are used as soon as they become available in the same iteration. That is, instead of use x_i from iteration k-1 in iteration k, the value of x_i from previous equation is used in the same iteration when available. The first equation is the only exception. As an example, for the first two equations, we have

$$\begin{aligned} a_{11}x_1^{(1)} &= b_1 - a_{12}x_2^0 - a_{13}x_3^{(0)} \cdots - a_{1n}x_n^{(0)} \\ a_{22}x_2^{(1)} &= b_2 - a_{21}x_1^{(1)} - a_{23}x_3^{(0)} \cdots - a_{1n}x_n^{(0)} \\ &\vdots \end{aligned}$$

which leads to

$$x_i^{(k)} = (b_i - \sum_{j=1}^{i-1} a_{ij} x_j^{(k)} - \sum_{j=i+1}^{n} a_{ij} x_j^{(k-1)}) \Big/ a_{ii} \tag{18}$$

Between iterations k-1 and k, the result converges to the final solution an amount given by $\delta x^{(k)}=x^{(k)}-x^{(k-1)}$. Thus, the solution at iteration k is given by $x^{(k)}=x^{(k-1)}+\delta x^{(k)}$. However, at iteration k-1 the result $x^{(k-1)}$ differs from the final solution by the amount of $\Delta x^{(k)}=x-x^{(k-1)}$, which is different from $\delta x^{(k)}$. Since $\delta x^{(k)} < \Delta x^{(k)}$, one may speed up the convergence rate by using the over-relaxation form (19) instead of simply computing $x^{(k)}$ as $x^{(k)}=x^{(k-1)}+\delta x^{(k)}$.

$$x^{(k)} = x^{(k-1)} + \omega x^{(k)}, \qquad \omega > 1 \tag{19}$$

where w is called the relaxation factor. Typically, this value is constant for all k and $1<w<2$. The iterative process expressed in (19) is called Successive Over-Relaxation, commonly abbreviated as SOR.

The basic concepts of linear algebra presented above are used in problems of voice signal reconstruction dealing with missing samples, such as those described in this chapter. These problems can be defined as linear system equations in which interpolation algorithms play an important role in finding their solutions. In this context, missing or unknown samples due to transmission errors or data loss are set to zero at the receiver, which in turn shall use reconstruction methods to find the best possible estimate of the original signal.

4. Two linear interpolation algorithms

This section describes two reconstruction algorithms capable of computing accurate estimates of missing samples in voice signals due to packet loss, transmission errors, etc. Therefore these algorithms are suitable to be implemented in receivers as error concealment methods to enhance the QoE delivered to users. Both algorithms are based on linear interpolation and operate on a sequence of voice samples of a predefined length, i.e., the number of samples under processing at a given time is constant. Let us define a $\boldsymbol{N}$-dimension signal vector with Fourier components x_1, x_2, … x_N, and the Fourier matrix $\boldsymbol{F}$ a unitary NxN matrix with components F_{mk} given by

$$F_{mk} = \frac{1}{\sqrt{N}} e^{-i\frac{2\pi}{N}mk} \tag{20}$$

where $\boldsymbol{i}$ is the imaginary unit. Therefore, the Discrete Fourier Transform DFT of $\boldsymbol{x}$, here represented by $\widehat{x}$, is the sequence $\widehat{x} = Fx$. In this context, sampling and band-limiting are two relevant linear operations defined in $\mathbb{C}^N$ which should be recalled. In this case, sampling is defined as a mapping function which converts a sequence of samples (i.e., a digital signal), into another one by setting to zero some of the original samples. This is used as an error modelling function by which the sampled version of the signal (i.e., the one with missing/lost samples) may be obtained by multiplying the original signal with a diagonal matrix D whose elements are comprised of zeros and ones (Ferreira, 1994a). The resulting signal is called the observed signal and it corresponds to a corrupted version of the original one. Therefore D is called the sampling matrix and its diagonal is the sampling set associated with the sampling operation. Considering $\boldsymbol{s}$ the number of nonzero entries in the sampling set, then s/N defines the density of sampling. Here it is assumed that $s<N$ and D is not the identity matrix, I.

Band-limiting can also be viewed as a sampling operation, in which the signal samples set to zero are in the Fourier domain, i.e., signal frequency components. In fact, by multiplying a diagonal matrix Γ by Fx, the resulting matrix ΓFx has zeros in those spectral components of x that correspond to the zeros of Γ. Then by left-multiplying F^{-1} by ΓFx returns the signal into the time domain, resulting in a filtering operation. Therefore, such band-limiting operation can be defined by a linear operator characterized by a matrix B defined as $B=F^{-1}\Gamma F$. As mentioned above, Γ is a sampling matrix different from the identity I. The bandwidth of the signal $y=Bx$ is defined as q/N, where q is the number of nonzero entries in Γ. The Nyquist sampling frequency is denoted as f_s while f_{os} is an oversampling frequency. In this case, an oversampling factor r is defined as $r=f_s/f_{os}$. Such oversampling factor is also given by $r=q/N$ and if $r<1$ then there is redundancy in the signal.

Considering N samples of a voice signal and n the number of corrupted samples, then the following condition holds: $n<N$. If the reconstruction algorithm has to solve N equations, i.e., using the whole space of dimension N, then it is called a maximum dimension algorithm. However, if the algorithm only needs to solve n equations concerning just the unknown samples, then it is called a minimum dimension algorithm. The error geometry is defined as the pattern of missing samples within the whole sequence of samples. Depending on the relative position between missing samples, three geometries are addressed: i) interleaved geometry, where the missing samples are equidistant and multiple of an integer $l\geq2$; ii) burst geometry where the missing samples occur in bursts of contiguous samples and iii) random geometry where the missing samples do not exhibit any special pattern but are randomly distributed along the original sequence. In this context a signal with bandwidth $\boldsymbol{b}$ means that the highest normalized frequency in the signal is $b/2$. The nonzero entries of the Γ diagonal define the so-called passband of B (Ferreira, 1994a).

Moreover, note that both sampling and band-limiting are idempotent operations. This means that repeating such operations over the same signal always produce the same result as that obtained from one single operation. Therefore, idempotence allows defining a passband signal $\boldsymbol{x}$ as follows:

$$x=Bx. \tag{21}$$

4.1 A maximum dimension algorithm – the discrete version of Papoulis-Gerchberg

The discrete version of Papoulis-Gerchberg algorithm is an iterative linear interpolation algorithm (Ferreira, 1994a). Its aim is to recover missing samples in a finite-length, band-limited data sequence x, given their positions within the sequence. In this case the data sequence of interest is a time segment of a voice signal. Fig. 1 and Fig. 2 show an example of both original and observed signals, x and y respectively, where the last one is obtained by setting to zero two of the original samples.

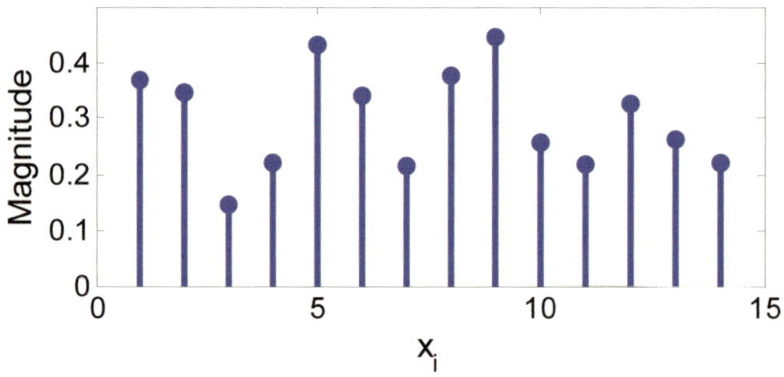

Fig. 1. Original time-domain signal x

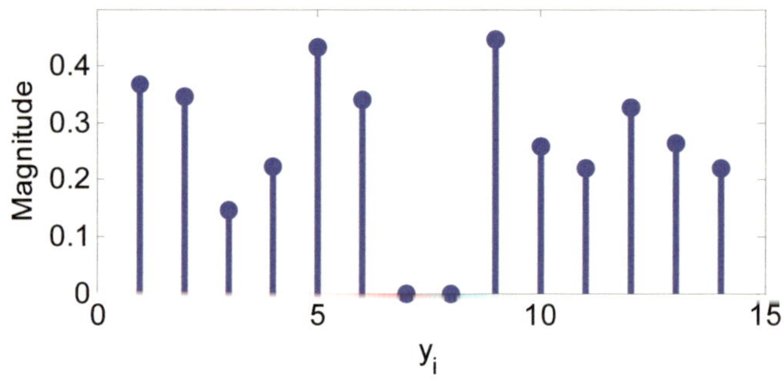

Fig. 2. Observed time-domain signal y

In this signal reconstruction algorithm, the known data are the samples of the observed signal, the position of the missing ones and the bandwidth of the original signal, as given by Equation (21). This is equivalent to know the vector y (Fig. 2), and the matrices D and B referred to above. Note that, in practice matrix D is obtained from the received signal with lost samples.

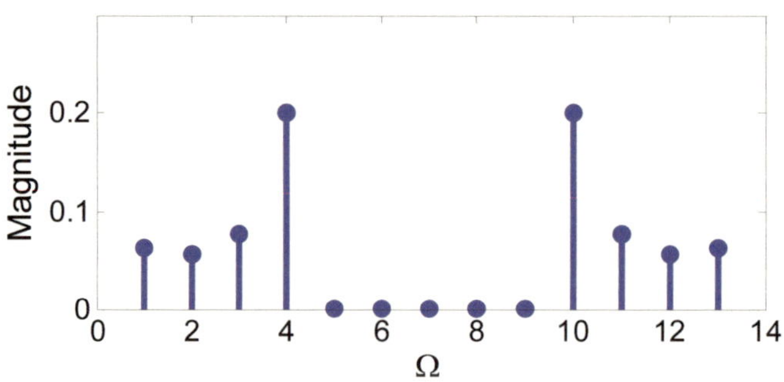

Fig. 3. Spectral components of the original signal, x

The aim of the reconstruction algorithm is to make the observed signal as close as possible to the original one. By knowing the original signal bandwidth, from which the spectral components are derived, it is possible to compare the observed signal with the original one as the iterative process converges. Fig. 3 shows the spectral components of the original signal x without the DC component.

Herein, the main algorithmic steps leading to the reconstructed signal are described as follows.

Step 1 - Compute the DFT of y: ***DFT(y)=Fy***

The first step in this algorithm is to transform y into the frequency domain, by computing its DFT, i.e., $DFT(y)=Fy$. In the subsequent iteration process, the observed signal y is subject to several operations. Let us define $y^{(0)}$ as iteration 0 of the reconstructed signal, $y^{(1)}$ the result of the first iteration, etc. Iteration 0 is obtained as $y^{(0)}=y=Dx$. As expected, whenever a signal incurs in sharp time-domain variations, such as those originated by loss of samples, this implies changes in the frequency domain. Therefore when losses occur in the original signal, high frequency components appear in the observed signal y, which lie outside the bandwidth of the original signal. Fig. 4 shows the result of such operation, where high frequency components (i.e., central components) appeared at locations where originally there were zeros (see Fig. 3).

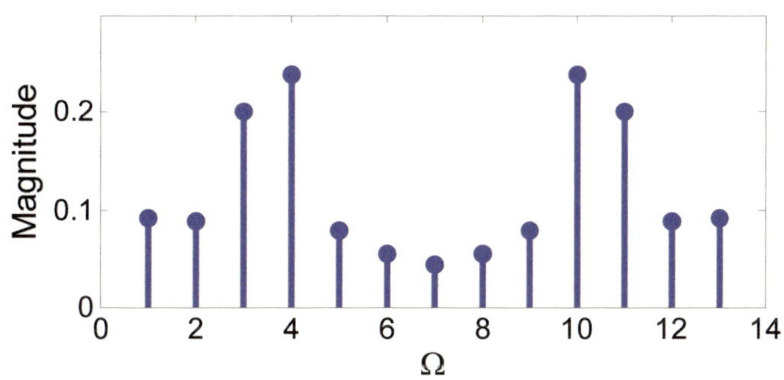

Fig. 4. Spectral components of the observed signal, y

Step 2 - Filter y according to the spectral characteristic of x: ***DFT(y')=ΓFy***

The underlying idea behind this process of signal reconstruction is to filter the observed signal y with the same spectral characteristics as those of the original signal. Then, the filtered signal, y', is closer to x than y, because its transform domain representation was also approximated to the original one.

Such filtering operation is achieved by left-multiplying matrix Γ by $DFT(y)$. It is given by $DFT(y')=\Gamma\, Fy$. Fig. 5 shows the result of this filtering operation, where the undesirable spectral components become zero while the others remain unchanged.

Step 3 - Return to the time-domain: ***y'=F⁻¹ΓFy*** ($y'=F^{-1}\Gamma Fy$)

The filtered signal y' can now be obtained in the time domain through the inverse of $DFT(y')$. Note that, as pointed out above, y' is closer to the original signal x than y, i.e., the effect of filtering is to approximate the missing samples towards their original values. Fig. 6 shows these new samples growing at the sampling instants where their previous values were zero. After few initial iterations, their amplitudes are not yet exactly the same as the original ones, but they tend to the original ones as the iterative process converges to a more accurate solution. This is because the values of such samples result from a filtering operation

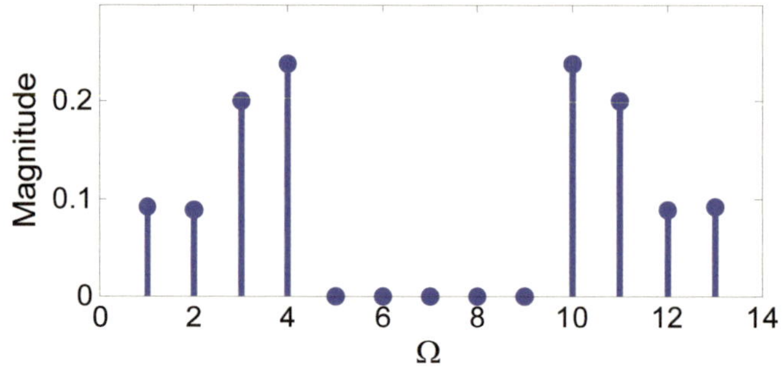

Fig. 5. Spectral components of y' after filtering y :$DFT(y')$

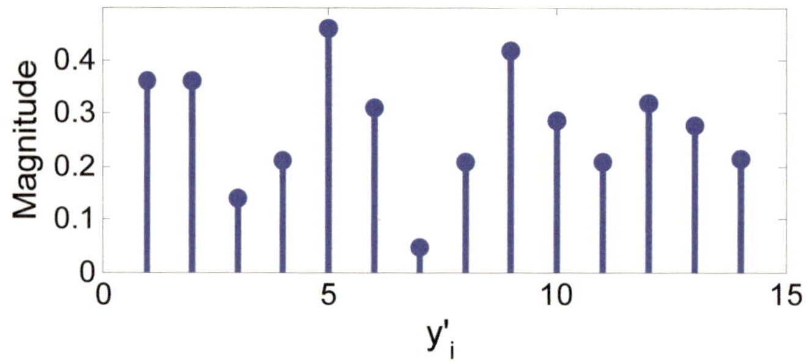

Fig. 6. Signal y' obtained after enforcing the original signal bandwidth through filtering.

that makes the corrupted signal closer to the original one by forcing it to have similar spectral components. However, the filtering operation also changes the values of the non-corrupted samples of y.

Step 4 - Extract the reconstructed samples from the others: $\boldsymbol{y''=(I-D)y'}$.

Although the previous process has the advantage of recovering sample values at sampling instants where they were zeros, it also slightly corrupts the good samples of the observed signal y. However, since the time locations of the missing samples are known through matrix D, in each iteration is possible to extract only the reconstructed samples through the following operation $y''=(I-D)y'$. The output of such extraction process is illustrated in Fig. 7 where only the new samples are left and all others are set to zero.

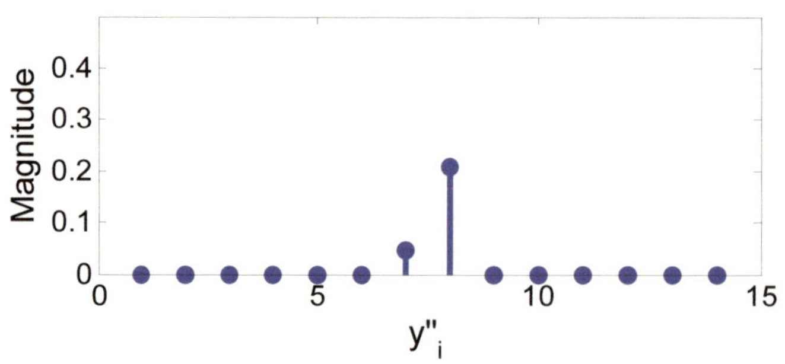

Fig. 7. Signal y'': samples extracted from y'.

Step 5 - Reconstructed signal composition: $\boldsymbol{y^{(1)}=y''+y}$

After the previous steps, on the one hand, signal y'' has only non-zero samples at those sampling instants where the missing samples were located in the observed signal. On the other hand, at the remaining sampling instants, the observed signal y contains all non-corrupted samples. This means that signals y and y'' contain non-zero samples at mutually exclusive temporal instants. So the sum of both signals results in the first approximation $y^{(1)}$ of the original signal x and acomplishes the first iteration of the reconstruction process. Fig. 8 shows the reconstructed signal $y^{(1)}$ after the first iteration.

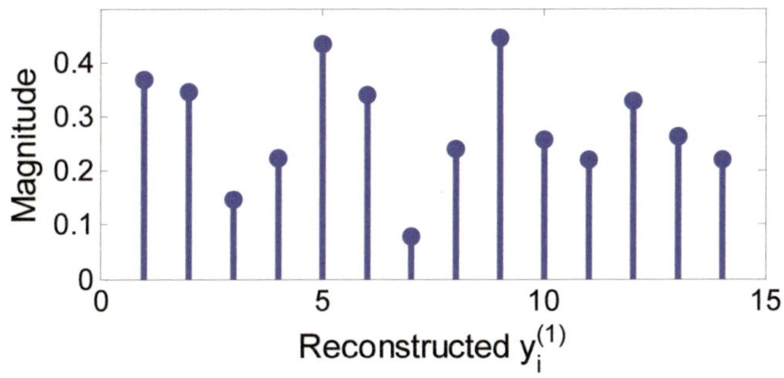

Fig. 8. Reconstructed signal $y^{(1)}$ after the first iteration.

Step 6 - Prepare next iteration: $\boldsymbol{y=y^{(1)}}$.

For the next iteration, the reconstructed signal $y^{(1)}$ appears as the new observed signal to enter into a new reconstruction cycle. Therefore, at this step $y=y^{(1)}$. Note that, since the non-corrupted samples of the original observed signal are needed in Step 5 of each iteration, y must be stored in memory at the startup of the process, i.e., before Step 1.

The algorithmic steps described above can be defined by a sequence of algebraic expressions, which are the basis for software implementation of the reconstruction method. The following expressions fully describe the reconstruction algorithm from Step 6 to Step 1.

$$y^{(1)}=y''+y \tag{22}$$

$$y^{(1)}=(I-D)y'+y \tag{23}$$

$$y^{(1)}=(I-D)F^{-1}\Gamma F\, y^{(0)}+y \tag{24}$$

From (24) it is possible to obtain the following expression for the reconstructed signal in the next iteration

$$y^{(k+1)}=(I-D)By^{(k)}+y \tag{25}$$

where $y^{(k)}$ represents the reconstructed signal at iteration k.

The iteration matrix is, thus, given by

$$A=(I-D)B \tag{26}$$

In order to improve convergence a relaxation constant, μ is used, thus Equation (25) becomes,

$$y^{(k+1)}=(I-\mu D)By^{(k)}+\mu y \tag{27}$$

and the iteration matrix is given by

$$A_\mu=(I-\mu D)B \qquad (28)$$

For an effective use of such a constant, values of μ belonging to the interval]0, 2[must be used (Ferreira, 1994a). More precisely, the optimum value of μ is given by

$$\mu_{opt}=\frac{2}{2-\lambda_{\max}}$$

where λ_{max} =ρ(S_1) with S_1 being $S_1=B(I-D)B$.

The algorithm converges if the density of sampling is greater than the signal bandwidth, i.e., $s/N>q/N$. Thus, convergence can be guaranteed by reducing the number of missing samples and/or the bandwidth.

An important issue concerning convergence are the error patterns (i.e., location of missing samples) which influence the asymptotic convergence rate of the algorithm, for a given density. The convergence rate partially depends on matrix B and on the error geometry. In fact, for low pass signals, the best possible error patterns are those in which the missing sample time positions are equidistant (Neves et al., 2008). The worst possible geometry is that of contiguous missing samples. In the middle there is the random geometry. This issue is important in order to obtain a well-conditioned problem. The fact that this is a maximum dimension method, the possibility of low convergence rates and the computing resources required per iteration (essentially a pair of FFTs) are disadvantages of this approach. Since this is a maximum dimension problem it is expected to exhibit a relatively low convergence rate due to the enormous computing resources required. This is further discussed in section 5.

4.2 A minimum dimension algorithm

As mentioned in previous sections, a minimum dimension algorithm is characterised by a system of only n equations corresponding to the n unknown samples. This subsection describes a minimum dimension algorithm which also requires band-limited signals of finite-dimension similarly to the Papoulis-Gerchberg algorithm described above, i.e., equation (21) must be valid.

To establish the basic concepts of this algorithm, the specific case of an original signal x_i with length N=5 is used, i.e., $x_i=\{x_1, x_2, x_3, x_4, x_5\}$. For this signal, Equation (21) becomes

$$\begin{aligned} x_1 &= b_{11}x_1+b_{12}x_2+b_{13}x_3+b_{14}x_4+b_{15}x_5 \\ &\vdots \\ x_5 &= b_{51}x_1+b_{52}x_2+b_{53}x_3+b_{54}x_4+b_{55}x_5 \end{aligned} \qquad (29)$$

where b_{ij} are the elements of the matrix B.

For reconstruction purposes let us assume that the 2nd and 4th samples of x_i are lost. Then the set of equations (29) are limited to those including the lost samples. In each of these equations, we are interested in separating the right side terms containing unknown samples (x_2, x_4) from those containing the known ones. This yields,

$$\begin{aligned} x_2 &= b_{21}x_1+b_{22}x_2+b_{23}x_3+b_{24}x_4+b_{25}x_5 \\ x_4 &= b_{41}x_1+b_{42}x_2+b_{43}x_3+b_{44}x_4+b_{45}x_5 \end{aligned} \qquad (30)$$

which is equivalent to

$$\begin{bmatrix} x_2 & x_4 \end{bmatrix} = \begin{bmatrix} b_{22} & b_{24} \\ b_{42} & b_{44} \end{bmatrix} \begin{bmatrix} x_2 \\ x_4 \end{bmatrix} + \begin{bmatrix} b_{21} & b_{23} & b_{25} \\ b_{41} & b_{43} & b_{45} \end{bmatrix} \begin{bmatrix} x_1 \\ x_3 \\ x_5 \end{bmatrix} \quad (31)$$

Let us denote by u the subset of the original signal x_i which contains the unknown values. In this case, $u=\{x_2, x_4\}$ is of cardinality $k=2$. Also, let us define $U=\{i_1, i_2, \ldots, i_k\}$ as the set of subscripts of k unknown samples in x_i. In the present case, $U=\{2, 4\}$. Therefore, equations (31) can be written as

$$x_i = \sum_{j \in U} b_{ij} x_j + \sum_{j \notin U} b_{ij} x_j; \qquad i \in U \quad (32)$$

or, in matricial form

$$u = Su + h \quad (33)$$

where S is a kxk principal submatrix of B, as defined in (31), and h, is the (N-k)-dimensional vector in the second sum of (32), which is a linear combination of the known samples of x_i.
The conditions under which these equations provide a solution for u can be found in (Ferreira, 1994b). In the case where a noniterative method is used, equation (33), becomes equivalent to

$$\begin{aligned} & u = Su + h \\ & u - Su = h \\ & Iu - Su = h \\ & (I - S)u = h \\ & (I - S)^{-1}(I - S)u = (I - S)^{-1}h \\ & u = (I - S)^{-1}h \end{aligned} \quad (34)$$

This result is valid, providing that $(I\text{-}S)^{-1}$ exists. Thus, theoretically, Equation (33) has a unique solution regardless the number and distribution of the lost samples. If equation (33) is solved through an iterative process, then the following form is suggested in the case where a non-relaxation method is used.

$$u^{(i+1)} = Su^{(i)} + h \quad (35)$$

Then $u^{(k)}$ is obtained at iteration k and the solution is given by the limit

$$u = \lim_{i \to \infty} u^{(i)} \quad (36)$$

regardless of $u^{(0)}$. The condition $\rho(S)<1$ guarantees that such limit exists, where S is the system matrix (Ferreira, 1994b).
Two different techniques can be used to solve (33): Direct calculation and iterative methods. Direct calculation of u as given in (34) has the advantage of being done in one single step, providing that $(I\text{-}S)^{-1}$ exists. In practice, there are several factors which may lead to serious difficulties in calculating the inverse of $I\text{-}S$. For example, if one of the eigenvalues of S is close enough to unity, then computation of $(I\text{-}S)^{-1}$ may become very difficult, or even impossible, leading to an ill-conditioned problem. In such cases, an iterative method may be

used to circumvent this difficulty and to find an accurate approximation for solution u. Despite the fact of having an ill-conditioned problem, in the case of direct calculation such problem is impossible to solve whereas in the case of iterative methods an approximation is always possible to be found, though its accuracy may not be very high.

The eigenvalues of the system matrix S depend on the distribution of the missing samples. In particular, its spectral radius is more likely be unitary for burst distributions rather than for equidistant missing samples (Ferreira, 1994c). In the case of signal reconstruction it is interesting to note that, if the distribution of the missing samples $U=\{i_1, i_2, \ldots, i_n\}$ is equidistant by some fixed integer $m\geq 1$, that is, $U=\{i_1m, i_2m, \ldots, i_nm\}$, then the eigenvalues λ_i of S have an upper bound given by $(\lfloor rm \rfloor+1)/m$ and a lower bound given by $\lfloor rm \rfloor/m$, i.e.,

$$\frac{\lfloor rm \rfloor}{m} \leq \lambda_i(S) \leq \frac{\lceil rm \rceil}{m} \leq 1 \tag{37}$$

where $\lfloor rm \rfloor$ denotes the greatest integer less than or equal to rm and $\lceil rm \rceil$ denotes the smallest integer equal or greater than rm. In the particular case of $r=\lfloor rm \rfloor/m$, the eigenvalues of S are all the same $\lambda_i(S)=r$, $\forall i$. In such case $S=rI$. In the particular case of $i_k=km$, the missing samples are equidistant and S becomes Toeplitz.

Given the above analysis, it is possible to put the problem into a well-conditioning point by properly selecting the gap between the missing samples. Then it is possible to put $\lambda_i(S)$ close to either r or its multiples, regardless of the number of missing samples. By using an appropriate choice of the oversampling and interleaving factors r and m (i.e., such that mxr is an integer) respectively, it is possible to put $\lambda_i(S)$ less enough than unity in order to control the reconstruction accuracy and processing speed.

In VoIP context, the use of an adequate interleaving factor m, not only makes such a signal to be more robust to possible degradations by transforming burst errors in equidistant ones, but also makes reconstruction easier because it leads to a well-conditioned problem. Therefore, when a packet is lost with n voice samples in its payload, this leads to a reconstruction problem where missing samples are equidistantly distributed, separated by m-1, and the matrix S of the resulting reconstruction problem is of dimension nxn.

Fig. 9 shows the maximum and the minimum eigenvalues of S as a function of the interleaving factor, m, for a given bandwidth, defined by r. As the figure shows, greater values of m lead to well-conditioning problems because λ_{max} decreases as m increases. Also, when the product rxm is an integer, all eigenvalues are equal since they are $\lambda_i(S)=r$, as stated before. In Fig. 9, this occurs for m=5 and m=10.

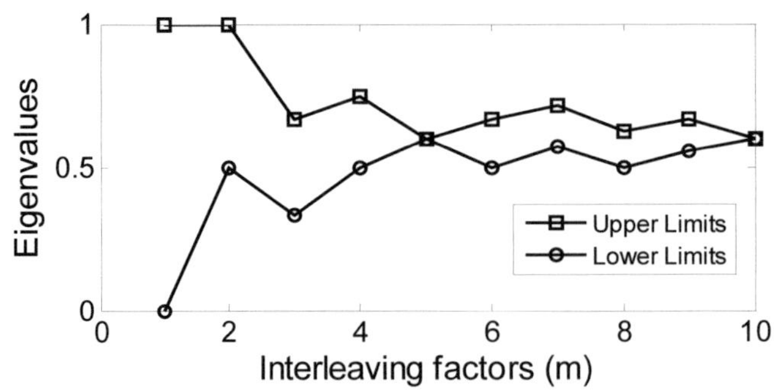

Fig. 9. Spectral radius vs. interleaving factor, r=0.6

Considering real time implementation issues, while the solution of (33) must be found in real time to be effective, the possibility to have a pool of different dimension system matrices *S*, previously calculated and stored in memory, turns the whole reconstruction process more expedite. Furthermore, its calculation may become as trivial as $S=rI$.

5. Simulation results

In this section, the reconstruction algorithms previously described are evaluated through simulation and the results are analysed and discussed. The simulation study is also aimed to provide a deeper understanding of the most important factors influencing the problem of signal reconstruction and to show how much a minimum dimension algorithm enhances the performance of the maximum dimension one.

In the case of the Papoulis-Gerchberg algorithm, it is important to analyse the factors that influence the conditioning of the reconstruction problem and how they influence its solution. These include the spectral radius of the iteration matrix, the distribution of the missing samples and the signal bandwidth. The performance is evaluated by measuring the number of iterations necessary to reach the solution, the percentage of lost samples, the iteration matrix spectral radius and the Root Mean-Squared Error (RMSE) between the original and reconstructed signals. The RMSE is given by the following expression, where $x[i]$ is the original signal, $\tilde{x}[i]$ the reconstructed signal and N the sequence length,

$$RMSE = \sqrt{\frac{1}{N}\sum_{i=1}^{N}\left(x[i]-\tilde{x}[i]\right)^2} \tag{38}$$

The stop criterion was defined as an upper bound for residual error between consecutive iterations, given by

$$residual = \sqrt{\frac{1}{N}\sum_{i=1}^{N}\left(y^{(k+1)}(i)-y^{(k)}(i)\right)^2} \leq 10^{-8} \tag{39}$$

where $y^{(k)}(i)$ is the signal at iteration k. In the case of random geometry tests, i.e., those where the loss pattern of voice samples is random, each simulation run uses more missing samples than the previous one, which in turn acts as a seed in order to guarantee an increasing spectral radius over successive runs. The same voice signal was used in all the tests. In all experiments, a voice signal with N=256 samples was used. In the case of the Papoulis-Gerchberg algorithm, three different error distributions, referred to as interleaved, random and burst geometries were used. These experiments run on a computer equipped with an Intel T2300@1.66 MHz processor and 1.5 GB RAM. Also, two different signal bandwidths were used, defined by two different factors r.

5.1 The maximum-dimension Papoulis-Gerchberg algorithm

The performance of Papoulis-Gerchberg algorithm was evaluated by carrying out three tests intended to find out how the spectral radius of the iteration matrix, the error geometry and the signal bandwidth influence the convergence of the algorithm.

5.1.1 The spectral radius of the iteration matrix

This test is intended to evaluate the influence of the spectral radius of the iteration matrix in the algorithm convergence. In the experiments the oversampling factor was set to r=0.6 and the relaxation constant μ=1. The percentage of missing samples varied from 0.4% to 25%. Fig. 10 shows the number of iterations necessary to obtain a residual error less than 10^{-8}, as a function of the spectral radius. As one can observe, as the spectral radius of the iteration matrix increases, the number of iterations also increases following approximately an exponential function. The absolute error of the approximated solution obtained after iteration k+1 is bounded by

$$\|e_{k+1}\| \leq \lambda_{\max}^{k} \|e_1\| \tag{40}$$

where λ_{max} represents the maximum eigenvalue of the system matrix (Ferreira, 1994a). This expression shows that in order to attain a given error, higher values of λ_{max} imply higher number of iterations, since λ_{max} is less than 1, k is greater than 1 and $\|e_1\|$ is constant. It is also possible to see that, if λ_{max}=1, the error after iteration k+1 will never decrease below to that of the first iteration, thus the algorithm does not converge. In the figure, it is evident that $\rho(\boldsymbol{A})$=1 leads to a non-convergence situation. Therefore, an important conclusion is that a spectral radius near to 1 can easily turn the problem into ill-conditioned making convergence difficult or even impossible. In this case an acceptable solution cannot be found.

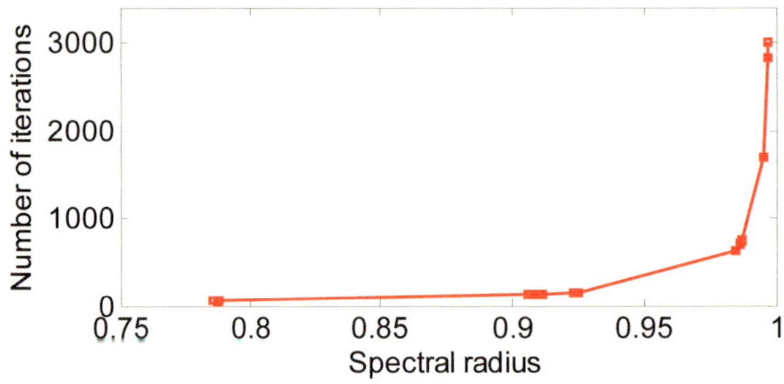

Fig. 10. Number of iterations *versus* the spectral radius (r=0.6)

5.1.2 Error geometry

This test is intended to evaluate the influence of the missing samples distribution on convergence and to identify the break even points, i.e., the maximum percentage of missing samples for which the algorithm is convergent. Note that each break even point also corresponds to a specific spectral radius because this is implicitly defined by the missing samples. In the experiments the values r=0.8 and μ=1 were used. Interleaved, random and burst distributions with loss percentages ranging from 1% to 50% were used. To determine break even points, spectral radii close to 1 were used.

Fig. 11 shows the spectral radius as a function of the percentage of missing samples, for the three error geometries under study. As the figure shows, the spectral radius depends on two factors: the percentage of missing samples and the error geometry. In regard to the percentage of missing samples, one can observe that the spectral radius increases as more samples are missing in the signal. This is common to all three geometries, which exhibit the same behaviour.

In the case of different error geometries, one can also see that for a given spectral radius, the interleaved geometry is the one which tolerates more missing samples and the burst geometry is the one that tolerates less missing samples, since just two or three missing samples make the spectral radius close to 1. The behaviour of the random geometry is between the other two. From another point of view, for the same number of missing samples, the interleaved geometry exhibits a lower spectral radius than the others and the burst geometry exhibits the greatest spectral radius. These results lead to the conclusion that interleaved geometry is the error pattern that tolerates a greater percentage of missing samples in the signal.

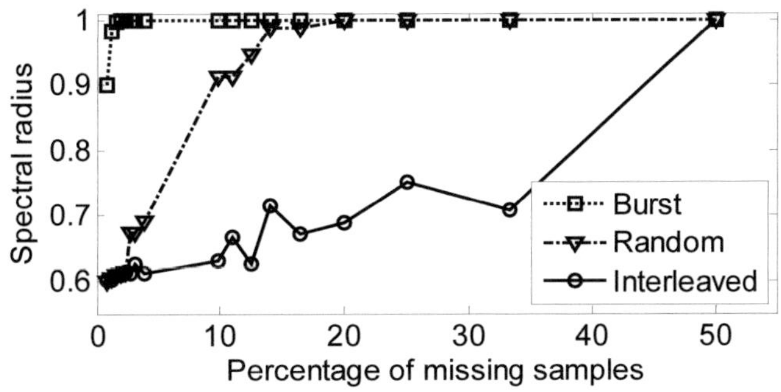

Fig. 11. Spectral radius *versus* percentage of missing samples, for three error geometries

Fig. 12 shows the break even points, for each type of error geometry defined by either the percentage of missing samples or its corresponding spectral radius. Note that these are the maximum values for which the algorithm still converges to a unique solution.

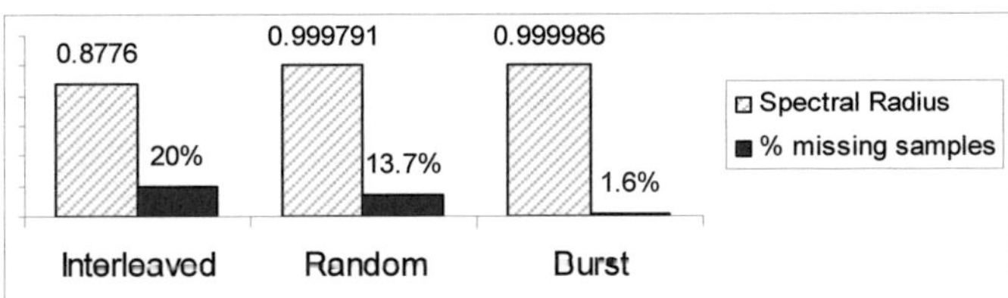

Fig. 12. Break even points for each geometry (r=0.8)

These results show that break even point positions vary according to the error geometry. In the case of the interleaved geometry, the maximum spectral radius that still leads to a well-conditioned problem is 0.8776. It corresponds to an interleaving factor of missing samples of m=5 (i.e., 1 out of 5) thus to 20% of missing samples. Other spectral radii between 0.8776 and 1 are possible, but the next value for the interleaving factor is four (m=4), which leads to a spectral radius of 1, thus to a ill-conditioned problem.

In the case of the random geometry, the maximum spectral radius that still leads to a well-conditioned problem is 0.999791 corresponding to lose 13.7% of the signal samples. Finally, the worst situation is the burst geometry in which the maximum possible spectral radius is 0.999986 corresponding to lose 1.6% of the signal samples.

Overall, these results confirm that the interleaved error geometry is the most tolerant to losses in the sense that more signal samples may be lost before the problem becomes ill-conditioned. On the opposite side, the burst error geometry was found to be the less tolerant to losses.

5.1.3 Influence of the signal bandwidth

This test is aimed to find out the influence of the signal bandwidth on the convergence of the algorithm. The test is similar to that of section 5.1.1 (see Fig. 10) except the signal bandwidth which was decreased through the oversampling factor, set to r=0.4. The results in Fig. 13 show that for spectral radii less than 0.8 the number of iterations required to converge is significantly reduced as compared with higher spectral radii.
Therefore, faster convergence is achieved for lower signal bandwidth.

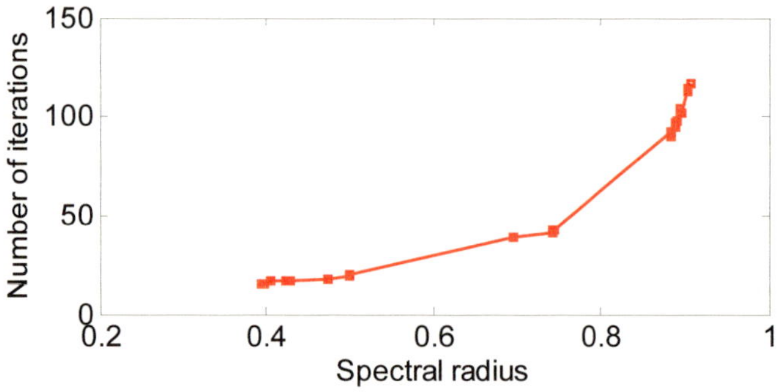

Fig. 13. Number of iterations as a function of the spectral radius (r=0.4)

Another relevant issue is to find out how the break even points are affected by decreasing the signal bandwidth. Fig. 14 shows that break even points are achieved at higher values than in the case of Fig. 12. This means that a greater percentage of missing samples is allowed in signals with lower bandwidth without reaching the non-convergence boundary.
For the interleaved geometry, the maximum spectral radius that still guarantees convergence is 0.5. Since the respective interleaving factor is m=2, then 50% of samples are allowed to be lost in this case. Comparing with results obtained in Section 5.1.1, where the signal bandwidth was greater (r=0.8), this corresponds to a significant improvement in tolerance to loss of samples. Note that in the previous case the maximum sample loss rate was just 20%. The same behaviour occurs for the random and burst error geometries. In the case of random losses, for the maximum spectral radius that still leads to a convergent situation (i.e., 0.999991), 50% of missing samples are still allowed against 13.7% in the case of r=0.8. In the case of error bursts, for the maximum allowed spectral radius of 0.999968, it is possible to have 3.9% of missing samples against 1.6% in the case of r=0.8.

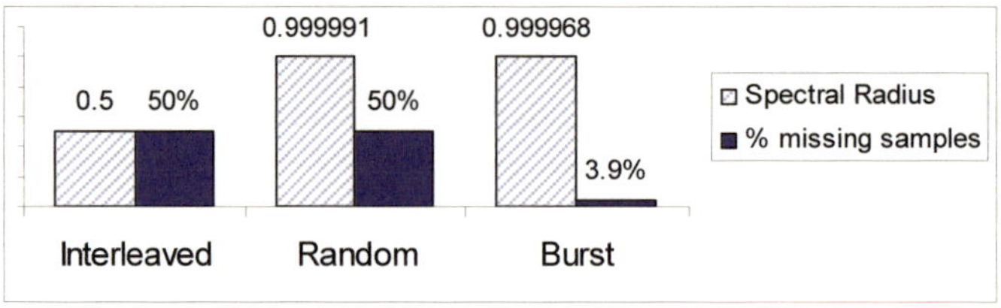

Fig. 14. Break even points for each geometry (r=0.4)

These results show that the signal bandwidth influences the convergence rate. A lower signal bandwidth leads to greater convergence rates. Also, the interleaved geometry is shown to be more tolerant to losses, which leads to the conclusion that such a mechanism is more adequate to improve error robustness and to ease signal reconstruction.

5.2 The minimum dimension interpolation algorithm

This experiments described in this subsection are intended to evaluate and compare the performance of the Papoulis-Gerchberg (PG) method with that of the minimum dimension method using both the iterative (MD Iterat) and direct computation (MD Direct) variants.

The performance metrics used in the study were the processing time obtained from Matlab© and the RMSE between the original and the reconstructed signals. Since the spectral radius plays an important role in the reconstruction accuracy and processing time, the dependence on the number of unknown samples was also studied.

Fig. 15 shows the dependency of the spectral radius from the percentage of missing samples for the various reconstruction methods. It is evident in the figure that the spectral radius increases with the number of missing samples, which means that in all methods more missing samples tend to result in ill-conditioned reconstruction problems. This is in line with the results of Section 5.1.2. Another important conclusion is that the spectral radius of the system matrix is independent from the reconstruction method for both oversampling factors r=0.8 and r=0.6. Moreover, it can be seen that greater bandwidth (i.e., greater r) implies greater spectral radii, which makes one to expect more processing time in the respective reconstruction. This is also in line with the conclusions of Section 5.1.3. Note that coincident lines in the figure means that for each value of r, the spectral radii are the same for all methods.

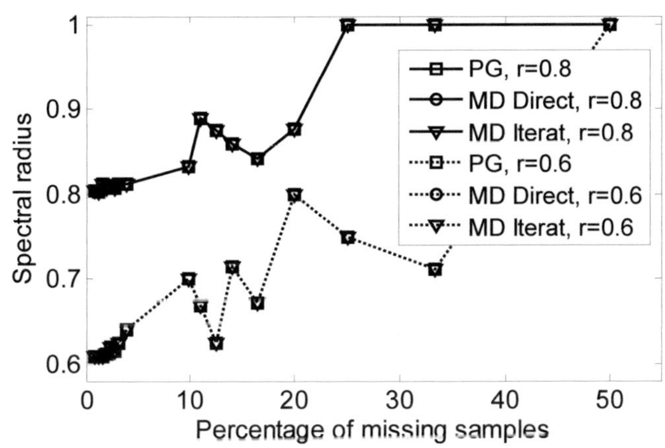

Fig. 15. Spectral radius *versus* missing samples for each method and oversampling factor

Fig. 16 shows how the RMSE between reconstructed signal and the original one depends on the number of missing samples. The break even points are also shown in the figure, separating the well-conditioning region (left side) from that of ill-conditioning (right side). In Fig. 16 one can also observe that for each oversampling factor r, both iterative methods achieve the same RMSE with the critical point occuring when the spectral radii $\rho(A)$ and $\rho(S)$ of the system matrices $\boldsymbol{A}$ and $\boldsymbol{S}$ are close to 1. $\rho(A)$ denotes the spectral radius of the maximum dimension algorithm matrix and $\rho(S)$ denotes the spectral radius of the minimum dimension algorithm matrix. For both methods, these spectral radii have the same value, $\rho(A)= \rho(S)=0.88$ corresponding to 20% of missing samples with an interleaving factor m=5.

Furthermore, for small percentages of missing samples, the direct computation variant (MD Direct) of the minimum dimension problem provides more accurate reconstructed signals than either maximum or minimum dimension iterative methods, i.e., the same accuracy is obtained from both methods when the number of missing samples is low. For large number of missing samples, iterative methods exhibit slightly higher reconstruction accuracy. Therefore, when the problem is well-conditioned, direct variant computation is more suitable whereas in the case of a ill-conditioned problem, iterative methods are preferable.

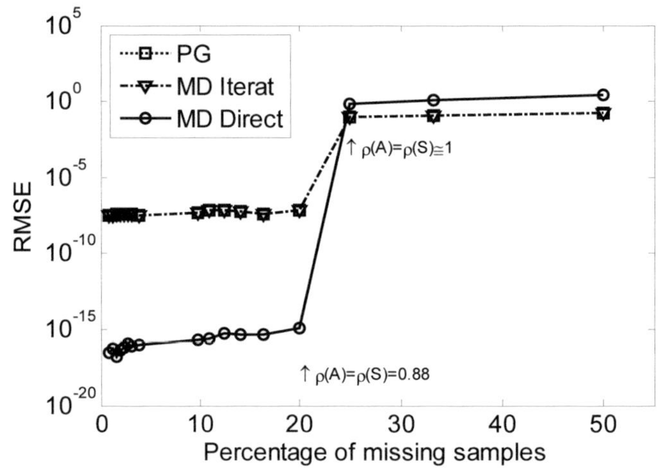

Fig. 16. RMSE *versus* number of missing samples for maximum and minimum dimension algorithms; r=0.8

Fig. 17 shows similar results as in Fig. 16, except that the signal bandwidth r is lower. The results in this figure confirm that, in the case where the number of missing samples is small, the direct variant of the minimum dimension algorithm (MD Direct) gives better reconstruction accuracy than iterative variants for both algorithms. However, for large number of missing samples, iterative variants exhibit slightly better reconstruction accuracy. The break even points are the same for both algorithms but in the figure they are shifted to the right, which means that more missing samples are allowed. In this case, it corresponds to a spectral radius of 0.71 and 33.2% of missing samples.

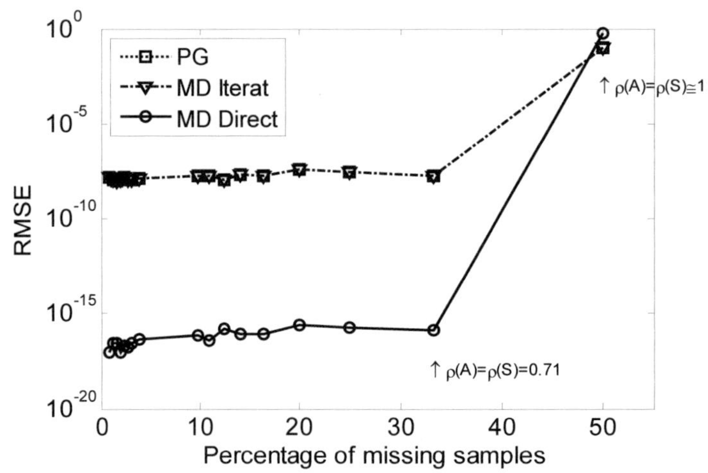

Fig. 17. RMSE *versus* missing samples; r=0.6

The computation time spent by the reconstruction algorithms are shown in Fig. 18 and Fig. 19, for the case of r=0.8 r=0.6, respectively. Both maximum and minimum dimension algorithms and the iterative and direct computation variants of the latter were evaluated. As it can be seen in these figures, for a small number of missing samples, direct computation of the minimum dimension problem is the fastest one and a lower bandwidth signal leads to smaller computation time, particularly when using an iterative method. However, for a large number of lost samples the direct method is more time consuming.

The processing time of the Papoulis-Gerchberg algorithm is always slower than that of the minimum dimension one, regardless of its variant, either iterative or direct computation. However the difference between them decreases when the number of missing samples increases. This is because is such case the problem dimension in the minimum dimension method approximates the maximum dimension of the Papoulis-Gerchberg.

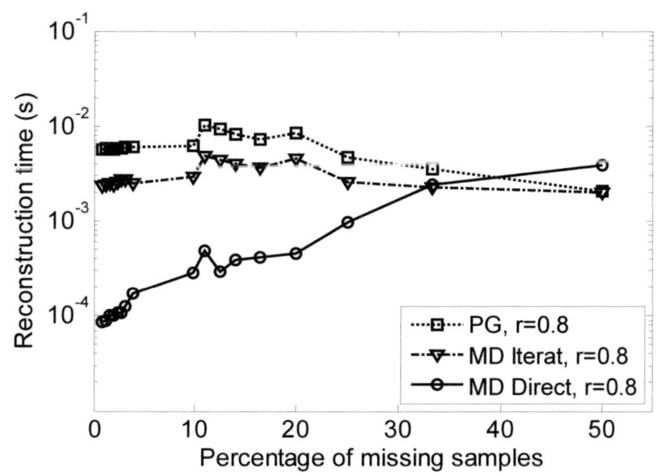

Fig. 18. Computation time of reconstruction; r=0.8

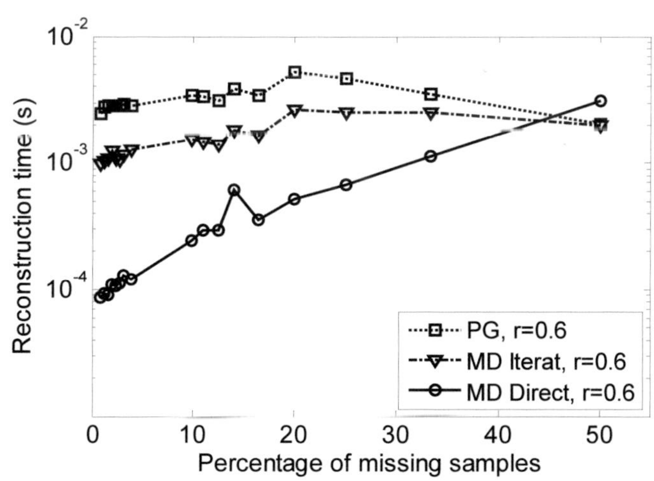

Fig. 19. Computation time of reconstruction; r=0.6

6. Case study

Whilst errors and data loss increase distortion in the received voice signals, reconstruction algorithms have a significant positive impact on the voice quality. Therefore proper evaluation of the quality experienced by users is extremely important to network and service providers. The study presented in this section is part of a R&D pilot project addressing voice quality evaluation currently running at Portugal Telecom Inovação, SA (PTIn). A non-reference voice quality model was derived and validated at PTin Labs using an IP Network and validated by using a specific probe and PESQ.

This experimental study was based on two ITU-T recommendations for voice quality evaluation: "Perceptual Evaluation of Speech Quality (PESQ)" Rec. ITU-T P.862 (ITU-T, 2001) and E-Model Rec. ITU-T G.107 (ITU-T, 2005). The E-Model was chosen as the basis for deriving the non-reference model used in the field trials, i.e., a modified E-Model.

In this trial, the impairments caused by both low bit-rate codecs and voice packet-losses of random distribution were under study. Thus, in the E-Model expression (1) ($R = R_0 - I_s - I_d - I_{e\text{-}eff} + A$), special attention has been paid to the term $I_{e\text{-}eff}$ which represents these type of impairments. The validation of the E-Model was done according to the conformance testing procedures described in the Rec. ITU-T P.564 (ITU-T, 2007a).

In the tests, the monitoring system platform ArQoS®, from PTIn, was used. This system permits to set up, maintain, monitoring and analyze telephony calls over technologies such as PSTN, GSM or IP. It provides QoS and QoE metrics such as MOS based on the PESQ algorithm. In the context of Rec. ITU-T P.564, the PESQ provides the reference for validation.

As depicted in the test scenario of Fig. 20, the main signal path includes coding and packetization, random packet-loss in an IP Network and decoding, from which the degraded signal is obtained. Thereafter, on one hand, both reference and degraded signals are given as inputs to the PESQ algorithm, whilst the output is the reference MOS used to calibrate the non-reference model. On the other hand, the degraded voice stream was collected and applied to a Gilbert modelling module whose output gives the probabilities necessary to calculate the *Ppl* and *BurstR* values for $I_{e\text{-}eff}$.

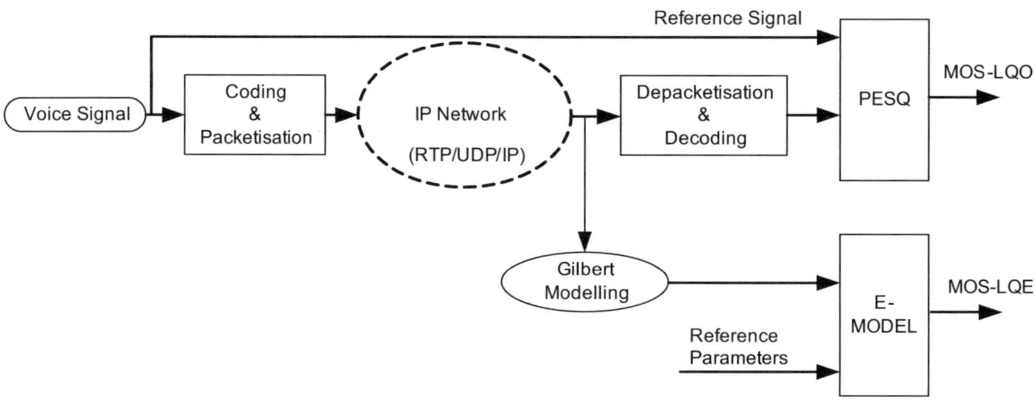

Fig. 20. Experimental setup for validation and calibration of the E-Model.

The first stage of this study aimed at achieving an accurate voice quality model based on the E-Model and using PESQ as reference for calibration. Note that both the E-Model and PESQ are sensitive to distortions caused by codecs and packet loss. The test samples defined in Rec. ITU-T P.501 (ITU-T, 2007b) were used in the trials. Two male and two female speaker sentences were used, comprising English and Spanish languages downsampled to 8 kHz (16 bits) as required by PESQ. Table 1 shows the samples used in this calibration stage.

Test sentences	Gender	Language
These days a chicken leg is a rare dish. The hogs were fed with chopped corn and garbage.	Female 1	English
The juice of lemons makes fine punch. Four hours of steady work faced us.	Male 1	English
No arroje basura a la calle. Ellos quieren dos manzanas rojas.	Female 1	Spanish
P - siéntate en la cama. El libro trata sobre trampas.	Male 1	Spanish

Table 1. Sentences used in the first stage of the trial.

The second stage was aimed to validate the results obtained in the previous stage by using a new set of sentences and new experiments. The test scenario and the test conditions were the same as in the calibration tests described above. Table 2 shows the test sentences used in this validation stage.

Test sentences	Gender	Language
Rice is often served in round bowls. A large size in stockings is hard to sell.	Female 2	English
The birch canoe slid on smooth planks. Glue the sheet to the dark blue background.	Male 2	English
No cocinaban tan bien. Mi afeitadora afeita al ras.	Female 2	Spanish
El trapeador se puso amarillo. El fuego consumió el papel.	Male 2	Spanish

Table 2. Used sentences on the validation stage

The codecs used in the trials for evaluation and calibration were G.711, G.729 8kbps and G.723.1 6.3kbps and six average packet loss ratios were selected to take the relevant results: 0%, 2.5%, 5%, 10%, 15% and 20%. The MOS_{LQO} values obtained from PESQ, as well as those obtained from the modified E-Model were collected for each packet loss rate, codec and sentence. This results in a total of 24 tests for each codec and 24 different MOS scores for each evaluation method, i.e, the modified E-Model and PESQ. Then for each codec, regression analysis was used to calibrate the intended voice quality model. Based on these two sets of scores (PESQ and modified E-Model), the coefficients of a polynomial $p(x)$ of degree n that fits p(E-Model MOS) to MOS_{LQO} were derived.

6.1 Results and discussion

Fig. 21 shows the results obtained from regression analysis, that models the relationship between MOS_{LQO} and the modified E-Model MOS scores for G.711 codec. The horizontal axis contains the scores obtained from the modified E-Model while the vertical axis represents the scores obtained from PESQ. For each point in the graph, the difference between the scores is the error between the modified E-Model and the reference PESQ. For instance, the second point from the left corresponds to E-Model MOS=1.5 and MOS_{LQO}=1.8, which means a MOS error of 0.3. In this case, the E-Model underestimates the MOS score in comparison with PESQ. In the graph, the points over the straight line correspond to no error cases in which both models produce the same result. In general, this figure shows that E-Model overestimates MOS relatively to PESQ. Therefore, a function to approximate the E-Model output to that of PESQ was derived. The figure shows the trend line that minimizes the RMSE between both MOS scores, which is the polynomial line that best approximates the E-Model to PESQ, for G.711 codec. Such line corresponds to the coefficients of a polynomial of degree 4 which gives the best approximation to PESQ. The resulting polynomial is given by

$$MOS_{LQO} = -0.0058MOS^4 + 0.1252MOS^3 - 0.6467MOS^2 + 1.9197MOS - 0.291 \quad (41)$$

which is the calibrating function of the E-Model MOS in order to get the corresponding MOS_{LQO} scores.

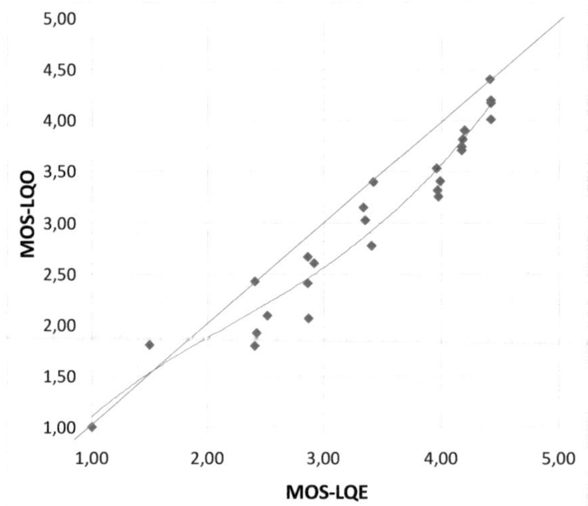

Fig. 21. Regression modelling of E-Model MOS scores as MOS_{LQO} for G.711

Fig. 22 shows the MOS scores obtained for G.729 codec under the same test conditions as in the previous case. The figure shows that in this case, the E-Model overestimates the MOS, when compared with MOS_{LQO} from PESQ. Fig. 22 also shows the trend line that best approximates the E-Model scores to MOS_{LQO} from PESQ algorithm, for G.729 codec. For this codec, the polynomial function to approximate the E-Model results to those of PESQ MOS_{LQO} is given by

$$MOS_{LQO} = 0.0554MOS^5 - 0.7496MOS^4 + 3.9507MOS^3 - 9.874MOS^2 + 11.939MOS - 3.8293 \quad (42)$$

Finally, Fig. 23 shows the results for G.723.1 codec. In this case, the E-Model underestimates MOS, in comparison with MOS_{LQO} from PESQ. The figure also shows the polynomial trend line that best approximates the E-Model scores to MOS_{LQO} from PESQ algorithm, for G.723.1 codec.

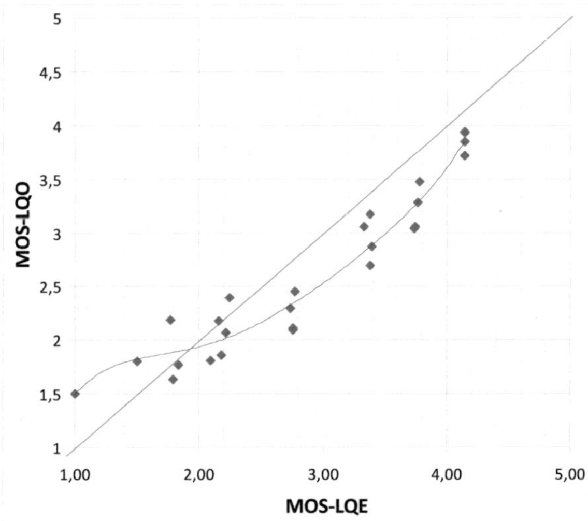

Fig. 22. Regression modelling of E-Model MOS scores as MOS_{LQO} for G.729

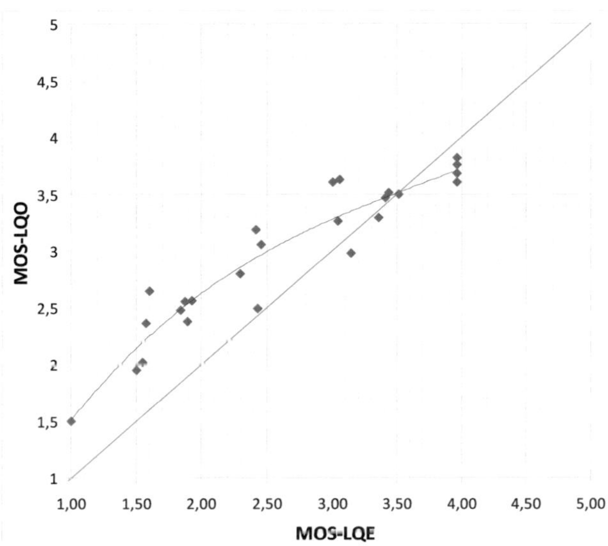

Fig. 23. Regression modelling of E-Model MOS scores as MOS_{LQO} for G.723.1

From these results, the function that best approximates MOS from E-Model to PESQ is given by:

$$MOS_{LQO} = 0.0018MOS^4 + 0.0248MOS^3 - 0.4262MOS^2 + 2.1953MOS - 0.2914 \qquad (43)$$

In the second stage, the sentences of Table 2 were used in the ArQoS® test system to obtain the respective PESQ MOS_{LQO} and E-Model MOS scores calibrated by using Equations (41), (42) and (43). Then the correlation factor, error and false positive/negative analysis between MOS_{LQO} scores and modified E-Model MOS were determined as defined in Recommendation ITU-T P.564. Table 3, Table 4 and Table 5 show the results obtained from the tests and the conformance accuracy requirements defined in ITU-T P.564. The tables show the correlation factor, percentage of errors and false negative/false positive measures, respectively.

Measure	Results			Requirements (P.564)	
	G.711	G.729	G.723.1	Class C1	Class C2
Correlation	0.956	0.964	0.887	>0.900	>0.850

Table 3. Results for the correlation factor

Measure	Results			Requirements (P.564)	
	G.711	G.729	G.723.1	Class C1	Class C2
Quality band B=1 ($MOS_{LQO} \geq 2.8$)					
Errors within boundary 1 (%)	81	90	67	≥97.9	
Errors within boundary 2 (%)	100	100	100	≥97.9	
Errors within boundary 3 (%)	100	100	100		≥95.0
Errors within boundary 4 (%)	100	100	100	≥99.0	
Errors within boundary 5 (%)	100	100	100		≥97.9
Errors within boundary 6 (%)	100	100	100		≥99.0
Quality band B=2 ($MOS_{LQO}<2.8$)					
Errors within boundary 7 (%)	75	86	78	≥90.0	
Errors within boundary 8 (%)	88	100	89		≥90.0
Errors within boundary 9 (%)	100	100	100	≥95.0	
Errors within boundary 10 (%)	100	100	100		≥95.0
Errors within boundary 11 (%)	100	100	100	≥99.0	
Errors within boundary 12 (%)	100	100	100		≥99.0

Table 4. Results for the percentage of errors.

Measure	Results			Requirements (P.564)	
	G.711	G.729	G.723.1	Class C1	Class C2
False negatives (%)	0	0	0	<5	<5
False positives (%)	0	0	0	<3	<3

Table 5. Results concerning false negatives/false positives

The results in Tabe 3 and Table 5, match both the correlation and false negative/false positive requirements for the Class 1. However, according to the results shown in Table 4, the percentage of errors falls within boundaries 7 and 8, which makes the modified E-Model to be included into Class 2.
Based on these results, the voice quality evaluation model based on the modified E-Model along with the respective calibration functions is currently in production at Portugal Telecom, SA.
Thus, satisfying these requirements, the voice quality evaluation model was integrated in the passive probes of ArQoS® system and is now in use at Portugal Telecom SA.

6.2 Practical application

While the ArQoS® active probes are meant to generate test calls on several type of networks, the ArQoS® passive probes are designed to analyse VoIP traffic, both signalling (SIP, Megaco, Radius, Diameter) and media stream (RTP) protocols. As passive probes, they analyse the existing traffic without any interference. They can be setup next to any element of the VoIP network, from the VoIP clients and Media Gateways to the core of the network. Collected data is gathered, analysed and processed automatically at the management system, providing many QoS statistics. The user can also use the system to trace a VoIP call in every probing point and in every protocol involved, allowing the end user to troubleshoot any possible problem.
The calibrated voice quality model of Portugal Telecom is of great use in the ArQoS® passive probes. It allows the translation of QoS metrics such as packet loss rate and jitter to a

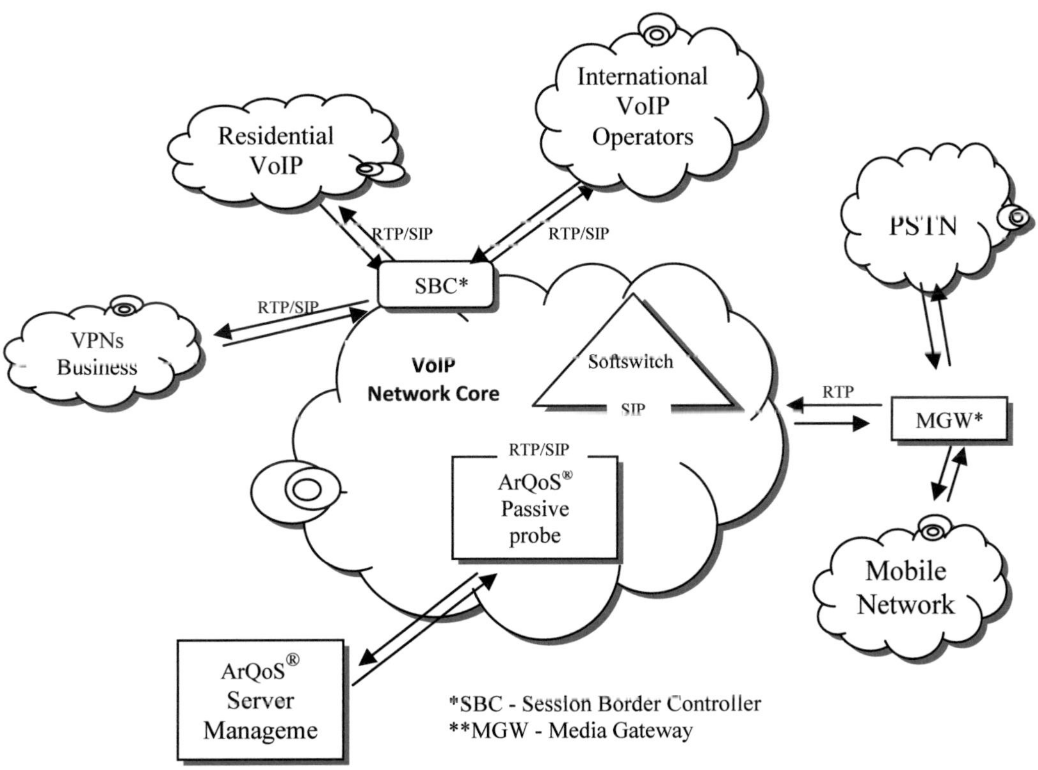

Fig. 24. Portugal Telecom VoIP network

more user friendly indicator as MOS. As depicted in Fig. 24 the ArQoS® passive probes are deployed in the Portugal Telecom VoIP Network core. All RTP streams are transmitted through the core, either in calls between VoIP and circuit-switch endpoints, or between just two VoIP clients. Our model is applied in every call then, resulting two MOS calculations, one for each way. On this application scenario, the network problems that affect the RTP stream after its passage through the core aren't really detected by the Probes. On the other hand, the reverse RTP stream that follows the same path should be affected to some extent before being analysed by the Probes. That means the user must always take into account both ways of each call. The calculated MOS values are also processed and shown in the ArQoS® statistics reporting tool, giving the users a good overview of the network voice quality.

7. Conclusion

Overall this chapter presented relevant problems of VoIP and described useful solutions, based on signal reconstruction, to overcome some of such problems. Special emphasis is given to a detailed description and comparison of two linear interpolation algorithms for voice reconstruction to cope with network errors and losses. A case study with VoIP field tests is described to evaluate the quality of VoIP services and a quality model is derived and validated.

8. Acknowledgements

This work was partially supported by Portugal Telecom Inovação in the context of Project E-VoIP (2008-2009).
The authors would like to thank Paulo Ferreira for helping in the revision of this chapter and also Simão Cardeal for providing some of the experimental data.

9. References

Aoki, N. (2004). VoIP packet loss concealment based on two-side pitch waveform replication technique using steganography, Proceedings of *TENCON 2004 - 2004 IEEE Region 10 Conference - Analog and Digital Techniques in Electrical Engineering*, 52-55, 0-7803-8560-8 Chiang Mai, Thailand 21-24 Nov. 2004 IEEE,

Becvar, Z.; Zelenka, J.; Brada, M. & Novak, L. (2007). Comparison of Common PLC Methods Used in VoIP Networks, Proceedings of *Systems, Signals and Image Processing, 2007 and 6th EURASIP Conference focused on Speech and Image Processing, Multimedia Communications and Services. 14th International Workshop on* 389 - 392, 978-961-248-029-5, Maribor, 27-30 June 2007 IEEE,

Bhute, V. P. & Shrawankar, U. N. (2008). Error concealment schemes for speech packet transmission over IP network, Proceedings of *15th International Conference on Systems, Signals and Image Processing*, 185-188, Bratislava, Slovak Republic, 25-28 June 2008,

Cheetham, B. (2006). Error Concealment for Voice over WLAN in Converged Enterprise Networks, *IST Mobile & Wireless Communications Summit 2006*, Mykonos, Greece, 4-8 June 2006,

Erdol, N.; Castelluccia, C. & Zilouchian, A. (1993). Recovery of missing speech packets using the short-time energy and zero-crossing measurements, *IEEE Transactions on Speech and Audio Processing*, 1, 3, (July 1993), 295-303, 1063-6676

Falk, T. H. & Chan, W.-Y. (2009). Performance Study of Objective Speech Quality Measurement for Modern Wireless-VoIP Communications, *EURASIP Journal on Audio, Speech, and Music Processing*, 2009, Article ID 104382, 11 pages,

Ferreira, P. J. S. G. (1994a). Interpolation and the discrete Papoulis-Gerchberg algorithm, *IEEE Transactions on Signal Processing*, 42, 10, (Oct 1994), 2596 - 2606, 1053-587X

Ferreira, P. J. S. G. (1994b). Noniterative and fast iterative methods for interpolation and extrapolation, *IEEE Transactions on Signal Processing*, 42, 11, (Nov 1994), 3278-3282, 1053-587X

Ferreira, P. J. S. G. (1994c). The Stability of a Procedure for the Recovery of Lost Samples in Band-Limited Signals, *IEEE Transactions on Signal Processing*, 42, 11, (Nov 1994), 3278 - 3282 1053-587X

Goodman, D.; Lockhart, G.; Wasem, O. & Wong, W.-C. (1986). Waveform substitution techniques for recovering missing speech segments in packet voice communications, *IEEE Transactions on Acoustics, Speech, and Signal Processing*, 34, 6, (December 1986), 1440-1448, 0096-3518

ITU-T (1996). Rec. P.800: *Methods for subjective determination of transmission quality* (Geneva 1996)

ITU-T (1999). Rec. G.109 *Definition of categories of speech transmission quality* (Geneva 1999)

ITU-T (2001). Rec. P.862: *Perceptual Evaluation of Speech Quality (PESQ)* (Geneva 2001)

ITU-T (2003). Rec. P.862.1: *Mapping function for transforming P.862 raw result scores to MOS-LQO* (Geneva 2003)

ITU-T (2004). Rec. P.563: *Single-ended method for objective speech quality assessment in narrow-band telephony applications* (Geneva 2004)

ITU-T (2005). Rec. G.107: *The E-Model, a computational model for use in transmission planning* (Geneva 2005)

ITU-T (2006). Rec. P.800.1: *Mean Opinion Score (MOS) terminology* (Geneva 2006)

ITU-T (2007a). Rec. P.564 *Conformance testing for voice over IP transmission quality assessment models* (Geneva 2007)

ITU-T (2007b). Rec. P.501: *Test signals for use in telephonometry* (Geneva 2007)

Jayant, N. & Christensen, S. (1981). Effects of Packet Losses in Waveform Coded Speech and Improvements Due to an Odd-Even Sample-Interpolation Procedure, *IEEE Transactions on Communications*, 29, 2, (Feb 1981), 101-109, 0096-2244

Kincaid, D. & Cheney, W. (2002). *Numerical Analysis: Mathematics of Scientific Computing*, The Brooks/Cole - Thompson Learning, 0-534-38905-08, Pacific Grove, CA, USA

Liu, F.; Kim, J. & Kuo, C.-C. J. (2001). Adaptive delay concealment for Internet voice applications with packet based time-scale modification, Proceedings of *ICASSP 2001-IEEE International Conference on the Acoustics, Speech, and Signal Processing*, 1461-1464, Washington DC, USA,

Neves, F.; Soares, S.; Reis, M. C.; Tavares, F. & Assuncao, P. (2008). VoIP reconstruction under a minimum interpolation algorithm, Proceedings of *IEEE International Symposium on Consumer Electronics, 2008. ISCE 2008*, 1-3, Vilamoura, Portugal, Apr. 2008,

Press, W. H.; Teukolsky, S. A.; Vetterling, W. T. & Flannery, B. P. (1994). *Numerical Recipes in C: The art of scientific computation*, Press Sybdicate of Cambridge University Press, 0-521-43108-5, Cambridge

Press, W. H.; Teukolsky, S. A.; Vetterling, W. T. & Flannery, B. P. (2007). *Numerical recipes: the art of scientific computing*, Cambridge University Press, 978-0-521-88068-8, Cambridge

Tang, J. (1991). Evaluation of double sided periodic substitution (dsps) method for recovering missing speech in packet voice communications, Proceedings of *IEEE Conference in Computers and Communications*, 454-458,

Tosun, L. & Kabal, P. (2005). Dynamically Adding Redundancy for Improved Error Concealment in Packet Voice Coding, Proceedings of *European Signal Processing Conf. EUSIPCO* 4, Antalya, Turkey, Sept. 2005,

Wah, B. W.; Su, X. & Lin, D. (2000). A survey of error-concealment schemes for real-time audio and video transmissions over the Internet, Proceedings of *Multimedia Software Engineering, 2000. International Symposium*, 17-24, Taipei, Taiwan,

Zourzouvillys, T. & Rescorla, E. (2010). An Introduction to Standards-Based VoIP: SIP, RTP, and Friends, *IEEE Internet Computing*, 14, 2, (March/April 2010), 69-73, 1089-7801

4

An Introduction to VoIP: End-to-End Elements and QoS Parameters

H. Toral-Cruz[1], J. Argaez-Xool[2], L. Estrada-Vargas[2] and D. Torres-Roman[2]
[1]*University of Quintana Roo (UQROO)*
[2]*Center of Research and Advanced Studies (CINVESTAV-IPN)*
Mexico

1. Introduction

In this chapter, two of the existing communication networks are studied: voice and data networks. Each network was created with the simple goal of transporting a specific type of information. For instance, the Public Switched Telephone Network (PSTN) was designed to carry voice and the IP network was designed to carry data.

In the PSTN, the main terminal device is a simple telephone set, while in the network, it is more complex, and it is provided with most of the intelligence necessary for providing various types for voice services. On the other hand, in the IP network the most of intelligence was placed in the terminal device, which is typically a host computer and the network only offers the best effort service (Park, 2005).

In mid 1990's, the two separate networks started to merge. A buzz word around this time is voice and data convergence. The idea is to create a single network to carry both voice and data.

However, with this convergence, a new technical challenge has emerged. In the converged network, the best effort services that are offered by the IP network is no longer good enough to meet requirements of real-time applications, such as Voice over Internet Protocol (*VoIP*).

VoIP refers to the transmission of voice using IP technologies over packet switched networks. It consists of a set of end-to-end elements, recommendations and protocols for managing the transmission of voice packets using IP. A basic *VoIP* system consists of three main elements: the *sender*, the *IP network* and the *receiver*.

VoIP is one of the most attractive and important service nowadays in communication networks and it demands strict *QoS* levels and real-time voice packet delivery. The *QoS* level of *VoIP* applications depends on many parameters, such as: bandwidth, One Way Delay (*OWD*), jitter, Packet Loss Rate (*PLR*), codec type, voice data length, and de-jitter buffer size. In particular, *OWD*, jitter, and *PLR* have an important impact.

This chapter presents an introduction to the main concepts and mathematical background relating to *communications networks*, *VoIP networks* and *QoS parameters*.

2. Communications networks

A communications network is a collection of terminals, links, and nodes which connect together to enable communication between users via their terminals. The network sets up a connection between two or more terminals by making use of their source and destination addresses (Fiche & Hébuterne, 2004).

Switched networks are divided into circuit-switched and packet-switched networks. The packet-switched networks are further divided into connection-oriented and connectionless packet networks (Kurose & Ross, 2003; Tanenbaum, 2003; Stallings, 1997). Figure 1 shows this classification.

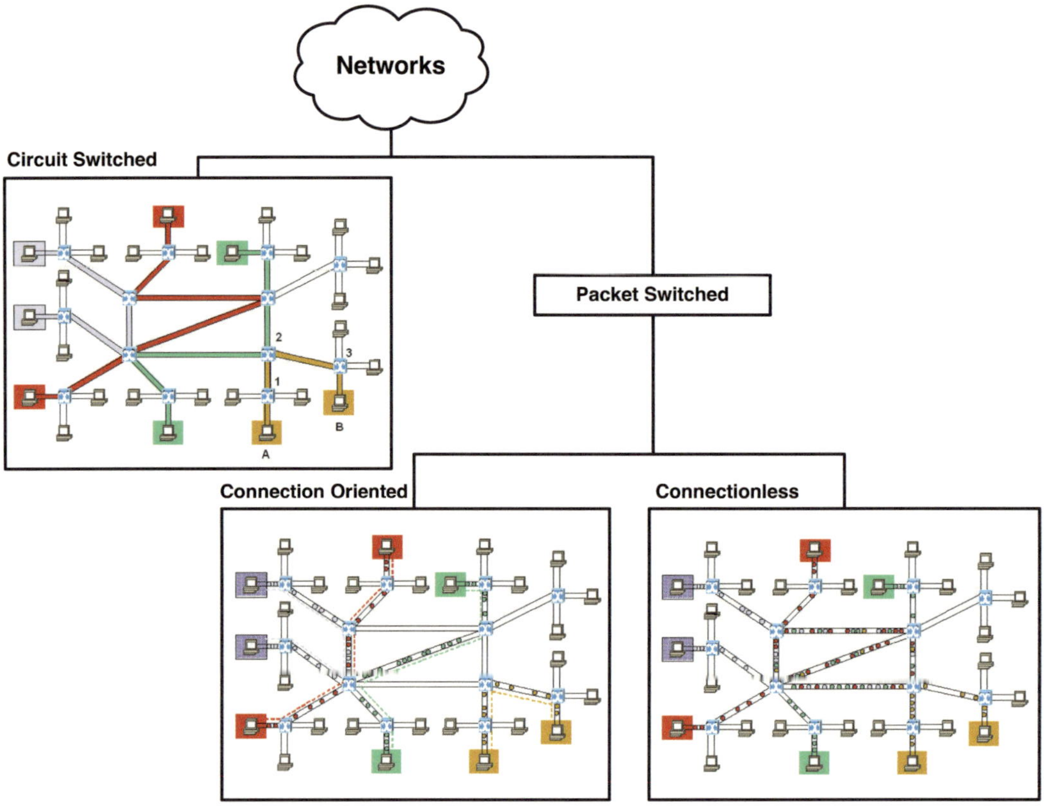

Fig. 1. Networks types

2.1 Circuit-switched network

Besides voice transport, circuit-switched networks are regularly used to transport different traffic types, such as data and control signals between computers and terminals, respectively. However, no matter which traffic type is transported, the user equipment and the set of nodes are called terminal and network, respectively. The network establishes the communication path between the terminals. The path is a connected sequence of links between nodes.

The communication via circuit-switched networks implies that there is a dedicated communication path between two or more terminals all through the communication session. Therefore, the resources (links and nodes) are reserved exclusively for information exchanges between origin and destination terminals. This communication involves three phases: circuit establishment, data transfer, and circuit disconnect. Before communication can occur between the terminals, a circuit is established between them. Thus, link capacity

must be reserved between each pair of nodes in the path, and each node must have available internal switching capacity to handle the requested connection. The nodes must have the intelligence to make these allocations and to devise a route through the network.
In circuit-switched networks, the nodes do not examine the contents of the information transmitted; the decision on where to send the information received is made just once at the beginning of the connection and remains the same for the duration of the connection. Thus, the delay introduced by a node is almost negligible. After the circuit has been established, the transmission delay is small and it is kept constant through the duration of the connection.
The circuit-switched networks can be rather inefficient. Once a circuit is established, the resources associated to it cannot be used for another connection until the circuit is disconnected. Therefore, even if at some point both terminals stop transmitting, the resources allocated to the connection remain in use.
The most common examples of circuit-switched network are the PSTN and the Integrated Services Digital Network (ISDN).

2.2 Packet-switched network

The data traffic is bursty and non-uniform. Terminals do not transmit continuously, i.e., are idle most of the time and very bursty at certain time. Data rates are not kept constant through the duration of the connection but they vary dynamically. A particular data transmission has a peak and average data rates associated to it and these are usually not the same. Therefore, employing dedicated circuits to transmit traffic with these characteristics is a waste of resources. The packet-switched network was first designed to fulfill the requirements of bursty traffic presented by data transmission.
In the packet-switched networks, the information is split up by the terminal into blocks of moderate size, called packets. These packets are autonomous, i.e., they are capable of moving on the network thanks to a header that contains the source and destination addresses. The packet is sent to the first node in this communication network.
The nodes are referred to as routers. When the router receives the packet, it examines the header and forwards the packet to the next appropriate router. This technique of inspection and retransmission is called store-and-forward, and it is accomplished in all routers of the path until the packet reaches its destination, unless the packet is lost. After reaching the destination, the destination terminal strips off the header of the packet to obtain the actual data that was originated at the source.
In this communication process, the terminal sends packets at its own rate, and the network multiplexes the packets from various origins in the same resources, to optimize their use. In this way several communications can share the same resources. The packet-switched network enables a better use of the transmission resource than circuit-switched network, in which the transmission resources are allocated without sharing. On the other hand, the multiplexing of different connections on the same resources causes delays and packet loss, which do not happen with circuit-switched network.
Finally it must be noted that in packet-switched networks a distinction is made between two modes of operation: connection-oriented mode and connectionless mode.
In connection oriented mode, a path is established before any packets are sent; this path is called virtual circuit. There is a prior exchange of initial signaling packets to reserve resources and to establish the path. The connection-oriented mode is modeled after the telephone system. In order to talk to someone, one has to pick up the phone, dial the

number, talk, and then hang up. Similarly, in connection-oriented mode, the user establishes a connection, uses the connection, and then releases the connection. The essential aspect of a connection is that it acts like a tube, the sender pushes objects (packets) in at one end, and the receiver takes them out at the other end. In most cases the order is preserved so that the packets arrive in the order they were sent.

In connectionless mode, each packet is treated independently, with no reference to packets that have gone before and the routing decisions are taken at each node. The connectionless mode is modeled after the postal system. Each message (packet) carries the full destination address, and each one is routed through the system independently of all the others. Normally, when two packets are sent to the same destination, the first one sent will be the first one to arrive. However, it is possible that the first one sent can be delayed so that the second one arrives first.

The connectionless mode has been popularized mainly by Internet protocol. The IP networks have progressed to the point that it is now possible to support voice and multimedia applications, but does not guarantee quality of service, because are based on "best effort" services.

3. *VoIP* networks

A communications network is a collection of terminals, links, and nodes which connect *VoIP* is the real-time transmission of voice between two o more parties, by using IP technologies over packet-switched networks. It consists of a set of recommendations and protocols for managing the transmission of voice packets using the IP protocol.

Current implementations of *VoIP* have two main types of architectures, which are based on H.323 (ITU-T Recommendation H.323, 2007; Sulkin A., 2002) and Session Initiation Protocol (SIP) frameworks (Rosenberg et al 2002; Sulkin, 2002; Camarillo, 2002), respectively. H.323, which was ratified by International Telecommunication Union (ITU-T), is a set of protocols for voice, video, and data conferencing over packet-based network. SIP, which is defined in request for comments 3261 (RFC 3261) of the Multiparty Multimedia Session Control (MMUSIC) working group of Internet Engineering Task Force (IETF), is an application-layer control signaling protocol for creating, modifying, and terminating sessions with one or more participants. Regardless of their differences, the fundamental architectures of these two implementations are the same. They consist of three main logical components: terminal, signaling server, and GW. They differ in specific definitions of voice coding, transport protocols, control signaling, GW control, and call management.

The current H.323 and SIP frameworks do not provide *QoS*. *VoIP* is one of the most *QoS* sensitive and demands strict *QoS* levels. The *QoS* level of *VoIP* applications depends on many parameters, such as: bandwidth, *OWD*, jitter, PLR, codec type, voice data length, and de-jitter buffer size. In particular, *OWD*, jitter, and PLR have an important impact.

3.1 H.323 architecture

ITU-T H.323 (ITU-T Recommendation H.323, 2007; Sulkin A., 2002) is a set of protocols for voice, video, and data conferencing over packet-switched networks such as Ethernet Local Area Networks (LANs) and the Internet that do not provide a guaranteed *QoS*. The H.323 protocol stack is designed to operate above the transport layer of the underlying network. H.323 was originally developed as one of several videoconferencing recommendations issued by the ITU-T. The H.323 standard is designed to allow clients on H.323 networks to communicate with clients on other videoconferencing networks. The first version of H.323 was issued in 1996, designed for use with Ethernet LANs and borrowed much of its multimedia conferencing aspects from other H.32.x series recommendations. H.323 is part of a large series of communications standards that enable videoconferencing across a range of networks. This series also includes H.320 and H.324, which address the ISDN and PSTN communications, respectively. H.323 is known as a broad and flexible recommendation. Although H.323 specifies protocols for real-time point-to-point communication between two terminals on a packet-switched network, also includes support of multipoint conferencing among terminals that support not only voice but also video and data communications. This recommendation describes the components of H.323 architecture. This includes terminals, Gateways (GW), Gatekeepers (GK), Multipoint Control Units (MCU), Multipoint Controller (MC), and Multipoint Processors (MP).

- *Terminal:* An H.323 terminal is an endpoint on the network which provides real-time, two-way communications with another H.323 terminal, GW, or MCU. This communication consists of control, indications, audio, moving color video pictures, and/or data between the two terminals. A terminal may provide speech only, speech and data, speech and video, or speech, data, and video.
- *Gateway:* The GW is a H.323 entity on the network which allows intercommunication between IP networks and legacy circuit-switched networks, such as ISDN and PSTN. They provide signaling mapping as well as transcoding facilities. For example, GWs receive an H.320 stream from an ISDN line, convert it to an H.323 stream, and then send it to the IP network.
- *Gatekeeper:* The GK is a H.323 entity on the network which performs the role of the central manager of *VoIP* services to the endpoints. This entity provides address translation and controls access to the network for H.323 terminals, GWs, and MCUs. The GK may also provide other services to the terminals, GWs, and MCUs such as bandwidth management and locating GWs.
- *MCU:* The MCU is an H.323 entity on the network which provides the capability for three or more terminals and GW to participate in a multipoint conference. It may also connect two terminals in a point-to-point conference which may later develop into a multipoint conference. The MCU consists of two parts, a mandatory MC, and an optional MP. In the simplest case, an MCU may consist only of an MC with no MPs. An MCU may also be brought into a conference by the GK without being explicitly called by one of the endpoints.
- *MC:* The MC is an H.323 entity on the network which controls three or more terminals participating in a multipoint conference. It may also connect two terminals in a point-to-point conference which may later develop into a multipoint conference. The MC provides the capability of negotiation with all terminals to achieve common levels of communications. It may also control conference resources such as who is multicasting video. The MC does not perform mixing or switching of audio, video, and data.
- *MP:* The MP is an H.323 entity on the network which provides for the centralized processing of audio, video and/or data streams in a multipoint conference. The MP provides for the mixing, switching, or other processing of media streams under the control of the MC. The MP may process a single media stream or multiple media streams depending on the type of conference supported.

The H.323 architecture is partitioned into zones. Each zone is comprised by the collection of all terminals, GW, and MCU managed by a single GK. H.323 is an umbrella recommendation which depends on several other standards and recommendations to enable real-time multimedia communications. The main ones are:

- *Call Signaling and Control:* Call control protocol (H.225), media control protocol (H.245), security (H.235), digital subscriber signaling (Q.931), generic functional protocol for the support of supplementary services in H.323 (H.450.1), supplemental features (H.450.2-H.450.11).
- *H.323 Annexes:* Real-time facsimile over H.323 (Annex D), framework, and wire-protocol for multiplexed call signaling transport (Annex E), simple endpoint types - SET (Annex F), text conversation and Text SET (Annex G), Security for annex F (Annex J), hypertext transfer protocol (HTTP)-based service control transport channel (Annex K), stimulus control protocol (Annex L), and tunneling of signaling protocols (Annex M).
- *Audio Codec's*: Pulse Code Modulation (PCM) audio codec 56/64 kbps (G.711), audio codec for 7 Khz at 48/56/64 kbps (G.722), speech codec for 5.3 and 6.4kbps (G.723), speech codec for 16 kbps (G.728), and speech codec for 8/13 kbps (G.729).
- *Video Codec's:* Video codec for ≥ 64 kbps (H.261) and video codec for ≤ 64 kbps (H.263).

3.2 SIP architecture

SIP was developed by IETF in reaction to the ITU-T H.323 recommendation. The IETF believed that H.323 was inadequate for evolving IP telephony, because its command structure is complex and its architecture is centralized and monolithic. SIP is an application layer control protocol that can establish, modify, and terminate multimedia sessions or calls (Rosenberg et al 2002; Sulkin, 2002; Camarillo, 2002). SIP transparently supports name mapping and redirection services, allowing the implementation of ISDN and intelligent network telephony subscriber services. The early implementations of SIP have been in network carrier IP-Centrex trials. SIP was designed as part of the overall IETF multimedia data and control architecture that supports protocols such as Resource Reservation Protocol (RSVP), Real-time Transport Protocol (RTP), Real-time Streaming Protocol (RTSP), Session Announcement Protocol (SAP), and Session Description Protocol (SDP). SIP establishes, modifies, and terminates multimedia sessions. It can be used to invite new members to an existing session or to create new sessions. The two major components in a SIP network are User Agent (UA) and network servers (registrar server, location server, proxy server, and redirect server).

- *User Agents:* Is an application that interacts with the user and contains both a User Agent Client (UAC) and User Agent Server (UAS). A user agent client initiates SIP requests, and a user agent server receives SIP requests and returns responses on user behalf.
- *Registrar Server:* Is a SIP server that accepts only registration requests issued by user agents for the purpose of updating a location database with the contact information of the user specified in the request.
- *Proxy Server:* Is an intermediary entity that acts both as a server to user agents by forwarding SIP requests and as a client to other SIP servers by submitting the forwarded requests to them on behalf of user agents or proxy servers.
- *Redirect Server:* Is a SIP server that helps to locate UAs by providing alternative locations where the user can be reachable, i.e., provides address mapping services. It responds to a SIP request destined to an address with a list of new addresses. A redirect server does not accept calls, does not forward requests, and does not it initiate any of its own.

The SIP protocol follows a web-based approach to call signaling, contrary to traditional communication protocols. It resembles a client/server model; where SIP clients issue requests and SIP servers return one or more responses. The signaling protocol is built on this exchange of requests and responses, which are grouped into transactions. All the messages of a transaction share a common unique identifier and traverse the same set of hosts. There are two types of messages in SIP; requests and responses. Both of them use the textual representation of the ISO 10646 character set with UTF-8 encoding. The message syntax follows HTTP/1.1, but it should be noted that SIP is not an extension to HTTP.

- *SIP Responses:* Upon reception of a request, a server issues one or several responses. Every response has a code that indicates the status of the transaction. Status codes are integers ranging from 100 to 699 and are grouped into six classes. A response can be either final or provisional. A response with a status code from 100 to 199 is considered provisional. Responses from 200 to 699 are final responses.

1. 1xx Informational: Request received, continuing to process request. The client should wait for further responses from the server.
2. 2xx Success: The action was successfully received, understood, and accepted. The client must terminate any search.
3. 3xx Redirection: Further action must be taken in order to complete the request. The client must terminate any existing search but may initiate a new one.
4. 4xx Client Error: The request contains bad syntax or cannot be fulfilled at this server. The client should try another server or alter the request and retry with the same server.
5. 5xx Server Error: The request cannot be fulfilled at this server because of server error. The client should try with another server.
6. 6xx Global Failure: The request is invalid at any server. The client must abandon search.

The first digit of the status code defines the class of response. The last two digits do not have any categorization role. For this reason, any response with a status code between 100 and 199 is referred to as a "1xx response", any response with a status code between 200 and 299 as a "2xx response", and so on.

- *SIP Requests:* The core SIP specification defines six types of SIP requests, each of them with a different purpose. Every SIP request contains a field, called a method, which denotes its purpose.

1. INVITE: INVITE requests invite users to participate in a session. The body of INVITE requests contains the description of the session. Significantly, SIP only handles the invitation to the user and the user's acceptance of the invitation. All of the session particulars are handled by the session description protocol used. Thus, with a different session description, SIP can invite users to any type of session.
2. ACK: ACK requests are used to acknowledge the reception of a final response to an INVITE. Thus, a client originating an INVITE request issues an ACK request when it receives a final response for the INVITE.
3. CANCEL: CANCEL requests cancel pending transactions. If a SIP server has received an INVITE but has not returned a final response yet, it will stop processing the INVITE upon receipt of a CANCEL. If, however, it has already returned a final response for the INVITE, the CANCEL request will have no effect on the transaction.
4. BYE: BYE requests are used to abandon sessions. In two-party sessions, abandonment by one of the parties implies that the session is terminated.
5. REGISTER: Users send REGISTER requests to inform a server (in this case, referred to as a registrar server) about their current location.

6. OPTIONS: OPTIONS requests query a server about its capabilities, including which methods and which session description protocols it supports.

SIP is independent of the type of multimedia session handled and of the mechanism used to describe the session. Sessions consisting of RTP streams carrying audio and video are usually described using SDP, but some types of session can be described with other description protocols. In short, SIP is used to distribute session descriptions among potential participants. Once the session description is distributed, SIP can be used to negotiate and modify the parameters of the session and terminate the session.

3.3 *VoIP* system structure

VoIP is a rapidly growing technology that enables transport of voice over data networks such as Ethernet LANs. A basic *VoIP* system consists of three parts: the sender, the IP networks, and the receiver, as shown in Figure 2.

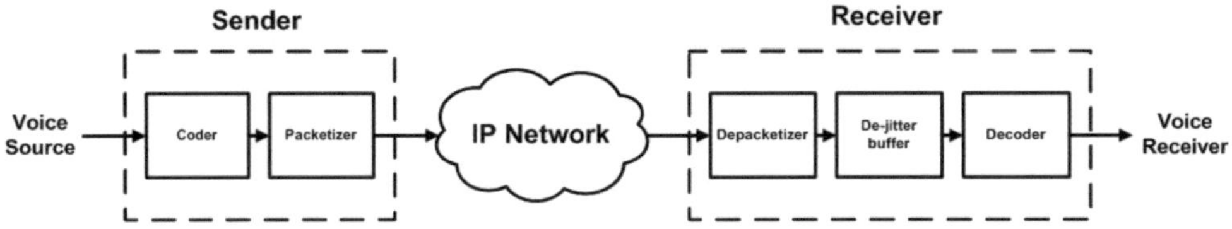

Fig. 2. *VoIP* system

Sender: The first component is the coder which periodically samples the original voice signal and assigns a fixed number of bits to each sample, creating a constant bit rate stream.

The voice stream from the voice source is first digitized and compressed by using a suitable coding algorithm such as G.711, G.729, etc. Various speech codec's differ from each other in terms of features such as coding bit-rate (kbps), algorithmic delay (ms), complexity, and speech quality (Mean Opinion Score - MOS). In order to simplify the description of speech codec's they are often broadly divided into three classes: waveform coders, parametric coders, or vocoders, and hybrid coders (as a combination thereof).

Typically waveforms codec's are used at high bit rates, and give very good quality speech. Parametric codec's operated at very low bit rates, but tend to produce speech which sounds synthetic. Hybrid codec's use techniques from both parametric and waveform coding, and give good quality speech an intermediate bit rates.

After compression and encoding into a suitable format the speech frames are packetized. The packetized process is implemented for gathering a set of voice data to be transmitted and adding the information needed for routing and handling those voice data across the IP network. The added bits are referred as the header, and the voice data to be delivered are referred as the payload. The structure of an IP packet over an Ethernet is shown in Figure 3.

The voice data length can be changed according to the *VoIP* transmission efficiency (*TE [%]*). The Media Access Control (MAC) header, IP header, User Datagram Protocol (UDP) header, RTP header, and Frame Check Sequence (FCS) are necessary for transmitting voice data over the Ethernet, while preamble and Inter Packet Gap (IPG) should be considered as occupied bandwidth on the transmission line. For instance, the total occupied bandwidth is 98 bytes including IPG, preamble, MAC header, IP header, UDP header, RTP header, and FCS when transmitting 20 byte voice data. The 78 bytes thus correspond to the overhead of IP transmission, so the ratio of voice data to the total is less than 25%, i.e. $TE\ [\%]=x/(x+y)*100$, where "x" is the voice data and "y" is the overhead.

The voice data length of an IP packet usually depends on the coding algorithm used. Eighty byte voice data is often used for G.711, whereas 20 byte voice data is used for G.729 in conventional *VoIP* communication. Table 1 shows the relationship between the voice data length in milliseconds and the voice data length in bytes, and Figure 4 shows the relationship between the voice data length and the bandwidth occupied by the *VoIP* frames of an Ethernet.

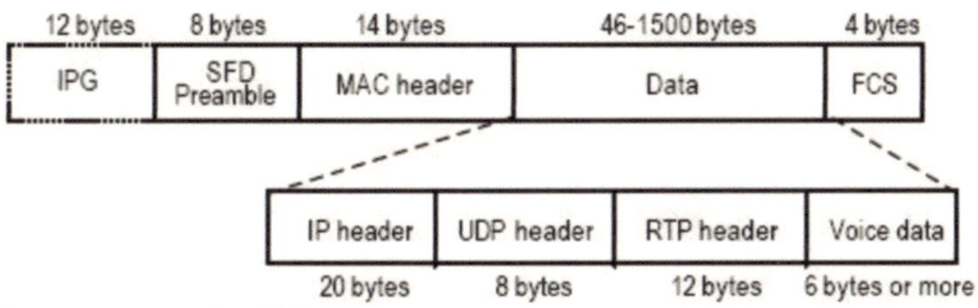

Fig. 3. *VoIP* packet structure for Ethernet

Voice Data Length (ms)	Voice Data Length (Bytes)	
	G.711	G.729
10	80	10
20	160	20
30	240	30
40	320	40
50	400	50
60	480	60
70	560	70
80	640	80
90	720	90
100	800	100

Table 1. Voice data length of *VoIP* packets

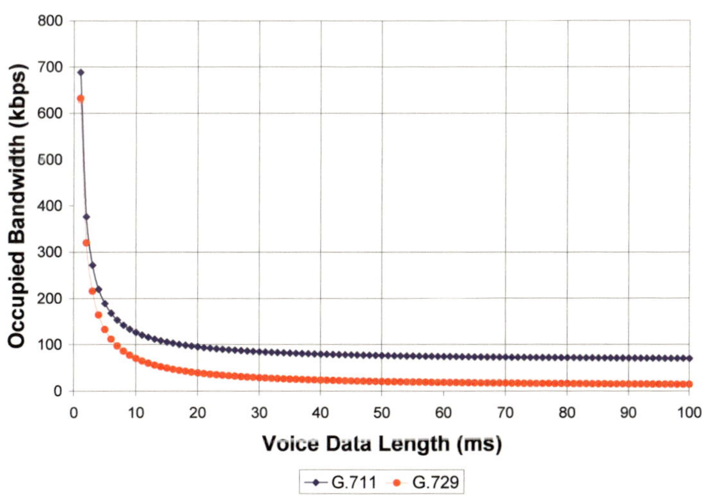

Fig. 4. Bandwidth occupied by *VoIP* frames

The longer the voice data length in a voice packet becomes, the more the transmission efficiency increases because the *VoIP* packet has overheads for the MAC header (in the case of the Ethernet), IP header, UDP header, and RTP header (see Figure 5). However, the longer one packet becomes, the more packet errors are likely to occur, so it is important to evaluate how the network traffic conditions affect the packet behavior and *QoS* in *VoIP* systems.

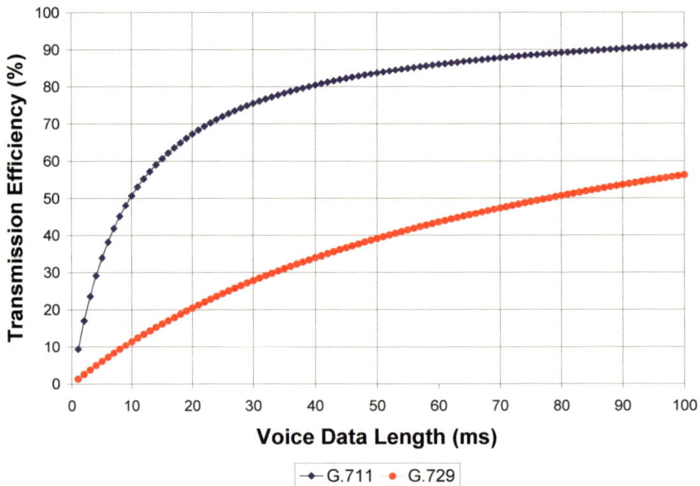

Fig. 5. Transmission efficiency

IP Network: Due to the shared nature of IP network, guaranteeing the quality of service of Internet applications from end-to-end is difficult. Since current IP networks are based on best-effort services, the packet may suffer different network impairments (e.g. packet loss, delay, and jitter), which directly impact the quality of *VoIP* applications.

Receiver: The packet headers are stripped off and voice samples are extracted from the payload by depacketizer. The voice samples must be presented to the decoder in such a way that the next sample is present for processing when the decoder has finished with its immediate predecessor. Such a requirement severely constrains the amount of jitter that can be tolerated in a *VoIP* system without having to gap the samples. When jitter results in an Inter-arrival Time (*IAT*) that is greater than the time required to re-create the waveform from a sample, the decoder has no option but to continue to function without the next sample information. Therefore, the effects of jitter will be manifested as an increase in the packet loss rate.

The buffer that holds the queued segments is called de-jitter buffer. The employment of such de-jitter buffers defines the relationship between jitter and packet loss rate in the receiver side. The delay variation that can be tolerated becomes therefore the essential descriptor of intrinsic quality that supplants jitter.

Therefore an important design parameter at the receiver side is the de-jitter buffer size or playout delay of a de-jitter buffer. Since, de-jitter buffer is used to compensate for network jitter at the cost of further delay (buffer delay) and loss (late arrival loss). Finally, the de-jittered speech frames are decoded to recover the original voice signal.

The playout delay is explained in the next few paragraphs. Figure 6 and Table 2 show a sample of packet delays. In the Figure6, the abscissa is the time at which a packet is sent, the ordinate is the time at which the packet is received, and the time here is measured by a globally synchronized clock. In an ideal network such as circuit switched network, the delay d for a given path is constant and low, so the (x,y) points form a line $y=x+d$ (e.g. $d=5ms$). This means packets can be played out as soon as they are received without having to pause (ideal playout time, $y=x+5$). In the packet switched network such as the Internet, delays are not constant, as queuing delays can vary significantly over time.

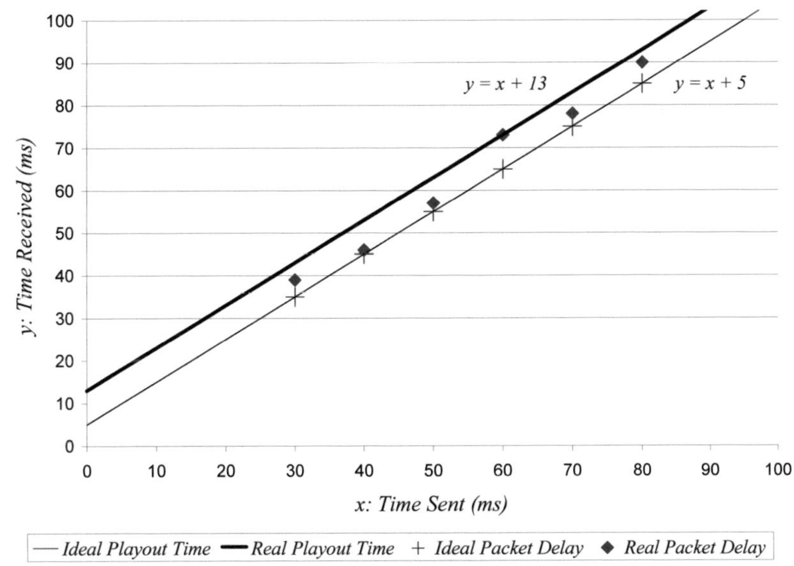

Fig. 6. Illustration of packet delay and playout delay

Time Sent (ms)	Ideal: Time Received (ms)	Real: Time Received (ms)
30	35	39
40	45	46
50	55	57
60	65	73
70	75	78
80	85	90

Table 2. Sample of packet delays

An example is the diamond-shaped plot in Figure 6. For *VoIP* applications, if the receiver plays out voice packets as they come in, it will have to generate a pause if the next packet delayed arrives. Therefore, in Figure 6, we must wait at least d_{play} time to prevent this situation. The term d_{play} is called the playout delay. Usually, d_{play} is calculated by subtracting the actual play time of the first packet from its receiving time. In this example, the first packets is sent at 30 ms, received at 39 ms, and played at 43 ms. Therefore, d_{play} is 4 ms, since the actual play times of all packets form a line $y=x+13$ (real playout time). An alternative definition of playout delay is the delay between sending time and playout time.

Many techniques have been developed for controlling the playout delay. Most existing playout adaptation algorithms work by taking some measurements on the delays experienced by packets and updating the playout delay.

4. *QoS* parameters

The voice quality of *VoIP* applications depends on many parameters, such as bandwidth, *OWD*, jitter, packet loss rate, codec, voice data length, and de-jitter buffer size. In particular, *OWD*, jitter, and packet loss have an important impact on voice quality.

4.1 One way delay

The delay experienced by a packet across a path consists of several components: propagation, processing, transmission, and queuing delays (Park, 2005). The Internet metric called one way delay (ITU-T Recommendation G.114, 2003) is the time needed for a packet to traverse the network from a source to a destination host. It is described analytically by Equation (1):

$$D^K(L)_{OWD} = \delta + \sigma + \sum_{h=1}^{s}\left(\frac{L}{C_h} + X_h^K(t)\right) \quad (1)$$

where $D^K(L)_{OWD}$ is the *OWD* of a packet K of size L, δ represents the propagation delay, σ the processing delay, s the number of hops, L/C_h the transmission delay, and $X_h^K(t)$ the queuing delay of a packet K of size L at hop h $(h=1,\ldots,s)$ with capacity C_h. The *OWD* variation between two successive packets, K and $K-1$ is called *OWD* jitter and is given by the Equation (2):

$$J^K(L) = D^K(L)_{OWD} - D^{K-1}(L)_{OWD} \quad (2)$$

4.2 Jitter

When voice packets are transmitted from source to destination over IP networks, packets may experience variable delay, called delay jitter. The packet *IAT* on the receiver side is not constant even if the packet Inter-departure Time (*IDT*) on the sender side is constant. As a result, packets arrive at the destination with varying delays (between packets) referred to as jitter. We measure and calculate the difference between arrival times of successive voice packets that arrive on the receiver side, according to RFC 3550 (Schulzrinne et al, 2003), this is illustrated in Figure 7.

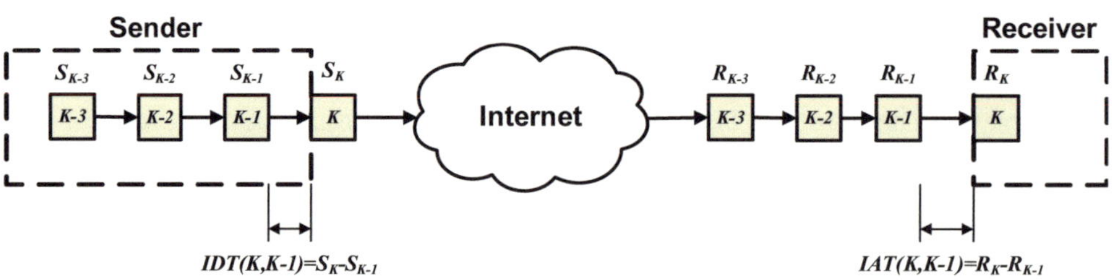

Fig. 7. Jitter experienced across Internet paths

Let S_K denote the transmission timestamp for the packet K of size L, and R_K the arrival time for packet K of size L. Then for two packets K and $K-1$, $J^K(L)$ may be expressed as:

$$J^K(L) = (R_K - S_K) - (R_{K-1} - S_{K-1}) = (R_K - R_{K-1}) - (S_K - S_{K-1}) \quad (3)$$

$$IDT(K,K-1) = (S_K - S_{K-1}) \quad (4)$$

$$IAT(K,K-1) = (R_K - R_{K-1}) \quad (5)$$

where, $IDT(K,K-1)$ is the Inter-departure Time (in our experiments, *IDT*= {10ms, 20ms, 40ms, and 60ms}) and $IAT(K,K-1)$ is the Inter-arrival Time for the packets K and $K-1$. In the current context, $IAT(K,K-1)$ is referred to as jitter. So, the *VoIP* jitter between two successive packets, i.e., packets K and $K-1$, is:

$$IAT(K,K-1) = J^K(L) + IDT(K,K-1) \quad (6)$$

4.3 Packet loss

There are two main transport protocols used in IP networks: UDP and TCP. While UDP protocol does not allow any recovery of transmission errors, TCP include an error recovery process. However, the voice transmission over TCP connections is not very realistic. This is due to the requirement for real-time operations in most voice related applications. As a result, the choice is limited to the use of UDP which involves packet loss problems.

Amongst the different quality elements, packet loss is the main impairment which makes the *VoIP* perceptually most different from the public switched telephone network. Packet loss can occur in the network or at the receiver side, for example, due to excessive network delay in case of network congestion.

Owing to the dynamic, time varying behavior of packet networks, packet loss can show a variety of distributions. The packet loss distribution most often studied in speech quality tests is random or Bernoulli-like packet loss. Uniform random loss here means independent loss, implying that the loss of a particular packet is independent of whether or not previous packets were lost. However, uniform random loss does not represent the loss distributions typically encountered in real networks. For example, losses are often related to periods of network congestion. Hence, losses may extend over several packets, showing a dependency between individual loss events. In this work, dependent packet loss is often referred to as bursty. The packet loss is bursty in nature and exhibits temporal dependency (Yajnik et al, 1999). So, if packet n is lost then normally there is a higher probability that packet $n + 1$ will also be lost. Consequently, there is a strong correlation between consecutive packet losses, resulting in a bursty packet loss behavior. A generalized model to capture temporal dependency is a finite Markov chain (ITU-T Recommendation G.1050, 2005).

2-state Markov Chain: Figure 8 shows the state diagram of a 2-state Markov chain.

In this model, one of the states (S_1) represents a packet loss and the other state (S_2) represents the case where packets are correctly transmitted or received. The transition probabilities in this model, as shown in Figure 8, are represented by p_{21} and p_{12}. In other words, p_{21} is the probability of going from S_2 to S_1, and p_{12} is the probability of going from S_1 to S_2. Different values of p_{21} and p_{12} define different packet loss conditions that can occur on the Internet.

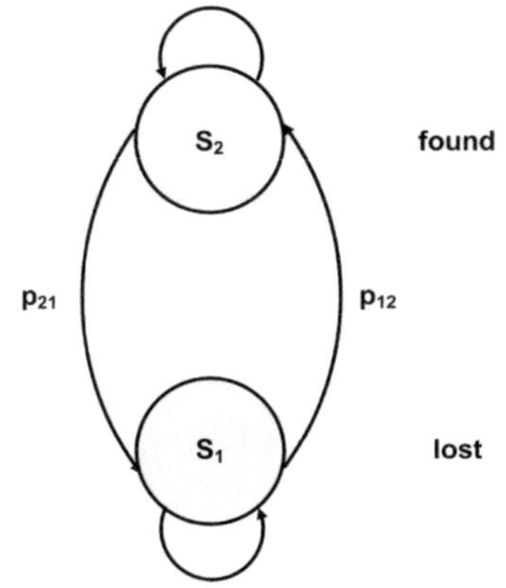

Fig. 8. 2-state Markov chain

The steady-state probability of the chain to be in the state *S1*, namely the *PLR*, is given by Equation (7):

$$PLR = S_1 = \frac{p_{21}}{p_{21} + p_{12}} \tag{7}$$

and clearly $S_2 = 1 - S_1$.

The distributions of the number of consecutive received or lost packets are called gap ($f_g(k)$) and burst ($f_b(k)$) respectively, and can be expressed in terms of p_{21} and p_{12}. The probability that the transition from S_2 to S_1 and S_1 to S_2 occurs after k steps can be expressed by Equations (8) and (9):

$$f_g(k) = p_{21}(1 - p_{21})^{k-1} \tag{8}$$

$$f_b(k) = p_{12}(1 - p_{12})^{k-1} \tag{9}$$

According to Equation (9), the number of steps *k* necessary to transit from S_1 to S_2, that is, the number of consecutively lost packets is a geometrically distributed random variable. This geometric distribution of consecutive loss events makes the 2-state Markov chain (and higher order Markov chains) applicable to describing loss events observed in the Internet.

The average number of consecutively lost and received packets can be calculated by $\bar{b}$ and $\bar{g}$, respectively, as shown in Equations (10) and (11).

$$\bar{b} = E\{f_b(k)\} = \frac{1}{p_{12}} \tag{10}$$

$$\bar{g} = E\{f_g(k)\} = \frac{1}{p_{21}} \tag{11}$$

4-state Markov Chain: Figure 9 shows the state diagram of this 4-state Markov chain.

In this model, a '*good*' and a '*bad*' state are distinguished, which represent periods of lower and higher packet loss, respectively. Both for the '*bad*' and the '*good*' state, an individual 2-state Markov chain represents the dependency between consecutively lost or found packets.

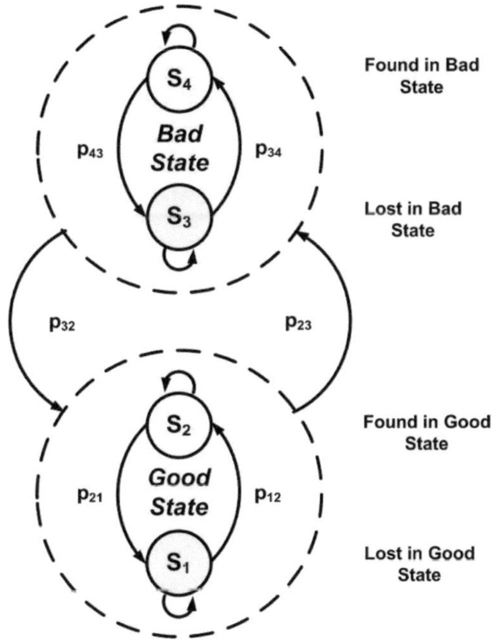

Fig. 9. 4-state Markov chain

The two 2-state chains can be described by four independent transition probabilities (two each one). Two further probabilities characterize the transitions between the two 2-state chains, leading to a total of six independent parameters for this particular 4-state Markov chain.

In the 4-state Markov chain, states S_1 and S_3 represent packets lost, S_2 and S_4 packets found and six parameters ($p_{21}, p_{12}, p_{43}, p_{34}, p_{23}, p_{32} \in (0,1)$) are necessary to define all the transition probabilities.

In the "*good state*" (G) packet loss occur with (*low*) probability P_G while in the "*bad state*" (B) they occur with (*high*) probability P_B. The occupancy times for states B and G are both geometrically distributed with respective means $\frac{1}{p_{32}}$ and $\frac{1}{p_{23}}$, respectively. The steady state probabilities of being in states G and B are $\pi_G = \frac{p_{32}}{p_{32} + p_{23}}$ and $\pi_G = \frac{p_{32}}{p_{32} + p_{23}}$, respectively.

The overall packet loss rates in the '*good*' and '*bad*' states P_G and P_B can be calculated by the following Equations:

$$P_G = \frac{p_{21}}{p_{21} + p_{12}} \tag{12}$$

$$P_B = \frac{p_{43}}{p_{43} + p_{34}} \tag{13}$$

The overall packet loss for the four-state Markov model is given by:

$$PLR = P_G \cdot \pi_G + P_B \cdot \pi_B \tag{14}$$

5. Conclusion

VoIP has emerged as an important service, poised to replace the circuit-switched telephony service in the future. However, when the voice traffic is transported over Internet, the packet based transmission may introduce degradations and have influence on the *QoS* perceived by the end users. The current Internet only offers best-effort services and was designed to support non-real-time applications. *VoIP* demands strict *QoS* levels and real-time voice packet delivery.

The voice quality of *VoIP* applications depends on many parameters, such as: bandwidth, *OWD*, jitter, *PLR*, codec, voice data length, and de-jitter buffer size. In particular, packet loss, *OWD* and jitter have an important impact on voice quality.

This chapter presents an introduction to the main concepts and mathematical background relating to communications networks, *VoIP* networks and *QoS* parameters.

6. References

Camarillo, G. (2002). *SIP Demystified.* USA: McGraw-Hill Companies, Inc.

Fiche, G., & Hébuterne, G. (2004). *Communicating Systems & Networks: Traffic & Performance.* London and Sterling, VA: Kogan Page Science.

ITU-T Recommendation G.114, (2003). *One-Way Transmission Time.* International Telecommunications Union, Geneva, Switzerland.

ITU-T Recommendation G.1050, (2005). *Network Model for Evaluating Multimedia Transmission Performance over Internet Protocol.* International Telecommunications Union, Geneva, Switzerland.

ITU-T Recommendation H.323, (2007). *Packet-Based Multimedia Communications Systems.* International Telecommunications Union, Geneva, Switzerland.

Kurose, J., & Ross, K. (2003). *Computer Networking: A Top-Down Approach Featuring the Internet.* USA: Pearson Education, Inc.

Park, K. I. (2005). *QoS in Packet Networks.* Boston, MA: Springer Science + Business Media, Inc.

Rosenberg, J., et al (2002). *SIP: Session Initiation Protocol (RFC 3261).* Internet Engineering Task Force.

Schulzrinne, H., et al (2003). *RTP: A Transport Protocol for Real-Time Applications (RFC 3550).* Internet Engineering Task Force.

Stallings. W. (1997). *Data and Computer Communications.* Upper Saddle River, NJ: Pearson Education, Inc.

Sulkin, A. (2002). *PBX Systems for IP Telephony: Migrating Enterprise Communications.* New York, NY: McGraw-Hill Professional.

Tanenbaum, A. S. (2003). *Computer Networks.* Upper Saddle River, NJ: Pearson Education, Inc.

Yajnik, M., Moon, S., Kursoe, J., & Towsley, D. (1999). *Measurement and Modelling of the Temporal Dependence in Packet Loss.* Paper presented at the 18th International Conference on Computer Communications (IEEE INFOCOM), New York, NY.

5

Influences of Classical and Hybrid Queuing Mechanisms on VoIP's QoS Properties

Sasa Klampfer[1], Amor Chowdhury[1], Joze Mohorko[2] and Zarko Cucej[2]
[1]*Margento R&D d.o.o.*
[2]*University of Maribor, Faculty of Electrical Engineering and Computer Science*
Slovenia

1. Introduction

Nowadays we can find many TCP/IP based network applications, such as: WWW, e-mail, video-conferencing, VoIP, remote accesses, telnet, p2p file sharing, etc. All mentioned applications became popular because of fast-spreading broadband internet technologies, like xDSL, DOCSIS, FTTH, etc. Some of the applications, such as VoIP (Voice over Internet Protocol) and video-conferencing, are more time-sensitive in delivery of network traffic than others, and need to be treated specially. This special treatment of the time-sensitive applications is one of the main topics of this chapter. It includes methodologies for providing a proper quality of service (QoS) for VoIP traffic within networks. Normally, their efficiency is intensively tested with simulations before implementation. In the last few years, the use of simulation tools in R&D of communication technologies has rapidly risen, mostly because of higher network complexity.

The internet is expanding on a daily basis, and the number of network infrastructure components is rapidly increasing. Routers are most commonly used to interconnect different networks. One of their tasks is to keep the proper quality of service level. The leading network equipment manufacturers, such as Cisco Systems, provide on their routers mechanisms for reliable transfer of time-sensitive applications from one network segment to another. In case of VoIP the requirement is to deliver packets in less than 150ms. This limit is set to a level where a human ear cannot recognize variations in voice quality. This is one of the main reasons why leading network equipment manufacturers implement the QoS functionality into their solutions. QoS is a very complex and comprehensive system which belongs to the area of priority congestions management. It is implemented by using different queuing mechanisms, which take care of arranging traffic into waiting queues. Time-sensitive traffic should have maximum possible priority provided. However, if a proper queuing mechanism (FIFO, CQ, WFQ, etc.) is not used, the priority loses its initial meaning. It is also a well-known fact that all elements with memory capability involve additional delays during data transfer from one network segment to another, so a proper queuing mechanism and a proper buffer length should be used, or the VoIP quality will deteriorate.

If we take a look at the router, as a basic element of network equipment, we can realise that we are dealing with application priorities on the lowest level. Such level is presented by waiting queues and queuing mechanisms, related with the input traffic connection interface.

The traffic which appears at the input connection is transferred to the queuing mechanisms and waiting queues. Which queuing mechanism from the set of available queuing mechanisms will be used depends on the network administrator's choice.

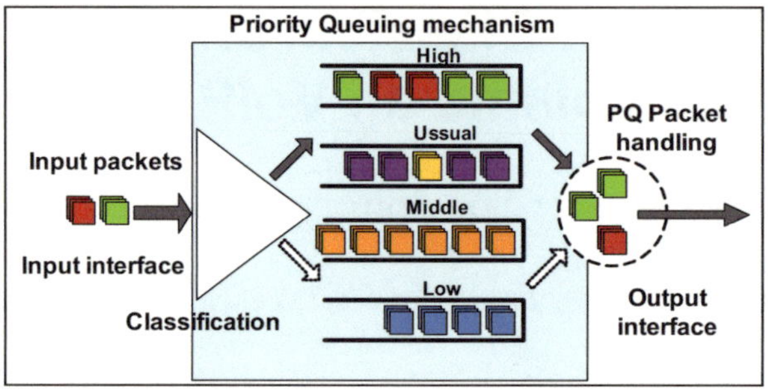

Fig. 1. Priority Queuing Mechanism

One of the QoS's most crucial components are waiting queues, where suitable queuing mechanisms take care of proper IP traffic treatment. The sophisticated queuing mechanisms also include traffic sorting and scheduling functionality. This group of regimes is called 'conscious', and includes the following queuing regimes:

- priority queuing (PQ) which sorts the packets according to their priority (see Fig. 1),
- weighted fair queuing (WFQ) which provides bandwidth fairness usage for all traffic types, and
- class-based weighted fair queuing (CBWFQ), which gives the advantage to the traffic for which the traffic class has been generated by the administrator.

First-in-first-out (FIFO) queuing and custom queuing (CQ) mechanisms belong to the old-fashioned queuing regimes, the so called 'unconscious' group. With such a group it does not matter which type of traffic appears at the input interface, but they treat the traffic as it actually is. In the FIFO case, the packet that came first in also goes first out, etc.

With individual analyses of queuing mechanism properties we get an idea of joining the advantages of two queuing mechanisms. This means that the positive properties of both mechanisms will be combined. Combining different queuing mechanisms and proving their new properties is a part of our scientific contribution. For the research we have been using a sophisticated simulation tool: OPNET Modeler. The result of our ideas and experiments are hybrid queuing mechanisms (except PQ-CBWFQ). The conclusion of our research is that the best solution of all the tested concepts is still the well-known PQ-CBWFQ method. From the set of tested hybrid methods the best results in terms of the VoIP jitter delay were obtained with our proposed WFQ-CBWFQ concept, which significantly reduces the jitter. The results of the WFQ-CBWFQ concept are according to our estimations in the VoIP jitter case even better than with the PQ-CBWFQ, but the disadvantage of the first concept reflects in a slightly higher VoIP delay in comparison to the PQ-CBWFQ.

Much similar research using simulations has been done in the area of VoIP's quality improvement; some of it is presented in the following literature: Mansour J. Karam & Fouad A. Tobagi, 2001, Velmurugan T. et al., 2009, and Fischer, M.J. et al., 2007. VoIP's quality improvement is a very popular research area, mostly focused on queuing aspects, and the problem of decreasing jitter influence as in our case. The hybrid queuing mechanism concept (except PQ-CBWFQ) is our original contribution, resulting from the research of the past three years.

2. Presentation of the quality of service and its connection to waiting queues

Here the basic terminology and facts about Quality of service and waiting queues will be explained; what QoS is, where it can be found (H. Jonathan Chao & Bin Liu, 2007), how it works, main parts of QoS (Kun I. Park, 2005), and QoS levels (M. Callea et al., 2005), how QoS handles congestions, etc. (L. L. Peterson & B. S. Davie, 2003 and Cisco Systems-Internetworking Technology Handbook, 2002). At this point, we will present the two most important areas corresponding to our research work; the so called fuzzy QoS area for distinguishing traffic, and the area which includes the mechanisms for traffic congestions management, to which the waiting queues belong.

2.1 What is QoS?

Quality of Service allows control of data transmission quality in networks, and at the same time improves the organization of data traffic flows, which go through many different network technologies. Such a group of network technologies includes ATM (asynchronous transfer mode), Ethernet and 802.1 technologies, IP based units, etc.; and even several of the abovementioned technologies can be used together.

An illustration of what can happen when excessive traffic appears during peak periods can be found in everyday life: an example of filling a bottle with a jet of water. The maximum flow of water into the bottle is limited with its narrowest part (throat). If the maximum possible amount of decantation (throughput) is exceeded, a spill occurs (loss of data). A funnel used for pouring water into a bottle, would in case of data transfer be in the waiting queues. They allow us to accelerate the flow, and at the same time prevent the loss of data. A problem remains in the worst-case scenario, where the waiting queues are overflowed, which again leads to loss of data (a too high water flow rate into the funnel would again result in water spills).

Priorities are the basic mechanisms of the QoS operating regime, which also affects the bandwidth allocation. QoS has an ability to control and influence the delays which can appear during data transmission. Higher priority data flows have granted preferential treatment and a sufficient portion of bandwidth (if the desired amount of bandwidth is available). QoS has a direct impact on the time variation of the sampling signals which are transmitted across the network. Such sampling time variation is also called jitter (T. & S. Subash IndiraGandhi, 2006). Both mentioned properties have a crucial impact on the quality of the data and information flow throughput, because such a flow must reach the destination in the strict real-time. A typical example is the interactive media market. QoS reflects their distinctive properties in the area of improving data-transfer characteristics in terms of smaller data losses for higher-priority data streams. The fact that QoS can provide priorities to one or more data streams simultaneously, and also ensure the existence of all remaining (lower-priority) data streams, is very important. Today, network equipment companies integrate QoS mechanisms into routers and switches, both representing fundamental parts of Wide Area Networks (WAN), Service Provider Networks (SPN), and finally, Local Area Networks.

Based on the abovementioned points, the following conclusion can be given: QoS is a network mechanism, which successfully controls traffic flood scenarios, generated by a wide range of advanced network applications. This is possible through the priorities allocation for each type of data stream.

2.2 How QoS works?

QoS mechanism, observed as a whole, roughly represents an intermediate supervising element placed between different networks, or between the network and workstations or servers that may be independent or grouped together in local networks. The position of the QoS system in the network is shown in Figure 2. This mechanism ensures that the applications with the highest priorities (VoIP, Skype, etc.) have priority treatment. QoS architecture consists of the following main fundamental parts: QoS identification, QoS classification, QoS congestions management mechanism, and QoS management mechanism, which handle the queue.

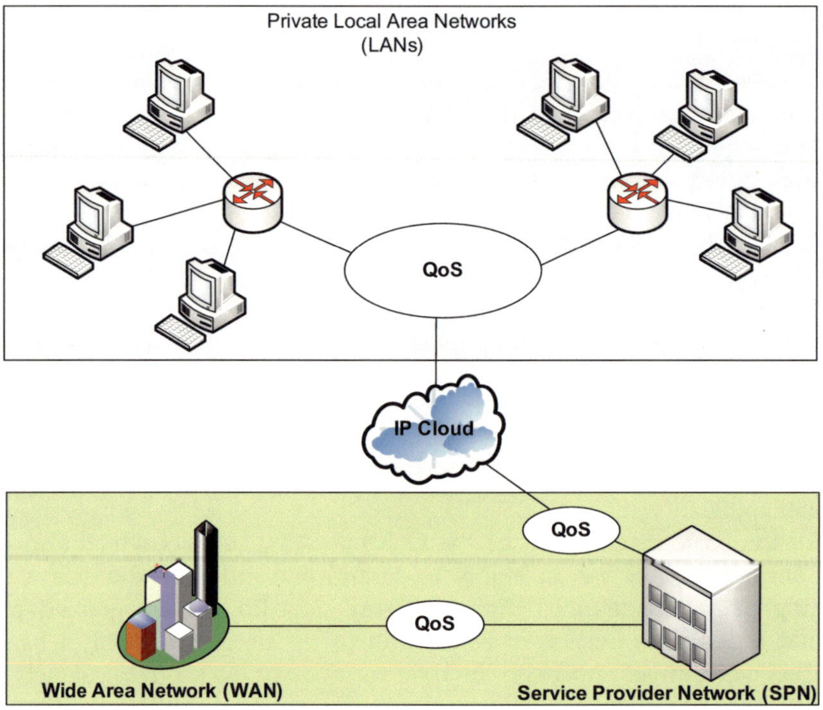

Fig. 2. QoS system's position in the network

2.2.1 QoS Identification

QoS identification is intended for data flows recognition and recognition of their priority. To ensure the priority a single data stream must first be identified and then marked (if this is needed). These two functions together partly relate to the classifying process, which will be described in detail in the next section. Identification is executed with access control lists (ACL). ACL identifies the traffic for the purpose of the waiting queue mechanisms, for example PQ - Priority Queuing or CQ - Custom Queuing. These two mechanisms are implemented into the router, and present one of its most important subparts. Their operation is based on the principle of "jump after a jump", meaning that the QoS priority settings belong only to this router and they are not transferred to neighboring routers, which form a network as a whole. Packet identification is then used within each router with QoS support. An example where classification is intended for only one router can be found with the CBWFQ (Class Based Queuing Weighted Fair) queuing mechanism. There are also techniques which are based on extended control access-list identities. This method allows considerable flexibility of priorities allocation, including the allocation for applications, users, destinations, etc. Typically, such functionality is installed close to the edge of the network or administrative domain, because only in this case each network element provides the following services on the basis of a particular QoS policy.

Network Based Application Recognition (NBAR) is a mechanism used for detailed traffic identification. For example, NBAR can identify URLs, which are located in the HTTP packet. When the packet is recognized, it can be marked with priority settings. If we look deeper into the structure of the HTTP packet, we can recognize URLs as well as the MIME type. This is a more than welcome feature of the WWW (World Wide Web)-based applications. NBAR can recognize various applications that use a variety of different ports/plugs. This functionality is performed with the procedure of checking control packets, where it finds the port through which the application will be sending the data. Such mechanism includes many useful features, which allow protocol identification and their statistical analysis at the interface entry point. The mechanism also contains a module for a linguistic description of the packet (Packet Description Language Modules - PDLM), where this functionality simplifies insertion of new protocols, which can be then identified.

2.2.2 QoS Classification

QoS classification is designed for executing priority services for a specific type of traffic. The traffic must first be pre-identified and then marked (tagged). Classification is defined by the mechanism for providing priority service, and the marking mechanism. At the point, when the packet is already identified, but it has not yet been marked, the classification mechanism decides which queuing mechanism will be used at a specific moment (for example, the principle of per-hop). Such an approach is typical in cases when the classification belongs to a particular device and is not transferred to the next router. Such a situation may arise in case of priority queuing (PQ) or custom queuing (CQ). When the packets are already marked for use in a wider network, the IP priorities can be set in the ToS field of the IP packet header. The main task of classification is identification of the data flow, allocation of priorities and marking of specific data flow packets.

2.2.3 QoS congestion management mechanism

Because of the nature of audio, video and data traffic, the whole traffic amount sometimes exceeds the maximum speed of the connection. In this situation the following question can be raised: what should the router do in such situations? Will it manage and insert the packets, or better yet series of packets, into a double queue or two single queues, which will be refreshing more often? For solving such problems, a tool for managing congestions is used nowadays. Congestion management mechanism ensures that the data flows are placed into corresponding and proper waiting queues. Depending on the application type and application priorities the mechanism decides into which queue the momentary packet will be inserted. As a classic example, we can take a look at an HTTP packet. For such a packet the mechanism will provide custom queuing discipline (CQ), where the packet will be assigned into one of 16 internal queues (see section 3). In case of priority queuing such a mechanism (PQ) would insert the HTTP packet into the lowest internal queue (*low*).

2.2.4 QoS queuing management mechanism

We have to be aware that the round-robin waiting queues (single, double) do not have an infinite length, meaning that sooner or later they are full or congested. Another disadvantage is that each memory structure involves additional delays during data transfer. When the queue is full, it cannot accept any new packets, meaning that a new packet will be rejected. The reason for rejection has been already discovered: the router simply cannot avoid discarding packets when the queue is full, regardless of which priority is applied in the ToS field of the packet. From this perspective the queue management mechanism must execute two very important tasks:

- Try to ensure a place in the round-robin queue or try to prevent the queue from becoming full. With this approach a queuing management mechanism provides the necessary space for high-priority frames;
- Enable the criterion for rejecting packets. The priority level applied in the packet must be checked at the beginning, after which the mechanism decides which packet will be rejected and which not. Packets with lower priority are rejected earlier in comparison to those with a higher priority. This allows undisturbed movement of high-priority traffic flows, and if there is some additional space at the available bandwidth, other low-priority traffic flows can also pass through the network.

Both described methods are included in the *Weighted Random Early Detect* mechanism, which can be found in various sources under the acronym WRED.

2.3 QoS service levels

Service levels are related to the QoS capabilities of the system, which help ensuring the proper delivery of specific traffic through the network to its destinations. QoS service levels differ in accuracy and consistency (QoS strictness). Such levels define how much bandwidth a certain application requires, how latency and jitter influence it, and how each service level manages the packet loss characteristics. Three basic service levels are provided across the entire heterogeneous network, as shown in Figure 2:

- Best effort service has no guaranteed service. A good example for this level is FIFO queue, which has no capability to differ individual traffic types.
- Differentiated service presents the so-called »soft« QoS. With its application all traffic types are treated in a better way, which also speeds up the treatment, improves the average threshold of bandwidth and reduces the low-priority traffic data loss. This type of service includes the traffic classification mechanism and QoS queuing mechanisms such as PQ, CQ, WFQ and WRED, which are going to be explained in detail in section 3. Basically, this level of service has a statistical advantage in comparison to the above-presented best effort service, but a guaranteed service, which is the main property of the last service level, is still not applied here.
- Guaranteed service level is representative of the so-called high-level QoS. It is primarily intended to maintain the network resources for specific traffic. Such level is provided by Resource Reservation Protocol (RSVP) and CBWFQ queuing mechanism.

To conclude: which service level is more appropriate for use in a particular network depends on the following factors:

- If a user tries to solve a communication problem for a particular application, each of the above mentioned levels could solve this problem. Performance which could be achieved depends on the requirements of the user applications.

- In everyday life, situations where users want to flexibly upgrade their communication infrastructure often appear. For this purpose there must be an upgrading technology, which offers support to all listed services which are tightly connected with each other.
- The cost of the guaranteed service implementation is slightly higher compared to implementing the differentiation service.

2.4 Congestions management concerning the waiting queues

One way how the network elements can manage and handle the transport routes and eliminate congestions and bottle-necks, is by using a queuing algorithm, which sorts the traffic and then decides which priority allocation method will be in use to dispatch packets to an output connection. A typical example is the Cisco's IOS software equipment, which includes the following queuing tools/mechanisms:

- FIFO queuing, which is based on the first-in first-out principle
- Priority Queuing (PQ)
- Custom Queuing (CQ)
- Weighted Fair Queuing (WFQ)
- Class-Based Weighted Fair Queuing (CBWFQ)

Each queuing algorithm is designed to solve a specific network traffic problem, and each algorithm also has an impact on the network performance. This will be described in more detail for each of the above mentioned queuing schemes in the next section.

3. Waiting queues used in present-day routers

Queues are very important parts of a router, and there are many different waiting queues. The basic waiting queues (FIFO, double FIFO, Custom Queuing (CQ), Priority Queuing (PQ), Weighted Fair Queuing (WFQ) (Yunni Xia† et al., 2007 and Anirudha Sahoo & D. Manjunath, 2007), and Class Based WFQ (CBWFQ) (T. Subash & S. IndiraGandhi, 2006 and L. L. Peterson & B. S. Davie, 2003) will be described and presented more precisely in this section. We will also describe the so-called 'worst case scenario' which can happen to VoIP when the traffic amount is high and the simplest queuing regime (FIFO) is in use.

To understand how waiting queues work, we have to say a few words about a single queue, as the simplest representative. Single waiting queue is a data structure that behaves as an ordered list, where data is inserted at one end, and output data comes out at the other end. This method is called FIFO (first-in first-out), and is presented below.

3.1 The FIFO waiting queue

The FIFO waiting queue can be illustrated with an example of people standing in a line in front of the cash register - who came first, will be the first to pay the cashier. Elements coming into a single queue from the left side in the serial order *a, b, c, d* can be removed from the queue in the same order (first *a,* then *b, c, d*). Figure 3 shows an example of a single line filling and emptying on the basis of the first-in first-out (FIFO) principle. FIFO queues are often implemented as round-robin queues, as shown in Figure 4.

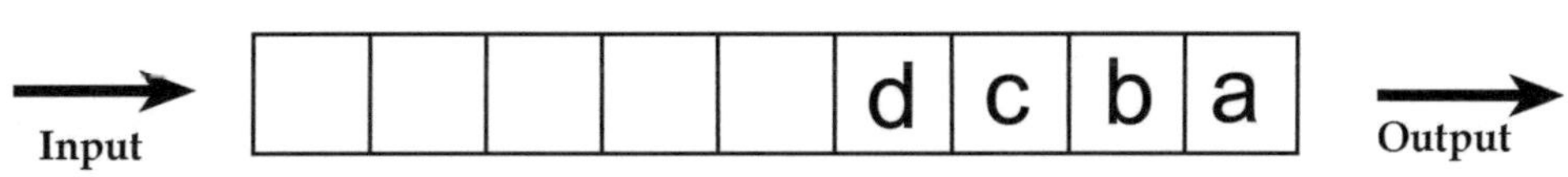

Fig. 3. The FIFO queue's filling and emptying procedure.

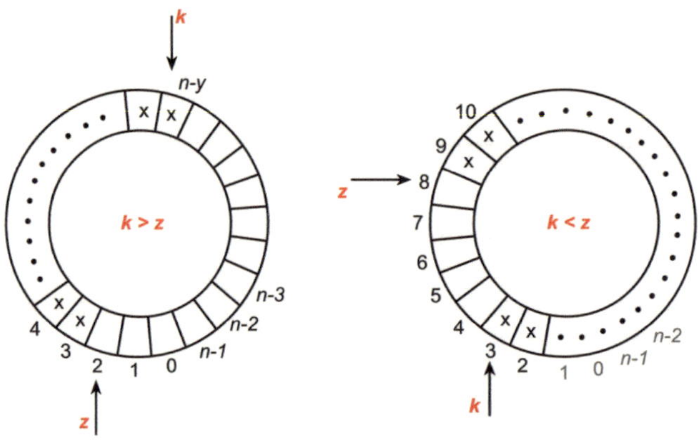

Fig. 4. The round-robin waiting queue with indexation.

Accessing items is quite limited when this method is in use. It is usable in situations where we need only the first element in the row - e.g., when printing documents. In networks, this type of a waiting queue is unsuitable for practical use, particularly with traffic flows with assigned priorities. A different and faster way than a regular FIFO is the double FIFO mechanism, where data is inserted and taken out on both sides. More about this concept is provided in the next sub-section.

3.2 The double FIFO waiting queue

The double FIFO waiting queue is a combination of two data structures (stack and single queue), which allows inserting and taking out elements on both sides. The advantage is in a faster data access, compared to a single queue or a stack. Since the circular structure operates in a round-robin mode of insertion and taking out, we are not limited with the end or the beginning of a permanently fixed structure. This is why such a concept is so flexible. Generally, we are only limited with the available size of the storage space. Operation of the double queue and its possible scenarios are illustrated in Figure 5:

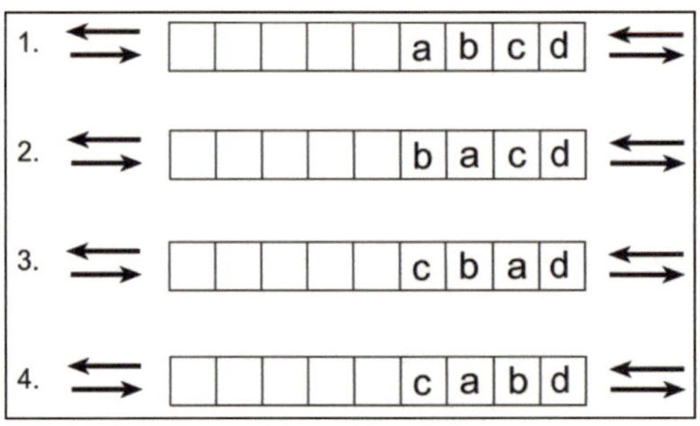

Fig. 5. The procedure of inserting the elements and the procedure of taking the elements out of the double waiting queue for the following scenarios: (1.) Element *a* is inserted from the right side, but all others are taken out on the left side in the following order; *b, c, d*. (2.) First we insert element *a* and then *b* from the left side, and then element *c* and *d* from the right side of the double waiting queue. (3.) The elements in the sequence *a, b, c* are inserted from the left side and the last element *d* from the right side. (4.) First we insert element *a* from the left side then *b* from right side, then again *c* from the left side, and finally *b* from the right side.

Operations executed upon the waiting queues must satisfy the conditions, which describe the behavior of the queue and the data in it. Operations should allow us to insert an element at the end of the queue, remove the element from the beginning, check which element is located at the beginning of the queue, and check if the queue is currently empty.

3.3 The CQ waiting queue

The primary purpose of custom queuing (CQ) is proportional sharing of the available network bandwidth among applications or organizations to avoid congestions in the network. CQ reserves the guaranteed bandwidth amount at a possible congestion point in the form of a constant ratio of bandwidth assurance, while the rest of the available bandwidth is left for other network traffic. Traffic management is performed by the allocating procedure according to the free space in the queue for each class of packets. It then starts the serving queue process in a circular manner, as shown in Figure 6. Furthermore, in each of the internal queue classes (up to 17), the amount of bandwidth, necessary for individual packets' transmission at the output connection is always calculated.

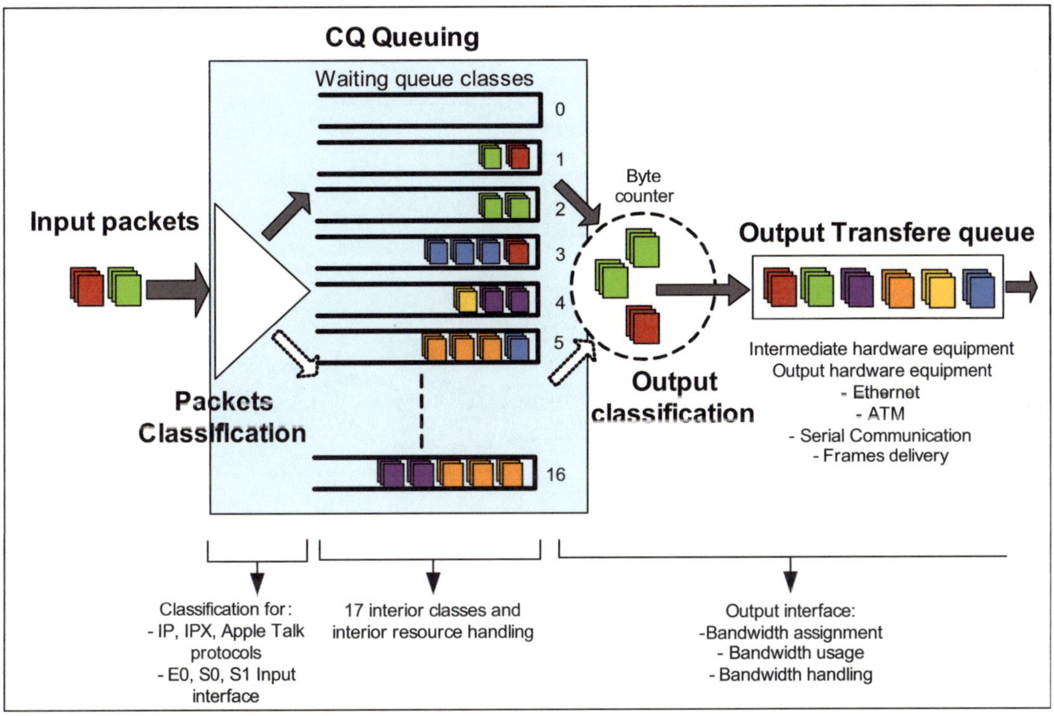

Fig. 6. Custom queuing (CQ) serves 17 internal queues in a circular manner.

Custom queuing algorithm places the packets in one of the seventeen internal waiting queues, where the queue with the index 0 is reserved for system messages, such as the so-called "keep-alive" messages and various warning messages. Queues discharging procedure is executed according to packets' weights. This means that the message with a higher priority has a smaller "weight" compared to the message with a lower priority (larger weight). The routers this way manage queues from 1 to 16 in a circular mode. Such functionality ensures an order, where no application (or group of applications) can take up more than a predetermined level of the overall bandwidth capacity, even in situations, where the link is over 90% full. CQ queuing mechanism is statically configured.

3.4 The PQ waiting queue

Priority queuing mechanism provides a smooth transition of important traffic (packets), through the network, using management at all intermediate points. PQ works by giving priority to the most important traffic. Priority queuing can be flexible regarding the allocation of different traffic parameters such as: the network protocols (IP, IPX, AppleTalk, etc.), input interfaces, the size of packets, source/destination addresses, and so on. In the PQ case, each packet (according to the entered priority in the ToS field), is classified into one of the four queues that are distinguished by different levels (priorities). The lowest level is marked with a label "low", and then the levels go up in the following subsequent order: "normal", "medium" and "high". Packets are individually sorted into appropriate queues according to the declared priority. Packets which are not classified or have not yet been classified (see the section on data flows classification) through the above described classification mechanism, automatically fall into the "normal" waiting queue as shown in Figure 7. During the data transmission the algorithm first handles the high-priority queues and then the low-priority queues.

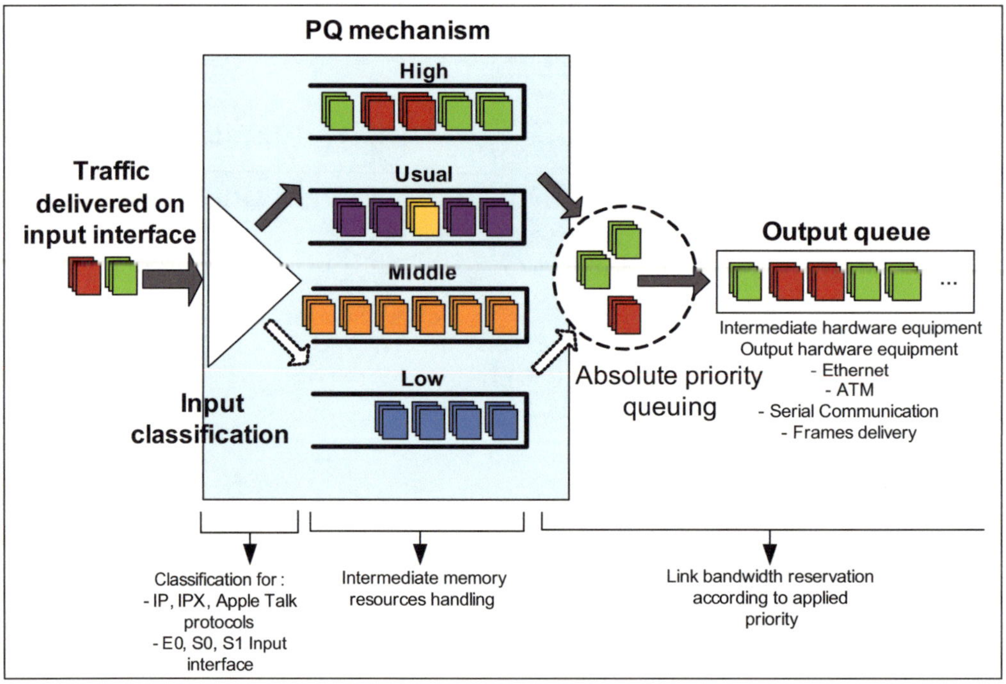

Fig. 7. Different priority classes into which the packets are inserted according to their priority.

PQ is particularly useful in situations, where the most important traffic must be treated and transmitted over different network types (WAN, LAN, etc.) first. PQ currently uses static configuration, and because of this it is not to able automatically adjust to the changing requirements in the network.

3.5 The WFQ waiting queue

In situations where it is desirable to provide a constant response time for more demanding users or applications without adding an excessive bandwidth, the ideal solution is the weighted fair queuing (WFQ) mechanism. This is an algorithm that provides bit-wise fairness, which allows each queue to be served fairly, where fairness is guaranteed by the number of bytes.

For example, let's take a closer look at two waiting queues below. The first queue has at the specific moment 100 inserted packets, while the other queue contains at the same moment 50 packets. In this situation the WFQ algorithm takes two packets from the second queue for each packet taken from the first queue. With this procedure both queues will be empty at the same time. WFQ ensures that no one queue suffers a lack of bandwidth. This way the low-level traffic can smoothly travel through the network, which represents a compromise for the majority of traffic. This increases the service efficiency, since an equal number of low-level and high-level packets are transmitted. The described operation is illustrated in Figure 8.

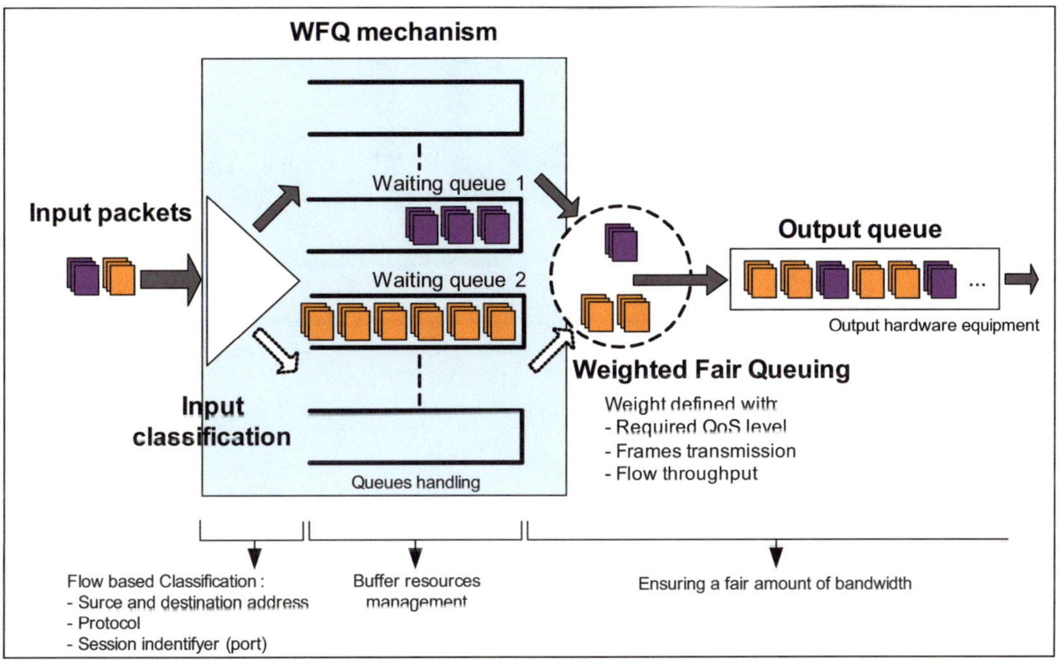

Fig. 8. The operating principle of the WFQ

The weighted fair queuing minimizes the configuration costs. Such mechanism can also automatically adapt to the changing temporary network traffic conditions. The fairness concept has been in practice very well established as the default mode on the majority of communication interfaces. The weighted amount is in the WFQ case calculated from IP priority bits, which provides a better performance for all queues. For IP priorities the values from 0 to 5 are in use (settings 6 and 7 are reserved), and the WFQ algorithm calculates how many additional services must be provided for every queue.

This method can use any available bandwidth for traffic transmission. Such operating principle is essentially different from the concept based on strict time-division multiplexing

(TDM), which simply increases the bandwidth and leaves it unused if the traffic is not present. WFQ can operate in association with the IP priority settings, as well as with the resource reservation protocol (RSVP).

WFQ algorithm also has the ability of addressing the problem of variable round-trip delay. This clearly improves the algorithms, such as SNA, LLC (logical link control) and transmission control protocol (TCP), as well removes congestions and speeds up slow connections. Results are much more predictable over the entire route, while the response time for each active flow can be reduced even for a multiple factor, as shown in simulation results in Figure 9. Time diagrams in the figure show round-trip delays for traffic without WFQ (left graph) and for the same traffic with WFQ (right graph) in milliseconds. The impact of the WFQ algorithm is more than evident.

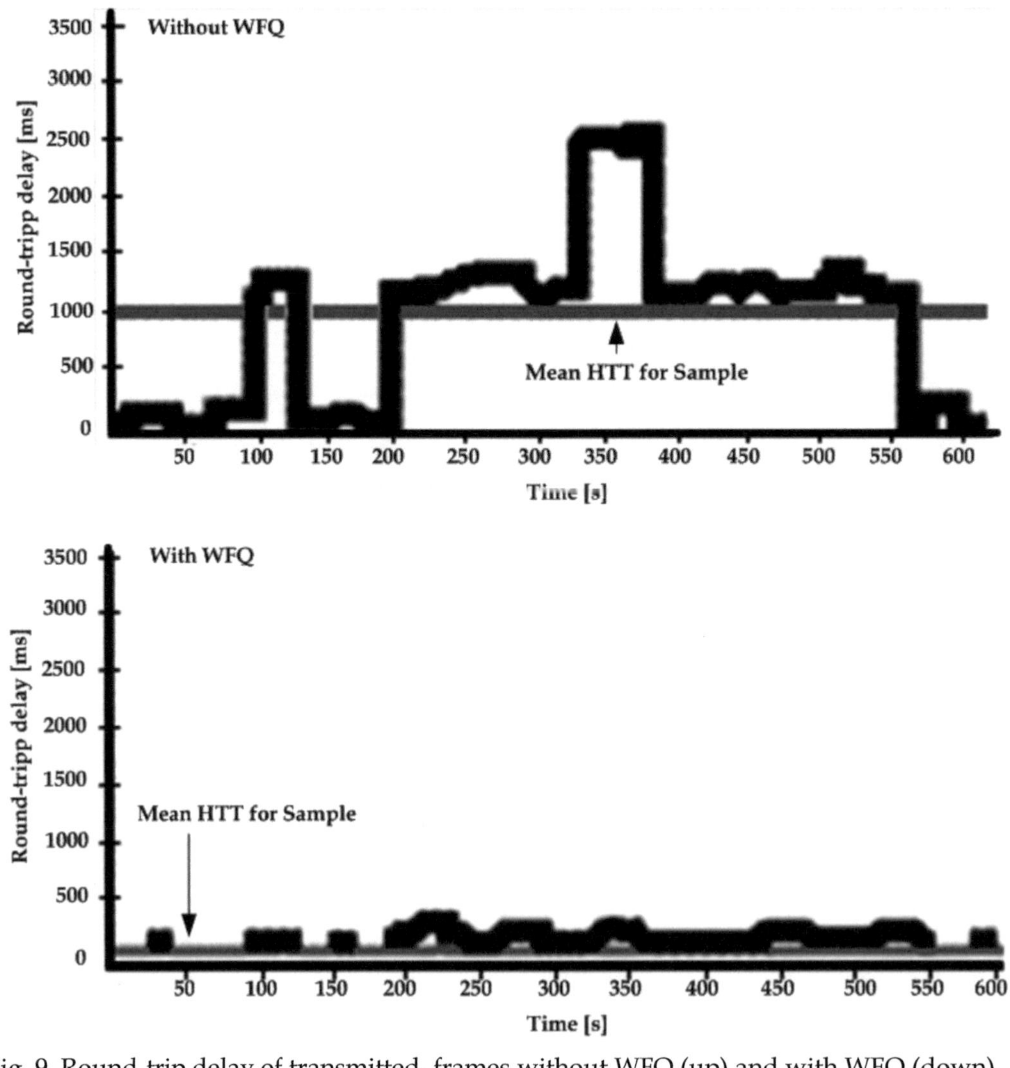

Fig. 9. Round-trip delay of transmitted, frames without WFQ (up) and with WFQ (down), using a WAN 128kbps connection.

3.6 The CBWFQ waiting queue

The Class-Based Weighted Fair queuing (CBWFQ) is a modern tool for managing congestions, and it provides a better flexibility in allocating a minimum bandwidth amount on the fair-queuing basis as well as on the basis of administrator-defined classes. Instead of providing a queue for every data stream, classes defined by the network administrator are used. If the traffic flow corresponds to an admin-defined class, it is immediately placed into such class, where it already has a reserved link bandwidth. If the traffic flow does not correspond to any of the admin-defined classes, it can use only the remaining link bandwidth, which is not reserved for any other class. For each defined class a minimum required bandwidth is guaranteed.

At this point, we could provide a concrete example, where the CBWFQ mechanism is very useful to avoid situations where more low-priority flows could overflow the high-priority data stream. A typical example is video-stream transmission, which requires almost half of the available bandwidth on the T1 connection. A sufficient amount of bandwidth could also be provided with the WFQ mechanism, but only in cases where only two data streams are present. In cases where more than two traffic flows are present at the same time, the video session will get less bandwidth (in the WFQ case), as the WFQ mechanism works on the principle of fairness. If, for example, 10 streams at the same time require T1 link bandwidth, the video session stream will get only one tenth (1/10) of the whole T1 link bandwidth, which is unacceptable for a video session. Even if IP priority 5 is set for the video session, the situation would not change significantly. The queuing mechanism must reserve at least half of the T1 link bandwidth for the video session. This can be ensured with the CBWFQ queuing mechanism. The network administrator determines the class, and places a video meeting into such class. This indicates that the router must provide 768 kbps service for such class, which is exactly half of the total bandwidth of the T1 connection. The needed bandwidth is thus allocated to the video. The remaining bandwidth is used for other (unclassified) data streams. These classes are serviced through the use of stream-based WFQ algorithm, which allocates the remaining bandwidth to other applications (in our case the remaining half of the T1 connection's bandwidth).

It should be noted that low latency queues (LLQ) can be marked so that the actual priority queue is differentiated. Such feature is known as the PQ-CBWFQ, which is a priority class-based weighted fair queuing. Low latency queuing allows a specific class to be served as a strict priority queue. Traffic in such classes will be serviced before all other traffic placed in other classes, and at the same time the necessary amount of bandwidth will be guaranteed. All traffic that is above the level of bandwidth reservation is simply discarded.

With the CBWFQ a minimum amount of bandwidth can be reserved for a given class. If there is some free bandwidth available, it can be used by such class. Similarly, when a class does not use all the guaranteed bandwidth, it can be used by other applications.

4. Hybrid waiting queues

Because different queuing mechanisms have different advantages, our idea was to combine different queuing mechanisms and join their positive (but also negative) properties into new hybrid queuing methods. The aim of hybrid methods is to concentrate the most possible positive properties of individual methods. Many different hybrid queuing methods are possible. This section provides descriptions of hybrid queuing disciplines for our proposed combinations CQ-CBWFQ and WFQ-CBWFQ (Sasa Klampfer et al., 2009 and Sasa Klampfer

et al. 2007) as well as for the known PQ-CBWFQ introduced by Cisco Systems. Each of these methods was evaluated with simulations, as described in section 6.
The negative side of hybrid methods is duplication of the memory of the mechanism which forms a queue. It is a well-known fact that every memory element and its size involve certain latency or delay for traffic which goes through these interfaces. The higher the number of these interfaces, i.e. waiting places, the bigger are the delays, which is not a desirable feature for time-sensitive applications (VoIP, video conference, etc.). This is why we have to make a compromise between the number, size and length of the intermediate buffers to avoid excessive data spillage (or data loss) when a buffer is too small, and to also avoid scenarios where the buffers are too big, and are increasing the delay. This aspect and the so-called jitter effect will be presented in detail in Section 5.

4.1 The CQ-CBWFQ hybrid waiting queue

This hybrid method combines the properties of the custom queuing (CQ) and the CBWFQ mechanisms (Figure 10). In the first phase the custom queuing allocates the available bandwidth among all active network applications so that congestion cannot appear. This is the main reason why we combined these two queuing schemes. In first phase we try to avoid congestions with custom queuing. In the CQ step traffic is managed by assigning weighted amounts, and is arranged into 16 queues. Once the packets are sent to the output CQ interface they arrive to the CBWFQ input interface. CBWFQ packet-classification mechanism, attached behind the custom queuing mechanism, arranges traffic into traffic classes defined by a class-based weighted fair queuing algorithm. Such classes are then ensured with fixed amounts of bandwidth. All the advantages of the CBWFQ are retained. With this method we reduce the delays within the network, which is not the case with the ordinary CQ scheme.

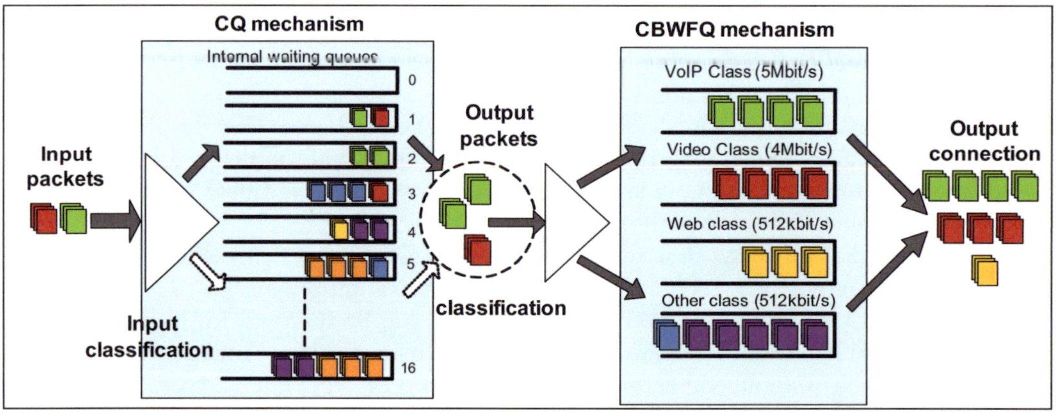

Fig. 10. The hybrid queuing mechanism consisting of the CQ and the CBWFQ regimes.

4.2 The PQ-CBWFQ hybrid waiting queue

This mechanism consists of two previously mentioned queuing mechanisms; the priority queuing mechanism and the admin class-defined queuing mechanism (CBWFQ). Since the properties of both mechanisms that construct the PQ-CBWFQ method have been already mentioned in previous sections, we should now take a look at the hybrid mode concept shown in Figure 11.

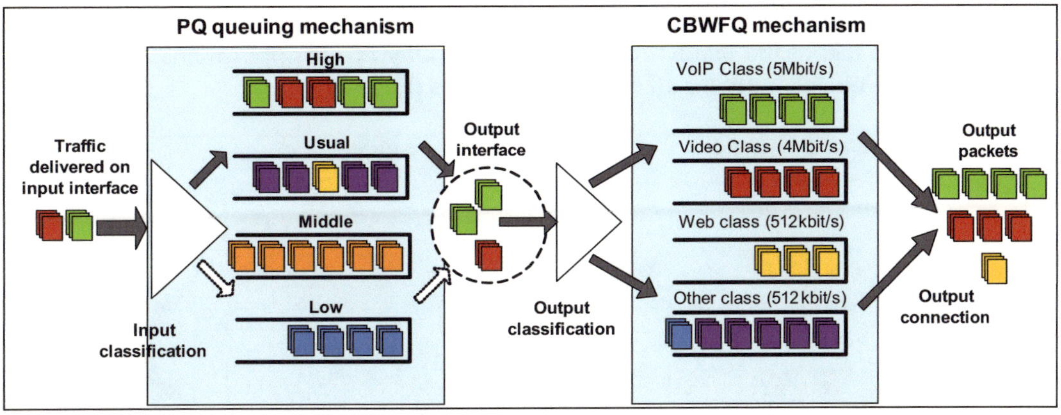

Fig. 11. The hybrid queuing mechanism consisting of the PQ and the CBWFQ regimes.

In the first step the traffic is arranged into waiting queues according to the priorities set in individual packets' ToS fields. According to the ToS priorities the packets are arranged by their importance to four different internal priority queues. In the second step, the output interface algorithm first serves the highest-priority data stream (packets that are in the queue with the highest importance) and then all other lower ranking queues. Once the packets appear at the outgoing interface of the priority queuing mechanism, they are again scheduled into admin-defined classes of CBWFQ mechanism. Such defined classes already have the needed bandwidth pre-reserved as set by the network administrator. This way the packets at the CBWFQ mechanism output interface do not need to fight for bandwidth, as it is guaranteed in advance. This accelerates the transfer of high-priority flows, and such flows become independent of all other lower-priority flows.

We can take the VoIP traffic as an example. VoIP traffic will already have provided a sufficient pre-allocated bandwidth, meaning that its pre-reserved bandwidth cannot be used by any other application or other traffic flow, whose classification does not fulfill the terms of class reservation. This way the output connection can transmit even the lower-priority traffic parallel to the high-priority traffic, but only in quantities and at rates established by the remaining bandwidth. This hybrid method (PQ-CBWFQ) is representative of low latency queues (LLQ) (S. Büchel, 2004). Low latency queuing mechanism allows a class that is served as a strict priority queue. Traffic in such class will be served before all other traffic in the remaining classes. Bandwidth-amount reservation is also guaranteed in this case. All traffic which is above the level of bandwidth reservation is simply discarded. Furthermore, the same hypotheses regarding the compromise between the choice of the size and the number of intermediate buffers mentioned in the above case are valid also with this method.

4.3 The WFQ-CBWFQ hybrid waiting queue

This mechanism consists of the weighted fair queuing (WFQ) and the class-based weighted fair queuing (CBWFQ). With this method we can show how important the first step is to ensure fairness for all applications where the internal WFQ queues are emptied by the principle of fairness (see section about the WFQ). At this step, we ensure undisturbed flow throughput for all active applications that appear at the WFQ mechanism's outgoing interface. In the next step the CBWFQ classification takes care of proper packets' assignment into admin-defined classes. This way every application at the first stage gets a fair treatment, and in the second phase high-priority applications get its own classes with the pre-reserved bandwidth. The rest of the bandwidth is left for all other active applications. The fairness and fluidity movement apply for all active applications (Figure 12).

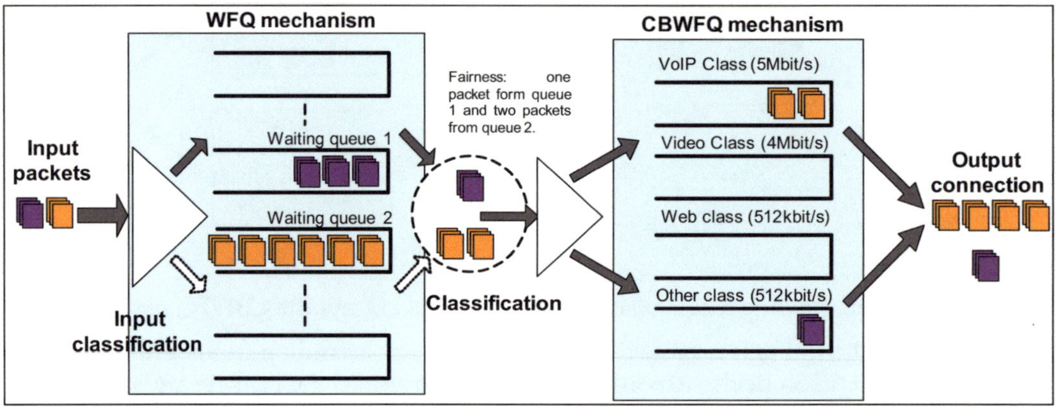

Fig. 12. The hybrid queuing mechanism consisting of the WFQ and the CBWFQ regimes.

WFQ is suitable for operating with IP priority settings, such as Resource Reservation Protocol (RSVP) (A. Kos & S. Tomazic, 2005), which is also capable of managing round-trip delay problems. This is the main reason, why we have combined the WFQ with the CBWFQ mechanism. Such queuing clearly improves algorithms such as SNA (Systems Network Architecture) - Cisco SNA (CSNA) which is an application that provides support for SNA protocols to the IBM mainframe. Using a Cisco 7000, 7200, or a 7500 Series router with a Channel Interface Processor (CIP) or Channel Port Adapter (CPA) and Cisco SNA (CSNA) support enabled, we can connect two mainframes (either locally or remotely), to a physical unit (PU) 2.0 or 2.1, or connect a mainframe to a front-end processor (FEP) in another Virtual Telecommunications Access Method (VTAM) domain (http://www.cisco.com/en/US/tech/tk331/tk332/tk126/tsd_technology_support_subprotocol_home.html), logical link control (LCC) (http://www.erg.abdn.ac.uk/users/gorry/course/lan-pages/llc.html), or transmission control protocol (TCP). WFQ-CBWFQ is at the same time capable of accelerating slow features and removing congestions in the network (merged positive properties of both queuing schemes). Results become more predictable over the whole routing path, while Ethernet delays can be greatly decreased (see the section with the simulation results) compared to other queuing disciplines (CQ, PQ, WFQ). The WFQ and the CBWFQ queuing combination can represent the best solution (merged positive properties of both methods) for reducing the Ethernet delay. This assumption is confirmed in Section 6, where the simulation results show the delays in the network are most reduced with the WFQ-CBWFQ combination.

5. Reducing the VoIP jitter by decreasing the router's buffer lengths

Our intention in this section is to show the reader how queuing combinations affect VoIP traffic quality, especially in terms of Ethernet delay and jitter (Mansour J. Karam & Fouad A. Tobagi, 2001). With the results of our simulation-based research (Section 6) we can prove the usefulness of our hybrid concept for decreasing Ethernet delay. Ethernet delay was rapidly decreased when the hybrid queuing combinations WFQ-CBWFQ and PQ-CBWFQ were used. Though the jitter is highly increased with such combinations the delay is still within the useful limits. By using the proposed queuing combination it is possible to minimize the Ethernet delay for IP-based time-sensitive applications, including VoIP (Cole R. Rosenbluth, 2000, and Frank Ohrtman, 2004). Because we combine different queuing disciplines, the waiting queues are also combined. This means that buffer lengths have been in many cases doubled or at least extended. This is why we have included this section about buffer length (L. Zheng & D. Xu, 2001, M. Kao, 2005, and TIPHON 22TD047, 2001) influence on the VoIP jitter. Jitter can also cause some VoIP packets falling out, because of which the quality of the conversation over VoIP can be significantly reduced. The use of such method results in an increased VoIP round trip delay as well as higher packet delay variation (jitter), which could with an improper buffer length exceed the limits of acceptability. The method is thus not acceptable in the VoIP case where limited delays are required. For this reason we also present the possibilities of reducing such delays by using proper buffer lengths. One approach involves reducing the buffer length, which however also must not be too short so that other packets do not fall out. The proper solution for such a case will be presented in this section.

5.1 Introduction to jitter

Jitter is defined as a variation in delays between the audio packets (VoIP), which can occur due to congestions in the network. On the transmitter side, the packets are sent in a continuous stream where they are equally time-gapped between each other. The jitter is caused by network congestions, improper selection of the queuing mechanism or improper network element's (router) configuration. Such a scenario is shown in Figure 13.

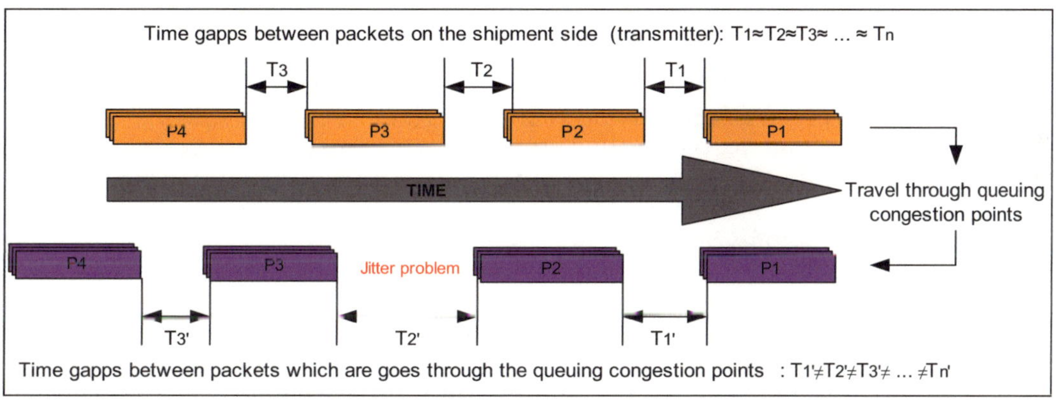

Fig. 13. Schematic description of the jitter

When a router accepts an audio data stream via real-time protocol (RTP-Real Time Protocol) which is provided for VoIP, it must ensure jitter compensation. To eliminate jitter effect, the so-called playout delay buffer must be used. Such an output memory is sometimes also called *de-jitter buffer* (Fig. 14). The packets are then sent in a regular sequence to the digital signal processor, which reproduces the sound.

In cases when the jitter is so big that the packets sent to the "de-jitter buffer" fall out of the allowed area, the packets are simply discarded. Rejecting packets leads to poor conversation quality. For smaller packet loss effect (e.g., individual packets) the DSP interpolation algorithm is provided; it replaces the lost packets with an alternative content, which is usual neighboring a successfully accepted packet (Cisco Systems, Jitter data sheet, 2003).

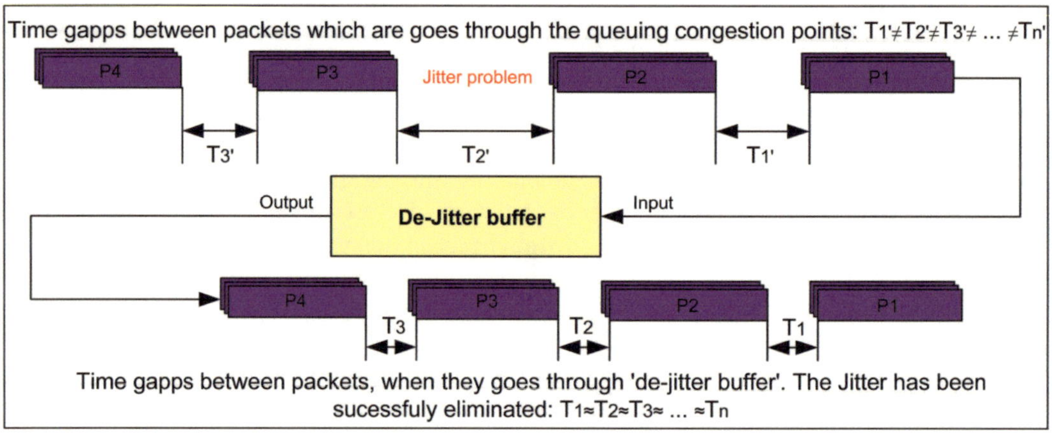

Fig. 14. De-jitter buffer's application

5.2 Encapsulation and its connection with jitter

Generally speaking the simplest way to detect jitter is at the interfaces of the existing routing equipment, because we there have full access. The success of eliminating this phenomenon is largely related to the packets and connection's encapsulation type. ATM networks are well known for being relatively robust regarding jitter occurrences. The main reason for this can be found in its asynchronous data transfer mode implementation. If the ATM is configured correctly, jitter practically does not occur. When we deal with point-to-point (P2P) applications, which use Point to Point Protocol (PPP) encapsulation, the jitter is always present in the form of serialization delay. Such delays can be controlled in a simple and easy way using fragmentation and interleaving in the PPP connection mechanism.

Recently, two queuing mechanism types came to be used within IP networks which are able to reduce the jitter in the VoIP session case. Both belong to the so-called low latency queuing mechanisms:

- IP RTP Priority Queuing
- PQ-CBWFQ (LLQ)
- PQ-WFQ (LLQ)

6. Examples of simulation for testing queuing mechanisms

In this section, we will first present the OPNET Modeler tool (OPNET Modeler Technical Documentation, 2005 and S. Klampfer - Diploma Thesis, 2007), used in our simulation experiments. The simulations include VoIP applications where we have used the G.729a voice encoder scheme. This is an 8 kbps Conjugate-Structure Algebraic-Code-Excited Linear Prediction (CS-ACELP) speech compression algorithm approved by ITU-T. G.729 (G.729 Datasheet, 2005).

In our experiments we prepare simulation examples with typical network topologies (Morgan Kaufmann, 2006 and Tadeusz Wysocki et al., 2005), network architecture, routers, connection types, used application types within the network, statistical distributions of the simulated application traffic, and number of users. These parameters influence traffic congestions according to their intensity and used application types (ITU-T Y.1541 Network Performance Objectives for IP Based Services, 2001 and ITU-T SG12 D74 IP Phones and Gateways: Factors impacting speech quality, 2002). In these simulation experiments, we have included three of the most useful queuing methods, where we combined priority queuing (PQ) with class-based weighted fair queuing (CBWFQ), custom queuing (CQ) with CBWFQ and weighted fair queuing (WFQ) with CBWFQ. Each hybrid method is compared with the basic method. For example, the PQ-CBWFQ method is compared with the priority queuing method, and so on.

Using the simulation results we will present the method with the best results on the simulation test bed regarding VoIP jitter and VoIP delay. We are going to make a comparison between the well known PQ-CBWFQ and the best of the proposed hybrid solutions (WFQ-CBWFQ). Our main goal is to determine the factor, which will tell us how much more suitable is a specific queuing method for VoIP traffic class, during whole routing procedure from end-to-end.

6.1 A short description of the OPNET modeler simulation tool

OPNET Modeler represents (OPNET Modeler Technical Documentation, 2005) one of the most useful simulation tools in the area of communications industry. The tool enables designing and studying telecommunication infrastructures, individual devices, protocols, applications, etc. It is based on object-oriented modeling. Individual modules included in specific libraries represents models of real building blocks used in real communication infrastructure. The created simulation models thus present a good approach compared to equivalent real networks. Support for modeling of all types of communication networks, included in advanced technologies such as Wi-Fi, UMTS, GSM, Fast Ethernet, etc. is also available. The tool allows modeling of PSTN, ISDN, xDSL, as well as optical networks. The user interface is based on a series of hierarchical graphic interfaces, which enable editing at each stage, as well illustrate the structure of protocols, devices and networks. The tool also supports animations, which can provide a better understanding of the simulation results and events appearing in the simulated networks. The user can also observe individual packets traveling during simulation execution (slow motion support). OPNET Modeler offers a rich existing model library of standard equipment and protocols, including the possibility of modeling new or upgrading existing ones, which can be done by using code level in C/C++ C/C++ programming languages.

6.2 Example 1: hybrid queuing mechanisms

Let's assume a company has VoIP quality problems in their communication infrastructure, and they call communication experts to solve these problems. The experts use the OPNET Modeler simulation tool to model a network structure of a private company's network on the level of links, equipment, applications, etc. Their goal is to find the optimal setup for communication equipment which would solve the problems.

Different queuing mechanisms and the proposed hybrid concepts were tested within a simulated network shown in Figure 15 for proving the advantages and the disadvantages of the proposed hybrid queuing methods. The main goal of these simulations is improving the network performance in terms of the VoIP end-to-end delay, Ethernet delay and jitter. Different queuing schemes are used in order to find the most appropriate one for the VoIP application's traffic.

VoIP traffic flows were set up randomly among all groups containing VoIP users ('3VoIP', '2VoIP', '5VoIP', 'VoIP' and 'Misc'). The network structure consists of servers, such as Web Server, FTP server, etc., which are connected through a 10BaseT connection and through a 16 port switch on the IP Cloud, as shown at the top of Figure 15. Four local-area segments (LANs) are connected to the routers, where different kinds of users (VoIP, Web users) are placed. Each Cisco router is connected with a 16 port switch, where it is then connected to an IP Cloud. Users use different application clients such as VoIP, Web, and FTP.

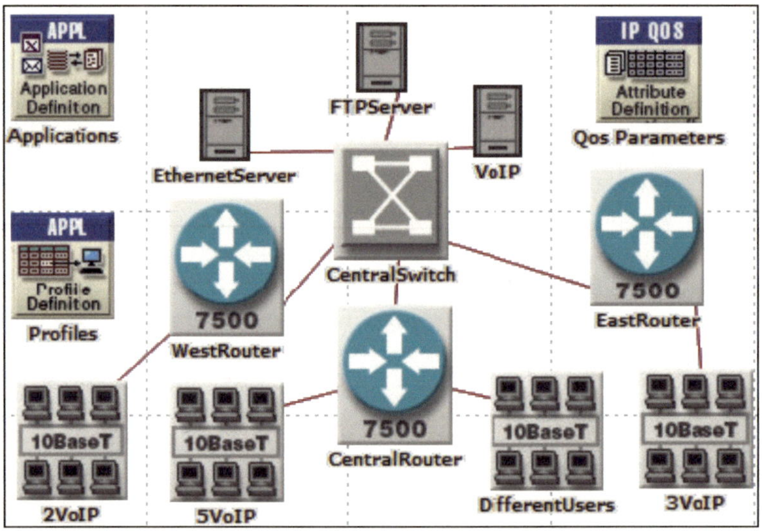

Fig. 15. The network simulation structure

Web and FTP applications are applied only for creating low-priority traffic flows. Such applications are defined with the 'Applications' node shown at the top right side of Figure 15. Using the 'Profiles' node (besides the applications node) the client profiles are defined, as well as the User Equipment's (UE's) tasks and which UE application can be used. In IP the QoS node (QoS parameters) defines the traffic policy for the network. Within each router, there are traffic classes, configured for the CBWFQ queuing method, where specific traffic flows (VoIP flow, Video session flow, Web browsing flow, etc.) are placed. Each router has three traffic classes, shown in Table 1, where the first-one, with 9Mbit/s, belongs to the VoIP traffic, and the second and the third-one belong to low-priority FTP and HTTP traffic flows with 512 kbit/s bandwidths defined for each class.

Application	Users	Class	Bandwidth
VoIP	10	1	9 Mbit/s
FTP	490	2	512 kbit/s
Web	10	3	512 kbit/s

Table 1. The application's traffic classes

6.2.1 Example 1: simulation results

Simulation results were collected after each successive simulation run, both for ordinary and hybrid queuing methods described above. The obtained results even in a graphical form clearly show the impact of each combination on Ethernet delay and jitter. The impact is obvious when each queuing combination is compared to a basic queuing scheme (PQ with PQ-CBWFQ).

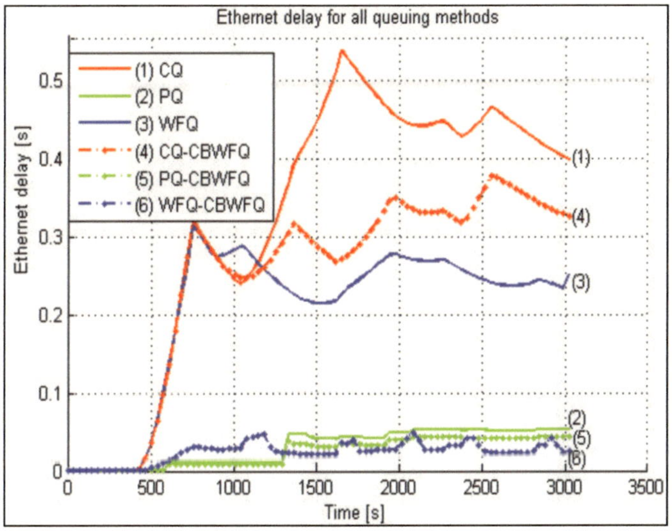

Fig. 16. The Ethernet delay for all queuing methods, where (1) presents Ethernet delay for custom queuing (CQ), (2) priority queuing (PQ) Ethernet delay, (3) Ethernet delay for weighted fair queuing (WFQ) method, (4) CQ-CBWFQ combination, (5) PQ-CBWFQ, and (6) Ethernet delay for WFQ-CBWFQ hybrid queuing method.

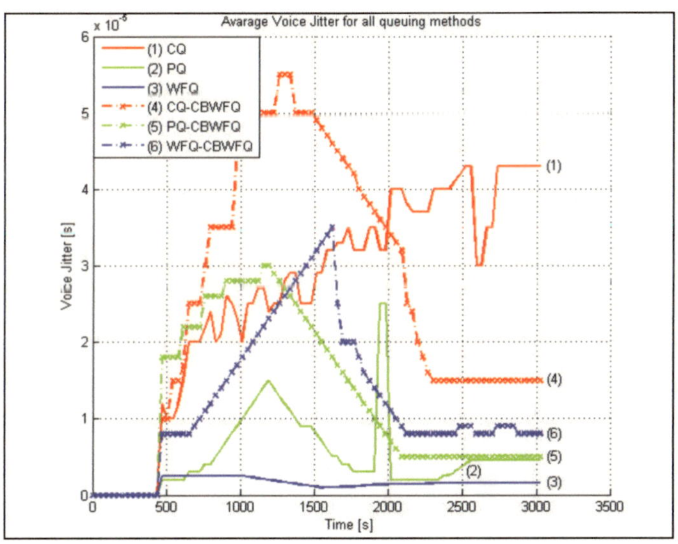

Fig. 17. The voice jitter for all queuing schemes, where (1) presents the custom queuing (CQ) jitter delay, (2) the priority queuing (PQ), (3) the weighted fair queuing (WFQ), (4) the CQ-CBWFQ, (5) the PQ-CBWFQ, and (6) voice jitter delay for the WFQ-CBWFQ hybrid queuing method.

Comparing a specific hybrid queuing method (Figure 16) with a specific ordinary queuing method (example: (1)-CQ with (4)-CQ-CBWFQ) we can see the Ethernet delay reduction in the CQ-CBWFQ case. The same is true for a comparison between (2)-PQ and (5)-PQ-CBWFQ, as well as between (3)-WFQ and (6)-WFQ-CBWFQ. WFQ-CBWFQ is obviously the best combination for reducing the average Ethernet delay within the network. Besides its advantages, the disadvantage of the method is the jitter issue. The best results are obtained with the PQ-CBWFQ queuing discipline (Fig. 16). Results of none of the other combinations satisfy our expectations for VoIP and other time-sensitive internet applications.

PQ-CBWFQ, which is usually known as LLQ (low latency queue), provides a strict priority queue for voice traffic and a weighted fair queue for any other traffic class. As we see in Figure 16, the PQ-CBWFQ combination works fine for the strict-priority traffic flows such as, for example, VoIP (tested in our case), video conferencing, video on demand, etc. High-priority traffic has in the case of PQ-CBWFQ the smallest delay, which is comparable with the WFQ queuing scheme.

Figure 17 presents voice jitter for all queuing schemes (hybrid and ordinary). In this case, the WFQ scheme is the smoothest and has the lowest jitter value. Speaking generally, the CQ-CBWFQ and WFQ-CBWFQ queuing schemes are the worst possibilities. The latter gives the best results in the Ethernet delay case. However, such jitter can negatively affect the VoIP speech quality. As we have expected; the PQ-CBWFQ also reaches low jitter values, which is desirable for VoIP and other real-time or near real-time applications. In any other queuing scheme, jitter values are higher but still acceptable in the VoIP case where the maximum value reaches only 40ms. The critical jitter limit is 150ms. Any delay in voice application larger than 150ms can be detected by the human ear. Voice packets must arrive at their destinations within 120ms, which is near the real-time frame defined as 100ms ± ΔT, where ΔT is equal to 20ms. The situation would be different if such jitter appeared between individual audio samples at 8 kHz sampling rate (Ts = 125us), but we focus only on jitter between audio frames. The reason for bad results in the jitter case for hybrid methods can be found in the buffer area. To minimize the adverse impact of jitter in media file downloads, the 'buffer' is usually employed. The buffer serves as the storage area in the system where incoming packets for digital audio or video are arranged before they are played back - the computer is given the time needed to ensure that the incoming data packets are complete before they can be played.

6.3 Example 2: PQ and CQ mechanisms compared to PQ-CBWFQ

The test network consists of remote servers, VoIP and Web clients (spread across specific geographic areas), switches, routers, etc. With the "IP Cloud" element we describe some properties of the entire wide area network, such as delay, packet loss, etc. The whole network structure (see Figure 18), public network, individual users, etc. is connected through an IP cloud to remote servers in the WAN network.

Four external LANs (LAN1, LAN2, LAN3 and LAN4), where each of them contains of 50 VoIP users, establish connections to the VoIP users at the other end of the WAN network using a 10 Mbit/s wired broadband connection. In each of the local area networks there are also World Wide Web (WWW) users, which exploit a part of the available bandwidth. These users can affect the VoIP traffic delay, but only in the cases, when inappropriate QoS and queuing mechanisms are used. A fast connection allows exchange of large amounts of data between units, and at the same time ensures small time delays, which is crucial for the VoIP sessions.

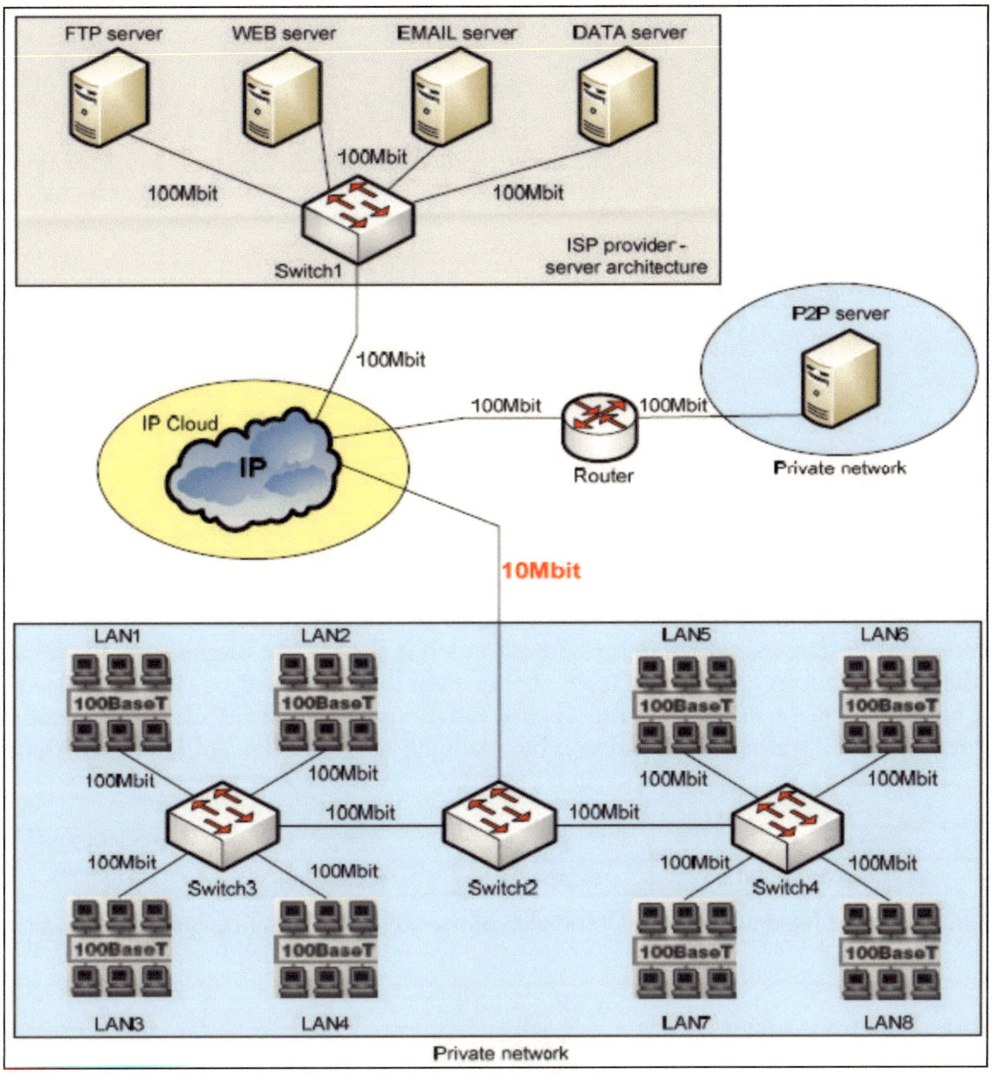

Fig. 18. Simulation structure of the wide area network

The wide area network (WAN) simulation structure is shown in Figure 18. All active applications are designed in the OPNET Modeler simulation tool in the form of three different scenarios. The first scenario consists of the CQ queuing method, second only of the PQ queuing method; while the third scenario consists of the PQ-CBWFQ queuing regime, which belongs to the low latency queuing group. Through a comparison of all mentioned scenarios we obtain the following results.

6.3.1 Example 2: simulation results

During network simulations where we used different queuing methods for IP traffic we have measured the traffic delays corresponding to each queuing method. Results are presented in Figure 19. Curves (1), (2) and (3) illustrate the average VoIP traffic delay for the used CQ, PQ and PQ-CBWFQ queuing mechanisms.

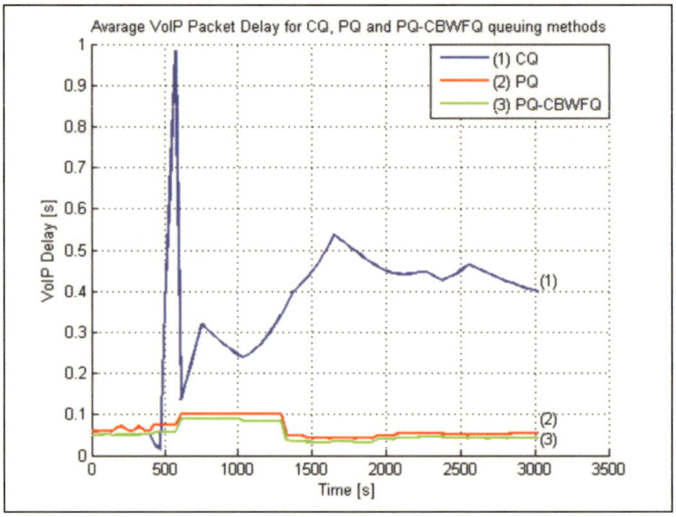

Fig. 19. The average VoIP traffic delay for the used CQ, PQ and PQ-CBWFQ queuing mechanisms.

Based on the simulation results shown in Figure 19, we have calculated and determined the relationship factors, which describe how much is the chosen method of classification for the specific observed network traffic better than the basic method. We have used CQ as a basic reference method in comparisons. Relationships were calculated by averaging CQ delay of VoIP traffic and dividing it by averaged delays of the VoIP traffic with other methods (Table 2).

Method	**CQ**	**PQ**	**PQ-CBWFQ**
Average delay [s]	0.346488	0.064444	0.052956

Table 2. The calculated average delay for each of the individual waiting queue methods.

Methods in comparison	$\frac{CQ}{PQ}$	$\frac{CQ}{PQCBWFQ}$	$\frac{PQ}{PQCBWFQ}$
Relationship factors	5.37	6.54	1.21

Table 3. Calculated relationship factors, which describe the usefulness of an individual method in comparison to others.

From the calculated factors we can see, that the PQ and PQ-CBWFQ queuing mechanisms are most suitable for time-sensitive applications such as for example VoIP. From their comparison we can conclude that the PQ method is better for a factor 5.37 than the custom queuing method, and PQ-CBWFQ combination is for a factor 6.54 better than the basic CQ method. In simulation results this can be observed in the form of the smallest delays for a specific application. In PQ and PQ-CBWFQ cases, the VoIP delay is lower than in the CQ case, and it does not exceed the critical delay (150ms), which represents the limit where the human ear can detect it. When both sophisticated methods are compared, the PQ-CBWFQ is for a factor 1.21 better than PQ queuing regime. Simulation results show how important the right choice and configuration of the queuing mechanisms are for time-sensitive traffic.

6.4 Example 3: testing ordinary queuing mechanisms (CQ, WFQ, CBWFQ, MWRR, DWRR)

Test simulation network architecture is an imitation of a real network belonging to a private company. Our main goal is to improve the network's performances. The highest level in Figure 20 represents the network server architecture offered by the internet service provider (ISP). Servers' subnet consists of five Intel servers where each of them has its own profile, such as; web profile (web server), VoIP, E-mail, FTP and video profile. These servers are connected through a 16 port switch and through a wired link to the private company's router. Company's network consists of four LAN segments including different kinds of users. In the west wing of the company are the VoIP users who represent technical support to the company's customers. In the south wing of the company is a conference room where employees have meetings. Two places here are meant for two simultaneous sessions. In the north wing there is a small office with only 10 employees who represent the development part of the company, and they use different applications needed for their work. For example, they are searching information on the web; calling their suppliers, exchanging files over FTP, and so on. The remaining east wing includes fifty disloyal employees who are surfing the net (web) during work time, downloading files, etc. (heavy browsing).

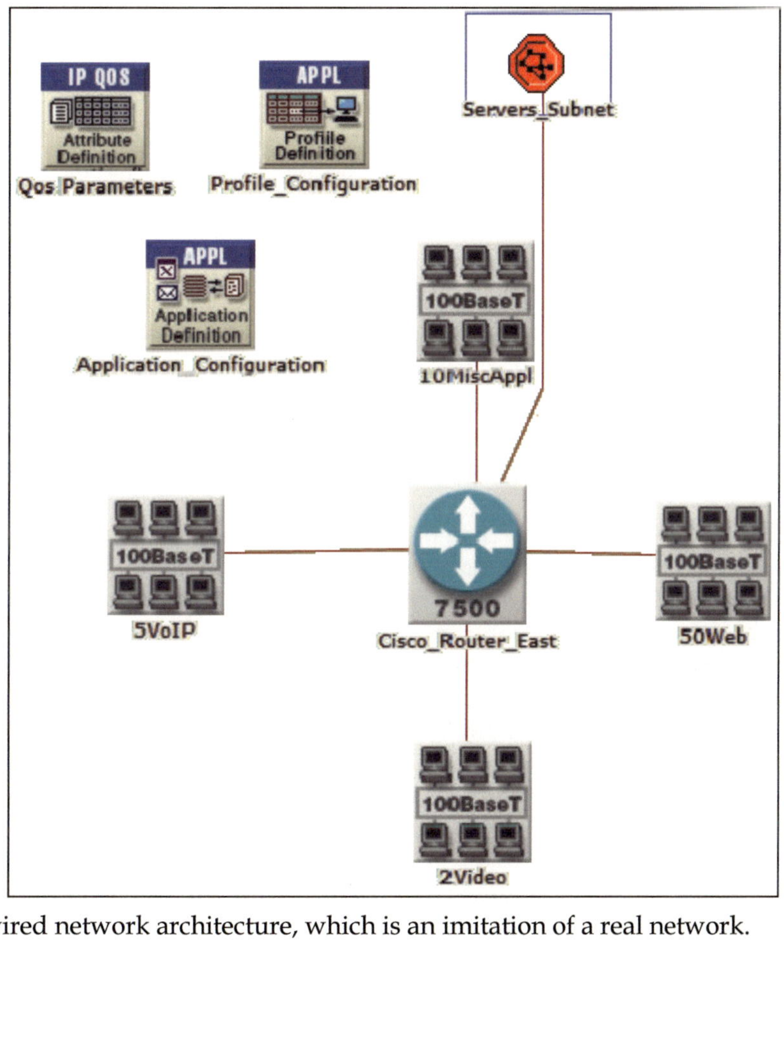

Fig. 20. A wired network architecture, which is an imitation of a real network.

Each of the company's wings is connected through a 100BaseT link to the Cisco 7500 router. This router is further connected to the ISP servers' switch through a wired (VDSL2) 10Mbit/s ISPs' link. Connections between servers and the switch are also type 100BaseT. The wired link in this case represents a bottleneck, where we have to involve a QoS system and apply different queuing disciplines.

Application	Number of users
Heavy web browsing	50 clients
FTP	4 clients
Video conferencing	7 clients
VoIP	5 clients
E-mail	1 client

Table 4. User distribution

We have created six scenarios; in the first scenario, we have tested the custom queuing discipline, which represents the basis for comparison with the WFQ (second), the MWRR (third), the DWRR (fourth), the CBWFQ (fifth) and with the combined hybrid PQ-CBWFQ (sixth scenario) queuing disciplines. The network topology remained the same in all scenarios; the differences are only in the used queuing disciplines. Through a comparison of simulation results for different scenarios we have tried to prove how each queuing discipline serves the used network applications. The obtained results are the following.

6.4.1 Example 3: simulation results

As we have mentioned before, we have collected delay statistics from six different queuing discipline scenarios (CQ, WFQ, MWRR, DWRR, CBWFQ and PQ-CBWFQ) for two different active applications (VoIP and HTTP) in the network and with different applied priorities by the ToS field of the IP packet header. We have defined VoIP traffic flows between clients where such flows represent high-priority traffic; while HTTP traffic represents low-priority flow, based on a best effort type of service. In our scenarios, we have 82.09% users who use lower-priority HTTP traffic and only 17.91% users who use the high-priority VoIP application.

In Figure 21, we can see that only 17.91% of users take up a majority part of bandwidth, so the lower-priority HTTP traffic, which represents a majority of all traffic, must wait. This is the reason why delays rapidly increase as can be clearly seen in Figure 21. Evidently VoIP traffic has lower delays in comparison with HTTP traffic. Best results are obtained with the custom queuing method, which ensures the required bandwidth at possible congestion points and serves all traffic fairly. After CQ queuing scheme follow WFQ, DWRR, MWRR, CBWFQ and PQ-CBWFQ. WFQ, DWRR, MWRR and CBWFQ have worse results in terms of delays because of fairness queuing discipline. Similar results are obtained also in case of HTTP. If the CBWFQ scheme is in use, high-priority traffic will be ensured with a fixed amount of available bandwidth defined by the network administrator. For example, the network administrator, using CBWFQ, defines 9Mbit/s for VoIP, in which case only 1Mbit/s remains for all other applications; so the majority of low-level traffic will be affected by rapid increasing of delays, as shown in Figure 22.

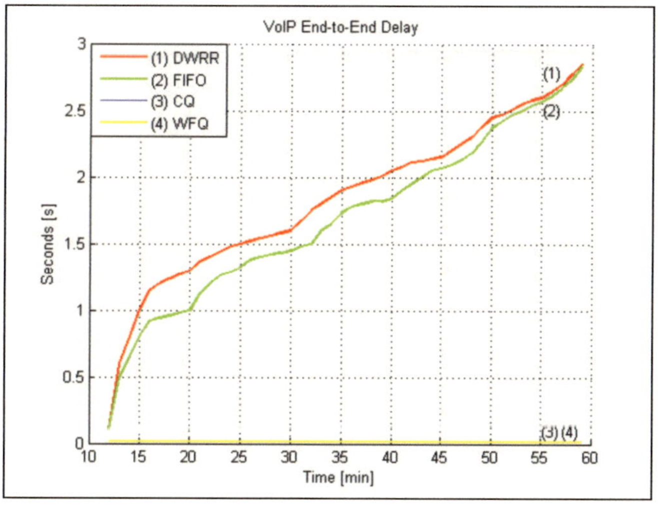

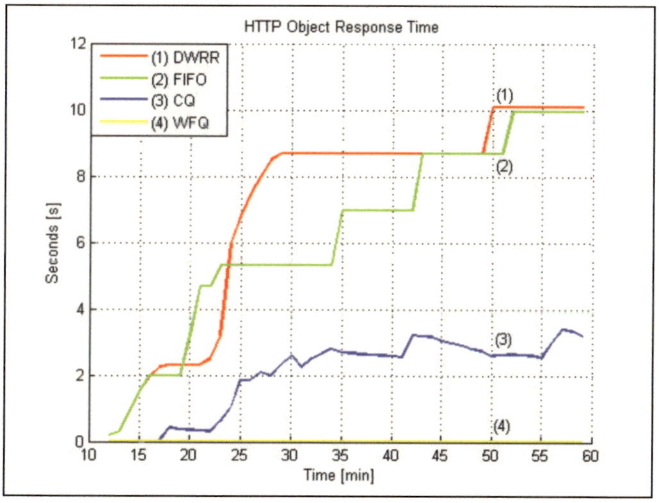

Fig. 21. VoIP End-to-End Delay (top) and HTTP Object Response Time (Bottom) when using different queuing disciplines upon VoIP and HTTP traffic.

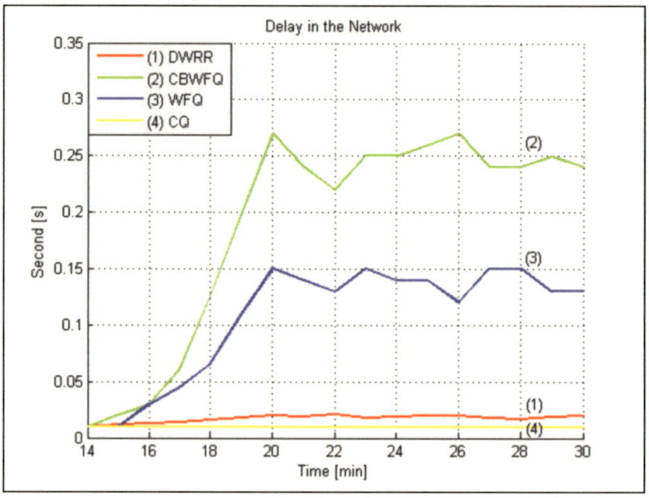

Fig. 22. Time average global delay in the network

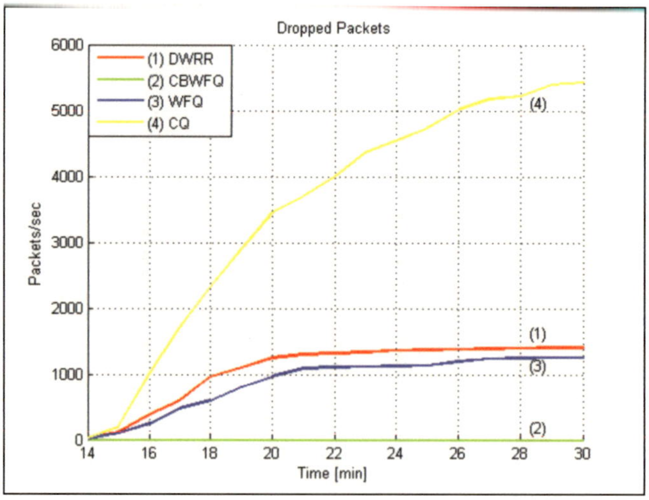

Fig. 23. Amount of VoIP dropped packets

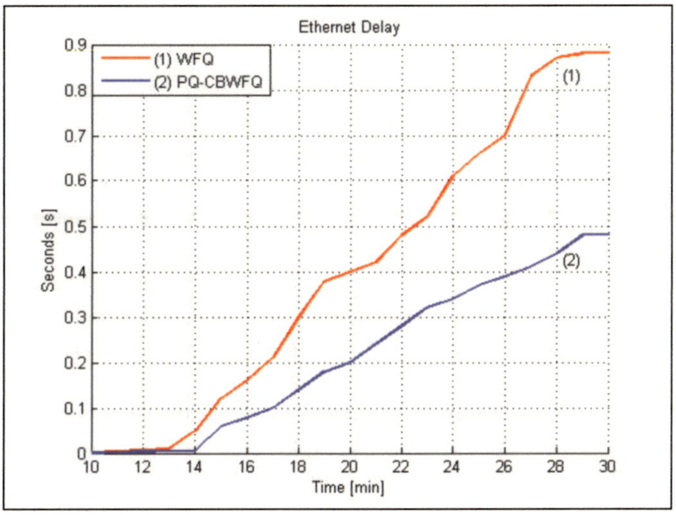

Fig. 24. Ethernet delay (in seconds) for combined PQ-CBWFQ method, compared with WFQ

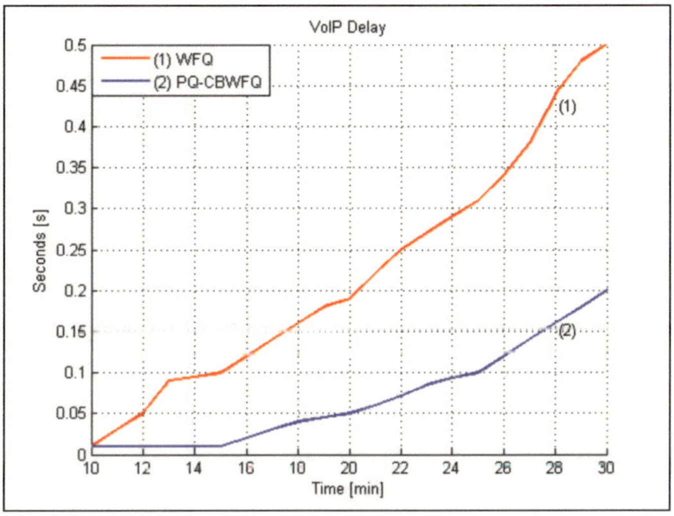

Fig. 25. VoIP delay (in seconds) for combined PQ-CBWFQ method in comparison with WFQ

Figure 23 shows the amount of VoIP dropped packets, when using different queuing schemes. As we have mentioned above, best results are in that situation obtained with CBWFQ method, which has a fixed guaranteed amount of bandwidth. WFQ, DWRR, MWRR and CQ queuing scheme follow. The situation is quite the opposite when we take delays into consideration. CBWFQ introduces the biggest delay, because a majority low level traffic must wait.

Figure 24 shows, how the combined queuing method PQ-CBWFQ improves the delays in comparison with the delays presented in Figure 22.

Using PQ-CBWFQ, the delay is smaller than with the WFQ, as we can see in Figure 24. However, the ordinary CBWFQ method involves a bigger delay than the WFQ, observed in whole Ethernet segment, as shown in Figure 22. Such combinations can perceivably improve network performance. Similar effect as shown in Figure 24 can also be seen in Figure 25 for VoIP delay.

Using the combined queuing method the delay for the VoIP traffic is also reduced in comparison with the ordinary WFQ queuing. In the VoIP application delays play an important role in the quality of perception. The smaller they are, the better voice quality can be offered.

After many simulation runs and graph analysis we can say that queuing policy discipline significantly influences the quality of service for network applications. In many cases CQ queuing discipline was the best choice; in case when we have only two traffic flows WFQ was the best choice; but when on the other hand we need to handle multiple traffic flows, the CBWFQ was the best solution. The CBWFQ method also has its disadvantages; in our case, we have defined only one class with a bandwidth amount 9Mbit/s reserved for VoIP, and the rest of the bandwidth is allocated to the majority of low-priority HTTP traffic. The majority traffic however does not have enough bandwidth and must wait, which causes delays. This is the main reason why CBWFQ has the highest average delays in the network. Regardless of that delays the VoIP delay is however constant during the simulation because of the bandwidth ensured by the defined class. Then again, if we want fairness queuing discipline, which serves all applications fairly, we should use WFQ or CQ mechanism. However, if we only want that the highest-priority traffic flows pass through the network, we should use priority queuing PQ.

Delays in CBWFQ case can be reduced using the PQ-CBWFQ hybrid queuing scheme (see examples 1 and 2). Our simulations show that we must look for solutions also in combined queuing methods. All other available combinations represent a challenge for further research in that area.

7. Conclusion

The results of the simulation examples presented in Section 6 show that when we deal with time-sensitive applications (like VoIP), we have to choose a member of the low latency queuing family. Regarding jitter and VoIP delays the PQ and PQ-CBWFQ queuing schemes are most suitable. In such cases also the voice quality is on a higher level, compared to those where ordinary queuing schemes (CQ, for example) are used. In cases where we have to make a compromise between important traffic and traffic of lower importance, the WFQ-CBWFQ hybrid method gives satisfying results. Our conclusion, according to the obtained simulation results, is to use the following queuing schemes for the following purposes:

- Time-sensitive applications (most recommended PQ-CBWFQ, CBWFQ, optionally PQ)
- Web and other low-importance applications (CQ, WFQ)
- Time-sensitive applications + low-importance applications (WFQ-CBWFQ)
- Other very-low-importance applications mutually equivalent according to the applied priority in the ToS field of the IP packet header (WFQ)

8. References

T. Subash, S. IndiraGandhi. Performance Analysis of Scheduling Disciplines in Optical Networks. MADRAS Institute of Technology, Anna University, 2006.

L. L. Peterson, B. S. Davie. Computer Networks. Edition 3, San Francisco 2003.

S. Bucheli. Compensation Modeling for QoS Support on a Wireless Network. Master degree thesis, 2004.

K. M. Yap, A. Marshall, W. Yu. Providing QoS for Multimodal System Traffic Flows in Distributed Haptic Virtual Environments. Queen's University Belfast, 2005.

Internetworking Technology Handbook - Quality of Service (QoS), Cisco Systems. OPNET Modeler Techical Documentation. G. 729 Data Sheet.

L. Zheng, D. Xu. Characteristics of Network Delay and Delay Jitter and its Effect on Voice over IP (VoIP) Communications. ICC 2001, IEEE International Conference, 2001.

M. Kao. Timing Jitter Control of an ADD/drop Optical Module in a convergent Network, Wireless and Optical Communications, 2005. 14th Annual WOCC 2005, International Conference.

http://en.wikipedia.org/wiki/Time-division_multiplexing

http://www.erg.abdn.ac.uk/users/gorry/course/lan-pages/llc.html

A. Kos in S. Tomazic. "Nov nacin zdruzevanja RSVP pretokov (The new method of merging RSVP flows)", ERK 2007, 26. - 28. september 2005, Portoroz, Slovenija, IEEE Region 8, Slovenska sekcija IEEE, 2005, zv. A, pg.. 175-178

http://www.cisco.com/en/US/tech/tk331/tk332/tk126/tsd_technology_support_sub-protocol_home.html

S. Klampfer. "Simulacija omrežij v Opnet Modeler-ju (Network simulations using OPNET Modeler", Diploma thesis, Faculty of Electrical Engineering and Computer Science, Univesity of Maribor, 2007.

I. Humar, J. Bešter, M. Pogačnik, M. Meža. Extending Differentiated Services with Flow Rejection Mechanism for Wireless IP Environments. Elektrotehniški Vestnik 1-2005.

Sasa Klampfer, Joze Mohorko, Zarko Cucej, "Simulation of Different Router Buffer Sizes which Influences on VoIP Jitter Delay within the routed Network", Informacije MIDEM, 2011 (confirmed but not published yet)

Sasa Klampfer, Joze Mohorko, Zarko Cucej, "IP packet queuing disciplines as basic part of QOS assurance within the network", Informacije MIDEM, junij 2009, letn. 39, št. 2(130)

Cole, R. Rosenbluth J. Voice over IP Performance Monitoring, AT&T Preprint September 2000

TIPHON 22TD047 Problems with the behavior of Jitter Buffers and their influence on the end-to-end speech quality, source KPN Research, March 2001

ITU-T Y.1541 Network Performance Objectives for IP Based Services RFC1889 Real Time Control Protocol

ITU-T SG12 D74 IP Phones and Gateways: Factors impacting speech quality, France Telecom, May 2002

Sasa Klampfer, Joze Mohorko, Zarko Cucej, "Impact of hybrid queuing disciplines on the VoIP traffic delay", Electrotechnical Review 2009

Sasa Klampfer, Joze Mohorko, Zarko Cucej, "Vpliv različnih načinov uvrščanja na karakteristiko prepustnosti omrežja (Influence of different queuing methods on the common permeability network characteristic)", ERK 2007, 24. - 26. september 2007, Portorož, Slovenija, IEEE Region 8, Slovenska sekcija IEEE, 2007, zv. A, pg.. 100-103

Frank Ohrtman, "Voice over 802.11", Artech House, Boston, London, 2004

Morgan Kaufmann, "Routing, Flow and Capacity Design in Communication and Computer Networks", Warsaw University of Technology, Warsaw, Poland, 2006

Kun I. Park, "QoS in packet networks", The mitre corporation USA, Springer 2005
Tadeusz Wysocki, Arek Dadej, Beata J. Wysocki, "Advanced wired and wireless networks", Florida Atlantic University, Springer 2005
H. Jonathan Chao and Bin Liu, "High performance switches and routers", John Wiley and Sons, 2007
Huan-Yun Wei, Ying-Dar Lin, "A survey and measurement - Based comparison of bandwidth management techniques, IEEE Communications Survey, 2003, Volume 5, No. 2
Mansour J. Karam, Fouad A. Tobagi, "Analysis of the Delay and Jitter of Voice Traffic Over the Internet", IEEE InfoCom 2001
Yunni Xia†, Hanpin Wang‡, Yu Huang, Wanling Qu, "Queuing analysis and performance evaluation of workflow through WFQN", IEEE Computer Society, First Joint IEEE/IFIP Symposium on Theoretical Aspects of Software Engineering (TASE'07)
Anirudha Sahoo and D. Manjunath, "Revisiting WFQ: Minimum Packet Lengths Tighten Delay and Fairness Bounds", IEEE COMMUNICATIONS LETTERS, VOL. 11, NO. 4, APRIL 2007
Velmurugan, T.; Chandra, H.; Balaji, S.; , "Comparison of Queuing Disciplines for Differentiated Services Using OPNET," Advances in Recent Technologies in Communication and Computing, 2009. ARTCom '09., Vol., no., pp.744-746, 27-28 Oct. 2009
Fischer, M.J.; Bevilacqua Masi, D.M.; McGregor, P.V.; "Efficient Integrated Services in an Enterprise Network," IT Professional, vol.9, no.5, pp.28-35, Sept.-Oct. 2007
Cisco Systems, Understanding Jitter in Packet Voice Networks (Cisco IOS Platforms), http://www.cisco.com/en/US/tech/tk652/tk698/tech_tech_notes_list.html
G.729 DataSheet, http://www.vocal.com/data_sheets/g729.pdf
M. Callea, L. Campagna, M.G. Fugini and P. Plebani. "Contracts for Defining QoS Levels In a Multichannel Adaptive Information System", IFIP International Federation for Information Processing, 2005, Volume 158/2005, 2005

6

VoIP System for Enterprise Network

Moo Wan Kim and Fumikazu Iseki
Tokyo University of Information Sciences
Japan

1. Introduction

This chapter describe VoIP system for the enterprise network (e.g. company, university) based on Asterisk(http://www.asterisk.org). Asterisk is a kind of open source software to implement IP-PBX system and supports various necessary protocols to realize the VoIP system such as SIP, H.323, MGCP, SCCP.
First the main ideas and development process are described based on the VoIP system that we have developed by using Asterisk in the Intranet environment. Then the new scheme to realize high security by using Open VPN is described when developing the large scale enterprise network.

2. Basic idea

The following are the main requirements to develop the VoIP system for the enterprise network (Yamamoto et al., 2008)

a. Scalability
   In the environment of the enterprize network, it is not easy to anticipate the traffic because there are lots of uncontrollable factors. So developing various scale systems based on the same architecture is necessary to meet the unpredictable change of traffic.
b. Cost
   It is obviously desirable to develop the system at reasonable cost because generally the budget is rather limited.
c. High security
   Also obviously high security is indispensable.

Considering the above requirements, the following are our basic ideas.

a. Developing VoIP system by using Asterisk as the open software
   Obviously considering development cost it is desirable to use the open software. So we have selected three open softwares as candidates, that is, OpenSIPS, FreeSwitch and Asterisk. As the SIP server's viewpoint, OpenSIPS and FreeSwitch are superior to Asterisk in terms of functions, but Asterisk support various protocols (e.g. H.323, MGCP, SCCP) other than SIP and also has lots of additional PBX services (e.g. Voice Conference, Automatic Call distributor). So we have decided to use Asterisk to development VoIP system for the enterprise network.
b. Realizing high security by using Open VPN

When we develop the large scale enterprise network by connecting multiple Asterisk servers located in different sites based on Asterisk proprietary protocol (i.e. IAX2), some method is necessary to realize the high security because the voice data among sites is not encrypted. For this purpose we have introduced a new scheme to establish VPN by using Open VPN.

3. Overview of Asterisk

Asterisk is a kind of open source software executed on Linux to implement IP-PBX system and support various VoIP protocols such as SIP, H.323, MGCP, SCCP. It can be connected with IP network and also can be connected with the existent telephone networks via analog/digital interfaces. Fig.1 shows the architecture of Asterisk. Channel portion in Fig.1 consist of various logical communication interface modules and Application portion consist of the additional PBX service modules. In the following the main modules of the channel and the application are described.

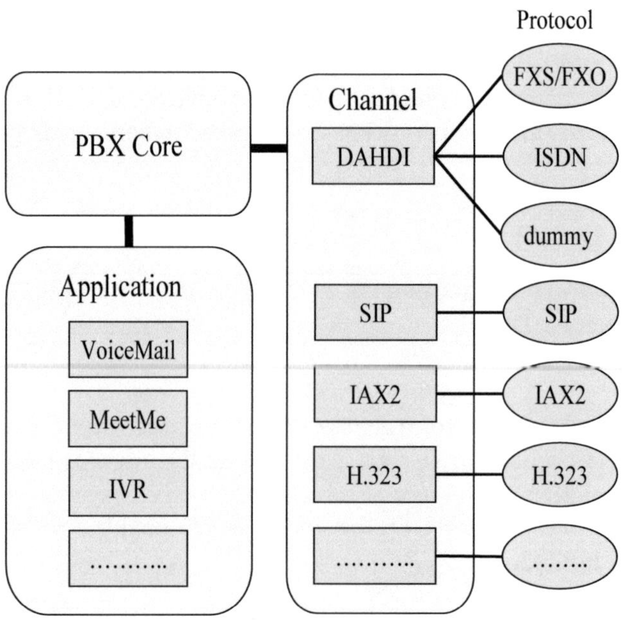

Fig. 1. Architecture of Asterisk

a. Channel modules
   - DAHDI (Digium/Asterisk Hardwae Device Interface): To connect with the ordinary existent telephone terminal it is necessary to insert the telephony card (e.g telephone card of Digium or of Voicetronix) as the physical interface and then the DAHDI interface module will be used. In case of connecting with existing POTS (Plain Old Telephone Service), FXS (Foreign eXchange Subsciber) and FXO (Foreign eXchange Office) interfaces will be used. In case of connecting with ISDN terminal it is necessary to insert the extension card as the physical interface.
   - SIP: This is the most basic signaling protocol to perform call processing in Asterisk and RTP/RTCP are used in order to transmit user data (e.g. voice data).

  - IAX2(Inter-Asterisk eXchange2): IAX2 is Asterisk proprietary protocol to conncet with multiple Asterisk servers located in the diffrent sites. The same port (i.e. 4569 as the default port) is used to transmit the call control signal and voice data.

b. Application modules
  - Voice Conference: The voice conference service in Asterisk is called as "MeetMe". User can join the conference by inputting the designated number as the service number.
  - Voice Mail: When the called user is absent or busy, voice message can be kept in the voice box as the voice mail.
  - IVR (Interactive Voice Response): The automatic voice response can be performed by integrating voice response data file and dial number plan.
  - ACD (Automatic Call Distributor): The call can be automatically terminated to some terminal in the group based on the registered distribution rule.
  - AGI (Asterisk Gateway Interface): AGI is an API to connect the outside program with Asterisk in order to include some additional functions. Various programming language (e.g. C, Java, Perl, PHP, Bone Shell) are supported.
  - SLA (Shared Line Appearances): Multiple telephone terminals can share a subscriber line.

More application modules (e.g. Call Parking, Call Queuing, Call Pickup, SNMP support) are also provided.

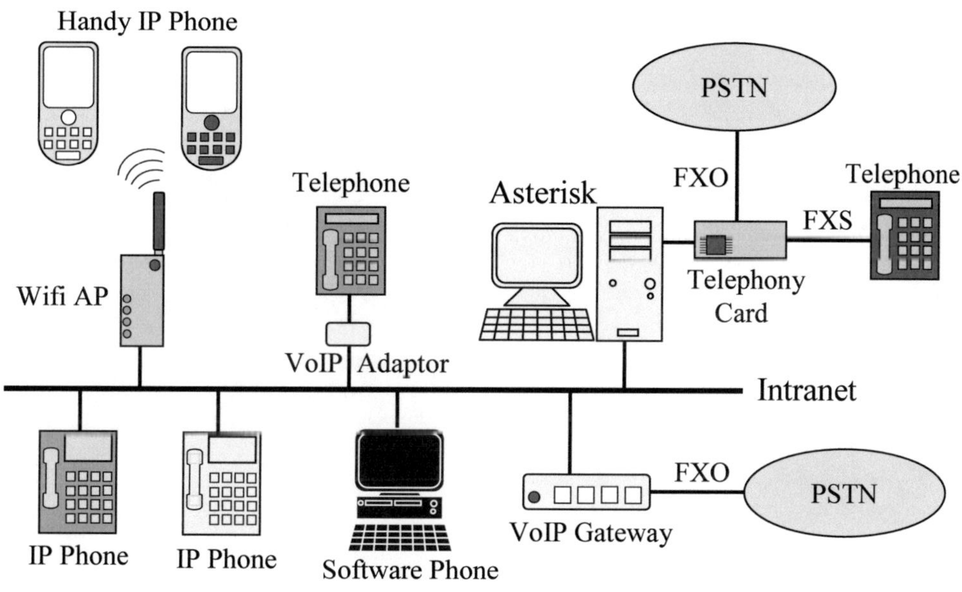

Fig. 2. VoIP system developed in Intranet

4. VoIP System based on Asterisk

4.1 VoIP system in Intranet

Fig.2 shows the VoIP system that we have developed by using an Asterisk in the Intranet environment (i.e. enterprise network).

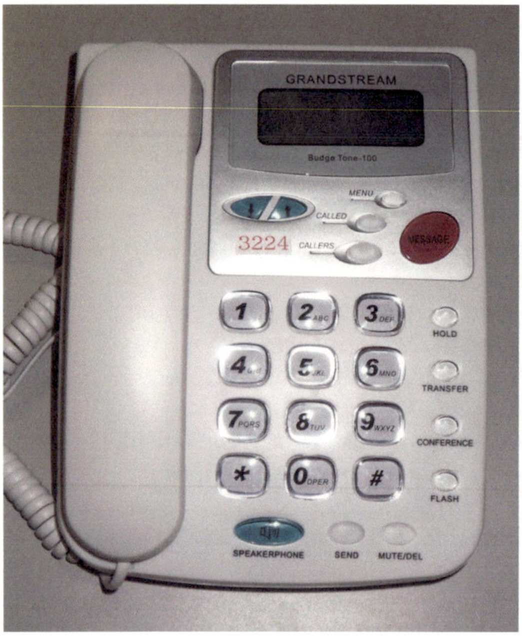

Photo 1. Grandstream BT101 as IP Phone

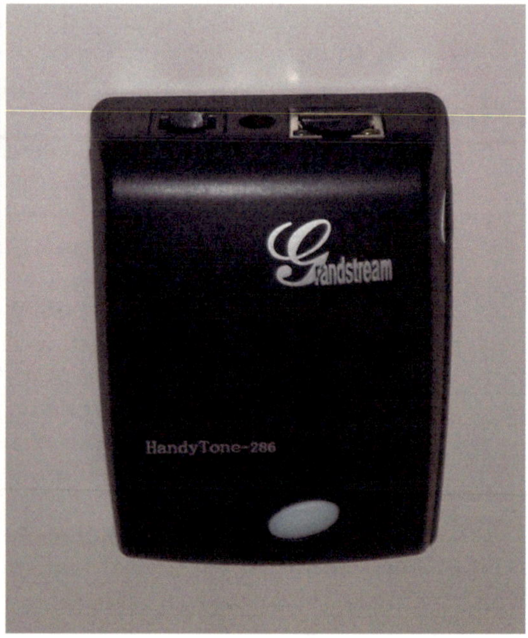

Photo 3. Grandstream HT286 as VoIP Adaptor

Photo 2. Snom 105 as IP Phone

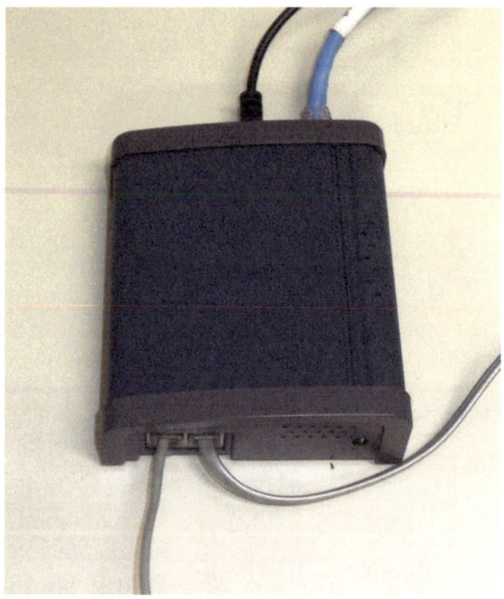

Photo 4. Sipura SPA1000 as VoIP gateway

In the Fig.2 all telephone terminals are connected to one Asterisk server, but it is possible to use multiple Asterisk servers depending on the scale of the Intranet (i.e. the number of terminals). As the IP phones, we have accommodated Grandstream BT101 (Photo 1) and Snom 105 (Photo 2), and also Grandstream HT286 (Photo 3) has been used as VoIP adaptor. Grandstrem HT488 and Sipura SPA1000 (Photo 4) have been used as VoIP gateways to connect with PSTN.

4.2 Connecting with SIP Server (Fig.3)

Asterisk can connect with existing SIP servers. When SIP server is located in the same network, it is easy to connect with each other. When SIP server is located in the different network (e.g. SIP server located in ISP network across Internet), it is possible to occur the NAT problem because the payload of SIP message can contain private information like private IP address. But even such case it is possible to connect with SIP server if we have selected some appropriate method to solve the NAT problem.

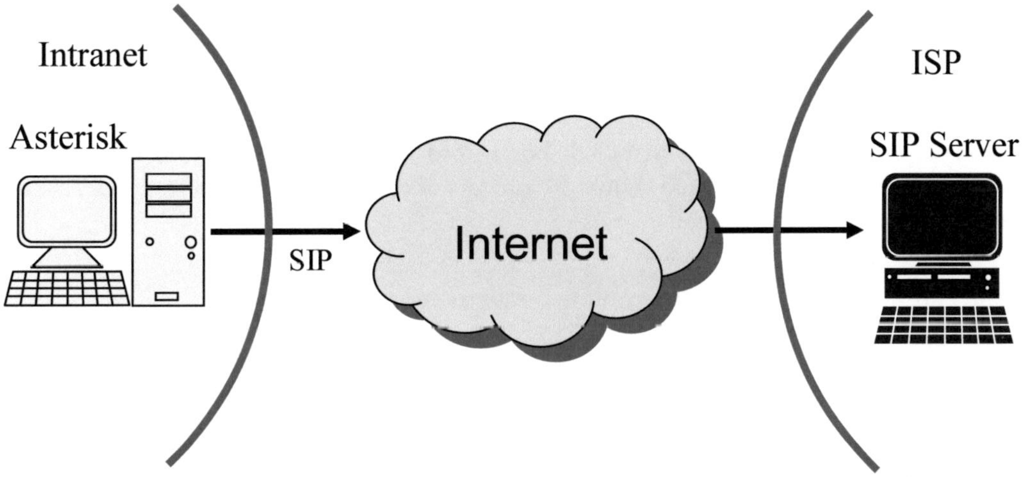

Fig. 3. Connecting with SIP server across Internet

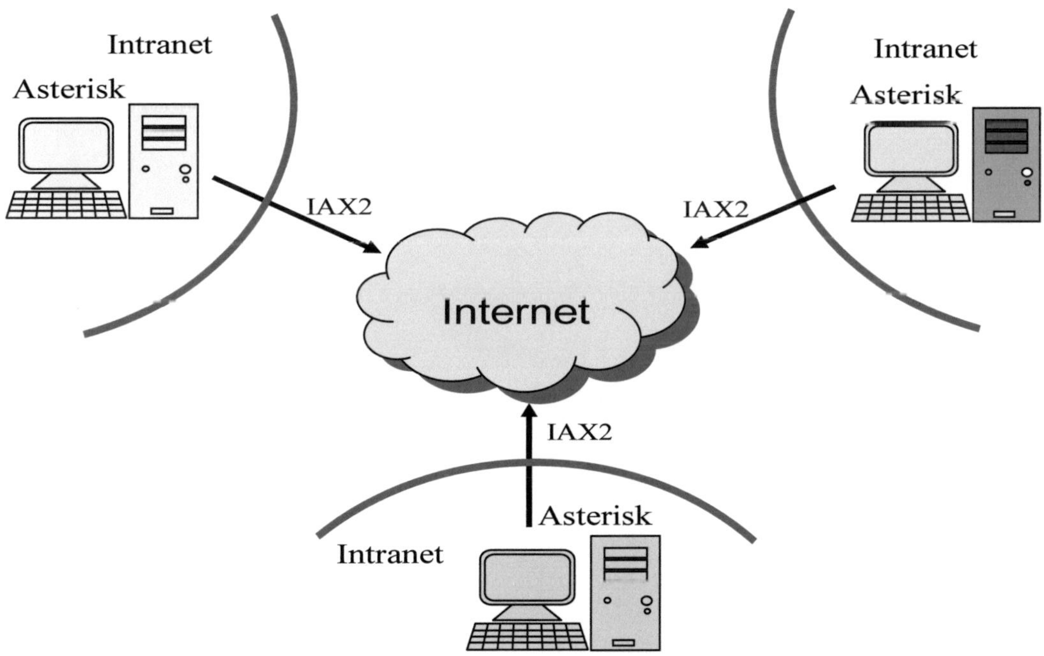

Fig. 4. Connecting with multiple Asterisks located in different Intranet

4.3 Multiple location connection by IAX2 (Fig.4)

As described previously IAX2 is the Asterisk proprietary protocol to connect with multiple Asterisk servers. So it is possible to connect with multiple Asterisk servers located in different Intranets easily.

5. Development process of VoIP system

In this section the detailed development process about the VoIP system we have developed is described.

5.1 Basic development process

a. DAHDI compile and install

First of all Asterisk should be installed, but before that it is necessary to complete the DAHDI compile and install. Fig.5 shows the process of compile and install from the Asterisk cite (http://www.asterisk.org/).

```
# export http_proxy=http://your.proxy.server:port-num/
# tar zfxv dahdi-linux-complete-2.3.0.1+2.3.0.tar.gz
# cd dahdi-linux-complete-2.3.0.1+2.3.0
# make all
# make install
```

Fig. 5. Process of DAHDI compile and install

b. Asterisk compile and install

Next Asterisk compile and install has been performed as shown in Fig.6.

```
# tar zxfv asterisk-1.6.2.10.tar.gz
# cd asterisk-1.6.2.10
# ./configure
# make
# make install
# make samples
# make config
```

Fig. 6. Process of Asterisk compile and install

Then after the necessary definition is completed, the access to Asterisk has been possible as shown in Fig.7.

c. Define Dial Plan

Dial Plan is the core portion of the call processing in Asterisk. Dial Plan is defined in /etc/asterisk/extensions.conf. Extensions.conf consist of general section, globals section and context blocks as follows;

- General section: General parametes to cover the whole Dial Plan are defined in this section.
- Globals section: Variables used in the content blocks are defined in this section.

- Context blocks: Multiple dial plan are defined in the context blocks independently. So Asterisk can realize flexible dail plan by selecting appropriate block based on the conditions. The format of each line in the context block is as follows;

exten => Extension, Priority, Application

Extension in the right side is generally telephone numer and Priority is the order of processing. Application is the processing to be perfoemed to the Extension.

```
# /etc/init.d/asterisk start
# asterisk -r
Asterisk 1.6.2.10, Copyright (C) 1999 - 2010 Digium, Inc. and others.
Created by Mark Spencer <markster@digium.com>
Asterisk comes with ABSOLUTELY NO WARRANTY; type 'core show warranty'
for details.
This is free software, with components licensed under the GNU General Public
License version 2 and other licenses; you are welcome to redistribute it under
certain conditions. Type 'core show license' for details.
================================================================
==============
Connected to Asterisk 1.6.2.10 currently running on star (pid = 2144)
Verbosity is at least 3
star*CLI>
```

Fig. 7. Backgound execution of Asterisk

Fig.8 shows the example of default context which is selected when no context is explictly defined.

```
exten => _1XXX,1,Dial(SIP/${EXTEN}, 30)
exten => _1XXX,n,GotoIf($["${DIALSTATUS}"="BUSY"]?busy)
exten => _1XXX,n,Hangup
exten => _1XXX,n(busy),Busy
```

Fig. 8. Default context in estensions.conf

X in _1XXX shows 0~9 and _ shows pattern matching. Dial(SIP/${EXTEN}, 30) in the first line shows to ring the SIP terminal during 30 seconds. GotoIf ($ ["$ {DIALSTATUS}" = "BUSY"] ?busy) in the second line shows that the processing will be terminated to the busy label if the call processing result is busy. ${EXTEN} shows the called party's telephone number and $ {DIALSTATUS} shows the variable to include the previous state.

Also it is necessary to define the channel file(e.g. /etc/asterisk/sip.conf in case of SIP, /etc/asterisl/chan_dahdi.conf in case of DAHDI, ip /etc/asteridk/iax.conf in case of IAX2). Fig.9 shows the call processing flows amoung channels.

d. Define SIP Terminal

As described previously, /etc/asterisk/extensions.conf and /etc/asterisk/sip.conf should be defined when SIP terminal is used. Fig.10 shows the example of /etc/asterisk/sip.conf. 1000 and 1001 shows the telephone number of SIP terminals and terminals with proper password can only be registered in Asterisk.

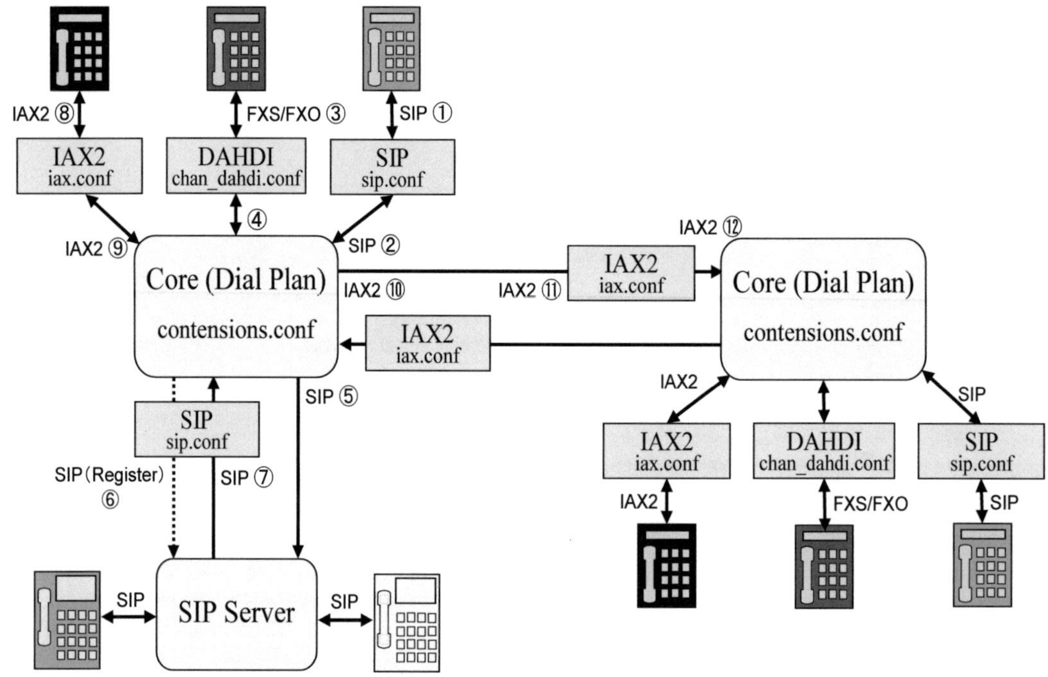

Fig. 9. Call processing flows among channels

```
[1000]
type=friend
secret=password1
host=dynamic

[1001]
type=friend
secret=password2
host=dynamic
```

Fig. 10. Example of /etc/asterisk/sip.conf.

Then the Dial Plan is defined for each SIP terminal by editing /etc /asterisk / extensions.conf. There is no context to describe Dial Plan in the example in Fig.10, so the default context is used. Thus it has been possible between 1000 SIP terminal and 1001 SIP terminal by using Asterisk server as the SIP server.

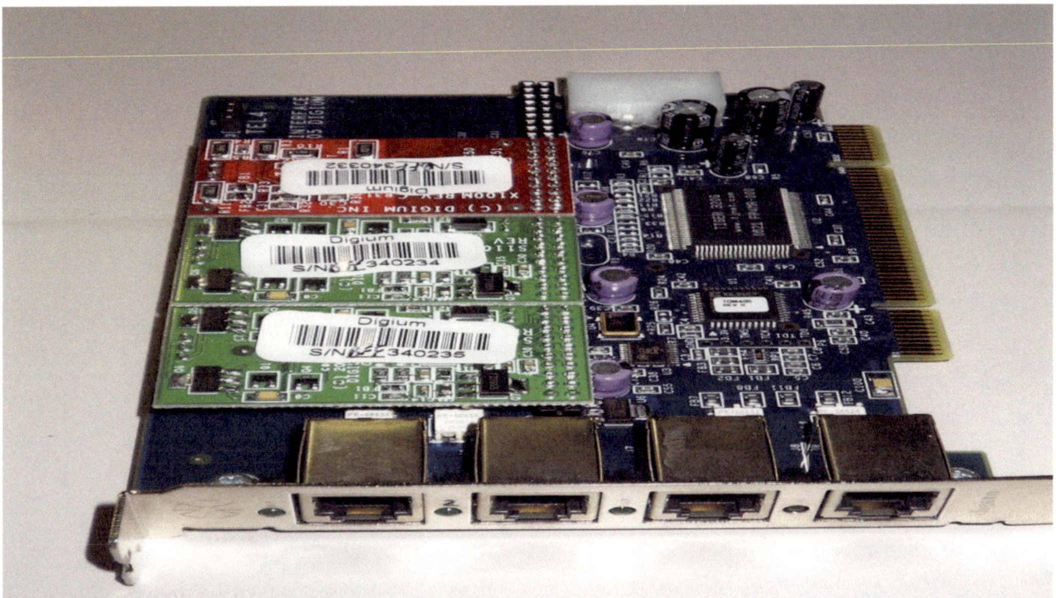

Photo 5. TDM410 as Telephony Card

e. Define Telephony Card

We have used the Digium's Telephony Card TDM410 (Photo 5) and AEX410 (Photo 6). 1~3 ports are FXS and 4 port is FXO.

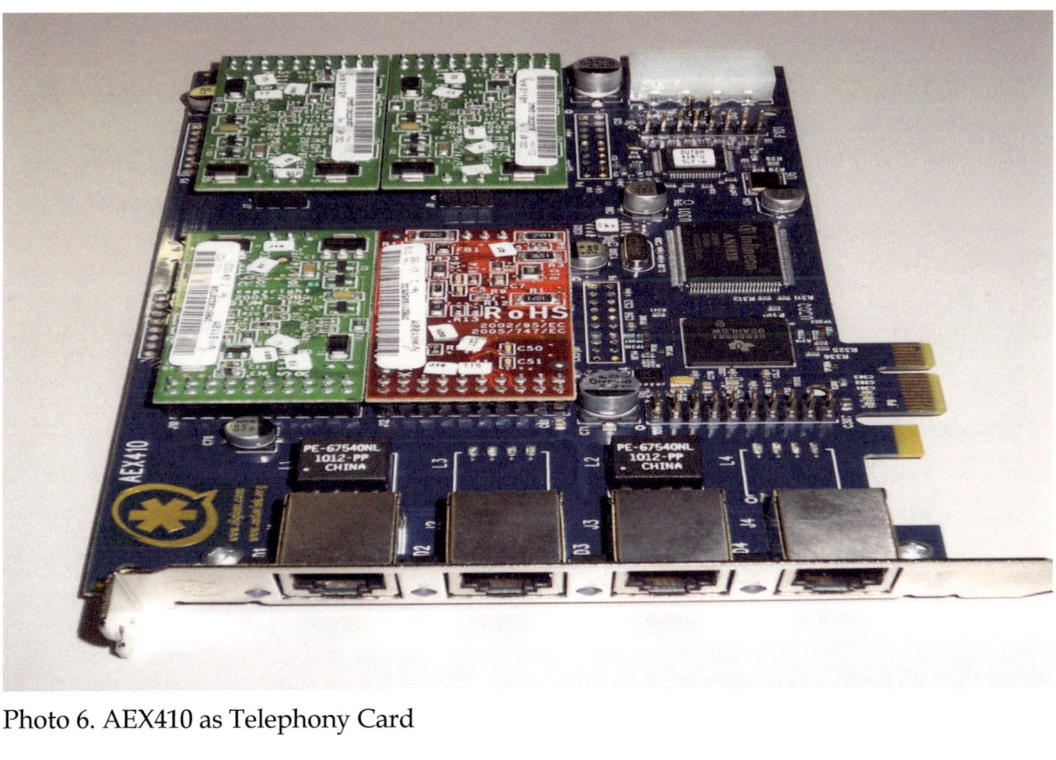

Photo 6. AEX410 as Telephony Card

Telephony Card has been defined in chan_dahdi.conf as shown in Fig.11.

```
context=default
signaling=fxo_ks
usecallerid=no
callwaiting=yes
echocancel=no
threewaycalling=yes
transfer=yes
channel => 1-3
;
context=incoming
signaling=fxs_ks
usecallerid=no
callwaiting=no
echocancel=no
transfer=no
channel => 4
```

Fig. 11. Example of chan_dahdi.conf

When the Dial Plan is defined in extensions.conf as shown in Fig.12, the call to 1 will be terminated to the terminal connected with port 1 and the call to 0 will be terminated to the port 4 (i.e. PSTN). That is, originating call to 0 means the call to connect ouside PSTN.

```
exten => 1,1,Dial(DAHDI/1, 30)
exten => 1,n,GotoIf($["${DIALSTATUS}"="BUSY"]?busy)
exten => 1,n,Hangup
exten => 1,n(busy),Busy

exten => 0,1,Dial(DAHDI/4, 30)
exten => 0,n,GotoIf($["${DIALSTATUS}"="BUSY"]?busy)
exten => 0,n,Hangup
exten => 0,n(busy),Busy
```

Fig. 12. Dial Plan in extensions.conf

When the call from PSTN should be terminated to the port 4, incoming context is defined in the extensions.conf as shown in Fig.13.

```
[incoming]
exten => s,1,Dial(SIP/1000)
exten => s,n,Dial(SIP/1001)
exten => s,n,Hangup
```

Fig. 13. incoming context for FXO port

f. Connecting with SIP server

As previously described, communication between Asterisk and SIP server can be possible. When terminal connected with Asterisk communicate with the terminal connected with SIP server, Dial Plan is defined as shown in Fig.14.

```
exten => _3XXX,1,Dial(SIP/${EXTEN}@sip.server.address,30)
exten => _3XXX,n,GotoIf($["${DIALSTATUS}"="BUSY"]?busy)
exten => _3XXX,n,Hangup
exten => _3XXX,n(busy),Busy
```

Fig. 14. Dial Plan for the call from Asterisk to SIP server

When terminal connected with SIP server communicate with the terminal connected with Asterisk, Asterisk should perform registration process as SIP client. So in order to perform the registration process, data is defined in the general section of sip.conf as shown in Fig.15. 4000 and 4001 are telephone numbers to be registered in the SIP server. 1000 and 1 are extensions to be used in the Dial Plan of Asterisk. Authid and password are ID and password to be registered in the SIP server, sip.server.address is IP address of the SIP server.

```
register => 4000:authid:password@sip.server.address/1000
register => 4001:authid:password@sip.server.address/1
```

Fig. 15. Data defined in general section for the registration process

g. Connecting with multi Asterisk based on IAX2

When IAX2 telephone terminal is registered in the Asterisk, /etc/asterisk/iax.conf is defined as shown in Fig.16.

```
[6000]
type=friend
host=dynamic
secret=iax2pass
[6001]
type=friend
host=dynamic
secret=iax2pass
```

Fig. 16. Example of iax.cong

When the call is terminated to the IAX2 terminal, Dial Plan is defined in extension.conf as shown in Fig.17.

```
exten => _6XXX,1,Dial(IAX2/${EXTEN},30)
exten => _6XXX,n,GotoIf($["${DIALSTATUS}"="BUSY"]?busy)
exten => _6XXX,n,Hangup
exten => _6XXX,n(busy),Busy
```

Fig. 17. Dial Plan for IAX2 terminal

As described previously, Asterisks located in multi Intranets can be connected with each other based on IAX2. In order to connect with Asterisk located in other Intranet, Dial Plan of the originating Asterisk should be defined as shown in Fig.18. Whole calls to 8XXX will transfer to the Asterisk whose address is defined as other.asterisk.address.

```
exten => _8XXX,1,Dial(IAX2/iax2id:iax2pass@other.asterisk.address/${EXTEN})
exten => _8XXX,n,GotoIf($["${DIALSTATUS}"="BUSY"]?busy)
exten => _8XXX,n,Hangup
exten => _8XXX,n(busy),Busy
```

Fig. 18. Dial Plan for originating Asterisk

Also Dial Plan of the terminating Asterisk located in other Intranet should be defined as shown in Fig.19.

```
exten => _8XXX,1,Dial(SIP/${EXTEN}, 30)
exten => _8XXX,n,GotoIf($["${DIALSTATUS}"="BUSY"]?busy)
exten => _8XXX,n,Hangup
exten => _8XXX,n(busy),Busy
```

Fig. 19. Dial Plan for terminating Asterisk

5.2 Application development process

a. MeetMe (Voice conference)

MeetMe, voice conference service, can be easily realized in Asterisk. In order to regist the service, first, registration data is defined in the [room] section of /etc/asterisk/meetme.conf as shown in Fig.20. The right side of => in Fig.20 include conference number, PIN, and PIN of administrator. PIN is the password to enter the conference and telephone number can be usually used as the conference number.

```
[room]
conf => 2000
conf => 2001,2456,7889
```

Fig. 20. Example of meetme.conf

Next in order to start the service, Dial Plan is defined as shown in Fig.21.

```
exten => _200X,1,Meetme(${EXTEN})
```

Fig. 21. Dial Plan for MeetMe

b. Voice Mail

When the called user is absent or busy, voice message can be kept as the voice mail. In order to start the voice mail service, first the mail box is defined in /etc/asterisk/voicemail.conf as shown in Fig.22. 1000 and 1001 show the numbers of mail boxes, and telephone number is used usually as the number of mail box. 1212 and 2875 in Fig.21 show the passwords.

```
[default]
1000 => 1212,SIP User1
1001 => 2875,SIP User2
```

Fig. 22. Example of voicemail.conf

Next the service function is defined in extensions.conf as shown in Fig.23. The argument of Voicemail shows the number of the mail box and ${EXTEN} means that telephone number can be used as the number of mail box.

```
exten => _1XXX,1,Dial(SIP/${EXTEN},5)
exten => _1XXX,n,GotoIf($["${DIALSTATUS}"="BUSY"]?busy)
exten => _1XXX,n,GotoIf($["${DIALSTATUS}"="NOANSWER"]?busy)
exten => _1XXX,n,Hangup
exten => _1XXX,n(busy),Voicemail(${EXTEN})
```

Fig. 23. Example of extensions.conf to define service function

In order to confirm the stored voice mail, the designated number is defined in extensions.conf as shown in Fig.24. If user input 999, the number of mail box and password, the stored voice messages can be confirmed.

```
exten => 999,1,VoiceMailMain()
```

Fig. 24. Example of extensions.conf to define the number to access voice mail

c. IVR (Interactive Voice Response)

In order to realize the automatic voice response service, detailed Dial Plan should be defined in /etc/asterisk/extensions.conf as shown in Fig.25. Answer in the [incoming] context shows that Asterisk will perform automatic response processing. The function of Background shows that the voice file of vm-enter-num-to-call will be played and that the control signal from the terminal can be processed even during the voice response. Playback is also a kind of function to play the voice file, but the user's signal cannot be processed during the voice response. WaitExtern is a function that suspend the signal processing for the defined time.

```
[default]
...............
exten => 9000,1,Goto(incoming,s,1)
...............

[incoming]
exten => s,1,Answer()
exten => s,n,Wait(1)
exten => s,n(again),Background(vm-enter-num-to-call)
exten => s,n,WaitExten(10)
exten => s,n,Playback(vm-goodbye)
exten => s,n,Hangup()
;
exten => i,1,Playback(invalid)
exten => i,n,Goto(s,again)
;
exten => 1,1,Dial(SIP/1000)
exten => 2,1,Dial(SIP/1001)
exten => 3,1,Dial(DAHDI/1)
```

Fig. 25. Example of IVR definition

6. Open VPN

In order to realize high security to connect multiple Asterisks located in different Intranets, we have implemented VPN capability. In this section the development process is described.

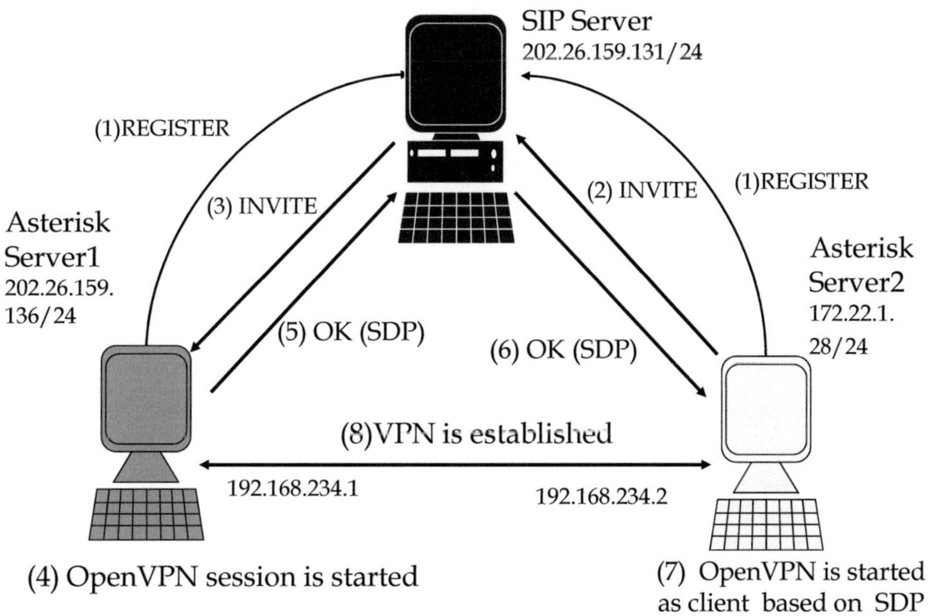

Fig. 26. VPN establishing procedure

Fig.26 shows the procedure to establish VPN between two Asterisk servers by using OpenVPN (http://openvpn.net/) based on the regular SIP sequence. To realize this procedure we have developed a program (i.e. sip_app) to have SIP client function with the function to invoke the external application. It is developed by using oSIP2 (http://www.gnu.org/software/osip) and eXosip2 (http://www.antisip.com/as/en/products.php) libraries in GNU, and has the SIP client function, SDP control function and the function to invoke the external process as child process. In the Asterisk server1, OpenVPN is registered as the external process and sip_app send the REGISTER message to SIP server (1). In the Asterisk server2, sip_app send the REGISTER message to SIP server (1) and send INVITE message to the Asterisk server1(2, 3). Asterisk server1 invoke the OpenVPN as the server mode (4) and reply 200 OK after inserting the necessary connection information into "a" record in SDP (5,6). Asterisk server2 invoke OpenVPN as the client mode after getting the necessary information from "a" record in SDP (7). OpenVPN in the Asterisk server2 communicate with OpenVPN in the Asterisk server1 and VPN between two servers has been established(8).

Table 1 shows the values of SDP at the process (6) in Fig.26. Record "m" shows media type (i.e. application/VPN) and the kind of protocol (i.e. OpenVPN). Record "a" is used by sip_app to control external process invoke. IP4 in Table1 is the IP address of the Asterisk server1 and PORT is the port to receive OpenVPN connection of Asterisk server1. VPN_LOCAL_ADDR is the IP address of Asterisk server1 and VPN_REMOTE_ADDR is the IP address of Asterisk server2.

Record Type	Value
v	0
o	2500 1169538046 1169538046 IN IP4 202.26.159.131
s	-
t	0 0
m	application/VPN 7084 OpenVPN 0
c	IN IP4 202.26.159.131
a	IP4:202.26.159.136
a	PORT:8000
a	VPN_LOCAL_ADDR:192.168.234.1
a	VPN_REMOTE_ADDR:192.168.234.

Table 1. Record value of SDP

Fig.27and Fig 28 show the detailed SIP messages at the process (5) , (6) in Fig.26.

```
SIP/2.0 200 OK
Via: SIP/2.0/UDP
202.26.159.131:5060;branch=z9hG4bKd5494712271eafdca196759bbcd82500
Via: SIP/2.0/UDP
202.26.159.131:5060;branch=z9hG4bKdf1ab35628fe284df07a0549b85b5d31
Via: SIP/2.0/UDP 172.22.1.28:5060;rport;branch=z9hG4bK1068437359
Record-Route:<sip:siproxd@202.26.159.131:5060;lr>
From:<sip:2501@202.26.159.131>;tag=1297171609
To:<sip:2500@202.26.159.131>;tag=1988095920
Call-ID: 1815073903@172.22.1.28
CSeq: 20 INVITE
Contact:<sip:2500@202.26.159.136:5060>
User-Agent: SIP for APP b1 rev.45
Allow: INVITE, ACK, OPTIONS, CANCEL, BYE, SUBSCRIBE, NOTIFY,MESSAGE,INFO,
REFER, UPDATE
Content-Type: application/sdp
Content-Length: 245

v=0
o=2500 1169538046 1169538046 IN IP4 202.26.159.136
s=-
t=0 0
m=application/vpn 8000 OpenVPN 0
k=DH:crypt code
c=IN IP4 202.26.159.136
a=IP4:202.26.159.136
a=PORT:8000
a=VPN_LOCAL_ADDR:192.168.234.1
a=VPN_REMOTE_ADDR:192.168.234.2
```

Fig. 27. SIP message at (5) in Fig.26

```
SIP/2.0 200 OK
Via: SIP/2.0/UDP 172.22.1.28:5060;rport;branch=z9hG4bK1068437359
Record-Route:<sip:siproxd@202.26.159.131:5060;lr>
From:<sip:2501@202.26.159.131>;tag=1297171609
To:<sip:2500@202.26.159.131>;tag=1988095920
Call-ID: 1815073903@172.22.1.28
CSeq: 20 INVITE
Contact:<sip:2500@202.26.159.131>
User-agent: SIP for APP b1 rev.45
Allow: INVITE, ACK, OPTIONS, CANCEL, BYE, SUBSCRIBE, NOTIFY, MESSAGE,INFO,
REFER, UPDATE
Content-Type: application/sdp
Content-Length: 245

v=0
o=2500 1169538046 1169538046 IN IP4 202.26.159.131
s=-
t=0 0
m=application/vpn 7084 OpenVPN 0
c=IN IP4 202.26.159.131
k=DH:crypt code
a=IP4:202.26.159.136
a=PORT:8000
a=VPN_LOCAL_ADDR:192.168.234.1
a=VPN_REMOTE_ADDR:192.168.234.2
```

Fig. 28. SIP message at (6) in Fig.26

7. Conclusion

This chapter describe VoIP system for the enterprise network (e.g. company, university) that we have developed based on Asterisk which is a kind of open source software to implement IP-PBX system. Through the development and evaluation, we have confirmed that VoIP system based on Asterisk is very powerful as a whole and most PBX functions to be required for the enterprise network can be realized.

Compared with the general SIP server, it can be said that Asterisk is more focused on providing basic functions. But Asterisk can connect with SIP server easily, so it is possible to implement the necessary additional functions by just connecting with other outside SIP servers. Also Asterisk can connect with the existent PSTN by using FXO telephony card, so it is possible to be used as the VoIP gateway.

When developing the large scale enterprise network by connecting multiple Asterisk servers located in different sites based on IAX2, to realize high security is the issue because the voice data is not encrypted. To solve this issue, we have proposed the method to establish VPN by using Open VPN and have also described the development process in detail.

8. References

http://www.asterisk.org
http://openvpn.net/
http://www.gnu.org/software/osip
http://www.antisip.com/as/en/products.php
Yamamoto et al.(2008). Validation of VoIP System for University Network, Proceedings of ICACT2008, 9C-2, Phoenix Park, Feb.2008, Korea

7

An Opencores /Opensource Based Embedded System-on-Chip Platform for Voice over Internet

Sabrina Titri, Nouma Izeboudjen, Fatiha Louiz, Mohamed Bakiri, Faroudja Abid, Dalila Lazib and Leila Sahli
Centre de Developpement des Technologies Avancées
Lotissement 20 Aout 1956 Baba Hassen, Algiers
Algeria

1. Introduction

Today, with the explosion of the IP network protocol, communication traffic is mainly dominated by data traffic, unlike in the past it was dominated by telephony driven voice. This phenomenon has lead to the emergence of voice over data (VOIP) equipment that can carry voice, data and also video on a single network. The idea behind VOIP is to use the IP network for voice services as an alternative to the public switched telecommunication network (PSTN). The advantages over traditional telephony include: lower costs per call, especially for long distance calls, and lower infrastructure cost compared to the PSTN. The market for VOIP equipment has increased dramatically and a lot of solutions are proposed to the research and industry communities. Each specialised paper that appears shows that VOIP has an important place in the telephony market, especially in enterprise and public domain areas. The main challenges in designing a VOIP application are the quality of service (QoS), the capacity of the gateways and real time computation. Factors affecting the QoS are line noise, echo cancellation, the voice coder used, the talker overlap and the Jitter factor. The capacity of the gateway is related to the number of lines that can be supported in an enterprise environment. An integrated hardware-software development environment is needed to deal with real time computation. (Dhir, 2001). Most important VOIP solutions proposed in the market are based on the use of a general purpose processor and a DSP circuit. In these solutions, parts of the application run on software on the general purpose processor and the other part of the application runs on the dedicated DSP hardware to meet some performances requirements. Recently, and with the advance of the microelectronic technology in one hand, and CAD tools in the other hand, it is possible to integrate a whole system into a single integrated FPGA chip. Ended, FPGAs have evolved in an evolutionary and revolutionary way. The evolution process has allowed faster and bigger FPGAs, better CAD tools and better technical support. The revolution process concerns the introduction of high performances multipliers, Microprocessors and DSP functions inside the FPGA circuit. Thus, a new field which integrates VOIP solutions into FPGAs based System on Chip (SoC) is emerging, particularly the field of embedded VOIP based FPGA platform. Contrarily to DSP and general purpose processors, FPGAs enable rapid, cost-effective product development cycles in an environment where target markets are constantly shifting and standards continuously evolving. Most of these offer processing capabilities, a programmable fabric, memory, peripheral devices, and connectivity to bring data into and out of the FPGA. Several approaches have emerged from industrial and academic research to design embedded systems into FPGA, such as the Xilinx approach which uses the Microblase processor (micro), the Altera (Altera) approach which is based on the use of the Nios processor, the IBM approach which uses the Power PC processor and the Opencores approach which uses the OpenRisc processor (Opencores). Each approach tries to promote its processor in the market. In this paper, we propose a SoC platform for VoIP application. This last one is composed of two parts: a software part which is related to configuration of the VOIP application and which is based on the Opensource Asterisk-PBX platform (Maeggelen & al.,2007) and a hardware part related to the VOIP Gateway and which is used to connect the traditional PSTN network to the Internet Network. We concentrate on the VIRTEX-5 FPGAs family from Xilinx to build the embedded SOC hardware. The final goal is to implement an embedded VOIP system and where part of Asterisk PBX software is embedded into FPGA. Due to the complexity of the system, we planed to achieve our objective in three phases:

- Phase1: Implementation of a simple VOIP application based on Asterisk and a commercial Digium TDM card.
- Phase2: Replace the Digium card and build a new VOIP Gateway based on FPGA and using the OpenRisc processor;
- Phase3: Build an embedded Asterisk into the proposed VOIP based FPGA Gateway.

The originality of our approach is the adoption of the OpenCores and Opensource concepts for the design and implementation of the whole SOC VOIP platform. With analogy to Opensource-Linux, Opencores is a new design concept which is based on publishing all necessary information about the hardware. The design specifications, hardware description language (HDL) at Register Transfer Level (RTL), simulation test benches, interfaces to other systems are documented. Usually, all this information is not available for free without any restriction. This new design concept is proposed as a bridge for the technological, educational and cultural gaps between developing and developed countries. The benefit of using such methodology is flexibility; reuse, rapid SoC prototyping into FPGA or ASIC and the entire software and hardware components of the VOIP application are available at free cost. This can also reduces the whole VOIP cost.

In section 2, general presentation of Voice over IP is given. Section 3 deals with presentation of the Opencores development platform. In section 4, presentation of the proposed VOIP Gateway architecture is given. Simulation and synthesis results are given in section 5. Followed by, presentation of the implementation results. In section 7 the PCB of the proposed SOC architecture is presented, followed by the presentation of the documentation phase; and finally, a conclusion.

2. General presentation of voice over IP

Voice over IP had its starts in February 1995 when a manufacturer started marketing software that enabled a conventional computer equipped with a sound card, microphone and loudspeaker to phone another PC via the internet. Initially, the voice quality achieved was unsatisfactory but the principle behind it drew a great attention of public, thus the first area of application for VoIP: PC-to-PC was established. Subsequent to this introduction a number of manufacturers concentrated on developing similar software and consequently raised the question of compatibility among different systems. In 1996, the International

Telecommunication Union (ITU-T),(ITU, 2007) responded by developing the H.323 standard. Afterwards, the focus was the possibility of placing long distance calls using voice over IP known as toll bypass; however this required setting up a connection between the telephone network (PSTN) and the data network, a task performed by the so called Gateways. The result has been additional application for VoIP including: PC-to-phone, Phone-to-PC and, when two gateways are used, Phone- to - phone communication is established. This last option was the catalyst in the establishment of a new provider group named ITSP (Internet Telephone Service Provider) that permits telephony over IP within the provider network using prepaid cards. To date, VoIP refers to the ability to transfer data and voice and also video on the single network. Figure 1 illustrates the basic operating principle of VoIP.
The human voice initially generates an analog signal. This signal is converted into a bit stream by an Analog/Digital (A/D) converter. And then submitted to a multiple compression process. The Voice frames are integrated into a voice packet. First RTP (Real time protocol) packet with a 12 address byte header is created. Then an 8-byte UDP packet with the source and destination address is added. Finally, a 20 byte IP header containing source and destination gateway IP address is added.The packet is sent through the internet where routers ands switches examine the destination address. When the destination receives the packet, the packet goes through the reverse process for playback. A minimal VoIP implementation requires two functionalities. First, it should be able to connect to other VoIP phones and, second, voice data should be carried by the Internet. The first requirement is fulfilled by using signaling.
The second one is achieved by using speech coding algorithms.

2.1 VOIP signaling

Signaling enables individual network devices to communicate with one another. Both PSTN and VoIP networks rely on signaling to activate and coordinate the various components needed to complete a call. In a PSTN network, phones communicate with a time-division multiplexed (TDM) Class 5 switch or traditional digital private branch exchange (PBX) for call connection and call routing purposes. In a VoIP network, the VoIP components communicate with one another by exchanging IP datagram messages. The format of these messages may be dictated by any of several standard protocols. The most commonly used signaling protocols -Session Initiation Protocol (SIP), H.323 and Media Gateway Control Protocol (MGCP). In this paper interest is given to the SIP protocol (Rosenberg & al, 2002).

2.1.1 Session Initiation Protocol (SIP)

SIP is a signalling protocol for initiating, managing and terminating sessions across packet networks. These sessions include Internet telephone calls, multimedia distribution, instant messaging, and multimedia conferences. SIP invitations are used to create session that allows participants to agree on a set of compatible media types. SIP makes use of elements called proxy servers to help route requests to the user's current location, authenticate and authorize users for services, implement provider call-routing policies, and provide features to users. SIP also provides a registration function that allows users to upload their current locations for use by proxy servers. SIP clients are referred to a SIP User Agents, and may make peer-to-peer calls, though usually they register and setup sessions via a SIP proxy. SIP can run on top of several different transport protocols though it most commonly uses UDP over Internet Protocol. Figure 2 shows the SIP session establishment.

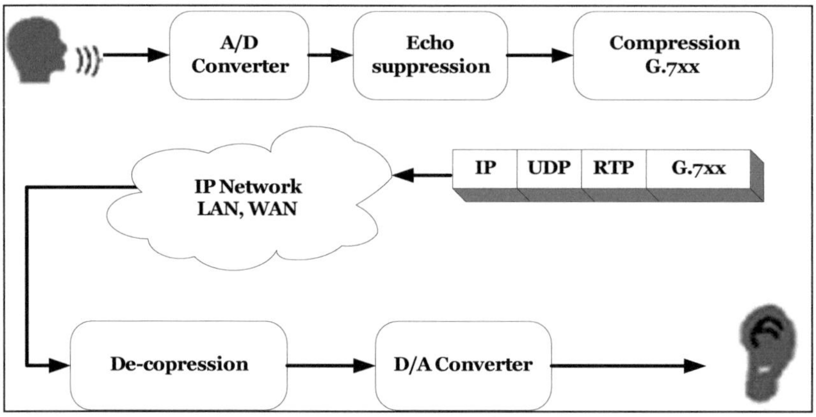

Fig. 1. Principle of VoIP

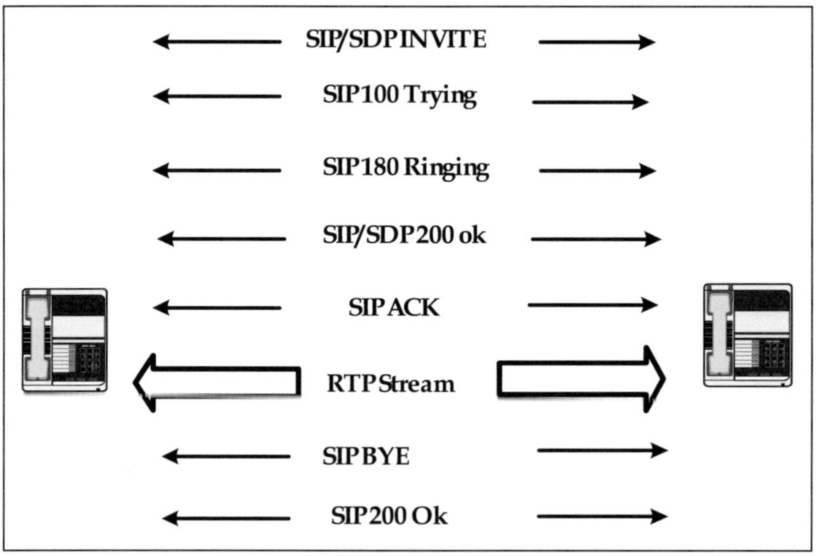

Fig. 2. SIP Session Establishment

2.2 Speech coding algorithm

The speech coding allows the reduction of transmission speech signal and communication channels to a limited bandwidth. The bandwidth of a transmission must be minimized while maintaining the quality of the voice signal. Most codecs are algorithms, used to reduce the bit rate of speech data incredibly, while maintaining the voice quality. The most commonly used codecs in VOIP systems are: G.711 PCM, G.726 (Chen, 1990)ADPCM , G.729 LD-CELP (ITU-T, 1996), and G. 729/G.729a CS-ACELP (Salami & al, 1998). PCM and ADPCM belong to the family of so called waveform codecs. These codecs simply analyze the input signal without any knowledge of the source. Most of these codecs work in time domain, like PCM. These codecs offer high quality speech at a low computational complexity. But if we try to get the bit rate below 16 kbps the quality decreases tremendously.

Coding algorithm		Bandwith (Kbps)	Algorithmic Delay (ms)	Complexity (MIPS)	MOS
G.711	PCM	64	0.125	0	4.3
G.726	ADPCM	16-40	0.125	6.5	2.0-4.3
G.728	LD-CELP	16	0.625	37.5	4.1
G7.29	CSACELP	8	10	17	3.4

Table1. Characteristics of the most coding algorithms

To get the bit rate really down another approach is necessary. Source coders need to know the characteristics about the input being coded. Out of these characteristics a model of the source is made. When an input is encoded the source coder tries to extract the exact parameters of this model from the input. Then these parameters and a two state excitation is transmitted. These codecs can simply transport the pure informational content of a speech sample and not the voice itself. Their big advantage is that they operate with bit rates as low as 2.4 kbit/s. Hybrid codecs try to combine the advantages of waveform codecs, which is good quality, with the advantages of the source codecs that is low bit rate. To get the best excitation signal all possible waveforms are tested and the one with the least error is then chosen. This involves a very high computational complexity for every analysis frame. The low bit rate codecs usually involve a high computational complexity and a delay and the waveform codecs have the advantage of low delay and excellent quality. In Table 1 there is an overview of the quality of the most common codecs according to the Mean Opinion Score (MOS). This score is derived from a large number of listeners who rated the quality of the played sample with a score from excellent (5) to bad (1). It should be understood that the various coding methods vary in the levels of complexity, delay characteristics and quality. The evaluation of speech quality is of critical importance in any VOIP application, mainly because quality is a key determinant of customer satisfaction. Traditionally, the only way to measure the perception of quality of a speech signal was through the use of subjective testing, i.e., a group of qualified listeners are asked to score the speech they just heard according to a scale from 1 to 5. This is most reliable method of speech quality assessment but it is highly unsuitable for online monitoring applications and is also very expensive and time consuming. Due to these reasons, models were developed to identify audible distortions through an objective process based on human perception. Objective methods can be implemented by computer programs and can be used in real time monitoring of speech quality. Algorithms for objective measurement of speech quality assessment have been implemented and the International Telecommunications Union has promulgated ITU-T P.862 standard (ITU, 2001), also known as Perceptual Evaluation of Speech Quality (PESQ), as its state of-the-art algorithm.

2.3 Presentation of asterisk

Asterisk is a complete IP PBX (Meggelen & al., 2007) in software. It runs on a wide variety of operating systems including Linux, Mac OS X, OpenBSD, FreeBSD and Sun Solaris and provides all of the features expect from a PBX including many advanced features that are often associated with high end (and high cost) proprietary PBXs. Asterisk supports Voice over IP in many protocols (SIP, H323, ADSI, MGCP, IAX), and can interoperate with almost all standards-based telephony equipment using relatively inexpensive hardware. Asterisk is released as open source under the GNU General Public License (GPL), meaning that it is available for download free of charge. Figure 3 shows different modules involved during routing an IP network to a PSTN one. Asterisk's core contains several engines that plays a critical role in the software. When asterisk is first started, the Dynamic Modular Loader loads and initializes each of the drivers which provide channel drivers, file formats, call detail record back-ends, codecs, applications and more, linking them with the appropriate internals APIs. Then Asterisk'PBX Switching Core begins accepting calls from interfaces and handling then according to the dialplan, using the Application Launcher for ringing phones, connecting to voicemail, dialing out outbound trunks, etc. The core also provides a standard Scheduler and I/OManager that applications and drivers can take advantage of Asterisk's Codec Translator permits channels which are compressed with different codes to seamlessly talk to one another. Most of of Asterisk's usefulness and flexibility come from the applications, codecs, channel drivers, file formats, and more which plug into Asterisk's various programming interfaces.

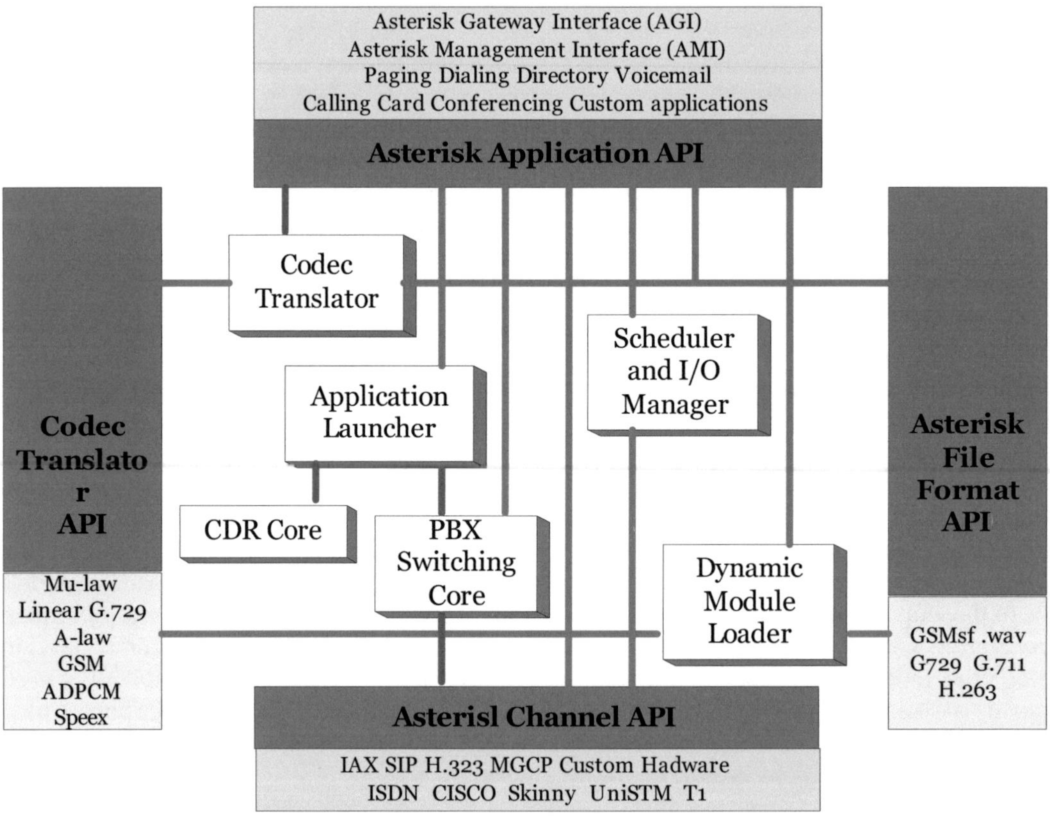

Fig. 3. Asterisk modules card

To provide call management, operation of Asterisk is reflected by a set of configuration files. The first configuration step is the definition of the user accounts and terminals. These are identified by the signalling protocol they use. We note particularly the file "***sip.conf***" which contains the parameters related to the SIP protocol. The first part is useful for the general options of SIP as the address IP and the corresponding port. The following part define the parameters of the client such the number of the user, his password, IP address, list of codecs allowed by the user, etc.Once the user account and terminal defined, we must assign phone numbers so that they are reachable, we must also determine the procedure which will hook on each call as well as the special services that we want to activate. This is done by dial numbering plan. This last one is the centrepiece of the configuration of the asterisk server. This dial plan contains all the intelligence and logic operation of a telephone network. It consists of a set of rules structured in a single file named *"extension.conf"*. The content of "extensions .conf" is organised in sections which can be either for static setting and definitions or for executable dial plan component in which case they are referred to as "contexts".

3. Presentation of the Opencores system on chip development platform

Using the OpenCores design methodology, we have developed our own SoC platform for VOIP applications (Titri & al., 2007),(Abid & al., 2009). Figure 4 gives an overview of the whole platform.

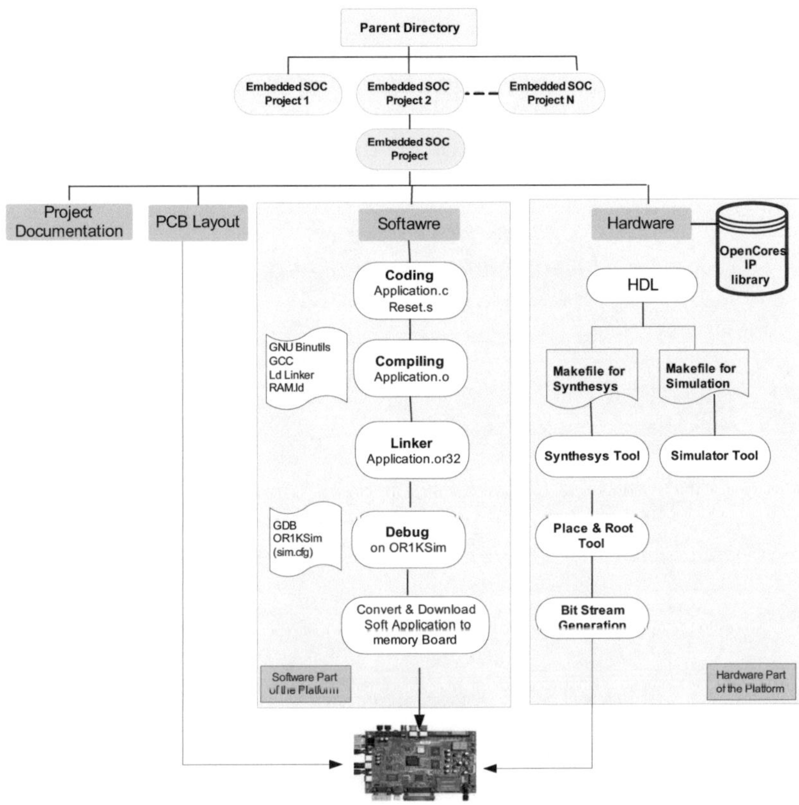

Fig. 4. Platform architecture

Creation of the platform begin by creating a library which is composed of the Wishbone interconnect standard bus, the OR1200 processor and other public cores suited for VOIP purposes such as the audio and video codec's, the MAC/Ethernet, the USB, the UART, memories, etc. In this library, all the cores are reusable and are described in the VERILOG language. As shown in figure 4, at a high level, a SoC designer specifies the Software and the hardware part of the project. In a SoC, software and hardware are related to each other by the RTOS (Real Time Operating System). After defining the architecture, different phases can be achieved in parallel: the simulation, the synthesis, the PCB layout and the project documentation phases.

3.1 Presentation of the hardware part of the platform

After defining the architecture, different phases can be achieved in parallel. First, we start by downloading from the opencores web site IP cores that constitute the architecture of the embedded SOC project. Figure 5 shows the structured embedded SOC project directories.

- **Lib***:* is a directory which contains all the IP cores ;
- **RTL**: is a directory which contains the source files of all IPs described in Verilog RTL (Register Transfer Level) which can be modified in the top level ;
- **Bench**: is a directory which contains test bench for all IPs core ;
- ***DOC***: is a directory which contains the specifications and design manual relating to each IPs core ;
- And finally a **CVS** (Concurrent Version Check) which is a directory who is automatically created when running the CVS. The Version control system software keeps track of all work and all changes in a set of files, and allows several developers (potentially widely separated in space and/or time) to collaborate each other. The repository stores a complete copy of all the files and directories which are under version.

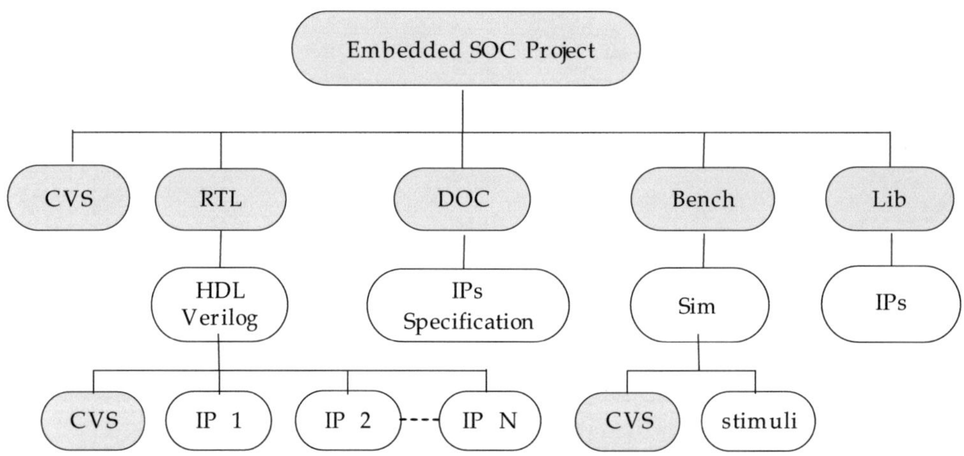

Fig. 5. The structured embedded SOC project directories

Once the HDL files of the architecture is downloaded and stored in the repository, the simulation and synthsis, the PCB layout and the project documentation phases can be achieved. Simulation and synthesis are done using the ISE design tool (ISE) and ModelSim simulator (ModelSim) respectively . These tools are executed at the back end plan of the platform. By using the Make language, a Makefile is created for simulation and another one for synthesis. These files contains the path/directory of the IP cores which are stocked in the library and the synthesis or simulations options (such as target FPGA device, surface/timing constraints, specific input/output, etc.). Figures 6 and 7 show respectively the contents of the makefile and its arborescence.

Thus, for each SoC architecture the Makefile is created once. With this way, a designer concentrate only in his design to avoid errors due to fault manipulation of the tools options,

```
DESIGN = Projet_SOC
PINS       = Projet_Soc_top.ucf
DEVICE = xc5vlx50-2ff1153
SRC       = VOIP_soc_top.v tc_top.v
# IP Debug interface
SRC+= dbg_interface/dbg_top.v \
 dbg_interface/dbg_sync_clk1_clk2.v \
 dbg_interface/dbg_registers.v \
 dbg_interface/dbg_crc8_d1.v \
# IP Processor
SRC += or1200/or1200_top.v    or1200/or1200.v
 or1200/or1200_wb_biu.v  or1200/or1200_immu_top.v
 or1200/or1200_ic_top.v  or1200/or1200_cpu.v \
 or1200/or1200_dmmu_top.v or1200/or1200_dc_top.v
# IP Memory
SRC+= mem_if/onchip_ram_top.v  mem_if/onchip_ram.v
        ...
```

Fig. 6. Contents of the Makefile

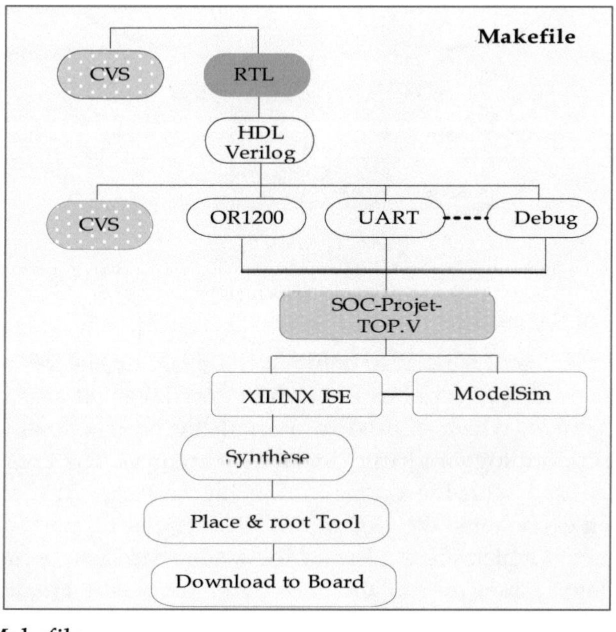

Fig. 7. Structured Makefile

hence the design time and further the time to market factor are reduced. The PCB layout is done using the ORCAD capture Ver9.6 tool. It is recommended to begin the PCB layout and the project documentation early in the design process to allow different members of a team working in the same project communicate and co-operate with each other. For example, each time a change is made within an IP or a new version is created, it is communicated to the PCB and documentation teams and vice-versa. This is done through the use of a CVS.

3.2 Presentation of the software part of the platform

The software part includes a set of development tools, all of them ported from GNU toolchain and an Architectural simulator *OR1KSim* developed by the Openrisc project team (Bennett 1,2008),(Bennett 2, 2008). The GNU toolchain consist of a GCC, GNU Binutils and GDB. In our project, the GNU Toolchains are used to compile, link programs, and generate the binary file. The Architectural simulator *OR1KSim* is a stand-alone C program which emulates the instruction set and behavior of an OR1200 processor OR1K. The simulator has also been expanded to include simulations of many OpenCores peripherals, including serial ports, memory controllers, etc. The simulator may be used to develop software for the target platform before the hardware becomes available or fully verified. This will allow the user to separate debugging of the hardware and software, rather than having to run untested software on uncertain hardware. As shown in figure 8, the first step consists on developing a C program "***application.c***", this file implements the main functions needed for the VOIP application.

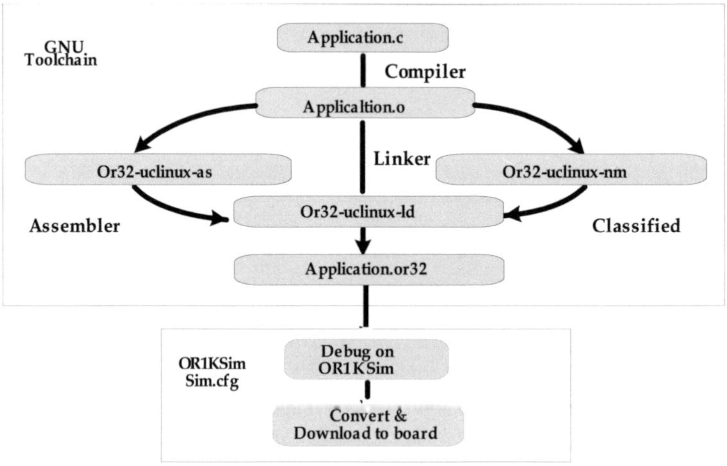

Fig. 8. Software flow of the platform

In the next step, the GCC tool is used to compile the program, in this phase the object file "**application.o**" is generated, in order to be used by the linker (*ld linker*). This file is linked with the linker file (*ram.ld*) which is used to map all the instructions, variables, data and stacks to the corresponding address in the memory. The resulting binary file "**application.or32**" is used with the configuration file "*sim.cfg*" in the debug on or1ksim step. The "*sim.cfg*" file contains the default configurations of peripherals and a set of simulation environments which are similar to the actual hardware situation. In this phase the or1ksim simulator and the GDB tools are invoked. Finally the binary file "**application.or32**" is converted to the memory initialization file and downloaded into the on-chip RAM configured in sim.cfg.

4. Presentation of the general VOIP architecture

Figure 9 illustrates the proposed SOC Platform architecture for VOIP application. This last one is composed of two parts : A software part which is related to configuration of the VOIP application and which is based on the Opensource Asterisk-PBX platform and a hardware part related to the VOIP Gateway and which is used to connect the traditional PSTN network to the internet Network. We concentrate on the VIRTEX-5 FPGAs family from Xilinx to build the embedded SOC architecture.

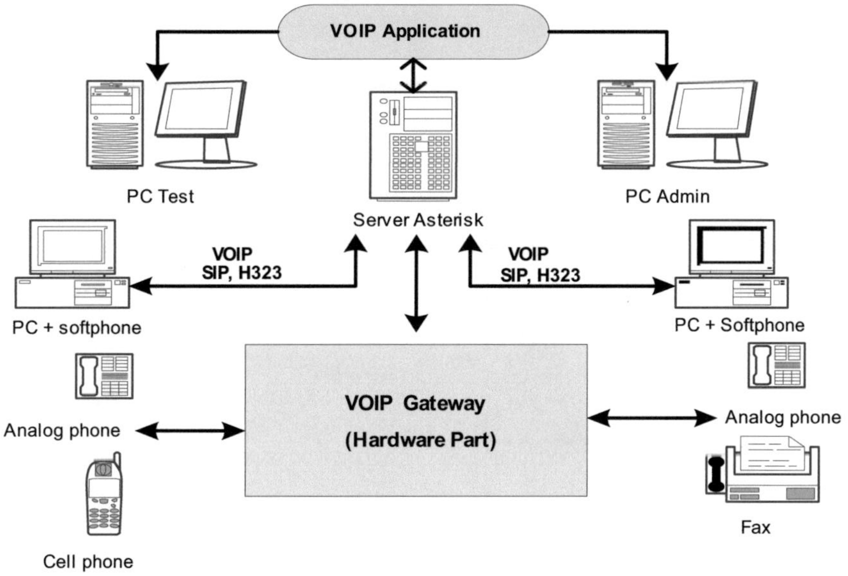

Fig. 9. Architecture of the VOIP application

4.1 Presentation of the software part

The software part of the application contains the following elements:

- A VOIP Asterisk server under Linux environment.
- An administrators "admin" under Windows environment to manage the system.
- A computer with a "softphone" under Windows to establish communications. The choice of Windows is justified by the simplicity of use and its convivial interface for the customer.
- Thanks to Ethreal (Eth, 2006) software which analyze the performance of the application on the VOIP network.
- An analogic phone in the case of the PC to phone and phone to phone application.
- A fax if one wants to send fax via internet protocol.

4.2 Presentation of the hardware part

Concerning the hardware part, we have developed an OpenRisc based SOC architecture that includes a 32 bits RISC processor core and a set of elements needed to provide a VOIP functionality, an OR1K debug system for debugging purpose, a memory controller that controls an external Flash and SDRAM memory, an Universal Asynchronous Receiver Transmitter (UART), an Audio codec for Voice coding, a standard Ethernet that transmit voice packets over The internet and an internal boot memory. All the cores are connected through the WISHBONE bus interface. We created a SOC verilog description for the integration of all the IP cores. The proposed VOIP gateway architecture is depicted in figure below.

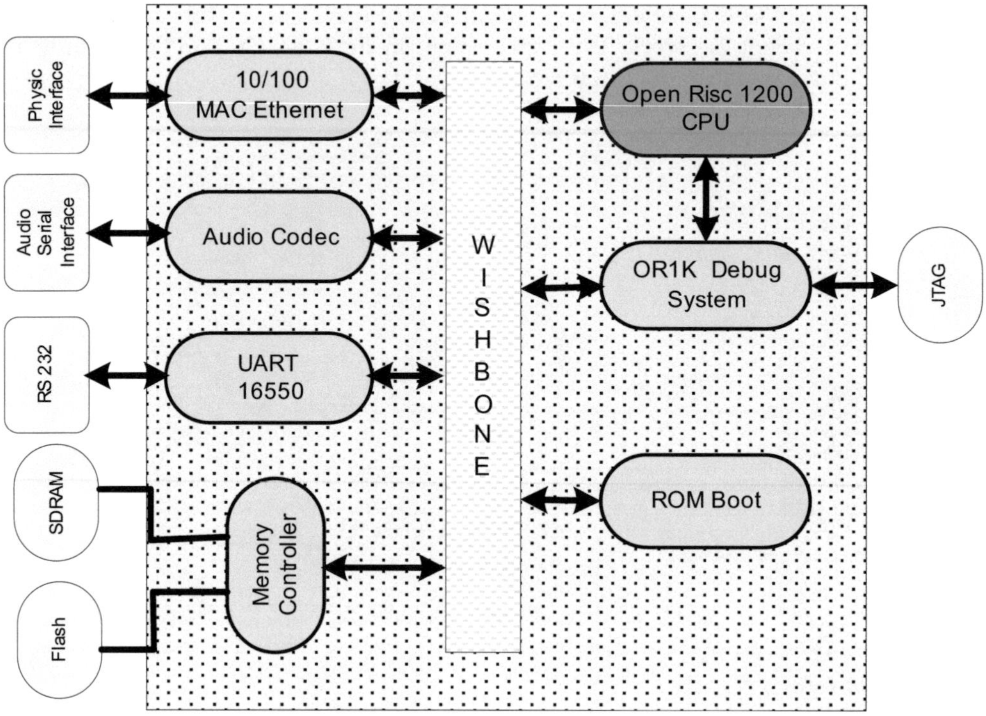

Fig. 10. VOIP gateway architecture

4.2.1 The WHISHBONE bus Interface

The WHISHBONE interconnect is a portable and flexible interface for use with semi conductor chips. It defines a common, logical interface between sections of the chip and allows them to communicate better. These sections known as "cores" can be developed and tested independently and later combined to form a complete system on chip. Currently WISHBONE is the only SoC specification in the public domain (Wishbone,2004). All other methodologies such the IBM Core Connect (IBM) bus and the AMBA Bus (AMBA) are proprietary. Figures 11 and 12, show the structure of the WISHBONE bus. The WISHBONE uses a master/slave architecture. That means that functional modules with MASTER interfaces initiate data transactions to participating SLAVE interfaces.
As shown in Figure 12, the master and slave communicate through an interconnection interface. Some signals are specific to the master core, others to the slave one and there are common signals shared between the master and the slave. the WHISHBONE bus can be configured in different ways depending on the application.

4.2.2 The OR1200 Processor

We use the OR1200 (Lampret, 2001), a publicly available processor for our development of SoC VOIP Gateway. This soft-core is freely distributed under an GPL license at OpenCores website, and fits for composition SoC in many ways. OpenRISC 1200, synthesizable core, is implemented with Verilog HDL, and has high flexibility because all configuration options for the processor are gathered together into a single file containing numerous define statements. A block diagram of the OR1200 architecture is depicted in Figure 13.

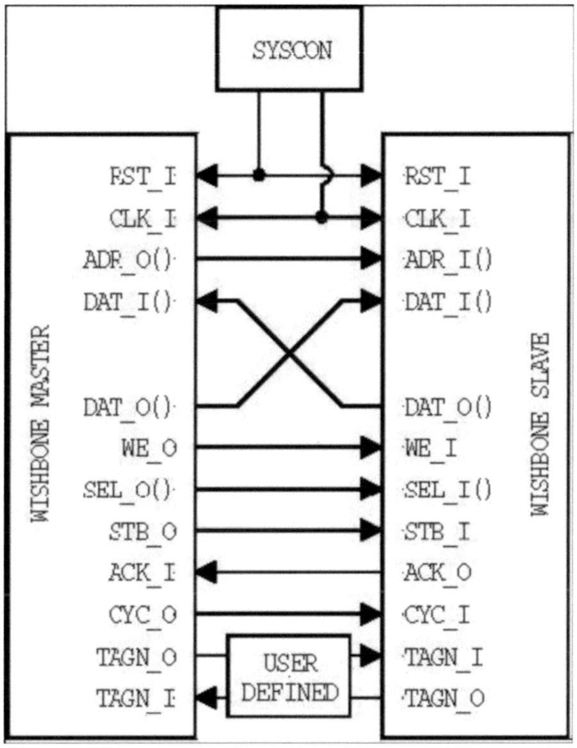

Fig. 11. Wishbone interconnection

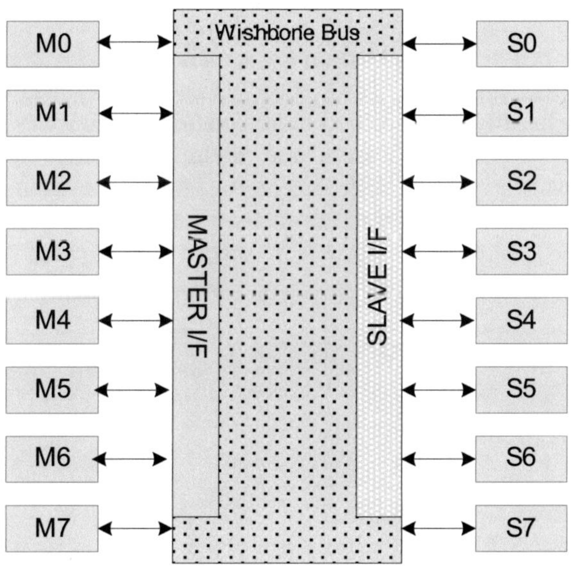

Fig. 12. Wishbone configuration

The OR1200 core is a 32-bit scalar RISC with Harvard micro-architecture, 5 stage integer pipeline, virtual memory support (MMU) and basic DSP capabilities. It includes a debug unit for real-time debugging, high resolution tick timer, programmable interrupt controller and power management support. OR1200 runs at 33 MHz on a Virtex FPGA. The OR1200 communicates with the WISHBONE interconnect (WBI). Documentation about the OR1K, HDL code and OR1K simulator under Linux and other tools for software debugging is available for free download. In our application we use the OR1200 processor, as it is well documented.

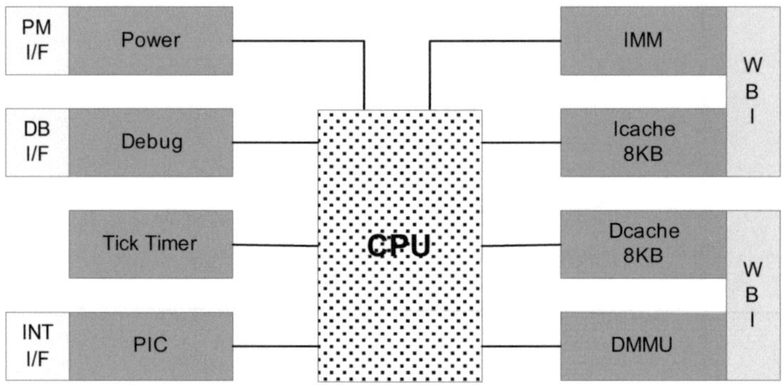

Fig. 13. The OpenRISC 1200 architecture

4.2.3 The OR1K debug system

The OR1K debug system (Yawn, 2009) allows controlling and observing the execution of the software running under the OR1200 processor. It acts as an interface between the host and the target system (SOC), communicating directly to the Openrisc 1200 CPU and the WishBone bus. Figure 14 shows the different modules involved in the OR1K debug system. These are: the "***Advanced debug Interface***" core (***adv_dbg_if***), the "***JTAG TAP"*** core and the "***Xilinx internal JTAG"***. The "***adv_dbg_if***" core controls transactions to the CPU and the WishBone bus, and provides clock domain synchronization between the CPU, the WishBone, and the JTAG TAP. The "***JTAG TAP"*** is used to connect directly with external debugger (software or hardware). Specified by the standard boundary scan IEEE 1149.1, It is accessed by four (or five) external pins, and includes mainly two main registers for instruction and data loading (IR and DR). This ***JTAG TAP*** is suitable for use in ASICs and all FPGAs. The ***Xilinx Internal JTAG* core** is used only when the system is implemented in a Xilinx FPGA which supports a BSCAN_* macro block (e.g. BSCAN_SPARTAN3, BSCAN_VIRTEX4, etc.).

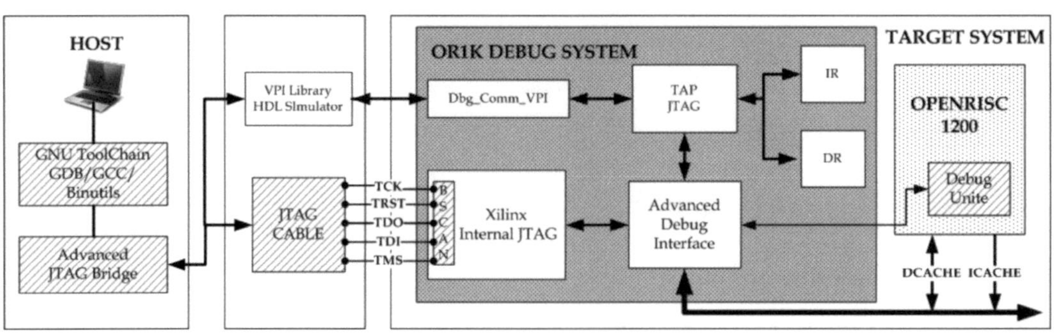

Fig. 14. The OR1K Debug System Architecture

4.2.4 The UART (Universal Asynchronous Receiver/Transmitter)

The UART core (Universal Asynchronous Receiver/Transmitter) from Opencores (Gorban, 2002), provides serial communication capabilities, which allow communication with a modem or other external devices, like another computer using a serial cable and a RS232 protocol. Figure 15 illustrates the overall architecture of the core. This core is designed to be maximally compatible with the industry standard National Semiconductors 16550A device.

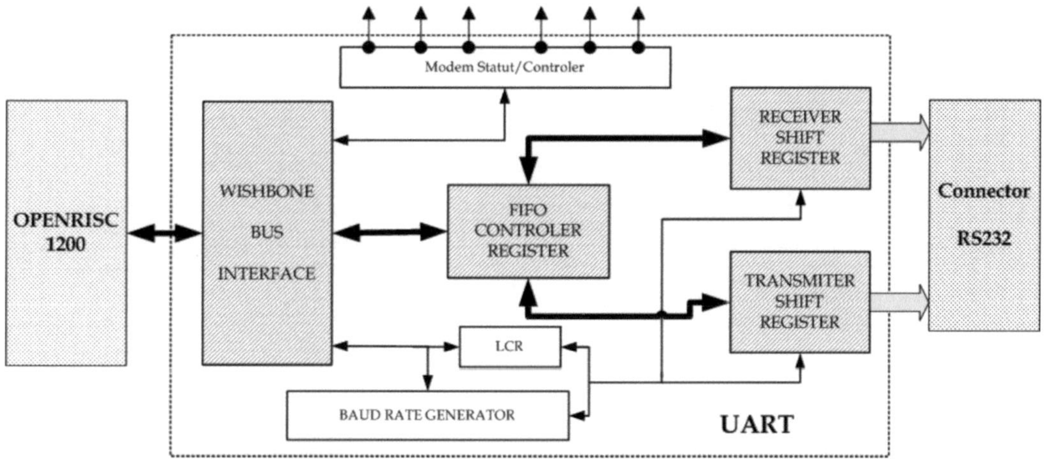

Fig. 15. The UART Architecture

and the other one is used to transmit or receive data from the UART port. All the data operations are FIFO (First In, First Out) and it requires one interrupt, 2 pads in the chip (serial in and serial out) and optionally another six modem Status/control signals. The Baud Rate Generator is a programmable Transmit and Receive bit timing device. Given the programmed value; it generates a periodic pulse, which determines the baud rate of the UART transmission. The transmitter module convertes the parallel data into serial form, the receiver unit process the serial data received from the RS232.

4.2.5 The memory controller

The memory controller (Usselman,2002) supports a variety of memory devices; flexible timing and predefined system start up from a Flash or ROM memory. Figure 16 illustrates the overall architecture of the core. It consists of a 32 bit bus WISHBONE interface, a power-on configuration, a refresh controller, an open bank and row tracking, an address MUX and Counter, a data latch packet and parity, a memory timing controller a memory interface and a configuration and status register.

4.2.6 The MAC/Ethernet unit

The Ethernet core (Mohor,2002) is a 10/100 Media Access Controller. It consists of synthesizable Verilog RTL core that provides all features necessary to implement the layer 2 protocol of the standard Ethernet. It is designed to run according to the IEEE 802.3 specification that defines the 10 Mbps and 100Mbps for Ethernet and Fast Ethernet applications respectively. In this work the Ethernet/MAC allows Internet connection. Figure 17 shows the general architecture of the IP.

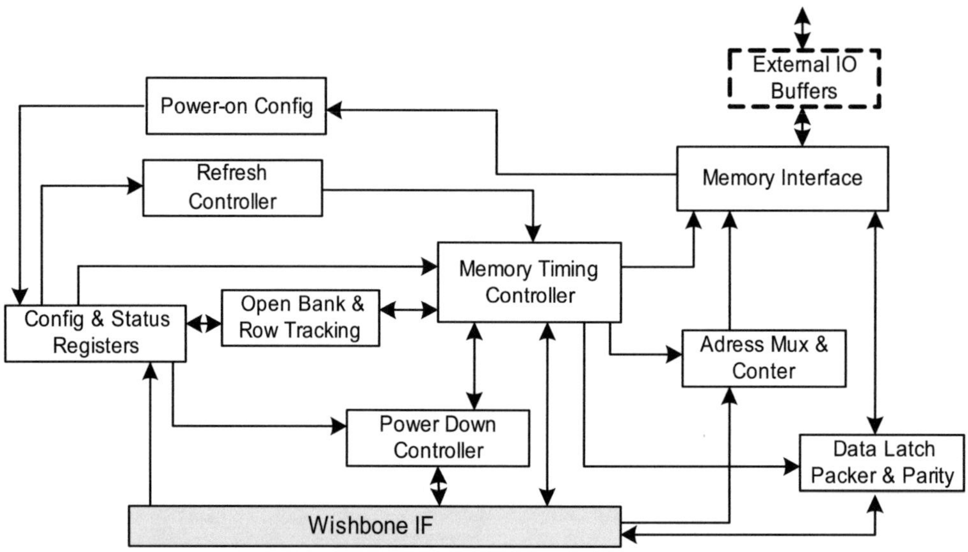

Fig. 16. The Memory Controller Architecture

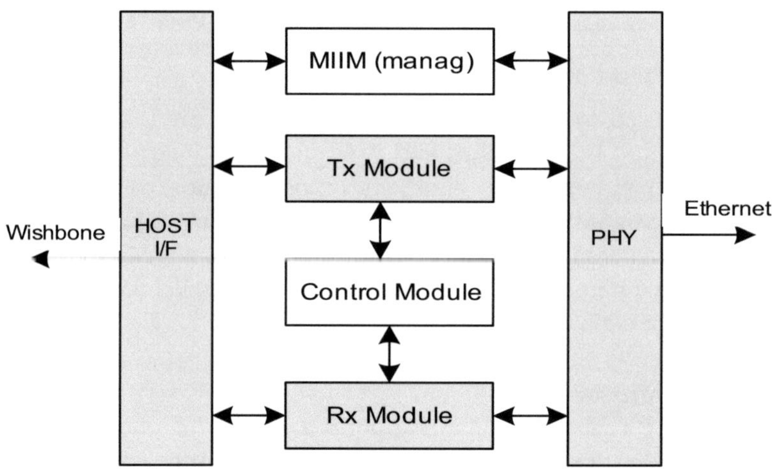

Fig. 17. The MAC Ethernet Architecture

It consists of several building blocks: a Tx module an RX module, a control module, a management block and a WISHBONE interface. The TX and RX modules provide full transmission and reception functionality respectively. Cyclic Redundancy Check (CRC) generators are incorporated in both modules for error detection purposes. The control module provides full duplex flow control. The management module provides the standard IEEE 802.3 Media Independent Interface (MII) that defines the connection between the PHY and the link layer. Using this interface, the connected device can force PHY to run at 10 Mbps with frequency of 2.5 MHz versus 100 Mbps (25 MHz) or to configure it to run at full or half duplex mode. The WISHBONE interface connects the Ethernet core to the RISC and to external memory. To adapt this IPs to our application we have determined the specification required to the VoIP application.

4.2.7 The audio codec

The Audio Codec core digitizes the analog voice from the headset, group data into packets and then transmits it across the network. Figure 18. shows the architecture of the G711.

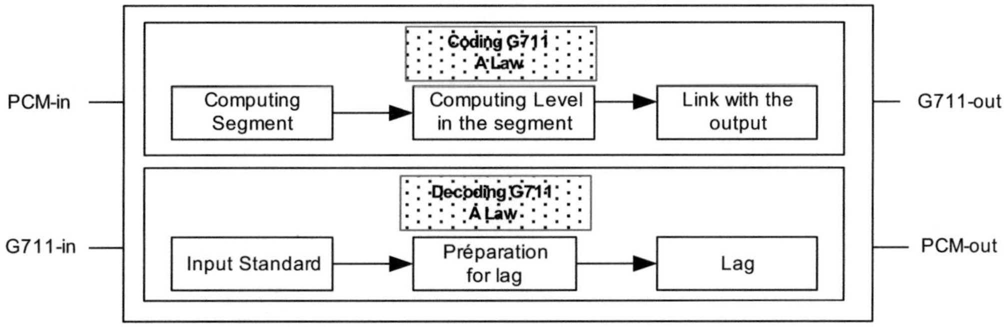

Fig. 18. Architecture of the G.711

We consider the G711 PCM, G726 ADPCM, G.728 LD-CELP and G729/G729a CS-ACELP. The programs codes for different Codec's are available free from ITU-T. They can easily adapted to our application. The two main encoding laws used nowadays are A law (a-law) and μ law (μ-law), that are also known as g.711 codec . A Law (a-law) is used mainly in European PCM systems , and the μ law is used in American PCM systems.

5. Simulation and synthesis results

5.1 Functional simulation

Although, most of the HDL cores at RTL level, are available freely for simulation and synthesis from OpenCores, the most difficult task in designing the SoC hardware is how to write an HDL code that integrates all the SoC components codes and how these components communicate each other through the WISHBONE interface bus. To do this, the first step is to define the MASTER from the SLAVE components in the architecture. The OR1200 processor is set as a MASTER of all components. Considering the complexity of the gateway system and to avoid problems of debugging, we set the goal to simulate and validate the functionality of each IP using the ModelSim simulator tool.

- Figure 19 shows the communication protocol between the processor OR1K, the bus Whishbone and different IPs. The processor is configured as "Master" and various IP As "Slave".
- Figure 20 shows the functionality of the memory controller and SDRAM .
- Figures 21 and 22 show the simulation results of the Transmission and Reception process of the 10/100 MAC/Ethernet .
- Figure 23 shows the simulation results of the encoder G711 .

5.2 Synthesis and implementation results

Having validated the various applications of the SOC, we performed the synthesis and system implementation through the ISE Foundation tool 10.3i Xilinx. Figure 24 shows the layout of the VOIP SOC Gateway. The whole Architecture is mapped into the ***XC5VLX50-1FF676*** FPGA circuit family. Mainly, the SoC occupies 60% of the FPGA surface in term of slice LUT, 27% of slices registers, 31 % of inputs/output , 8% of integrated DSP48E.

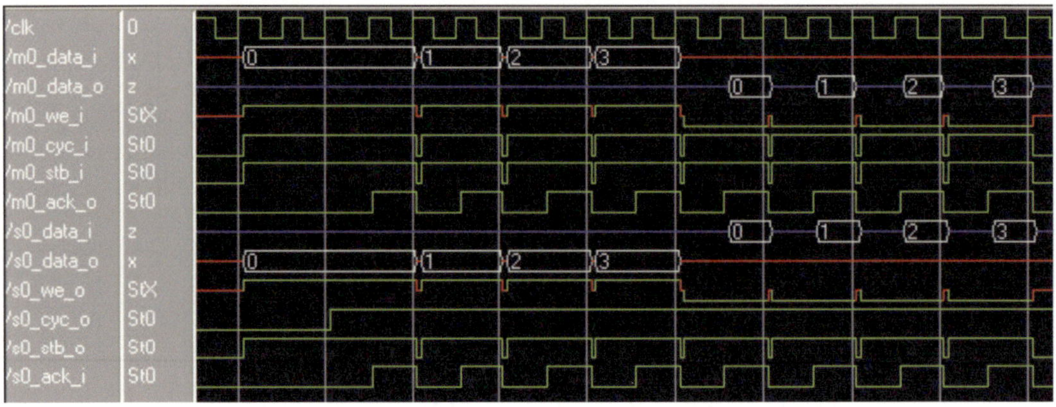

Fig. 19. Wishbone simulation result

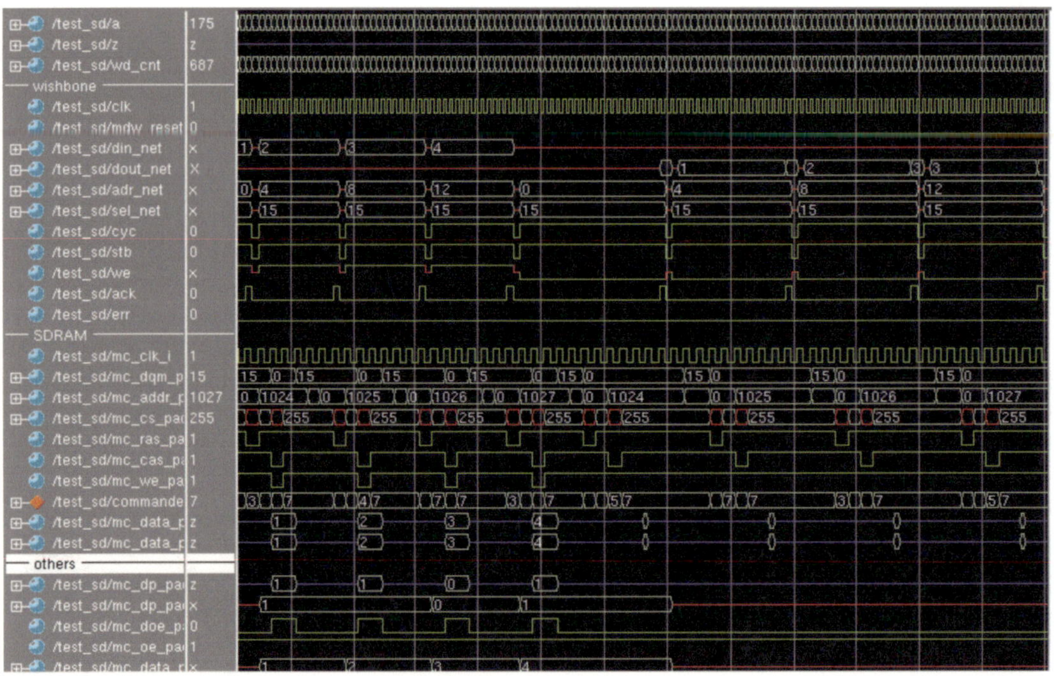

Fig. 20. Memory Controller simulation results

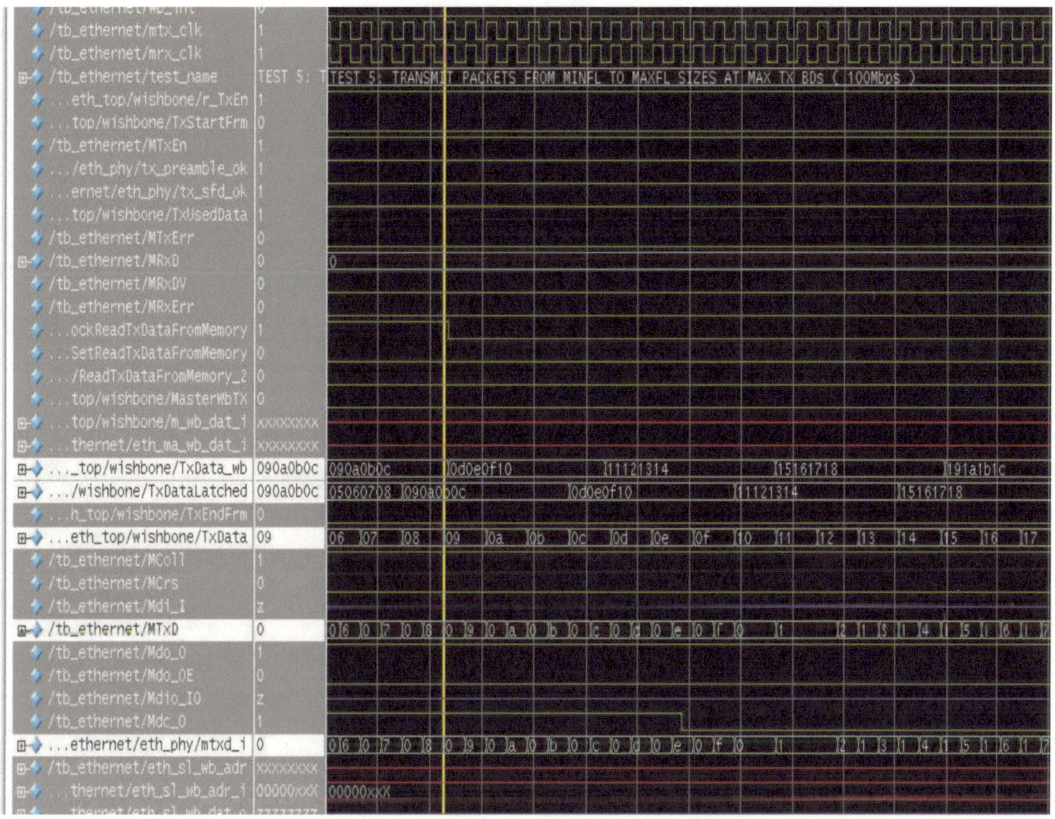

Fig. 21. MAC Ethernet Transmit simulation result

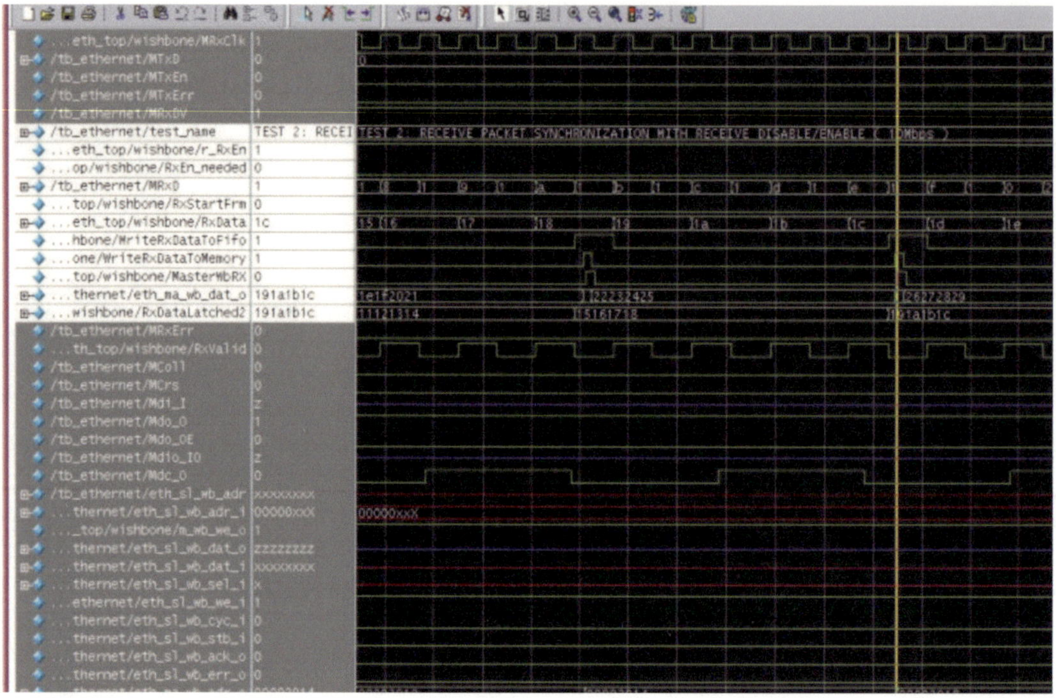

Fig. 22. MAC Ethernet Reception simulation result

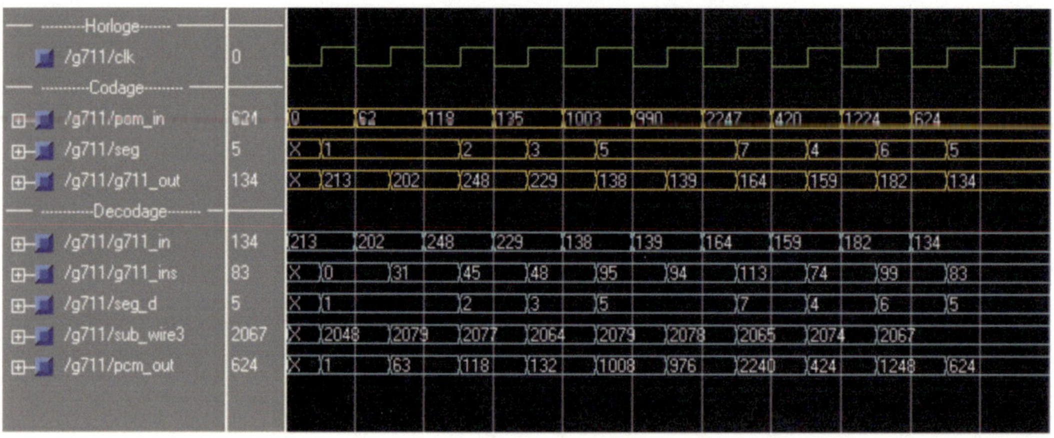

Fig. 23. G711 simulation result

6. Test results

Due to the complexity of the system, we have adopted a strategy in order to achieve our goal, several steps are necessary in order to validate the embedded VOIP application. These are: (1) Test of the VOIP application using Asterisk, (2) Test of the proposed SOC gateway architecture, (3) Running Uclinux/Asterisk under OR1Ksim to load and run the whole VOIP application.

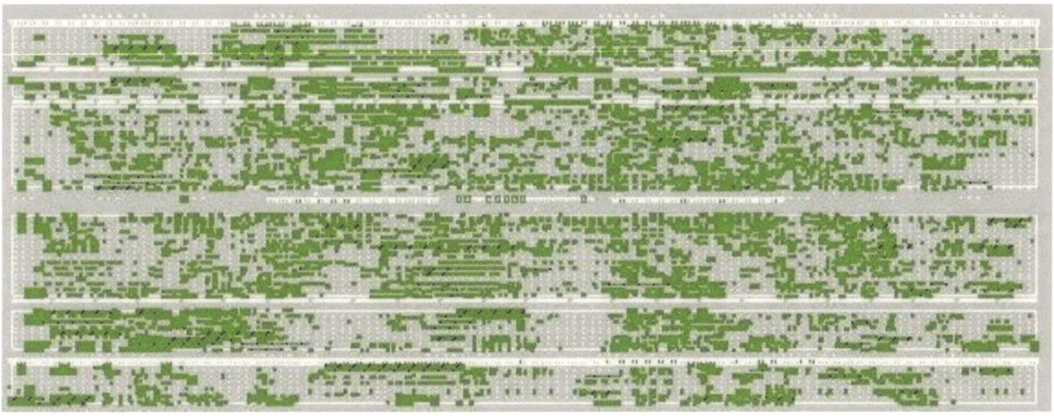

Fig. 24. Layout of the VOIP SOC Gateway

6.1 Test of the VOIP application using Asterisk

In this section, we have used a TDM Digium card TDM11B (Digium) as gateway to connect to Asterisk. Three applications tests are done in order to test the VOIP application:

The first application is to test the network traffic. To do this, we have used the software Ethereal. Figure 25 represents the results obtained in the PC observer regarding the timing of a telephone call as follows:

- **Signalling:** The first three queries are repeated twice: the customer has not yet hanged up;
- **Communication**: as soon as the customer picks up the handset called his phone, a SIP message (200 OK) is sent to the server call: the customer has accepted the appeal request. In the same way, the call server sends a message SIP (200 OK) to the customer to inform him that the client accepted his appeal. The acquittal of the customer

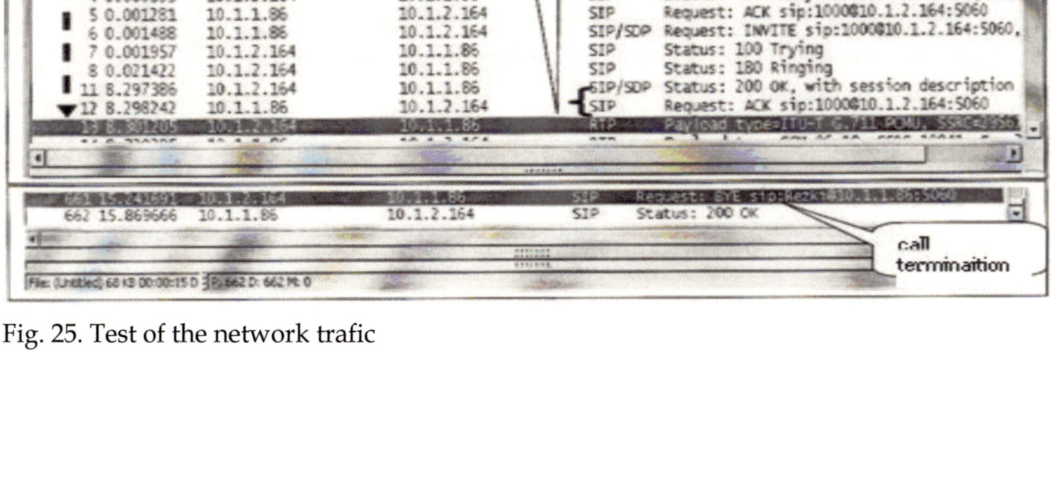

Fig. 25. Test of the network trafic

(Message: ACK SIP: 1000@10.1.2.164: 5060) has triggered the session between two clients. The role of SIP is completed successfully. He leaves his place for the following two steps namely coding and transmission of voice. The selected black frame shows the beginning of trade flow between the two RTP correspondents (voice packets encoded in the standard G711 standard of the International Telecommunication Union (ITU).

- **End of the call**: exchange SIP message: BYE.

The second application is to test the hierarchy of different communication protocols involved in a VOIP application. Figure 26 shows the order of the various protocols in a VOIP call session, after analyzing the available statistics in the Ethereal program for each call made. Figure 26 shows that the first protocol involved in a communication VOIP is the SIP signalling protocol. The number of packets exchanged via SIP is eight. Thereafter, the encapsulation IP/UDP/RTP, to arrive at the Ethernet physical layer.

The third application is to test the establishment of a call between two analogue phones via VoIP gateway. Figure 27 shows that communication is well established.

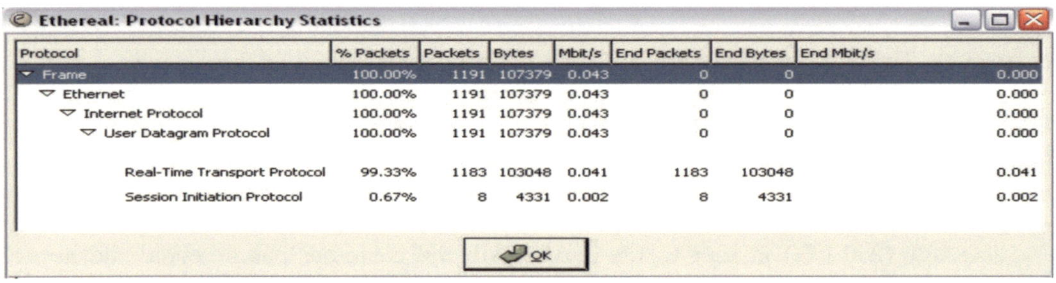

Fig. 26. The hierarchy of protocols involved in the appeal

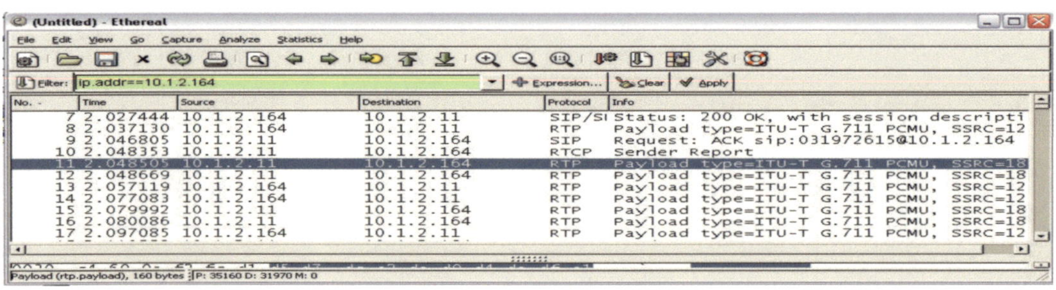

Fig. 27. Call establishment

6.2 Test of the proposed SOC gateway architecture

In this section the following tests are done: (1) Serial transfer test , (2) Boot Uclinux under OR1ksim, (3) Embedded network emulation and test.All these applications are done using the software part of the opencores development platform. The application of the serial transfer test in the FPGA is done through the GDB. The communication protocol between the host and the architecture implemented on FPGA is done through the JTAG Proxy Server.

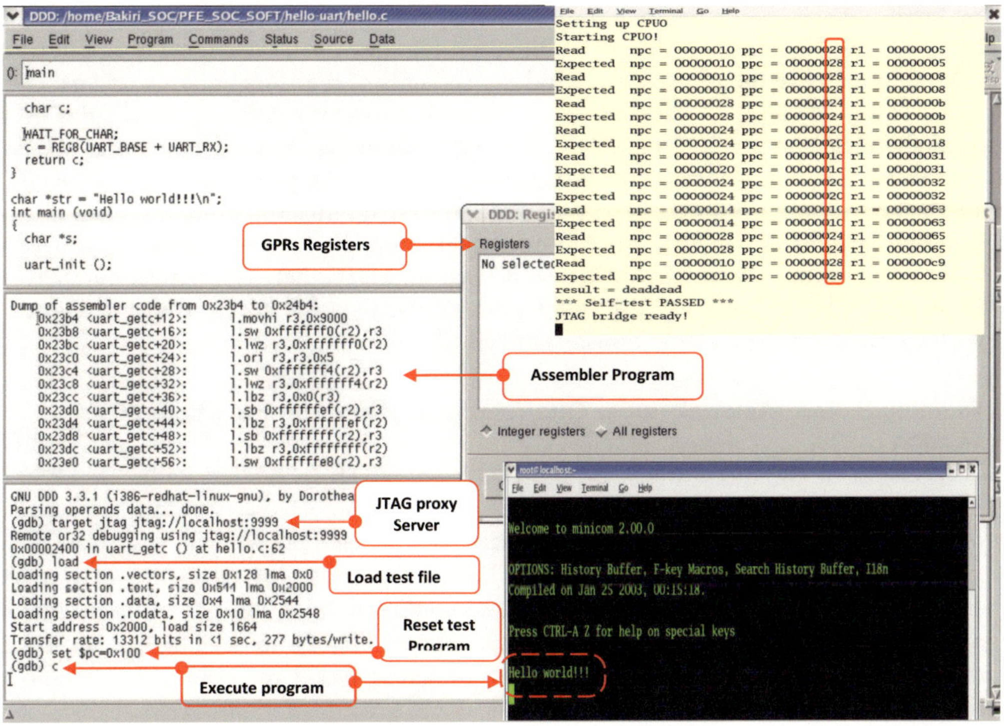

Fig. 28. Results of the serial transfer test

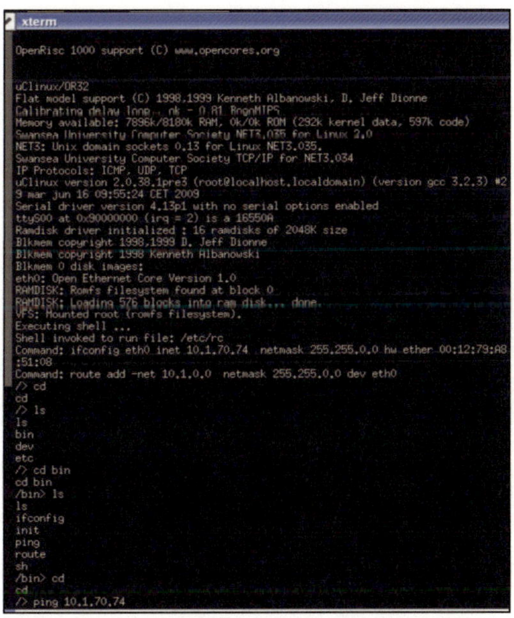

Fig. 29. Boot of Uclinux under OR1ksim

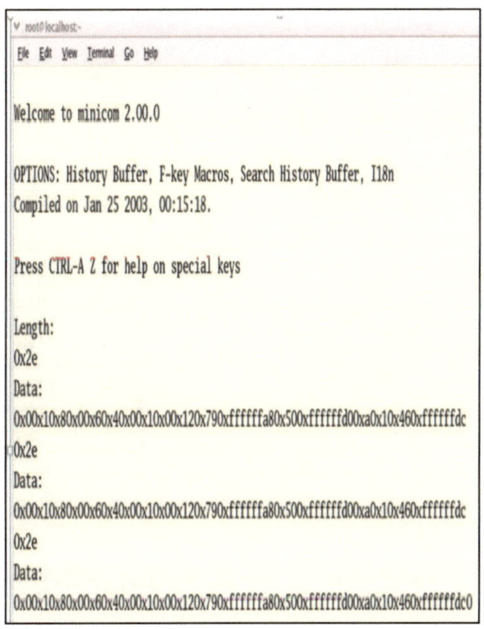

Fig. 30. FPGA board-PC Frame tansfer test result

Figure 28 summarize all the commands executed by the Display Data Debuger (DDD)which is the graphical interface of the GDB.Different windows are displayed (application.c program window, assembler program window, contents of registers window and execution program window). The execution of these commands allows the debugger to display on the terminal the message *"HELLO WORLD"*. The visualization of the "Hello World" message allowed us to validate the communication protocol between the processor and the UART.
Figure 29 shows results of booting Uclinux under the OR1kSim simulator.
To test the embedded network emulation, the Ethernet IP core is chosen as a network controller. The Ethernet frame from Ethreal is used to test the network application between FPGA board and PC. We used the serial port to visualize the frame transfer. Figure 30 shows the FPGA board-PC frame transfert test result.

6.3 Running Uclinux/Asterisk under OR1Ksim to load and run the whole VOIP application

In this section, we aim to build a VOIP application in which Asterisk is embedded into the FPGA. The advantage of using such solution, is to realize a portable system while reducing power dissipation, chip interconnects and device size. Embedded Asterisk is state of the art design. To our best knowledge two works have been proposed. The first one is from Asterisk "Astlinux" which provides an Asterisk installation on a linux distribution that has been build from scratch and optimized for small format of hardware format. The second one is from the OPSIS company (Koroneos, 2008) which is based on FPGA, and where the processor is Power PC instead of OpenRisc. The main advantage of our approach is that the software and the hardware involved in the design are all opensource, this reducing the coast of the VOIP application.

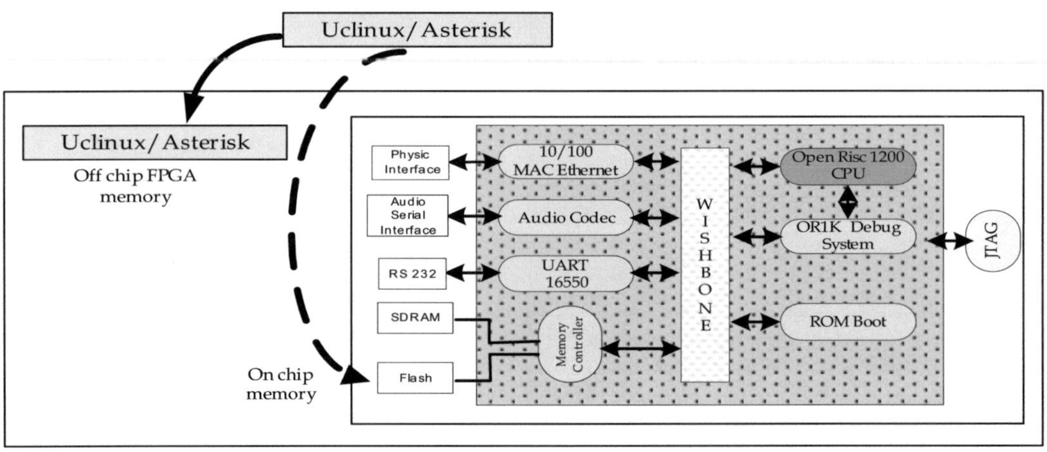

Fig. 31. Embedded Asterisk into the FPGA

7. Prototyping Circuit Board (PCB) of the proposed SOC architecture

To lead the project until its term, we planned to construct a prototype board using the Orcad CAD tool (ORCAD, 2004). Figure 32 shows the different steps involved in PCB design. Orcad gives the possibility to create electronics diagrams and trace the physical part of the design (layout) starting from the footprints of the components. Internet is essentially used to retrieve technical documentation of the components. Capture-CIS is one of the many components which give the possibility to create electric diagrams. Digi-Key is an Internet provider of electronic components who is entirely compatible with Orcad. We have the possibility of configuring Orcad-CIS to access the database of components and suppliers of the site of Digi-key. This allows selection directly from the library of Digi-Key to insert a component in our diagram. The tool has a much expanded database in which it only remains to find the selected components. Despite such a database, it is possible that we will not find all the components because some may be very specific. In this case it is requested to produce its own library because most of the map items are too specific to be part of Orcad libraries and Digi-Key. Once the diagram is finished, we move to the checking of the electrical characteristics (Design Rules Check) of our scheme in order to be sure that everything is connected and no errors in terms of electrical. We can then generate the list of components used: BOM (Bill of Materials). Layout Plus is another component of the Orcad family. From Netlist, we trace the mechanical part of the board (footprints). For that must be associated with each component of the diagrams a physical footprint which defines the size that makes the element on the board. It is often necessary to create its own library as for capture. Indeed, as it uses very specific components, the footprints do not necessarily exist. However, the physical characteristics are provided in the datasheets or all at least their reference because they are standardized. Once all the footprints were associated with the components, Layout Plus puts them on the sheet. Then we go to the routing, we put the components inside the framework which represents the physical limits of the module. Figure 33 shows the PCB block diagram of VOIP Gateway

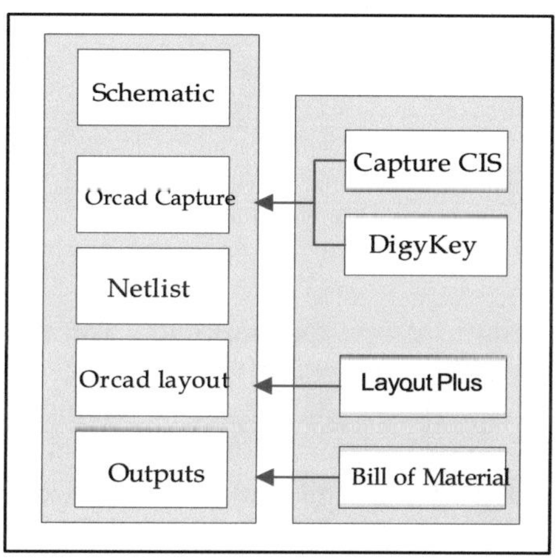

Fig. 32. Steps involved in PCB design

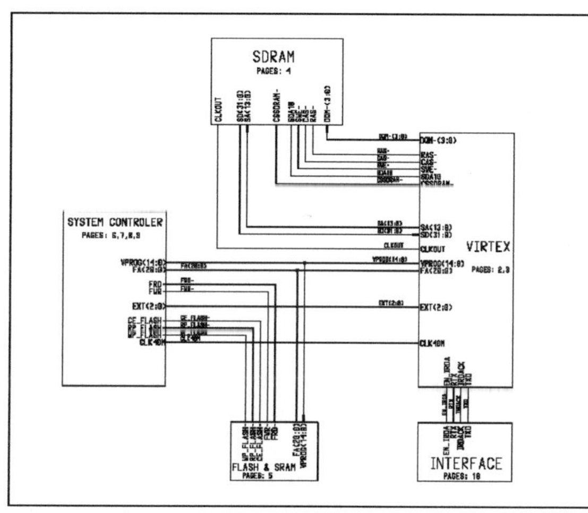

Fig. 33. PCB Bloc diagram of the VOIP Gateway

8. Documentation

As shown in section 3.1, the documentation is an important phase to achieve a design. Designers must start writing the document specific to the project early in the design process. This must be done in parallel with hardware design, software design and PCB design of the project. Generally speaking, writing a design document follows a specific model. In

Figure bellow, we propose an organization chart which resumes all the steps involved in writing the project documentation.

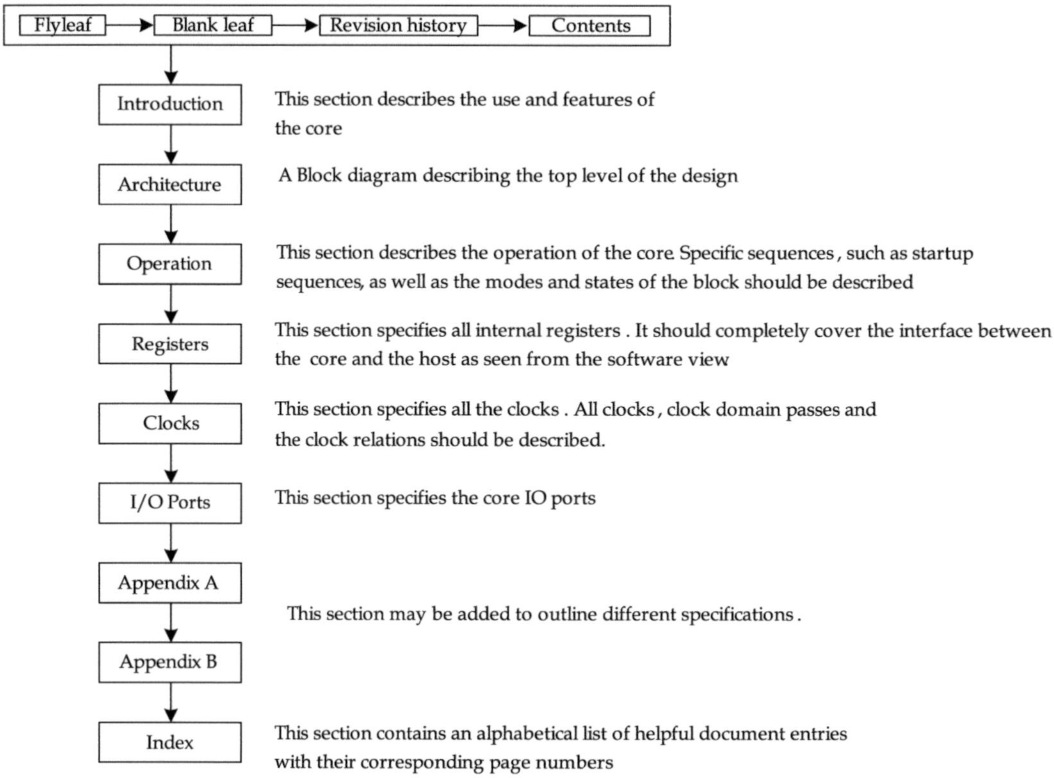

Fig. 34. Steps involved in writing the project documentation

9. Conclusion and perspectives

In conclusion, by adopting the Opencores/Opensource design methodology, we have successfully implemented a SOC Platform which is suited for VOIP applications. The proposed design methodology takes into account all the phases of project development, from specifications to Prototyping board (PCB) and documentation, depending on the designer objective. Up to now, the gateway has been successfully implemented and tested. It remains that Asterisk is not yet embedded into the FPGA based OpenRisc processor. This work constitutes the last step for the whole VOIP platform. Concerning the SOC development platform, it could be extended to other system on chip embedded applications, and the target hardware can be an FPGA or an ASIC circuit. The whole platform can constitutes a basic know how in the field of VOIP and embedded systems.

10. References

Altera, www.altera.com/

ARM, http://www.arm.com

Abid, F. , Izeboudjen, N., Titri, S., Salhi, L., Louiz, F., Lazib, D., "Hardware /Software Development of System on Chip Platform for VoIP Application ", International Conference on Microelectronics (ICM), pp. 62-65, pp 62-65. Marakech (Morocco), December 19-22, 2009

Bennett , J., "Or1ksim User Guide", Embecosm, 2008.

Bennett, J., "The Opencores Openrisc 1000 simulator and toolchain installation guide" Embescom, Novembre, 2008.

Chen, J.H, "High Quality 16 kb/s Speech Coding with a One Way Delay less than 2 ms", Proceedings of the IEEE International Conference on Acoustic. Speech Signal Processing, pp. 453-456,.April, 1990.

Digium www.digium.com

Dhir, A., "Voice- Data- Convergence- Voice over Ip », WP138 (V1.0) www.xilinx.com

Eth, "Ethereal, the world's most popular network protocol analyze", May, 2006, available on line: www.ethereal.com

Gorban, J., "UART IP Core Specification ", Rev. 0.6 August 11, 2002.

IBM, www.ibm.com/chips/techlib/techlib.nsf/products/PowerPC_405_Embedded _Cores/.

ISE , "ISE 7.1 user manual". www.xilinx.com.

ITU-T, Recommendation G.729 " Coding of speech at 8 kbit/s using conjugate structure algebraic code excited linear prediction (CS-ACELP), (March 1996).

ITU-T, Recommendation P.862 "Perceptual evaluation of speech quality (PESQ), an objective method for end-to-end speech quality assessment of narrow-band telephone networks and speech codecs" , February, . 2001.

ITU-T Software Tool Library 2000 user's manual Geneva,

Koroneos, S. stelios., "Asterisk on Embedded systems ", AstriCon 2008 www.astricon.net

Lampret, D., "OpenRISC 1200 IP Core Specification", Rev. 0.7 Sep 6, 2001.

Meggelen, J.V, Smith, J., & Madsen,L., "Asterisk The Future of Telephony". O'Reilly, August 15, 2007.

Micro , www.xilinx.com/ise/embedded/mb_ref_guide.pdf.

Modelsim "Model Sim User manual", www.modelsim.com

Mohor, I., "Ethernet IP core specifications", Rev04 octobre 2002;

Opencores, www.opencores.org

ORCAD, "Orcad capture user guide" , www.cadence.com

Rosenberg, J.,Schulzrinne, H., Camarillo, G., Johnston,A., Peterson, A., Sparks,R., Handley, M., & Schooler,E., " SIP: Session Initiation Protocol. RFC 3261", June 2002. www.rfc-editor.org/rfc/rfc3261.txt

Salami, R., Laflamme, C., Adoul, J.P, kataoka, A., Hayashi, S., Moriya, T., Lamblin, C. , Massaloux, Proust, Kroon, P., Shoham, Y., " Design and description of CS-ACELP: A toll quality 8 kb/s speech coder", IEEE Transaction on Speech and Audio Processing, vol. 6, pp. 116- 130, March, 1998

Titri, S., Izeboudjen, N., Sahli, L., Lazib, D., Louiz, F., "OpenCores Based System on chip Platform for Telecommunication Applications: VOIP". DTIS'07, International Conference on design & Technology of Integrated Systems in Nanoscale Era, pp. 253-256, Rabat (Morocco), Sep. 2-5, 2007.

Usselmann, R., "Memory Controller IP Core ", Rev. 1.7 January 21, 2002.
Whishbone, "WISHBONE System-on-Chip (SoC) Interconnection Architecture for Portable IP Cores". OpenCores, September 7, 2002
Yawn, N. , "Advanced Debug System", 2009 http://www.opencores.org/project,adv_debug_sys

8

Experimental Characterization of VoIP Traffic over IEEE 802.11 Wireless LANs

Paolo Dini, Marc Portolés-Comeras,
Jaume Nin-Guerrero and Josep Mangues-Bafalluy
IP Technologies Area
Centre Tecnològic de Telecomunicacions de Catalunya (CTTC)
Av. C. F. Gauss 7 – 08860 Castelldefels, Barcelona,
Spain

1. Introduction

Voice over Internet Protocol (VoIP) technology has become a potential alternative to and also a supplement of the traditional telephony systems over the Public Switched Telephone Network (PSTN), providing a versatile, flexible and cost-effective solution to speech communications. VoIP allows the transmission of voice signals from one party to another one digitally, i.e., the analog voice signal is coded into small packets of digital data and sent over a network.

The traditional telephone network, PSTN, uses the circuit switching technique, in which the network establishes a dedicated end-to-end connection between two hosts. The resources needed to support the communication between these end systems are reserved for the whole duration of the communication, so as to guarantee a given quality of the communication. The main drawback of circuit switching is its lack of flexibility due to the fact that dedicated circuits are idle during silent periods and thus network resources are wasted during these contemplation periods. Unlike PSTN, VoIP networks use packet switching, which sends digitized voice data packets over the networks using many possible paths. The packets are reassembled at their destination to generate the voice signals. Network resources are not reserved in VoIP networks, i.e. voice packets are sent into the network without reserving any bandwidth. On the one hand this method provides more flexibility to the network but, on the other hand, it suffers from congestions. Voice applications are delay intolerant services, therefore voice quality at the end host is not guaranteed in VoIP networks.

Nowadays, the pervasiveness of WLAN networks together with the spread of VoIP capable wireless devices has motivated an extensive use of VoIP applications over WLAN networks. However, the interaction between these two technologies (VoIP and WLAN) is still not well understood and has received much attention from the research community during recent years. When the VoIP communication has to travel through a WLAN link congestion problems are hardened due to the shared nature of radio medium, the error prone channel and the limited bandwidth of the link, which can cause a further degradation of the voice quality.

This chapter focuses on the transmission of VoIP traffic over IEEE 802.11 WLAN networks and it takes an experimental approach to the topic. The objective of the chapter is double-fold. Firstly it aims at illustrating, from a practical perspective, the challenges that VoIP communications face when transmitted over WLAN networks. Secondly, it has the objective of providing experimental evidence of the requirements and practicality of some of the solutions that have been proposed in recent literature to optimize user experience in these scenarios.
Basically, the chapter illustrates the performance of VoIP technology over single-hop and multi-hop WLAN settings using the EXTREME Testbed® experimentation platform (Portolés-Comeras et al., 2006). Throughout the text we show how there exists a fundamental relation between the quality of VoIP calls and the capacity of WLAN networks. Even more, the experimental results show that this relation is difficult to handle in practice as this relation suffers from a sudden 'breakdown' by which when the number of calls exceeds a certain volume, most of communications sharing the WLAN network are severely degraded.
Beyond these results the chapter provides elements and hints on how to deal with experimentation settings to study VoIP over WLANs, and validates some state-of-art results and hypotheses from a practical perspective.
The structure of the chapter is as follows. First the background on VoIP networks and IEEE 802.11 WLAN is presented. Then, the problem of transmitting VoIP traffic over WLAN is stated in the two typical WLAN topologies: single-hop and multi-hop, also listing the literature on such topics. Section 4 describes the methodology used for analyzing the problem and the experimental framework is presented. After that, the experimental results are reported in Section 5. Finally, conclusions are drawn in Section 6.

2. Background

2.1 Voice over IP networks

Commonly voice over IP (VoIP) networks allows phone to phone, PC to PC and PC to phone communications through an IP backhaul as depicted in Figure 1. PC to PC is a call in which one PC communicates with another PC. In phone to phone an IP phone communicates with an analog phone. PC to phone is a type of communication in which a PC communicates with an analog phone.

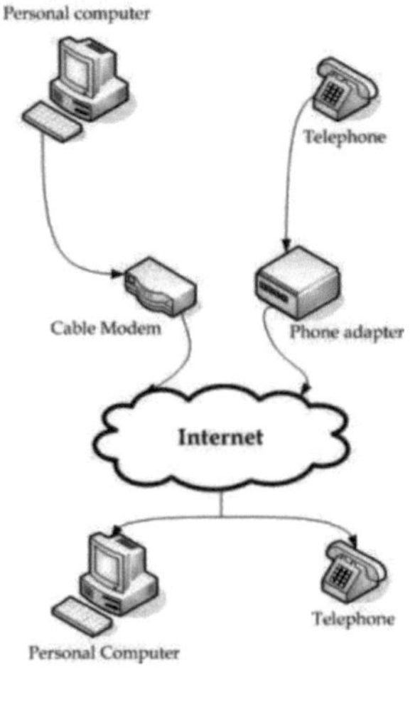

Fig. 1. VoIP network

In the user plane the communication takes place as follows.
At the sender, the voice stream from the voice source is first digitized and compressed by the encoder. Then, several coded speech frames are packetized to form the payload part of a RTP packet. The headers (e.g. IP/UDP/RTP) are added to the payload to compose the packet which is sent to IP networks. The packet may suffer different network impairments (e.g. packet loss, delay and jitter) in IP networks. At the receiver, packet headers are stripped off and speech frames are extracted from the payload by the depacketizer. Playout buffer compensates network jitter at the cost of further delay (buffer delay) and loss (late arrival loss). The de-jittered speech frames are decoded to recover speech with lost frames concealed (e.g. using interpolation) from previous received speech frames. For a better comprehension, Figure 2 reports the different block diagrams involved in a communication in a VoIP system.

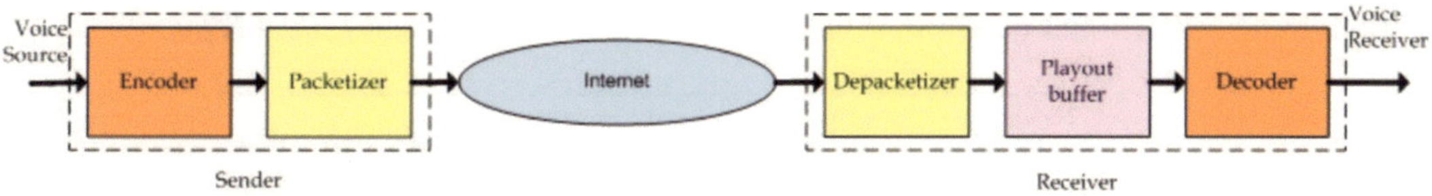

Fig. 2. VoIP System block diagram

As far as the control plane of a VoIP system is concerned, it has to perform the following tasks:
1. Find out the destination (e.g. IP address)
2. Establish the communication with that party and negotiate the parameters needed for the correct use of the session by the involved parties.
3. Potentially send quality reports to the sender to improve the quality of the communication (e.g., using RTCP).

Normally VoIP networks utilize H.323 [H.323] or SIP [RFC-3261] to perform the signaling functions described above.

2.2 Voice quality assessment

One of the most important metrics in VoIP systems is the speech quality experienced by the end users, also referred to as Quality of Experience (QoE) in the following sections.
Voice quality assessment methods can be classified in two main classes: subjective and objective methods.
The most known subjective method is the Mean Opinion Score (MOS). MOS value is obtained as an average opinion of the voice perceived quality based on asking people the grade of the service they received on a five-point scale, i.e. Excellent, Good, Fair, Poor, Bad. This method is internationally accepted and recommended by ITU [P.800]. Nevertheless it suffers from several problems such as highly time consuming, expensiveness, lack of repeatability.
Objective methods can be intrusive or non-intrusive. A typical intrusive method is the Perceptual Evaluation of the Speech Quality Measurement Algorithm (PESQ) based on the P.862 ITU-T standard. It is based on the comparison of a reference and the degraded speech signals to obtain a predicted one way MOS score. Such method is of course accurate, but it is unsuitable for monitoring live traffic because of the need of reference data to generate the reference signal. On the other hand, non-intrusive methods do not need of a reference signal

and seem more appropriate to monitor live traffic. E-Model [G.107] is the most used non-intrusive method. It determines voice quality directly from IP network and terminal parameters.
In our studies we adopted such method to assess perceived voice quality. Next subsection gives an overview of the main characteristics of such method.

2.2.1 E-Model

The European Telecommunications Standards Institute (ETSI) Computation Model (abbreviated in E-Model) has been developed by ETSI in the framework of the ETR 250 and it is used to predict the voice quality non-intrusively for VoIP applications.
The primary output from the E-Model is the "Rating Factor" R, which represents a measure of the perceived quality by the user during a VoIP call. According to ITU-T Recommendation 03/2005, the E-Model defines a region of acceptable quality when R is higher than 70. In Table 1 is reported the relationship between values of R and MOS.

R-value	MOS	User Satisfaction
90	4.34	Very satisfied
80	4.03	Satisfied
70	3.60	Some users dissatisfied
60	3.10	Many users dissatisfied
50	2.58	Nearly all users dissatisfied

Table 1. Relationship between R-factor and MOS values

The value of R is calculated as follows:

$$R = R_0 - I_S - I_d - I_e + A \tag{1}$$

where R_0 represents the basic signal-to-noise ratio, including noise sources such as noise and room noise. I_S is a combination of all impairments which occur simultaneously with the voice signal (e.g. quantization noise, received speech level and sidetone level). I_d represents the impairments that are delayed with respect to speech (e.g. talker/listener echo and absolute delay). I_e represents the effects of special equipments or equipment impairments (e.g. codecs, packet losses and jitter). A is an advantage factor (e.g. it is 0 for wireline and 10 for GSM).
The present chapter, as explained in the introduction, aims at analyzing how well an IEEE 802.11 WLAN can support VoIP service. Therefore our interest is on the impairments due to codec, delay, losses and jitter introduced by the WLAN, for that reason we can consider the simplified formula below to calculate the R-factor.

$$R = 93.2 - I_d - I_e - I_C \tag{2}$$

with

$$I_d = 25\left\{(1 - X^6)^{1/6} - 3(1 + \left[\frac{X}{3}\right]^6)^{1/6} + 2\right\} \tag{3}$$

where $X = \log_2 \frac{delay(ms)}{100\ ms}$

I_c, codec impairment

and

$$I_e = I_C + (95 - I_C) \cdot \frac{P_{Pl}}{P_{Pl} / (R_{Burst} + B_{Pl})} \quad (4)$$

where

- P_{Pl}: packet loss probability
- B_{Pl}: packet loss robustness (codec dependant)
- R_{Burst}: models the burstiness of the losses

by assuming that impairments are mainly due to network conditions.

2.3 Background on WLAN

This section will describe the basic mechanisms of the Distributed Coordination Function (DCF) used in IEEE 802.11 WLAN standard. For a detail description, please refer to [ANSI/IEEE Std, 1999].

DCF uses carrier sense multiple access with collision avoidance (CSMA/CA) as medium access protocol. The CSMA/CA protocol is designed to reduce the collision probability between multiple STAs accessing a medium, at the point where collisions would most likely occur. It also assures equal access priority to all stations competing for the radio resource in a given period of time.

In Figure 3 is illustrated a typical scenario when a transmitter and a receiver communicate using CSMA/CA:

- transmitting station has to sense the medium idle for a certain time, called DIFS, before sending its data ;
- receiving station acknowledges the reception after waiting for a different period of time, called SIFS, if the packet was received correctly (CRC is used to check the correctness of the received frames);
- automatic retransmission of data packets is used in case of transmission errors.

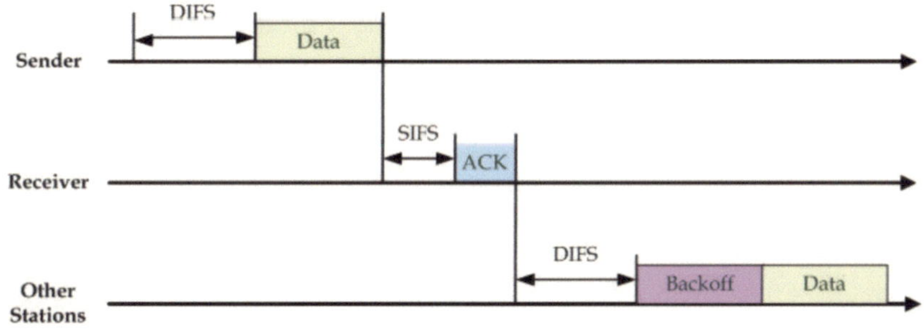

Fig. 3. Sending unicast packets using CSMA/CA

As it can be seen from Figure 3, different inter frame spaces (IFS) are used to provide the priority levels for access to the wireless media. In DCF, two different IFSs are defined; they are listed in the following from the shortest to the longest:

- Short Inter-Frame Space (SIFS), used for an ACK frame;
- DCF Inter-Frame Space (DIFS), used before to transmit data frames and management frames.

The entire process of transmission is as follows.

A STA, desiring to initiate transfer of data, senses the medium to determine the busy/idle state of the medium. As different STAs can sense idle medium, they could simultaneously access to the channel, generating a collision. Therefore, a backoff procedure is implemented in DCF. Before starting a transmission, each node performs a backoff procedure, with the backoff timer uniformly chosen from [0;*CW*] in terms of time slots, where *CW* is the current contention window. If the channel is determined to be idle for a backoff slot, the backoff timer is decreased by one. Otherwise, it is suspended. When the backoff timer reaches zero, the node transmits a data packet. If the receiver successfully receives the packet, it acknowledges the packet by sending an acknowledgment (ACK) after a SIFS. If no acknowledgment is received within a specified period, the packet is considered lost; in this case the transmitter will double the size of *CW*. After attending a DIFS, every station shall generate a random backoff period for an additional deferral time before transmitting and choose a new backoff timer, and start the above process again. When the transmission of a packet fails for a maximum number of times, the packet is dropped.
Figure 4 presents the various step of the previous procedure.

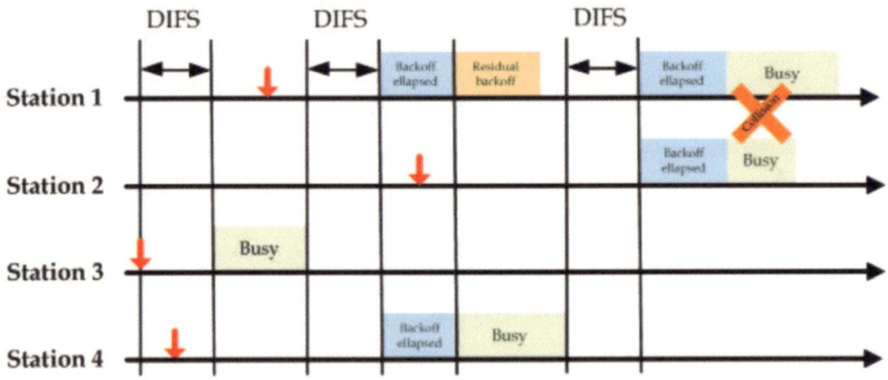

Fig. 4. Backoff procedure using CSMA/CA

According to the IEEE 802.11 standard, the network can be configured into two modes: infrastructure mode or ad hoc mode. In the infrastructure mode, an access point (AP) is needed to participate in the communication between any two nodes, whereas in the ad hoc mode, all nodes can directly communicate with each other without the participation of an AP.

3. VoIP over Wireless LAN

3.1 Introduction

In recent years there has been a growing interest in the use of WLANs based on IEEE 802.11 because of its low cost, simple deployment and free band access. As a matter of fact, nowadays the employ of WLAN in home, in offices and in public sites is a normal practice to provide customers with intranet and Internet access. In particular, WLANs are very popular among enterprises and universities to give workers and students greater flexibility to access the corporate/campus network without being tied to the network by a wire, so that they can access and contribute data far more quickly than before, boosting the productivity of all others who depend on critical information and, hence, increasing the overall agility of the organization.

Meanwhile also Voice over IP is gaining popularity as alternative to the traditional phone line thanks to its lower cost of infrastructure, easier integration of voice and data applications and lower call cost.

It is then easy to understand the increasing interest in studying the way the IEEE 802.11 can support VoIP services.

The main benefits of using VoIP over WLAN are basically three:

- WLAN can offer mobile voice services within a local area such as a campus or organization's facilities. In theory such service is already provided by cell phones, but many facilities experience cell interference or poor interior coverage, making cell phones unusable.
- extend VoIP services such as presence, push-to-talk, localization, conference calling, call transfer, do not disturb, on-line voice mail to WLAN environment
- convergence of data and voice in the same handheld device.

However VoIP applications are real-time services, then impose upper limits on delay and jitter in addition to usual requirements on packet loss and throughput to achieve an adequate quality. Ensuring the quality of service for VoIP in WLANs is a big concern as the performance characteristics of their physical and MAC layers is much worse than their wireline counterparts. In particular, lower peak transmission rate, lossy medium, interference problems, are some drawbacks of the physical layer. Moreover the DCF mechanism used by IEEE 802.11 WLANs, described in the previous section, can cause frame collisions during the communication, which is another issue to take into account in such environment.

The following two sections aim at giving an overview of the state-of-the-art on the VoIP over WLAN in the two typical WLAN topologies, namely Single-hop and Multi-hop topology.

3.2 VoIP over single hop WLAN

3.2.1 Background and state of the art

An extensive literature on 802.11 WLAN performance evaluation exists, though it is essentially based on theoretical studies for the characterization of the DCF in general conditions.

Stochastic Petri Nets are used in (Heindl & German, 2001) to model the behavior of DCF and then performance measures such as effective channel throughput are derived. In [Bianchi, 2000] the author used a Markov chain to model DCF and evaluate throughput and packet loss as a function of the number of wireless stations. This work does not take care of what type of protocol is above the MAC, hence the assumptions on traffic load do not correspond to load generated by VoIP traffic. In particular, the hypothesis of working in saturated condition is not correct for VoIP traffic as demonstrated in (Zhai et al., 2005).

Prior work that pertains to study VoIP over IEEE 802.11 has focused mainly on Point Coordination Function (PCF) as access protocol, for instance in (Crow et al., 1997) and in (Veeraraghavan et. al., 2001).

The first experimental studies at our knowledge on VoIP over WLAN is in (Garg & Kappes, 2003), where a study on the maximum number of VoIP users supported by a single WLAN access point is presented in a real scenario. They analyze basically how many VoIP users can an access point support, varying the codec. No reference to the QoE perceived by users is given.

Another interesting experimental work is in (Elaoud et al., 2005). The authors introduce an evaluation metric to quantify the performance of a voice call that takes into account both packet losses and delay, thus providing a study on WLAN voice capacity with and without background traffic. Differences in performance evaluation due to the different VoIP codecs are not taken into account. No comparison with standard voice perceived quality assessment methods is presented.

In (Narbutt & Davis, 2006) the authors analyze experimentally the relationship between voice call quality (using the E-Model) and wireless resource usage by introducing three WLAN bandwidth components, namely load bandwidth, access bandwidth and free bandwidth. However an analysis on the effects of IEEE 802.11 PHY and MAC layer over VoIP quality is missed.

In (Zhai et al., 2006) authors claim that the optimal working point for a WLAN supporting VoIP traffic is when collision probability (p) is equal to 0.1. In that point throughput is maximum and packet delay and jitter are small enough to support voice quality requirements. They also introduce a metric called Channel Busyness Ratio (Rb) for measuring radio resource usage. They claim that in their working region ($p<0.1$), Rb is proportional to the throughput, so as concluding that channel busyness ratio is a suitable metric also to assess VoIP quality. No reference to standard voice quality assessment methods is provided in the paper as well as no measurement of packet loss is presented.

3.3 VoIP over Multi Hop WLAN

3.3.1 Background and state of the art

Studies around the use of VoIP in multi-hop WLAN scenarios aroused together with the popularity of Wireless Mesh Networks (WMNs). Even more, since the very beginning these studies rapidly became highly experimental (e.g. see Armenia, 2005). Among those seminal studies, the work by the authors of (Niculescu, 2006) constitutes an important reference for research studies that followed. The authors illustrate some of the main challenges associated with the transmission of VoIP over WMNs and analyze the performance of some practical solutions to cope with these challenges. Examples of this are the aggregation of flows, header compression, multi-interface configuration studies, and label-based forwarding of packets.

Beyond these initial efforts the literature has focused on some of the challenges that were identified since the beginning.

The study of the capacity of wireless networks received much attention in the beginnings of the decade after the seminal work by Gupta and Kumar (Gupta, 2000). This trend extended to studies related to WMNs and ultimately to studies of VoIP applications over wireless multihop networks. The findings show how the number of hops that flows traverse as well as the number of active nodes in a network affect the overall capacity of the system and, ultimately, the throughput of the applications that run over it. This has fostered the development of practical solutions that predict the utilization that VoIP calls represent to the capacity of a multihop network (see Kashyap, 2007) and used to implement effective call admission control mechanisms such as in (Wei,2006) and (Kashyap, 2007).

A method commonly used in order to make a more effective use of the bandwidth is that of packet aggregation (Niculescu, 2006). VoIP flows generally use constant sized packets to transmit information that make an inefficient use of the bandwidth resources (due to transmission overheads). Aggregation strategies try to mitigate these negative effects aggregating packets from different flows that share common paths of the wireless network. Examples of this are (Kim,2006) (Zhuang, 2006) and (Kassler, 2007).

Finally, also related to optimizing the utilization of bandwidth resources, some authors have worked in header compression solutions together with the aggregation strategy. Examples of this are (Niculescu, 2006) and (Nascimiento, 2008)

Besides optimizing the utilization of bandwidth resources other studies have also paid attention to analyzing which is the impact of the chosen routing strategy on the quality of VoIP calls (Ksentini, 2008) and have designed access strategies (MAC) that are VoIP aware and can help improve the quality of the calls (Yackoski, 2010).

4. Methodology

The work carried out in the framework of this chapter is based on the analysis of experimental tests performed within the laboratory of the IP Technologies area of the CTTC. This section aims at furnishing basic input to understand the operation of the test platform used for characterizing VoIP over WLAN.

The testbed is called EXTREME, which stands for EXperimental Testbed for Research Enabling Mobility Enhancements (EXTREME Testbed®). However, its flexibility has allowed broadening its scope from mobility to any networking scenario that could be of interest to both industrial and research communities. Particular emphasis has been put on those scenarios having a remarkable wireless component, including technologies such as UMTS/HSPA, and 802.11 WLAN.

The main architectural blocks of EXTREME are depicted in Figure 5 as well as its internal and external connections. The core of the EXTREME Testbed® lies on a Central Server. It is the interface between the experimenter/user and the Testbed, hiding its complexity and offering high-level experimentation services to the user. A serie of reconfigurable network nodes can be customized and used as network nodes for experimentation purposes (e.g. traffic emulation, routing, switching, acting as access points, wireless clients, capturing packets...). Each of these machines is connected to both a control network and a data

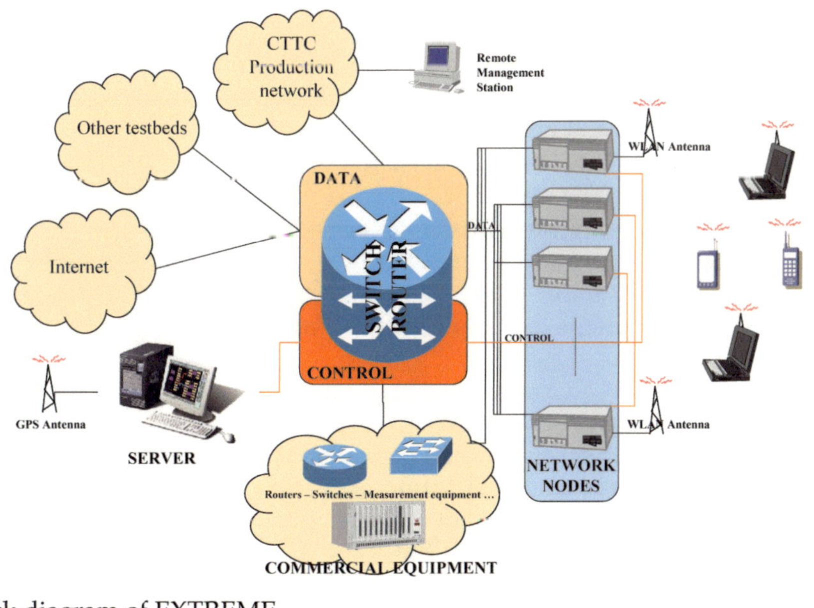

Fig. 5. Block diagram of EXTREME

network. Through the control network they interact with the central server for set up, configuration and data collection purposes (e.g. status, experiment results, etc.). The data network is used during experimentation to support communications. The interconnection pattern of nodes for each experiment is configured in the backbone switch-router.
Commercial equipment (traffic generators, networks emulators, and measurement equipment) is integrated in the testbed. External connectivity is offered through the CTTC production network and through connections to external production and research networks.
Regarding operating system (OS) and application software, for control and core development purposes mainly open source software is used, but any type of software can be integrated in the platform.
In the context of networking experimentation, an experimenter in the EXTREME Testbed® follows the following phases:

- Experiment design. The researcher defines the experiment at a high-level using some description files.
- Autoconfiguration software maps this high-level description into a physical topology.
- Experiment load and configuration. The autoconfiguration tools are in charge of controlling the node booting process, disk image loading, and execution of configuration files into the nodes.
- Execution of the experiment. The experiment execution control software is in charge of executing, at the chosen instant, the applications, in selected nodes, to follow the intended experimentation.
- Data collection for the EXTREME Measurement Architecture (EMMA) analysis, which can also be programmed using the execution control software.

The EXTREME Measurement Architecture (EMMA) provides a framework for the researcher to monitor the system under test while freeing him/her from the low-level details of the configuration of the traffic generation and capture tools.
A control server is at the core of EMMA, carrying out a series of functions:

- Interaction with the user. It provides a single point of interaction between the user and EMMA.
- Configuration of all transmit, receive, and monitoring (wired and wireless) nodes, i.e. the user is able to configure sources and destinations, flow characteristics, parameters to measure for both active and passive measurements.
- Scheduling of measurement events by the user.
- Gathering of traces and/or computations carried out at monitoring and/or end-nodes.
- Presentation of graphical results based on information gathered.
- Rapid evaluation and integration of new hardware and software monitoring tools.

EMMA allows multiple instances to be created, each monitoring a different experiment when more than one scenario/experiment are running concurrently in the reconfigurable testbed.
Active measurements, based on injecting synthetic traffic flows, serve to characterize paths segments, and potentially end-to-end paths.
Passive measurements, based on analyzing a copy of the traffic at a given point or observing certain variables without affecting real traffic, serve to characterize the traffic or other operational parameters at a particular point in the network.
The experimenter can specify how many flows are generated, source and destination of these flows, their characteristics, and where the monitoring machines are placed in the network, capturing and/or analyzing these flows.

5. Experimental results

5.1 VoIP over single hop WLAN

5.1.1 Introduction

The following section aims at explaining by showing numerical results achieved through experimental tests, how well an IEEE 802.11 WLAN in infrastructure mode (i.e. single hop) can support VoIP services. The analysis studies the effects of network congestion due to a high number of transmitting nodes and of wireless channel errors on the voice quality perceived by the user.

In the infrastructure mode, all nodes send and receive their traffic through an Access Point (AP). In section 2.3, IEEE 802.11 access protocol has been introduced. It is important to highlight here that the AP has no preferential access to the medium with respect to the other nodes. Taking this into account, as the number of nodes grows, different events which can damage the user QoE occur in the network:

- the number of contending stations rise, then causing increase in packet collision probability and consequently in packet error probability and packet delay because of the back-off procedure and packet retransmissions.
- the high number of packets to be delivered by the AP, i.e. downlink packets, suffer higher delay than in the uplink as well as possible losses due to AP transmission buffer overflow. For that reason, downlink is considered the bottleneck in VoIP over WLAN systems.

Moreover in a real scenario, the error prone nature of wireless channel (due to path loss, multipath and fading) can increase the packet error probability; also several WLANs can coexist in the same area, interfering each other and worsening the general network performance.

As introduced in section 2.2, several network metrics have a combined impact in the voice quality perceived by the users. In particular, the weight of packet delay, packet losses and codec impairment on the user QoE (modeled through the E-Model) is analyzed in the following subsections.

5.1.2 Voice quality performance on congested networks

This subsection intends to experimentally study the effect of network congestion due to a high number of nodes on the voice quality experienced by the users of such network. EXTREME testbed, detailed in section 4, has been configured for such experiments. The network under test has been built with ten nodes running Fedora 10 Linux OS with 2.6.17.11 kernel version. Each node is equipped with two Atheros based WLAN cards using MadWifi driver. Test traffic is generated using MGEN software [MGEN] and the synchronization of all the machines is achieved with high frequency NTP updates through the control network. This mechanism provides accuracies up to 200 μs in average and 400 μs as maximum value. One node acts as an AP and the other nine can act as a maximum of eighteen VoIP users, one per card. For each sender–receiver pair, packets are captured in both sides, so the end to end delay can be calculated and lost packets detected.

Table 2 resumes the traffic generated by each considered codec, namely G711, G723.1 and G729. A voice call is composed of one constant bit rate uplink flow and one constant bit rate downlink flow.

Codec	Bitrate (kbps)	Packet inter-arrival time (msec)	RTP Packet size (bytes)
G711	64	20	160
G723.1	6.3	30	24
G729	8	20	20

Table 2. Characteristics of the traffic generated by the voice codecs

The three codecs has been tested with the built network configured to work at 1Mbps and 2Mbps physical rate. Basically, for any given codec-data rate pair, tests with incremental number of voice users have been performed until reaching the voice capacity threshold for that pair. We refer to voice capacity as the maximum number of voice users the WLAN can support with R-factor higher than 70.

Results are shown in form of piled bar diagrams. The darkest bar represents the average R-factor experienced by all the users in downlink, which is considered the bottleneck of the system, as stated in the above. As mentioned in section 2.2.1, the highest this value can get is 93.2. Several impairments can produce the experienced R-factor to be lower than the maximum value, namely delay, codec and packet loss impairments. Codec impairment models the speech degradation due to compression in the voice codification and is represented by a white bar. Delay and packet loss effects are modelled in their respective impairments, represented in dark colour (delay) and light colour (packet loss). The impairments and R-factors are only plotted when they are higher than 0.

Figure 6, Figure 7 and Figure 8 show respectively the results obtained for the G711, G723.1 and G729 codec. In all the cases studied, the R-factor has a sudden breakdown in a given point: the input of only one user more generates an abrupt falling in the QoE of all the active users, regardless of the codec in use. This behaviour is typical in systems where no mechanism to guarantee quality of service (e.g., packet scheduler, congestion control) is implemented, as in the IEEE 802.11 standard. Another important result that can be noticed in the three figures is that the impairment due to packet losses is higher than the impairment due to packet delay at the breakdown, with the exception of the scenario of G711 codec at 1 Mbps. Such scenario can be considered a border line situation due to its very low number of nodes in the network that implies a very low number of contending stations and consequently a very low value of collision probability and packet error probability. Therefore, in general, it can be claimed that packet error delivery due to collisions and AP buffer overflow have a great impact on the performance of the network. Methods to control packet losses have to be introduced to allow WLAN to guarantee voice user QoE also in congested situations.

Finally, from the three figures, different values of the R-factor can be observed in a non-congested situation. These values strongly depend on the codec impairment. G723.1 has the highest and G711 the lowest in our set up.

5.1.3 Field trials

In this section the effect of the wireless channel errors is experimentally analyzed. Wireless channel can introduce errors in the network for two reasons basically:

- path loss, multipath and fading
- interference from other networks transmitting at the same carrier and residing in the neighbourhood

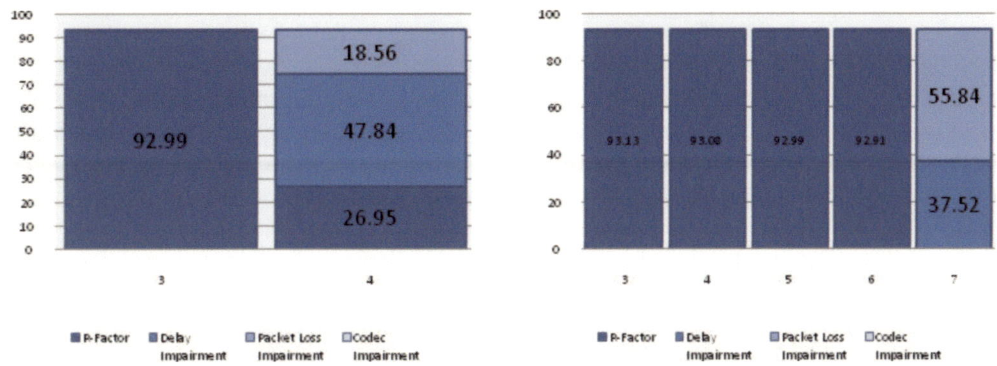

Fig. 6. R-Factor vs Number of users at 1 Mbps (left) and 2 Mbps (right) for G711 codec

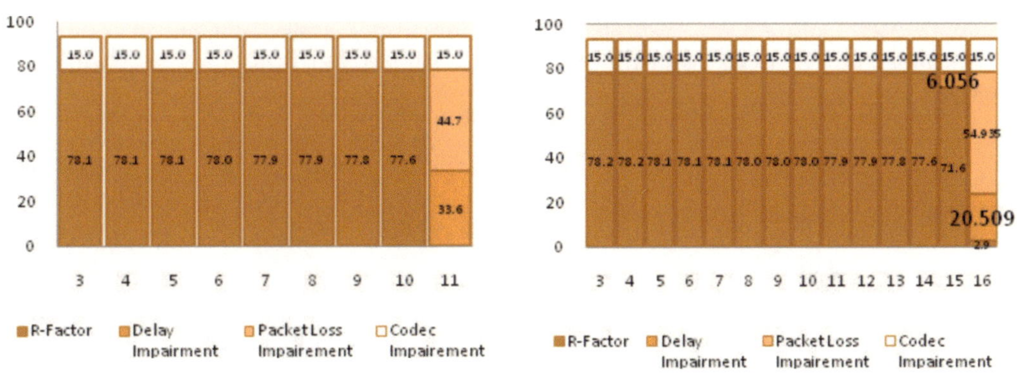

Fig. 7. R-Factor vs Number of users at 1 Mbps (left) and 2 Mbps (right) for G723.1 codec

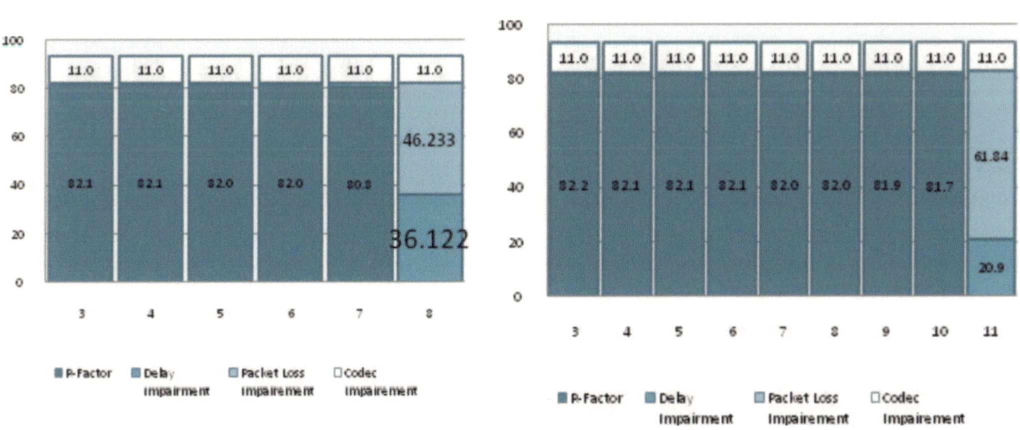

Fig. 8. R-Factor vs Number of users at 1 Mbps (left) and 2 Mbps (right) for G729 codec

For this scope the test platform has been modified. As a matter of fact, the results presented in section 5.1.1 have been measured in an in-lab controlled environment and using RF cables. Those cables isolate the system under test from external interferences and provide an almost ideal radio channel. Then, we decide to remove those cables and expose the test platform to the several production WLANs running in our campus, both in adjacent and overlapped channels and to a real radio channel. Only G711 codec has been tested, since in these trials we were not interested in studying the difference among different voice codecs. The tests have been run during several mornings, with no control on the interfering networks.

Results of the field trials are shown in Figure 9. Performance is reduced in general. Especially in 2Mbps scenario voice capacity is reached with three voice users less than in the case described in the previous subsection. Also, the R-factor breakdown is deeper than in the previous case: both delay and losses impairment increase in these trials due to wireless channel errors that produce retransmission and back-off procedure with higher frequency. It is important to highlight that even in the scenario considered in this subsection, loss impairment is the one with more weight on the quality experienced by the user. This result confirms the necessity to introduce methods to control network congestion in WLANs to guarantee user QoE. As an example we mention Call Admission Control, which is a successful scheme that has been used in cellular network to provide high quality voice services.

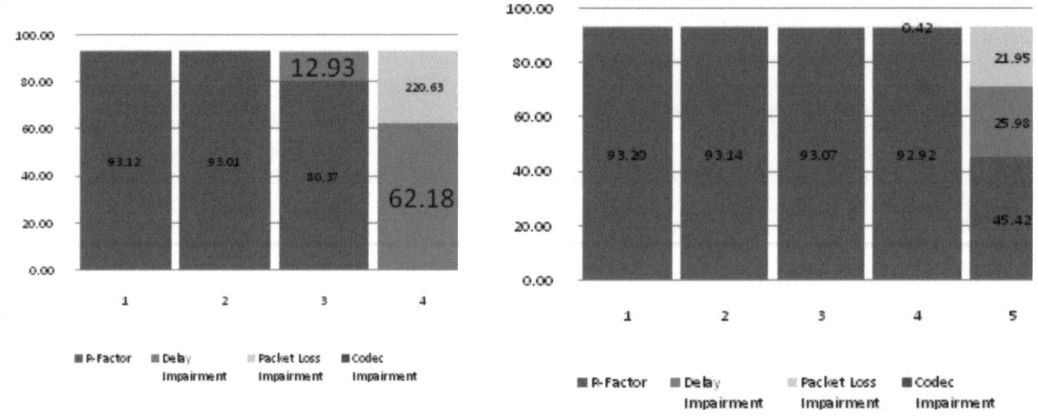

Fig. 9. R-Factor vs Number of users at 1 Mbps (left) and 2 Mbps (right) for G711 codec

5.2 VoIP over multi-hop WLAN

5.2.1 Scenario considered

As mentioned before, studies in wireless multihop networks highly depend on the scenario considered. This section proposes a target scenario for the study. The results obtained may be extended to several other scenarios but generalization is beyond the purpose of this paper.

Figure 10 presents the targeted scenario. A number of VoIP terminals collaborate in order to route individual VoIP calls between each one of the rest of terminals and peers residing in an external network. A wireless gateway is the one interconnecting the rest of the network and the terminals holding VoIP calls.

There are a number of considerations to be taken into account to completely define the scenario. Firstly, all VoIP communications are established between a wireless terminal and a node that resides somewhere in the backbone side of the network in the figure. Secondly, all terminals support establishing a single VoIP communication but are able to forward VoIP calls from other terminals. This can be thought as the communications infrastructure inside an office, where, in order to reduce costs, a single wireless gateway is installed and its coverage is extended through collaborative relaying. Third, the mobility of terminals is reduced. In general, users holding each one of the terminals remain in the same position for a reasonably long time. However, they might occasionally move, which leads to triggering a route re-discovery process. Fourth, VoIP terminals use the IEEE 802.11 WLAN protocol to form the multi-hop network. Finally, the mean duration of a call is considered to be of 2.6 minutes, as reported in (Lam, 1997).

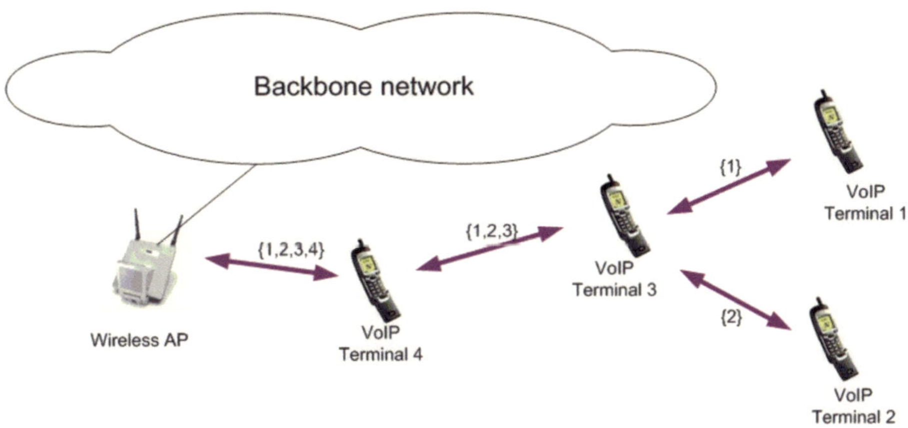

Fig. 10. Scenario: call relaying

The following sections present a study of the relation between VoIP quality and this multihop scenario. First, the section introduces the experimentation setup, then experimental data is used to show the relation between VoIP quality and number of hops and users. Finally, the section analyses the impact of state-of-art aggregation strategies on the quality of VoIP calls and the inter-relation between the disconnection time caused by route-rediscoveries and quality degradation from an end-user perspective.

5.2.2 Experimentation setup

All experiments have been carried out within the EXTREME framework described in section 4. All computers involved in this scenario are Pentium IV PCs with 512MB of RAM memory. They all run Linux operating system with Kernel 2.4.26.

Figure 11 shows the experimental setup used to obtain the results described in this section. Several nodes of the EXTREME cluster are each equipped with a PCI based wireless card carrying the popular Prism chipset (specifically, Z-COM ZDC XI-626 WLAN cards). All wireless cards are interconnected using coaxial wiring and propagation losses are emulated using RF attenuators, as depicted in the figure. This serves a double purpose. Firstly, it isolates the experimentation environment from external interferences. Secondly, it allows us to build a highly controlled environment where transmission range and carrier sense range can be adjusted in accordance to our needs for each one of the stations. Specifically, we adjust attenuations so that each one of the stations can only transmit to its neighboring ones but can 'sense' those stations that are two hops away.

When required wireless terminals start UDP traffic flows emulating VoIP traffic and with destination the VoIP sink in the figure. At the same time the VoIP sink starts an equal flow in the reverse direction completing the bidirectional VoIP communication. VoIP flows are emulated using the MGEN tool (MGEN). The reason to choose this application is double fold. On one side the traffic source can activate an option called "precise on" that efficiently controls real-time generation of packets. On the other side the traffic sink is able to store received packets in a format that allows convenient packet loss count and latency computation afterwards.

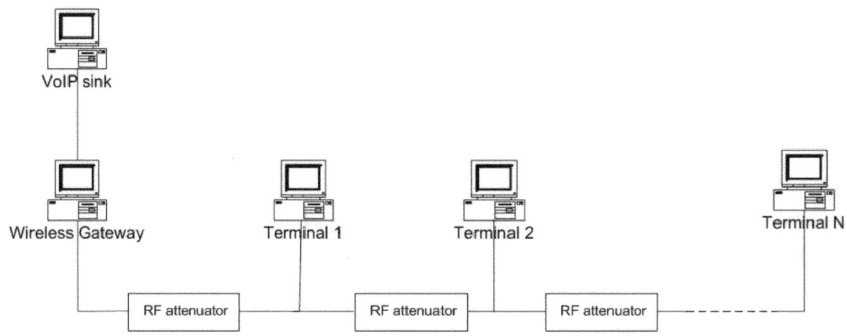

Fig. 11. Experimental Setup

5.2.3 VoIP capacity constraints due to number of hops and users

Since the seminal work by Gupta and Kumar (Gupta, 2000), the research community has put large efforts into optimizing the use of resources in wireless networks in order to optimize their utilization. The capacity of wireless networks highly depends on factors such as the density of wireless nodes and the distance between communicating nodes (e.g. the number of hops that a flow may traverse). Even more, when working with practical systems, frequency reuse distances as well as the applications that are being used play a very important role in order to make an efficient use of network resources.

This section illustrates, experimentally, the inter-dependence between the capacity of a wireless multihop network and various configuration options of WLAN devices in the presence of VoIP applications. The results give some insights into the effects of configuration options (such as carrier sense range, VoIP codec chosen, WLAN hardware used, number of active users, etc.) to the quality of VoIP calls supported.

Impact of the number of hops on a single-flow VoIP quality

Here we analyze the impact of the number of hops traversed on the quality of a VoIP call. Figure 12 shows the R-factor obtained when computing the E-model at the VoIP sink when the terminal it communicates with is located from 1 to 7 hops away. Note that, while it is a bidirectional communication, we do not print the curve obtained at the wireless terminal, as it is practically the same as the one obtained at the VoIP sink node. Note also, that all nodes are configured to transmit at 2Mbps physical rate.

This figure differs from the results reported in (Ganguly, 2006) as here a single VoIP flow can be sent over a larger number of hops. The main reason for this lies in the following observation. With the interference model adopted here (carrier sense range only reaches two hop distance) we assure that, at any time, any node only contends for channel access with at most four other terminals (those within carrier sense range), so its available channel

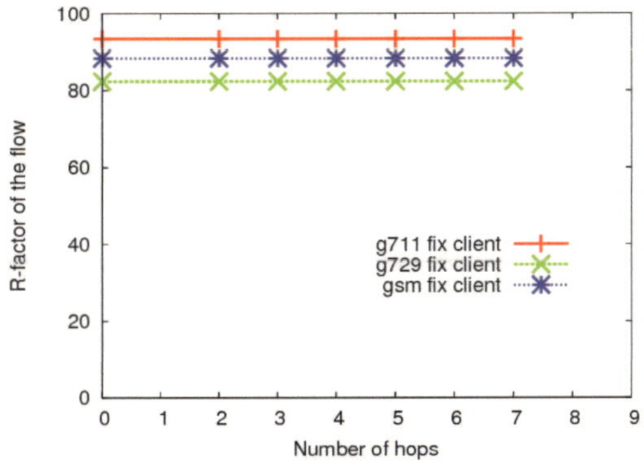

Fig. 12. R-factor vs number of hops traversed by a single flow as observed at the VoIP sink node

resources (bandwidth) will, at most, be divided by four (Jangeun, 2003). The resulting per node throughput capacity is constant and sufficient to support a VoIP call, no matter the number of hops packets have to traverse.

As a result, one can say that a conscious interference-aware deployment of a wireless multihop network can help, in the absence of other background traffic, increasing the maximum number of hops that a VoIP flow can traverse without suffering any quality degradation.

Impact of the number of hops on multi-flow VoIP quality

In this case we study the quality of voice conversations when each one of the terminals present in the network starts a VoIP call with the VoIP sink node. Going back to section 5.2.1, each one of the terminals communicates with the VoIP sink node via the neighboring node closest to the wireless gateway, which relays all VoIP messages in both directions. The idea is to study the maximum number of terminals supported in such a scenario. Note that this is a chain topology, so that there is only one route possible from each one of the terminals and the VoIP sink node.

Figure 13a and figure 13b, plot the quality of the VoIP call between the last terminal and the VoIP sink, at the VoIP sink node(a) and the wireless terminal(b) respectively. They plot the

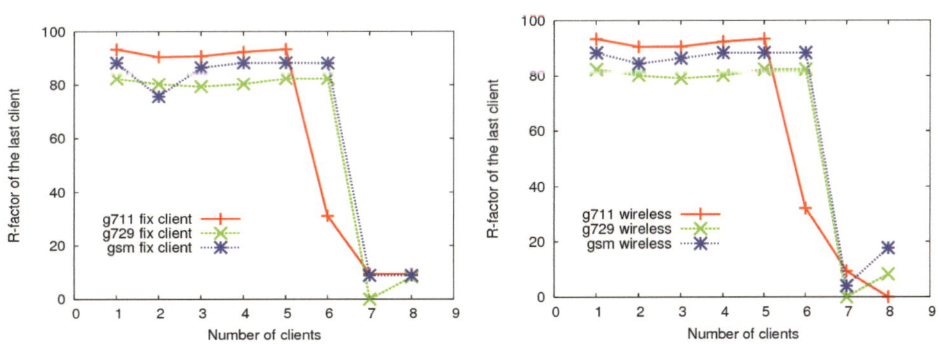

(a) (b)

Fig. 13. R-factor of the last terminal call, as observed (a) at the VoIP sink and (b) at the wireless terminal for a different amount of active terminals

voice quality versus the total number of terminals (clients) maintaining a VoIP conversation with the VoIP sink node. Note that the number of terminals is equivalent to the number of hops traversed by the VoIP flows going to (and from) the last wireless terminal.
The figures show how, when using the G.711 codec, the system can only sustain up to 5 VoIP calls in the scenario described with an acceptable quality (R>70). This raises when using G.729 or GSM codecs, as the system can sustain up to 6 calls.
Two observations can be raised from the figures. Firstly, the breakdown previously reported in (Falconio, 2006) is shown experimentally. When the network saturates, the R-factor suffers a sudden breakdown preventing any communication between the last node and the VoIP sink. Secondly, when using different voice codecs, a different number of hops is reached. This suggests that a voice codec adaptation might be an efficient strategy to support a higher number of voice calls in saturated wireless multihop environments.
It is worth mentioning here, that not only communications with the last terminal in the chain but practically all the rest of the VoIP communications fall into unacceptable voice quality situation when the network enters saturation (i.e. when the last terminal starts VoIP transmission). This change is also abrupt, in a breakdown manner, which challenges the design of admission control mechanisms.

A side observation: Impact of the hardware used

Figure 14 compares the performance of two different card models when working in the multi-hop scenario. The figure shows how a multi-hop network built using Atheros based cards can support a lower number of nodes than when built using Prism cards. Such results can be explained using the results in (Portoles-Comeras, 2007), where it was shown that Atheros cards when detecting the absence of stations competing for the medium, does not perform backoff with the objective of increasing the throughput. However, in this case such a mechanism leads to having a more unbalanced multi-hop network that can sustain a lower number of VoIP calls.

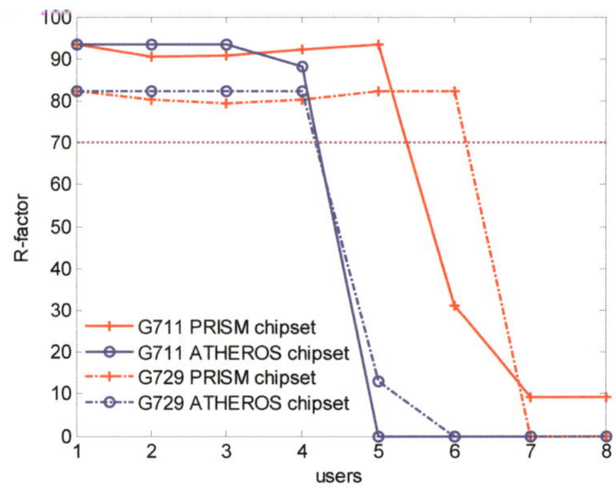

Fig. 14. Comparison of the number of VoIP calls supported in a multi-hop WLAN scenario when using the g711 and g729 codec

5.2.4 Benefits of aggregation: an illustrative example

In order to increase the number of VoIP calls supported in a mesh networking deployment, the authors in (Niculescu, 2006) propose using an aggregation strategy to be applied at the networking stack of each one of the wireless mesh nodes. While this strategy presents promising results, some considerations should be taken, regarding its application in our targeted scenario. Firstly, this solution implies modifying the networking stack of all the terminals to be used in order to include the proposed algorithm. This modification must be done at the OS level which increases complexity of the task. Secondly, considering that short buffering capacity is expected in the relaying terminals, no much forwarding opportunities might arise for packet aggregation.

Here we propose, as an alternative, doing the aggregation at the VoIP application itself. When the quality of the call being maintained is detected to have poor quality (e.g. through RTCP notification and run-time R-factor computation) the application can alternatively choose to aggregate various voice packets into one, prior to the send process. This process reduces the amount of resources required to keep the communication. The number of packets to be sent is reduced and this leads to reducing the amount of overhead to send them. This strategy has, however, an impact on the end-to-end delay of packets. In order to conduct aggregation some packets are delayed in purpose. However, as explained above, the end-to-end delay is not, generally, an issue in the targeted scenario, so there exists a margin of tolerance.

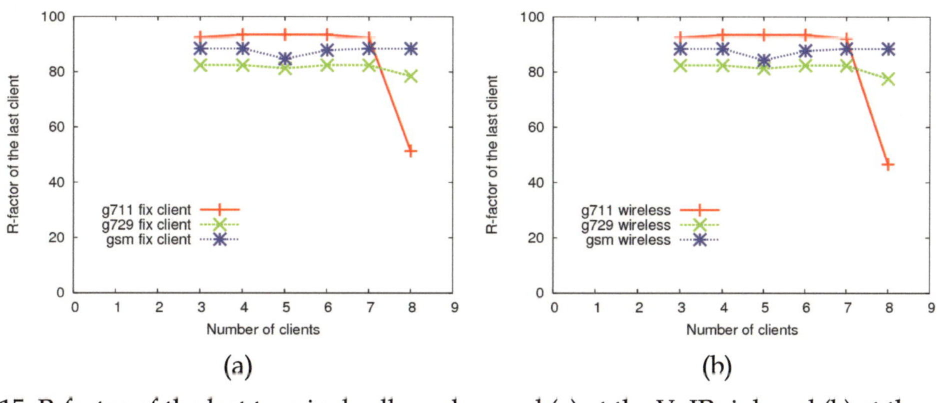

Fig. 15. R-factor of the last terminal call, as observed (a) at the VoIP sink and (b) at the wireless terminal for a different amount of active terminals

Figure 15a and Figure 15b show similar plots as those in figure 13. In this case, however, stations are applying the aggregation strategy proposed. Each one of the terminals aggregates at the application layer two VoIP packets into one and sends them together to the next hop towards the VoIP sink node. The extra delay suffered by some packets due to the aggregation process is accounted for in the computation of the R-factor value. However one might notice that as the end-to-end delay is still low (<150ms) the R-factor value does not reflect any change. The figures show, however, how the aggregation effectively serves the purpose of supporting a higher number of active VoIP terminals in the network chain. These results suggest the possibility of including aggregation strategies at the application layer instead of the lower layers, as this extends the maximum number of terminals supported in our target scenario.

5.2.5 The impact of route-rediscovery latency on voice quality

The bursty loss resulting from the transient disconnection suffered by the VoIP terminal during a route re-discovery process, and the regency of the user after re-establishing regular communications, are factors to be considered in order to analyze the appropriateness of a route re-discovery process.

Figure 16 plots the R-factor value perceived by a VoIP versus the time elapsed since the route discovery disconnection finished[1]. This is plotted for various disconnection times, ranging from 200ms (typical in infrastructure based WLAN networks) and 5 seconds (a value considered well beyond acceptance for real time communications). Plotted curves show that when the disconnection time is below one second the user does not perceive unacceptable quality degradation. Even when the disconnection takes around 2 seconds the user 'forgets' about the disturbance at about 15 seconds after the VoIP communication is re-established. Note, however that this values do not account for mean end-to-end packet losses and delays that should be included for completeness in the curve.

Observing the curve one can notice that a long disconnection is preferable to several shorter frequent ones, as the user may rapidly forget about a single disconnection but would not tolerate frequent shorter ones. Once a protocol and route rediscovery have been designed, curves in this plot may serve to evaluate the possibility to support quality VoIP calls.

For completeness, figure 17 plots similar curves for the G.729 codec case. When using this codec the user is less tolerant to disconnection times and a maximum of 1 second occasional disconnections is tolerated after which it takes around 15 seconds for the user to 'forget' about the annoyance. These plots suggest again the use of codec adaptation strategies in order to adapt the communication to the network conditions. While G.729 might be more attractive in order to support a higher number of calls in a network, it is less recommended when the route re-discovery process incurs high latency.

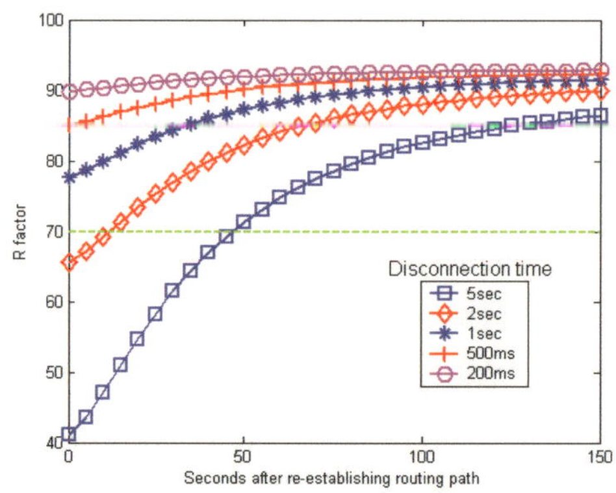

Fig. 16. Impact of route rediscovery disconnections on the quality of VoIP calls when using the G.711 codec

[1] Note that in order to introduce the time component in the calculation of the R-factor in figures 16 and 17, we have used the number of samples correctly received depending on the time elapsed since the route-rediscovery process. The E-model Standard definition does not include this way of using it but, currently, there does not exist any suitable subjective VoIP metric that includes time as an input parameter.

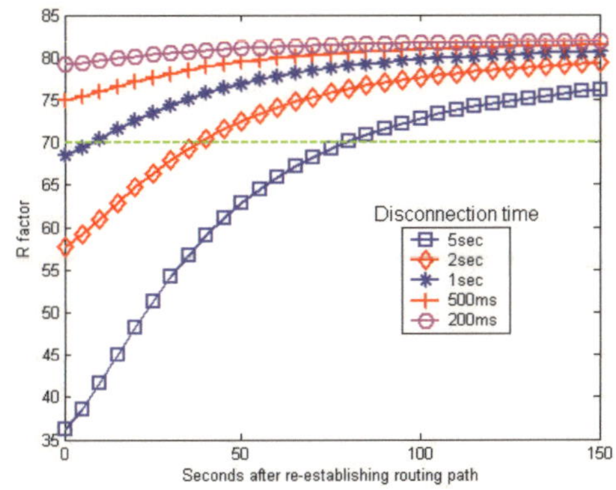

Fig. 17. Impact of route rediscovery disconnections on the quality of VoIP calls when using the G.729 codec

6. Conclusions

The main aim of this chapter has been to study the problem of the transmission of VoIP traffic over the IEEE 802.11 WLANs. The approach of the chapter has been practical and experimental: the challenge that VoIP communication faces when transmitted over WLAN networks has been pointed out by providing experimental evidence of the requirements and practicality of some of the solutions that have been proposed in the literature to optimize user experience in such environment.

Single-hop and multi-hop WLAN topologies have been experimentally studied using the EXTREME Testbed®. The objective of the experiments has been to show the relation between the quality of the voice calls and the capacity of the WLAN in terms of VoIP users supported with a acceptable quality (R>70).

In the single-hop scenario the effect of congestions and of channel errors on voice quality has been analyzed. The tests showed the decisive impact of packet losses due to collisions and to errors introduced by the wireless medium on the quality experienced by the user, which has been always higher than the impairment due to delay, regardless the codec used for the communication. This result supports the necessity of the introduction of methods to control congestions in WLANs. Recently, the "802.11e" standard has been introduced by IEEE to manage QoS in WLANs. Anyway, the new proposed access protocol is more oriented to the assignment of different priority to different types of traffic based on the service requirements than to the introduction of a congestion control mechanism. The definition of Call Admission Control schemes, as in cellular networks, is a valid alternative to guarantee VoIP quality in WLANs.

The results, gathered using the multi-hop set up, reveal that beyond the overhead that IEEE 802.11 WLAN protocol introduces, the number of users, the number of hops to traverse and also the specific deployment strategy (taking into account the carrier sense range) constitute determinant factors affecting the capacity of the network in terms of VoIP users supported.

The experimental results also show how a deployment strategy has to take into account the specific hardware used to support wireless communications, as this decision may also have effects on the VoIP quality perceived by end-users.

Using the multi-hop scenario, the chapter also shows how the aggregation of VoIP packets is a suitable strategy to reduce the impact of IEEE 802.11 overhead on the global network capacity as it can effectively increase the number of VoIP calls supported without penalizing the VoIP quality perceived by end users.

Finally, the multi-hop analysis presented introduces a methodology to determine the impact on VoIP quality of the route re-discovery process usually associated to wireless multi-hop deployments. Depending on the specific multi-hop scenario this process will occur with higher or lower frequency. The methodology introduced allows tuning any engineering as it provides some bounds on the maximum time route-rediscoveries can take.

7. Acknowledgement

This work has been partially funded by the Catalan Regional Government under grant 2009SGR-940.

8. References

M. Portolés, M. Requena, J. Mangues, M. Cardenete, *EXTREME: Combining the ease of management of multi-user experimental facilities and the flexibility of proof of concept testbeds*, in Proc. of IEEE TRIDENTCOM, 2006

H.323 ITU-T Recommendation *Packet-based multimedia communications systems* available at http://www.itu.int/rec/T-REC-H.323-200912-I/en

RFC-3261 *SIP: Session Initiation Protocol* available at http://www.ietf.org/rfc/rfc3261.txt

P.800 ITU-T Recommendation *Methods for subjective determination of transmission quality* available at http://www.itu.int/rec/T-REC-P.800-199608-I/en

G.107 ITU-T Recommendation *The E-model: a computational model for use in transmission planning* available at http://www.itu.int/rec/T-REC-G.107-200904-P/en

ANSI/IEEE Std 802.11-1999 *Wireless LAN Medium Access Control (MAC) and Physical Layer (PHY) Specifications*, 1999.

L. Kleinrock and F. A. Tobagi, *Packet switching in radio channels: Part 2 the hidden node problem in carrier sense multiple access modes and the busy tone solution*, IEEE Transactions on Communications, vol. COM 23, no. 12, pp. 1417 - 1433, 1975.

G. Bianchi, *Performance Analysis of the IEEE 802.11 Distributed Coordination Function,* IEEE J-SAC, Vol 18 No 3, Mar. 2000.

A. Heindl and R. German. *Performance modeling of IEEE 802.11 wireless LANs with stochastic Petri nets.* Performance Evaluation, 44 (2001), 139-164.

H. Zhai, X. Chen, Y. Fang, *How Well Can the IEEE 802.11 Wireless LAN Support Quality of Service?*, IEEE Trans. On Wireless Comm., vol.4, n.6, November 2005.

P. Crow, I. Widjaja, J. G. Kim and P. Sakai, *Investigation of the IEEE 802.11 medium access control (MAC) sublayer functions*, In Proceedings of INFOCOM'97, volume 34, pages 126-133, April 1997.

M. Veeraraghavan, N. Cocker and T. Moors *Support of voice services in IEEE 802.11 wireless LANs*, In Proceedings of INFOCOM'01, 2001.

S. Garg, M. Kappes, *Can I Add a VoIP Call?*, Proc. ICC 2003, Seattle, USA, May 2003.

M. Elaoud, D. Famolari, A. Ghosh, *Experimental VoIP Capacity Measurements for 802.11b WLANs*, Proc. CCNC 2005, Las Vegas, USA, January 2005.

M. Narbutt, M. Davis, *Gauging VoIP Call Quality from 802.11 WLAN Resource Usage*, Proc. WoWMoM 2006, Niagara Falls, USA, June 2006.

H. Zhai, X. Chen, Y. Fang, *A Call Admission and Rate Control Scheme for Multimedia Support over IEEE 802.11 Wireless LANs*, Springer Wireless Networks, vol.12, n.4, August 2006.

MGEN, The Multi-Generator Toolset available at http://mgen.pf.itd.nrl.navy.mil/

IXIA Test Application IxChariot http://www.ixiacom.com/products/display.php?skey=ixchariot

S. Armenia, L. Galluccio, A. Leonardi, S. Palazzo, "Transmission of VoIP Traffic in Multihop Ad Hoc IEEE 802.11b Networks: Experimental Results", IEEE WICON'05, Budapest, Hungary, 2005.

D. Niculescu, S. Ganguly, K. Kim, and R. Izmailov, "Performance ofVoIP in a 802.11 Wireless Mesh Network" , IEEE INFOCOM 2006, Barcelona, Spain, 2006.

P. Gupta and P. R. Kumar, "The capacity of wireless networks", IEEE Trans. Inform. Theory, vol. 46, no. 2, pp. 388–404, 2000.

A. Kashyap, S. Ganguly, S. R. Das, and S. Banerjee, "Voip on wireless meshes: Models, algorithms and evaluation", in IEEE INFOCOM 2007, Anchorage, Alaska, US, 2007

H. Wei, K. Kim, A. Kashyap, and S. Ganguly, "On Admission of VoIP Calls Over Wireless Mesh Network". IEEE ICC '06, Instambul, Turkey, 2006

K. Kim, R. I. S. Ganguly, and H. Sangjin, "On packet aggregation mechanisms for improving VoIP quality in mesh networks", IEEE VTC 2006-Spring, Melbourne, Australia, May 2006

Y. Zhuang, K. Tan, V. Shen, and Y. Liu, "VoIP aggregation in wireless backhaul networks", IEEE ICC 2006, Instambul, Turkey, 2006.

A. J. Kassler, M. C. Castro, and P. Dely, "Voip packet aggregation based on link quality metric for multihop wireless mesh networks", FTC 2007, Beijing, China, October 2007.

A. Nascimento E. Mota, S. Queiroz, E. Nascimento, "Header compression for VoIP over multi-hop wireless mesh networks", IEEE ISCC 2008, Marrakech, Morocco, July 2008

A. Ksentini ,O. Abassi, "A comparison of VoIP performance over three routing protocols for IEEE 802.11s-based wireless mesh networks (wlan mesh)", ACM MobiWac '08, Vancouver, British Columbia, Canada, October, 2008

J. Yackoski, C. Shen, "Managing End-to-End Delay for VoIP Calls in Multi-Hop Wireless Mesh Networks", IEEE INFOCOM 2010 San Diego, CA, US, March 2010

D. Lam, D. Cox, J. Widom, “Teletraffic Modeling for Personal Communications Services”, IEEE communications magazine 1997

S. Ganguly, V. Navda, K. Kim, A. Kashyap, D. Niculescu, R. Izmailov, S. Hong, S. Das, “Performance Optimizations for Deploying VoIP Services in Mesh Networks”, in IEEE JSAC, November 2006

J. Jangeun, M.L. Sichitiu , "The nominal capacity of wireless mesh networks," IEEE Wireless Communications , vol.10, no.5, Oct 2003

P. Falconio, J. Mangues-Bafalluy, M. Cardenete-Suriol, M. Portoles-Comeras, "Performance of a multi-interface based wireless mesh backbone to support VoIP service delivery", in proceedings of the WiMob 2006, Montreal, Canada, 19-21 June, 2006

M. Portoles-Comeras, M. Requena-Esteso, J. Mangues-Bafalluy, “Framework for characterizing hardware deployed in Wireless Mesh Networking Testbeds”, IEEE TridentCom 2007, Orlando, Florida, May 2007

9

VoIP Over WLAN: What About the Presence of Radio Interference?

Leopoldo Angrisani[1], Aniello Napolitano[1] and Alessandro Sona[2]
[1]*University of Naples Federico II*
[2]*University of Padua*
Italy

1. Introduction

The use of Voice over IP (VoIP) is rapidly accelerating around the world and becoming familiar to an increasing number of people using Skype routinely (Douskalis, 1999). VoIP is also becoming more and more deployed through the so-called Voice over Wireless Local Area Network (VoWLAN) technology (Lin & Chlamtac, 2000), which integrates wired and wireless telephony in the same Internet Protocol (IP) structure, reducing the cost of calls and avoiding the typical problems of the highly variable coverage of the cell phone networks inside buildings. This vivacious scenario is giving to VoWLAN technology an increasing importance, entitled to become even greater in the future with the diffusion of new-kinds of portable devices (e.g. PDAs and social phones) and the availability of more and more Wi-Fi zones everywhere in the world.

In this chapter attention is focused on one of the most critical problems affecting VoWLAN operation, which, if not properly taken into account and controlled, may severely degrade the overall quality of service perceived by the final user. Such an important issue is radio interference in the wireless channel, which may affect the integrity of the signal received by a WLAN terminal and, consequently, cause misinterpretation of the carried digital information. The phenomenon is nowadays becoming more and more critical because of the increasing use of radio terminal equipment deploying the typical frequency band in which WLANs operate, i.e. the so-called unlicensed 2.4 GHz Industrial Scientific and Medical (ISM) band. In the related frequency range, in fact, IEEE 802.11 WLANs (informally known collectively as Wi-Fi) (IEEE 802.11, 1999) must coexist with IEEE 802.15.4 (IEEE 802.15.4, 2003) and IEEE 802.16 (IEEE 802.16, 2001) apparatuses. Moreover, they have to operate in the presence of unintentional spurious signals from electronic devices that either use this band, like cordless phones, microwave ovens, baby monitors, security cameras, or operate in adjacent frequency bands, like a number of wireless appliances whose distribution in modern houses, public and professional contexts is by now widespread.

Some authors tried to investigate on the effects of interference on voice quality in a VoWLAN conversation (Wang & Mellor, 2004; Wang & Li, 2005; Garg & Cappes, 2002; 2003; El-fishawy et al, 2007; Prasat, 1999; Hiraguri et al, 2002). For instance, in (Wang & Li, 2005) the coexistence of Transmission Control Protocol (TCP) and VoIP traffic in a WLAN has been studied in terms of delays and performance loss. In (Garg & Cappes, 2003), experimental studies have been shown on the throughput of IEEE 802.11b wireless networks for user diagram protocol (UDP) and VoIP traffic. In all these contributions, attention is essentially

focused only to interference at network/transport layer, due to the presence of competitive traffic in the same WLAN. Few information is instead typically available in terms of physical layer interference.
In this chapter, the performance of VoIP over WLAN is analyzed under the effect of physical layer interference, in the presence and absence of cross-traffic. The goal is twofold: first to underline the importance of radio interference in the behavior of a WLAN when supporting VoIP applications; second to outline solutions to avoid interference and thus optimizing a VoIP call over a WLAN. To this aim, an experimental approach based on cross-layer measurements is adopted (Angrisani & Vadursi, 2007), describing and commenting meaningful results obtained from a number of experiments conducted by the authors on a testbed operating in a semi-anechoic chamber and emulating two typical real life scenarios. In particular, different network architectures and voice codec typologies are emulated, such as G.711 (ITU-T G.711, 1972), G.729 (ITU-T G.729, 1996), G.723.1 (ITU-T G.723.1, 2006), usually utilized in VoIP applications over WLAN. Experiments are conducted according to a cross-layer approach and monitoring the following parameters: (i) signal to interference ratio (SIR) and jitter at physical layer, (ii) packet loss at network/transport layer, and (iii) mean opinion score (MOS) and R factor at application layer. For each investigated scenario, the presented outcomes will allow the reader to clearly identify and understand the origin of some typical interference phenomena on VoIP services over WLAN. They also allow to experimentally verify the effectiveness of practical and helpful rules, addressed in the chapter, for improving quality losses in a VoWLAN application in the presence of interference at physical and network/transport layer.

2. Preliminary notes

In this section, preliminary notes concerning VoIP and VoWLAN technology, IEEE 802.11 standard and voice quality metrics are introduced with the purpose of recalling some of the terms and parameters used in Sections 4 and 5.

2.1 VoIP

VoIP is a family of transmission technologies for the real-time delivery of voice calls over IP networks such as the Internet or other packet-switched networks. It is playing a fundamental role in the development and use of Internet in the world. It is also greatly contributing to the convergence of different technologies and applications over the same hardware infrastructures. The success of VoIP is especially due to the Internet itself, and in particular to its emerging use all over the world. Internet is in fact becoming a need of primary importance in an increasing number of countries. It is radically modifying styles and behaviors of people, communities and companies in their everyday relationships, activities and businesses. User mobility, real-time interaction, instant messaging, text paging, social networks, voice services, internet access during travels, multimedia exchanging, are only few examples of common needs and applications required by modern people, professionals and industries.
In a traditional VoIP call, terminals are connected through a local area network (LAN), made of cables, switches, hubs, and other similar apparatuses. This topology ensures efficient and reliable communication with strong immunity levels against radio interference; cables are in fact frequently covered by metallic shields and properly connected to the ground in order to avoid the influence of external perturbing radio interference. Nevertheless, many problems still arise, making the use of VoIP services not yet fully reliable. One problem can be attributed to the fact that voice calls require real-time procedures, which cannot fully

be satisfied in an IP-based context. In a IP network, in fact, two terminals are not linked through a physical circuit like in a public switched telecommunication network (PSTN). They instead communicate through a set of data packets, each of which containing a destination address and a fragment of the digitalized voice conversation. The addressed terminal collects the received packet, extracts the useful information, and reconstructs the original signal. This mechanism has to be completed without loss of packets or too long delays, so that to avoid failures in the real-time reconstruction procedure, and consequently artifacts in the voice conversation. Another problem is the use of a cabled infrastructure, which requires a non-negligible effort in terms of installation, reconfiguration and maintenance. In particular, an high number of cables are needed to connect a building, through walls and pipes in the walls and under ground floors or even roads. This means very high costs and long times to wire large areas and buildings. In the design of new buildings, LANs require to accurately predict all the possible needs of future users in such a way as to reduce as well as possible further modifications of the wired plant. This typically leads to an high risk of oversizing the whole infrastructure, and a consequent increase of costs. LANs are also a limiting infrastructure for voice applications; in particular, it obliges users to be physically connected to a personal computer, thus strongly limiting their mobility within the covered area.

2.2 From VoIP to VoWLAN

VoWLAN (Voice over WLAN) is a method of sending voice information in digital form over a wireless broadband network. It represents the conjunction of two important emerging technologies: VoIP and WLAN. In a VoWLAN call, terminals are connected to the Internet through a wireless link and an access point. It consists in the use of a wireless broadband network according to the IEEE 802.11 set of specifications for the purpose of vocal conversation (IEEE 802.11, 1999). VoWLAN is leading to an increasing importance and use of WLANs, which are rapidly wide spreading everywhere in the world, through an increasing number of public and private hot-spots located in public areas, university campuses, factories, sport arenas, and so on. This is also increasing the use of VoIP through an emerging community of people and professionals using Skype routinely and daily.

The use of radio communications allows to efficiently solve the above quoted mobility disadvantages of LANs; in particular they offer the following benefits:

1. a complete absence of cables between terminals and access points;
2. a complete mobility of terminals inside a covered area without the need of interrupting the connection between terminals and server;
3. an higher productivity of employers due to the gained higher mobility;
4. an easy and quick installation of new terminals, without cables to connect; a new user can be added simply by supporting the terminal with a wireless card;
5. a quite null effort to manage the infrastructure and its modifications;
6. cheaper local and international calls, free calls to other VoWLAN units and a simplified integrated billing of both phone and Internet service providers.

The convergence of voice and data over the same wireless devices (*e.g.* laptop, VoIP cordless phones, portable digital assistants PDAs) requires specific solutions to be applied at the following levels:

1. ***Hardware*** An high-speed control processing unit (CPU) is needed in each wireless terminal, able to adequately manage voice streams compression and de-compression tasks. High performance microphones and speakers are also needed to adequately support voice quality.
2. ***Software*** A number of typical problems due to the use of the wireless medium must be solved through the design of proper algorithms. For instance, these algorithms must guarantee the required quality of service (QoS) or to correct the effects of the typical latency of wireless communications.
3. ***Network*** A strong and reliable interaction between WLAN and the traditional telephony network is needed. In this task, real-time is an essential requirement to be satisfied.
4. ***Interference*** The effect of interference can be detrimental on a WLAN performance operating in the already crowded 2.4 GHz ISM band. In this case, no shielding or filtering solutions can be applied. The incoming external signal may lead to the loss of some data packets, hence reducing the possibility to reconstruct the original voice sequence.

Hereinafter, attention will mainly be paid to the effects of radio interference which, as quoted in Sec. 1, represent one of the most critical VoWLAN problems up to now still not completely investigated. The effect of the interference on a WLAN communication can be different and classified into two main classes: (i) the effects arising when interference occupies the frequency band on which the WLAN is starting to transmit. In this case, the network is forced to wait until the interference stops and the channel becomes free again; this phenomenon delays the delivery of packets and may cause disruptive effects on the voice call. (ii) The effects arising when interference acts during a WLAN communication; in this case the interference signal superimposes to the useful one causing errors in the delivered and received data stream. This kind of effect may lead to errors in the de-codification process of data packets with consequent loss of packets and artifacts in the voice call.

2.3 IEEE 802.11g standard

IEEE 802.11 is a standard used to provide wireless connectivity to fixed, portable, and moving stations within a local area (IEEE 802.11, 1999). It applies to the lowest two layers of the Open System Interconnection (OSI) protocol stack, namely the physical layer and the data link layer. The physical layer (PHY) is the interface between the upper media access control (MAC) layer and the wireless media where frames are transmitted and received. The PHY layer essentially provides three functions. First, it interfaces the upper MAC layer for transmission and reception of data. Second, it provides signal modulation through direct sequence spread spectrum (DSSS) techniques, or orthogonal frequency division multiplexing (OFDM) schemes. Third, it sends a carrier sense indication back to the upper MAC layer, to verify activity on the media. The data link layer includes the MAC sub-layer, which allows the reliable transmission of data from the upper layers over the wireless PHY media. To this aim, it provides a controlled access method to the shared wireless media called carrier-sense multiple access with collision avoidance (CSMA/CA). It then protects the data being delivered by providing security and privacy services. The 802.11 family includes multiple extensions to the original standard, based on the same basic protocol and is essentially different in terms of modulation techniques. The most popular extensions are those defined by the IEEE 802.11a/b/g amendments, on which most of the today manufactured devices are based. Nowadays, 802.11g is becoming the WLAN standard more widely accepted worldwide. It works in the 2.4 GHz band, like 802.11b, but operates at a maximum data rate of 54 Mbps, like 802.11a, with net throughput of about 19 Mbps. In practice, it provides the benefits of 802.11a but in the 2.4 GHz band. The 802.11g hardware is then backwards compatible with 802.11b hardware. It uses the OFDM scheme for the data rates of 6, 9, 12, 18, 24, 36, 48, and 54 Mbit/s, and reverts to complementary code keying (CCK) (like 802.11b) for 5.5 and 11 Mbit/s, and DBPSK/DQPSK+DSSS for 1 and 2 Mbit/s. 802.11g suffers from the same problem of 802.11b, namely it operates in the already crowded 2.4 GHz ISM band (2.4 - 2.4845 GHz). In this band, the standard defines a total of 14 frequency channels, each of which is characterized by a 22 MHz bandwidth. This implies that channels are partially overlapped, and that the number of non-overlapping usable channels is only 3 in FCC nations (ch 1, 6, 11) or 4 in European nations (ch 1, 5, 9, 13). Hereinafter, attention will mainly be paid to IEEE 802.11g standard.

2.4 Voice quality

In a VoIP call, the voice signal is fragmented into a set of data packets and delivered over an IP-based infrastructure. The quality of the voice call at the receiver side depends on the arrival order of the received packets, and on the presence of possible errors. If some packets are erroneously received, or characterized by a too long delay, all the process is delayed. For ordinary applications such as email or web, delays may not represent a critical problem. But, for the case of voice calls, like VoIP, where strict real-time constraints are required, delays can strongly degrade the voice quality perceived by end users.
Voice quality can be subdivided into the following two contributions:

***Listening quality (LQ)*:** the clearness of the voice message perceived by the listener in a given time interval;

***Conversional quality (CQ)*:** the quality of the conversation, including bi-directional phenomena like message delays at the receiver side and echoes.

It also depends on two main factors: (i) distortion, *i.e.* difference of the received signal and the transmitted one, (ii) overall delay, also known as "mouth to ear" delay, which includes all the collected delays. These two factors are strictly related to the network on which the call is sent. For example, a PSTN is typically rather immune to distortion and delays, while an IP network has the drawback to be more susceptible to such phenomena, and ultimately, in the specific case of wireless networks, to interference. A VoIP network has also addition delay contributions due to a number of performed intermediate operations like data coding, packets organization, queue management, de-jitter, etc. Another source of vocal distortion is the use of low bit-rate audio codec. More insights about the most typical impairments affecting voice quality in a VoWLAN conversation will be given in Sec. 3.
Voice quality can be analyzed in two different manners: (a) subjective or (b) objective measurements. Subjective measurements are conducted in terms of mean opinion score (MOS), which is the average result of opinion scores obtained by a group of listeners according to a rating scheme defined in (ITU-T P.800, 1996). The MOS is expressed as a single number in the range 1 to 5, where 1 (bad) is the lowest perceived quality, and 5 (excellent) is the highest perceived quality. It can be estimated only through in-laboratory conducted tests. MOS scores are attributed according to the voice quality perceived by the listeners who participated in tests. Tests are also to be executed in different boundary conditions, *i.e.* by changing the sentences, the deployed language and some listening conditions, which can lead to different MOS values. In fact, MOS scores achieved in different conditions can never be compared one with another. In (ITU-T P.800, 1996), four different test typologies are mentioned:

Conversation opinion test The test is carried out by couples of users using the phone system under test. At the end of conversations, a judgment is expressed by each user, and the average score, called MOSc (conversational MOS), is evaluated;

Listening Test/ACR (Absolute Category Rating) The test is performed by a group of listeners who give a judgment to a set of short sentences listened through the system under test. At the end of test, the average score, called MOS, is evaluated;

Listening Test/DCR (Degradation Category Rating) The test is performed by a group of listeners who analyze the differences between some short sentences taken as reference and the corresponding ones obtained by using the system under test. The result of the test is an average score, called DMOS (degradation MOS), accounting for the degradation effects effectively perceived;

Listening Test/CCR (Comparison Category Rating) The test is the same of DCR, but with the difference that listeners are here not informed about the type of message they are listening, *i.e.* if it is the reference or the corrupted one. The result of the test is an average score, called CMOS (comparison MOS).

Subjective measurements have the drawback to be very expensive and time consuming: they require a laboratory with characteristics satisfying specific requirements, and a number of people to be involved in the tests. This has lead to the development of new measurement techniques based on objective procedures and aimed at giving results similar to those obtainable with subjective measurements.
Objective quality measurements are performed through algorithms and can be intrusive or not intrusive. They are typically easy to implement, low cost and efficient in terms of measurement repeatability. Intrusive methods provide estimates of MOS introducing a voice sample in the network under test. In well-known algorithms like Perceptual Evaluation of Speech Quality (PESQ) or Perceptual Speech Quality Measure (PSQM) the measurement is performed by comparing the original sample with the received one. Non-Intrusive algorithms are instead based on the analysis of the only received voice stream, providing a transmission quality metric that can be used to estimate a MOS score. This method has the advantage that all calls in a network can be monitored without any additional network overhead, but the disadvantage that the effects of some impairment can not be measured. The most known non-intrusive method is the E-model defined in (Schulzrinne et al, 2003), based on the R factor, also known as *Transmission Rating Factor*. The objective of the model is to determine a quality rating incorporating the "mouth to ear" characteristics of a speech path. The range of the R factor is nominally 0-100, even if <50 values are generally unacceptable and typical telephone connections are never higher than 94, giving a typical range of 50-94. In the basic model, the R factor is expressed as follows:

$$R = R_0 - I_s - I_d - I_e + A, \tag{1}$$

where R_0 stands for the signal-to-noise ratio, i.e. the factor R in an ideal case with no disturbances and distortions, I_s is the simultaneous impairment factor, which accounts for the degradation due to simultaneous events like spurious tones and quantization distortions, I_d is the delay impairment factor, due to the delays and echoes, I_e is the equipment impairment factor due to some used devices like the icodec, and A is the advantage factor, which accounts for the tolerance of users to impairments. For instance, the typical tolerance is in the range 5-10 in a cell phone call, and null in a PSTN call. In Table 1, the typical MOS scores and R factors associated to some specific user opinions are shown for the case of a G.711 codec.

Listener Opinion	R Factor	MOS Score
Maximum obtainable for G.711	93	4.4
Very satisfied	90-100	4.3 - 5.0
Satisfied	80-90	4.0 - 4.3
Some users satisfied	70-80	3.6 - 4.0
Many users dissatisfied	60-70	3.1 - 3.6
Nearly all users dissatisfied	50-60	2.6 - 3.1
Not recommended	< 50	1.0 - 2.6

Table 1. MOS and R factor scores

3. Typical impairments

In-channel radio interference can strongly degrade the quality of a VoWLAN voice conversation as found experimentally and documented in Section 5. In order to better understand how interference can provoke this effect, basic notes about the most typical impairments affecting VoWLAN communications are here recalled.

3.1 Delay

One first impairment is due to the presence of delays (also called latency) in the arrival of data packets from the transmitter. In Fig. 1 a simplified scheme of a VoWLAN system architecture is reported, along with a symbol representing the interference.
As shown, a microphone is used to convert the incoming voice message into an analogue voltage signal. The signal is then converted into a digital data flow by means of an analog to digital converter (A/D); this data flow is subsequently fragmented, compressed and organized by a suitable encoder according to an IP-based scheme. Data packets are then modulated and converted into a radio frequency signal compliant with the IEEE 802.11 standard and delivered through an antenna to an access point. This latter one demodulates the incoming radio signal, collects and ordinates the received data packets. Data packets are subsequently delivered to a receiver terminal, which extracts the useful (payload) information, converts it into an analogue signal (digital to analogue, D/A, conversion) and

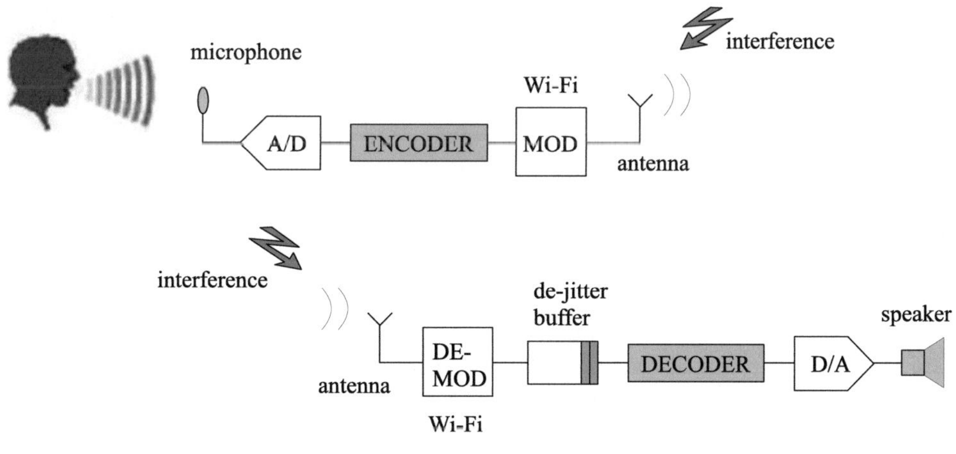

Fig. 1. Simplified architecture of a VoWLAN system under the effect of interference

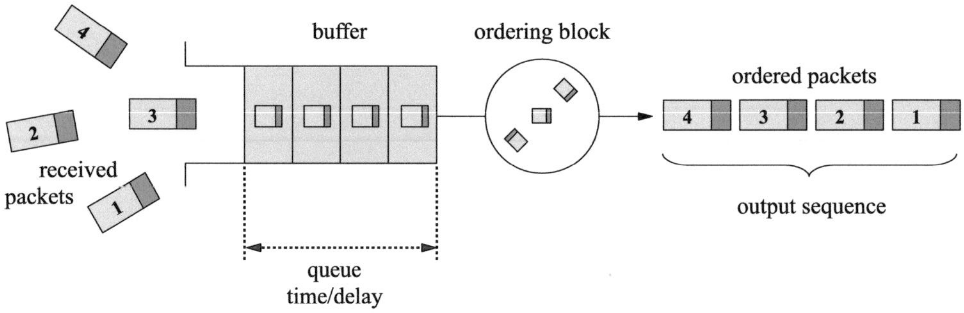

Fig. 2. Procedure deployed to order the data packets at the receiver side

reproduces the voice through a final speaker. In all this mechanism, interference acts on the "on-air" communication between the transmitter (*e.g.* a portable terminal) and the receiver (*e.g.* the access point) antennas.
In case of delays in the arrival of data packets, an unordered sequence of packets approaches the receiver, leading to the possibility of errors and impairments in the reconstruction of the original message. Therefore, a buffering stage is usually adopted at the receiver side, which keeps in memory the packets for a limited time interval, called *queue time*. In the queue time, the buffering stage orders the packets and reconstructs the original sequence. In Fig. 2, a sketch representing this mechanism is shown, in which four unordered data packets are finally arranged according to the desired sequence.
The described queuing mechanism requires the availability of buffers able to process the incoming data flow at a speed faster than the flow rate itself. The adopted queuing strategy is also important to avoid impairments especially in terminals characterized by poor capacity levels (bandwidth). To this aim, different data packet scheduling techniques are commonly adopted:

First in First Out (FIFO) It represents the simplest technique: packets are scheduled according to the arrival order, without any modification;

Weighted Fair Queuing (WFQ) It allows different bandwidths to each data flow according to a pre-assigned queing weight. Each data flow has a separate FIFO queue; this allows an ill-behaved flow (who has sent larger packets or more packets per second than the others) to only degrade itself and not other sessions;

Custom Queuing (CQ) Similar to WFQ, it shares the bandwidth between packet flows proportionally to a pre-assigned traffic class;

Priority Queuing (PQ) It ensures that highest priority data packets are scheduled before the lower priority ones, to which service can even be not guaranteed.

The final overall delay accounts for different contributions, among which we recall:

Propagation delay is the amount of time that a signal takes to travel from the transmitting to the receiving antennas over a medium. It can be computed as the ratio between the link length and the propagation speed over the specific medium. It becomes significant only in the case of long radio link distances;

Processing delay is the amount of delay due to the encoder and decoder processing activities, *i.e.* compression and decompression task, data fragmentation and data packets switching;

Queing delay is the amount of delay occurring both at transmitter and receiver side in the presence of data congestion. At the transmitter side, it occurs when packets are not processed and delivered with sufficient speed. At the receiver side, it occurs when the buffer capacity is not sufficient to manage all the received data;

End-to-end delay is the sum of the previous delays, which, in some particular cases, can be even greater than 500 ms, that is so high to cause superposition of users voices.

These delay terms, along with the ones of microphone, speaker, A/D and D/A converters, compose the so called *mouth-to-ear* delay, which value should never overpass a 150 ms threshold, over which the human ear perceives the presence of delays. In the end-to-end delay a number of parameters and phenomena can act, for instance the length of packets, interference, network traffic. For instance, longer packets are preferable in order to have a less compression of data, hence a shorter processing delay and a overall lower presence of header information. On the other side, shorter packets are preferable in order to obtain a reduced quieting delay to the detriment of processing delay and header size. This latter choice is just that more commonly adopted in a VoWLAN communication.

3.2 Jitter

Jitter is a critical phenomenon affecting communication systems and provoking impairments especially in those operating in real-time mode. It consists of a variation in packet transit delay typically caused by queuing processes at the transmitter and/or receiver side or by defects in the radio channel. It can be measured as the difference between the expected arrival time of a packet and the one effectively observed. The quality of a signal and in particular of a VoWLAN conversation can strongly be degraded by jitter. In order to mitigate jitter effects, a suitable time delay q is commonly added to each packet so that to equalize the time between packets. This task is commonly performed by a device at the receiver side, the so-called *dejitter buffer*, as sketched in Fig. 3, which adds to any received packet a suitably modulated time delay q. These intervals q make uniform the time cadence of arrival data packets, mitigating the effects of jitter.
The size of the dejitter buffer and the maximum delay q are typically chosen in such a way as to minimize the overall delay d among output packets and enhance the receiver ability to compensate the jitter. For instance, high q levels typically means a better ability of the

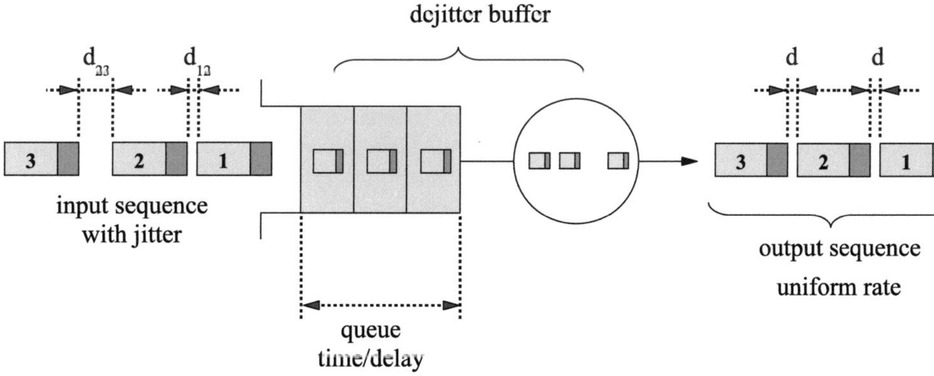

Fig. 3. Procedure deployed to compensate the non-uniform delays (jitter) of incoming data packets

device to compensate the jitter, but also longer *d*. Similarly, high buffer sizes typically mean a better ability to compensate jitter, but also the introduction of longer delays due to the dejitter operation. An efficient solution is typically the use of dynamic buffers, which size can be modulated according to the network status and the jitter value. This control is typically realized by measuring the delay introduced by the network (in particular its variance) and by stretching or reducing the length of the silence interval between consecutive packets. A typical measure of the dejitter time interval is instead 50 ms.

3.3 Packet loss

Packet loss is a frequent and critical phenomenon affecting data communication networks. In these networks, in fact, packet losses and errors are not typically tolerated. This requires the use of suitable and known mechanisms and strategies to replace missing data or to avoid/correct errors.

In the case of VoIP, the loss of one or more data packets or voice samples, as well as the presence of errors in the received stream, can be more tolerated. In fact, the final voice quality must be sufficient to satisfy a good listener, which means that one or more errors as well as packet or sample losses can be tolerated. This makes the two above quoted impairments (*i.e.* delays and jitter) more critical than packet loss in VoIP and VoWLAN networks.

A commonly adopted solution to mitigate packet loss is the so-called *packet loss concealment*. It consists of repeating the latest obtained sample in spite of the missing (not arrived) one. In particular, a time interval is assigned to each expected sample, at the end of which if the sample has not arrived yet the previous one is reproduced. For the G.729 codec, an overall 5% of average loss per call can be tolerated. Further and more sophisticated strategies conceal the missing samples by interpolating tha values assumed by the adjacent received ones.

The data packets structure should carefully be chosen by taking into account the following two issues: (i) the use of buffer queue of high dimensions reduces the effect of packet loss; (ii) long packets and buffer queue increase the overall delay, causing voice degradation.

In case of vocal code schemes like G.711, holes of 32-64 ms or longer may provoke loss of phonemes, and thus lead to disruptive voice degradation. Shorter holes in the range 4-16 ms or lower can instead be tolerated by any listener. The decrease of packet size below forty bytes is not always applicable because of the protocols IP, UDP and RTP and in particular of the size of the header they require. On the other hand too long packets may lead to too long delays, even beyond the ITU recommended levels.

3.4 Echoes

Echoes is a typical effect of phone conversation consisting in a series of delayed repetitions of voice sequences provoking distortions at the listener's ear. The phenomenon can be considered tiresome for delays longer than 25 ms. Due to a non-ideal impedance matching of the communication system elements, it is typically generated inside the gateway and the listener terminal. It can also be due to the resonance effect between microphone and speakers of a user VoIP or VoWLAN terminal when placed and operating close one with another. Echoes can be reduced by optimizing the system impedance matching: in these cases, echoes levels 50 dB lower than the useful signal one can be considered a very good target. They can also be mitigated by using efficient echo cancelers, *i.e.* digital devices implementing adaptive finite impulse response (FIR) filters and compensating the effects of echoes.

4. Measurement testbed

A number of experiments have been conducted with the aim of investigating on the effects of radio interference in the behavior of a WLAN when supporting VoIP applications. Experiments have been carried out by using a real testbed, operating in two different scenarios, in the following denoted as *A* and *B*. The testbed enlists an IEEE 802.11g wireless network (WLAN) supporting VoIP applications. Additional interference sources have been introduced in the proximity of the WLAN to emulate typical in-channel interference arising in real-world environment. Tests have been conducted within a protected and controlled environment, i.e. a shielded semi-anechoic chamber compliant with electromagnetic compatibility requirements for radiated emission tests.

In Figs. 4 and 5 the testbed deployed in the two analyzed scenarios is sketched; an its photograph is also shown in Fig. 6. It enlists the following elements:

1. an 802.11g access point, AP, D-link DI-624+;
2. a notebook, NB1, from Hewlett Packard, equipped with a Intel Pentium III processor, 296 MB RAM, Windows XP, and a 802.11g D-link DWL-G650 adapter+;
3. a notebook, NB2, from ACER, equipped with a 1.4 GHz Intel Centrino processor, 512 MB RAM, Windows XP, and a 802.11g D-link DWL-G650 adapter;
4. a notebook, NB3, from IBM, equipped with a Intel Pentium IV, Linux Ubuntu, and a 802.11g D-link DWL-G650 adapter;

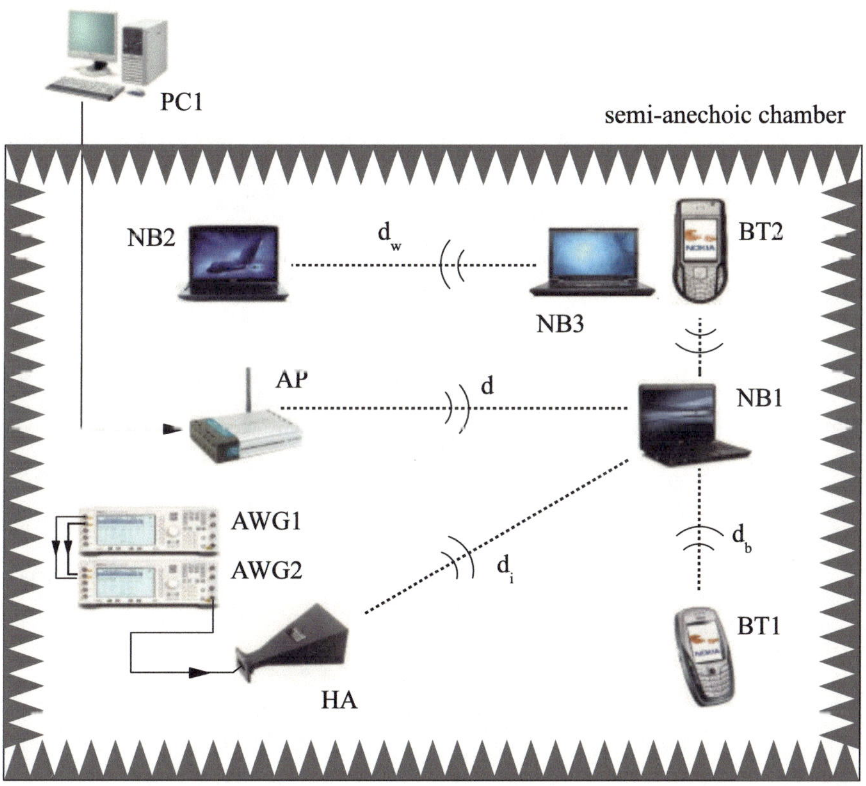

Fig. 4. Testbed configuration deployed in scenario A: wired-wireless VoIP communication

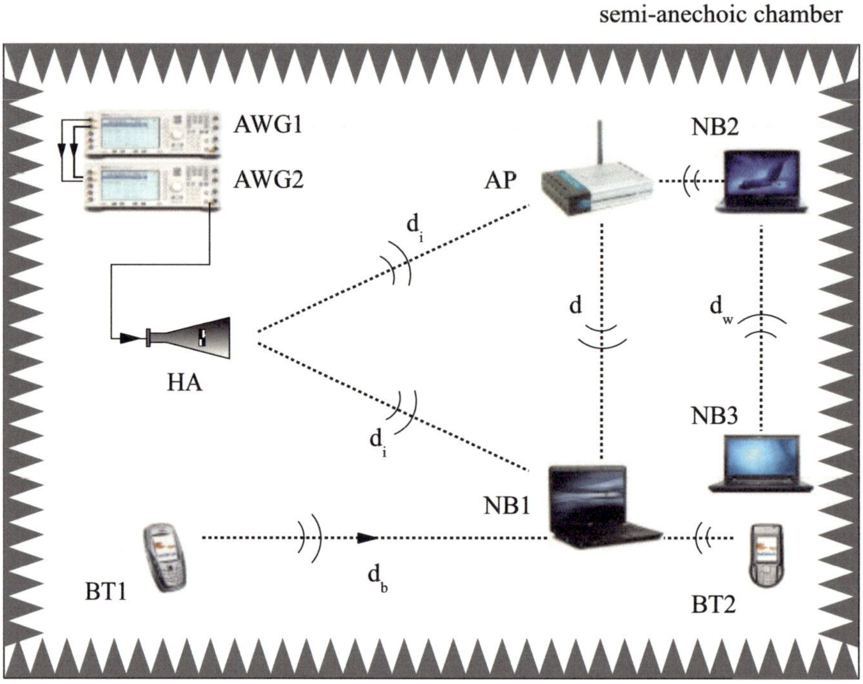

Fig. 5. Testbed configuration deployed in scenario B: wireless-wireless VoIP communication

Fig. 6. Test site and adopted instrumentation

5. a computer desktop, PC1, equipped with a 1,4 GHz Intel Pentium IV, 1-3 GB MB RAM;
6. two mobile phones: a Nokia 6600, BT1, and a Nokia 6630, BT2, each equipped with a 1.1/class 2 Bluetooth transmitter;
7. two arbitrary waveform generators, AWG, Agilent Technologies E4431B ESG-D (250 kHz - 6 GHz frequency range) and E4438C ESG (250 kHz - 6 GHz frequency range);
8. a microwave horn antenna, HA, from Amplifier Research with 0.8-5 GHz frequency range;
9. a real-time spectrum analyzer, RSA, Tektronix RSA 3408, connected with a receiving microwave horn antenna Schwarzbeck BBHA9120D (1 - 18 GHz frequency range).

4.1 Scenario A

In this first measurement scenario, a wired-wireless configuration is emulated between two VoIP terminals: PC1 and NB1. As can be seen in Fig. 4, PC1 is placed outside the camber and communicates to the AP, inside the chamber, by means of a wired link. AP subsequently forwards the received data stream to NB1 by means of a WLAN connection. In this context, the use of VoIP over IEEE 802.11g is only analyzed in the download stage. The analyzed voice signals are pre-recorded voice messages suitably generated in order to let the voice quality measurement algorithms easily and efficiently detect the presence of voice impairments in the message such as latency, jitter, and packet loss. In particular, NB1 is placed at a distance d = 2.25 m from AP, while PC1, outside the chamber, is located within a shielded room. This allows the analysis of the effect of the interference, purposely generated inside the room, acting on the only wireless link. At the position of NB1, in case of null interference, the measured power level from AP is nearly -25 dBm.
The following interference are instead considered:

a. Bluetooth signal, generated by the couple BT1 and BT2, communicating with each other at a reciprocal distance $d_b = 4$ m, and with BT2 placed close to NB1. The power levels they generate provide a signal to interference ratio (SIR) at the WLAN receiver side (NB1) equal to 4 dB;

b. Additive White Gaussian Noise (AWGN), radiated by the antenna HA at a distance $d_i =$ 1.3 m. In this case, the SIR level at NB1 is suitably varied changing the power at the AWG generator output connector;

c. Wi-Fi data traffic over the same frequency channel, generated by the couple of Wi-Fi terminals NB2 and NB3, placed at a reciprocal distance of $d_w = d$ and in the proximity of AP and NB1, respectively. In particular, NB3 is used to generate and transmit data traffic, at different data rate, and NB2 to receive it.

4.2 Scenario B

In this second measurement scenario, a wireless-wireless configuration is emulated between the following two terminals: NB1 and NB2. As represented in Fig. 5, NB2 generates VoIP traffic that NB1 receives through the intermediate AP. In this case, the VoIP over IEEE 802.11g call is analyzed at both upload and download stage. The architecture of the testbed is very similar to that of scenario A, with the exception of: PC1, here not considered, NB2, which generates VoIP traffic toward AP and receives interfering data traffic from NB3, and HA, placed at a distance $d_i = 3$ m from both AP and NB1 and oriented as shown in Fig. 5. The same interference sources of scenario A are instead considered.

4.3 Measurement instrumentation and software tools

Measurements have been conducted according to a cross-layer approach, which consists of several measurements, to be concurrently carried out at different layers of the ISO/OSI stack. The approach aims at experimentally correlating the major physical layer quantities to those characterizing key higher layer parameters (e.g. network/transport layer, application layer), allowing an efficient assessment of communication networks performance and drawbacks (Angrisani & Vadursi, 2007) and (Angrisani et al, 2007). In particular the following three layers have been considered: physical layer, through estimates of in-channel power and signal to interference ratio (SIR) at the receiver side, network/transport layer, by means of jitter and packet loss (percentage of lost packets) measurements, and application layer, through R factor and MOS estimates.

To the purpose, suitable measurement instrumentation and software tools have been deployed. In particular, physical layer measurements of in-channel power and SIR have been executed by using the RSA, in channel power mode, and the 1 - 18 GHz horn antenna (Bertocco & Sona, 2006). Network/transport and application layer estimates have instead been carried out by means of specific software tools, *e.g.* D-ITG, WRAPI+ and D-Link Air Plus Xtreme G Wireless Utility. D-ITG is a distributed Internet traffic generator (Botta et al, 2007), whose architecture allows to generate traffic and vary parameters such as inter-departure time, packet length, etc. It also allows measuring several QoS parameters at both the sender and receiver sides, and reporting a complete report of measured parameters over the entire measurement time. WRAPI+ is a real-time monitoring tool that enables a user to assess the values assumed by some performance parameters of a WLAN. In particular, it provides a complete report of information concerning the IEEE 802.11b/g network behavior in a given time interval. D-Link Air Plus Xtreme G Wireless Utility is a tool available from the D-Link DWL-G650 board allowing the monitoring of further parameters of the WLAN like for instance bit-rate and the received power level at both AP and NB1.

5. Experimental results

The two measurement scenarios have been investigated in five different configurations: 1) without interference, 2) Bluetooth interference, 3) AWGN interference, 4) WLAN concurrent data traffic, and 5) both AWGN interference and WLAN concurrent data traffic. Tests have been performed by considering only one audio codec for 1-4 configurations (G.711), and three different ones for the case of both AWGN interference and WLAN concurrent data traffic (G.711, G.723.1, G.729).

5.1 No interference

In the first experiment, a VoWLAN communication has been emulated in the absence of interference. VoIP calls have been generated by using pre-registered messages delivered from PC1 to NB1 (scenario A), and from NB2 to NB1 (scenario B). Measurements have been executed at the only receiver side. The obtained results show that:

- jitter is negligible;
- packet loss is nearly equal to zero;
- R factor reaches the value of 93, i.e. the maximum level for G.711 compression mode;
- MOS is equal to 4.4, i.e. the quality of the voice calls, at the received side, is more than satisfactory.

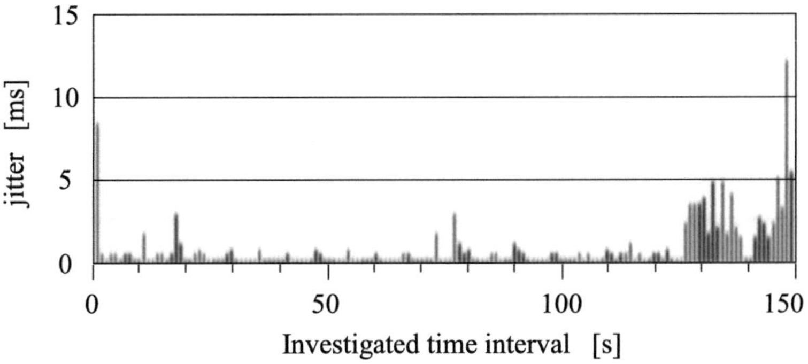

Fig. 7. Jitter estimated in the absence of interference

A diagram of the measured jitter levels in the case of scenario A is shown in Fig. 7 for an investigated time interval of 150 s length. Quite similar values have been obtained in scenario B. Fig. 7 shows the presence of delays, which origin can be attributed to the impairments in the deployed devices. However, the values they assume can be considered very low with respect to the maximum threshold of 150 ms that can be tolerated in a voice conversation, without significant loss of perceived quality (Douskalis, 1999).

5.2 Bluetooth interference

In the second experiment, the behavior of a VoWLAN communication has been studied under the effect of Bluetooth interference. As well known, Bluetooth devices radiate small power levels, *i.e.* typically in the range 0 through 20 dBm. Nevertheless the distance at which they commonly operate from computers and Bluetooth devices, like printers, mouse, and keyboards, is typically rather small, below 1 m, and the frequencies they use belong to the same ISM band, partially occupied by Wi-Fi networks. Therefore, despite the low levels of power, the effects of Bluetooth terminals on the analyzed VoWLAN application can not be a priori excluded.

Table 2 summarizes the results of the experiments conducted in the two scenarios. The table shows that in both the scenarios, the effects of interference are negligible both in terms of network/transport layer parameters, *i.e.* packet loss and jitter, and of application layer parameters, i.e. R factor and MOS. In fact, despite a reduction of the R factor and MOS with respect to the case of non-interference, the quality of the VoIP call is in the class "very satisfied". Quite the same values have been obtained at different positions of the Bluetooth terminals within the room and locating BT1 close to AP.

	Scenario A mean value	Scenario A st. dev	Scenario B mean value	Scenario B st. dev
packet loss [%]	0.060	0.003	0.100	0.009
jitter [ms]	0.100	0.003	0.600	0.003
R factor	90.090	0.010	90.090	0.010
MOS	4.380	0.020	4.370	0.050

Table 2. Effects of Bluetooth interference and R factor scores

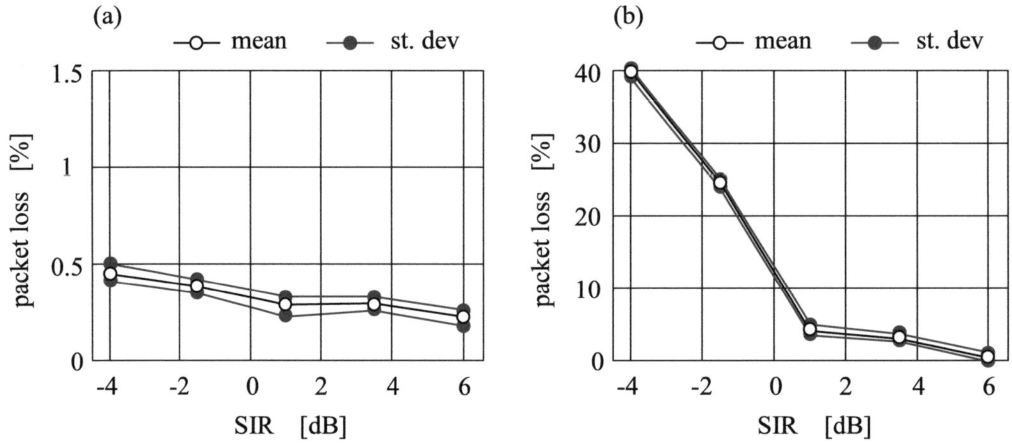

Fig. 8. Measured packet loss vs signal to interference ratio (SIR): (a) scenario A, (b) scenario B

5.3 AWGN interference

A third set of experiments have been conducted by considering the only effect of AWGN interference, affecting the VoWLAN streaming. The obtained results are summarized in Figs. 8, 9, and 10.

In Fig. 8, a relevant effect of interference in terms of packet loss can be noted in the case of scenario B and for $SIR < 1$ dB. Below this threshold, here denoted as SIR_{max}, packet loss grows rather quickly upon the decreasing of SIR, while for greater values it slowly lowers from 5 to 0 %. Much smaller values have instead been obtained in the case of scenario A, for any investigated SIR value. A similar difference between scenario A and B and for $SIR < 1$ dB can be observed in Figs. 9 and 10. Specifically, in the scenario A, for any considered SIR, the estimated values of jitter are rather low (below 2 ms) with respect to the tolerated limit of 150 ms, and the obtained R factor and MOS scores belong to the highest Table 1 category, *i.e.* "very satisfied". The only exception is for $SIR = -4$ dB, for which the voice quality can be considered "satisfied". In the scenario B, an abrupt growing of the estimated jitter levels

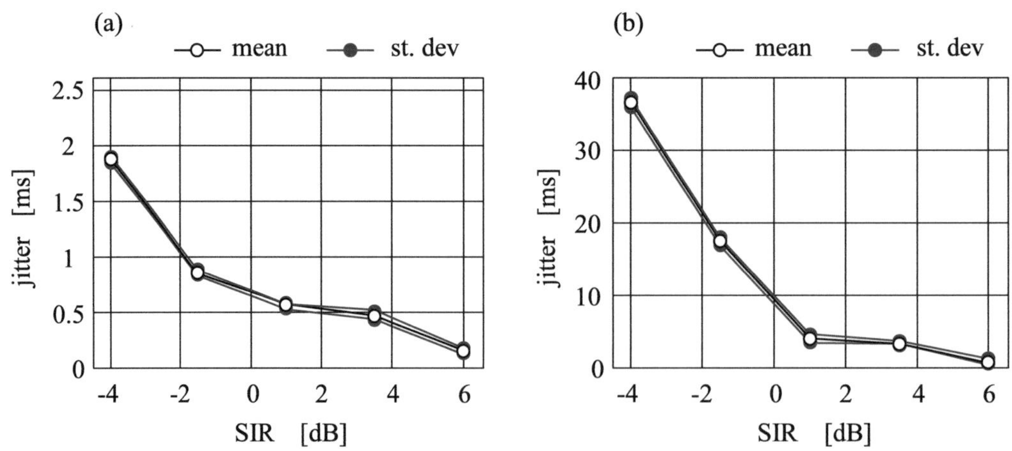

Fig. 9. Measured jitter vs signal to interference ratio (SIR): (a) scenario A, (b) scenario B

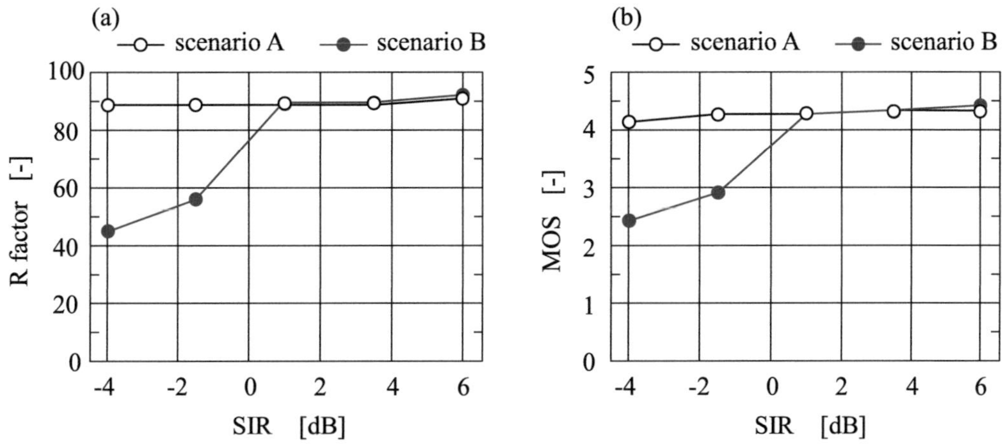

Fig. 10. Measured R factor (a) and MOS (b) vs signal to interference ratio (SIR)

can be noted for SIR levels below the threshold $SIR_{max} = 1$ dB. When $SIR = -4$ dB, the jitter assumes a non-negligible value (37 ms) with respect to the tolerated limit (150 ms), and even greater values are expected for $SIR < -4$ dB. Also in this case, R and MOS belong to the "very satisfied" category.

5.4 WLAN data traffic

In the fourth set of experiments, measurements have been conducted in the presence of a second interfering WLAN, here denoted as WLAN*, constituted by the couple of terminals NB2 and NB3 of Figs. 4 and 5. When WLAN* transmits, the WLAN under test is forced to wait until the end of the interference, and thus to defer the delivery of VoIP packets. The obtained results are summarized in Figs. 11, 12, and 13 for different WLAN* data rate from nearly 22 up to 46 Mbit/s. In the diagrams, the vertical line represents the maximum allowed data rate of the WLAN under test at medium access control (MAC) layer.
In the experiments, the power radiated by NB3 has been chosen higher than the reference

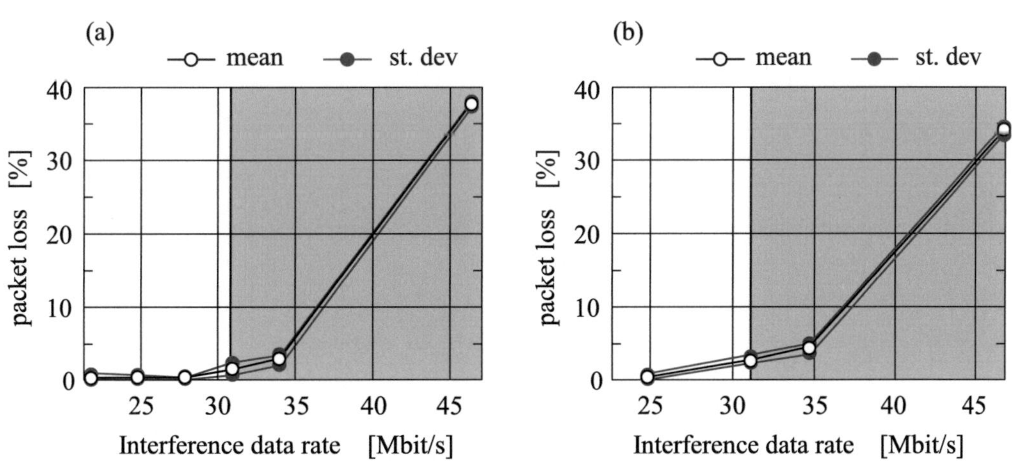

Fig. 11. Measured packet loss vs WLAN* traffic data rate: (a) scenario A, (b) scenario B

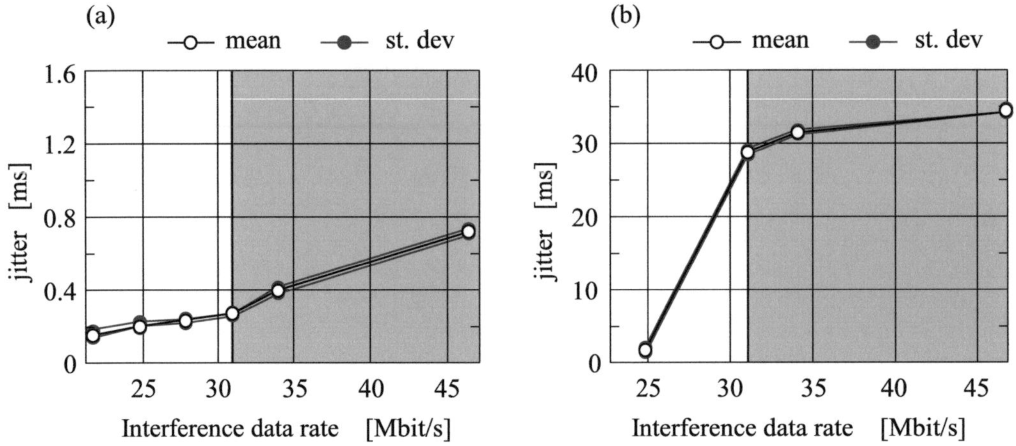

Fig. 12. Measured jitter vs WLAN* traffic data rate: (a) scenario A, (b) scenario B

threshold used by the AP to verify the status of the channel (free or busy). In Fig. 11, the detrimental effects of interference can be noted only for high data rates, beyond the vertical line, in the grey region (overload network). Beyond this limit, packet loss abruptly increases upon the growing of the data rate in both the scenarios, up to maximum values of 40 and 35 ms, respectively. In terms of jitter, Fig. 12 shows that the competitive data traffic can degrade the jitter but only in the scenario B. In fact, in the wired-wireless configuration, the estimated jitter is negligible (lower than 1 ms), while in the wireless-wireless setup it rapidly grows when the interference data rate approaches the network capacity at MAC layer. It can also be noted that for data rates lower than a threshold R_{max} of nearly 25 Mbit/s, the jitter is quite negligible. Fig. 13 finally confirms that also at application layer the effect of competitive WLAN data traffic is perceivable only at the highest data rates (greater than R_{max}). Below this threshold, a maximum voice quality can be obtained, while beyond R_{max} abrupt degradations are observed.

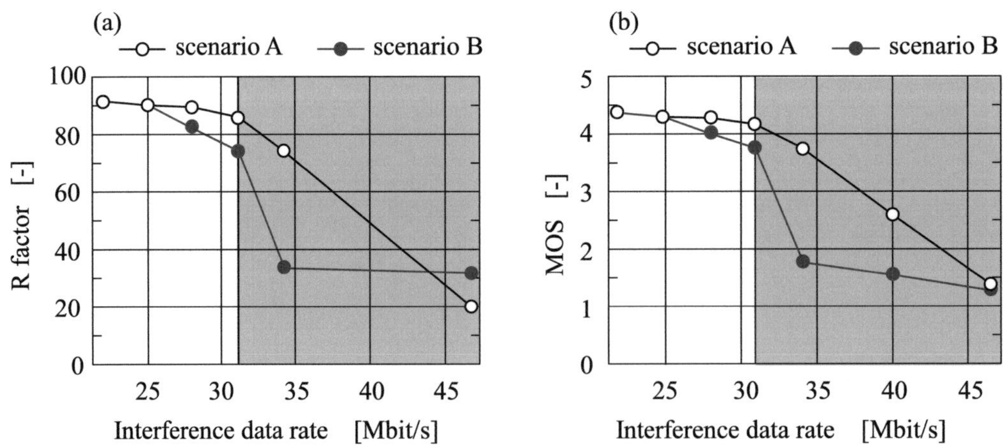

Fig. 13. Measured R factor (a) and MOS (b) vs WLAN* traffic data rate

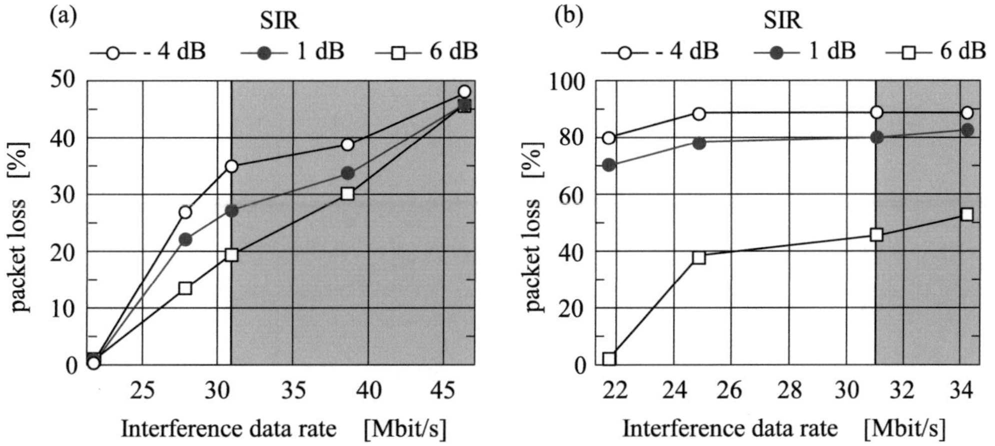

Fig. 14. Measured packet loss vs WLAN* traffic data rate for different SIR: (a) scenario A, (b) scenario B

5.5 AWGN interference and WLAN data traffic

A final group of experiments has involved the case of both AWGN interference and concurrent WLAN data traffic simultaneously operating. To this aim, the interfering sources, *i.e.* the AWGN generator and WLAN*, have been set in the same way as described in subsections 5.3 and 5.4. Measurements have been executed once again at different layers, specifically in terms of packet loss, jitter, R factor and MOS upon the varying of WLAN* traffic data rate in the range from nearly 22 up to 46 Mbit/s and for three different SIR levels: -4, 1, and 6 dB. The obtained results for both scenarios A and B and G.711 audio codec are summarized in Figs. 14, 15, and 16.

From the comparison of Figs. 11 and 14 results, some considerations can be drawn:

1. in the scenario A, the maximum data rate R_{max} beyond which packet loss abruptly increases, changes from 25 to nearly 22 Mbit/s. In the scenario B, this effect is even more

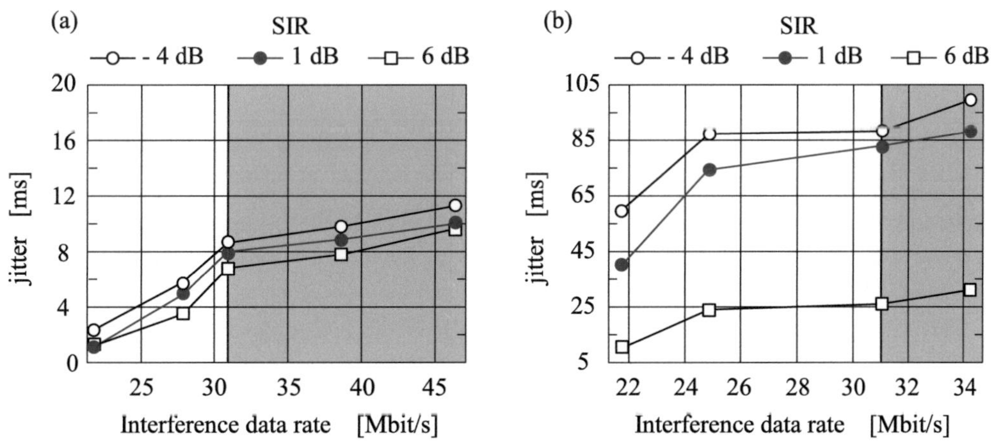

Fig. 15. Measured jitter vs WLAN* traffic data rate for different SIR: (a) scenario A, (b) scenario B

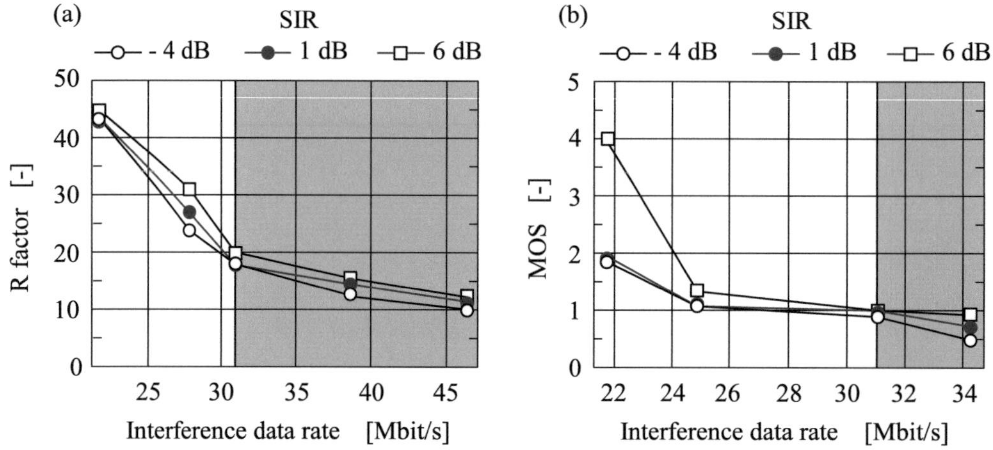

Fig. 16. Measured R factor (a) and MOS (b) vs WLAN* traffic data rate for different SIR

visible; in fact, R_{max} is nearly 22 Mbit/s for $SIR = 6$ dB and $<< 22$ Mbit/s for $SIR \leq 1$ dB, as shown by the two upper curves, which, in the range 22 - 34 Mbit/s, assume very high values (≥ 70 dB). In this case, further measurements should be performed at lower data rate to determine the corresponding values R_{max} below which packet loss becomes negligible or even null;

2. in terms of jitter, Fig. 15 shows that scenario A is rather immune even to the simultaneous presence of AWGN interference and concurrent data traffic. In fact, the estimated jitter curves appear very close one with another with values not higher than 12 ms, that means quite negligible with respect to the 150 ms threshold. A different effect can instead be noted in the wireless-wireless setup, where packet loss significantly worsens upon the increasing of AWGN interference intensity. Also in this case, the effect of AWGN interference is clearly visible for SIR valures equal to or lower than 1 dB;
3. Fig. 16 finally shows that at application layer the simultaneous presence of both competitive WLAN data traffic and AWGN interference is very detrimental even with data rate values in the range 22 – 25 Mbit/s and for any considered SIR value. The obtained R factor highlights that "very satisfied" levels of voice quality cannot be obtained for concurrent data rate levels higher than 22 Mbit/s.

Further tests have been performed at the same setup conditions but with different audio codecs, i.e. the aforementioned G.723.1 and G.729. The following results have been observed:

A. In terms of packet loss, G.711 is the audio codec that provides better results. In particular, a nearly 10% worsening of packet loss is observed for both G.723.1 and G.729 regardeless of the considered intereference data rate.

B. G.711 is also better in terms of jitter, which, for the G.729 codec, assumes very high values, even up to nearly 75 ms for an interference data rate equal to 35 Mbit/s.

C. The R factor is quite the same for G.723.1 and G.729 codecs, and much higher for G.711. For instance, in the scenario B and with 25 Mbit/s of interference data rate, the estimated R factor is 85 for G.711 and nearly 67 for G.723.1 and G.729 codecs.

D. Similarly, MOS is quite the same for G.723.1 and G.729 codecs, and much higher for G.711. For instance, in the scenario B and with 25 Mbit/s of interference data rate, the estimated MOS is 4.3 for G.711 and nearly 3.8 for G.723.1 and G.729 codecs.

6. Conclusion

A number of experimental results have been presented in order to investigate on the interference effects of Bluetooth signals, AWGN and WLAN competitive data traffic on IEEE 802.11g WLAN supporting VoIP applications. Cross layer measurements performed in terms of SIR, jitter, packet loss, R factor and MOS have been carried out with the aim of analyzing the best configurations of parameters like the interfering WLAN data rate and the measured SIR at the receiver side. For instance, in both the analyzed scenarios, i.e. wired-wireless and wireless-wireless WLAN, the maximum interfering WLAN data rate R_{max} and the minimum SIR, SIR_{min}, values have been estimated.

It has been demonstrated that the use of VoIP over WLAN can strongly be interfered by the presence of in-channel noise-like signals, such as AWGN, and of competitive data traffic generated by a near operating WLAN exploiting the same frequency channel. Therefore, parameters like SIR and WLAN interference data rate should always be carefully monitored and, if possible, adjusted beyond or below the thresholds R_{max} and SIR_{min}, respectively, to be estimated as suggested in the chapter. The use of G.711 codec is also suggested against the simultaneous effect of both concurrent data traffic and radio interference.

Many other measurement sessions could be performed to investigate on further interference phenomena here not considered for more conciseness. For instance, the analysis could be extended to the study of the interference effects due to burst-like signals or real life ones. It could also be very interesting extending the study to many other system parameters, like for instance those concerning system's quality of service.

7. References

Lin, Y. B. & Chlamtac, I. (2000). *Wireless and Mobile Network Architectures*, John Wiley and Sons, ISBN 978-0-471-39492-1, New York, US.

Douskalis, B. (1999). *IP Telephony: The Integration of Robust VoIP Services*, Prentice Hall, ISBN 978-0-13-014118-7, New Jersey, US.

IEEE Standard 802.11 (1999). *Wireless LAN Medium Access Control (MAC) and Physical Layer (PHY) Specifications*, IEEE computer society.

IEEE Standard 802.15.4 (2003). *Wireless Medium Access Control (MAC) and Physical Layer (PHY) Specifications for Low-Rate. Wireless Personal Area Networks (LR-WPANs)*, IEEE computer society.

IEEE Standard 802.16 (2001). *IEEE Standard for Local and Metropolitan Area Networks - Part 16: Air Interference for Fixed Broadband Wireless Access Systems*, IEEE computer society.

Garg, S. & Cappes, M. (2003). An Experimental Study of Throughput for UDP and VoIP Traffic in IEEE 802.11b Networks, *Proceedings of Wireless Communications and Networking*, pgs 1748-1753, New Orleans, LA, US, March 2003.

Angrisani, L. & Vadursi, M. (2007). Cross-layer Measurements for a Comprehensive Characterization of Wireless Networks in the Presence of Interference, *IEEE Trans. on Instrumentation and Measurement*, Vol. 56, No. 4, 2007.

Wang, X. G.& Mellor, G.M. (2004). Improving VOIP application's performance over WLAN using a new distributed fair MAC scheme, *Proceedings of Advanced Information*

Networking and Applications, pgs 126-131, ISBN: 0-7695-2051-0, March 2004, Fukuoka, Japan.

Wang, W. & Li, S.C.L. (2005). Solutions to Performance Problems in VoIP Over a 802.11 Wireless LAN, *IEEE Trans. on Vehicular Technology*, Vol. 54, No. 1, Jan 2005, pgs 366-384.

Garg, S. & Cappes, M. (2002). *On the Throughput of 802.11b Networks for VoIP*, TechnicalReport ALR-2002-012, Avaya Labs, 2002.

El-fishawy, N. A. & Zahra, M. M. & El-gamala, M. (2007). Capacity estimation of VoIP transmission over WLAN, *Proceedings of Radio Science Conference*, pgs 1-11, March 2007, Cairo, Egypt.

Prasat, A. R. (1999). Performance comparison of voice over IEEE 802.11 schemes, *Proceedings of Vehicular Technology Conference*, pgs 2636-2640, Vol. 5, Sept. 1999, Houston, Tx, US.

Hiraguri, T. & Ichikawa, T. & Iizuka, M. & Morikura, M. (2002). Novel Multiple Access Protocol for Voice over IP in Wireless LAN, *IEEE Int. Symp. on Computers and Communications*, pgs 517-523, ISBN: 0-7695-1671-8, July 2002, Taormina, Italy.

ITU-T Recommendation G.711 (1972). *Pulse Code Modulation (PCM) of Voice Frequencies*, 1972.

ITU-T Recommendation G.729 (1996). *Coding of Speech at 8 kbit/s Using Conjugate-Structure Algebraic-Code-Excited Linear Prediction (CS-ACELP)*, 1996.

ITU-T Recommendation G.723.1 (2006). *Digital Terminal Equipments - Coding of Analogue Signals by Methods Other Than PCM. Dual Rate Speech Coder for Multimedia Communications Transmitting at 5.3 and 6.3 kbit/s*, 2006.

ITU-T Recommendation P.800 (1996). *Methods for Subjective Determination of Transmission Quality*, 1996.

Schulzrinne, H. & Casner, S. & Frederick, R. & Jacobson, V. (2003). *RTP: A Transport protocol for Real-Time Applications*, RFC 3550, July 2003.

Angrisani, L. & Bertocco, M. & Fortin, D.& Sona, A. (2007). Assessing coexistence problems of IEEE 802.11b and IEEE 802.15.4 wireless networks through cross-layer measurements, *IEEE International Instrumentation and Measurement Technology Conference*, paper n. 7326, ISBN: 1-4244-0588-2, May 2007, Warsaw, Poland.

Botta, A. & Dainotti, A. & Pescape, A. (2007). Multi-protocol and multi-platform traffic generation and measurement, *INFOCOM 2007 DEMO Session*, May 2007, Anchorage, Alaska, USA.

Bertocco, M, & Sona, A. (2006). On the power measurement via a superheterodyne spectrum analyzer, *IEEE Trans. on Instrumentation and Measurement*, pgs. 1494-1501, ISSN: 0018-9456., Vol. 55, No. 5, 2006.

10

VoIP Features Oriented Uplink Scheduling Scheme in Wireless Networks

Sung-Min Oh and Jae-Hyun Kim
School of Electrical and Computer Engineering, Ajou University
Republic of Korea

1. Introduction

VoIP services have been considered as one of the most important services in the next generation wireless systems. VoIP service requires the same quality of service (QoS) requirement as constant bit rate services. For this reason, the IEEE 802.16 standard has defined an unsolicited grant service (UGS) to guarantee the QoS. However, the UGS is inadequate to support VoIP services with silence suppression because of the waste of radio bandwidth in the silent-periods. In the UGS, a base station (BS) periodically allocates a maximum-size radio bandwidth (grant) during the silent-periods even though a subscriber station (SS) does not have a packet to transmit in the silent-periods. To solve this problem, (Lee et al., 2005) proposed an extended real time polling service (ertPS) to support VoIP services with silence suppression. The ertPS can manage the grant-size according to the voice activity in order to save the radio bandwidth in silent-period. Unfortunately, the waste of radio bandwidth and the increase of access delay can still exist when the ertPS is applied to the system because the grant-size and grant-interval used by the ertPS cannot correspond with the packet-size and the packet-generation-interval of the VoIP services in the application layer.
Recently, the IEEE 802.16's Task Group m (TGm), which was approved by IEEE to develop an amendment to IEEE 802.16 standard in 2006, published the draft evaluation methodology document in which several kinds of VoIP speech codecs are considered such as G.711, G.723.1, G.729, enhanced variable rate codec (EVRC), and adaptive multi-rate (AMR) (Srinivasan, 2007). These VoIP speech codecs generate packets with different packet-size and packet-generation-interval as shown in Table 1. However, the IEEE 802.16 standard does not define the QoS parameter generation method, because they have focused on only medium access control (MAC) and physical (PHY) layer. For this reason, IEEE 802.16 based systems need the QoS parameter mapping algorithm to obtain the features of the VoIP services in the application layer. Hong and Kwon (Hong & Kwon, 2006) proposed the QoS parameter mapping algorithm to exploit the feature of the VoIP services in IEEE 802.16 systems which statistically measures the peak data rate of VoIP services and calculates the QoS parameters. However, the algorithm needs significant time to measure the VoIP traffic to perform the statistical analysis, and the QoS parameters cannot correspond to the features of the VoIP services when the number of samples of the VoIP traffic is not sufficient to analyze the features of the VoIP service. To overcome these problems, this chapter designs a cross-layer QoS parameter mapping scheme which exploits the information of the VoIP speech codec included in the session description protocol (SDP) to generate the QoS parameters for VoIP scheduling algorithms.

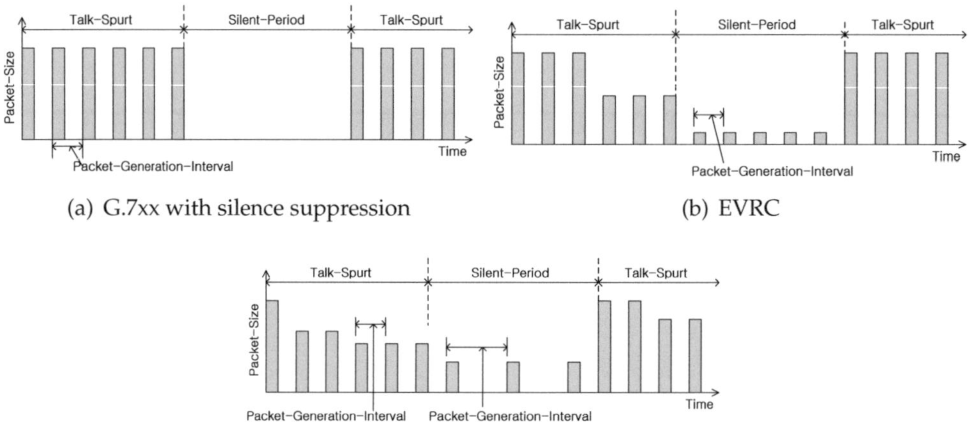

(a) G.7xx with silence suppression

(b) EVRC

(c) AMR

Fig. 1. Traffic models for various VoIP speech codecs

Moreover, this chapter proposes a new cross-layer VoIP scheduling algorithm which exploits the QoS parameters generated by the proposed QoS parameter mapping scheme. The conventional VoIP scheduling algorithms have been designed considering a specific VoIP speech codec. The UGS has been designed to guarantee a QoS for G.7xx (i.e. G.711, G.723.1, and G.729) without silence suppression, and the ertPS has been developed to support EVRC. In particular, the ertPS is designed to compensate for the resource inefficiency of the UGS in the silent-periods. Unfortunately, the ertPS is not an optimal VoIP scheduling algorithm for the whole VoIP speech codecs. In the ertPS, a BS periodically allocates a minimum-size grant to a SS every 20 msec regardless of the voice activity in the silent-period. However, the AMR speech codec generates a packet every 160 msec in the silent-period. Thus, the ertPS can cause the waste of radio bandwidth in the silent-period when it supports the AMR speech codec. To overcome this inefficiency of the ertPS, Oh et al (Oh et al., 2008) proposed a new VoIP scheduling algorithm, which is called as a hybrid VoIP (HV) algorithm in this chapter. The HV algorithm adapts a random access scheme in the silent-period to save radio bandwidth. However, it can suffer from an overhead occurred in the silent-period when the EVRC is applied in the application layer. The problems of VoIP scheduling algorithms according to the VoIP speech codecs are detailed in section 3. Consequently, this chapter proposes the cross-layer VoIP scheduling algorithm to support all available VoIP speech codecs. The main feature of the cross-layer VoIP scheduling algorithm is that it can dynamically adjust the grant-interval in the silent-period according to the VoIP speech codec applied in the application layer. By this feature, the proposed scheduling algorithm can save radio bandwidth guaranteeing a QoS for all VoIP speech codecs in the silent-period. The description of the proposed scheduling algorithm is presented in section 4.

2. Traffic models for various VoIP speech codecs

This section describes traffic models for various VoIP speech codecs which are presented in Fig. 1 where each VoIP speech codec has individual features in their packet generation policy (ITU-T-G711, 2000; ITU-T-G7231, 1996; ITU-T-G729, 2007; 3GPP2-EVRC, 2004; 3GPP-TS-26201, 2001; 3GPP-TS-26092, 2002; 3GPP-TS-26071, 1999). Fig. 1 (a) represents a traffic model for

VoIP Speech Codec	PS (bytes)	PGI (msec)
G.711	160	20
G.723.1	19.88	30
G.729	10	10
EVRC	21.375, 10, 2	20
AMR	Voice frame: 11.875, 12.875, 14.75, 16.75, 18.5, 19.875, 25.5, 30.5 SID frame: 5	Talk-spurt: 20 Silent-period: 160

Table 1. Features of VoIP Speech Codecs (PS: Packet-Size, PGI: Packet-Generation-Interval)

G.7xx with silence suppression. In the silent-period, this model does not generate any packets so as to save radio bandwidth but a receiver side can suffer from deterioration in the QoS performance in these situations when the background noise at the transmitter side is high. The reason for this is that the source controlled rate (SCR) switching in a VoIP speech codec of the receiver side can take place rapidly so that the EVRC and AMR speech codecs periodically send packets which include the information of the background noise at the transmitter side every grant-interval in the silent period. However, these speech codecs have different grant-interval; namely the EVRC generates the packets every 20 msec, whereas the AMR speech codec generates silence indicator (SID) frames every 160 msec in the silent-periods, as depicted in Fig. 1 (b) and (c).

In talk-spurts, the G.7xx generates fixed-size packets, whereas the EVRC and AMR speech codecs generate variable-size packets according to the wireless channel or the network condition. The packet-size is as specified in Table 1. The EVRC generates packets according to three data rate which are full rate (21.375 bytes), half rate (10 bytes), and eighth rate (2 bytes), where the eighth rate is for the background noise. The AMR speech codec generates variable-size packets every 20 msec in the talk-spurts and Table 1 represents the variable packet-sizes for the AMC speech codec.

IEEE 802.16e/m systems can suffer from several problems in supporting these various features of the VoIP speech codecs. These problems are detailed in the following section.

3. Challenges for VoIP services in IEEE 802.16e/m systems

IEEE 802.16 defined UGS and ertPS to support VoIP services with a QoS guarantee. However, the conventional VoIP scheduling algorithms can suffer from the waste of radio bandwidth and the increase of access delay. These problems can be caused by two challenges in the IEEE 802.16e/m systems such as the absence of a QoS parameter mapping scheme and the resource inefficiency of the conventional VoIP scheduling algorithms.

3.1 Absence of the QoS parameter mapping scheme

The convergence sublayer (CS) defined in (Handley & Jacobson, 1998) connects the MAC layer with the IP layer. When a session is generated in the application layer, a connection identifier (CID) is created in the CS. At this time, QoS parameters are needed to guarantee the QoS of the session. However, the IEEE 802.16 standard does not define a QoS parameter generation method and hence mismatches between QoS parameters in the MAC layer and the features of a session in the application layer can occur. Such mismatch problems can cause the waste of

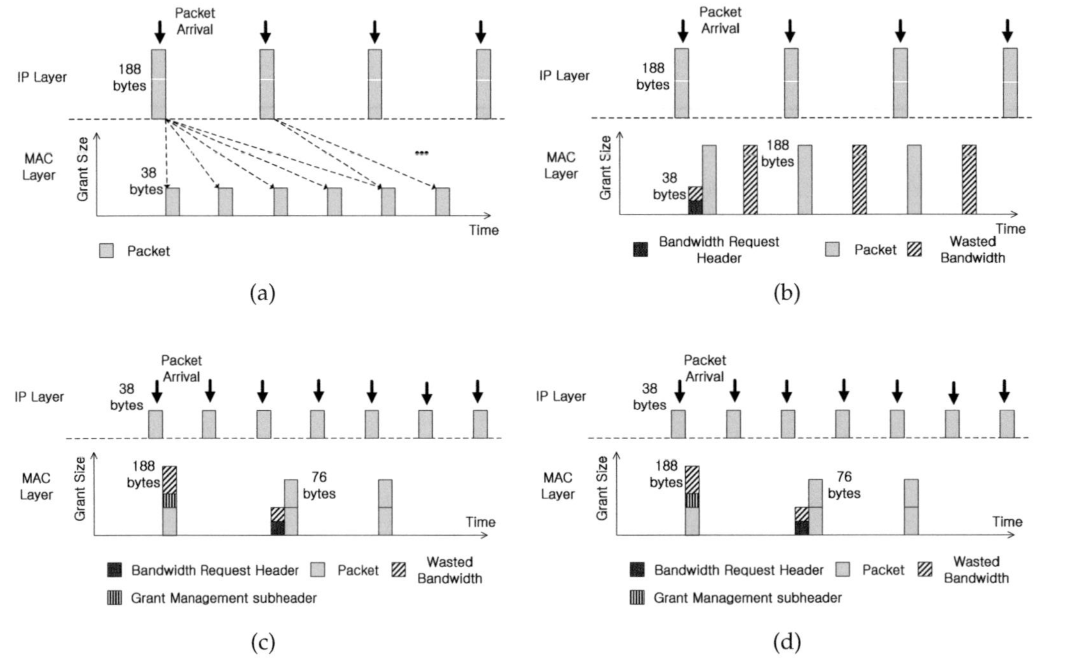

Fig. 2. Examples of the mismatch problem between the QoS parameters in the MAC layer and the features of VoIP services in the application layer; default QoS parameters (grant-size: 38 bytes and grant-interval: 10 msec), VoIP speech codec (G. 711 without silence suppression), and VoIP scheduling algorithm ((a) UGS and (b) ertPS), {default QoS parameters (grant-size: 188 bytes and grant-interval: 20 msec), VoIP speech codec (G. 729 without silence suppression), and VoIP scheduling algorithm ((c) UGS and (d) ertPS)}

radio bandwidth or the increase of access delay. To describe the mismatch problems in detail, this chapter gives examples as shown in Fig. 2.

Figs. 2 (a) and (b) represent the mismatch problems. In this case, the default values of the QoS parameters are set by considering the G.729 . In addition, VoIP scheduling algorithms, as shown in Fig. 2 (a) and (b), are UGS and ertPS, respectively. As depicted in Fig. 2 (a), the access delay increases by 40 msec to transmit a packet due to the mismatch problem. A BS periodically allocates a fixed-size grant (38 bytes) every 10 msec even though a SS needs additional bandwidth to transmit a packet, because the UGS cannot request any additional bandwidth. Due to this problem, the access delay can increase linearly when the system continuously receives data packets from the upper layer. This anomalistic phenomenon can cause serious deterioration of the QoS performance for VoIP services. Unlike UGS, the ertPS can prevent the increase of access delay, as shown in Fig. 2 (b). The reason is that the ertPS can request additional bandwidth by the bandwidth-request-header. However, the radio bandwidth (188 bytes) can be wasted every 20 msec; because a BS periodically allocates a grant (188 bytes) every 10 msec even though data packets are generated every 20 msec.

Figs. 2 (c) and (d) also represent the mismatch problem. In this case, the default values of the QoS parameters are set by considering the G.711. As depicted in Fig. 2 (c), a packet can experience an access delay of 10 msec every 20 msec. In addition, 112 bytes of bandwidth is wasted every 20 msec when UGS is applied to the system. The ertPS can save the waste of radio bandwidth as shown in Fig. 2 (d). However, the access delay still exists because of the mismatch between the grant-interval and the packet-generation-interval.

As mentioned above, the mismatch problem can cause the waste of radio bandwidth or the increase of access delay. To solve the mismatch problem, this chapter proposes a new cross-layer QoS mapping scheme, which will be described in section 4.

3.2 Resource inefficiency of the conventional VoIP scheduling algorithms

The UGS and ertPS methods are inefficient in their use of the wireless resource. In UGS, a BS periodically allocates the maximum-size grant to a SS regardless of the voice activity even though the data rate of the VoIP services with silence suppression decreases in the silent-periods. Because of this resource inefficiency of the UGS, the ertPS has been designed to support VoIP services with silence suppression. The ertPS can manage the grant-size according to the voice activity. In order to change this, the ertPS has two main features. Firstly, it exploits a generic-MAC-header to inform a BS of the SS's voice activity. Lee et al (Lee et al., 2005) defined a Grant-Me (GM) bit using a reserved bit in the generic-MAC-header. When in a silent-period the voice activity indicated by the GM bit is '0' whereas in a talk-spurt, the GM bit is '1'. Secondly, a BS periodically allocates a grant to transmit a generic-MAC-header in the silent-period. By using this feature, a SS can transmit a generic-MAC-header even though there is no packet to transmit in the silent-period.

On the other hand, the grant for a generic-MAC-header is wasted during the silent-period from considering the wireless resource aspects. As shown in Fig. 3 (a), a grant is wasted every 20 msec when the G.7xx situation with silence suppression is applied to the system. When the AMR speech codec is applied to the system, seven grants are wasted every 160 msec during the silent-period, as shown in Fig. 3 (b).

To overcome this inefficiency of the ertPS, (Oh et al., 2008) proposed a HV algorithm with three main features. Firstly, a BS does not periodically allocate a grant to a SS in the silent-period in order to save the uplink bandwidth. Secondly, the HV adopts the random access scheme to transmit a packet in the silent-period. Thirdly, it also uses the random access scheme when the voice activity changes from a silent-period to a talk-spurt, because the transition time from one to the other is unpredictable. The HV exploits a bandwidth-request-and-uplink-sleep-control (BRUSC) header in order to inform a BS of the SS's voice activity and request the required bandwidth. The BRUSC header has a reserved bit which is defined as a silence talkspurt (ST) bit in (Oh et al., 2008), and this has a bandwidth request (BR) field which can be specified as a required bandwidth in bytes. In the HV method, the SS transmit a BRUSC header by using the random access scheme when a packet to transmit is generated in a silent-period, or when the voice activity changes from being in a silent-period to a talk-spurt. At this time, the grant-size is the same with the bandwidth required by the BRUSC header.

Unfortunately, the HV algorithm can suffer from collisions when the EVRC is applied to the system. In case of the AMR speech codec and G.7xx with silence suppression, the collision cannot affect the QoS performance for the VoIP services, because the transmission rate of a BRUSC header is very low. However, a SS transmits a BRUSC header every 20 msec during a silent-period by the random access scheme when the EVRC is applied to the system as shown in Fig. 3 (c). For this reason, the message overhead required to transmit a packet rapidly increases because the transmission rate of a BRUSC header increases. For this problem, the HV algorithm may be inadequate for EVRC. Consequently, this chapter proposes the cross-layer VoIP scheduling algorithm to support the whole VoIP speech codecs with efficient use of radio

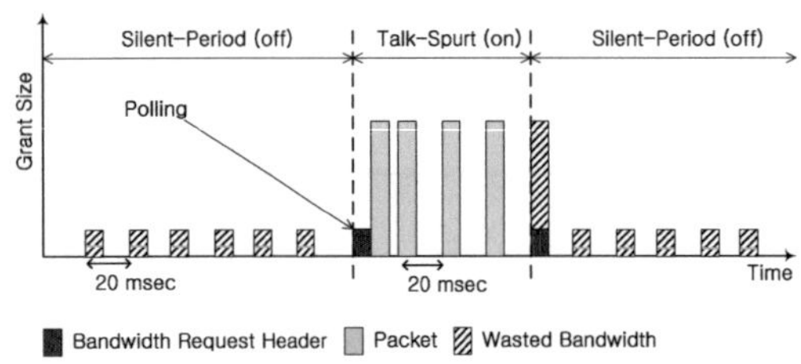

(a) ertPS for G.7xx with silence suppression

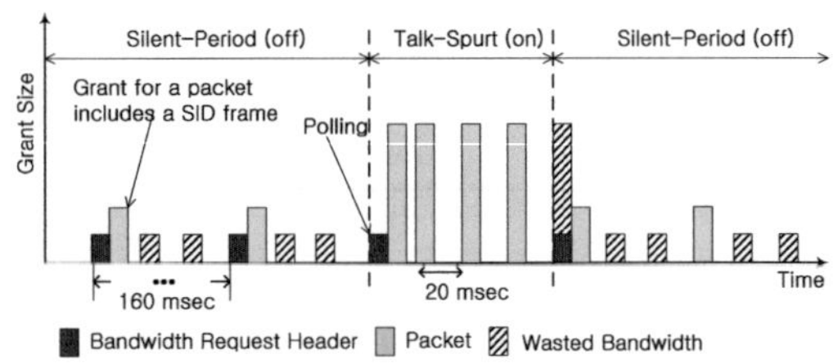

(b) ertPS for AMR speech codec

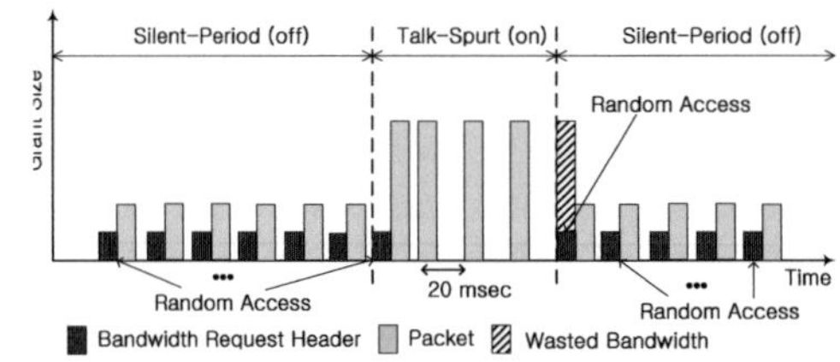

(c) HV algorithm for EVRC

Fig. 3. Resource inefficiency of the conventional VoIP scheduling algorithms

bandwidth.

4. Proposed cross-layer framework for VoIP services

In order to overcome the challenges of the VoIP services in IEEE 802.16e/m systems mentioned in section 3, we design the cross-layer framework for VoIP services which is shown in Fig. 4. It consists of the cross-layer QoS parameter mapping scheme and the new cross-layer VoIP scheduling algorithm. The description of the cross-layer QoS parameter mapping scheme and the cross-layer VoIP scheduling algorithm are as follows.

4.1 Cross-layer framework for VoIP services

We propose the cross-layer QoS parameter mapping scheme to compensate for the absence of the QoS parameter mapping scheme in IEEE 802.16e/m systems. The cross-layer QoS parameter mapping scheme consists of three functions such as the QoS parameter creation function, CID creation function, and CID mapping function as shown in Fig. 4.

4.1.1 QoS parameter creation function

The QoS parameter creation function is the main function in the cross-layer QoS parameter mapping scheme. It generates the QoS parameters using the session information in the application layer. When a VoIP session is opened in the application layer, the session initiation function activates a session initiation protocol (SIP) to connect a session between the end devices. At this time, the SIP message includes a SDP to deliver the session information, e.g. media type, transport protocol, media format, and so on, for guaranteeing the required QoS. In SDP, a field 'm' presents the media information such as m= (media) (port) (transport) (format list). For example, 'm=audio 49170 RTP/AVP 0' means that media is audio, port number is 49170, transport protocol is real time protocol (RTP) with audio video profile (AVP), and

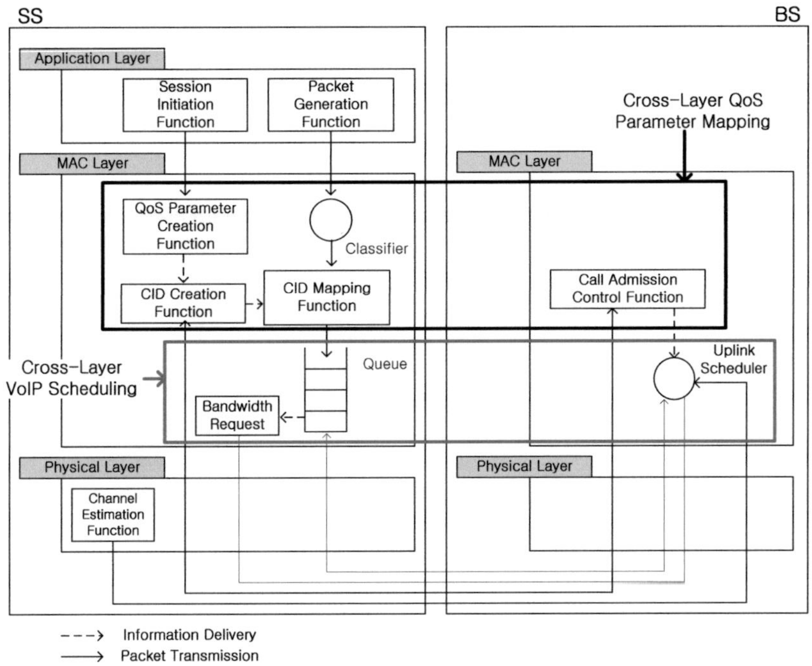

Fig. 4. Cross-layer framework for VoIP services

voice codec is G.711 (0) (Handley & Jacobson, 1998). In this chapter, the proposed scheme uses the field 'm' to identify the kinds of VoIP speech codec applied in the application layer. The features of VoIP services can be identified by the kinds of VoIP speech codec as shown in Table 1. For this reason, the QoS parameter creation function can obtain the features of the VoIP services such as the packet-size and packet-generation-interval from the SDP. Therefore, the QoS parameter creation function can generate the QoS parameters using the features of VoIP services as shown in Table 2.

4.1.2 CID creation function

The CID creation function generates a CID between a BS and a SS. It transmits a dynamic service addition request (DSA-REQ) message which includes the QoS parameter set, as shown in Table 2, to a call admission control function in a BS. The call admission control function decides whether the system supports the VoIP service or not based on the QoS parameter set

QoS parameter set	Values
Maximum sustained traffic rate	PS × PGI
Maximum traffic burst	PS
Minimum reserved traffic rate	PS × PGI
Minimum tolerable traffic rate	PS × PGI
Unsolicited grant interval	PGI
Unsolicited polling interval	PCI
SDU inter-arrival interval	PGI

Table 2. QoS Parameter Mapping Example for the VoIP Scheduling Algorithms

in the DSA-REQ message, and it sends a DSA response (DSA-RSP) message which includes a CID if the system can support the VoIP services. The CID creation function delivers the CID to the CID mapping function, when it receives the DSA-RSP message from the call admission control function.

4.1.3 CID mapping function

When the CID mapping function receives a CID from the CID creation function, it updates a CID table which consists of CID and the information of the user datagram protocol (UDP)/IP header such as the source/destination UDP port number, source/destination IP address, and protocol, and so on. The CID mapping function identifies a packet received from the IP layer using the information of the UDP/IP header, and it searches the CID which corresponds with the information of the UDP/IP header. For examples, the CID mapping function can identify a packet which includes a SIP message using the UDP port number because the UDP port number of SIP is 5060 or 5061. In addition, it can identify a VoIP packet using a source/destination IP address. The reason is that the source/destination IP addresses of the packets in a VoIP session are fixed. After the packet identification and CID mapping, the CID mapping function stores the packets in a queue which corresponds with the CID. The IEEE 802.16 systems transmit the packets stored in the queue by using VoIP scheduling algorithms.

4.2 Cross-layer VoIP scheduling algorithm

In order to solve the inefficiency of the conventional VoIP scheduling algorithms mentioned in section 3, we propose the new cross-layer VoIP scheduling algorithm. This proposed algorithm has three main features. Firstly, it exploits the QoS parameters, e.g. the grant-size and the grant-interval, generated by the cross-layer QoS parameter mapping scheme. Secondly, it adjusts the grant allocation policy according to the kinds of VoIP speech codec in the silent-period to save the uplink bandwidth. When the G.7xx with silence suppression is applied in the application layer, a BS stops the periodic grant allocation during the silent-periods in the proposed algorithm. When the EVRC or AMR speech codecs are applied in the application layer, a BS periodically allocates a grant every 20 msec or 160 msec during silent-periods, respectively. Thirdly, it adopts the random access scheme only when the voice activity changes from a silent-period to a talk-spurt. In addition, the proposed algorithm uses a BRUSC header to inform a BS of the SS's voice activity, as in the HV algorithm. In this chapter, we define that the ST bit '0' means a silent-period, whereas the ST bit '1' means a talk-spurt.

4.2.1 In case of silent-period

Figs. 5 (a), (b), and (c) represent the cross-layer VoIP scheduling algorithm for G.7xx, AMR speech codec, and EVRC, respectively. As shown in Fig. 5, a SS sends a BRUSC header with the ST bit '0' by using the polling scheme when the voice activity changes from a talk-spurt to a silent-period. When a BS receives a BRUSC header with the ST bit being '0', the BS stops the grant allocation or periodically allocates the grant. In case of G.7xx, the BS stops the periodic grant allocation in order to save radio bandwidth in the silent-period. In case of the AMR speech codec and EVRC, the BS periodically allocates a grant every 160 msec and 20 msec during the silent-period, respectively. The grant-size corresponds with the bandwidth specified in the BR field of the BRUSC header.

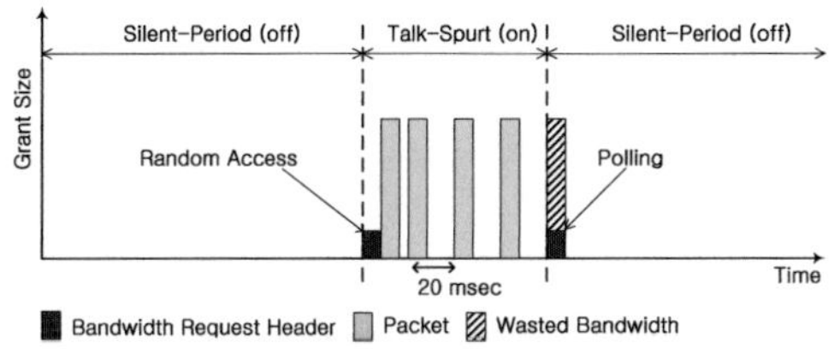

(a) for G.7xx with silence suppression

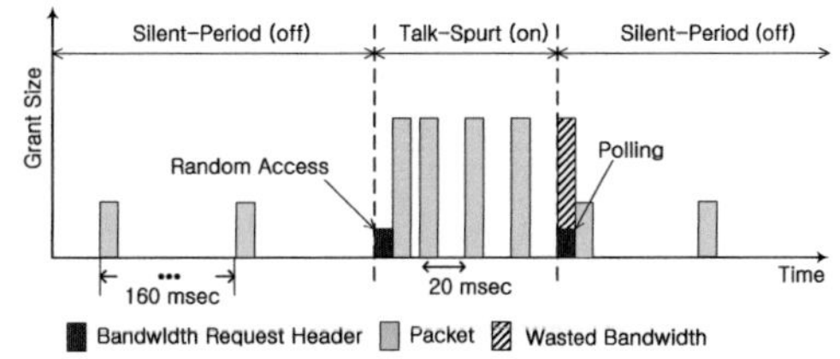

(b) for the AMR speech codec

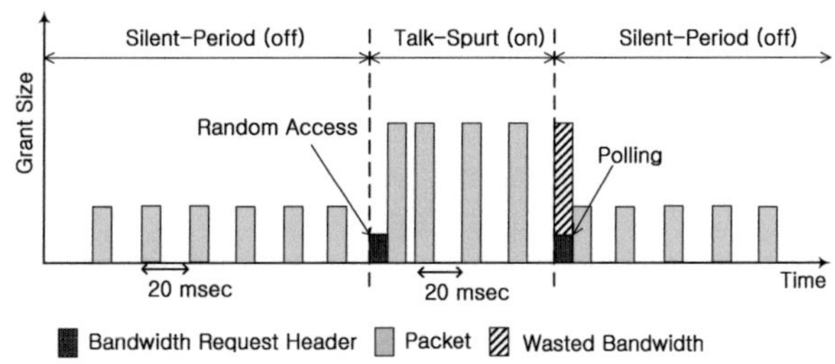

(c) for EVRC

Fig. 5. Cross-layer VoIP scheduling algorithm

4.2.2 In case of talk-spurt

A BS periodically allocates a grant to a SS. The grant-size can be variable according to the data rate of the AMR speech codec. The proposed algorithm uses a BRUSC header or grant-management subheader for the variable data rate in the talk-spurt, similar to the HV algorithm. When the voice activity changes from a silent-period to a talk-spurt, a SS transmits a BRUSC header with the ST bit '1' by the random access scheme, as shown in Fig. 5. In the random access scheme, a SS transmits a ranging-request (RNG-REQ) message through a ranging subchannel to obtain the radio bandwidth in order to transmit a BRUSC header. A RNG-REQ message includes an orthogonal ranging code randomly selected by the SS. The grant-size is determined by the packet-size. When a BS receives the BRUSC header with the ST bit as '1', the BS allocates a grant to the SS at the next frame, and it periodically assigns a grant to the SS every grant-interval.

5. Performance evaluation

This section represents the performance evaluation results for the cross-layer QoS parameter mapping scheme and cross-layer VoIP scheduling algorithm. In order to compare the resource efficiency and QoS performance, we evaluate the system performance in terms of the average number of the allocated subchannel and average access delay. The average number of the allocated subchannel indicates the total number of subchannels, which is allocated by a BS per second. The average access delay means the average time to transmit a packet from a SS to a BS. In addition, we analyze the VoIP capacity according to the VoIP scheduling algorithms where the VoIP capacity means the maximum tolerable number of VoIP users.

VoIP speech codecs in application layer	Scenarios	Default values Grant-size	Default values Grant-interval
G.723.1 without silence suppression	Scenario 1	188	20
	Scenario 2	30	10
G.11 without silence suppression	Scenario 1	40	30
	Scenario 2	30	10
G.729 without silence suppression	Scenario 1	188	20
	Scenario 2	40	30

Table 3. Simulation Scenarios for the QoS Parameter Mapping Scheme

5.1 Simulation results for the cross-layer QoS parameter mapping scheme

The end-to-end performance evaluation simulator for the cross-layer framework has been built as shown in Fig. 4. In the end-to-end performance evaluation simulator, the whole functional blocks are modeled, and these are represented in Fig. 4. In addition, we considers the IEEE 802.16e/m orthogonal frequency division multiple access (OFDMA) system that uses 5msec time division duplex (TDD) frame size, 10 MHz bandwidth, and 1024 fast Fourier transform (FFT). In order to implement the channel variation, we consider the path loss, log-normal shadowing, and frequency-selective Rayleigh fading according to the user's mobility. To evaluate the performance for the QoS parameter mapping scheme, we consider one VoIP user in a cell. In addition, we assume that the IEEE 802.16 systems define the QoS parameters related to the VoIP services as the default values considering a specific VoIP speech codec, because the IEEE 802.16 standard does not mention the QoS parameters generation method. The default values are defined as shown in Table 3 and we consider the VoIP speech codecs as G.723.1, G.711, and G.729 without silence suppression, and defines two scenarios for each VoIP speech codec applied in the application layer, as shown in Table 3.

Fig. 6 presents the simulation results for the QoS parameter mapping scheme. Figs. 6 (a) and (b) show the simulation results when the UGS is applied to the system, whereas Figs. 6 (c) and (d) indicates the simulation results when the ertPS is applied to the system. As shown in Fig. 6 (a), the average access delay can go to infinity when the UGS is applied to the system, if the grant-size is smaller than the packet-size which is specified by the VoIP speech codec. The reason is that the access delay linearly increases when the number of transmitting packets increases because of a queuing delay of the whole VoIP packets, see Fig. 2 (a). On the other hand, the proposed algorithm can reduce the access delay to 3 msec. In case of G.723.1 and G.729, the average access delay of scenario 1 and 2 increases by 4 8 msec compared to that of the proposed algorithm. This increase of the access delay is caused by the mismatch of the QoS parameters and features of the VoIP services. However, the average access delay can not affect the QoS of the VoIP services because the maximum tolerable delay is defined, in (Srinivasan, 2007), as 50 msec. Unfortunately, these cases can suffer from resource inefficiency in term of the average number of allocated subchannel, as shown in Fig. 6 (b). Except for the G.729 with scenario 2, the average number of allocated subchannel increases by 400 $\sim$ 1200 subchannels per second compared to that obtained for the new proposed algorithm. In case of G.711, the average number of allocated subchannels for scenarios 1 and 2 are much smaller than that of the proposed algorithm. However, the SS experiences long access delays to transmit packet in scenarios 1 and 2. These cases can cause a serious deterioration of the QoS performance for VoIP services. Consequently, the system can waste wireless resources as well as increase the access delay, if the system uses the default values for the QoS parameters of VoIP services when the UGS is applied to the system. As shown in Figs. 6 (a) and (b), the

proposed algorithm can save the waste of wireless resources and as well as reduce the access delays.
Unlike the UGS, the ertPS can manage the grant-size according to the packet-size. For this reason, the ertPS can improve the system performance even though the system exploits the default values for the QoS parameters of VoIP services. As shown in Figs. 6 (c) and (d), the access delay and the average number of allocated subchannels when using the conventional algorithm with the ertPS decrease compared to those obtained for the conventional algorithm with the UGS. The average access delay can be reduced from "infinity" to less than 10 msec in the case of G.711. However, the waste of radio bandwidth and the increase of access delays still exist because of the mismatch of the grant-interval and the packet-generation-interval. In the case of G.723.1, the SS has to wait for a grant in scenario 1 because a BS periodically allocates a grant every 20 msec even though a packet is generated every 30 msec in the application layer. In scenario 2 of G.723.1, the SS does not need to wait for a grant because a BS allocates a grant every 10 msec. However, this case can waste two grants every 30 msec. For this inefficiency, the average number of allocated subchannel increases by about 200 % compared to the proposed algorithm as shown in Fig. 6 (d). In the case of G.729, a transmitting packet is delayed because the grant-interval is larger than the packet-generation-interval. For this reason, the average number of allocated subchannel decreases in scenarios 1 and 2 compared to that of the proposed algorithm whereas the average access delay increases by 10 16 msec. Therefore, the cross-layer QoS parameter mapping scheme can improve the system performance in terms of the number of allocated subchannels and access delays.

5.2 Numerical results for the cross-layer VoIP scheduling algorithm

This subsection represents the system performance for the new cross-layer VoIP scheduling algorithm in terms of the VoIP capacity. The VoIP capacity means the maximum supportable number of VoIP users. In order to analyze the system performance, the voice traffic has been modeled as an exponentially distributed ON-OFF system with mean ON-time $1/\lambda$ and mean OFF-time $1/\mu$. Fig. 7 represents the one-dimensional Markov chain for N independent VoIP users (Oh et al., 2008). In Fig. 7, each state indicates the number of VoIP users in the ON state. Since the sum of the whole steady-state probability is unit, the steady-state probability is derived as

$$\begin{aligned} p_N(k) &= \binom{N}{k}\left(\frac{\mu}{\lambda+\mu}\right)^k\left(\frac{\lambda}{\lambda+\mu}\right)^{(N-k)}, \\ & \quad k=0,1,2,\cdots,N. \end{aligned} \tag{1}$$

The average number of VoIP users in the silent-period (N_{OFF}) is

$$N_{OFF}(N) = \frac{N\lambda}{\lambda+\mu}, \tag{2}$$

where N is the number of VoIP users.
In this chapter, the unit of the grant-size is defined as the number of slots. The average number of uplink slots required every grant-interval for a VoIP user in each scheduler is given by

$$S_{UGS} = S_{ON\_max}, \tag{3}$$

$$S_{ertPS} = \left(\frac{S_{ON}}{\lambda} + \frac{S_{GMH}}{\mu}\right), \tag{4}$$

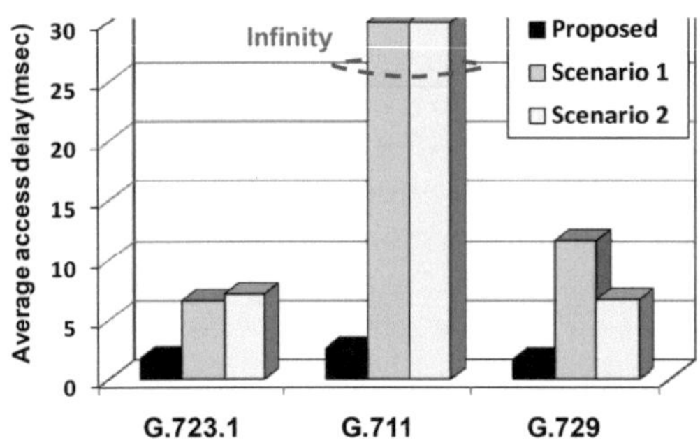

(a) average access delay with UGS

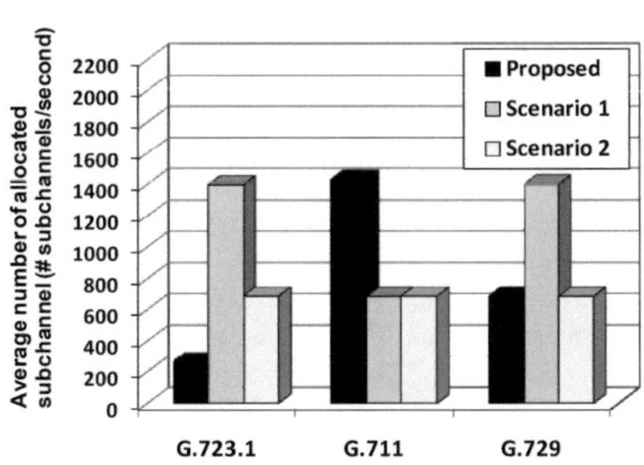

(b) average number of allocated subchannels with UGS

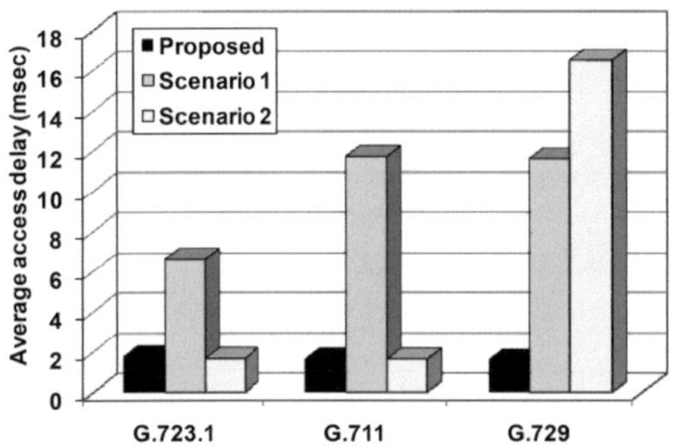

(c) average access delay with ertPS

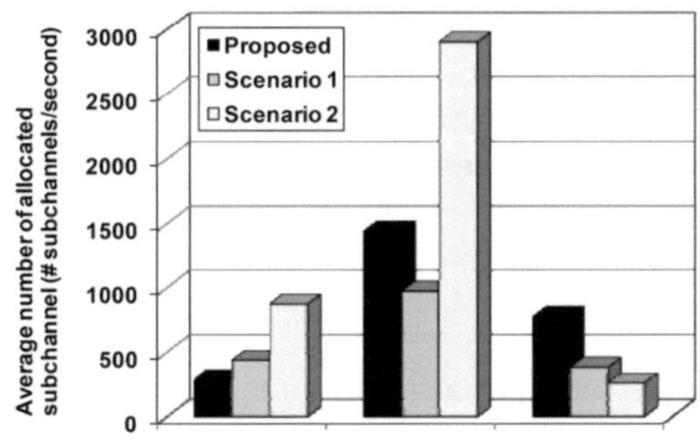

(d) average number of allocated subchannels with ertPS

Fig. 6. Simulation results for the cross-layer QoS parameter mapping scheme

$$S_{HV}(N,F) = \left(\frac{S_{ON}}{\lambda} + \frac{S_{SI} + S_{BRUSC}R_{HV}(N,F)}{(T_{GIS}/T_{GIT})\mu}\right), \quad (5)$$

$$S_{pro}(N,F) = \left(\frac{S_{ON}}{\lambda} + \frac{S_{SI} + S_{BRUSC}R_{pro}(N,F)}{(T_{GIS}/T_{GIT})\mu}\right), \quad (6)$$

where S_{ON_max}, S_{ON}, S_{SI}, and S_{GMH} are the number of uplink slots required to send a maximum-size speech frame, variable-size speech frame, silence(or noise) frame, and generic-MAC header, respectively. F is the number of bandwidth request ranging codes. Note that the S_{GMH} in (4) can be changed to S_{SI} in the EVRC, because the EVRC generates a noise frame every packet-generation-interval. T_{GIT} (sec) and T_{GIS} (sec) indicate the grant-interval during the talk-spurts and the grant-interval during the silent-periods, respectively. In (5) and (6), R_{HV} and R_{pro} represent the average number of retransmissions for a BRUSC header in the HV algorithm and the new proposed algorithm, respectively.

The average number of uplink slots required every grant-interval for a VoIP user in the UGS and ertPS is independent on the number of VoIP users and the number of bandwidth

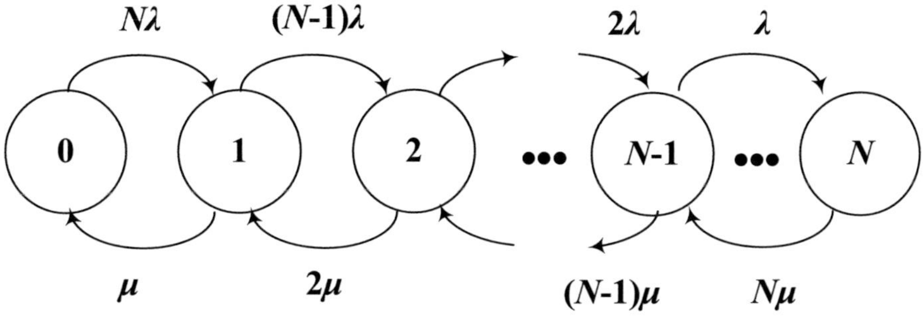

Fig. 7. Markov chain model for N independent VoIP users with exponentially distributed ON-OFF system

request ranging codes, because a BS periodically allocates a grant to a SS every grant-interval. However, in the HV, a SS sends a BRUSC header to transmit a SID frame every TGIS by the random access scheme in the silent-period. For this reason, the average number of contending users ($N_C(N)$) in a frame is

$$N_{C\_HV}(N) = N_{OFF}(N) \times \frac{T_{MF}}{T_{GIS}}, \tag{7}$$

where T_{MF} is the MAC frame size. In (7), the second term on the right side means the transmission rate of one user in a frame. In the random access scheme, the SS transmits a ranging-request (RNG-REQ) message through a ranging subchannel to obtain the radio bandwidth to transmit a BRUSC header. A RNG-REQ message includes an orthogonal ranging code randomly selected by the SS. When several SSs simultaneously choose the same orthogonal ranging code in a ranging subchannel, they experience a collision. In the random access scheme, other SSs should not select the ranging code which is already selected by a SS in a frame. Thus, the success probability ($P_{SUC}(N,F)$) in a frame is given by

$$P_{SUC}(N,F) = \left(1 - \frac{1}{F}\right)^{N_{C\_HV}(N)-1}. \tag{8}$$

The average number of retransmissions in the HV algorithm is given by

$$\begin{aligned} R_{HV}(F) &= \sum_{k=0}^{\infty} kP_{SUC}(N,F)(1 - P_{SUC}(N,F))^{k-1} \\ &= \frac{1}{P_{SUC}(N,F)}. \end{aligned} \tag{9}$$

By using (2), (7), and (8), the average number of retransmission in the HV can be derived as

$$R_{HV}(N,F) = \left(1 - \frac{1}{F}\right)^{1 - \frac{N\lambda}{\lambda+\mu} \times \frac{T_{MF}}{T_{GIS}}}. \tag{10}$$

In the proposed algorithm, a SS transmits a BRUSC header by the random access scheme only when a voice activity changes from a silent-period to a talk-spurt, unlike in the HV algorithm.

Thus, the average number of contending users in a frame is equal to $N_{OFF}(N) \times T_{MF}$. For this reason, the average number of retransmissions in the new proposed algorithm is

$$R_{pro}(N,F) = \left(1 - \frac{1}{F}\right)^{1-\frac{N\lambda}{\lambda+\mu}\times T_{MF}}. \tag{11}$$

At this time, the VoIP capacity (m) for each VoIP scheduling algorithm can be defined as follows.

$$m(N,F) = \frac{T_{GIT}}{T_{MF}} \times \frac{S_{TOT}}{S(N,F)}, \tag{12}$$

where S_{TOT} is the total number of uplink slots in a frame (Srinivasan, 2007) and $S(N,F)$ means the average number of uplink slots required every T_{GIT} for each VoIP scheduling algorithm such as S_{UGS}, S_{ertPS}, S_{HV}, and S_{pro}. In (12), the term on the right side represents the product of the number of frame during the grant-interval of the talk-spurt and the maximum supportable number of VoIP users in a frame. Unfortunately, the $S(N,F)$ of HV and proposed algorithm is given with respect to the number of VoIP users and the number of bandwidth request ranging codes as shown in (5), (6), (10), and (11). For this reason, it is difficult to analyze the VoIP capacity in the HV and proposed algorithms.
For the simple analysis process, we approximately analyze the average number of retransmission as follows.

$$\begin{aligned} R_{HV}(N,F) &= \left(1 - \frac{1}{F}\right)^{1-\frac{N\lambda}{\lambda+\mu}\times\frac{T_{MF}}{T_{GIS}}} \\ &= 1 + \frac{\lambda T_{MF} N}{(\lambda+\mu)T_{GIS}} \times \frac{1}{F} + \frac{\left(\frac{\lambda T_{MF} N}{(\lambda+\mu)T_{GIS}}\right) \times \left(\frac{\lambda T_{MF} N}{(\lambda+\mu)T_{GIS}} + 1\right)}{2} \times \left(\frac{1}{F}\right)^2 + \cdots \end{aligned} \tag{13}$$

By using MacLaurin series, $R_{HV}(N,F)$ can be written as (13). Here, IEEE 802.16 defines the number of orthogonal ranging codes as 256 where the ranging code consists of initial, handover, bandwidth request, and periodic ranging codes. However, the number of ranging codes in a frame can be above 256 because the number of ranging slots which consists of 256 ranging codes can be one or more. Thus, F can be a sufficiently large number. For this reason, $R_{HV}(N,F)$ can be approximately given by

$$R_{HV}(N,F) \approx 1 + \frac{\lambda}{\lambda+\mu} \times \frac{T_{MF}}{T_{GIS}} \times \frac{1}{F} \times N, \tag{14}$$

where $1/F$ is much less than one. Here, (14) is substituted for (5). Fig. 8 depicts the average number of uplink slots required every grant-interval for a VoIP user ($S_{HV}(N,F)$) according to the number of VoIP users and number of bandwidth request ranging code when VoIP speech codec is the EVRC. As shown in Fig. 8, N and F can be neglected in terms of $S_{HV}(N,F)$. In addition, this result is similar to the case of the AMR speech codec and G.7xx, because those speech codecs generate packets by using the lower transmission rate in the silent-period. Therefore, $S_{HV}(N,F)$ can be approximately represented as

$$S_{HV} \approx \left(\frac{S_{ON}}{\lambda} + \frac{S_{SID} + S_{BRUSC}}{(T_{GIS}/T_{GIT})}\right). \tag{15}$$

As in the HV algorithm, the new proposed algorithm can approximately analyze the $S_{pro}(N,F)$ as (16), because the proposed algorithm transmits a BRUSC header only when the

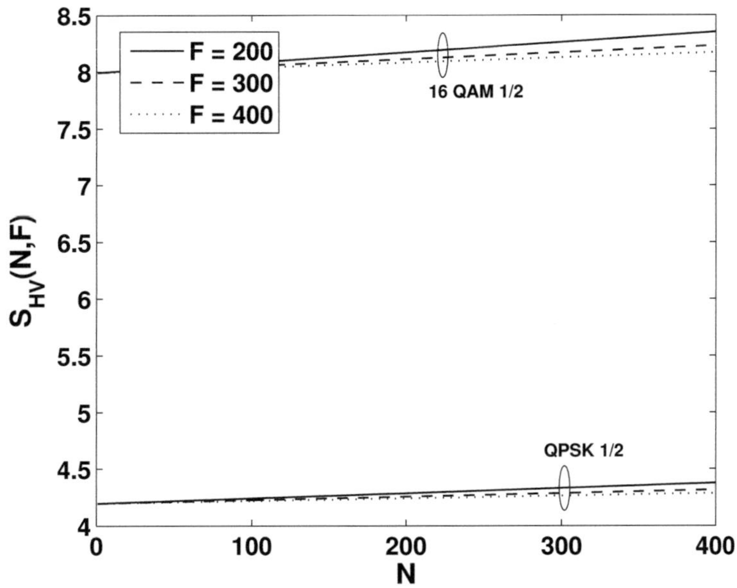

Fig. 8. $S_{HV}(N,F)$ vs. N and F (MCS level = QPSK 1/2 and 16 QAM 1/2, VoIP speech codec = EVRC, S_{TOT} = 144 slots, T_{MF} = 5 msec, FFT size = 1024, λ = 2.5, μ = 1.67, and bandwidth = 10 MHz)

voice activity changes from silent-period to talk-spurt.

$$S_{pro} \approx \left(\frac{S_{ON}}{\lambda} + \frac{S_{SID} + S_{BRUSC}}{(T_{GIS}/T_{GIT})} \right). \tag{16}$$

By using (14) and (15), (12) can be derived as

$$m = \frac{T_{GIT}}{T_{MF}} \times \frac{S_{TOT}}{S}, \tag{17}$$

where S is the average number of uplink slots required every T_{GIT} for each VoIP scheduling algorithm. In (17), the VoIP capacity can be easily analyzed, because m is not dependent on the N and F.

Fig. 9 presents numerical results for the VoIP capacity according to the modulation and coding scheme (MCS) levels. It can be seen that the HV and the proposed algorithm can increase the VoIP capacity except for the EVRC compared to the conventional ertPS and UGS, respectively. The reason is that the algorithms can save the uplink bandwidth in the silent-period by using the random access or the adaptation of the grant-interval. However, the HV and the proposed algorithm could not obtain the gain in terms of VoIP capacity when the VoIP speech codec is the EVRC, as shown in Fig. 9 (e). The HV is particularly inefficient in using the radio bandwidth compared to the ertPS when the VoIP speech codec is the EVRC, because the HV transmits a BRUCS header to send a noise frame of the EVRC every 20 msec. By using this feature of the HV, the VoIP capacity decreases by 29 % compared to when the ertPS is used. Unlike the HV, the proposed algorithm can efficiently use the radio bandwidth because of the adaptation of the grant-interval when the VoIP speech codec is the EVRC as well as the G.711 and AMR speech codec.

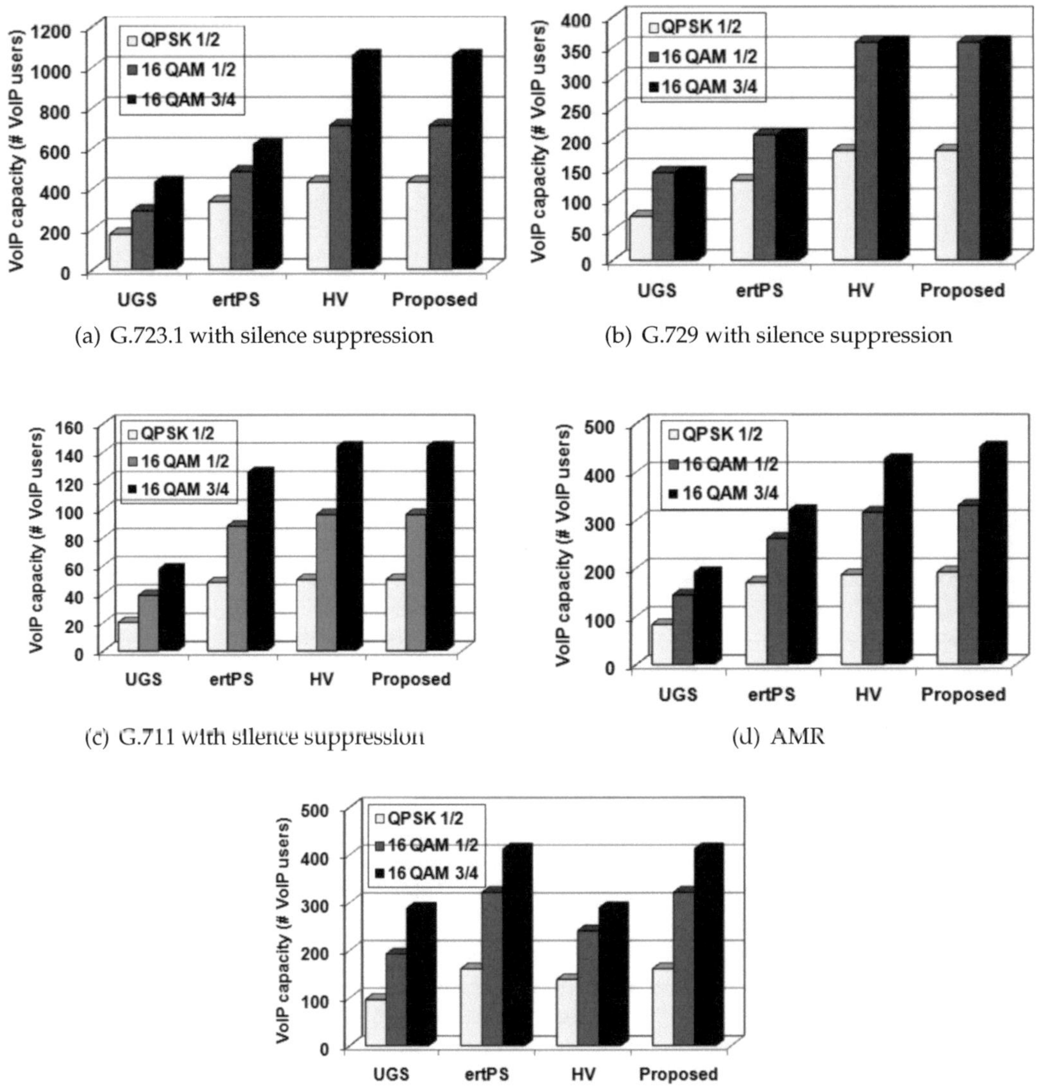

(a) G.723.1 with silence suppression

(b) G.729 with silence suppression

(c) G.711 with silence suppression

(d) AMR

(e) EVRC

Fig. 9. VoIP capacity vs. VoIP scheduling algorithms and MCS levels (S_{TOT} = 144 slots, T_{MF} = 5 msec, FFT size = 1024, λ = 2.5, μ = 1.67, compressed RTP/UDP/IP header size = 3 bytes and bandwidth = 10 MHz)

As shown in Fig. 9, the gain of the HV and the proposed algorithm depends on the kinds of VoIP speech codec in the application layer. The gain increases by 70 % when the VoIP speech codec is G.723.1 or G.729, as shown in Figs. 9 (a) and (b). The G.723.1 and G.729 generate a small-size voice frame in talk-spurt, whose size is 19.88 bytes and 10 bytes, respectively. For this reason, the number of supportable VoIP users increases with respect to other VoIP speech codecs due to the saved bandwidth in the silent-periods. From these numerical results, the HV and the proposed algorithm can support 150 $\sim$ 400 VoIP users more than the other algorithms. Consequently, the HV and the proposed algorithm, which do not periodically allocate a grant in the silent-period, can increase the VoIP capacity and the proposed algorithm can in particular increase the VoIP capacity by 15 % $\sim$ 70 % regardless of the kinds of VoIP speech codec in the application layer.

6. Conclusion

VoIP traffic can have various features according to the kinds of VoIP speech codecs, hence wireless systems need to consider the features of VoIP speech codec. In this chapter, we have considered variable packet-size and packet-generation-interval for main VoIP speech codecs, and proposed a new cross-layer framework to efficiently support a VoIP service in IEEE 802.16 systems. The cross-layer framework for a VoIP service consists of a cross-layer QoS parameter mapping scheme and a cross-layer VoIP scheduling algorithm. The cross-layer QoS parameter mapping scheme directly obtains the QoS parameters for a VoIP service using the QoS information of the application layer. The cross-layer VoIP scheduling algorithm efficiently supports a VoIP service based on the QoS parameters generated by the proposed cross-layer QoS parameter mapping scheme. By the performance evaluation results, it has been shown that the new algorithm can efficiently support a VoIP service regardless of the kinds of VoIP codec in the application layer.

7. References

3GPP-TS-26071 (1999). 3GPP TS 26.071 v3.0.1: Mandatory speech codec speech processing functions AMR speech codec; general description.

3GPP-TS-26092 (2002). 3GPP TS 26.092 v5.0.0: AMR speech codec; comfort noise aspects.

3GPP-TS-26201 (2001). 3GPP TS 26.201 v5.0.0: AMR wideband speech codec; frame structure.

3GPP2-EVRC (2004). 3GPP2 C.S0014-A v1.0: Enhanced variable rate codec.

Handley, M. & Jacobson, V. (1998). RFC 2327 - SDP: Session description protocol.

Hong, S. E. & Kwon, O. H. (2006). Considerations for voip services in IEEE 802.16 broadband wireless access systems, *Proceedings of IEEE VTC spring*, pp. 1226–1230.

IEEE (2006). IEEE standard for local and metropolitan area networks - part 16: air interface for fixed and mobile broadband wireless access systems amendment 2.

ITU-T-G711 (2000). ITU-T recommendation G.711 appendix II: A comfort noise payload definition for ITU-T G.711 use in packet-based multimedia communication systems.

ITU-T-G7231 (1996). ITU-T recommendation G.723.1 appendix A: Silence compression scheme.

ITU-T-G729 (2007). ITU-T recommendation G.729: Coding of speech at 8 kbit/s using conjugate-structure algebraic-code-excited linear prediction.

Lee, H. W., Kwon, T. S. & Cho, D. H. (2005). An enhanced uplink scheduling algorithm based on voice activity for voip services in IEEE 802.16d/e systems, *IEEE Commun. Lett.* Vol. 9: 691–692.

Oh, S. M., Cho, S. H., Kwun, J. H. & Kim, J. H. (2008). VoIP scheduling algorithm for AMR speech codec in IEEE 802.16e/m system, *IEEE Commun. Lett.* Vol. 12(No. 5).

Oh, S. M. & Kim, J. H. (2005). The analysis of the optimal contention period for broadband wireless access network, *Proceedings of IEEE PWN 05*, pp. 215–220.

Srinivasan, R. (2007). Draft IEEE 802.16m evaluation mothodology document.

11

Scheduling and Capacity of VoIP Services in Wireless OFDMA Systems

Jaewoo So
Sogang University
Republic of Korea

1. Introduction

The voice over Internet protocol (VoIP) service is widely supported in wireless orthogonal frequency division multiple access (OFDMA) systems such as a mobile worldwide interoperability for microwave access (WiMAX) system and a long term evolution (LTE) system. In wireless OFDMA systems, a base station (BS) broadcasts information to users about new resource assignments for every frame, where each resource is represented by time symbols and subchannels (IEEE, 2009; Ghosh et al., 2005). The representations of the allocated resources are usually broadcast at the level of a low modulation and coding scheme (MCS) because the BS must ensure that all users can receive the signaling information. The allocation process generates a substantial signaling overhead that influences the system resource utilization. In particular, the performance of VoIP services is seriously affected by the signaling overhead because of following reasons: First, the amount of signaling information is too large compared with the small-sized VoIP packets. Second, the symmetry between the downlink and uplink causes immense downlink overheads. Third, a BS may periodically allocate resources to VoIP users because the voice traffic are periodically generated and the voice traffic is delay sensitive.

In OFDMA-based systems such as IEEE 802.16e/m or 3GPP LTE, a BS allocates resources to users on a frame-by-frame basis and does not remember allocation information from one frame to next. This type of scheduling is referred to as *dynamic scheduling*. Dynamic scheduling allows the BS to schedule each frame independently. However, the signaling overhead increases with the increase of users that are served in the frame. As a means of reducing the signaling overhead, *persistent scheduling* has been proposed for VoIP services which has a periodic traffic pattern and a relatively fixed payload size. The persistent scheduling allows a BS to allocate resources persistently for multiple frames and therefore the BS can reduce the signaling overhead by obviating the need to send signaling information in every frame. The IEEE 802Rev2, the IEEE 802.16m and the 3GPP LTE standards support the persistent scheduling for efficient VoIP services.

Many researchers have evaluated the performance of VoIP services in wireless OFDMA systems. In (Kwon et al., 2005), the capacity of VoIP services was evaluated through a simulation framework in the IEEE 802.16e OFDMA system but without the development of an analytical model. The performance of wireless OFDMA systems was studied in (Niyato & Hossain, 2005a;b). None of these studies, however, considered the signaling overhead. Although other studies have evaluated how the signaling overhead affects the system performance in the wireless OFDMA system, they failed to consider the algorithm for reducing the signaling overhead (Gross et al., 2006; So, 2008). In (Ben-Shimol et al., 2006), persistent scheduling was introduced for constant bit rate voice sessions; however, no analytical model was used and no consideration was given to the adaptive modulation and coding (AMC) scheme for data transmissions. In (Wan et al., 2007), a cross-layer packet scheduling and subchannel allocation scheme was proposed for IEEE 802.16e OFDMA systems. Each packet is prioritized in relation to its channel quality but no consideration is given to the signaling overhead. Furthermore, scheduling based on channel quality is problematic when applied to delay-sensitive VoIP services. In (Jiang et al., 2007) and (Shrivastava & Vannithamby, 2009b), the performance of persistent scheduling in wireless OFDMA systems was evaluated in terms of the VoIP capacity but no analytical model was developed. In (Shrivastava & Vannithamby, 2009a) and (McBeath et al., 2007), group scheduling was proposed as a solution to the problem of persistent scheduling. Users are clustered into multiple groups, and the resource allocation for individual users has some persistence within each group's resources. However, none of these studies developed an analytical model. In (So, 2009), the performance of persistent scheduling was mathematically analyzed but the downlink resources for data transmissions and the signaling message transmissions were assumed to be separated. In a practical system, the downlink resources are shared by the data transmissions and the signaling message transmissions.

This chapter introduces the concepts of two scheduling schemes for VoIP services, dynamic scheduling and persistent scheduling, in terms of resource allocations. Moreover, we develop an analytical model to evaluate the capacity of VoIP services according to the scheduling schemes by considering the AMC scheme in data transmission. The remainder of the chapter is organized as follows: Section 2 gives a description of the system model; Section 3 introduces the dynamic scheduling and the persistent scheduling for VoIP services; Section 4 analyzes the capacity of VoIP services in view of the throughput and the signaling overhead; Section 5 shows the numerical and simulation results; and finally, Section 6 presents conclusions.

2. System model

2.1 System description

We considers a downlink (DL) VoIP transmission from a BS to users in a time division duplex (TDD)-based mobile WiMAX system of the IEEE 802.16Rev2 standard. In an OFDMA-based WiMAX system, each resource is represented in slot units; a slot is a two-dimensional entity with a time symbol space and a subchannel space. One slot carries 48 data subcarriers (IEEE, 2009). The TDD-based mobile WiMAX system is operated on a frame basis, where each frame consists of a DL subframe and an uplink (UL) subframe (IEEE, 2009). The DL subframe consists of a preamble, a frame control header (FCH), a DL-MAP message, a UL-MAP message, and data bursts. By broadcasting a MAP message, the BS indicates the location, size, and encoding of data bursts. The duration of a frame is denoted by T_f.

2.2 Channel model

The probability density function of the instantaneous received signal-to-noise ratio (SNR), γ, at the user is denoted by $f_\gamma(\gamma)$. If N denotes the total number of MCS levels available in the downlink, there are N regions defined by the thresholds $\gamma_1 < \gamma_2 < \cdots < \gamma_{N+1}$. When the instantaneous received SNR, γ, falls in region n, that is, when $\gamma_n \leq \gamma < \gamma_{n+1}$, the MCS level n is used, where $n \in \mathcal{N} = \{1,2,\cdots,N\}$. When $\gamma < \gamma_1$, no data is assumed to be sent. The probability that the SNR γ falls in the nth region is given by (Alouini & Goldsmith, 2000)

$$P_\gamma(n) = \int_{\gamma_n}^{\gamma_{n+1}} f_\gamma(\gamma)d\gamma = \frac{\Gamma(m, m\gamma_n/\overline{\gamma}) - \Gamma(m, m\gamma_{n+1}/\overline{\gamma})}{\Gamma(m)}, \quad (1)$$

where $\Gamma(m)$ is the gamma function which equals $\Gamma(m) = \int_0^\infty t^{m-1}\exp(-t)dt$, $\Gamma(m,x)$ is the complementary incomplete gamma function which equals $\Gamma(m,x) = \int_x^\infty t^{m-1}\exp(-t)dt$, m is the Nakagami fading parameter, and $\overline{\gamma}$ is the average SNR.

Wireless channel is described by a finite state Markov chain taking the discrete adaptive modulation and coding into consideration, as shown in Fig. 1. Assuming slow fading conditions, the state transition probability of the MCS level during the frame duration T_f is given by (Liu et al., 2005; Razavilar et al., 2002)

$$P_t(i,j) = \begin{cases} (N_{i+1}T_f)/P_\gamma(i), & \text{if } j = i+1, j \in \mathcal{N} \\ (N_i T_f)/P_\gamma(i), & \text{if } j = i-1, j \in \mathcal{N} \\ 1 - P_t(i,i+1) - P_t(i,i-1), & \text{if } j = i, j \in \mathcal{N} \\ 0, & \text{otherwise,} \end{cases} \quad (2)$$

where i is the MCS level in the current frame and j is the MCS level in the next frame. The level crossing rate, N_i, is expressed as follows (Liu et al., 2005):

$$N_i = \sqrt{2\pi \frac{m\gamma_i}{\overline{\gamma}}} \frac{f_d}{\Gamma(m)} \left(\frac{m\gamma_i}{\overline{\gamma}}\right)^{m-1} \exp\left(-\frac{m\gamma_i}{\overline{\gamma}}\right), \quad (3)$$

where f_d is the maximum Doppler shift given in hertz.

2.3 VoIP traffic model

The G.729 codec generates a 20 byte encoded voice frame every $T_v = 20$ milliseconds (Bi et al., 2006). Hence, the average size of voice data per a medium access control (MAC) packet can be expressed as follows:

$$L_v = \frac{T_s}{20 \text{ milliseconds}} \times 20 \text{ bytes}, \quad (4)$$

where T_s is the scheduling period. For example, if the BS schedules voice frames every $T_s = 40$ milliseconds, the value of L_v becomes 40 bytes. The constant overhead at the MAC layer is 13 bytes including a 6 byte generic MAC header, a 4 byte cyclic redundancy check (CRC), and a 3 byte IP header, because the IP header can fit into 3 bytes as a result of robust header compression. The packet structures are depicted in Fig. 2. The VoIP packets are assumed to be transmitted in accordance with a simplified first-in-first-out scheduling model. Moreover, the VoIP packet uses an AMC scheme at the physical layer.

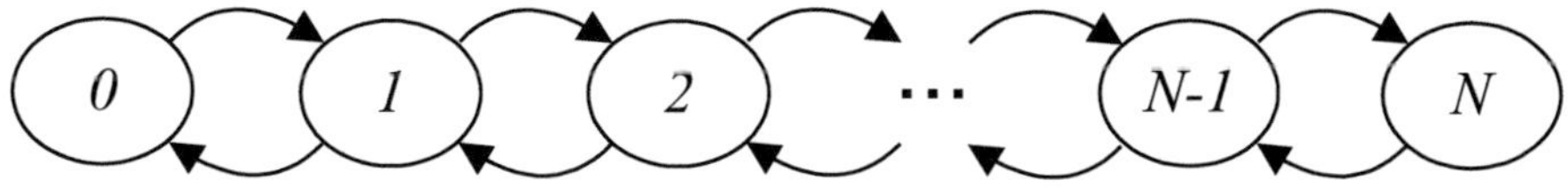

Fig. 1. Finite states Markov channel model

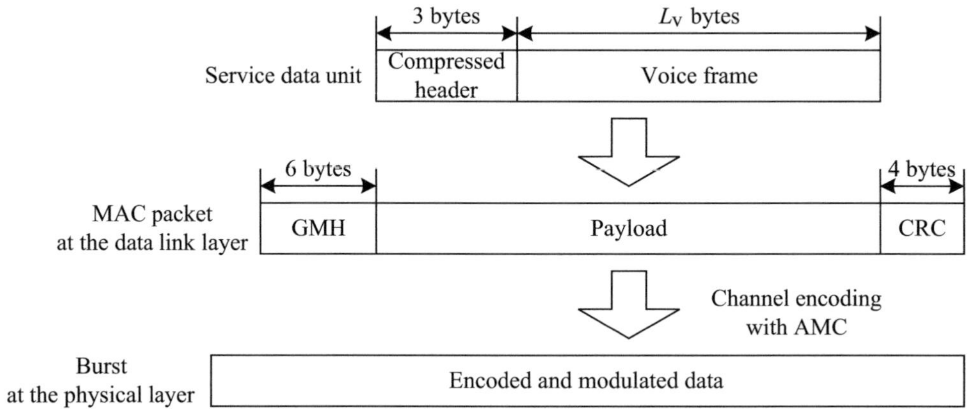

Fig. 2. Packet structure

The VoIP traffic has been modeled as an exponentially distributed on-off model with a mean on-time of $\alpha^{-1} = 1$ second and a mean off-time of $\beta^{-1} = 1.5$ second (Ozer et al., 2000). We use the two-state Markov-modulated Poisson process (MMPP) to model the aggregate VoIP traffic requested from N_v users (Heffes & Lucantoni, 1986; Shah-Heydari & Le-Ngoc, 1998). The two-state MMPP is represented by the transition rate matrix, $\mathbf{R}$, and the Poisson arrival rate matrix, $\mathbf{\Lambda}$, as follows:

$$\mathbf{R} = \begin{bmatrix} -r_1 & r_1 \\ r_2 & -r_2 \end{bmatrix}, \qquad \mathbf{\Lambda} = \begin{bmatrix} \lambda_1 & 0 \\ 0 & \lambda_2 \end{bmatrix}. \tag{5}$$

We determine the four parameters, λ_1, λ_2, r_1, and r_2, by using the index of dispersion for counts (IDC) matching technique as follows (Shah-Heydari & Le-Ngoc, 1998; Baiocchi et al., 1991; Huang et al., 1996):

$$\lambda_1 = A\frac{\sum_{j=0}^{M_v} j\pi_j}{\sum_{i=0}^{M_v} \pi_i}, \qquad \lambda_2 = A\frac{\sum_{j=M_v+1}^{N_v} j\pi_j}{\sum_{i=M_v+1}^{N_v} \pi_i}, \tag{6}$$

where $\pi_j = \binom{N_v}{j} p^j (1-p)^{N_v-j}$, $p = \beta/(\alpha+\beta)$, $M_v = \lfloor N_v \cdot p \rfloor$, and A, which is the emission rate in the on state, equals $1/T_v$. The transition rates are as follows:

$$r_1 = \frac{2(\lambda_2 - \lambda_{avg})(\lambda_{avg} - \lambda_1)^2}{(\lambda_2 - \lambda_1)\lambda_{avg}(\text{IDC}(\infty) - 1)} \tag{7}$$

$$r_2 = \frac{2(\lambda_2 - \lambda_{avg})^2(\lambda_{avg} - \lambda_1)}{(\lambda_2 - \lambda_1)\lambda_{avg}(\text{IDC}(\infty) - 1)}, \tag{8}$$

where $\lambda_{avg} = N_v \cdot A \cdot p$ and $\text{IDC}(\infty)$ is taken from (Heffes & Lucantoni, 1986).

3. Scheduling schemes

3.1 Dynamic scheduling

In the conventional mobile WiMAX system, the BS broadcasts a DL-MAP message for every frame to inform the allocations of radio resources in the downlink. A DL-MAP message

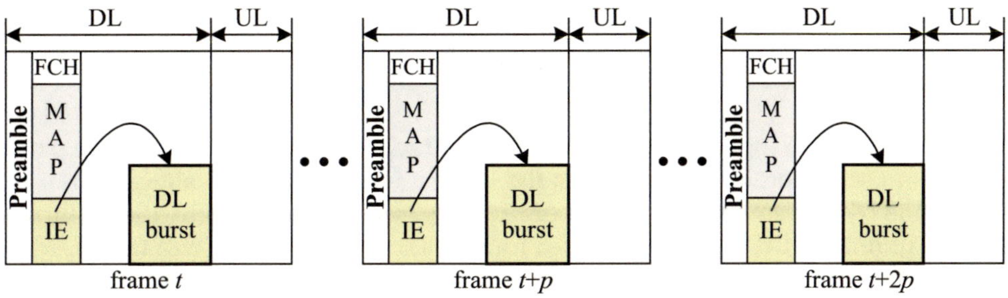

(a) Dynamic scheduling

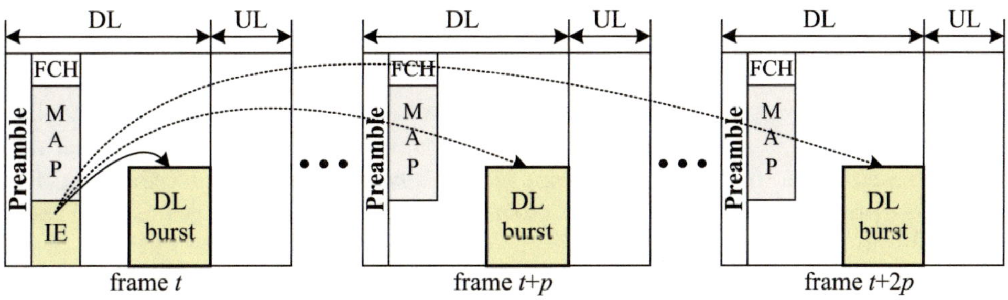

(b) Persistent scheduling

Fig. 3. Dynamic scheduling and persistent scheduling

contains DL-MAP information elements (IEs) that indicate the location, size, and encoding of data bursts directed to the users. The flow between the BS and a user is identified by a connection identifier (CID). Packets directed to different users are integrated into a single burst if the MCS levels of the packets are identical. Let all VoIP packets scheduled for the downlink frame t be denoted by $\mathbf{X}^{(t)} = (x_1^{(t)}, x_2^{(t)}, \cdots, x_N^{(t)})$, where $x_n^{(t)}$ is the number of packets modulated with the nth MCS level and N is the total number of MCS levels available in the downlink. The superscript (t) can be omitted for the steady state analysis. In dynamic scheduling, a DL-MAP IE uses a constant 44 bits to indicate the location, size, and encoding of a data burst; it also uses a 16 bit CID field. Accordingly, in dynamic scheduling, the size of the DL-MAP IEs can be expressed as follows (IEEE, 2009):

$$h_{\mathrm{IE}}^{(ds)}(\mathbf{X}) = \sum_{n=1}^{N} (44 + 16x_n) \cdot J(x_n) \text{ [bits]}, \tag{9}$$

where $J(x_n)$ is an index function expressed as follows: if $x_n > 0$, $J(x_n) = 1$; otherwise $J(x_n) = 0$.

3.2 Persistent scheduling

For VoIP services, the packet arrival rate is somewhat predictable. Hence, the BS can reduce the signaling overhead by transmitting an initial assignment message, which is valid in a periodic sequence of future frames. This type of scheduling is referred to as *persistent scheduling* (IEEE, 2009; 2010).

Figure 3 illustrates a high-level concept of dynamic scheduling and persistent scheduling for when a BS transmits a burst for every p frame in a downlink. In dynamic scheduling, as shown in Fig. 3(a), the BS broadcasts a DL-MAP IE in the MAP message for frame t, frame $t + p$, frame $t + 2p$, and so on, where p is the period of the allocation. The DL-MAP IEs indicate the location, size, and encoding of the DL burst in each frame. Because the BS allocates resources by using the DL-MAP IEs for every frame, the BS can change the modulation and coding schemes from frame to frame. However, in persistent scheduling, the BS allocates a persistent resource to a user when it first schedules the user in frame t; and the allocated resource is valid in frame $t + p$, frame $t + 2p$, and so on. Hence, as shown in Fig. 3(b), the BS broadcasts a DL-MAP IE in the MAP message only for frame t and does not broadcast the DL-MAP IEs for frame $t + p$, frame $t + 2p$, and so on. Accordingly, the signaling overhead decreases and the effective downlink resource increases. However, persistent scheduling may result in some inefficiency because the BS cannot change both the MCS level and the locations of persistently allocated resources on a frame-by-frame basis.

The main problems of persistent scheduling are the resource hole and the MCS mismatch. The term *resource hole* is used to describe sets of successive slots that are not allocated between persistently allocated resources. A resource hole is generated whenever an already allocated burst is deallocated because the resource hole can be completely filled by the new user with the exact same resource requirements. The term *MCS mismatch* is used to describe the difference between the optimized MCS level at the current frame and the latest MCS level indicated by the BS through the persistent scheduling. The MCS mismatch is caused by variation of the radio channel during the session. The MCS mismatch causes a link adaptation error or an additional overhead due to signaling the change to the user (Shrivastava & Vannithamby, 2009a). The resource hole and the MCS mismatch both degrade the efficiency of the resource utilization.

We propose a new format of a DL-MAP IE for persistent scheduling. The format is shown in Table 1. The proposed persistent DL-MAP IE follows the format of the standard DL-MAP extended-2 IE (IEEE, 2009). The format of the proposed DL-MAP IE has two parts. The first part indicates the location, size, and encoding of a burst that the BS transmits to a user every p frames. The allocation of the bandwidth starts from the *slot offset* of the last zone, and the allocated bandwidth is represented by the *allocation size*. The encoding is implicitly determined by the mapping relation between the MCS level and the size of the burst, as shown in Table 2. The second part is the adjustment part. The BS performs an adjustment procedure to eliminate the problems of persistent scheduling by configuring the two fields shown in Table 1: the *adjustment offset* and the *adjustment size*. The user, which uses a persistent allocation, updates its location and size in relation to these two fields. If the value of the adjustment offset is not equal to its slot offset, the user increases or decreases its slot offset by the value of the adjustment offset; otherwise the user does not update its slot offset. If the value of the adjustment offset is equal to the slot offset of an user, the user increases or decreases its bandwidth by the value of the adjustment size and changes its MCS level in accordance with the mapping relation between the MCS level and the burst size. Hence, through these adjustments, the proposed DL-MAP IE prevents the resource hole and the MCS mismatch from degrading the performance.

Although the IEEE 802.16Rev2 and the IEEE 802.16m standard include a format for a persistent DL-MAP IE (IEEE, 2009; 2010), the proposed persistent DL-MAP IE has the advantage of being able to reduce the size of the standard persistent DL-MAP IE. The size reduction is as follows: first, the proposed DL-MAP IE eliminates the CID field whenever the BS adjusts the persistently allocated resources because the CID information can be implicitly determined by the location of the allocated resources. Second, as shown in Table 2, the

Syntax	Bits	Notes
DIUC	4	if (DIUC==14) Extended-2
Extended-2 DIUC	4	
Length	8	Length in bytes of the following data
Allocation Flag	1	Indicate a resource allocation
if (Allocation Flag == 1) {		
N_Alloc	4	Number of allocations
for (i=0; i<N_Alloc; i++) {		
CID	16	Connection indentifier
Slot Offset	8	Offset from the last of zone
Allocation Size	8	Bandwidth in units of slots
Allocation Period	4	Allocation period, p
}		
}		
Adjustment Flag	1	Indicate an adjustment
if (Adjustment Flag == 1) {		
N_Adj	6	Number of adjustments
for (i=0; i<N_Adj; i++) {		
Adjustment Offset	8	Offset from the last of zone
Adjustment Size	8	Increase/decrease of bandwidth in units of slots (signed value)
}		
}		

Table 1. Format of the proposed persistent DL-MAP IE

proposed DL-MAP IE eliminates the encoding fields because the MCS level can be implicitly determined by the mapping relation between the MCS level and the allocated size.
The size of the proposed persistent DL-MAP IE depends on the number, u, of new allocations and the number, v, of existing allocations that changed in size during the p frames. The signaling overhead due to new allocations can be neglected because the talk spurt time is relatively long compared to the frame time, usually in hundreds of milliseconds in contrast to several milliseconds. The proposed persistent DL-MAP IE uses constant 18 bits to indicate the extended-2 IE and flags; it also uses 6 bits to indicate the number of adjustment bursts. In addition, two adjustment fields use 16 bits to adjust the location, size, and encoding of a persistently allocated burst. Accordingly, in persistent scheduling, the size of the DL-MAP IEs can be approximated as follows:

$$h_{\mathrm{IE}}^{(ps)}(v) \approx \left\{18 + (6 + 16v)\right\} \cdot J(v) \text{ [bits]}, \tag{10}$$

MCS level, n	Modulation and Coding	bits/ symbol	Burst size (slots), l_n when $T_s = 20$ ms	Burst size (slots), l_n when $T_s = 40$ ms	Threshold, dB
1	QPSK 1/12	0.17	36	54	-5.6
2	QPSK 1/8	0.25	24	36	-3.8
3	QPSK 1/4	0.5	12	18	-1.4
4	QPSK 1/2	1.0	6	9	2.1
5	QPSK 3/4	1.5	4	6	6.6
6	16-QAM 1/2	2.0	3	5	7.2
7	16-QAM 3/4	3.0	2	3	12.5

Table 2. Modulation and coding schemes for VoIP traffic

where $J(v)$ is an index function expressed as follows: if $v > 0$, $J(v) = 1$; otherwise $J(v) = 0$.

4. Performance analysis

4.1 MCS variation in persistent scheduling

In the persistent scheduling, the last allocation is used to transmit a VoIP packet without any notification of a DL-MAP IE if the MCS level is unchanged. However, the MCS level may vary in every frame in accordance with the time-varying channel conditions. The probability of staying at the same MCS level, n, during p frames is

$$\begin{aligned} \Omega_p(n) &= \sum_{\forall m_i} \left\{ P_t(n,m_2)P_t(m_2,m_3)\cdots P_t(m_p,n) \right\} \\ &= \sum_{m_i \in \mathcal{Z}} \prod_{i=1}^{p} P_t(m_i,m_{i+1}), \end{aligned} \tag{11}$$

where $\mathcal{Z} = \{\forall(m_i,m_{i+1}) \mid m_i \le m_{i+1} \le m_i + 1, m_1 = m_{p+1} = n, m_i \in \mathcal{N}, m_{i+1} \in \mathcal{N}\}$ and the state transition probability of the MCS level during the frame duration, $P_t(m_i,m_{i+1})$, is obtained from (2). Hence, the average probability of staying at the same MCS level during p frames is

$$\xi = \sum_{n=1}^{N} \Omega_p(n) P_\gamma(n), \tag{12}$$

where $P_\gamma(n)$ is obtained from (1). When the MCS levels of all the users are distributed with $\mathbf{X} = (x_1, x_2, \cdots, x_N)$, the probability of the MCS levels of v users being changed during the p frames is given by

$$P_c(v|\mathbf{X}) = \sum_{\forall \mathcal{Y}} \prod_{n=1}^{N} \binom{x_n}{y_n} (1 - \Omega_p(n))^{y_n} (\Omega_p(n))^{x_n - y_n}, \tag{13}$$

where $\mathcal{Y} = \{(y_1, y_2, \cdots, y_n) \mid \sum_{n=1}^{N} y_n = v, y_n \le x_n\}$.

4.2 Scheduling feasibility condition

For simplicity, the UL-MAP message and the UL bursts are not considered. In the MAP message, a BS may transmit a 12 bit CID-switch IE to toggle the inclusion of the CID parameter. With the subsequent inclusion of a 88 bit constant overhead and a 32 bit CRC, the size of the compressed MAP message in units of bits can be expressed as follows (IEEE, 2009):

$$h_{\mathrm{MAP}}(\cdot) = \left\lceil \frac{88 + 12 + h_{\mathrm{IE}}(\cdot) + 32}{8} \right\rceil \cdot 8, \tag{14}$$

where $h_{\mathrm{IE}}(\cdot)$, which is the size of the DL-MAP IEs, is obtained from (9) or (10) according to the scheduling scheme. The MAP message is generally modulated with a QPSK rate of 1/2 and broadcast after six repetitions; and one slot carries 48 data subcarriers (IEEE, 2009; So, 2008). Accordingly, when the MCS levels of all the users are distributed in the manner of $\mathbf{X} = (x_1, x_2, \cdots, x_N)$ in dynamic scheduling, the size of the MAP message in units of slots is given by

$$H_{\mathrm{MAP}}^{(ds)}(\mathbf{X}) = \lceil h_{\mathrm{MAP}}(\mathbf{X})/48 \rceil \cdot 6. \tag{15}$$

Similarly, in persistent scheduling, the average size of the MAP message in units of slots is given by

$$H_{\mathrm{MAP}}^{(ps)}(\mathbf{X}) = \sum_{v=0}^{\sum_{n=1}^{N} x_n} \Big(\lceil h_{\mathrm{MAP}}(v)/48 \rceil \cdot 6 \Big) P_c(v|\mathbf{X}). \tag{16}$$

The DL scheduling is feasible if the resources occupied by the FCH, the MAP message, and the data bursts are less than or equal to the total available resources in units of slots, N_{tot}. Then, when the MCS levels of all the scheduled users are distributed in manner of $\mathbf{X} = (x_1, x_2, \cdots, x_N)$, the feasibility condition is

$$\begin{aligned} \Gamma(\mathbf{X}) &= H_{\mathrm{FCH}} + H_{\mathrm{MAP}}(\mathbf{X}) + \sum_{n=1}^{N} (x_n \cdot l_n) \\ &\leq N_{\mathrm{tot}}, \end{aligned} \tag{17}$$

where H_{FCH}, which denotes the number of slots used to transmit the FCH, is 4 (IEEE, 2009); x_n denotes the number of packets modulated by the nth MCS level; and l_n denotes the size of the data burst, which is modulated with the nth MCS level, after the encoding and repetition in units of slots. The value of l_n is shown in Table 2.

4.3 Queuing analysis

The performance of VoIP services is analyzed with a discrete time Markov chain model. A discrete-time MMPP can be equivalent to an MMPP in continuous time (Niyato & Hossain, 2005a). Arrival and service process of the queue is depicted in Fig. 4. The queueing analysis is based on our earlier work (So, 2008).

4.3.1 Arrival process

We define the diagonal probability matrix, $\mathbf{D}_k$. Each diagonal element of $\mathbf{D}_k$ is the probability of k packets transmitting from users during the frame duration, T_f, and this probability is given by $(\lambda_i T_f)^k e^{-\lambda_i T_f}/k!$ for $i = 1, 2$ where λ_i is obtained from (6). Furthermore, the average packet arrival rate at the queue during the frame duration is

$$\rho = \mathbf{s} \left(\sum_{k=0}^{N_v \cdot A_{\max}} k \, \mathbf{D}_k \right) \mathbf{1}, \tag{18}$$

where $A_{\max}$ is the maximum number of packets that can be transmitted during T_f per user; $\mathbf{1}$ is a column matrix of ones; and $\mathbf{s} = [s_1, s_2]$ is obtained by solving $\mathbf{sU} = \mathbf{s}$ and $s_1 + s_2 = 1$, where the matrix $\mathbf{U}$ is given by (Heffes & Lucantoni, 1986)

$$\mathbf{U} = (\mathbf{\Lambda} - \mathbf{R})^{-1} \mathbf{\Lambda}, \tag{19}$$

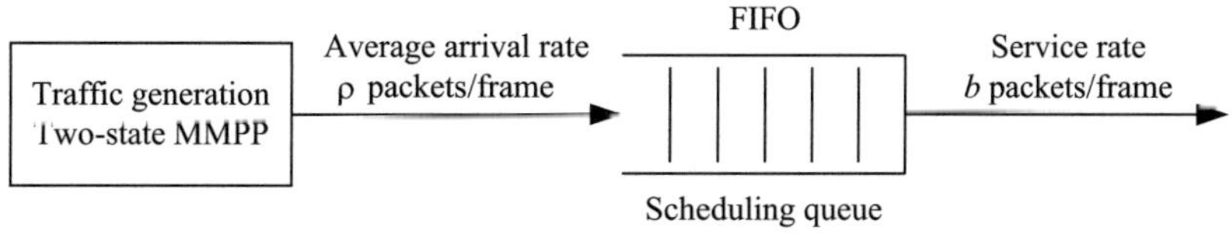

Fig. 4. Arrival and service process of the queue

where $\mathbf{\Lambda}$ and $\mathbf{R}$ are obtained from (5). The transition probability matrix $\mathbf{U}$ keeps track of the phase during an idle period. Each element U_{ij} of the matrix $\mathbf{U}$ is the transition probability that the first arrival to a busy period arrives with the MMPP in phase j, given that the last departure from the previous busy period departs with the MMPP in phase i (Heffes & Lucantoni, 1986).

4.3.2 Service process

The BS schedules VoIP packets from the queue in accordance with the FIFO policy. The number of the scheduled VoIP packets depends on the channel condition of each VoIP packet. Let b denote the number of VoIP packets scheduled at frame time t, i.e., $b = x_1 + x_2 + \cdots + x_N$, where x_n is the number of VoIP packets modulated with the nth MCS level. At frame time t, if the (17) is satisfied when the BS services the b packets and the (17) is not satisfied when the BS services the $(b+1)$ packets, then the BS will schedule b packets in the frame. Let the parameters $\mathbf{X}_b$ and $\mathbf{X}'_{b+1}$ be denoted as follows: $\mathbf{X}_b = \{\forall(x_1, x_2, \cdots, x_N) \mid \sum_{n=1}^{N} x_n = b, x_n \geq 0\}$; and $\mathbf{X}'_{b+1} = \{\forall(x'_1, x'_2, \cdots, x'_N) \mid \sum_{n=1}^{N} x'_n = b+1, x_n \leq x'_n \leq x_n + 1\}$. The cases where the BS schedules b packets are then represented by

$$\psi_b = \{\forall \mathbf{X}_b | \Gamma(\mathbf{X}_b) \leq N_{\text{tot}} \text{ and } \Gamma(\mathbf{X}'_{b+1}) > N_{\text{tot}}\}. \tag{20}$$

Let the index function be defined as follows:

$$I_n(\mathbf{X}_b) = \begin{cases} 1, & \text{if } \mathbf{X}_b \notin \psi_b \text{ when } x_n \text{ increases} \\ 0, & \text{otherwise.} \end{cases} \tag{21}$$

Two conditions should be satisfied for the BS to schedule b VoIP packets from the queue: the first condition is that the MCS-level distribution of b packets satisfies (17) and the second condition is that the MCS-level distribution of $(b+1)$ packets does not satisfy (17) when the BS schedules the $(b+1)$th packet. Thus, the probability of the BS scheduling b VoIP packets from the queue is (So, 2008)

$$\begin{aligned} P_s(b) &= \Pr\{\text{the number of scheduled packets} = b\} \\ &= \Pr\{\mathbf{X}_b \in \psi_b \text{ and } \mathbf{X}_{b+1} \notin \psi_{b+1}\} \\ &= \sum_{\forall \mathbf{X}_b \in \psi_b} \left[\left(b! \prod_{n=1}^{N} \frac{P_\gamma(n)^{x_n}}{x_n!} \right) \left(1 - \sum_{n=1}^{N} (P_\gamma(n) I_n(\mathbf{X}_b)) \right) \right], \end{aligned} \tag{22}$$

where $P_\gamma(n)$ is obtained from (1). The probability $P_s(b)$ is the sum of the products of two equations. The left side of the equation is the probability that b packets are distributed with a specific MCS-level distribution, $\mathbf{X}_b$. The right side of the equation is the probability that the $(b+1)$th packet is not a specific MCS level.

4.3.3 State transition probability

The state is defined as the number of packets in the queue and is expressed as follows: $\boldsymbol{\pi} = [\pi_0\, \pi_1 \cdots \pi_{2K+1}]$. Then, the state transition matrix $\mathbf{P}$ of the queue can be expressed as follows:

$$\mathbf{P} = \begin{bmatrix} \mathbf{p}_{0,0} & \mathbf{p}_{0,1} & \cdots & \mathbf{p}_{0,K} \\ \mathbf{p}_{1,0} & \mathbf{p}_{1,1} & \cdots & \mathbf{p}_{1,K} \\ \vdots & \vdots & \vdots & \vdots \\ \mathbf{p}_{K,0} & \mathbf{p}_{K,1} & \cdots & \mathbf{p}_{K,K} \end{bmatrix} \tag{23}$$

where K is the maximum size of the queue. The element $\mathbf{p}_{i,j}$ represents the transition probability that the number of packets in the queue will be j at the next frame when the number of packets is i at the current frame. If the number of packets in the queue of the current frame is i and the BS schedules b packets during the frame duration, a new batch of $\{j - \max(i - b, 0)\}$ packets should arrive so that the number of packets in the queue of the next frame is j. Hence, each element of the matrix $\mathbf{P}$ is obtained as follows:

$$\mathbf{p}_{i,j} = \sum_{b=b_{\min}}^{b_{\max}} \mathbf{U}\,\mathbf{D}_{j-\max(i-b,0)} P_s(b). \tag{24}$$

The matrix $\boldsymbol{\pi}$ is obtained from the equations $\boldsymbol{\pi}\mathbf{P} = \boldsymbol{\pi}$ and $\boldsymbol{\pi}\mathbf{1} = 1$. The probability of k packets being in the queue is $\pi(k) = \pi_{2k} + \pi_{2k+1}$.

4.4 Throughput analysis

The average number of VoIP packets transmitted to users during the frame duration is

$$\overline{b} = \sum_{b=b_{\min}}^{b_{\max}} \sum_{k=0}^{K} \min(k, b)\pi(k)P_s(b), \tag{25}$$

where K is the maximum queue size, $b_{\min}$ is the minimum number of scheduled packets, and $b_{\max}$ is the maximum number of scheduled packets in the downlink. Accordingly, the average throughput, which is defined as the average amount of voice data successfully transmitted per second, is

$$S = \overline{b} \cdot L_v / T_f, \tag{26}$$

where L_v, which is the size of voice data in a VoIP packet, is obtained from (4).

4.5 Signaling overhead

Let the signaling overhead be defined as the size of the DL-MAP IEs. In dynamic scheduling, the average signaling overhead can then be expressed as follows:

$$\begin{aligned} H_{\text{sig}}^{(ds)} = & \sum_{b=b_{\min}}^{b_{\max}} \sum_{k=0}^{b-1} \sum_{\forall \mathbf{X}_k} \left[\left(k! \prod_{n=1}^{N} \frac{P_\gamma(n)^{x_n}}{x_n!} \right) P_s(b)\pi(k) h_{\text{IE}}^{(ds)}(\mathbf{X}_k) \right] \\ & + \sum_{b=b_{\min}}^{b_{\max}} \sum_{k=b}^{K} \sum_{\forall \mathbf{X}_b \in \psi_b} \left[\left(b! \prod_{n=1}^{N} \frac{P_\gamma(n)^{x_n}}{x_n!} \right) \right. \\ & \left. \times \left(1 - \sum_{n=1}^{N} P_\gamma(n) I_n(\mathbf{X}_b) \right) \pi(k) h_{\text{IE}}^{(ds)}(\mathbf{X}_b) \right]. \end{aligned} \tag{27}$$

Similarly, when persistent scheduling is applied, the average signaling overhead is given by

$$\begin{aligned} H_{\text{sig}}^{(ps)} = & \sum_{b=b_{\min}}^{b_{\max}} \sum_{k=0}^{b-1} \sum_{v=0}^{k} \sum_{\forall \mathbf{X}_k} \left[\left(k! \prod_{n=1}^{N} \frac{P_\gamma(n)^{x_n}}{x_n!} \right) P_s(b)\pi(k) h_{\text{IE}}^{(ps)}(v) P_c(v|\mathbf{X}_k) \right] \\ & + \sum_{b=b_{\min}}^{b_{\max}} \sum_{k=b}^{K} \sum_{v=0}^{b} \sum_{\forall \mathbf{X}_b \in \psi_b} \left[\left(b! \prod_{n=1}^{N} \frac{P_\gamma(n)^{x_n}}{x_n!} \right) \right. \\ & \left. \times \left(1 - \sum_{n=1}^{N} P_\gamma(n) I_n(\mathbf{X}_b) \right) \pi(k) h_{\text{IE}}^{(ps)}(v) P_c(v|\mathbf{X}_b) \right], \end{aligned} \tag{28}$$

where $P_c(v|\mathbf{X})$ is obtained from (13).

5. Numerical and simulation results

The downlink performance of VoIP services is evaluated in a mobile WiMAX system with a Rayleigh channel environment of $f_\gamma(\gamma) = 1/\overline{\gamma}\exp(-\gamma/\overline{\gamma})$, where $\overline{\gamma}$ is the average received SNR. On the assumption of a partial usage of subchannels (PUSC), a diversity subcarrier permutation is used to build a subchannel. For a downlink PUSC, one slot consists of one subchannel and two OFDMA symbols and one slot carries 48 data subcarriers (IEEE, 2009). The total number of MCS levels available in the downlink is assumed to be $N = 7$ with the thresholds as shown in Table 2. The thresholds were obtained by computer simulation under a practical environment with the channel ITU-R recommendation M.1225 (Leiba et al., 2006). For a mobile WiMAX system with a bandwidth of 8.75 MHz, the simulation uses a frame structure of $T_f = 5$ milliseconds and $N_{\text{tot}} = 390$ slots (IEEE, 2009; So, 2008). Figure 5 and Figure 6 assume that the BS schedules the voice frames every 20 millisecond, i.e., $T_s = 4$ frames. Accordingly, in persistent scheduling, the persistent allocation period is $p = 4$ frames. Figure 5 shows the average throughput as the number of active voice users increases. The average throughput linearly increases when the number of active voice users is less than a certain number of active voice users. However, the throughput approaches an asymptotic limit after the offered load overwhelms the system capacity. The asymptotic limit of the average throughput is higher in the persistent scheduling than in the dynamic scheduling because persistent scheduling increases the effective downlink resources by reducing the signaling overhead. For example, for $\overline{\gamma} = 9$ dB, the asymptotic limit of the average throughput is about 1.41 Mbps in persistent scheduling and 1.14 Mbps in dynamic scheduling.

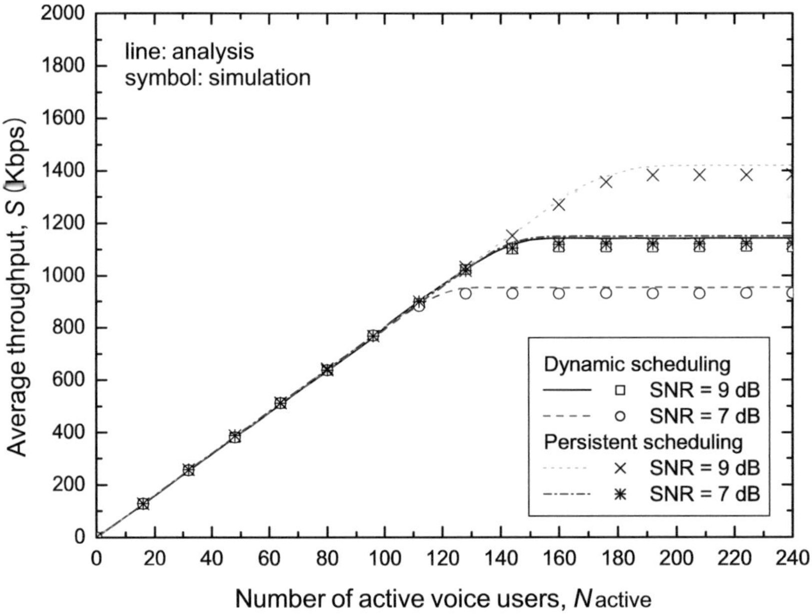

Fig. 5. Average throughput versus the number of active voice users when $T_s = 40$ milliseconds

Figure 6 shows the average signaling overhead for both dynamic scheduling and persistent scheduling. In dynamic scheduling, the signaling overhead linearly increases as the number of scheduled VoIP packets increases. Under high loading conditions, the signaling overhead of dynamic scheduling is about 772 bits when $\overline{\gamma} = 9$ dB and about 685 bits when $\overline{\gamma} = 7$ dB.

However, in persistent scheduling, the signaling overhead is not dependent on the number of scheduled packets but on the number of packets whose MCS levels change during the allocation period. In the simulation environments, the average probability of staying at the same MCS level when $p = 4$ frames is about $\xi = 0.64$, regardless of the value of $\overline{\gamma}$. The value of ξ directly decreases the signaling overhead. Under high loading conditions, the signaling overhead of persistent scheduling is approximately 235 bits, regardless of the value of $\overline{\gamma}$.

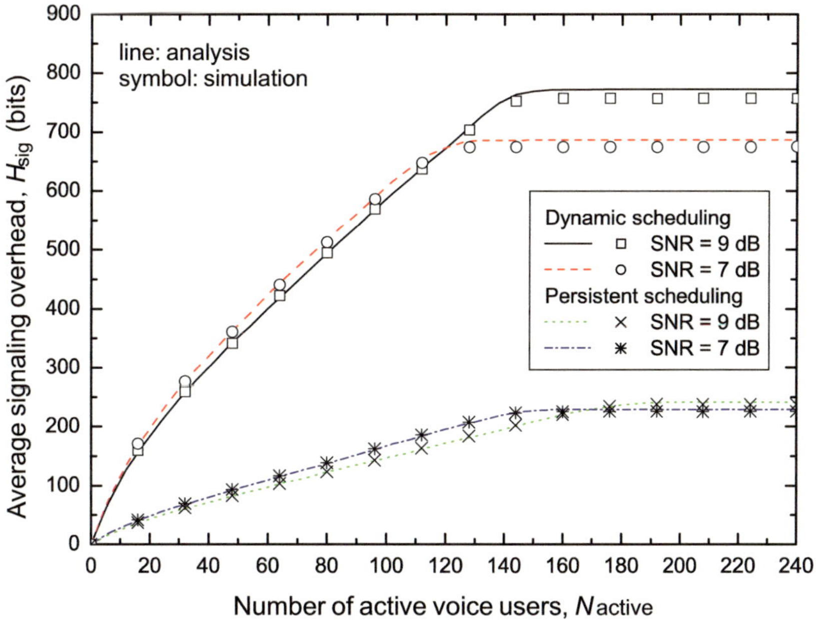

Fig. 6. Average signaling overhead versus the number of active voice users when $T_s = 40$ milliseconds

Figure 7 and Figure 8 assume that the BS schedules the voice frames every 20 milliseconds or 40 milliseconds; that is, $T_s = 4$ or 8 frames. Accordingly, in persistent scheduling, the persistent allocation period is $p = 4$ or 8 frames. Figure 7 shows the average throughput in relation to the scheduling period for when $\overline{\gamma} = 9$ dB. As the scheduling period increases, the average throughput increases because the MAC overhead decreases by about 38%. The signaling overhead also decreases as the scheduling period increases because the number of scheduled bursts decreases when the scheduling period increases. However, the increment in the scheduling period increases the scheduling delay. Under high loading conditions, the average throughput of dynamic scheduling is about 1.14 Mbps when $T_s = 4$ frames and about 1.61 Mbps when $T_s = 8$ frames. That is, the average throughput of the dynamic scheduling increases by about 41.2% when the scheduling period increases from 20 milliseconds to 40 milliseconds. Under high loading conditions, the average throughput of persistent scheduling is about 1.41 Mbps when $p = 4$ frames and about 1.88 Mbps when $p = 8$ frames. That is, the average throughput of the persistent scheduling increases by about 33.3%. In the simulation environments, the average probability of staying at the same MCS level is about $\xi = 0.64$ when $p = 4$ frames and $\xi = 0.54$ when $p = 8$ frames. The decrement of the value of ξ directly increases the signaling overhead. Hence, when the scheduling period increases from 20 milliseconds to 40 milliseconds, the throughput increase is smaller in persistent scheduling less than in dynamic scheduling.

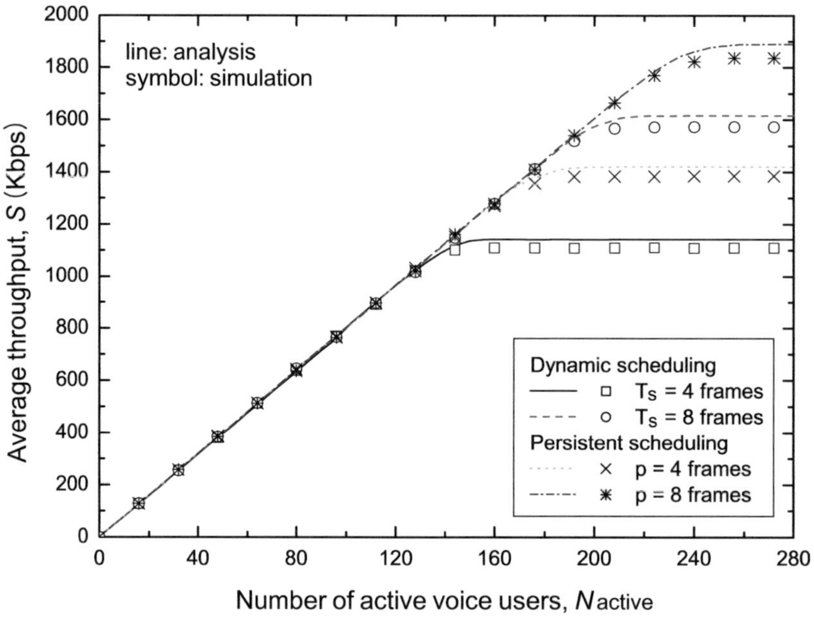

Fig. 7. Average throughput in relation to the allocation period for when $\overline{\gamma} = 9$ dB

Figure 8 shows the average signaling overhead in relation to the scheduling period for when $\overline{\gamma} = 9$ dB. Under high loading conditions, the average signaling overhead of dynamic scheduling decreases by about 23.1% as the scheduling period increases because the number of scheduled bursts decreases with the increase of the scheduling period. Similarly, under high loading conditions, the average signaling overhead of persistent scheduling decreases by about 10.5% as the scheduling period increases although the average probability of staying at the same MCS level increases with the increase of the persistent allocation period.

6. Conclusion

The chapter introduced two scheduling schemes, dynamic scheduling and persistent scheduling, for VoIP services in wireless OFDMA systems. Additionally, we developed analytical and simulation models to evaluate the performance of VoIP services in terms of the average throughput and the signaling overhead according to the scheduling schemes. The integrated voice traffic from individual users is used to construct a queueing model at the data link layer, and each VoIP packet is adaptively modulated and coded according to the wireless channel conditions at the physical layer. In VoIP services, the signaling overhead causes serious spectral inefficiency of wireless OFDMA systems. In dynamic scheduling, the signaling overhead depends on the number of scheduled VoIP packets; it also depends on the MCS-level distributions of the data bursts. However, in persistent scheduling, the signaling overhead is not dependent on the number of scheduled packets but on the number of packets whose channel states change during the allocation period. Under high loading conditions, when the average SNR is 9 dB, the average throughput is roughly 23.6% higher in persistent scheduling than in dynamic scheduling because persistent scheduling significantly reduces the signaling overhead by eliminating the notification of the resource allocation. When the allocation period is 4 frames, the signaling overhead is roughly 68.7% less in persistent scheduling than in dynamic scheduling. Hence, a reduction in the signaling overhead is

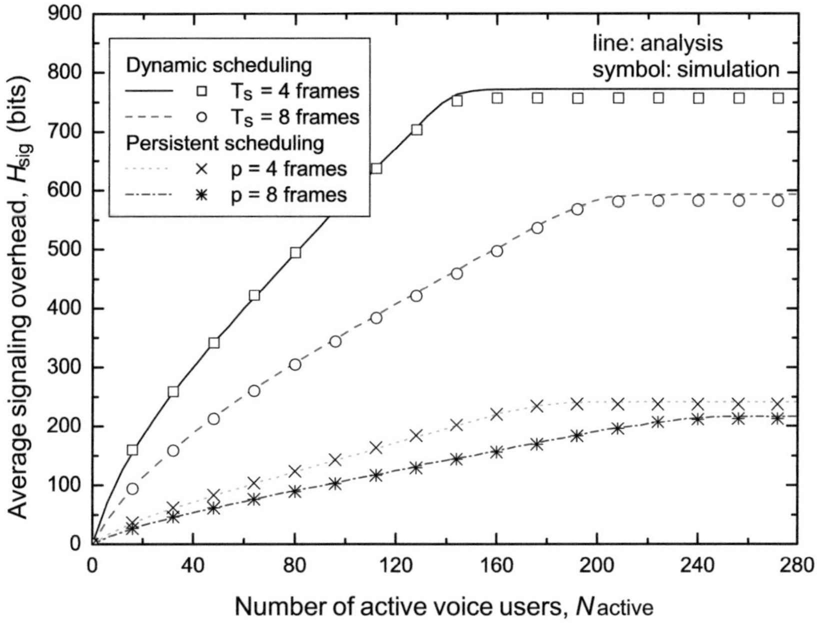

Fig. 8. Average signaling overhead in relation to the allocation period for when $\overline{\gamma} = 9$ dB

crucial for effective servicing of small packets such as VoIP packets. When the allocation period increases from 4 frames to 8 frames, the average throughput increases because the MAC overhead ratio and the signaling overhead both decrease while the scheduling delay increases. The proposed analytical model, though limited to the downlink in this study, can also be applied to the uplink.

7. References

Alouini, M.-S. & Goldsmith, A. J. (2000). Adaptive modulation over nakagami fading channels, *Wirel. Pers. Commun.* 13(1/2): 119–143.

Baiocchi, A., Melazzi, N. B., Listanti, M., Roveri, A. & Winkler, R. (1991). Loss performance analysis of an ATM multiplexer loaded with high-speed ON-OFF sources, *IEEE J. Select. Areas Commun.* 9(3): 388–393.

Ben-Shimol, Y., Chai, E. & Kitroser, I. (2006). Efficient mapping of voice calls in wireless OFDMA systems, *IEEE Commun. Lett.* 10(9): 641–643.

Bi, Q., Chen, P.-C., Yang, Y. & Q.Zhang (2006). An analysis of VoIP service using 1xEV-DO revision A system, *IEEE J. Sel. Areas Commun.* 24(1): 36–44.

Ghosh, A., Wolter, D. R., Andrews, J. G. & Che, R. (2005). Broadband wireless access with WiMax/802.16: Current performance benchmarks and future potential, *IEEE Commun. Mag.* pp. 129–136.

Gross, J., Geerdes, H.-F., Karl, H. & Wolisz, A. (2006). Performance analysis of dynamic OFDMA systems with inband signaling, *IEEE J. Sel. Areas Commun.* 24(3): 427–436.

Heffes, H. & Lucantoni, D. M. (1986). A Markov modulated characterization of packetized voice and data traffic and releated statistical multiplexer performance, *IEEE J. Select. Areas Commun.* SAC-4(6): 856–868.

Huang, J., Le-Ngoc, T. & Hayes, J. F. (1996). Broadband satcom system for multimedia services,

Proc. IEEE ICC, pp. 906–909.

IEEE (2009). IEEE standard for local and metropolitan area networks, part 16: Air interface for fixed broadband wireless access systems, *IEEE 802.16-2009 Std.* .

IEEE (2010). IEEE standard for local and metropolitan area networks, part 16: Air interface for fixed broadband wireless access systems, Advanced air interface, *IEEE 802.16m/D4 Std.* .

Jiang, D., Wang, H., Malkamaki, E. & Tuomaala, E. (2007). Principle and performance of semi-persistent scheduling for VoIP in LTE system, *Proc. IEEE WiCom*, pp. 2861–2864.

Kwon, T., Lee, H., Choi, S., Kim, J., Cho, D.-H., Cho, S., Yun, S., Park, W.-H. & Kim, K. (2005). Design and implementation of simulator based on a cross-layer protocol between MAC and PHY layers in a WiBro compatible IEEE 802.16e OFDMA system, *IEEE Commun. Mag.* pp. 136–146.

Leiba, Y., Segal, Y., Hadad, Z. & Kitroser, I. (2006). Coverage/capacity simulations for OFDMA PHY in ITU-T channel model including MRC, STC, AAS results, *IEEE C802.16e-04/16* .

Liu, Q., Zhou, S. & Giannakis, G. B. (2005). Queuing with adaptive modulation and coding over wireless links: cross-layer analysis and design, *IEEE Trans. Wireless Commun.* 4(3): 1142–1153.

McBeath, S., Smith, J., Reed, D., Bi, H., Pinckley, D., Rodriguez-Herrera, A. & O'Connor, J. (2007). Efficient signaling for VoIP in OFDMA, *Proc. IEEE WCNC*, pp. 2247–2252.

Niyato, D. & Hossain, E. (2005a). Queue-aware uplink bandwidth allocation for polling services in 802.16 broadband wireless networks, *Proc. IEEE Globecom*, pp. 3702–3706.

Niyato, D. & Hossain, E. (2005b). Queueing analysis of OFDM/TDMA systems, *Proc. IEEE Globecom*, pp. 3712–3716.

Ozer, S. Z., Papavassiliou, S. & Akansu, A. N. (2000). On performance of switching techniqueues for integrated services in CDMA wireless systems, *Proc. IEEE VTC*, pp. 1967–1973.

Razavilar, J., Liu, K. J. R. & Marcu, S. I. (2002). Jointly optimized bit-rate/delay control policy for wireless packet networks with fading channels, *IEEE Trans. Commun.* 50(3): 484–494.

Shah-Heydari, S. & Le-Ngoc, T. (1998). MMPP modeling of aggregated ATM traffic, *Proc. IEEE Canadian Conference on Electrical and Computer Engineering*, pp. 129–132.

Shrivastava, S. & Vannithamby, R. (2009a). Group scheduling for improving VoIP capacity in IEEE 802.16e networks, *Proc. IEEE VTC*, pp. 1–5.

Shrivastava, S. & Vannithamby, R. (2009b). Performance analysis of persistent scheduling for VoIP in WiMAX networks, *Proc. WAMICON*, pp. 1–5.

So, J. (2008). Performance analysis of VoIP services in the IEEE 802.16e OFDMA system with inband signaling, *IEEE Trans. Veh. Technol.* 57(3): 359–363.

So, J. (2009). Performance analysis of a semi-fixed mapping scheme for VoIP services in wireless OFDMA systems, *Proc. International Conference on Wireless and Mobile Communications*, 13–17.

Wan, L., Ma, W. & Guo, Z. (2007). A cross-layer packet scheduling and subchannel allocation scheme in 802.16e OFDMA system, *Proc. IEEE WCNC*, pp. 1867–1872.

12

Reliable Session Initiation Protocol

Harold Zheng, Ph.D., and Sherry Wang, Ph.D.
Johns Hopkins University/
Applied Physics Laboratory
U.S.A.

1. Introduction

The IP Multimedia Subsystem (IMS) is a maturing technology. It has the potential to be used in Mobile Ad Hoc Networks (MANETs) to provide multimedia Internet experience for much diversified users with a variety of applications in a highly mobile environment. The introduction of the IMS into MANETs and futuristic mobile networks face unique challenges and needs.

The underlying signalling protocol for the IMS is the Session Initiation Protocol (SIP). In this chapter, we first investigate the "unreliable signalling" problem of using SIP for mobility support. Based on the investigation and the analysis, this chapter introduces an enhanced SIP signalling mechanism called Chain-Based SIP signalling (CBS) to mitigate the problem. The analytical performance analysis results will be given in the chapter as well.

1.1 Session Initiation Protocol (SIP)

The Session Initiation Protocol (SIP) (Rosenberg, J. et al., 2002) is an application-layer signalling and control protocol that performs user location, session setup, and session management. It works independently of underlying transport protocols and the type of sessions that are being established. The SIP is a core protocol for initiating, managing, and terminating peer-to-peer communication sessions on the Internet. These sessions may be text, voice, video, or a combination of these. SIP sessions involve one or more participants and can use unicast or multicast communications.

The SIP proposal began in 1995 in IETF Multiparty Multimedia Session Control (MMUSIC) Working Group (WG), then from February 1996 (draft-ietf-mmusic-sip-00, 15 ASCII pages with one request type) to March 1999 (RFC 2543, 153 ASCII pages, 6 methods) the first RFC was proposed. In November 1999, SIP WG was formed. In December 2000, it was recognized that the amount of work at SIP WG was becoming unmanageable, and consequently, numerous individual subsections were formed. In April 2001, a proposal for splitting SIP WG into SIP and SIPPING was announced. In June 2002, the RFC 2543 was obsolete and replaced by RFC 3261 (Rosenberg, J. et al., 2002). Today, there are over 100 IETF RFCs related to SIP and SIP implementations widely available. The SIP Status can be found at:

http://tools.ietf.org/wg/sip/.

The Table 1 lists some commonly used SIP related IETF RFCs.

RFCs	Description
RFC 2326: Real-Time Streaming Protocol (RTSP)	An application-level protocol for control over the delivery of data with real-time properties
RFC 2327: Session Description Protocol (SDP)	Describes multimedia sessions for the purposes of session announcement, session invitation, and other forms of multimedia session initiation.
RFC 2976: The SIP INFO Method	Adds INFO method to the SIP protocol
RFC 3050: Common Gateway Interface for SIP	Defines a SIP CGI for providing SIP services on a SIP server
RFC 3261: Session Initiation Protocol (SIP)	The core SIP specification. It baselines the SIP protocol for multimedia session handling.
RFC 3262: Reliability of Provisional Responses in the SIP	Specifies an extension to provide reliable provisional response messages.
RFC 3263: SIP: Locating SIP Servers	Uses the DNS procedures to allow a client to resolve a SIP Uniform Resource Identifier (URI) into an IP address, port, and transport protocol of the next hop to contact for locating a server.
RFC 3264: An Offer/Answer Model with the SDP	Defines Offer/Answer model for the SDP use with the SIP.
RFC 3265: Session Initiation Protocol (SIP)-Specific Event Notification	Describes an extension of the SIP, by which SIP nodes can request notification from remote nodes indicating that certain events have occurred.
RFC 3266: Support for IPv6 in SDP	Describes the use of Internet Protocol Version 6 (IPv6) addresses in conjunction with the SDP.
RFC 3311: The Session Initiation Protocol (SIP) UPDATE Method	Adds an UPDATE method to the SIP protocol.
RFC 3312: Integration of Resource Management and SIP	Defines a generic framework for preconditions and discusses how network quality of service can be made in a precondition for the establishment of sessions initiated by the SIP.
RFC 3313: Private Session Initiation Protocol (SIP) Extensions for Media Authorization	Defines a SIP extension that can be used to integrate QoS admission control with call signalling and help guard against denial of service attacks.
RFC 3320: Signalling compression (SigComp)	Defines a solution for compressing messages generated by application protocols such as the SIP and the RTSP.
RFC 3323: A Privacy Mechanism for the SIP	Defines new mechanisms for the SIP in support of privacy.
RFC3329: Security Mechanism	defines new functionality for negotiating the security

RFCs	Description
Agreement for the SIP	mechanisms used between a the SIP user agent and its next-hop SIP entity.
RFC3372: Session Initiation Protocol for Telephones (SIP-T): Context and Architectures	Taxonomies the use of PSTN-SIP gateways, provides uses cases, and identifies mechanisms necessary for interworking.
RFC3407: SDP simple Capability Declaration	Defines a set of SDP attributes that enables SDP to provide a minimal and backwards compatible capability declaration mechanism.
RFC3428: Session Initiation Protocol (SIP) Extension for Instant Messaging	Defines SIP extensions for Instant Messaging.
RFC3515: The Session Initiation Protocol (SIP) Refer Method	Adds REFER method to the SIP protocol.
RFC3550: RTP: A Transport protocol for Real-Time Applications	A replacement of RFC 1889 (RTP). It describes the RTP and enhances the scalable timer.
RFC3605: Real Time Control Protocol (RTCP) Attributes in Session Description Protocol (SDP)	Describes the parameters of media streams used in multimedia sessions.
RFC3702: AAA Requirement for SIP	Provides basic authentication, authorization, and Accounting requirements for the SIP.
RFC3711: The Secure Real-time Transport Protocol (SRTP)	Describes the SRTP that can provide confidentiality, message authentication, and replay protection to the RTP traffic and to the RTCP.
RFC3840: Indicating User Agent Capabilities in the SIP	Defines mechanisms by which a SIP user agent can convey its capabilities and characteristics to other user agents and to the registrar for its domain.
RFC 3853: S/MIME Advanced Encryption Standard (AES) Requirement for the Session Initiation Protocol (SIP)	Updates the normative guidance of RFC 3261 to require the Advanced Encryption Standard (AES) for S/MIME.
RFC3856: A Presence Event Package for the SIP	Describes the usage of the SIP for subscriptions and notifications of presence. Presence is defined as the willingness and ability of a user to communicate with other users on the network.
RFC4028: Session timers in the SIP	Defines an extension to the SIP for a periodic refresh of SIP sessions through a re-INVITE or UPDATE request.
RFC4032: Update to the Session Initiation Protocol (SIP) Preconditions Framework	Updates RFC 3312, which defines the framework for preconditions in SIP.

RFCs	Description
RFC4083: Input 3GPP Release 5 Requirements on the SIP	Describes the requirements identified by 3GPP to support the SIP for Release 5 of the 3GPP IMS in cellular networks.
RFC 4168: SCTP as a Transport for SIP	Specifies a mechanism for usage of SCTP (the Stream Control Transmission Protocol) as the transport mechanism between SIP entities.
RFC 4189: Requirements of End-to-Middle Security for the SIP	Defines a set of requirements for a mechanism to achieve end-to-middle security.
RFC 4320: Actions Addressing Identified Issues with the Session Initiation Protocol's (SIP) Non-INVITE Transaction	Describes modifications to the SIP to address problems that have been identified with the SIP non-INVITE transaction.
RFC 4353: A Framework for Conferencing with the SIP	Defines a framework for how conferencing can occur. This framework describes the overall architecture, terminology, and protocol components needed for multi-party conferencing.
RFC 4354: A SIP Event Package and Data Format for various settings in support for the PoC Service	Defines a SIP event package to support publication, subscription, and notification of additional capabilities required by the Push-to-Talk over Cellular (PoC) service.
RFC 4412: Communications Resource Priority for the SIP	Provides support for precedence handling within the SIP protocol
RFC 4780: Management Information Base for the Session Initiation Protocol (SIP)	Defines a portion of the Management Information Base (MIB) for use with SIP. It describes a set of managed objects that are used to manage SIP entities, which include User Agents, Proxy, Redirect, and Registrar servers.
RFC 4916: Connected Identity in the Session Initiation Protocol (SIP)	Provides a means for a SIP User Agent that receives a dialog-forming request to supply its identity to the peer User Agent by means of a request in the reverse direction, and for that identity to be signed by an Authentication Service.
RFC 5027: Security Preconditions for Session Description Protocol (SDP) Media Streams	Defines a new security precondition for the Session Description Protocol (SDP) precondition framework described in RFCs 3312 and 4032.
RFC 5367: Subscriptions to Request-Contained Resource Lists in the Session Initiation Protocol (SIP)	Specifies a way to create subscription to a list of resources in SIP.
RFC 5393: Addressing an Amplification Vulnerability in Session Initiation Protocol (SIP) Forking Proxies	Normatively updates RFC 3261, the Session Initiation Protocol (SIP), to address a security vulnerability identified in SIP proxy behaviour.

RFCs	Description
RFC 5621: Message Body Handling in the Session Initiation Protocol (SIP)	Specifies how message bodies are handled in SIP.
RFC 5626: Managing Client-Initiated Connections in the Session Initiation Protocol (SIP)	Defines behaviours for User Agents, registrars, and proxy servers that allow requests to be delivered on existing connections established by the User Agent.
RFC 5630: The Use of the SIPS URI Scheme in the Session Initiation Protocol (SIP)	Provides clarifications and guidelines concerning the use of the SIPS URI scheme in the Session Initiation Protocol (SIP).
RFC 5922: Domain Certificates in the Session Initiation Protocol (SIP)	Describes how to construct and interpret certain information in a PKIX-compliant certificate for use in a SIP over Transport Layer Security (TLS) connection.
RFC 5954: Essential Correction for IPv6 ABNF and URI Comparison in RFC 3261	Corrects the Augmented Backus-Naur Form (ABNF) production rule associated with generating IPv6 literals in RFC 3261.

Table 1. Commonly Used SIP RFCs

1.2 SIP design

SIP is a text-based and transaction oriented (i.e. using request-response sequences) signalling protocol using a client/server model and relying on HTTP like messages that communicate between end-users and SIP servers. It is independent of lower layer protocols or media. SIP is suitable for applications that have a notion of session. SIP uses Uniform Resource Identifier (URI) to identify users. The URI associates the user and the carrying platform that uses an IP address. With this mechanism, it is convenient to support mobility for hosts, sessions, and users.

1.2.1 SIP methods

SIP uses Methods / Requests / Responses to establish sessions. There are six basic methods:

- INVITE - To initiate a session
- ACK - To confirm that the client has received a final response to an INVITE request
- BYE - To terminate a session
- CANCEL - To terminate any pending session but not terminate a session that has already been connected
- OPTIONS - To query for the capabilities support by other side (either a server or a client)
- REGISTER - To register contact information

There are other SIP-methods extensions:

- INFO - To allow for the carrying of session related control information that is generated during a session (RFC 2976). For example, carrying wireless signal strength information in support of mobility
- NOTIFY - To request notification from remote nodes indicating that certain events have occurred (RFC 3265)
- PRACK - To provide reliable provisional acknowledgement (RFC 3262)

- REFER – To ask the recipient to issue a SIP request (e.g. call transfer) for contacting a third party (RFC 3515)
- SUBSCRIBE – To request asynchronous notification of an event or set of events (RFC 3265)
- UPDATE – To update parameters of a session (RFC 3311)

1.2.2 SIP responses

The SIP uses specific messages to exchange information. These messages are classified into six groups:

- **Provisional (1xx)** – This is a type of informational response to indicate that the request is received and is continuing to be processed. For example:
    - 100 Trying (i.e. The request has been received by the next-hop server and an action is being taken on behalf of this request.)
    - 180 Ringing (i.e. The UA receiving the INVITE is trying to alert the user.)
    - 181 Call forwarded (i.e. To indicate that the call is being forward to a different destination)
    - 182 Queued (i.e. The called party is temporarily unavailable, the server queue the request instead of reject it.)
    - 183 Session in progress
- **Successful (2xx)** – Successful in terms of action, message received, and message understood. For example, 200 OK (i.e. The request has succeeded.)
- **Redirection (3xx)** – Extra actions are necessary in order to finish the request. For example:
    - 300 Multiple Choices (i.e. The request is resolved to several choices.)
    - 301 Moved Permanently (i.e. The user can no longer be found.)
    - 302 Moved Temporarily (i.e. The requesting client should try a new address.)
    - 380 Alternative Service (i.e. The call was not successful, but alternative services are possible.)
- **Request failure** (4xx) – It indicates a definite failure of a request from a particular server. For example,
    - 400 Bad Request (i.e. The request cannot be understood.)
    - 401 Unauthorized (i.e. The request requires user authentication.)
    - 403 Forbidden (i.e. The server understood the request, but refused to fulfill it.)
    - 404 Not Found (i.e. The server has definitive information that the user does not exist at the domain specified in the request.)
    - 486 Busy Here (i.e. The callee is currently not willing or able to take the call.)
- **Server failure (5xx)** – The server itself has erred and cannot process valid request. For example,
    - 500 Server Error
    - 501 Not Implemented (i.e. The server does not support the functionality required to fulfill the request.)
    - 503 Unavailable (i.e. The server is temporarily unable to process the request due to a temporary overloading or maintenance of the server.)
    - 504 Timeout (i.e. the server did not receive a timely response from an external server to process the request.)

- **Global failure (6xx)** - It indicates that a server has definitive information about a particular user's unsuccessful call and none of the requests can be fulfilled. For example,
  - 600 Busy Everywhere
  - 603 Decline
  - 604 Doesn't Exist (i.e. The server has authoritative information that the user indicated in the request does not exist anywhere.)
  - 606 Not Acceptable (i.e. the UA is contacted successfully but some aspects of the session such as requested media, bandwidth, etc. are not acceptable.)

These messages are designed to fulfill all signalling requirements. These messages and the process of these messages build the core of the SIP protocol (Rosenberg, J. et al., 2002).

1.2.3 SIP-based network entities

SIP defines a number of logical entities as described as the follows:

- *User Agent (UA)*

  A UA is a SIP-enabled end system that consists of two components: a User Agent Client (UAC) and a User Agent Server (UAS). A UAC initiates SIP requests or originates calls and a UAS listens to incoming calls and responses to the UAC's requests. A UA communicates with other UAs directly or indirectly via an intermediate server (e.g. a proxy server). A typical UA is a SIP phone or a voice mail server. Generally, UAs are the only elements where media and signalling converge.
- *Network Servers*
  - **Proxy server** - It decides next hop, forwards request, and relays call signalling. It performs routing function, i.e., determine to which hop, (UA/proxy/redirect) signalling should be relayed. It serves as a rendezvous point at which callees are globally reachable. It has a Forking function, which means that several destinations may be tried for requests sequentially or in parallel.

    A proxy server can be either stateless or stateful. A stateless proxy only forwards incoming requests without ensuing the request's reliability. A stateful proxy remembers the requests and related processes (*transaction*) so that it can reliably deliver a SIP request either sucessfully or return a response code. Only the stateful proxy can fulfill Forking function, which sends copies of the requrest to different destinations.

    A proxy cannot (usually) control media path because a proxy does not know all routing hops along an end-to-end media path. Unless route recording is used, subsequent SIP requests (including ACK with SDP) may take different paths.
  - **Redirect server** - It receives requests and return a response that indicates where the SIP requestor should send to in next step. That is, the redirect server does not forward incoming requests; instead, it sends the address of the next hop back to the caller, and then redirects the caller to other servers.
  - **Registrar** - It stores SIP URIs and associated contacts of SIP users. It accepts REGISTER requests from SIP users and maintains user's whereabouts at a location server.
  - **Location server** - It provides users' location details.

- **Application server** – It provides advanced services for users.

- *Gateways*

  A SIP gateway is an application that implements protocol translation, which is used to connect a SIP network to a network that uses different signalling protocols. A SIP gateway may only terminate signalling path, such as in the case of connecting to a H.323 enabled network. The SIP gateway translates SIP signalling messages to the H.323 format, while the media (using the Real-time Transport Protocol) can still run over the media path. A SIP gateway may also terminate both signalling and media paths, such as in the case of connecting to a Public Switched Telephony Network (PSTN) network. In this case, a SIP gateway converts signalling messages and a PSTN media gateway converts media data flows.

1.3 SIP security

The SIP security is based on 3GPP standards (23.228 IP Multimedia (IM) Subsystem - Stage 2, 33.203 Access Security for IP-Based Services, and 33.210 Network Domain Security) and IETF RFCs such as Security Mechanism Agreement for the Session Initiation Protocol (RFC 3329). SIP security should be able to fulfill the following goals (Arkko, J. et al. 2003):

1. The entities involved in the security agreement process need to find out exactly which security mechanisms to apply, preferably without excessive additional message exchanges.
2. The selection of security mechanisms itself needs to be secure.
3. The entities involved in the security agreement process need to indicate success or failure of the security agreement process.
4. The security agreement process should not introduce any additional state to be maintained by the involved entities.

1.3.1 SIP signalling security

The SIP signalling security uses both end-to-end signalling security and hop-by-hop signalling security mechanisms to satisfy the requirements. The end-to-end signalling security uses SIP authentication and SIP message body encryption. However, it cannot cover entire signalling messages since some fields need to be visible for routing purpose. Consequently, intermediate proxies can compomise security. The Hop-by-hop signalling security relies on transport-layer or network-layer security mechanisms, such as Transport Layer Security (TLS) and Internet Protocol Security Architecture (IPSec), to protect signalling messages. It may allow covering entire signalling message within a hop. A more appealing solution is to combine both mechanisms. Table 2 lists both security mechanisms and their related RFCs.

1.3.2 SIP signalling security threats

Network security is usually categorized into: authentication, confidentiality, integrity, and availability (Knuutinen, 2003), (Rantapuska, 2003), (Sawda & Urien, 2006). The text-based SIP messages are vulnerable to security attacks such as spoofing, hijacking, and message tampering (Geneiatakis, D. et al. 2006). Table 3 summarizes some threats, their impacts, and possible solutions.

SIP Security Mechanisms		Description	Standards
End-to-end security	Digest Authentication	Authentication of signalling message using HTTP digest	RFC 2617
	S/MIME	Authentication and encryption messages	RFC 2633
Hop-to-hop security	The Transport Layer Security (TLS) Protocol Version 1.1	Prevent eavesdropping, tampering, or message forgery at the transport layer	RFC 4346
	Internet Protocol Security (IPSec)	Authentication and encryption at the network layer	RFC 2412 RFC 4301 RFC 4303 RFC 4308 RFC 4835

Table 2. SIP Signalling Security

Threats	Security Aspects	Examples of Impacts	Possible Solutions
Denial-of-service (DoS) attacks, e.g. using • CANCEL • BYE • 4xx, 5xx, 6xx	Availability	Interrupt sessions, force servers unusable	Traffic filtering, access control, DoS protection, etc.
Hijacking, e.g. • Registration • Using 3xx redirect responses • Mid-session re-INVITE	Availability	Register malicious device as the contact address of the victim and deregister all connected contacts	Authenticate the originators of requests
Message tampering	Integrity	Change SDP message body to direct RTP stream to an eavesdrop device	Encryption
Replay messages to cause DoS	Availability	Overload a server	Sequencing message
Snooping	Confidentiality	Gain information on users' identities, services, media, network topology, etc. With the information, other attack can be further triggered.	Encryption, Privacy protection
Spoofing REGISTER	Confidentiality	Call redirection	Authenticate the originators of requests
Spoofing INVITE	Confidentiality	Bypass call filtering	Authenticate the originators of requests
Spoofing ICMP "port unreachable"	Availability	Interrupt sessions	Traffic filtering, access control

Table 3. Some Identified Threats, Impacts, and Solutions

2. SIP mobility support and signalling reliabilities

The mobility involves user devices and network equipment movement, sometimes at a high speed, which causes rapid changes in network topology and attachment points. A mobile node should be accessible by other nodes even when a network attachment point is changed. In addition, the ongoing communication should be reliable and the performance of the communication should be kept at a constant level before, during, and after the node movement. All these requirements present significant challenges to the usability of a signalling protocol such as the SIP.

2.1 SIP mobility

There are four types of mobility supported by the SIP (Schulzrinne, H. & Wedlund, E. 2000).

- Terminal Mobility - It allows Mobile Hosts (MHs) move between subnets without interrupting communications.
- Session Mobility - It allows a user to maintian a media session even while changing terminals.
- Personal Mobility - It allows to address a single user located at different terminals by the same logical address. A user can use more multiple devices to send and receive calls.
- Service Mobility - It allows a user to maintain access to their services while the user is moving or changing devices and network service providers.

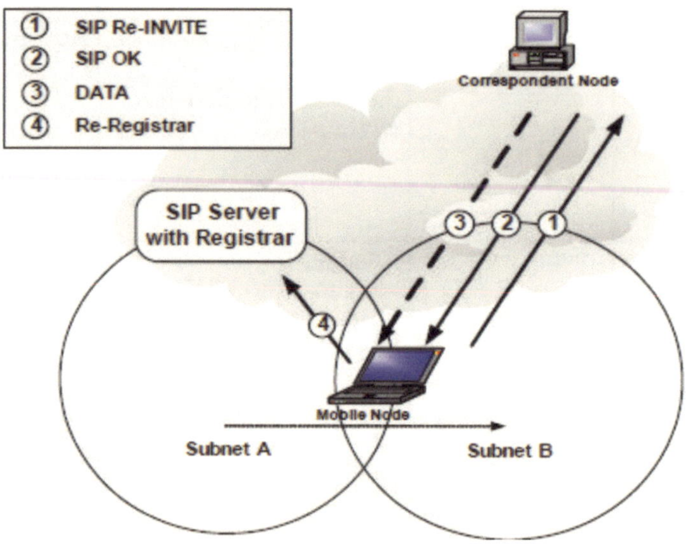

Fig. 1. An Notional Example of SIP Terminal Mobility Support

This chapter focuses on the terminal mobility and the associated unreliable signalling problem in its possible movement scenarios.

2.2 SIP mobility support scenario

The SIP mobility support usually has two challenging cases: 1) one of the two mobile hosts (MHs) moves during a session and 2) both hosts simultaneous move during a session (Wong and Woon, 2007). Details are discussed in next section.

2.2.1 Move during A Session

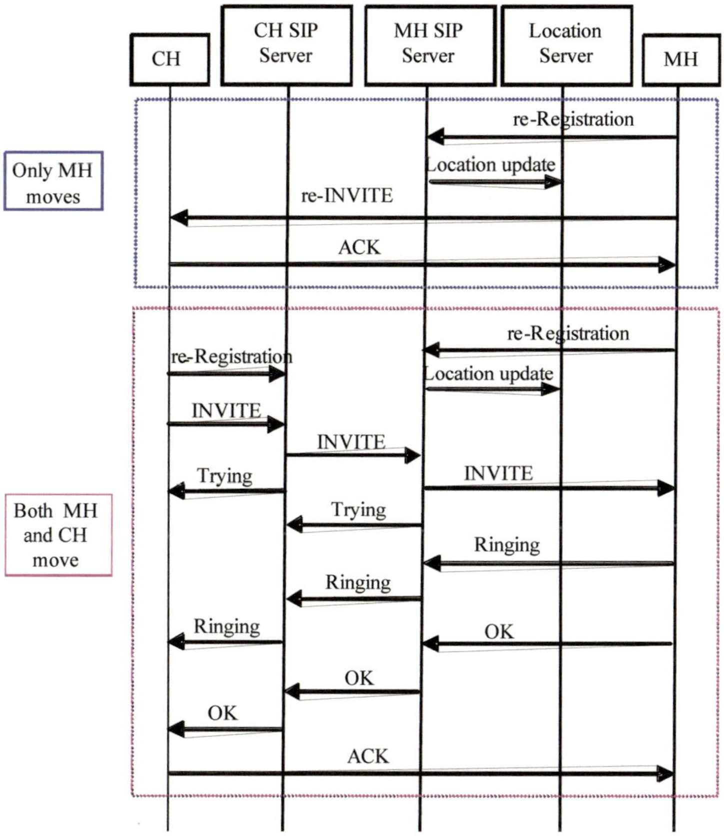

Fig. 2. SIP Message Flows for Move during A Call

This case happens when the MH (the caller) is moving during a session. It has been suggested (Wedlund and Schulzrinne, 1999) to use a "re-invited" message to inform the Correspondent Host (callee) when the caller is moving during a session. This is done via a registration process. The caller's home SIP register updates the MH's location server. This procedure keeps tracking the moving caller and provides possible lost-session reconnection when the SIP "re-INVITE" message does not arrive to the callee. The MH needs to update its current address to its home SIP server registrar and location server to let them know where it is, which provides the updated information for future communications. The Correspondent Host (CH) then acknowledges the message and the session re-starts (please refer to the case of "only MH moves (in blue)" in Figure 2).

2.2.2 Simultaneous move

The simultaneous move (Wong and Woon, 2007) is a special situation of the case "move during a session" (or "move during a call") where both MH and CH move at the same time. Neither of them can receive the "re-INVITE" message from the other party since both of them are changing their locations. In this case, after each host arrives to its new location, it registers its new location (IP address) to its home SIP servers (to both registrar and location server). After registration, either one of them or both of them will send a "re-INVITE" message to each of the host-home SIP servers. The home SIP server will contact the other party's home SIP server to get an updated location address. After that, another "INVITE" message will be sent out either from the MH or from the CH to the other party to start the communication. Figure 2 shows the message exchange flow for the case of "both MH and CH move". It is noticeable that there are many message exchanges for supporting mobile hosts maintaining an ongoing session.

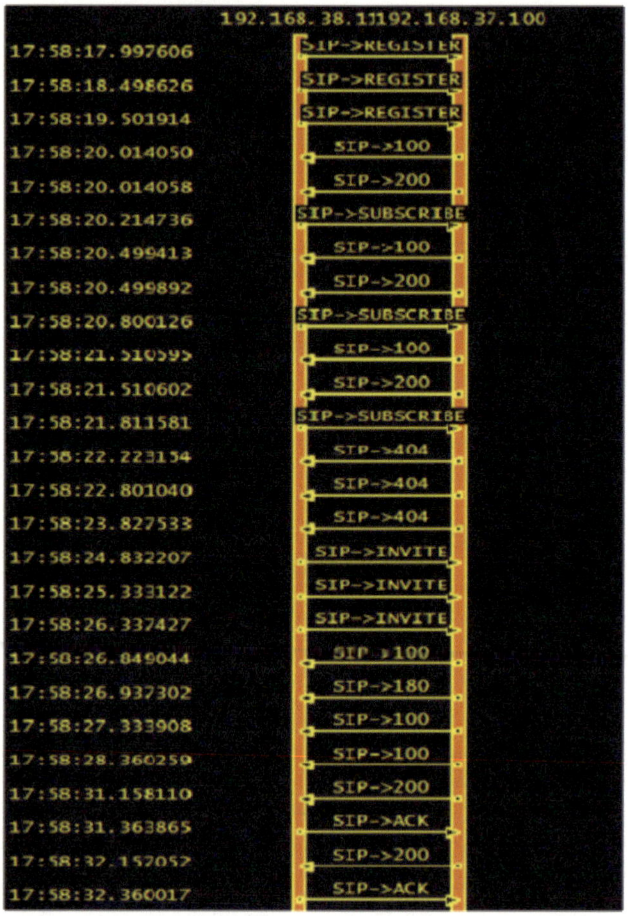

Fig. 3. Delay Causes SIP Message Repetitions

2.2.3 Fragility of SIP signalling

The scenario depicted in Figure 2 shows that without correct and on-time registrations for a mobile host, a mobile network is at risk of losing communications. In a mobile environment, it may not be practical for a mobile host to update its location to a remote SIP server frequently. Home SIP servers (including a registrar and a location server) are usually located far away from an edge network. The connections between an edge network and its home network can be fragile due to many factors.

In addition, when both mobile hosts are constantly moving, the registration requests from each host may be triggered more frequently. The connectivity between an edge network and a SIP server may span a large geographic distance by using satellite links, which could cause a long delay for message exchanges (e.g. registration and call setup). Moreover, the network link capacity can be limited and a link could be unreliable because of unintentional interferences, hostile actions, terrain, foliage, weather, or other factors. Failure or delay of SIP registrations will significantly impact SIP mobility handling.

From our previous SIP performance study (Wang, S. & Zheng, H. 2009), we have observed that network delays, delay variations (jitter), and packet loss affect signalling quality and voice quality (measured by Mean Opinion Score) considerably. Figure 4 and Figure 5 show some examples. One disturbing observation was that when network delay increased, the number of SIP messages increased proportionally. This was caused by re-sending messages due to messages time out as shown in Figure 3. This repetition wastes radio resource and may result in a self-generated Denial of Service (DoS). It is evident that we need to modify the message forwarding mechanism in order to reduce redundant messages, to improve signalling reliability, and to enhance mobility support.

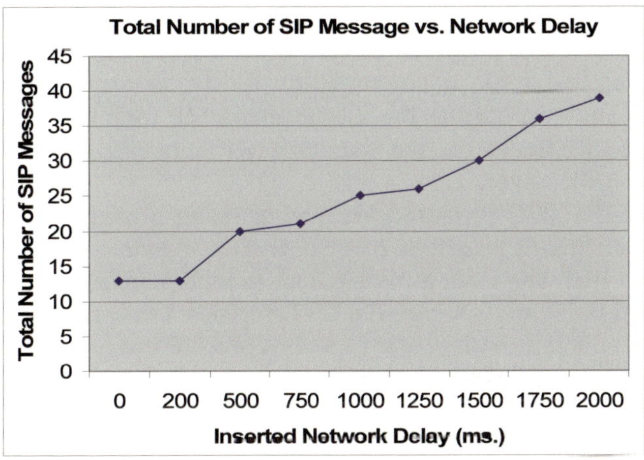

Fig. 4. Network Delay Impact on SIP

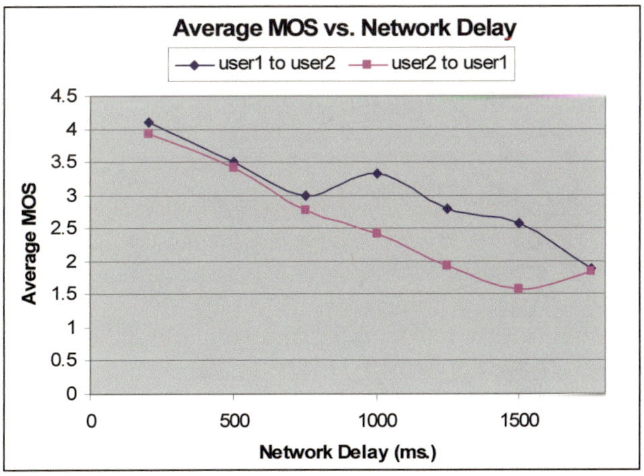

Fig. 5. Network Delay Impact on Voice Quality

Since the main function of the SIP is to provide signalling between two communication hosts, the challenges include how to let each host know where the other host is, how to connect to each other, and how to keep a session alive with or temporarily without the help from its home network. To solve this problem, a reliable SIP message forwarding mechanism [Zheng and Wang, 2007] has been proposed. The next section will present the details.

3. Reliable Chain-Based SIP (CBS)

In order to overcome the problem of unreliable registration in the SIP mobility support, a chain-based SIP signalling (CBS) mechanism has been proposed (Zheng, H. & Wang, S. 2007), which increased the signalling reliability by adopting Mobility Agent(s) to construct a signalling chain that facilitated a reliable signalling.

3.1 Chain-based signalling

Some existing studies have shown that it is feasible to have hierarchical mobility support by using SIP. Vali, D. et al. (2003) proposed the use of an intermediate SIP server called the SIP Mobility Agent (MA) to handle micro mobility. A MA is responsible for handling SIP message forwarding and supporting the intra-domain SIP mobility. The inter-domain SIP mobile handling is still based on the standard SIP mobility by sending "re-INVITE" messages to the home SIP server.

(Zheng, H. & Wang, S. 2007) proposed an idea of using a chain of mobility agents that traverse multiple domains. It proposed that SIP mobile agents could exist in each domain along a routing path that was from a mobile host to its Home SIP Server. The chain-based signalling is depicted in Figure 6, where the CBS employs a new network component called Mobile Agent (MA), which provides basic functions of a SIP proxy server.

In this proposal, a MA locally holds the information of mobile hosts resided in its reachable subnets and domains. The MA periodically updates the users' information to synchronize

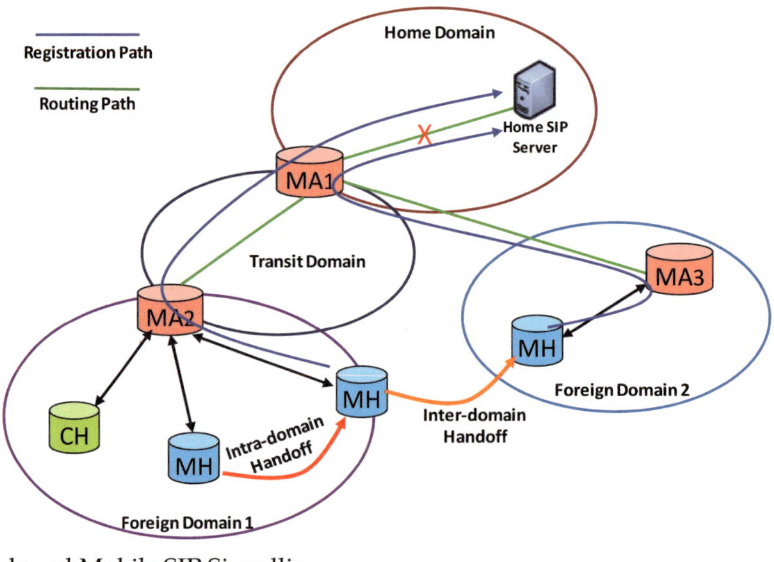

Fig. 6. Chain-based Mobile SIP Signalling

with the home network. The MAs can reside within routers along the routing path from the MH to the SIP home server. Usually, a MA is collocated with a domain border edge router. Since MAs are located within a standard routing path, it is not necessary for a Mobile Host (MH) to find where MAs are. The SIP messages naturally interact with MAs when these messages are traversed on the routing path to the Home SIP server.

Using the SIP registration as an example, the CBS signalling procedure can be explained as following. Each mobile host is required to register to its home SIP server before it can access to any application services. When a mobile host registers itself, it sends a registration message to its Mobility Agent (MA) in the current domain. After it registers the SIP mobile locally, the MA forwards the mobile registration request to the next domain that is in the path towards the home SIP server. This process continues until the request reaches the home SIP server. This type of registration is called "chained registration". The registration message forwarding within a registration chain is not the duty of the mobile host. Instead, it becomes a duty of the MAs. Therefore, as long as a mobile host registers itself to a local domain MA, the registration is considered as being finished. The rest of the registration processes will be completed at each MA along the routing path. It is not necessary to finish the whole registration process at once; instead, it can be done in a pair-wised fashion. As long as there is connectivity available between a pair of MAs, the registration process can continue forwarding the request. Therefore, this method significantly improves the survivability of a registration request.

In addition, each involved MA updates the hosts' registration requests referring to a time stamp. If a MA receives multiple registration requests, it saves the one with the latest time stamp. It also checks the SIP request ID. Multiple registration requests can be either from the mobile host or from lower chain rings of the MA registration chain. These two types of request are treated equally at each MA. In a registration chain, the home SIP server is the last ring of the chain. It always gets an updated host registration with the host location information when the connectivity between registration chain MAs is available. The link availability between a MA pair does not need to exist simultaneously. Instead, as long as a network link between two MAs exists, an updated registration is forwarded. In this fashion, the mobile host request can propagate to the home SIP server. Using this method, the intermittent link availability between a mobile host and its home SIP server is less of a hindrance. Figure 6 illustrates an example of forwarding SIP registration messages using the CBS. The details are given in the next section.

In addition to forwarding user SIP messages, MAs can potentially be functional as light-weighted SIP servers. SIP messages, such as SIP registrations, are kept within a MA in case the MA is selected as a SIP server. This mechanism eliminates extra user SIP registration request messages when the home SIP server is unavailable and a substitution of MA is elected.

3.2 Message-forwarding modes

The CBS SIP message forwarding has two modes. One is called ***forced forwarding***. In this mode, whenever a MA receives a registration request, it updates its own database, then immediately forwards the request to an upper ring if a communication link is available.

The other forwarding mode is called ***periodic forwarding***. An MA re-sends unsuccessfully forwarded requests to an upper ring based on a preset time interval. The forced forwarding normally happens the first time the MA receives a fresh registration request. If the forced forwarding fails, then the periodic forwarding will continue re-sending the request to the upper ring up to the maximum numbers of retrials. However, if there is a newer registration request arrives from the same mobile host, the MA resets the forwarding timer and abandons the older request. This happens when the current request is timed out and the host sends a new request.

If there is a broken link within the request-forwarding path, the MA at a lower part of the chain will serve as a SIP server to fulfil the SIP signalling functions locally relevant to the caller. The purpose is avoiding host request time out, thereby, to avoid redundant request messages. For example, in Figure 6, the link between the MA1 and the home SIP server is broken; then, the MA1 is served as an acting SIP server. Using this CBS request-forwarding mechanism, every server within the chain has the possibility to be an acting SIP server and may perform SIP signalling functions.

The choice of a server as an acting SIP server depends on the MA's logical location in the registration chain. In Figure 6, it is assumed that the link between the home SIP server (on the top of the figure) and MA1 is a satellite link. When the satellite link is broken, since MA1 is located at the top of registration chain, therefore, MA1 is designated as an acting SIP server. In this way, the SIP signalling process is not blocked by a broken link.

3.3 Intra-domain and Inter-domain soft handoff

Another advantage of using the chain structure is that it provides potential for fast handoffs. A handoff is a process of transferring an ongoing session from one network attachment to another. A seamless handoff (unnoticed by a user) will significantly improve communication quality during host movements. During a handoff, the transition period needs to be short. The quicker a handoff can be completed, the higher velocity a mobile user can achieve (Banerjee, N. et al. 2005).

The server that is responsible for performing the SIP procedures is at the lowest level (towards the CH) of the signalling chain. It knows both CH and MH addresses. In our case, it is MA2 in Figure 6.

In an intra-domain mobility situation as shown in Figure 6, the MH gets a new IP address before relinquishing its old IP address. It obtains the new IP address from an intra-domain visiting sub-network (see the red line in Figure 6). The MH registers itself at MA2 and sends a "re-INVITE" to MA2. The MA2 sends the "re-INVITE" message to the CH. The CH sends OK and it is ACKed by the MH. Then a new session is established and the communication continues.

If only the MH moves, it sends the "re-INVITE" message directly to the CH since the MH knows the CH location via the old connection. However, the MH still needs to register its new location to the MA2. For the sake of reducing handoff time, the MH can send two "re-INVITE" requests to both old CH address and MA2 (Wong, K. D. & Woon, W. L. 2007). If CH does not move, it can receive both messages. The CH can reject the message from the MA2 to avoid duplication. Since the handover process in this proposal does not need to send all the SIP messages to the home SIP server, the overall performance is improved.

Using signalling-server chain for inter-domain mobility handling is different from the standard SIP mobility support. The proposal uses a SIP proxy server (MA1 in our case) that is closer (physically) to the mobile host than the home SIP server is, which avoids using the original home SIP server that is far away and the satellite link may be broken. The inter-domain soft handoff procedure is similar to the intra-domain soft handoff for setting up a session. The improvement is to have a much shorter signal path than the one used by the standard SIP, which reduces the handoff time and increases the signalling reliability.

3.4 CBS performance assessment

Using a signalling chain can significantly improve the SIP request success probability and reduce message delay. These claims are proved in the following sections.

3.4.1 Message forwarding success probability analysis

We will analyze SIP message forwarding success probability in two cases. In case 1, a SIP client sends a SIP message only once; in case 2, a client can re-transmit the message *N* times. The results from both cases show that the CBS increases the success probability of SIP message transmission significantly, especially when the link reliability decreases. The definitions of parameters are as follows:

P_{CBS}: The SIP registration success probability using chain-based mechanism
P_{SIP}: The SIP registration success probability using standard SIP mechanism
M: Number of domains
N: Maximum number of times SIP registration request forwarding by each MA
p_i: Packet transmission success probability in domain *i*.

3.4.1.1 Message forwarding success probability analysis - single try

In this simple situation, by using the standard SIP without re-transmission, the probability that a message successfully traverses M domains and reaches its destination can be expressed as:

$$P_{sip} = \prod_{i=1}^{M} p_i \tag{1}$$

While using the CBS, because of its "forced forwarding" and "periodical forwarding" mechanisms, the success probability is:

$$P_{CBS} = \prod_{i=1}^{M} (1-(1-p_i)^N) \tag{2}$$

Where a message success transmission probability is $1-(1-p_i)^N$ in Chain *i* for a maximum of N retransmissions.

$$Let\ q_i = 1 - p_i;$$

Since $0 < q_i \le 1$, then $\frac{1-(1-p_i)^N}{p_i} = 1 + q_i + q_i^2 + \cdots + q_i^{N-1} \geq 1$, therefore,

$$\frac{P_{CBS}}{P_S} = \prod_{i=1}^{M} \frac{1-(1-p_i)^N}{p_i} \ge 1,$$

Thus, $P_{CBS} \ge P_S$.

3.4.1.2 Message forwarding success probability analysis - multiple try

In this case, the probability of successfully using SIP is changed to:

$$P_{SIP} = 1 - \left(1 - \prod_{i=1}^{M} p_i\right)^N \tag{3}$$

Now, comparing Eq.2 and Eq.3, we can prove that P_{CBS} is still larger than P_{SIP}. The proof is as the followings.

Let a be a ratio between P_{CBS} and P_{SIP}, that is:

$$\alpha = \frac{\prod_{i=1}^{M}(1-(1-p_i)^N)}{1-\left(1-\prod_{i=1}^{M}p_i\right)^N} \tag{4}$$

Let's consider a special situation, in which each "chain" has the same message transmission success probability. Therefore, each $p_i = p$;

$$\begin{aligned}\hat{\alpha}(p) &= \frac{\prod_{i=1}^{M}(1-(1-p)^N)}{1-\left(1-\prod_{i=1}^{M}p\right)^N} = \frac{\prod_{i=1}^{M}(1-(1-p)^N)}{1-(1-p^M)^N} \\
&= \frac{(1-(1-p)^N)^M}{1-(1-p^M)^N} = \frac{\left(1-\left(1-\binom{N}{1}p+\binom{N}{2}p^2-\ldots+(-1)^N\binom{N}{N}p^N\right)\right)^M}{\binom{N}{1}p^M-\binom{N}{2}p^{2M}+\ldots(-1)^{N-1}\binom{N}{N}p^{NM}} \\
&= \frac{\left(\binom{N}{1}p-\binom{N}{2}p^2+\ldots+(-1)^{N+1}\binom{N}{N}p^N\right)^M}{\binom{N}{1}p^M-\binom{N}{2}p^{2M}+\ldots+(-1)^{N+1}\binom{N}{N}p^{NM}} \\
&= \frac{\left[\binom{N}{1}p\right]^M\left(1-\frac{\binom{N}{2}}{\binom{N}{1}}p^1+\ldots+(-1)^{N+1}\frac{\binom{N}{N}}{\binom{N}{1}}p^{N-1}\right)^M}{\left[\binom{N}{1}p^M\right]\left(1-\frac{\binom{N}{2}}{\binom{N}{1}}p^M+\ldots+(-1)^{N+1}\frac{\binom{N}{N}}{\binom{N}{1}}p^{(N-1)M}\right)} \\
&= \frac{\left[\binom{N}{1}\right]^{M-1}\left(1-\frac{\binom{N}{2}}{\binom{N}{1}}p^1+\ldots+(-1)^{N+1}\frac{\binom{N}{N}}{\binom{N}{1}}p^{N-1}\right)^M}{\left(1-\frac{\binom{N}{2}}{\binom{N}{1}}p^M+\ldots+(-1)^{N+1}\frac{\binom{N}{N}}{\binom{N}{1}}p^{(N-1)M}\right)}\end{aligned} \tag{5}$$

When p is small, we can have

$$\alpha(0)=\lim_{p\to 0^+}\frac{\left[\binom{N}{1}\right]^{M-1}\left(1-\frac{\binom{N}{2}}{\binom{N}{1}}p^1+\ldots+(-1)^{N+1}\frac{\binom{N}{N}}{\binom{N}{1}}p^{N-1}\right)^M}{\left(1-\frac{\binom{N}{2}}{\binom{N}{1}}p^M+\ldots+(-1)^{N+1}\frac{\binom{N}{N}}{\binom{N}{1}}p^{(N-1)M}\right)} \tag{6}$$

$$=\left[\binom{N}{1}\right]^{M-1}=N^{M-1}\quad>1$$

Similarly, when p is large or even close to 1, we have

$$\alpha(1)=\lim_{p\to 1^-}\frac{\left[\binom{N}{1}\right]^{M-1}\left(1-\frac{\binom{N}{2}}{\binom{N}{1}}p^1+\ldots+(-1)^{N+1}\frac{\binom{N}{N}}{\binom{N}{1}}p^{N-1}\right)^M}{\left(1-\frac{\binom{N}{2}}{\binom{N}{1}}p^M+\ldots+(-1)^{N+1}\frac{\binom{N}{N}}{\binom{N}{1}}p^{(N-1)M}\right)}$$

$$=\frac{\left[\binom{N}{1}\right]^{M-1}\left(1-\frac{\binom{N}{2}}{\binom{N}{1}}+\ldots+(-1)^{N+1}\frac{\binom{N}{N}}{\binom{N}{1}}\right)^M}{\left(1-\frac{\binom{N}{2}}{\binom{N}{1}}+\ldots+(-1)^{N+1}\frac{\binom{N}{N}}{\binom{N}{1}}\right)} \tag{7}$$

$$=\frac{\left(\binom{N}{1}-\binom{N}{2}+\ldots+(-1)^{N+1}\binom{N}{N}\right)^M}{\left(\binom{N}{1}-\binom{N}{2}+\ldots+(-1)^{N+1}\binom{N}{N}\right)}$$

$$=\left(\binom{N}{1}-\binom{N}{2}+\ldots+(-1)^{N+1}\binom{N}{N}\right)^{M-1}=(1-(1-1)^N)^{M-1}=1.$$

In summary, when the message transmission success probability is low, which is represented by a small value of p, $p \approx 0$, the chain-based message delivery mechanism has a much higher probability (NM-1 times) to be successful as indicated by Eq. 6. When a link is reliable, this means that the $p \approx 1$, both chain-based and the original SIP mechanisms have a similar performance.

For a 3-chain network infrastructure, we can have the reliability depicted in Figure 7. By using UDP as the transport protocol, SIP only sends the "invite" message 7 times[1], so we set N=7. We can see that the chain-based message transmission mechanism is much more reliable than the original SIP messaging does.

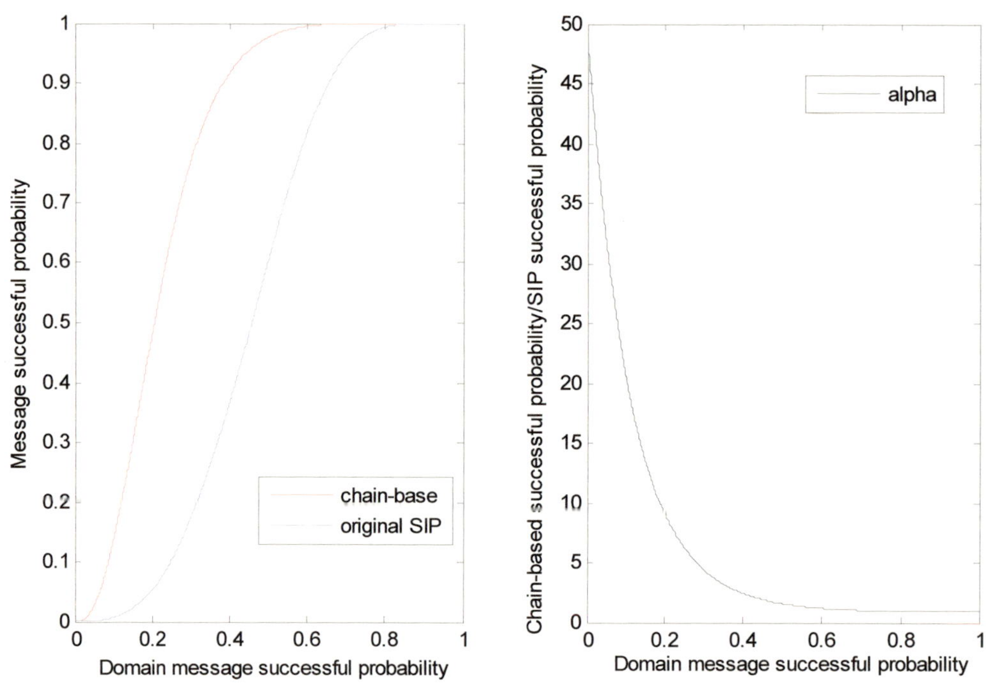

Fig. 7. Reliability Comparison of CBS and standard SIP

3.4.2 Delay analysis

Let p_i be the successful transmission probability at the chain domain i. Also, let d_i be the transmission delay for a message to be transmitted across different domains, which includes propagation delay and processing delay. It is assumed that the transmission delay is the same for both directions of a path. If a message is only retransmitted N times, the expected delay for a message to be transmitted over one "chain" can be considered as the following.

---

[1] A SIP UAC stops retransmitting a request after 7 tries without receiving a response. The first retransmitting is sent after 500 ms, the rest of are sent at a 1-second interval.

$$T_i = d_i p_i + 2d_i p_i(1-p_i) + 3d_i p_i(1-p_i)^2 + \cdots$$
$$+ (N-1)d_i p_i(1-p_i)^{N-1} + D_{large}(1-p_i)^N$$
$$= d_i(p_i + 2p_i(1-p_i) + 3p_i(1-p_i)^2 + \cdots$$
$$+ (N-1)p_i(1-p_i)^{N-1}) + D_{large}(1-p_i)^N$$
$$= d_i p_i \sum_{k=1}^{N} k(1-p_i)^{k-1} + D_{large}(1-p_i)^N$$

$$Let \ q = 1 - p_i;$$

$$T_i = d_i(1-q)\sum_{k=1}^{N} k \cdot q^{k-1} + D_{large}q^N$$
$$= d_i(1-q)\frac{\partial}{\partial q}\sum_{k=1}^{N} q^k + D_{large}q^N = d_i(1-q)\frac{\partial}{\partial q}\left(\frac{1-q^N}{1-q}\right) + D_{large}q^N \tag{8}$$
$$= d_i(1-q)\frac{(1-q)(-Nq^{N-1}) - (1-q^N)(-1)}{(1-q)^2} + D_{large}q^N$$
$$= d_i\frac{(1-q^N) - N(1-q)(q^{N-1})}{1-q} + D_{large}q^N$$
$$= d_i\left(\frac{1-(1-p_i)^N}{p_i} - N(1-p_i)^{N-1}\right) + D_{large}(1-p_i)^N$$

Eq. 8 assumes that the message can be delivered within N times of re-transmissions. The delay is the expected value of the re-transmissions. However, if the message cannot be successfully sent within N re-transmissions, the delay will be infinity since the chain-based mechanism stops sending it to save network resources. There is a small probability for such a case. Each message has a probability equal to $(1-p_i)^N$ that it will not be sent. The delay for the message is infinity. We use a large number D_{large} to represent the large delay.

The total expected delay for using the chain-based message transmission mechanism can be expressed as a summarization of delays from each chain, assuming there are a total of M chains.

$$T_{CBS} = \sum_{i=1}^{M} T_i = \sum_{i=1}^{M}\left(d_i\left(\frac{1-(1-p_i)^N}{p_i} - N(1-p_i)^{N-1}\right)\right) + D_{large}(1-p_i)^N \tag{9}$$

As a comparison, the expected delay based on the traditional SIP message transmission can be expressed as:

$$T_{SIP} = \left(\sum_{i=1}^{M} d_i\right)\cdot\left(\frac{1-\left(1-\prod_{i=1}^{M} p_i\right)^N}{\prod_{i=1}^{M} p_i} - N\left(1-\prod_{i=1}^{M} p_i\right)^{N-1}\right) + D_{large}\left(1-\prod_{i=1}^{M} p_i\right)^N \tag{10}$$

We need to compare Eq. 9 and Eq. 10 to determine which one has a longer delay. To reduce the calculation complexity, it is assumed that the transmission success probability p_i is the same in all chains. Therefore, Eq. 9 and Eq. 10 become

$$T_{CBS} = \sum_{i=1}^{M} T_i = \left(\sum_{i=1}^{M} d_i\right) \cdot \left(\frac{1-(1-p)^N}{p} - N(1-p)^{N-1}\right) + D_{large}(1-p)^N \quad (11)$$

$$T_{SIP} = \left(\sum_{i=1}^{M} d_i\right) \cdot \left(\frac{1-(1-p^M)^N}{p^M} - N(1-p^M)^{N-1}\right) + D_{large}(1-p^M)^N \quad (12)$$

The last items in Eq. 11 and Eq. 12 represent the probabilities of messages that are not successfully transmitted. The probability $(1-p^M)^N$ in Eq. 12 is larger than $(1-p)^N$ from Eq. 11. This means that using the chain-based mechanism yields a smaller probability of non-successful transmission than what the traditional SIP mechanism does. This echoes the conclusion from the reliability analysis.

For delay analysis, we focus on the time used for the messages that have been successfully transmitted. In that term, we only compare the first items in Eq. 9 and Eq. 10. Again, it is assumed that each "chain" domain has the same success transmission probability. Hence, it has

$$T_{CBS} = \left(\sum_{i=1}^{M} d_i\right) \cdot \left(\frac{1}{p}\right), \quad \text{and} \quad (13)$$

$$T_{SIP} = \left(\sum_{i=1}^{M} d_i\right) \cdot \left(\frac{1}{p^M}\right) \quad (14)$$

Eq. 11 converges to Eq. 13 when p is relative large. Similarly, Eq. 12 converges to Eq. 14. Comparing Eq. 13 and Eq. 14, we conclude that Eq. 13 yields a smaller value than Eq. 14, hence, T_{CBS} is smaller than T_{SIP}. The simulation result is shown in Figure 8. The simulation is based on M=3, N=20 and D_{large} = 4N.

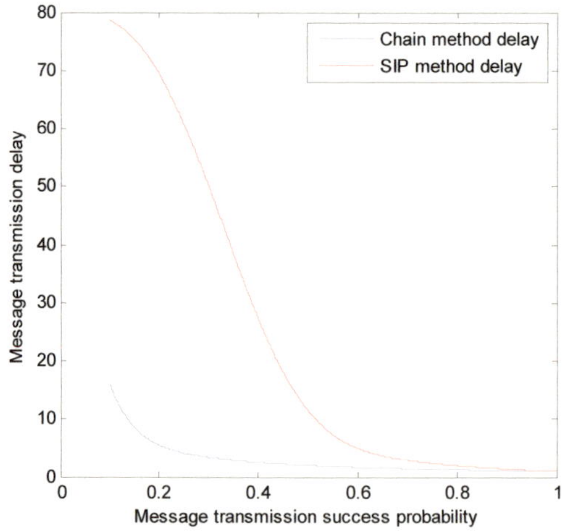

Fig. 8. SIP Message Forwarding Delay Comparisons

5. Conclusion

In this chapter, the problem of unreliable signalling caused by the deficiency of the standard SIP in an ad hoc mobile network environment was investigated. To mitigate the problem, several innovative ideas from protocol and network architecture perspectives have been introduced, which are important for furthering the SIP development and performance improvement.

6. References

Handley, M. & Jacobson, V. (1998). IETF RFC 2327, "SDP: Session Description Protocol"

Kent, S. & Atkinson, R. (1998). IETF RFC 2401, "Security Architecture for the Internet Protocol"

Orman, H. (1998). IETF RFC 2412, "The OAKLEY Key Determination Protocol"

Franks, J. et al., (1999). IETF RFC 2617, "HTTP Authentication: Basic and Digest Access Authentication"

Ramsdell, B. (1999). IETF RFC 2633, "S/MIME Version 3 Message Specification"

Schulzrinne, H. & Wedlund, E. (2000) Application-Layer Mobility Using SIP, *ACM SIGMOBILE Mobile Computing and Comminications Review, Vol. 4, Issue 3, pp47-57, July 2000, ISSN: 1559-1662*

Rosenberg, J. et al., (2002). IETF RFC 3261, "SIP: Session Initiation Protocol"

Cisco. (2002) Security in SIP-Based Networks *http://www.cisco.com/warp/public/cc/techno/tyvdve/sip/prodlit/sipsc_wp.pdf*

Arkko, J. et al. (2003) IETF RFC 3329, "Security Mechanism Agreement for the Session Initiation Protocol (SIP)"

Knuutinen, S. (2003). Session Initiation Protocol Security Consideration, *T-110.551 Seminar on Internetworking*

Rantapuska, O. (2003). SIP Call Security in an Open IP Network, *T-110.551 Seminar on Internetworking*

Vali, D. et al. (2003). An Efficient Micro-Mobility Solution for SIP Networks *Proceedings of IEEE 2003 Global Communications Conference (GLOBECOM 2003)*

Wong, K. D. et al. (2003). Managing Simultaneous Mobility of IP Hosts *Proceedings of IEEE Military communications Conference 2003 (MILCOM 2003)*

Banerjee, N. et al. (2005) SIP-based Mobility Architecture for Next Generation Wireless Networks *Proceedings of IEEE 3rd International Conference on Pervasive computing and communications, 2005 (PerCom 2005)*

Kent, S. (2005). IETF RFC 4303, "IP Encapsulating Security Payload (ESP)"

Geneiatakis, D. et al. (2006). SIP Security Mechanisms: A state-of-the-art Review *Proceedings of 2nd IEEE International conference on Information and Communication Technologies: from Theory to Applications (ICTTA'06)*

Avaya, (2006). Enterprising with SIP – A Technology Overview *https://www.avaya.com/usa/resource/assets/whitepapers/lb2343.pdf*

Dierks, T. & Rescorla E. (2006). IETF RFC 4346, "The Transport Layer Security (TLS) Protocol Version 1.1"

Sawda, S. & Urien P. (2006). SIP Security Attacks and solutions: a state-of-the-art review *Proceedings of 2nd IEEE International Conference Information & Communication Technologies from Theory: to Applications,* ICCTA'06.

Manral, V. (2007). IETF RFC 4835, "Cryptographic Algorithm Implementation Requirements for Encapsulating Security Payload (ESP) and Authentication Header (AH)"

Wong, K. D. & Woon, W. L. (2007). Analysis of Simultaneous Mobility under Asymmetric Mobility Conditions, *Proceedings of IEEE MILCOM 2007.*

Zheng, H. & Wang, S. (2007). Mobility Management in Disadvantaged Tactical Environments, *Proceedings of IEEE MILCOM 2007.*

Wang, S. & Zheng, H. (2008) Enhanced IP Multimedia Subsystems (IMS) for Futuristic Tactical Networks, *Proceedings of IEEE MILCOM 2008.*

Wang, S. & Zheng, H. (2009). SIP-based VoIP Experiment for Disadvantaged Tactical Edge Networks, Proceedings of ICST / ACM The 5th International Conference on Testbeds and Research Infrastructures for the Development of Networks and Communities (TRIDENTCOM) 2009.

13

Multi-path Transmission, Selection and Handover Mechanism for High-Quality VoIP

Jingyu Wang, Jianxin Liao and Xiaomin Zhu
Beijing University of Posts and Telecommunications
State Key Laboratory of Networking and Switching Technology
P.R. China

1. Introduction

With the development of audio encoding standards and IP technology, voice over IP (VoIP) is becoming quite popular. However, high-quality voice data over current networks without QoS Support, such as Internet and UMTS, still posses several challenging problems because of the adverse effects caused by network bandwidth restrictions and complex dynamics. One approach to provide QoS for VoIP applications over the wireless networks is to use multiple paths to deliver VoIP data destined for a particular receiver, i.e., this data is fragmented into packets and the different packets take alternate routes to the receiver. One advantage of this approach is that the complexity of QoS provision can be pushed to the network edge and hence improve the scalability and deployment characteristics while at the same time provide a certain level of QoS guarantees.

The common view among researchers of the next generation mobile communication is that it will be a heterogeneous network environment, offering seamless services such as VoIP across multiple wireless access technologies. In the future there will be more multimode devices which can access multiple radio access networks. Moreover in the future we will see greater overlap between the coverage provided by the differing access technologies as Fig. 1. A host is multi-homed if it can be addressed by multiple IP addresses, as is the common case when the host has multiple network interfaces. Multi-homing is increasingly economically feasible and can be expected to be the rule rather than the exception in the near future.

This chapter proposed a novel transport layer solution cmpSCTP that aims at exploiting SCTP's multi-homing capability by selecting several paths among multiple available network interfaces to improve data transfer rate to the same multi-homed device. As such, it is naturally leads to another two new issues: (1) How to select most appropriate paths for CMT. As different paths are likely to overlap each other and even share bottleneck which lurks behind the IP/network layer topology, it is necessary to fall back on end-to-end probes to estimate this correlation by analyzing path characteristics so that we can select multiple independent paths as much as possible; (2) How to seamless handover paths for mobility.

Using cmpSCTP's flexible path management capability, we may switch the flow between multiple paths automatically to realize the seamless handover called Latent Handover, which is flow-oriented and switches the traffic to the new path progressively to make the handover process unconscious to users or upper layer applications, especially for real-time

VoIP application. The theoretical analysis evaluated the multipath transmission model and verified that the Latent Handover can efficiently optimize the handover process and enhance transmission efficiency during handover. Extensive simulations under different scenarios verified that the multipath mechanism can effectively enhance VoIP transmission and mobility efficiency.

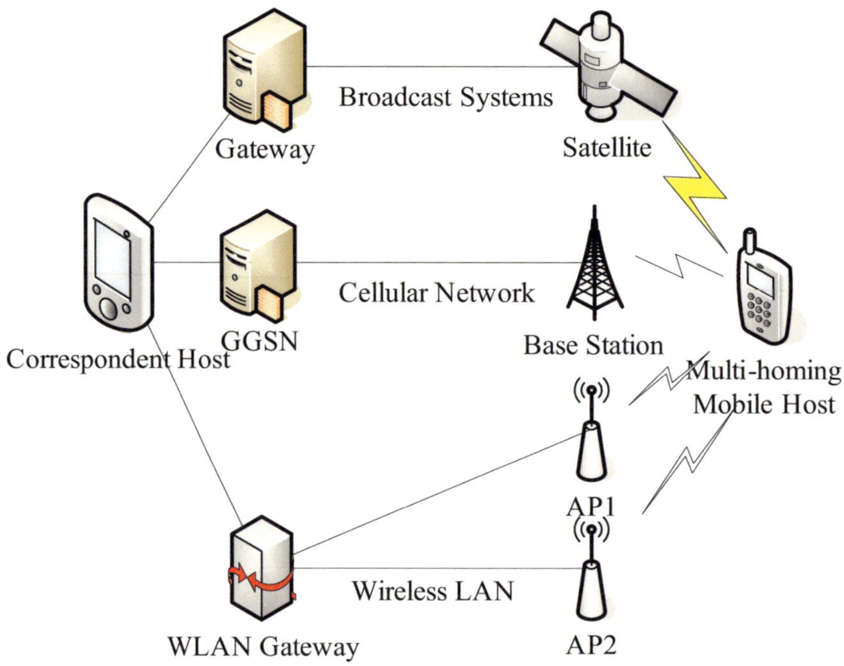

Fig. 1. Heterogeneous overlapping radio environment

2. Extension of SCTP to support multi-path transmission

2.1 Advance of multi-path transmission

Stream Control Transmission Protocol (SCTP) is the third transport layer protocol to be ratified by the Internet Engineering Task Force (IETF). SCTP provides reliable, connection oriented communication to endpoints that may have multiple IP addresses. Allowing a connection to span across multiple IP addresses is known as multi-homing, and it is just one of the features of SCTP which has researchers interested in using it as more than a signalling transport protocol. Yet, the multi-homing feature of SCTP can only exploit at most one of the available paths at any given time.

The work (Iyengar et al., 2006), by the original SCTP proposers, suggests to change the SCTP sender operation to compensate for the problems introduced by using a unique sequence-number space for tracking packets sent over multiple paths. The sender maintains a set of per-destination virtual queues and spreads the packets across all available paths as soon as the congestion window allows it. Retransmissions are triggered only when several Selective ACKnowledgments (SACKs) report missing chunks (SCTP protocol data units) from the same virtual queue.

(Al et al., 2004) proposes Load-Sharing SCTP (LS-SCTP), a mechanism to aggregate the bandwidth of all the paths connecting the endpoints and dynamically add new paths as they become available. (Hsieh & Sivakumar, 2002) proposes pTCP (parallel TCP) based on the Transmission Control Protocol (TCP). pTCP has two components - Striped connection Manager (SM) and TCP-virtual (TCP-v). This decoupling of functionality allows for intelligent scheduling of transmissions and retransmissions.

However, none of the previous proposals fully addresses the case in which the paths comprised in the SCTP association exhibit widely-different bandwidths and round trip times (RTTs). In such scenario, the packets reach the destination out of order, which is bound to trigger a lot of unnecessary retransmissions.

2.2 cmpSCTP design

Similar to LS-SCTP, cmpSCTP is also based on the idea of separating the association flow control from congestion control. In cmpSCTP the flow control is on an association basis; thus both the sender and receiver endpoints use their association buffer to hold the data chunks regardless of the path on which these data chunks were sent or received. On the other hand, congestion control is performed on a per path basis; thus the sender has separate congestion control for each path.

To support the decoupling of functionalities, cmpSCTP uses several novel mechanisms including multi-buffer structure, multi-state management, two-level sequence number, and cooperative SACK strategy to realize effective bandwidth aggregation. Also cmpSCTP includes an overall retransmission technique that prevents the side effects of simultaneous transmission of data on paths with different characteristics, including unnecessary fast retransmissions, which ensures fast delivery of lost data chunks to prevent stalling the association.

Through extending dynamic address reconfiguration, cmpSCTP keeps ongoing end-to-end paths alive and provides adaptive load sharing on multiple paths. In addition, cmpSCTP extends the SCTP path-monitoring feature, through regular transmission of actual effective data chunks to update the list of unstable paths suitable for load sharing. The detailed design of cmpSCTP may be found in [Liao et al., 2008].

3. Correlation-aware multi-path selection

The most researches about CMT have the assumption that multiple paths are independent (Iyengar et al., 2006), but this assumption is rarely warranted at real network. For example, two different paths are likely to overlap one or more joint links somewhere in the network, even share similar bottleneck. So it is necessary to diminish this assumption and take into account the correlation between paths (Apostolopoulos & Trott 2004). Furthermore, the benefits of path diversity do not just depend on whether paths are absolutely independent or dependent, but rather on their correlated degrees in actual networks. Evaluating correlation degrees of available paths and selecting relative independent paths if possible is an important element in effective use of path diversity, which is partly motivated by the observation that packets sent over dependent paths are likely to suffer simultaneously from large packet delays, and otherwise not. Therefore, we can conclude that if the delay patterns on different paths are strongly (or weakly) correlated, the internal shared congestions are

more (or less) likely to occur. It is reasonable to model the path correlation based on the path delay patterns, and what we need to do is to collect a history of delay values of each path through external end-to-end measurements, without cooperation from the network routers.
Intuitively, we can view the selection of a highly reliable set of end-to-end paths as the problem of maximizing the effect of path diversity for a parallel-series network. Path bottleneck points are the most critical to impact the performance of the entire path, and their relative locations directly affect the degree of path correlation. Therefore it is crucial to identify bottlenecks in the large-scale network so as to evaluate path correlation.

3.1 Effect of path diversity

The exploitation of path diversity has attracted much attention recently, and a broad overview of the general area is provided by (Apostolopoulos & Trott 2004). We note that the existence of multiple disjoint paths can result in many benefits including: (1) increased bandwidth, and (2) improved loss characteristics. There are a number of approaches [3-5] to accomplishing multipath data delivery, the path diversity-based approach is considered in this paper.
There are other similar works in interface (Casetti et al., 2008), access network (Alkhawlani & Ayesh, 2008) and IP address (Iyengar et al., 2006) selection for multihomed wireless host. Historically, this was good, as the first link was usually the bottleneck which had the least bandwidth. Often now, however, it is a "backhaul" rather than the access link that has the most constrained bandwidth - an example of this could be a satellite or 3G link which connects a train WLAN to the internet. Therefore, the target should be how to select end-to-end complete paths instead of merely part of them. Another work in (Fracchia et al., 2007) aims at selecting the best path among several available end-to-end paths through the use of bandwidth estimation techniques, which is more suited to the single path selection.
Multipath selection needs to take advantage of the benefits of path diversity, so discovering the correlation characteristics of multiple paths is the most key problem. It can be done either by internal nodes or by end systems. The aforementioned approaches attempt to learn about single path characteristics, but do not address directly the problem of identifying the correlations between multiple paths. Unlike others, the work (Rubenstein et al., 2002) attempt to detect whether two flows share the same bottleneck through end-to-end measurement. However, their goal is to exploit the relation between the flows rather than the paths.

3.2 Problem statement

Consider the multihomed networks are constituted by the multihomed end-devices (see Fig. 2). The source and the destination are connected via a network of communication links. An end-to-end path is a virtual link directly connecting two IP addresses which come from source and destination device respectively. It can be mapped to the IP path. For example, the Path P_{12} started from IP_s^1 and ended with IP_d^2 consists of the nodes N_S, N_m, N_k, and N_D. Characteristics of two end-to-end paths may be correlated because they may share some IP links or nodes. For example, the P_{12} and P_{13} share the IP links (N_S, N_m) and (N_m, N_k).
An *M-by-N* multihomed network topology can be abstracted as a directed acyclic graph $G=(V,E)$ between M source addresses in the source device and N destination addresses in the destination device, along with a given single-path routing policy that maps each source-destination pair to a single route from the source to the destination. Ignoring the topology

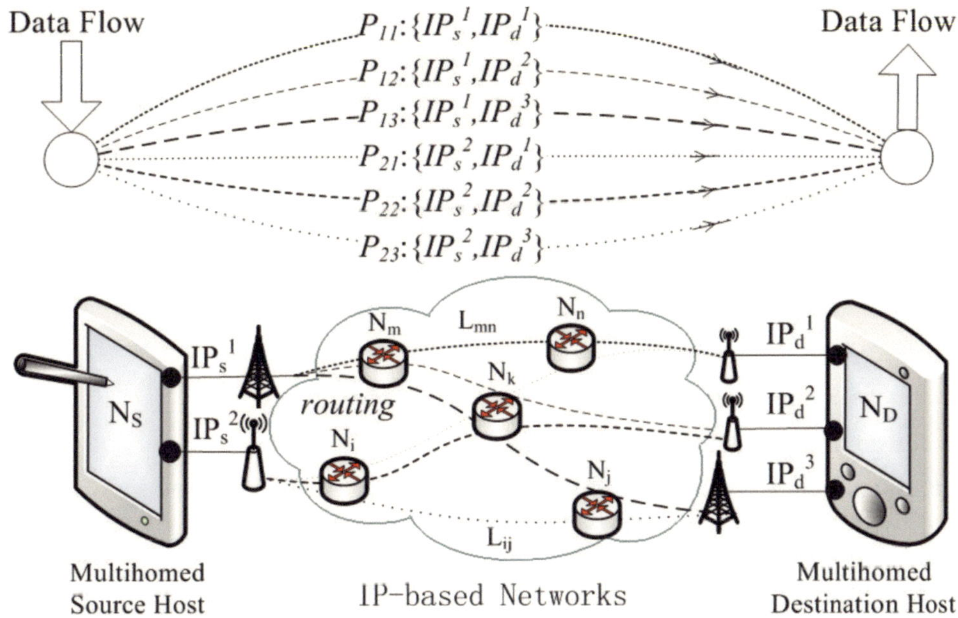

Fig. 2. An example path graph mapping to connectivity graph

and physical links of the network, we let P_{ij} simply denote any one path connecting source address IP_s^i and destination addresses IP_d^j. We assume that drops at congestion points are burst due to the Drop-tail nature of most routers, and the packets are dropped in an i.i.d. fashion. Moreover the packet drop processes in different links are independent of each other. We ignore quantization issues, data corruption or random delays.

Our goal is to select the number of paths required by the upper application and at the same time to minimize the correlation of selected path set. Nevertheless, the attempt to select correlation-minimization path set directly is an *Integer Quadratic Programming* problem (Garey & Johnson, 1979), which is an exponential exhaustive search to select paths. In addition, we observe that path bottleneck is the most critical congestion to impact the performance of the entire path, and their location relationship affect the degree of path correlation directly. Thus, we introduce a pre-grouping process according to whether they exist shared bottleneck or not, and then perform multipath selection among groups which is solvable in a reasonable amount of time. The proposed GMS solution consists of the following three steps: (1) grouping based on whether these paths exist shared bottleneck or not; (3) simple selection of the best path from each group; (4) precise selection of the required number of paths based on the paths obtained in step 3, if necessary. In GMS, we get rid of the strongly correlated paths and carry out the multipath selection on a smaller number of candidate paths, since the benefit of path diversity is never gained from the paths with shared bottleneck.

3.3. Grouping process

When sufficient samples are usable, path correlation computation can be performed for any two paths to determine whether exists shared bottleneck or not. This information is used to classify paths and produce a series of groups with each containing a set of highly correlated paths. The group list is the final output of the classification process.

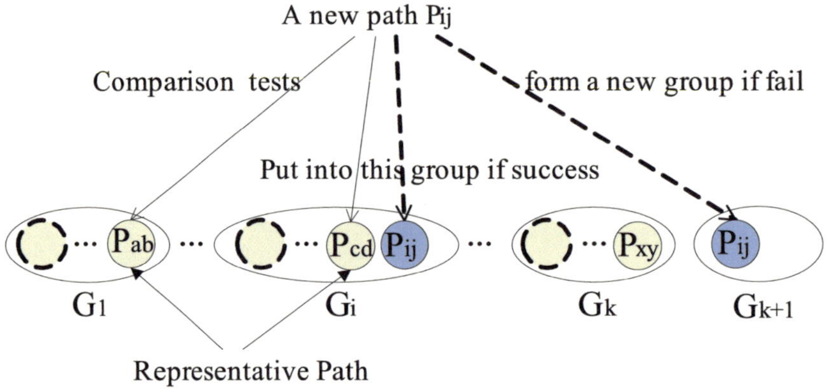

Fig. 3. The grouping method for a new path

The grouping process starts with empty group lists and a set of target paths (with sufficient samples) to be grouped. It first selects the first path P_{11} in a group. Then the second path P_{12} is compared with P_{11} to determine whether it should join the group or create a new group. Next for a new path P_{ij} to be grouped, we propose a "representative" path which is the first path in a group. The grouping method for a new path is shown in Fig. 3. A new path is only compared with the representative path to determine whether it should join the group or create a new group. This ensures that all paths that are grouped together are highly correlated with the same shared bottleneck.

3.4 Selection process

In the second step, it is necessary to find the best paths (Fracchia et al., 2007) within each group firstly. The best path is the path which yields minimum expected transmission time for the requested data given the concurrent transmissions. This path selection just need consider the observable performance of the path, not involving the complex routing mechanism. Different from the correlation between paths used for multi-path selection, the intrinsic performance of path is more important for the single path selection within each group. The motivation behind this is to give preference to high-bandwidth low-latency path, for instance we can simply choose it on their bandwidth whose complexity is linear. This kind of selection, no restricted by the number of paths, upper-layer application and so on, is called *free selection*.

Additionally, it may happen that the upper layer application or end system may impose specific requirements on the number of paths. In this case, we need to select the required number of paths among groups as the selection output. To differentiate from *free selection*, this additional selection is called *restrained selection*. The candidate paths are the within-group optimal paths selected in *free selection*. In fact, these paths have *weak* correlation among individuals, and may use for multipath transmission straightly to provide the maximum flow as much as possible.

For the number of paths required s is greater than the number of candidate paths (or groups) k, i.e. $s \geq k$, more paths are needed to be selected as transmission paths. The actual strategy can depend on the specific scenarios, and the final results can still use the output results of *free selection*, or append several other paths by random selection. For the other cases of $s<k$, further selection is needed to find fewer paths as required. These candidate

paths do not have shared bottleneck, but they are likely to share some ordinary congestion events which still present a certain correlation. In *restrained selection,* we adopt the *cross-measure* value of $M_x = \rho(P_{ij}, P_{xy})$ to quantify path correlation and select several paths with minimum correlation, which can be formulated as an optimization problem.

3.5 Evaluation results

In this section, we evaluate the effectiveness of our scheme in selecting optimal multiple paths, and also compare several strategies related to path selection. We construct a topology that the source is provided with 2 addresses and the destination with 3, so there will be 6 parallel paths. Six concurrent TCP-like flows are generated as foreground traffic, accompanied by the same number of multiplexed self-similar flows generated as background traffic. Here, to interpret the paths more easily, we express a path on its order as pk to identify the path from IP_s^i to IP_d^j rather than the form of P_{ij} on the interface. The transform rule is: k=(i-1)*N+j.

In the simulation results presented next, SPS denotes the original single best path selection scheme; RMS denotes the random multiple better paths selection scheme without the consideration of path correlation, which selects paths according to the priority of their Bandwidth-Delay Product; GMS-Free denotes *free selection* scheme in order to achieve the maximum flow based on GMS algorithm; GMS-Restrained denotes *restrained selection* scheme subject to some restrictions, here only considering the number of paths.

As different selection schemes can affect the performance, we compare the effect of aggregating throughput between GMS and other schemes. In this experiment, we demonstrate the effect of aggregating throughput based on four schemes separately in Fig. 4. We use FTP applications as our foreground traffic along with probing packets through all available paths. All six paths are all used to send data to collect the path delay, evaluate the path correlation, and consequently, select suitable path sets with different selection schemes. For GMS-Restrained, the number of paths required s is all set to 3, i.e. s=3. The possible selected path sets are {p4} of SPS, {p2, p3, p6} of RMS, {p1, p3, p4} of GMS-Restrained, and {p1, p3, p4, p5} of GMS-Free.

After finding suitable path set, the sender transmits the application data over the selected paths. The simulation results, shown in Fig. 4, demonstrate that aggregating throughput of

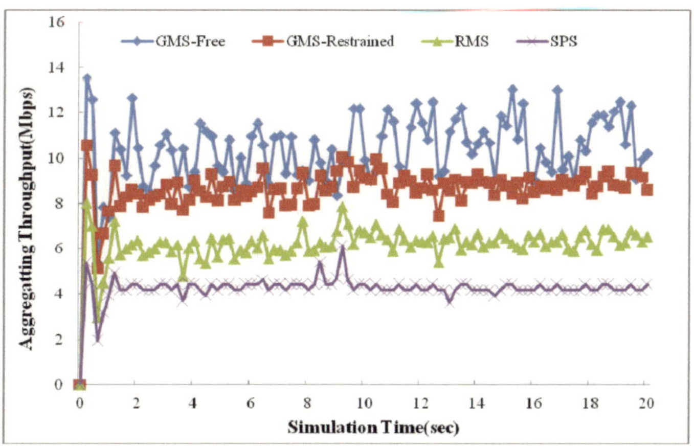

Fig. 4. Effect of different selection schemes

GMS-Free attained is the highest achieved by fully independent multiple paths, which is attributed to the exploitation of path correlation. Moreover, comparing the curves for GMS-Restrained and RMS, we observe that the aggregating throughput based on RMS is significant lower than GMS-Restrained, though both of them have the same number of selected paths. This is because RMS is a *correlation blind* scheme that cannot exploit path-diversity.

4. Flow-oriented latent handover

Handover management in wireless overlapping networks that have fully overlapping coverage should be paid more attention. Handover management techniques should allow mobile users to roam among multiple wireless networks in a manner that is completely transparent to applications and keep service continuity as much as possible. A number of handover management techniques have been proposed in the literatures (Nasser et al., 2006), (Ma et al., 2004), but the existing handover schemes all possess three inherent characteristics. One is that these handover schemes are connection-oriented, where exist connection intervals unavoidably even if they have already been cut down to a very low level. As such, it is difficult to realize seamless handover indeed; the second one is that their flow-control mechanisms are not aware of handover process, which causes the traffic flow to fluctuate remarkably and inevitable packet loss; the third one is that these schemes don't take into consideration the differences in the paths characteristics, which can lead to a situation where a slow path can drag down the performance of the handover.

In this paper, we proposed and designed a new handover scheme called Latent Handover, which is flow-oriented and switches the traffic to the new path progressively to hidden the handover process unconscious by user and upper layer application especially for real-time service. The basic idea of Latent Handover is to exploit IP diversity to keep the multiple paths alive during the process of setting up the new path to achieve a seamless handover. At the same time, flow-control is integrated with the process of handover to switch traffic progressively during the process of falling off the old path to achieve a smooth handover.

In order to avoid drastic performance degradation, the proposed Latent Handover greatly reduces the packet loss during handover by implementing the redundant transmission through old and new paths to maintaining former traffic, and by monitoring the available bandwidth of the new path and then selecting the qualified paths to concurrent transfer different packets.

4.1 Latent handover description

In this section, the architecture of Latent Handover in heterogeneous overlapping network is described, and how to use cmpSCTP for Latent Handover in the transport layer with the help of the concurrent multihoming feature is also described.

4.1.1 Architecture

The proposed Latent Handover need to acquire multiple paths from the sender to the receiver during handover, estimate the available bandwidth on each path through an end-to-end congestion control algorithm, calculate the number of flows and the target rate of each fragment, and assign different flows to different paths for transmission. Fig. 5 illustrates the overall system architecture of the proposed Latent Handover.

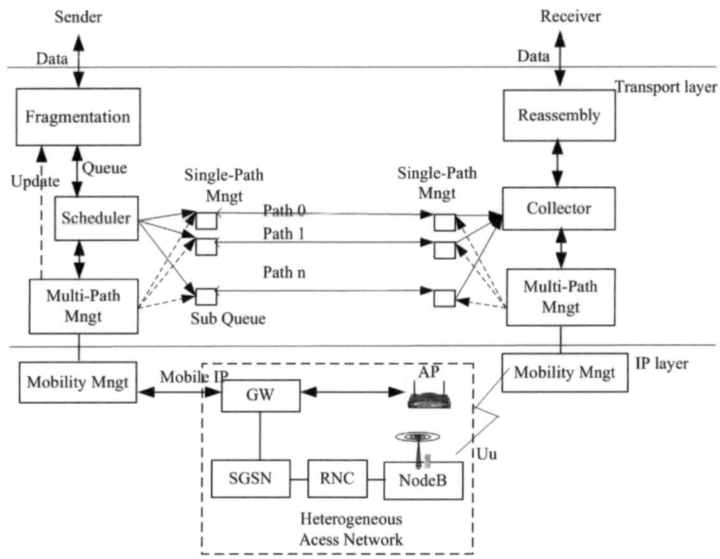

Fig. 5. System architecture of Latent Handover

The Multi-Path Management module at each end of the transport protocol manages the currently available paths, using CoA (Care of Address) binding update messages in the mobile IP protocol. The Multi-Path Management modules report the existence of multiple paths to the Scheduler and the Collector. The Multi-Path Management module also assigns a Single-Path module to a new path and removes a Single-Path module from an old path during handover. The Scheduler module calculates and reports the number of flows and the flow rate for each flow to the Fragmentation at the sender. The Collector module at the receiver accepts incoming packets from multiple paths, the out-of-order chunks is filtered and reordered by the Reassembly module before delivering to the application.

4.1.2 Handover process

The simple handover process of Latent Handover between two cells can be described by the following four steps using the cmpSCTP protocol, which is shown in Fig. 6.

Step 1. Obtain new IP address : The handover preparation procedure begins when MH moves into the overlapping wireless coverage area of two adjacent cells. Once the MH receives the router advertisement from the new Access Point (AR2), it should begin to obtain a new IP address generated by a DHCP server ,

The cmpSCTP association get the new IP address to maintain two paths simultaneously through two methods: standard IP and Mobile IP. The main difference lies in cmpSCTP over Mobile IP allows both MH and CH to simultaneous binding multiple addresses in network layer, So cmpSCTP over Mobile IP is a preferred method for Latent Handover to obtain a new address since it might reduce the required signalling time in cmpSCTP layer.

Step 2. Add new path to association: When the cmpSCTP association is initially setup, only the CH's IP address and the MH's first IP address (Path1) are exchanged between CH and MH. After the MH obtains another IP address (Path2 in STEP 1), MH should bind Path2 into the association (in addition to Path1) and notify CH about the availability of the new path.

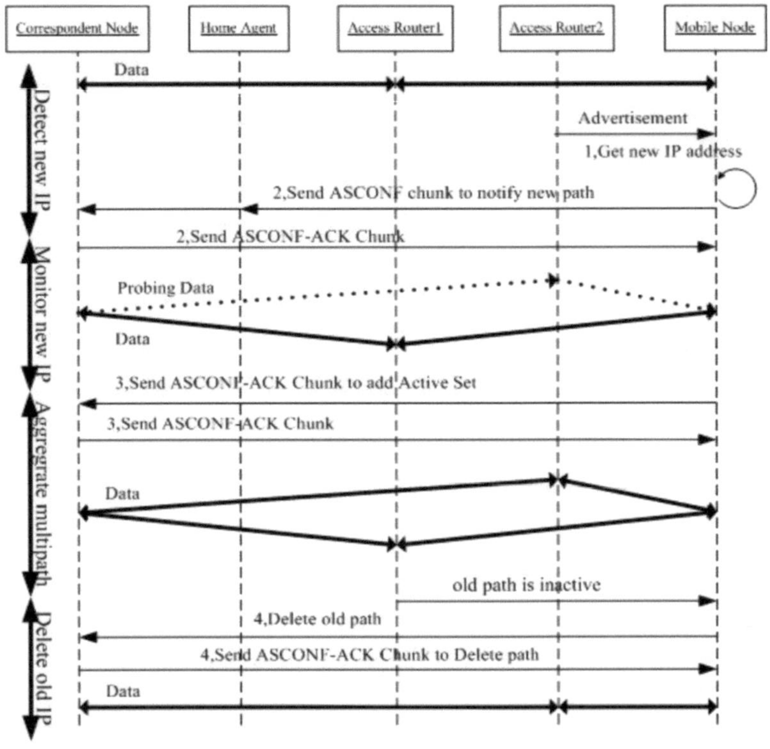

Fig. 6. Timing diagram of Latent Handover

In Latent Handover, cmpSCTP provides a graceful method to modify an existing association when the MH wishes to notify the CH that a new Path will be added to the association and this has no impact on existing active Path1.. MH notifies CH that Path2 is available for data transmission by sending an ASCONF chunk to CH. On receipt of this chunk, CH will add Path2 to its local control block for the association and reply to MH with an ASCONF-ACK chunk indicating the success of the IP addition. At this time, Path1 and Path2 are both ready for receiving data transmitted from CH to MH, but transmission strategy is a little different.

Due to Path2 likely presents instable in a period of time, which needs go through a probing stage. In this stage, Path2 are monitored utilizing the amount of actually significative data originally ready to be transmitted in path1 as probing packet. This kind of redundant transmission guarantees the smoothness of handover and increases the possibility of data being delivered successfully to the MH.

Step 3. Add monitored path to *Active_Set*: When MH moves further into the coverage area of wireless access network2, Path2 becomes increasingly so as reliable to take on the task of transmission data of its own. This task can be accomplished by the MH sending an ASCONF chunk with the ActivePath parameter, which results in CH adding Path into the *Active_Set*.

Then CH can partition data traffic into the Path1 and Path2 to increase the association throughput of data. During Latent Handover, CH will update the fragmentation and schedule strategy according real-time status of each path to optimize the total transmission efficiency. Once MH detects the quality of any path drops down below the threshold of *Active_Set*, the path will put into the *Monitored_Set*. By deactivating instead of deleting the path, Latent Handover can adapt more gracefully to MH's zigzag (often referred to as ping pong) movement patterns and reuse the previously obtained Path1, as long as the lifetime of Path1 has not expired. This will reduce the latency and signalling traffic that would have otherwise been caused by obtaining a new IP address.

Step 4. Delete obsolete Path: When MH moves out of the coverage of wireless access network1, no new or retransmitted data packets should be directed to Path1. In Latent Handover, MH can notify CH that IP1 is out of service for data transmission by sending an ASCONF chunk to CH (Delete Path). Once received, CH will delete Path1 from its local association control block and reply to MH with an ASCONF-ACK chunk indicating the success of the Path deletion.

4.1.3 Multi-path management

During handover, to allow the multi-path management module at the sender to maintain multiple paths simultaneously, the mobile IP (Johnson et al., 2004) simultaneous binding and route optimization options are used. The simultaneous binding option allows the receiver to simultaneously register multiple CoAs, and the route optimization option allows the sender to be informed of the current CoA registrations. When a new CoA is reported, the Multi-Path Management module assigns a flow control module to the new path and notifies the local multi-path transmitter/receiver of the new path; when a loss of a CoA is reported, the Multi-Path Management module removes a flow control module and notifies the local multi-path transmitter/receiver of a loss of a path.

Based on the cmpSCTP, the new paths are put into the *Monitored_Set* to detect their available network conditions. These paths are periodically checked against the so called "triggering conditions". If a triggering condition is fulfilled, the MH decides if a path should be added to the *Active_Set*. Then, MH creates a report which is sent to the CH. The rest of the candidate paths are kept in a *Monitored_Set*, from which replacement paths will substitute failed or degraded paths from the *Active_Set*.

The Multi-Path Management is responsible for updating the active paths list, which includes all the paths that can be used for load sharing, as well as for monitoring the status of the active paths. The Multi-Path Management updates the active paths list as it gets a feedback from the network regarding the failure of an exiting path or the availability of a new path. For example, when mobile IP protocol reports a new Care Of Address (CoA), with a PATH-ADD message, the Path Monitor performs the following actions: 1) It adds the new path to the existing association, using the Address Configuration Change (ASCONF) chunk [28]; 2) It creates a logical buffer for the new path; 3) Finally, it adds the new path to the active paths list. On the other hand, when the Multi-Path Management receives a PATH-LOSS message from the mobile IP, it performs the following: 1) It removes the path from the active paths list; 2) It deletes the logical buffer that corresponds to the path; 3) Finally, it removes the path from the association using the ASCONF chunk.

In addition, the Multi-Path Management removes a path from the active paths list when the number of consecutive retransmission time-outs on the path exceeds Path.Max.Retrans, which is set to 5, or when the path quality deteriorate to a limit that could affect the performance of the whole association. Currently, we are using a reasonable default threshold for the average loss rate on each path, and basing the path membership in the active paths list on that specified value. Inactive paths remain as a part of the association, and the sender keeps monitoring them through special copy of one of the data chunks for probing the path, on the contrary the standard SCTP, that through Heartbeat control chunks, as will be described in the next section. As soon as a path recovers, the Multi-Path Management adds it again to the active paths list.

4.2 Simulation model

In this section, we describe the simulation topology and parameters applied for evaluating the performance of the Latent Handover scheme. The purpose of the extensive simulations is two-fold: first to investigate the performance of the proposed scheme with various network parameters, and second to compare the proposed scheme with other existing handover schemes.

In our simulation, we created the network topology consisting two hosts as shown in Fig. 7. We assumed that an cmpSCTP association is already initiated between the two multihomed cmpSCTP hosts: cmpSCTP source and destination, and the association is unidirectional, which means that data chunks will only be sent from the Corresponding Host (CH) to Mobile Host (MH). Our simulation experiments concentrate on analyzing a single handover instance shown in Fig. 7 since a more general scenario with a sequence of handovers consists of individual handovers with different parameter settings. The mobile The following network configurations is used in the simulations. The coverage radius of each WLAN AP or UMTS base station is 300 meters, and the distance between two neighboring UMTS base stations is 400 meters. In each cell, a host is placed to simulate the background traffic. Wireless links are 802.11b WLAN 2Mbps links, while UMTS links are 1Mbps with *RTT* = 60ms. The bit error rate on a link dynamically changes within the range between 1×10-3 to 1×10-5 (with the average of 2×10-5), and all wireless links have the same bit error rate characteristics. All wired links are 155Mbps with *RTT* = 100ms, with 1×10-12 bit error rate, and 10μs propagation delay, unless otherwise noted. The path MTU at each path is 1 Kbytes, and each data chunk also has size of 1 Kbytes. We set the application packets inter-arrival time so as to insure that the application will always have packets for transmission.

Existing schemes chosen to compare against the proposed Latent Handover scheme use a single path from the sender to the mobile host (i.e., the receiver). In order to evaluate the performance of Latent Handover to perform vertical handover, we have performed three simulation scenarios and derived various performance measures, the goodput especially. The first one, the sender would send over all networks by concurrent multi-streaming the packets using Latent Handover, in the second scenario, the sender will achieve its sending with performing multi-path based on mSCTP, the last one, we utilize the original handover mechanism without performing multi-path. In our performance study we used the association throughput as a performance metrics, which is defined as the amount of data delivered to the receiver's application layer per second.

Available bandwidth in the new cell (i.e., the cell that the mobile host is entering) is varied by changing the average of the Poisson distribution used to generate background traffic in the new cell. Available bandwidth of the old cell (i.e., the cell that the mobile host is leaving) is assumed to be 2Mbps. In some simulations, a mobile host leaves an old cell (2Mbps) and enters a new cell which has a large amount of available bandwidth (5Mbps). In other simulations, a mobile Host enters a new cell with a lesser amount of available bandwidth (1Mbps). In this case, congestion occurs in the new cell. RTT from the sender to the mobile host is varied by changing the transmission delay from the mobile host to the backbone router.

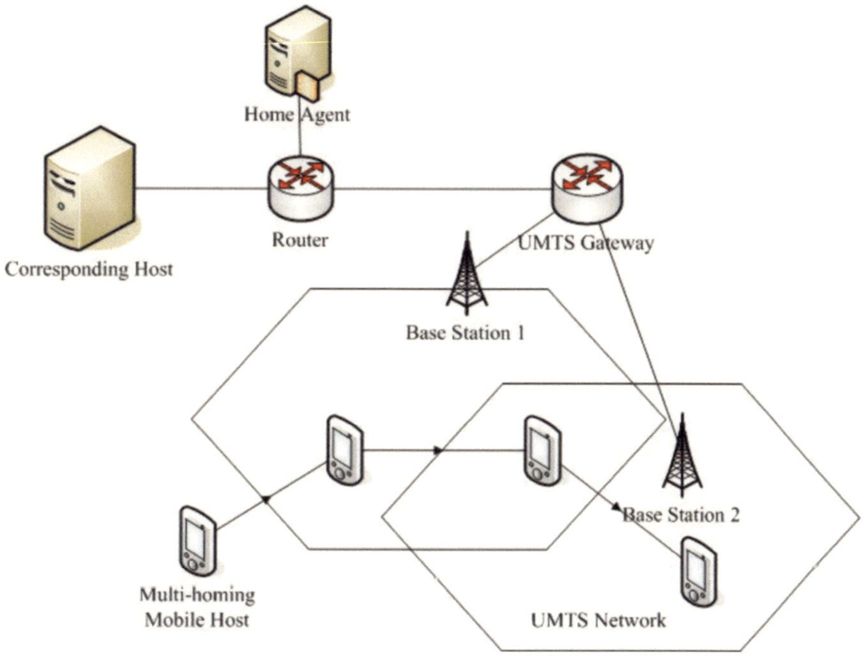

Fig. 7. Simulation scenario

4.3 Numerical results

In this section, simulation results are presented to evaluate the performance of the Latent Handover scheme. All the figures will be presented in this section, SP denotes the single-path handover scheme; MP_mSCTP denotes the multi-path handover scheme based on mSCTP. MP_cmpSCTP denotes the proposed multi-path Latent Handover scheme. Each result is an average of multiple simulation runs under the same set of parameters.

4.3.1 Throughput

In this experiment we assumed that we have two paths, namely path 1 and path 2 in order to examine the performance of cmpSCTP under the condition of paths with diverse capacities. The speed of mobile host movement is assumed to be 15 m/s (meters per second) and the RTT is assumed to be 60 ms. Fig. 8 shows the throughput during handoff. The x-axis in Fig. 8 represents the time, while the y-axis represents the effective throughput excluding the duplicate packets. In Fig. 8(a), the mobile host moves from a cell with a larger amount of available bandwidth (2Mbps) to a cell with a smaller amount of available bandwidth (1Mbps). In Fig. 8(b), a mobile host moves between two homogeneous cells with the same amount of available bandwidth (2Mbps). In Fig. 8(c), a mobile host moves from a cell with a smaller amount of available bandwidth (2Mbps) to a cell with a larger amount of available bandwidth (5Mbps).

As can be seen from Fig. 8, that despite the difference in the bandwidths of the paths, the throughput achieved by cmpSCTP is close to the ideal throughput. The high throughput achieved by cmpSCTP is due to its striping mechanism that is based on the rate of the bandwidth of the paths. This is because the Latent Handover scheme allows utilization of all available paths as soon as a mobile Host enters an overlapping area, making it possible to utilize the maximum available bandwidth throughout the duration of handover. The single path scheme and the multiple path scheme based on mSCTP switch to a path in a new cell in the middle of the handover period, making it not possible to use the path with the maximum available bandwidth throughout the duration of handover.

In Fig. 8 (b), no congestion occurs in the new cell since it has the same amount of available bandwidth with the old cell. As a result, all three schemes show relatively small fluctuations in the throughput. In Fig. 8(a), on the other hand, the other two schemes show a drastic drop in the throughput due to congestion loss in the new cell. This is because the rate control at the source is not aware of the handoff and continues sending data packets at a high rate that matches the available bandwidth in the old cell, resulting in congestion loss. The proposed Latent Handover scheme in Fig. 8(c) shows smooth changes in the throughput due to the TFRC rate control in the new cell and redundant transmission of the partial packets.

From Figures 8 (a) through (c), it is shown that the Latent Handover scheme achieves the highest throughput in almost all cases that have been simulated.

4.3.2 Handover latency

In this section, we simulation the latency of handover for MH. The handover latency is defined as the gap between 'the time that the MH has received the last DATA chunk over the old IP address', and 'the time that the MH has received the first DATA chunk over the new IP address'. For handover analysis, we consider the handover latency is the length of time interval between new path acquisition time and the receiving time of the last packet from the old path. For the single-homing MH, the new path acquisition time can be calculated by summing up the time TDHCP (for the configuration of a new IP address from a DHCP server), the handover delay of the underlying link layer Tlink_handover (for the processing time of the link-down and link-up in the underlying link layer), and the other signal negotiation latency. For the multihoming MH based on mSCTP, the new path acquisition time will be more affected by the signal negotiation latency, the primary factor is TASCONF (for the Add-IP and Primary-Change and Delete-IP operations in the mSCTP handover). TASCONF corresponds to the Round Trip Time (RTT) for exchange of ASCONF and ASCONF-ACK chunks between MH and CH. It is noted that the RTT is proportional to the distance between two endpoints and also inversely proportional to the bandwidth of the link. We also note that the mSCTP handover requires three times of exchanges of ASCONF and ASCONF-ACK chunks for ADD-IP, Primary-Change, Delete-IP, respectively. Accordingly, for Latent Handover scheme, the above operations are performed in advance before MH cuts off the old path, therefore the handover latency of cmpSCTP is much lower so much as close to zero. Fig. 9 show the handover latency for different moving speed of MH. For this experiment, all of the handover approaches are applied in order to compare and investigate the impact of MH moving speed to the performance of the different handover schemes.

As the moving speed of MH becomes faster, handover latency increases in all the handover schemes If two MHs with different moving speed start transiting the cell overlapping area at the same time, the faster MH should escape from the overlapping area earlier, i.e., the faster MH stops receiving packets from the previous path earlier. Since the path acquisition time is not affected by the moving speed of MH, the time to start receiving packets through the new

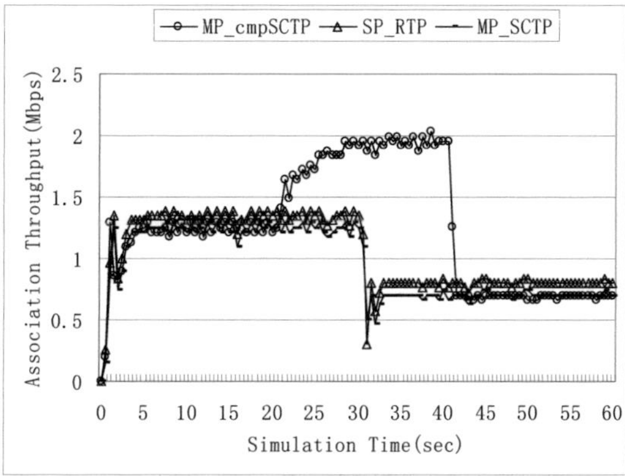

(a) The new cell has smaller available bandwidth

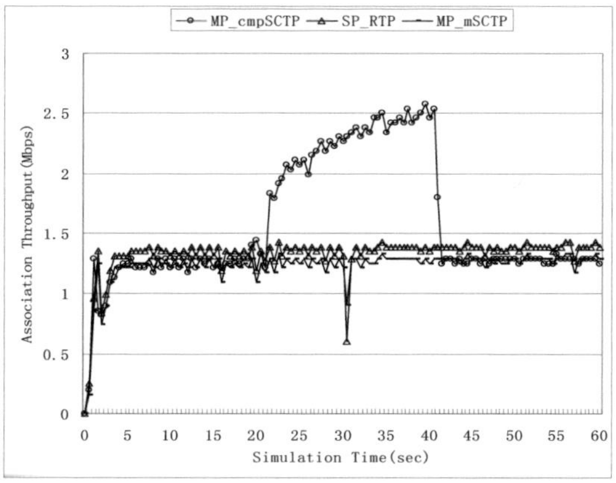

(b) The new cell has the same available bandwidth

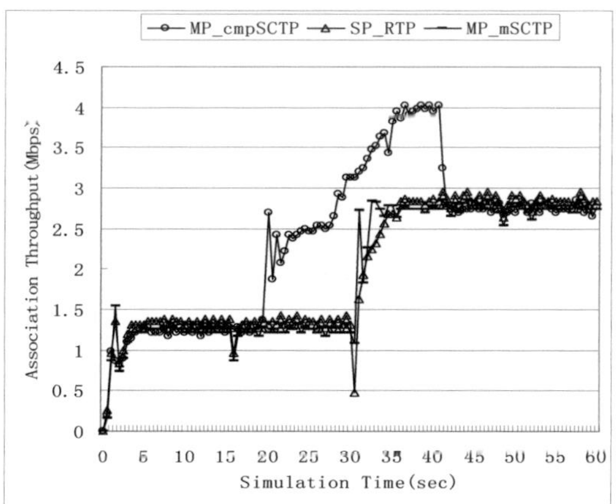

(c) The new cell has larger available bandwidth

Fig. 8. Association throughput during handover

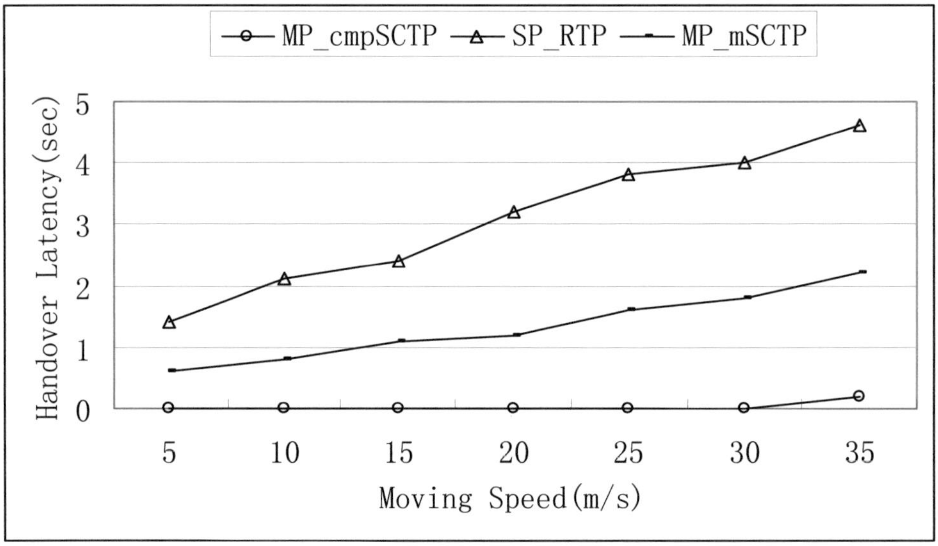

Fig. 9. Impact of moving speed on handover latency.

path is almost the same regardless of the moving speed. Therefore, handover latency becomes larger as the moving speed becomes faster, and the Latent Handover scheme always has the handover latency close to zero for all moving speeds, which explained for Fig. 9. Until the speed of MH movement increases to the degree that MH's overlapping area transiting time is smaller than the new path acquisition time, cmpSCTP will cause some amount of handover latency.

5. Conclusion

In future wireless access networks, CMT can enhance aggregating throughput and enable the network resource to be utilized efficiently. In this chapter, we proposed a new cmpSCTP protocol to better support high-quality VoIP applications over heterogeneous wireless networks. The cmpSCTP keeps two or more end-to-end paths concurrent, transferring new data from a source to a destination host.

More sophisticated network deployments mean that there may be some topologically shared or joint links between different transport paths. Thus, we propose a multipath selection strategy to exploit the path diversity by taking into account the potential path correlation. The probing and grouping mechanism can select the path set with minimum correlations, thus enabling the subsequent selection to avoid underlying shared bottleneck.

There is another demand for mobility between networks with maintained connectivity which requires the ability to switch the transmission path. Thus, we discuss the issue of handover in heterogeneous wireless networks. Our simulation results demonstrate that the Latent Handover leads to satisfactory performance due to appropriate treatment with the flow switch.

Further investigation is planned to address some of the issues associated with the media coding of VoIP applications, forward error correction (FEC) and hybrid strategies on CMT. The analysis and evaluation of these issues are our future work.

6. Acknowledgments

This work was jointly supported by: (1) National Science Fund for Distinguished Young Scholars (No. 60525110); (2) National 973 Program (No. 2007CB307100, 2007CB307103); ((3) National Natural Science Foundation of China (No. 61072057, 60902051); (4) Fundamental Research Funds for the Central Universities (BUPT2009RC0505); (5) Development Fund Project for Electronic and Information Industry (Mobile Service and Application System Based on 3G); (5) Development Fund Project for Electronic and Information Industry (Mobile Service and Application System Based on 3G).

7. References

Alkhawlani, M. & Ayesh, A. (2008). Access network selection based on fuzzy logic and genetic algorithms, *Advanced Artificial Intelligence (AAI)*, Vol.8, No.1, pp.1-12, ISSN 1687-7470.

Al, A. Saadawi, T. & Lee, M. (2004). LS-SCTP: a bandwidth aggregation technique for stream control transmission protocol, *Computer Communications*, Vol. 27, No.10, pp. 1012–1024, ISSN 0140-3664.

Apostolopoulos, J. & Trott, M. (2004). Path diversity for enhanced media streaming, *IEEE Communications Magazine, Special Issue Proxy Support Streaming Internet*, Vol. 42, No. 8, pp. 80–87, ISSN 0163-6804.

Casetti, C. Chiasserini, C. Fracchia, R. & Meo, M. (2008). Autonomic interface selection for mobile wireless users, *IEEE Transactions on Vehicular Technology*, Vol. 57, No. 6, pp. 3666-3678, ISSN 0018-9545.

Fracchia, R. Casetti, C. Chiasserini, C. & Meo, M. (2007). WiSE: best-path selection in wireless multihoming environments, *IEEE Transactions on Mobile Computing*, Vol. 6, No. 10, pp. 1130-1141, ISSN 1536-1233.

Garey, M. & Johnson, D. (1979). Computers and intractability: A guide to the theory of NP-Completeness, *W. H. Freeman Company*, ISBN 071678158, San Francisco, CA.

Hsieh, H. & Sivakumar, R. (2002). A transport layer approach for achieving aggregate bandwidths on multi-homed mobile hosts, *Proceedings of ACM International Conference on Mobile Computing and Networking (MobiCom), pp. 83-94,* Atlanta, Georgia, USA.

Iyengar, J. R Amer, P. & Stewart, R. (2006). Concurrent multipath transfer using SCTP multihoming over independent end-to-end paths, *IEEE/ACM Transactions on Networking*, Vol. 14, No. 5, pp. 951–964, ISSN 1063-6692.

Johnson, D. Perkins, C. & Arkko, J. (2004). Mobility support in IPv6, *IETF RFC 3775*.

Liao, J. Wang, J. & Zhu. X. (2008). A multi-path mechanism for reliable VoIP transmission over wireless networks, *Computer Networks*, Vol. 52, No. 13, pp. 2450-2460, ISSN 1389-1286.

Ma, L. Yu, F. & Leung, V. (2004). A new method to support UMTS/WLAN vertical handover using SCTP, *IEEE Wireless Communications*, Vol. 11, No. 4, pp. 44-51, ISSN 1536-1284.

Nasser, N. Hasswa, A. and Hassanein, H. (2006). Handoffs in Fourth Generation Heterogeneous Networks, *IEEE Communications Magazine,* Vol. 44, No. 10, pp. 96-103, ISSN 0163-6804.

Rubenstein, D. Kurose, J. & Towsley, D. (2002). Detecting shared congestion of flows via end-to-end measurement, *IEEE/ACM Transactions on Networking*. Vol. 10, No. 3, pp. 381–395, ISSN 1063-6692.

14

End-to-End Handover Management for VoIP Communications in Ubiquitous Wireless Networks

Shigeru Kashihara[1], Muhammad Niswar[2], Yuzo Taenaka[3], Kazuya Tsukamoto[4], Suguru Yamaguchi[1] and Yuji Oie[4]
[1]*Nara Institute of Science and Technology*
[2]*University of Hasanuddin*
[3]*The University of Tokyo*
[4]*Kyushu Institute of Technology*
[1,3,4]*Japan*
[2]*Indonesia*

1. Introduction

With the development and widespread of diverse wireless network technologies such as wireless local area networks (WLANs) and worldwide interoperability for microwave access (WiMAX), the number of mobile internet users keeps on growing. This rapid increase in mobile internet users accelerates the further spread of these wireless networks, and thus various wireless service providers (WSPs) and individuals will provide many different wireless networks. These networks then will be the underlying basis of ubiquitous wireless networks, as illustrated in Fig. 1. Thus, ubiquitous wireless networks will provide stable Internet connectivity at anytime and anywhere. At the same time, voice over IP (VoIP) is expected to become a killer application in the ubiquitous wireless networks, i.e., the next generation cell-phone. Recently, many users have easily used VoIP communication such as Skype (Skype, 2003) in wireless networks. However, users cannot seamlessly traverse wireless networks during VoIP communication due to various factors such as the inherent instability of wireless networks, a limited communication area and changes of IP addresses.
This chapter focuses on what is needed to maintain VoIP communication quality during movement in the ubiquitous wireless networks. If you are a subscriber of a WSP, the WSP will provide for your mobility inside the WSP's wireless network. Unfortunately, as described above, in ubiquitous wireless networks consisting of wireless networks provided by various WSPs and individuals, because each wireless network has a different network address, a mobile station (MS) needs handovers with changes of IP addresses. However, in the current Internet architecture, VoIP communication is broken when changing IP addresses. Furthermore, since ubiquitous wireless networks consist of wireless networks provided by various providers, it is next to impossible for a single provider to support mobile service for users in the ubiquitous wireless networks. Hence, an MS needs a method to traverse wireless networks managed independently by different providers without communication termination. Then, even if an MS can avoid communication termination at handover, the following problems must also be resolved to maintain VoIP communication quality during movement. First, when an MS executes handover to a wireless network with a different

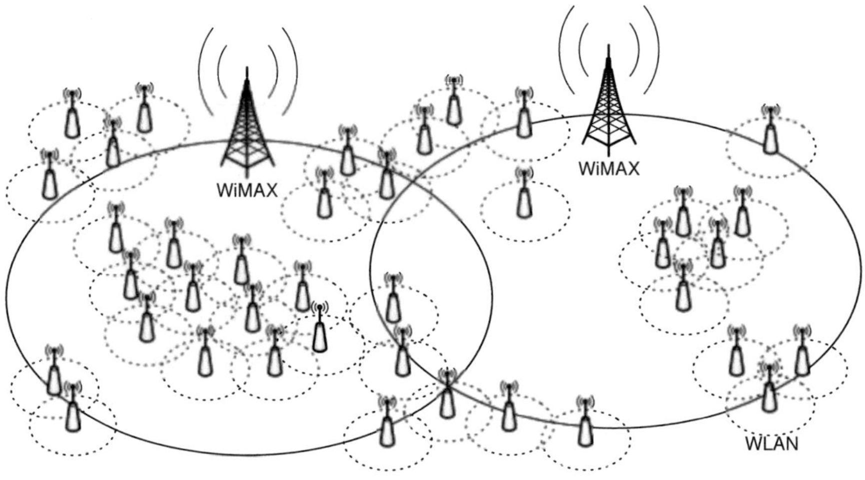

Fig. 1. Ubiquitous wireless networks

network address, layer 2 and 3 handover processes inevitably lead to interruption of VoIP communication. Second, the timing to initiate handover is also a critical issue. In fact, late handover initiation severely affects VoIP communication quality because the wireless link quality suddenly degrades. Third, how to recognize which network will be the best choice among available networks is an issue of concern. Thus, to maintain VoIP communication quality during movement, the following requirements must be satisfied.

1. Keep VoIP communication from communication termination by change of IP address
2. Eliminate communication interruption due to layer 2 and 3 handover processes
3. Initiate appropriate handover based on reliable handover triggers
4. Select a wireless network with good link quality during handover

This chapter introduces end-to-end handover management methods satisfying all of the above requirements, to maintain VoIP communication quality during movement. As illustrated in Fig. 1, since we assume that the ubiquitous wireless networks consist of a large number of WLANs and WiMAX, we focus on two mobility scenarios, i.e., WLAN-WLAN and WLAN-WiMAX scenarios. Note that the concept of our proposed methods also will be suitable for other new wireless networks such as 3GPP Long Term Evolution (LTE).
This chapter is organized as follows. Section 2 surveys related work. Section 3 presents an end-to-end handover management method in a WLAN-WLAN scenario and the implementation of the prototype system. In Section 4, to consider a more realistic environment, we extend our handover management method to apply for multi-rate and congested WLANs. Section 5 presents a handover management method among different wireless access technologies, i.e., WLAN and WiMAX. Finally, Section 6 presents concluding remarks and future work.

2. Related Work

There have been numerous discussions about supporting an MS's mobility among wireless networks with different network addresses. In this section, we focus especially on handover management needed to keep VoIP communication quality during such movement. As described in Section 1, in the ubiquitous wireless networks, an MS may experience many handovers with changes of IP addresses. Mobile IPv4 (MIPv4) (Perkins, 2002) and Mobile IPv6 (MIPv6) (Johnson et al., 2004) have received significant interest as a network-based mobility management method to support mobility with changes of IP address. To avoid communication termination due to a change of IP address, MIPv4/v6 employs agent servers in the wireless networks, and the agent servers manage the location of MSs and control packet transmission between an MS and a corresponding station (CS). Although the agent servers do keep communication connections even when the IP address of the MS is changed, MIPv4/v6 is not enough to provide a seamless handover. To move to another wireless network, an MS has to perform layer 2 and 3 handover processes and it cannot send and receive any packets during that time. Furthermore, location registration with the agent servers also introduces an interruption delay. Thus, such interruptions lead to degradation of VoIP communication quality.

To support seamless handover with MIPv4/v6, many extension methods have been studied. In Hierarchical Mobile IPv6 (HMIP) (Soliman et al., 2008), an additional server reduces the registration period inside the same domain. However, when an MS moves between different domains, the HMIP eventually requires layer 2 and 3 handover processes and a location update like the original MIPv4/v6. In Fast handover for Mobile IPv6 (FMIP) (Koodli, 2005), additional functions are added to allow an MS to update the location before executing handover. However, FMIP also needs layer 2 and 3 handover processes after updating the location. Therefore, it does not completely eliminate communication interruption due to layer 2 and 3 handover processes (Kim et al., 2005) (Montavont & Noel, 2003). In addition, since MIP-based methods require special agent servers, they cannot easily be used in ubiquitous wireless networks because a different provider independently manages each wireless network. Thus, it is desirable to provide an end-to-end handover management method without extra network facilities.

As for end-to-end handover approaches, the mobile Stream Control Transmission Protocol (mSCTP) (Xing et al., 2002) and the Media Optimization Network Architecture (MONA) (Koga et al., 2005) have been proposed. The mSCTP is a mobile extension of the Stream Control Transmission Protocol (SCTP) (Stewart, 2007), and allows an MS to simultaneously use two or more wireless interfaces for communications, i.e., multi-homing architecture. Compared with the single-homing architecture, the multi-homing architecture can contribute to elimination of communication interruption due to layer 2 and 3 handovers because an MS can connect with another wireless network by using an idle interface before breaking off the current communication. However, the mSCTP supports only non-real-time communications such as a file transfer; real-time communications such as VoIP are not supported. On the other hand, MONA also has a multi-homing function and it can handle both real-time and non-real-time communications. However, MONA does not focus on handover management for maintaining VoIP communication quality.

3. End-to-end handover management in WLAN-WLAN scenario

This section focuses on a case where an MS traverses WLANs with different network addresses. As illustrated in Fig. 1, with the proliferation of free WLAN hotspots such as FON (FON, 2005), so that the overlapping WLANs provide wide coverage as ubiquitous WLANs, an MS will be able to access the Internet via the ubiquitous WLANs everywhere. However, the coverage of each access point (AP) is relatively small and each AP also independently provides wireless connectivity, i.e., they have different network addresses. Thus, in what follows, we focus on end-to-end handover management to enable an MS to maintain VoIP communication while traversing WLANs with different network addresses. In Section 3.1, to maintain VoIP communication quality during movement, we first discuss a handover trigger needed to appropriately detect degradation of wireless link quality. We then introduce our handover management architecture and the implementation design in Sections 3.2 and 3.3, respectively. Section 3.4 shows the basic performance of our prototype system.

3.1 Handover trigger for WLAN

A handover trigger plays an important part in maintaining VoIP communication quality during movement. In fact, late handover initiation severely affects VoIP communication quality because the wireless link quality suddenly degrades. Prevention of such degradation requires a handover trigger that promptly and reliably detects degradation of the wireless link quality. The received signal strength indication (RSSI) is generally employed as a common index of wireless link quality. However, the RSSI fluctuates drastically due to various complicated effects such as distance to an AP, multi-path fading, and intervening objects. Moreover, the values obtained from each WLAN interface depend on a vendor, e.g., the RSSI range of Atheros's chipset is from 0 to 60 and that of Cisco's chipset is from 0 to 100 (Muthukrishnan et al., 2006). Therefore, since it is very difficult to set an optimal handover threshold for the RSSI, the RSSI cannot serve as a reliable handover trigger.

Because RSSI cannot serve as a reliable handover trigger, we focused on the number of data frame retries as a new handover trigger to promptly and reliably detect degradation of wireless link quality due to movement (Kashihara & Oie, 2007). In a WLAN, a sender can detect successful packet transmission by receiving an ACK frame in response to a transmitted data frame. If a data or an ACK frame is lost, the sender transmits the same data frame until the number of data frame retries reaches a predetermined retry limit. Note that when Request-to-Send (RTS)/Clear-to-Send (CTS) is applied, the retry limit is set to four, otherwise, the retry limit of seven is applied. If the number of data frame retries reaches the retry limit, the sender treats the data frame as a lost packet. Thus, since data frame retries mainly occur for the following two reasons: (i) reduction of RSSI and (ii) collision with other frames, we can suppose that the number of data frame retries indicates how much wireless link quality is degraded before packet loss actually occurs.

To show the effectiveness of data frame retries as a handover trigger, we investigated RSSI and data frame retries in a real environment (Tsukamoto et al., 2007). The paper discussed the characteristics of RSSI and data frame retries for FTP and VoIP applications in an open-space and an indoor environments. We here introduce only the results of VoIP communication in the indoor environment. In Fig. 2, the MS has VoIP communication with the CS via the AP, and then it goes away from the AP. In the experiment, we employed the ORiNOCO AP-4000 (Proxim, 2007) as an AP. The transmission speed of the WLAN (802.11b) is set to a fixed 11Mb/s, and RTS/CTS is activated. As a WLAN interface of the MS, the ORiNOCO 802.11a/b/g Combo Card Gold (Proxim, 2007) is used. Note that the RSSI ranges from 0 to 60 because the WLAN interface has the Atheros's chipset. An analyzing station (AS) captures transmitted frames over the WLAN by using Ethereal 0.10.13 (Ethereal, 1998).

The graph shows the results of packet loss ratio, RSSI, and the number of data frame retries for VoIP communication when the MS actually moves away from the AP at a walking speed. "Retry: n" indicates that a packet experiences frame retries "n" times, and its associated symbol marked in the graph shows when that occurs. From the graph, we can see that since the RSSI drastically fluctuates and decreases abruptly with the movement of the MS,

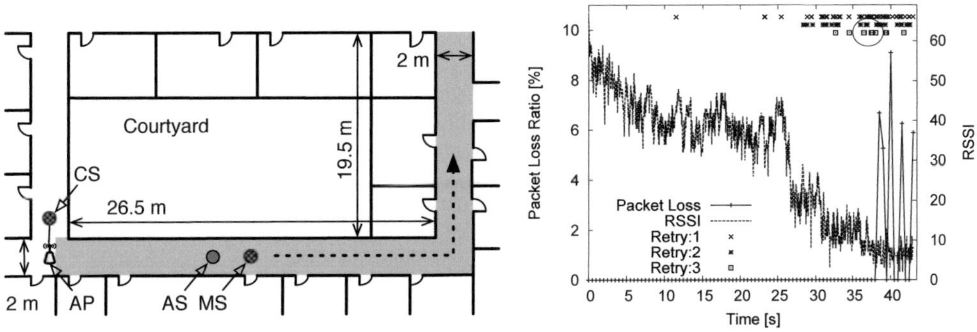

Fig. 2. Experimental environment and result

it is difficult to determine a threshold value to appropriately initiate handover. On the other hand, as for data frame retries, in particular, "Retry: 3" occurs just before appearance of lost packets. Thus, the number of data frame retries can be used to promptly and reliably detect deterioration of the wireless link quality.

3.2 Handover management architecture

As described in Section 1, in order to maintain VoIP communication quality during movement, we need to satisfy the following requirements.

1. Keep VoIP communication from communication termination by change of IP address
2. Eliminate communication interruption due to layer 2 and 3 handover processes
3. Initiate appropriate handover based on reliable handover triggers
4. Select a wireless network with good link quality during handover

Moreover, to freely traverse wireless networks without special network facilities, a handover management on an end-to-end basis is also required. We then proposed a handover management method on an end-to-end basis for ubiquitous WLANs (Kashihara & Oie, 2007) (Kashihara et al., 2007).

We outline here our handover management method. Figure 3 illustrates our architecture design for seamless handover. To satisfy requirements (1) and (2), we employed a multi-homing architecture and a handover manager (HM) on the transport layer. The multi-homing architecture enables an MS to handle two or more wireless interfaces simultaneously. If an MS with a single WLAN interface moves among WLANs with different network address, inherently it can never avoid communication termination and interruption because a single interface cannot access more than one AP at a time. On the other hand, since a multi-homing MS can execute layer 2 and 3 handover processes using an idle WLAN interface in advance before breaking off communications on the active WLAN interface, it can seamlessly switch to a candidate AP without communication termination and interruption. Moreover, to control handover without additional agent servers, the handover should be managed over the transport layer because the transport layer is the lowest layer that controls an end-to-end flow. Therefore, in our architecture, we implemented the HM, which controls handovers according to wireless link condition, on the transport layer.

To satisfy requirement (3), we employed the number of data frame retries as a new handover trigger because data frame retries inevitably occur before occurrence of packet loss in wireless networks. Thus, to control handover, the HM needs to obtain information from the MAC layer

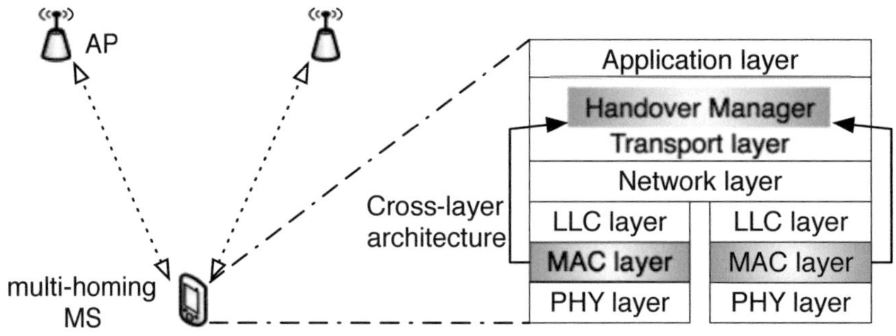

Fig. 3. Architecture design for seamless handover

based on the cross-layer architecture. As for requirement (4), the HM needs to select a WLAN with better link quality to avoid an inappropriate handover to an AP with poor link quality. In our proposed method, when performing handover in an overlap area, an MS starts to transmit duplicated packets via both APs; that is, the MS switches to multi-path transmission. During multi-path transmission, the HM investigates the wireless link quality of both APs based on the number of data frame retries and then selects the better one. After that, it reverts to single-path transmission via the selected AP. Therefore, the HM achieves a seamless handover by appropriately switching between single-path and multi-path transmissions.

3.3 Design and implementation

As described above, to achieve an end-to-end seamless handover, we need to implement a multi-homing architecture, cross-layer architecture, and multi-path transmission function. In this section, since we actually implemented our prototype system on a real system (Taenaka et al., 2007), we introduce its design and implementation.

In our implementation, we first employed MONA (Koga et al., 2005) as the base system enabling an MS to handle multiple wireless interfaces. That is, our multi-homing architecture basically depends on MONA. Next, we explain how to exploit the cross-layer architecture, which enables the HM to obtain the number of data frame retries from the MAC layer. In the previous simulation study (Kashihara & Oie, 2007), although the number of data frame retries is directly passed from the MAC layer to the HM at every packet through the cross-layer architecture, we found that it actually causes significant deterioration of kernel performance due to frequent interruptions. Therefore, in the paper (Taenaka et al., 2007), we proposed an asynchronous process between the HM and the MAC layer. In the design, as illustrated in Fig. 4, the MAC layer for each WLAN interface writes the number of data frame retries into its own shared memory, and the HM retrieves the information from the shared memory. The shared memory consists of (1) index and (2) retry count. The retry count region consists of an array containing 100 elements with a ring buffer. Actually, the MAC layer records the number of data frame retries for one data packet in the shared memory whenever each data packet is successfully transmitted or else discarded due to maximum frame retries. Then, the MAC layer also writes the latest array position of the retry count region into the index region.

To achieve a seamless handover, our proposed method also employed two transmission modes, i.e., single-path and multi-path transmission modes. Next, we describe the details of the switching procedures. An MS usually communicates by single-path transmission. When the number of data frame retries exceeds the Multi-Path Threshold (MP_TH) in the HM, the

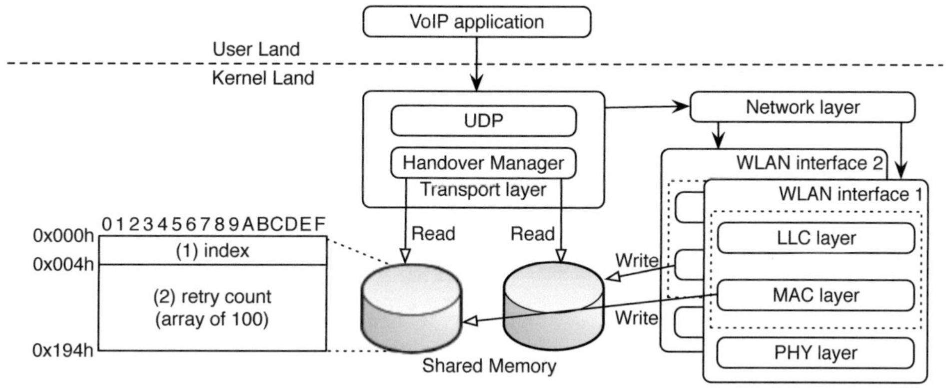

Fig. 4. Design of cross-layer architecture and shared memory

HM switches to multi-path transmission to prevent packet loss and to investigate the wireless link quality of both WLANs. Figure 5 illustrates the flowchart for switching to multi-path transmission. Note that the process is executed at every packet transmission. The flowchart is divided into two parts: (a) reading the information from the shared memory, and (b) switching to multi-path transmission according to the wireless link quality. In the flowchart, "italic letters" and "bold letters" indicate variable and system parameters, respectively. In our proposed method, since the HM and the MAC layer work asynchronously, some packets may already be sent at the MAC layer when the HM checks the number of data frame retries, i.e., the HM needs to check past packet transmissions (see Fig. 5(a)). Then, the HM first checks the range of elements (*get_cnt*) updated in the retry count region after the previous execution. This procedure is depicted in Fig. 6. In the procedure, two position indexes are employed: *start_pos* indicates an array position where the HM starts to obtain the number of data frame retries in the retry count region, and *end_pos* indicates the latest array position. To get *start_pos*, the process first checks whether this is a first-time execution or not. If so, *start_pos* is set to 0. Otherwise, *start_pos* has already been set to the latest array position in the previous execution. On the other hand, *end_pos* is set to the value of the index region in the shared memory. Therefore, updated elements (*get_cnt*) are calculated by *start_pos* and *end_pos*.

In Fig. 5(b), the HM compares the number of data frame retries (*retries*) with the MP_TH, which is a threshold to switch to the multi-path transmission, *get_cnt* times. In the comparison, if a value obtained from the retry count region exceeds the MP_TH, the HM immediately escapes

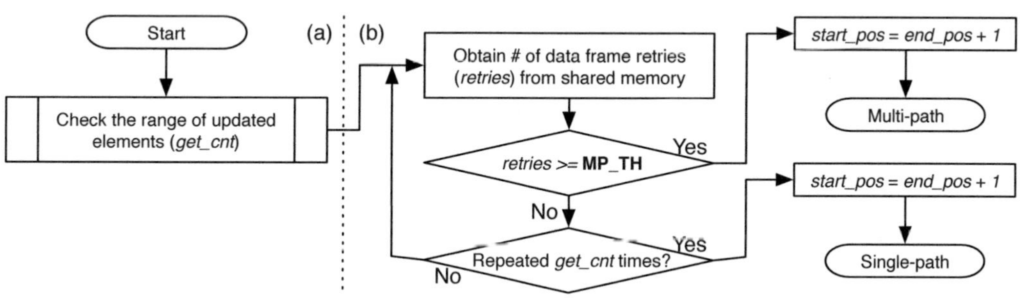

Fig. 5. Switching to multi-path transmission

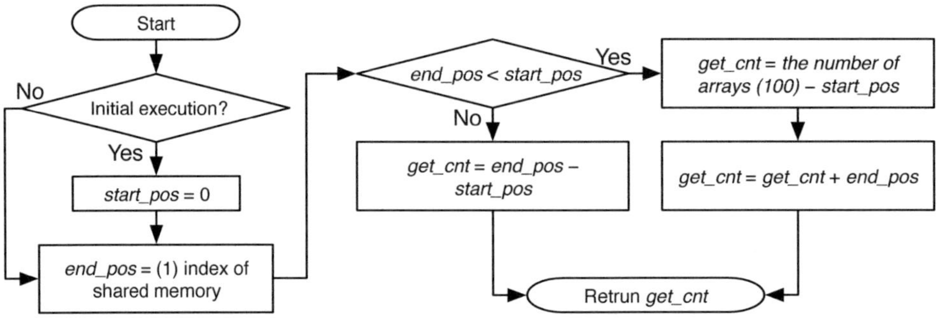

Fig. 6. Calculation of the range of updated elements

from the loop and switches to the multi-path transmission. Then, *start_pos* is set to *end_pos* + 1 for the next execution. Otherwise, the HM continues to compare it with the MP_TH. If any element does not exceed the MP_TH, single-path transmission continues. Then, after the process, *start_pos* is set to *end_pos* + 1 for the next execution.

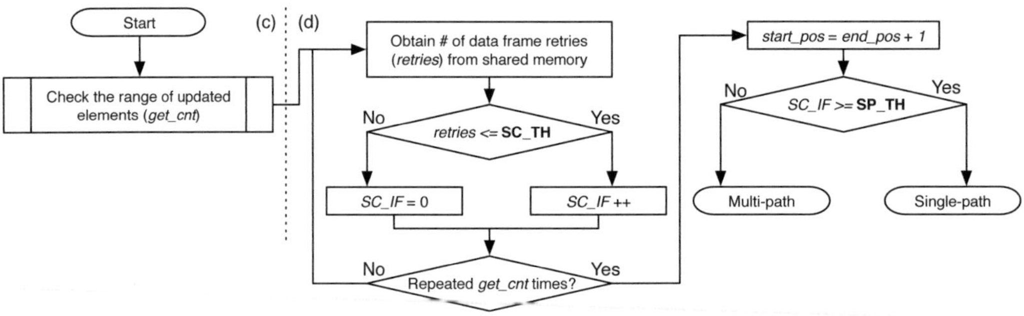

Fig. 7. Switching to single-path transmission

In multi-path transmission, since an MS sends duplicated data packets through the two WLANs, the network traffic load doubles. Thus, an MS needs to return to single-path transmission as soon as possible to reduce the extra network traffic. Figure 7 illustrates a switching operation to single-path transmission. In Fig. 7(c), the HM first calculates the range of updated elements (*get_cnt*) in the retry count region for each WLAN, as does the single-path transmission operation. In Fig. 7(d), the HM then obtains the updated *retries* for each WLAN interface from the shared memory. The HM continuously compares the obtained value with the SC_TH, which is a threshold to check the stability of wireless link condition, for each WLAN interface *get_cnt* times. If the value is smaller than the SC_TH, the *SC_IF*, which is a counter for the network stability, is incremented by one. Otherwise, *SC_IF* is reset to zero because the HM decides that the wireless link quality for the WLAN interface is still unstable. After the loop, the HM updates *start_pos* for the next execution and compares the *SC_IF* of each WLAN interface with the SP_TH, which is a threshold to return to single-path transmission. If the *SC_IF* exceeds the SP_TH, the HM switches back to single-path transmission. Otherwise, the HM continues multi-path transmission.

Next, we describe our implementation environment. Our handover management architecture is implemented in the Cent OS 4.3 (Linux kernel version 2.6.9) on Lenovo ThinkPad X60 (CPU: Core Duo 1.66 GHz, Memory: 512 MB). Since an MS has two WLAN interfaces for a multi-homing architecture, it employs a built-in WLAN interface (P/N: 40Y7028) and a PC card WLAN interface (ORiNOCO 802.11 a/b/g Combo Card Gold). Then, to extract the number of data frame retries from the WLAN interfaces with Atheros chipset, the MadWifi driver (MadWifi, 2004) is employed. The cross-layer architecture is implemented only on the MadWifi driver.

3.4 Performance evaluation

This section demonstrates the basic performance of our prototype system described in Section 3.3 (Bang et al., 2009). Our proposed method employs the following three thresholds, MP_TH of three, SP_TH of two, and SC_TH of one, to control handover. The three values are determined based on the results in our paper (Kashihara & Oie, 2007).

Figure 8 shows the experimental topology and the result. In the topology, we employed five PCs for an MS, a CS, two APs, and a router. The router belongs to three networks with different network addresses and directly connects to the CS and the two APs by wired connection. Since we assume that ubiquitous WLANs consist of many WLANs provided by various providers, the paths to the CS have different delays to reproduce a realistic environment; that is, the path delay through AP1 is 10 ms and that through AP2 is 30 ms. The delays are intentionally added at the router using dummynet of FreeBSD (FreeBSD, 1995). The two APs are constructed on two identical laptops (HP nx6120) with a PC card WLAN interface (ORiNOCO 802.11 a/b/g combo Card Gold) in which Fedora Core 6 with MadWifi driver is installed. Then, both APs are configured as the master mode of the MadWifi driver to stand as an AP. In the wireless settings, the data rate is fixed at 11 Mb/s of IEEE 802.11b and the RTS/CTS function is disabled. The distance of APs is 45 meters.

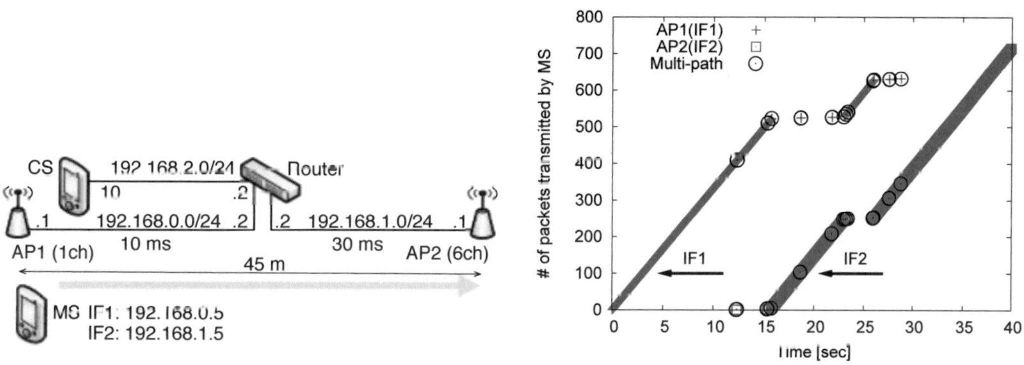

Fig. 8. Experimental topology and result

Now we describe our experimental scenario. Since we focus on the VoIP communication performance during handover, the two WLAN interfaces of the MS are assumed to associate with the two APs before starting an experiment. That is, WLAN interface 1 (IF1) associates with AP1, and, likewise, WLAN interface 2 (IF2) associates with AP2. This means that the MS is in an overlap area of two APs and has already connected to them. Then, after starting to capture traffic using tcpdump (TCPDUMP, 2000), the MS walks from AP1 to AP2 while communicating with the CS using VoIP (G.711). When it arrives at AP2, we stop capture of the traffic. The graph shows the number of packets transmitted by the MS over time. The AP1 and AP2 marks indicate when single-path transmission through AP1 and AP2 are executed, respectively, while that of multi-path shows when multi-path transmission is employed. The graph shows that the MS initiates handover at approximately 15 seconds according to the

Maximum	Minimum	Average	Median
11	0	4.7	5

Table 1. Packet loss for nine experiments

Maximum	Minimum	Average	Median
2.1 %	0.4 %	1.3 %	1.2 %

Table 2. Multi-path transmission ratio for nine experiments

change of the wireless link condition. After that, the MS repeats the handovers two more times: it returns back to AP1 at approximately 23 seconds and switches again to AP2 at approximately 26 seconds. Note that we here define switching to single-path transmission on the next WLAN as a handover. Table 1 shows the number of lost packets from the MS to the CS throughout the nine experiments. From the result, we can see that the prototype system can execute handover seamlessly. Table 2 lists the multi-path transmission ratios during the nine experiments. The result shows that our prototype system has extremely few redundant packets. Therefore, our prototype system can achieve seamless handover while appropriately switching between single-path and multi-path transmissions.

4. End-to-end handover management for multi-rate and congested WLANs

In the previous section, we introduced a prototype system of our handover management method to maintain VoIP communication quality during movement in ubiquitous WLANs. Although we focused on degradation of wireless link quality during movement in Section 3, we also need to consider the impact of multi-rate function and congestion at an AP to apply for a more realistic environment. Section 4.1 first discusses the handover triggers for multi-rate and congested WLANs. We next introduce our handover management method and show the basic performance in Section 4.2 and 4.3, respectively.

4.1 Handover triggers for multi-rate and congested WLANs

In Section 3, we introduced the number of data frame retries as a handover trigger for movement in WLANs with a fixed transmission rate (11 Mb/s). However, in a real environment, almost all WLANs employ a multi-rate function that can change the transmission rate according to the wireless link condition. If the transmission rate is dropped by the multi-rate function, a more robust modulation type is selected and thus data frame retries are decreased. As a result, since an MS cannot properly detect degradation of wireless link quality only from data frame retries in multi-rate WLANs, we need to consider more reliable handover triggers.

Next, we consider an RTS frame retry ratio as an alternative metric of data frame retries. Since an RTS frame is always transmitted at the lowest rate (e.g., 6 Mb/s in 802.11a/g and 1 Mb/s in 802.11b), an MS can appropriately detect changes in wireless link quality by utilizing it. Moreover, the RTS frame also prevents collisions due to hidden nodes in a wireless network. However, as the RTS threshold is set to 2,347 bytes in the IEEE802.11 standard, an RTS frame is not sent because of the VoIP packet size (e.g., 160 bytes). Therefore, in our proposal, all MSs must set the RTS threshold to 0 to enable MSs to send RTS frames. To show the effectiveness of the RTS frame retry, we investigated the behavior of RTS retry ratio when an MS moves away from an AP using Qualnet 4.0.1 (Scalable Network Technologies, 2006) (see Fig. 9(a)). In the study, RTS frame retry ratio is employed instead of the frequency of data frame retries for reliable detection of degradation of wireless link quality. Actually, an instantaneous increase of RTS frame retries may lead to more misdetection of wireless link quality. The RTS retry ratio is calculated as follows:

$$RTS\ frame\ retry\ ratio = \frac{the\ number\ of\ RTS\ frame\ retries}{total\ transmitted\ RTS\ frames} \tag{1}$$

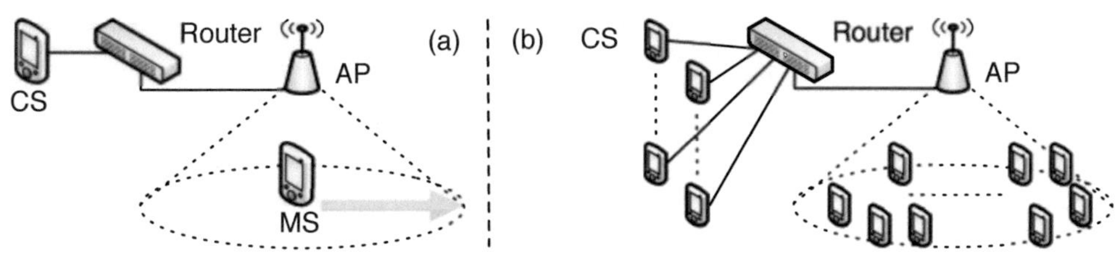

Fig. 9. Simulation model

Figure 10 shows the relationships between the MOS and the RTS frame retry ratio over distances between the AP and the MS. We here employ MOS (ITU-T G.107, 2000) to assess the VoIP quality. Note that MOS of more than 3.6 indicates an adequate VoIP call quality. The graph shows that the MOS tends to degrade with increase in the RTS frame retry ratio when the MS moves away from the AP. Since the RTS frame retry ratio is fluctuating due to the unstable wireless link quality, we employed a least-squares method to grasp their trend and estimate the best fit of the occurrences of RTS frame retry ratio over the distance, shown as a straight line in the graph. The line shows that the RTS frame retry ratio of 0.6 indicates the starting point of VoIP quality degradation. Hence, we employ the RTS frame retry ratio of 0.6 as one of the thresholds to initiate handover in this study.

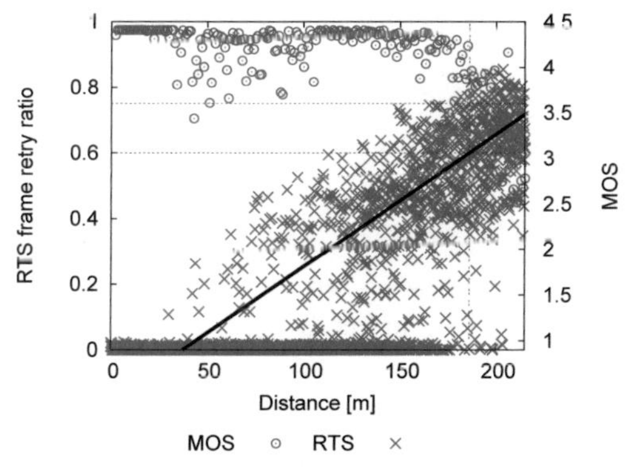

Fig. 10. RTS frame retry ratio vs. MOS over distance

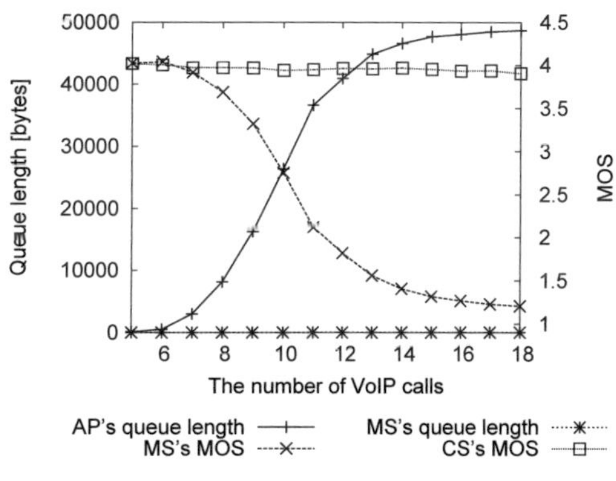

Fig. 11. Relationship among the number of VoIP calls, queue length, and MOS

We next consider a problem in a congested WLAN. In a congested WLAN, with the increase of VoIP calls, the AP queue length also increases. This is because the transmission opportunity of an AP is the same as that of each MS. That is, when the number of VoIP calls increases, the transmission probability from an AP to MSs decreases. As a result, packets routed to the MS are queued in the AP buffer, and they may experience large queuing delays or packet losses due to an increase in the queue length or the buffer overflow. Consequently, the increase in an AP's queue length severely affects the VoIP quality at MSs. However, an AP based on the IEEE802.11 (a/b/g/n) standard unfortunately does not provide a mechanism that can inform MSs of the AP's queue length. Therefore, to maintain VoIP quality, each MS needs to autonomously detect the congestion of the AP.

Next we investigated the relationship between the number of VoIP calls and an AP's queue length through simulation experiments (see Fig. 9(b)). In the simulation scenario, we randomly locate from one to 18 MSs in a WLAN. Each MS communicates with a CS using VoIP. Figure 11 shows the relationships between the number of VoIP calls, AP's and MS's queue length, and MS's and CS's MOS. The graph shows that although the CS's MOS is kept adequate even if the AP's queue length increases with the increase of VoIP calls, the MS's MOS degrades significantly. Although the results indicate that the AP's queue length has a large impact on VoIP communication quality, how can MSs detect the increase in the AP's queue length without modifying an AP? We then proposed estimating the AP's queue length based on the RTT between an MS and an AP (Niswar et al., 2009a). Note that in this chapter the RTT between the MS and the AP is called Wireless RTT (WiRTT). As depicted in Fig. 12, to calculate the WiRTT, an MS periodically sends a probe request packet (ICMP message) to an AP and receives a probe reply packet from an AP. When there is an increase in the AP's queuing delay, the WiRTT also increases because the probe reply packet inevitably experiences queuing delay in the AP buffer. Therefore, the WiRTT can be used to derive information about the AP's queue length.

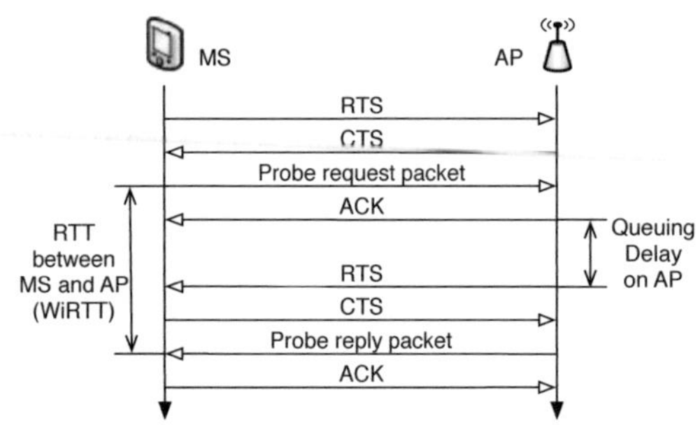

Fig. 12. RTT between MS and AP (WiRTT)

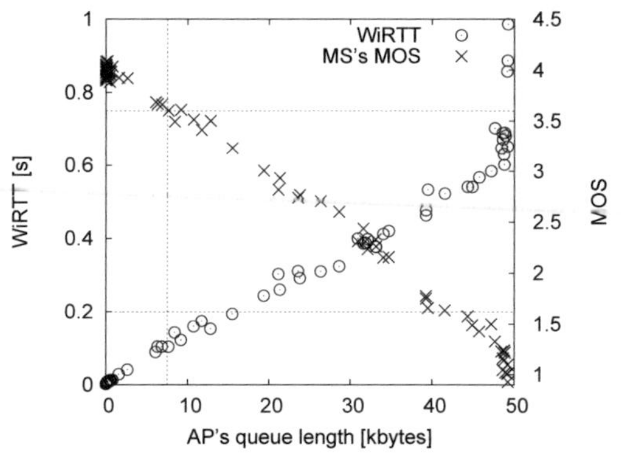

Fig. 13. Relationship among AP's queue length, WiRTT and MOS

Figure 13 shows the relationships between the AP's queue length, WiRTT and MOS in the simulation model of Fig. 9(b). The graph shows that to satisfy adequate VoIP quality (MOS of 3.6), the AP's queue length should be kept less than 7,500 bytes. That is, a WiRTT that is less than 200 ms can keep adequate VoIP quality. Therefore, in our proposed method, we employ WiRTT to estimate the AP's queue length and set the WiRTT threshold (WiRTT_th) at 200 ms to maintain an adequate VoIP quality.

The WLAN also supports a multi-rate function, which can automatically change the transmission rate based on the wireless link condition. In the case where the wireless link quality degrades, for example when the transmission rate is degraded by a change in the modulation type, packets sent at the lower transmission rate occupy more wireless resources, i.e., longer transmission period. As a result, the lower transmission rate is likely to cause congestion of an AP. Therefore, to avoid congestion of an AP, the transmission rate should also be treated as a handover trigger.

4.2 Handover management for multi-rate and congested WLANs

As described above, to achieve seamless handover among multi-rate and congested WLANs, we employ RTS frame retry ratio, WiRTT, and transmission rate as handover triggers. We then proposed an extended handover management method based on these triggers (Niswar et al., 2009a). To support soft handover on an end-to-end basis, the handover management method also supports multi-homing, cross-layer architectures, a multi-path transmission function, and a handover manager (HM) similar to the previous method (Kashihara & Oie, 2007).

Figure 14 shows an algorithm for switching to single/multi-path transmission when an MS moves within the overlap area of two APs (AP1 and AP2). In the proposed method, an HM transmits a probe packet to the two associated APs at 500 ms intervals to estimate each AP's queue length. If *WiRTTs* of both WLAN interfaces (IF1 and IF2) are below the WiRTT_th, the HM detects that both APs are not congested. The HM then investigates the RTS frame retry ratio (*retry_ratio*) of the current active IF to detect degradation of the wireless link condition due to movement. If the *retry_ratio* reaches the threshold to switch to multi-path transmission (R_Mth), the HM switches to multi-path transmission to investigate both the wireless link conditions and avoid packet loss. On the other hand, if the *WiRTT* of IF1 reaches WiRTT_th, i.e., detection of congestion at the AP1, the HM switches to the AP2 directly without switching to multi-path transmission because the multi-path transmission leads to more serious congestion in WLANs, and vice versa. Finally, if both measured *WiRTTs* reach WiRTT_th, the HM then investigates the wireless link condition indicated by the *retry_ratio* of the active single WLAN interface.

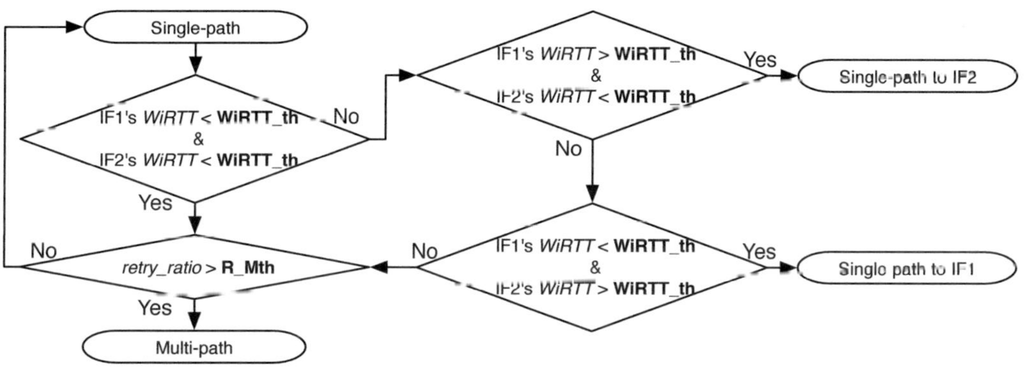

Fig. 14. Switching to single/multi-path transmissions

In multi-path transmission, to maintain VoIP quality and investigate both wireless link qualities, an HM sends the same data packets via both IFs. Hence, the HM needs to switch back to single-path transmission as soon as possible to prevent redundant network overload. Figure 15 illustrates an algorithm for switching back to single-path transmission. The HM measures *WiRTTs* of both IFs at all times. If either of the *WiRTTs* is below the WiRTT_th, the HM switches to the IF with the smaller *WiRTT*. If both *WiRTTs* are simultaneously below the WiRTT_th, the HM then compares the *retry_ratio* of both IFs. Figure 16 shows an algorithm to compare RTS retry ratios of both IFs. If both *retry_ratio* of the IFs are equal, the HM continues multi-path mode. On the other hand, if either of the *retry_ratio* is below the threshold to switch back to single-path transmission (R_Sth), the HM switches back to single-path transmission through the IF with the smaller *retry_ratio*.

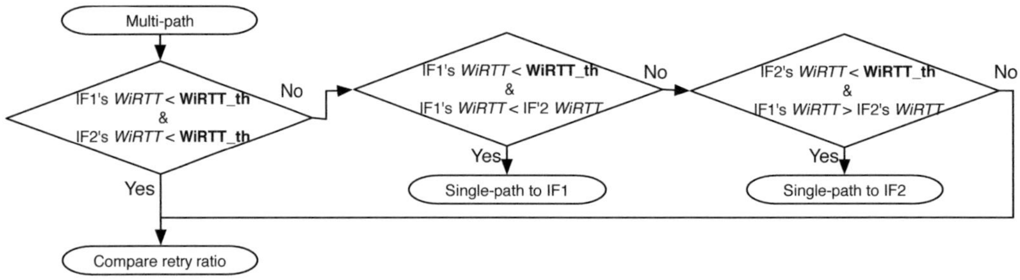

Fig. 15. Switching from multi-path transmission to single-path transmission

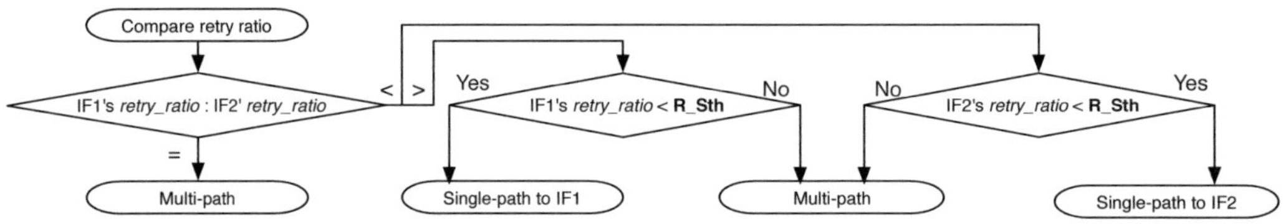

Fig. 16. Comparing RTS retry ratios

If all MSs send probe packets to measure *WiRTT*, the probe packets may contribute to the congestion of the AP. As a result, they may unfortunately detect congestion of the serving AP (e.g., AP1) at nearly the same time. Then, they may switch the communication to a neighbor AP (e.g., AP2) and leave the AP1. As a result, AP2's queue length drastically increases, and then they switch back to the AP1 again. This phenomenon, typically known as the ping-pong effect, leads to degradation of all VoIP quality due to fluctuations in both APs' queue length. To avoid the ping-pong effect, an MS executes handover based on its own current transmission rate, as shown in Fig. 17. As mentioned earlier, since an MS with lower transmission rate occupies more wireless resources, it is more liable to lead to congestion in the AP. Moreover, as MSs with a lower transmission rate typically are farther away from the connected AP, they should execute handover as soon as possible to maintain their VoIP communication quality. Hence, in our proposed method, MSs start to execute handover in order based on transmission rates. The process actually works as follows. When the serving AP is congested, all MSs detect the congested AP through *WiRTT*. Then, MSs with the lowest transmission rate of 6Mb/s first execute the handover since transmission rate number (*TR_num*) is set to zero by default. Note that *TR_num* of zero indicates 6 Mb/s. After that, if the AP's queue length is still congested after Time_th seconds, the remaining MSs increase the *TR_num* by one, i.e., the *TR_num* of one indicates 9 Mb/s. Then, MSs with transmission rates under 9 Mb/s execute handover. This handover process is repeated until congestion of the AP is alleviated. If the congestion is alleviated, *TR_num* of all MSs are set back to the default value, i.e., zero. That is, each MS can autonomously execute handover without knowing whether another MS with lower transmission rate has executed the handover or not. Therefore, to execute handover, all MSs monitor only their own transmission rate and compare the rate with the current *TR_num*.

If every MS sends a probe packet to measure *WiRTT*, these probe packets may aggravate congestion in a WLAN. To eliminate redundant probe packets, we further extended the

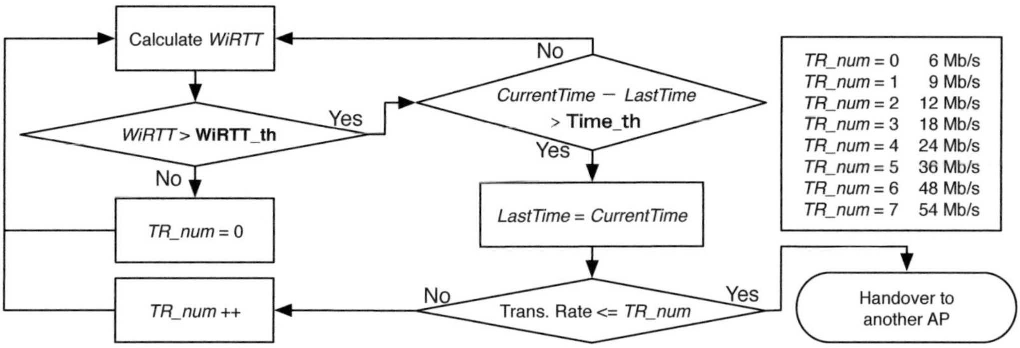

Fig. 17. Handover based on transmission rate

handover management method. In the extension, only one representative MS sends a probe request packet to an AP, and then other MSs measure *WiRTT* by capturing the probe packets that the representative MS sends and receives. Figure 18 shows how to calculate *WiRTT* from captured probe packets. Each MS first monitors all packets over a WLAN before sending a probe packet by itself. If it receives a probe request packet sent by another MS, it cancels the transmission of a probe request packet and tries to measure *WiRTT* by capturing the probe and probe reply packets that the representative MS exchanges with the AP. Each MS can identify whether a captured packet is a probe packet or not by checking the probe packet size (64 bytes). An MS can also identify whether a probe packet is a request (ICMP Request) or a reply (ICMP Response) by observing the MAC address of the captured probe packet because all MSs can identify the MAC address of the connecting AP. If the destination MAC address of the captured probe packet is that of the AP, each MS can judge the packet is a probe request packet. On the other hand, if the source MAC address is an AP's, then each MS judges the packet is a probe reply packet. In Fig. 18, *ProbeReq_Time* and *ProbeReply_Time* are the receiving time of a probe request packet transmitted by another MS and that of a probe reply packet transmitted by the AP, respectively. As every MS can identify whether a captured packet is a probe request or probe reply, it can calculate the *WiRTT* (= *ProbeReply_Time* - *ProbeReq_Time*) properly. In this way, our proposed method can eliminate redundant probe packets.

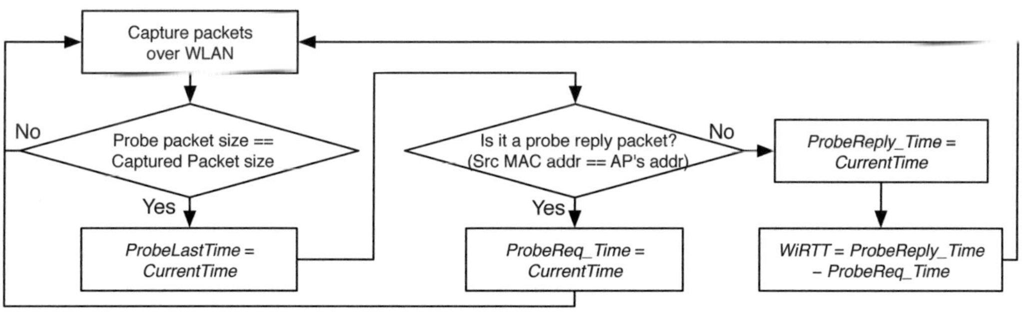

Fig. 18. Calculate *WiRTT* from captured probe packets

If the representative MS leaves a WLAN, one of the remaining MSs needs to start periodically sending a probe packet as a representative MS. Figure 19 shows how a representative MS is selected. First, all MSs always examine the difference between the last received time of a probe packet (*ProbeLastTime*) and the current time (*CurrentTime*). If the difference is greater than probeAbsenceTime, that is, if an MS cannot capture a probe packet for probeAbsenceTime seconds, MSs with the lowest transmission rate in a WLAN try to send a probe packet. This is because almost all MSs in the WLAN can capture a probe packet transmitted at the lowest transmission rate. Thus, the timing to send a probe packet among MSs is based on *WaitingTime*. Basically, an MS with the smallest *WaitingTime* will be the representative MS because *WaitingTime* is calculated based on *TR_Weight*, which indicates the weight of the transmission rate. Thus, if *TR_Weight* is lower, then an MS gets a small *WaitingTime*. If there are several MSs with the same transmission rate, then a random value in *WaitingTime* helps to stagger the timing to send a probe packet.

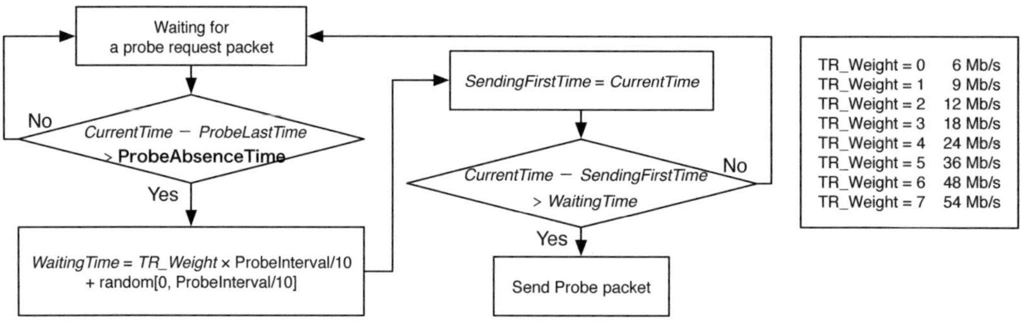

Fig. 19. Selection of a representative MS

4.3 Performance evaluation

This section shows the basic performance of the proposed method. The proposed method was implemented on Qualnet 4.0.1. Figure 20 shows a simulation model and the system parameters. In the simulation, 15 multi-homing MSs randomly move within a coverage area between two APs at the speed of 1 m/s. We employed a G.711 VoIP codec that sends a 160-byte packet at 20-ms intervals.

Figure 21 shows the MOS and the AP1's queue length over time for the previous method using only the data frame retries and the extended method. In the left graphs (the previous method), the average of AP1's queue length is extremely high and MS's MOS does not satisfy adequate VoIP quality (3.6) at all. On the other hand, in the right figure (the extension method), the extension method almost always maintains adequate VoIP quality. Also, even though MOS did degrade at times, it recovered promptly because each MS investigated the wireless link quality, congestion state, and its own transmission rate. Therefore, MSs can promptly and reliably execute handover among multi-rate and congested WLANs based on the handover triggers.

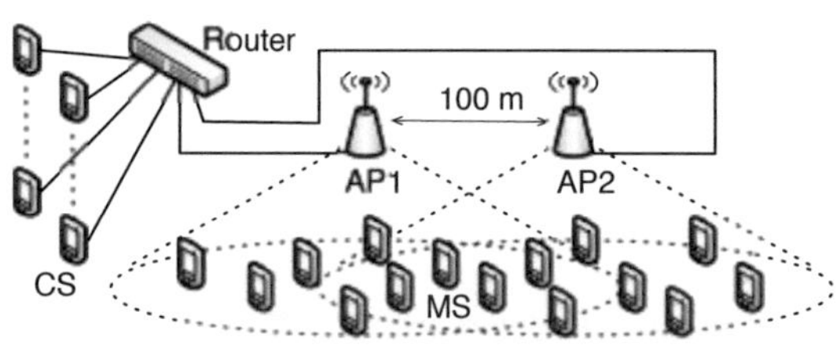

WiRTT_th	200 ms
R_Mth	0.6
R_Sth	0.4
ProveAbsenceTime	1 second
Time_th	2 seconds

Fig. 20. Simulation model

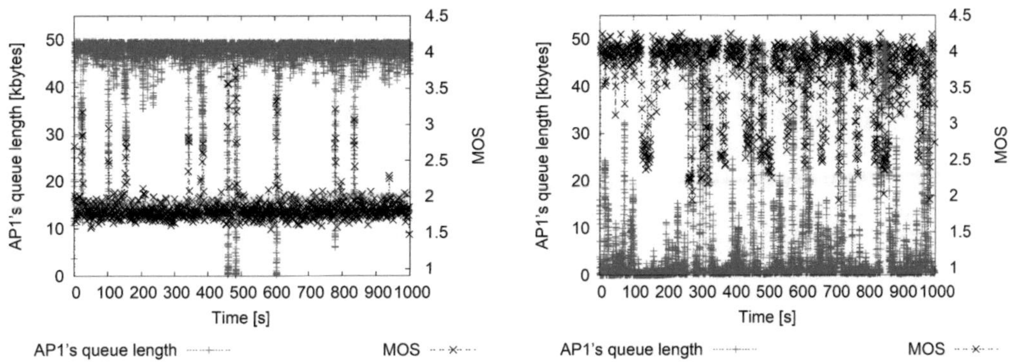

Fig. 21. Relationships among AP1's queue length and MOS for the previous (left graph) and the extension (right graph) methods

5. End-to-end handover management in WLAN-WiMAX scenario

The previous sections introduced handover management methods in a WLAN-WLAN scenario. However, as shown in Fig. 1, mobile users also have opportunities to connect with different types of wireless networks such as WiMAX and LTE. This section focuses on an end-to-end handover management method in a WLAN-WiMAX scenario. This section contributes to selection of appropriate handover triggers and development of handover management methods among different wireless technologies. This concept will be applied to other future wireless networks. Section 5.1 first discusses the handover triggers for WiMAX. We then introduce our handover management method and the basic performance in Section 5.2 and 5.3, respectively.

5.1 Handover triggers for WiMAX

In a WLAN-WiMAX scenario, unlike a WLAN-WLAN scenario, an MS connects to wireless networks with different wireless technologies over time. However, since these wireless networks have different wireless characteristics, we cannot use the same handover triggers and handover management to maintain VoIP communication quality during movement. Thus this section discusses appropriate handover triggers for WiMAX. Note that for a WLAN we use RTS retry ratio, WiRTT, and transmission rate as the handover triggers described in Section 4.

Since we focus on handover management on an end-to-end basis, handover triggers should be basically obtained on the MS side. Furthermore, handover triggers also need to detect both wireless link conditions and congestion states in a WiMAX network. WiMAX supports high-data rates and multi-service types; hence, it is a strong contender for wireless broadband access technologies to support real-time applications such as VoIP over wireless networks. However, since WiMAX employs best effort (BE) service during the initial phase of deployment, VoIP applications must contend with various types of applications over WiMAX. To maintain bi-directional VoIP communication, then, we need to consider handover triggers indicating both downlink and uplink transmission conditions.

To maintain VoIP communication quality over WiMAX, we proposed a combined use of the following two handover triggers, Carrier to Interference plus Noise Ratio (CINR) and an MS's interface queue length (Niswar et al., 2009b). We first describe the CINR. As described before, RSSI is generally employed as a handover trigger. However, since RSSI provides only signal strength at a receiver side, it cannot actually detect noise, interference, and other channel effects (e.g., multi-path fading and shadowing). Hence, a high RSSI does not always mean that the wireless link quality is good. On the other hand, as CINR indicates signal effectiveness including noise, it can provide an appropriate index of wireless link quality.

We then investigated the characteristics of CINR and MOS over WiMAX through a simulation experiment. Figure 22(a) depicts the simulation model. In the simulation model, we employ a Rayleigh fading model because we assume an urban environment. For an application, a VoIP application of G.711 that sends a 160-bytes packet every 20 ms is employed. In the simulation, the MS moves away from the base station (BS).

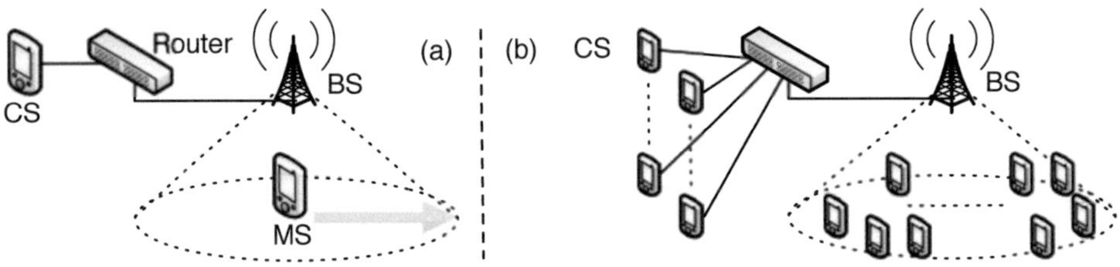

Fig. 22. Simulation model in WiMAX

Figure 23 shows the relationship between CINR and MOS. From the graph, when CINR goes below 50 dB, MOS starts to degrade with dynamic fluctuation. To estimate the CINR's threshold (CINR_th) for initiating handover from the trend of CINR, we employ the solid line by a loess method. The solid line indicates that MOS is 3.6 when CINR is 26 dB. Thus, in this study, we set a CINR of 26 dB as the CINR_th.

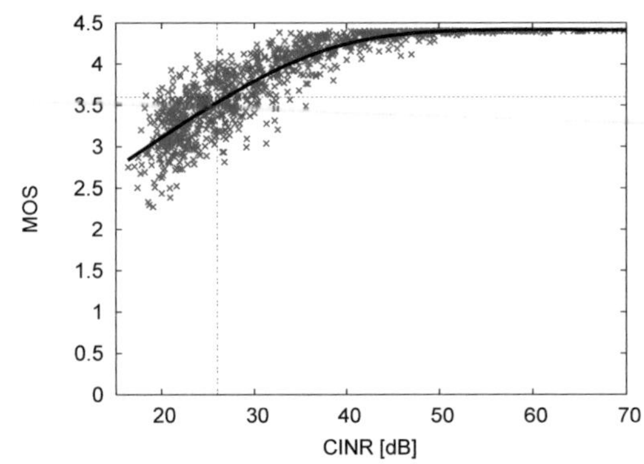

Fig. 23. Relationship between MOS and CINR

In WiMAX, although the bandwidth (BW) scheduler of a BS thoroughly manages downlink BW, uplink BW is allocated as described below. As illustrated in Fig. 24, a BS first tries to allocate BW to MSs through Downlink Map (DL MAP), Downlink Channel Descriptor (DCD), Uplink Channel Descriptor (UCD), and Uplink Map (UL MAP). Then, an MS transmits a BW request in response to the allocated time slot in UL_MAP. After the MS obtains an Uplink (UL) Grant from the BS, it can transmit data packets with the allocated uplink grants. Hence, the end-to-end uplink delay (T_{E2E}) from sending a data packet at an MS to reaching a CS is calculated as follows:

$$T_{E2E} = T_{queue} + T_{BWreq} + T_{Sch} + T_o \tag{2}$$

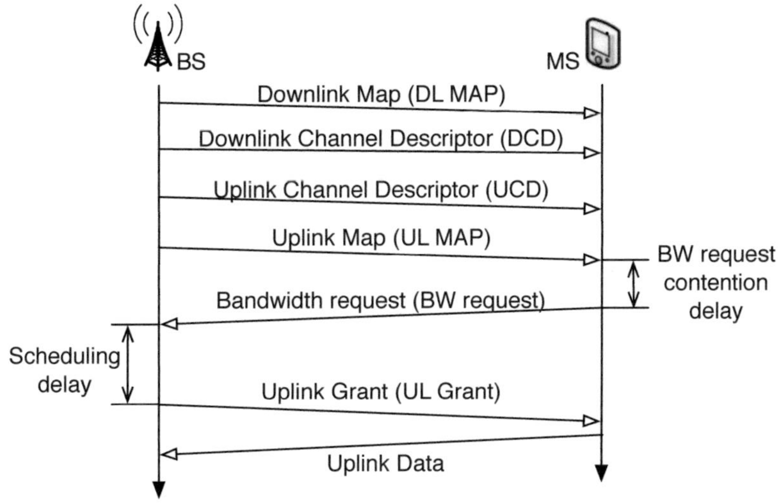

Fig. 24. Uplink transmission process over WiMAX

where T_{queue} represents queuing delay in the interface buffer at an MS. T_{BWreq} and T_{Sch} indicate BW request contention delay and BS's scheduling delay, respectively. T_o represents additional delays, e.g., transmission delays over wired and wireless link. Although the BW request contention and the BS scheduling delay may become longer with the increase in MSs, eventually they lead to the increase of queue length at an MS's interface. Therefore, the MS's interface queue length has a potential to be a handover trigger to detect wireless network congestion in a WiMAX.

We then investigated the relationship between the number of VoIP calls and MS's queue length. As illustrated in Fig. 22(b), up to 30 MSs are randomly located within the coverage area of a BS. Each MS randomly moves at a speed of 1 m/s during VoIP communication with a CS. Figure 25 shows the relationship among the number of VoIP calls, MOS, and MS's queue length. The graph shows that although uplink MOS decreases as the number of VoIP calls increases, downlink MOS is kept at an adequate value. Moreover, the MS's queue length increases as the number of VoIP calls. Therefore, we can see that uplink MOS decreases with the increase of the MS's queue length, which leads to the large queuing delay. Then, in terms of accommodation of VoIP calls in a single BS, Fig. 25 shows that up to 20 VoIP calls can be accepted to maintain appropriate VoIP communication quality. That is, not all VoIP communication quality can be maintained when the MS's queue lengths are more than 12,000 bytes. Thus, we employ 12,000 bytes as a threshold of MS's queue length (QL_th).

5.2 Handover management among different wireless technologies

This section introduces a handover management method in a WLAN-WiMAX scenario (Niswar et al., 2010). The proposed method also implements an HM on the transport layer of an MS like our previous method (Kashihara & Oie, 2007). A multi-homing MS has two wireless interfaces, WLAN and WiMAX. Note that since we assume that each wireless network has a different network address, each wireless interface has a different IP address. Then the proposed handover management method also employs multi-homing, cross-layer architectures, and multi-path transmission mode to maintain VoIP quality during handover.

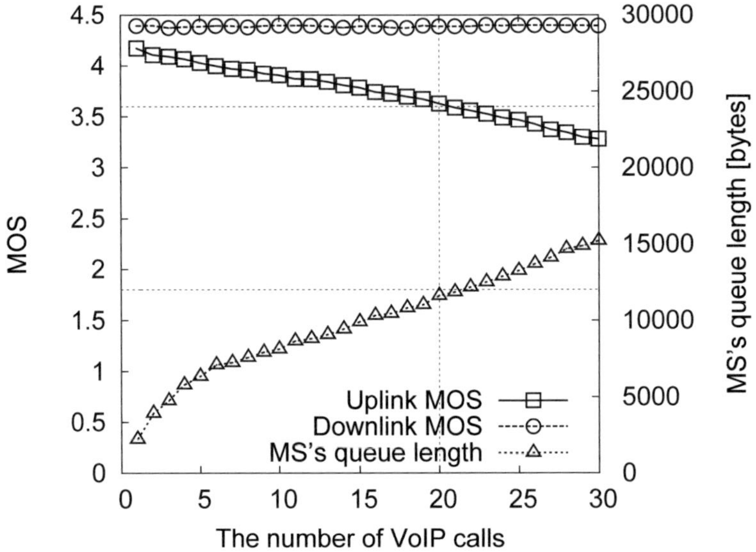

Fig. 25. Relationship among the number of VoIP calls, MOS, and MS's queue length

Figure 26 depicts an algorithm for switching from single-path transmission to multi-path transmission when an MS is in the overlap area of WLAN and WiMAX. Our handover management method first examines the wireless link conditions and then investigates wireless network congestion. For example, when an MS communicates through a WLAN, the HM monitors the RTS frame retry ratio (*retry_ratio*) to detect the wireless link quality at sending of every packet. If the *retry_ratio* exceeds R_Mth of 0.6, the HM switches to multi-path transmission; otherwise, it next examines *WiRTT* to detect the congestion state of the WLAN. If the *WiRTT* exceeds the WiRTT_th of 200 ms, multi-path transmission starts; otherwise, the HM continues single-path transmission via the WLAN. On the other hand, in WiMAX, the HM first monitors *CINR*. If *CINR* is less than the CINR_th of 26 dB, the HM switches to multi-path transmission to maintain the VoIP quality and investigates the condition of both wireless networks; otherwise, it next examines the MS's queue length (*MS's QL*) to detect the congestion state of WiMAX. If the *MS's QL* exceeds the QL_th of 12,000 bytes, the HM switches to multi-path transmission; otherwise it keeps using single-path transmission via the WiMAX.

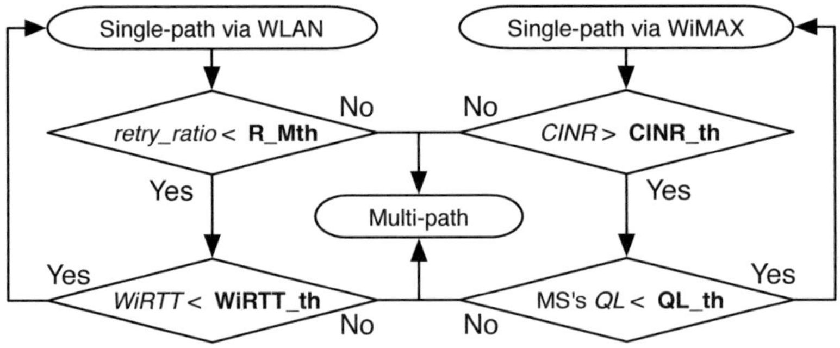

Fig. 26. Switching from single-path to multi-path

When multi-path transmission is applied, the HM monitors all handover triggers and compares them. Figure 27 illustrates a switching process from multi-path transmission to single-path transmission. First, an HM evaluates handover triggers for wireless link quality, i.e., RTS retry ratio (WLAN) and CINR (WiMAX). If the *retry_ratio* exceeds R_Sth as well as the *CINR* is below the CINR_th, the HM continues multi-path transmission because both wireless link qualities are unstable. If the *CINR* exceeds the CINR_th, the HM switches back to single-path transmission via WiMAX. On the other hand, if the *retry_ratio* is below the R_Sth, it switches back to single-path transmission via WLAN. If both the wireless link conditions indicate good conditions at the same time, the HM next examines handover triggers indicating the congestion states of the wireless networks, i.e., *WiRTT* (WLAN) and *MS's QL* (WiMAX). If both the handover triggers exceed the thresholds, the HM continues multi-path transmission. If the *MS's QL* is below the QL_th, the HM switches to single-path transmission via the WiMAX. On the other hand, if the *WiRTT* is below the WiRTT_th, the HM switches to single-path transmission via the WLAN. If both handover triggers are below the thresholds at the same time, the HM returns to single-path transmission via the previous wireless network.

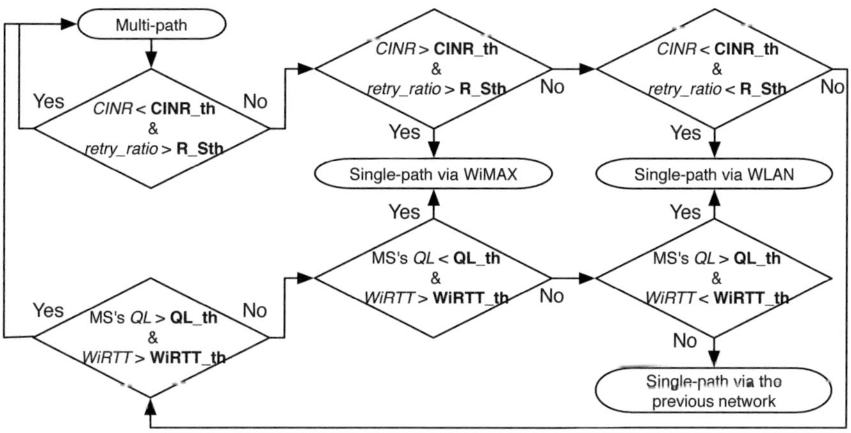

Fig. 27. Switching from multi-path to single-path

5.3 Performance evaluation

This section shows the basic VoIP communication performance of the proposed method through simulation experiments. We first investigated the VoIP communication quality when an MS moves between WLAN and WiMAX. We then evaluated the VoIP communication quality in congested wireless networks.

Figure 28(a) illustrates a simulation model in a movement environment. In the scenario, an MS conducting VoIP communication with a CS moves between WLAN and WiMAX at a speed of 1 m/s. Figure 29 shows that our proposed method can obtain an average uplink MOS of 4.29 and downlink MOS of 4.28 when an MS moves from WLAN to WiMAX. On the other hand, in movement from WiMAX to WLAN, Fig. 30 shows our proposed method can obtain an average uplink MOS of 4.06 and downlink MOS of 4.29.

Figure 28(b) illustrates a simulation model in a congested environment. The simulation experiments have the following two scenarios; one is a congested WLAN, the other is a congested WiMAX. In a congested WLAN scenario, 13 MSs are randomly distributed in the

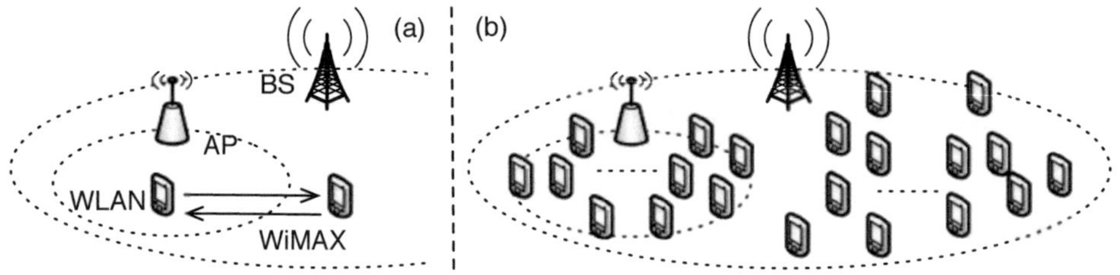

Fig. 28. Simulation model

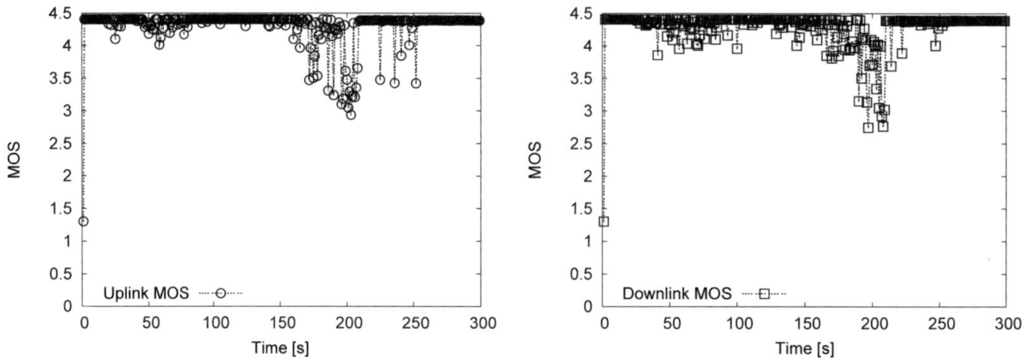

Fig. 29. MOS during movement (from WLAN to WiMAX)

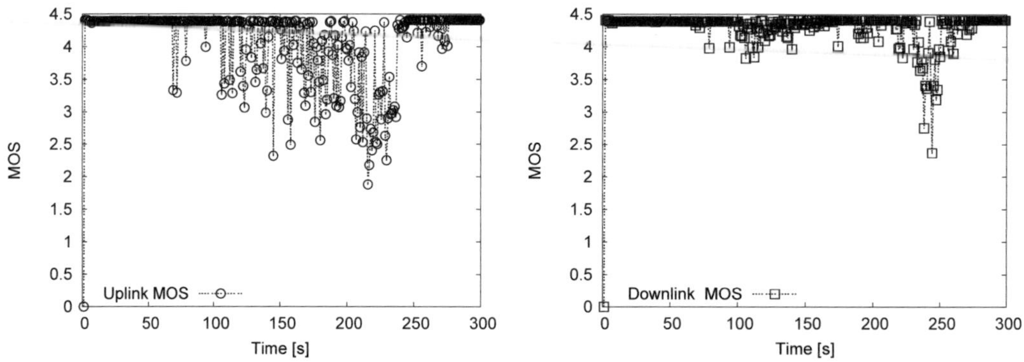

Fig. 30. MOS during movement (from WiMAX to WLAN)

WLAN and no MS is in the WiMAX. Only one MS employs our proposed handover method, and it establishes a VoIP call via the WLAN at the start of the simulation. Then, the remaining MS, which does not employ the proposed method, establishes a VoIP call with a CS every five seconds. That is, the traffic in the WLAN gradually increases. From Fig. 31, the simulation results show that the MS which employs our proposed method obtains the average uplink MOS of 4.26 and downlink MOS of 4.25.

Furthermore, we also evaluated the basic performance of our proposed method in a congested WiMAX as depicted in Fig. 28(b). In the simulation scenario, 30 MSs are randomly distributed

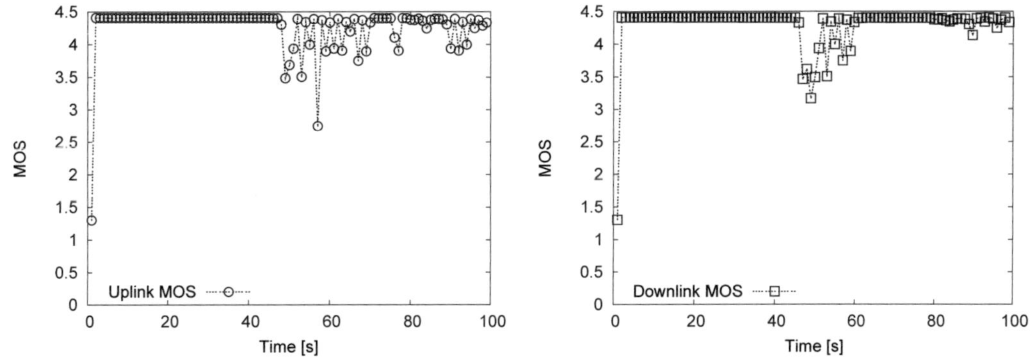

Fig. 31. MOS over congested wireless network (WLAN)

within WiMAX, but no MS is in the WLAN. In this study, since the acceptable number of VoIP calls in the WiMAX is 20 MSs, all VoIP quality is degraded if each MS does not autonomously execute appropriate handover according to the wireless network condition. Here also, only one MS employs our proposed method and it establishes a VoIP call through WiMAX at first. After that, a new VoIP call is established through WiMAX every three seconds. Figure 32 shows that the MS which employs our proposed method obtains the average uplink MOS of 3.88 and downlink MOS of 4.34. Therefore, our proposed method can maintain VoIP communication quality during movement among different types of wireless networks.

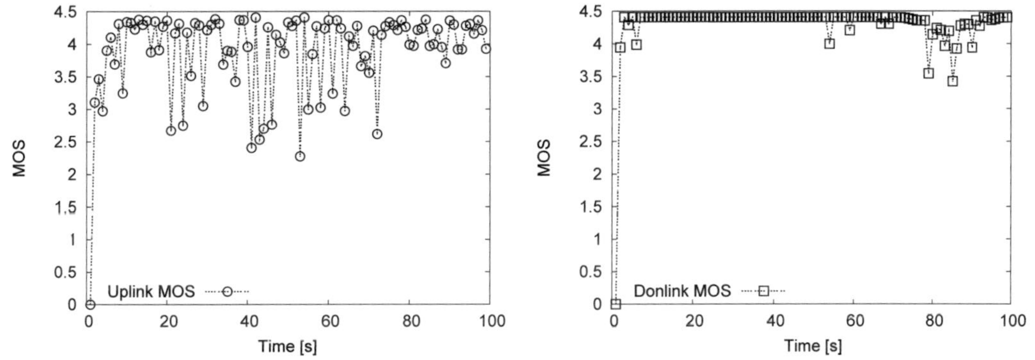

Fig. 32. MOS over congested wireless network (WiMAX)

6. Conclusion

In this chapter, we introduced end-to-end handover management methods for VoIP communication in ubiquitous wireless networks. As described in Section 1, since current and future wireless networks have different network addresses, an MS will need to move among wireless networks while maintaining VoIP communication. To achieve seamless handover among such wireless networks, the following requirements should be satisfied.

1. Keep VoIP communication from communication termination by change of IP address
2. Eliminate communication interruption due to layer 2 and 3 handover processes
3. Initiate appropriate handover based on reliable handover triggers
4. Select a wireless network with good link quality during handover

First, to satisfy requirements (1) and (2), we employed a multi-homing architecture and the HM on the transport layer. A multi-homing architecture is indispensable when moving among wireless networks with different network addresses to avoid communication termination and interruption. On the other hand, the HM can control handovers among the multiple IP addresses on an end-to-end basis, i.e., it needs no special network agent like MIP. Then, to satisfy requirement (3), we employed reliable handover triggers considering VoIP communication quality in WLAN and WiMAX. To maintain VoIP communication quality during movement in ubiquitous wireless networks, we need to consider wireless link quality and congestion states in a wireless network. For wireless link quality, we proposed handover triggers that quickly grasp characteristics of a wireless network, i.e., RTS frame retry ratio in WLAN and CINR in WiMAX. On the other hand, we also proposed handover triggers to detect congestion states in a wireless network, i.e., WiRTT and transmission rate in WLAN, and MS's queue length in WiMAX. The HM can promptly and reliably detect the wireless network condition by using the handover triggers. Finally, to satisfy requirement (4), the HM employed multi-path transmission. When the wireless network condition is degraded, the HM switches to multi-path transmission. Multi-path transmission avoids packet loss during handover while investigating the wireless network condition. Thus, multi-path transmission contributes to achieve seamless handover.

Although this chapter focused on end-to-end handover management, the following problems still must be solved to achieve seamless mobility. First, to execute handover to an AP with a good network condition, an MS needs to locate and connect with a candidate AP with a better network condition among many APs. Although RSSI is commonly employed to select a candidate AP, as described in Section 3.1, RSSI cannot appropriately detect wireless network condition. Actually, we also proposed and implemented an AP selection method to solve this problem (Taenaka et al., 2009), but due to the lack of space here, we cannot describe the details. Moreover, when the number of VoIP calls exceeds the acceptance limit of the wireless networks, all VoIP communication quality degrades. In this situation, the network should not accept a new VoIP call. Thus, to avoid such the degradation, APs and BSs should have an admission control method. Also, our proposed handover methods have no location management function. To manage MSs' location, our proposed method needs to cooperate with some location management functions. For example, we can utilize a dynamic DNS and an overlay network like Skype as network and application level approaches, respectively. Once a VoIP communication is established between an MS and a CS through a location management function, our proposed handover method can maintain VoIP communication during handovers.

7. Acknowledgements

This work was supported by the Kinki Mobile Radio Center Inc. and the Japan Society for the Promotion of Science, Grant-in-Aid for Scientific Research (S)(18100001).

8. References

Skype Limited. (2003), http://www.skype.com

Perkins, C. (Ed.) (2002). IP Mobility Support for IPv4, IETF RFC 3344

Johnson, D.; Perkins, C. & Arkko, J. (2004). IP Mobility Support for IPv6, IETF RFC 3775

Soliman, H.; Castelluccia, C.; ElMalki, K. & Bellier, L. (2008). Hierarchical Mobile IPv6 (HMIPv6) Mobility Management, IETF RFC 5380

Koodli, R. (Ed.) (2005). Fast Handovers for Mobile IPv6, IETF RFC 4068

Kim, Y.; Kwon, D.; Bae. K. & Suh, Y. (2005). Performance Comparison of Mobile IPv6 and Fast Handovers for Mobile IPv6 over Wireless LANs, Proceedings of IEEE Vehicular Technology Conference 2005-fall (VTC2005-fall), pp. 807-811, September 2005

Montavont, N. & Noel, T. (2003). Analysis and Evaluation of Mobile IPv6 Handovers over Wireless LAN, Mobile Networks and Applications, Vol. 8, No. 6, pp. 643-653, December 2003

Xing, W.; Karl, H.; Wolisz, A. & Muller, H. (2002). M-SCTP: Design and Prototypical Implementation of an End-to-End Mobility Concept, Proceedings of 5th International Workshop The Internet Challenge: Technology and Application, October 2002

Koga, H.; Haraguchi, H.; Iida, K. & Oie, Y. (2005). A Framework for Network Media Optimization in Multi-homed QoS Networks, Proceedings of ACM First International Workshop on Dynamic Interconnection of Networks (DIN2005), pp. 38-42, September 2005

Stewart, R. (Ed.) (2007). Stream Control Transmission Protocol, IETF RFC 4960

FON wireless Ltd. (2005), http://www.fon.com

Muthukrishnan, K.; Meratnia, N.; Lijding, M.; Koprinkov, G. & Havinga, P. (2006). WLAN location sharing through a privacy observant architecture, Proceedings of 1st International Conference on Communication System Software and Middleware (COMSWARE), pp. 1-10, January 2006

Kashihara, S. & Oie, Y. (2007). Handover management based on the number of data frame retransmissions for VoWLANs, Elsevier Computer Communications, Vol. 30, No. 17, pp. 3257-3269, November 2007

Tsukamoto, K.; Yamaguchi, T.; Kashihara, S. & Oie Y. (2007). Experimental evaluation of decision criteria for WLAN handover: signal strength and frame retransmissions, IEICE Transactions on Communications, Vol. E90-B, No. 12, pp. 3579-3590, December 2007

Proxim Wireless Corporation (2007), http://www.proxim.com

Ethereal (1998), http://www.ethereal.com

Kashihara, S.; Tsukamoto, K. & Oie. Y. (2007) Service-oriented mobility management architecture for seamless handover in ubiquitous networks, IEEE Wireless Communications, Vol. 14, No. 2, pp.28-34, April 2007

Taenaka, Y.; Kashihara, S.; Tsukamoto, K.; Kadobayashi, Y. & Oie, Y. (2007). Design and implementation of cross-layer architecture for seamless VoIP handover, Proceedings of The Third IEEE International Workshop on Heterogeneous Multi-Hop Wireless and Mobile Networks 2007 (IEEE MHWMN'07), October 2007

MadWifi (2004), http://madwifi.org

Bang, S.; Taenaka, Y.; Kashihara, S.; Tsukamoto, K.; Yamaguchi, S. & Oie, Y. (2009). Practical performance evaluation of VoWLAN handover based on frame retries, Proceedings of IEEE Pacific Rim Conference on Communications, Computers and Signal Processing (PACRIM'09), CD-ROM, August 2009.

FreeBSD (1995), http://www.freebsd.org

TCPDUMP/LIBCAP public repository, http://www.tcpdump.org

Scalable Network Technologies (2006), http://www.scalable-networks.com

ITU-T G.107 (2000), The E-model, a computational model for use in transmission planning (ITU-T Recommendation G.107), Telecommunication Standardization Sector of ITU, Series G: Transmission systems and media, digital systems and networks, 2000

Niswar, M.; Kashihara, S.; Tsukamoto K.; Kadobayashi Y. & Yamaguchi S. (2009a). Handover management for VoWLAN based on estimation of AP queue length and frame retries, IEICE Transactions on Information and System, Vol. E92-D, No. 10, pp. 1847-1856, October 2009

Niswar, M.; Kashihara, S.; Taenaka, Y.; Tsukamoto, K.; Kadobayashi, Y. & Yamaguchi, S. (2009b). MS-initiated handover decision criteria for VoIP over IEEE 802.16e, Proceedings of IEEE Pacific Rim Conference on Communications, Computers and Signal Processing (PACRIM'09), CD-ROM, August 2009

Niswar, M.; Kashihara, S.; Taenaka, Y.; Tsukamoto, K.; Kadobayashi, Y. & Yamaguchi, S. (2010). Seamless vertical handover management for VoIP over intermingled IEEE 802.11g and IEEE 802.16e, Proceeding of 8th Asia-Pacific Symposium on Information and Telecommunication Technologies (APSITT 2010), CD-ROM, June 2010

Taenaka, Y.; Kashihara, S.; Tsukamoto, K.; Yamaguchi, S. & Oie, Y. (2009). Proactive AP selection method considering the radio interference environment, IEICE Transactions on Information and System, Vol. E92-D, No. 10, pp. 1867-1876, October 2009

15

Developing New Approaches for Intrusion Detection in Converged Networks

Juan C. Pelaez
U.S. Army Research Laboratory
APG, MD 21005,
USA

1. Introduction

An Intrusion Detection System (IDS) is an important evidence collection tool for network forensics analysis. An IDS operates by inspecting both inbound and outbound network activity and identifying suspicious patterns that may be indicative of a network attack.

For each suspicious event, IDS software typically records information similar to statistics logged by firewalls and routers (e.g., date and time, source and destination IP addresses, protocol, and basic protocol characteristics), as well as application-specific information (e.g., username, filename, command, and status code). IDS software also records information that indicates the possible intent of the activity [Gra05].

IDS data is often the starting point for examining suspicious activity. Not only do IDSs typically attempt to identify malicious network traffic at all transmission control protocol/Internet protocol (TCP/IP) layers, they also can log many data fields (including raw packets) that can be useful in validating events and correlating them with other data sources [Ken06].

IDSs are classified into two categories—anomaly detection and misuse (knowledge-based) detection. Anomaly detection systems require the building of profiles for the traffic that commonly traverses a given network. This profile defines an established baseline for the communication and data exchange that is normally seen over a period of time. These systems have several drawbacks: the IDS alerts are not well adapted for forensics investigation (i.e., sometimes vague), they are complicated (i.e., cannot be communicated easily to nontechnical people), and have a high false negative rate.

In contrast, misuse detection methods, also known as signature-based detection, look for intrusive activity that matches specific signatures. These signatures are based on a set of rules that match typical patterns and exploits used by attackers to gain access to a network [Fer05].

The disadvantage with misuse detection systems is that without a signature, a new attack method will not be detected until a signature can be generated and incorporated.

VoIP has had a strong effect on tactical networks by allowing human voice and video to travel over existing packet data networks with traditional data packets. Among the several issues that need to be addressed when deploying this technology, security is perhaps the most critical. General security mechanisms, such as firewalls and Intrusion Detection Systems (IDS), cannot detect or prevent all attacks. Current techniques to detect and counter attacks against the converged infrastructure are not sufficient; in particular, they are deficient with respect to real-time network intrusion detection, especially where very high dimensional data are involved, because of computational costs. In addition, they are unable to stop/detect unknown, internal attacks, and attacks that come in the body of the messages (e.g., steganophony attacks [Pel09]). It is indispensable to analyze how an attack happened in order to counter it in the future.

In order to effectively counter attacks against the converged network, a systematic approach to network forensic collection and analysis of data is necessary. In conducting network forensics investigations in a VoIP environment, the collection of voice packets in real time and the use of automatic mechanisms are fundamental. In this chapter we will study how attacks against the converged network can be automatically detected in order to create a more secure VoIP system. Our primary focus is on attacks that target media and signaling protocol vulnerabilities.

To effectively study new approaches for intrusion detection in VoIP, this chapter starts by analyzing the attacks against the VoIP infrastructure from a hybrid architecture perspective, which will give a clear set of use cases to which we can relate these attacks. Then, network forensic challenges on converged networks are analyzed based on the Digital Forensics Research Workshop framework and on the forensic patterns approach. Further, an analysis of the protocol-based intrusion detection method is presented. Then, statistical methods for intrusion detection, such as stream entropy estimation and dimensionality reduction, are discussed. Finally, the converged experimentation testbed used for prototype tools and commercial software testing is introduced. This chapter ends with some conclusions and ideas for future work.

2. Attacks against the VoIP network

As VoIP operates on a converged (voice, data, and video) network, voice and video packets are subject to the same threats than those associated with data networks. In this type of environment not only is it difficult to block network attackers but also in many cases, examiners are unable to find them out [Fer07]. Likewise, all the vulnerabilities that exist in a VoIP wired network apply to VoIPoW technologies plus the new risks introduced by weaknesses in wireless protocols.

Figure 1 shows a Use Case diagram for a simplified VoIP system with typical use cases and internal and external roles. For example, the subscriber role can be classified as internal or remote, and also according to the type of device used. In addition to these roles, the use case diagram can be used to systematically analyze the different types of attacks against the VoIP network, following the approach in [Fer06].

Based on the Use Case Diagram of Figure 1, we can identify potential internal and external attackers (hackers). Internal attackers could be a subscriber with a malicious behavior. Therefore, this Use Case Diagram will help us to determine the possible attacks against the VoIP infrastructure.

Most of the possible attacks against the VoIP infrastructure will be listed systematically. Although completeness cannot be assured, we are confident that at least all important possible attacks were considered. This research does not guarantee to provide a complete list of every possible threat in VoIP. The threats that we assume are based on the knowledge of the VoIP application, and from the study of similar systems.

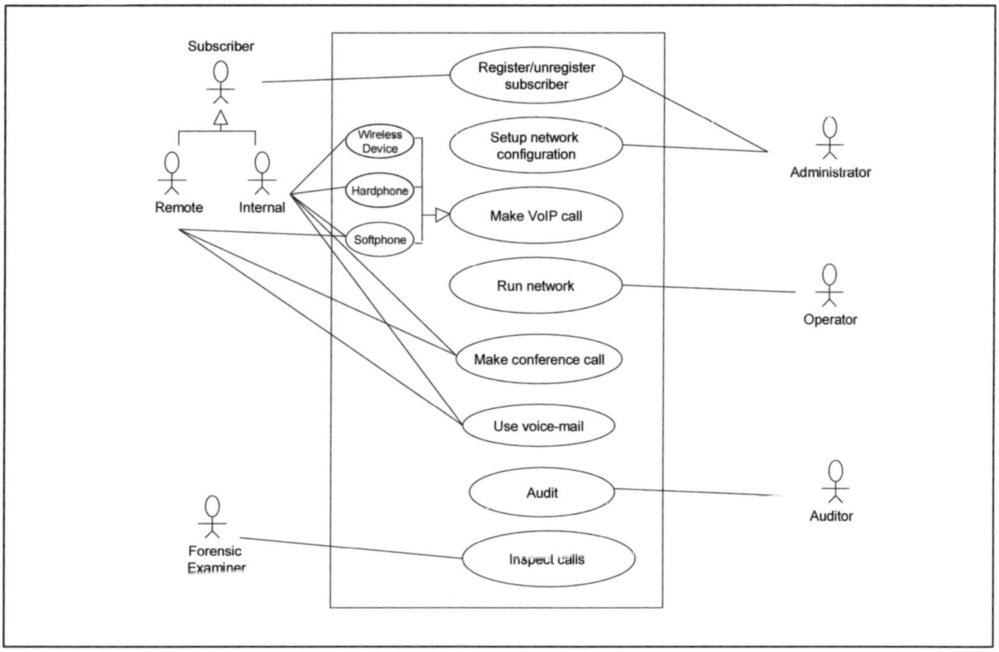

Fig. 1. Use case diagram for a VoIP system

It should be noted that only attacks against the VoIP system are considered. Attacks to systems that collaborate with this system are beyond our control (e.g. attacks against radio networks). Additional security issues relevant to telecom, physical networks, and switches are beyond the scope of this dissertation.

Based on the Use Case Diagram of Figure 1, we can determine the possible attacks against the VoIP infrastructure and classified as: Registration Attacks, Attacks when Making/Receiving a voice call and attacks against Audit.

2.1 Attacks when making/receiving a VoIP Call

Many of the already well-known security vulnerabilities in data networks can have an adverse impact on voice communications and need to be protected against [Pog03]. The attacks when making/receiving a voice call can be classified as follows:

Theft of service is the ability of a malicious user to place fraudulent calls. In this case the attacker simply wants to use a service without paying for it, so this attack is against the service provider.

Masquerading, occurs when a hacker is able to trick a remote user into believing he is talking to his intended recipient when in fact he is really talking to the hacker. Such an attack typically occurs with the hacker assuming the identity of someone who is not well-known to the target. A masquerade attack usually includes one of the other forms of active attacks [Sta02].

IP Spoofing, occurs when a hacker inside or outside a network impersonates a trusted computer.

Call Interception is the unauthorized monitoring of voice packets or RTCP transmissions. Hackers could capture the packets and decode their voice packet payload as they traverse a large network. This kind of attack is the equivalent of wiretapping in a circuit-switched telephone system.

Repudiation attacks can take place when two parties talk over the phone and later on one party denies that the conversation occurred.

Call Hijacking or Redirect attacks could replace a voice mail address with a hacker-specified IP address, opening a channel to the hacker [Gre04]. In this way, all calls placed over the VoIP network will fail to reach the end user.

Denial-of-service (DoS) attacks prevent legitimate users of a network from accessing the features and services provided by the network.

Signal protocol tampering occurs when a malicious user can monitor and capture the packets that set up the call. By doing so, that user could manipulate fields in the data stream and make VoIP calls without using a VoIP phone [Pog03]. The malicious user could also make an expensive call, and mislead the IP-PBX into believing that it was originated from another user.

Attacks against Softphones occur because as they reside in the data VLAN, they require open access to the voice VLAN in order to access call control, place calls to IP phones, and leave voice messages. Therefore, the deployment of Softphones provides a path for attacks against the voice VLAN. VoIP systems are capable of handling large volumes of calls using both IP phones and Softphones. Unlike traditional phones, which must be hardwired to a specific PBX port, IP phones can be plugged into any Ethernet jack and assigned an IP address. These features not only represent advantages but also they may make them targets of security attacks.

Note that all these attacks apply also to conference calls and some may apply to the use of voice mail.

2.2 Registration attacks

Brute Force attacks are simply an attempt to try all possible values when attempting to authenticate with a system or crack the crypto key used to create ciphertext [Bre99]. For example, an attacker may attempt to brute-force attack a Telnet login, he must first obtain the Telnet prompt on a system. When connection is made to the Telnet port, the hacker will try every potential word or phrase to come up with a possible password.

Reflection attacks are specifically aimed at SIP systems. It may happen when using http digest authentication (i.e. challenge-response with a shared secret) for both request and response. If the same shared secret is used in both directions, an attacker can obtain credentials by reflecting a challenge in a response back in request. This attack can be eliminated by using different shared secrets in each direction. This kind of attack is not a problem when PGP is used for authentication [Mar01].

The *IP Spoofing* attacks described earlier can also be classified as registration attacks.

2.3 Attacks against Audit (IP-PBX and operating systems)

Due to their critical role in providing voice service and the complexity of the software running on them, IP PBXs are the primary target for attackers. Some of their vulnerabilities include:

- *Operating system attack.* Exploits a vulnerability in an operating system. An attack that makes use of this vulnerability, while perhaps not directed toward a VoIP system, can nevertheless create issues.

- *Support software attack.* Exploits a vulnerability in a key supporting software system, such as a database or web server. An example is the SQL Slammer worm, which exploited a vulnerability in the database used on a specific IP PBX.
- *Protocol attack.* Exploits a vulnerability in a protocol implementation, such as SIP or H.323. An example is the vulnerability in the H.323 implementation in Microsoft's ISA Server.
- *Application attack.* Exploits a vulnerability in the underlying voice application, which is not filtered by the protocol implementation.
- *Application manipulation.* Exploits a weakness in security, such as weak authentication or poor configuration, to allow abuse of the voice service. For example, registration hijacking or toll fraud.
- *Unauthorized access.* Occurs when an attacker obtains administrative access to the IP PBX.
- *Denial of Service.* Either an implementation flaw that results in loss of function or a flood of requests that overwhelms the IP PBX [Col04].

3. Network forensic challenges

3.1 Reference forensic model

Several models are used for investigation in forensic science. We chose the framework from the Digital Forensics Research Workshop (DFRWS) because it is comprehensive and more oriented to our research approach. The DFRWS model shows the sequential steps for digital forensic analysis [DFRWS01]. These steps are shown in table 1.

Identification	Preservation	Collection	Examination	Analysis	Presentation
Event/crime detection	Case management	Preservation	Preservation	Preservation	Documentation
Resolve Signature	Imaging technologies	Approved methods	Traceability	Traceability	Expert testimony
Profile detection	Chain of custody	Approved software	Validation techniques	Statistical	Clarification
Anomalous detection	Time synchronization	Approved hardware	Filtering techniques	Protocols	Mission impact statement
Complaints	–	Legal authority	Pattern matching	Data mining	Recommended countermeasure
System monitoring	–	Lossless compression	Hidden data discovery	Timeline	Statistical interpretation
Audit analysis	–	Sampling	Hidden data extraction	Link	–
–	–	Data reduction	–	Spatial	–
–	–	Recovery techniques	–	–	–

Table 1. DFRWS digital investigative framework ([DFRWS01])

The preservation phase involves acquiring, seizing, and securing the digital evidence; making forensic images of the evidence; and establishing the chain of custody. The middle phases of the forensic process (i.e., the collection, examination, and analysis of the evidence) provide network investigators with a structured method to collect more and better evidence and to reduce the analysis time in VoIP networks.

The presentation phase involves the legal aspects of the forensic investigation—presenting the findings in court and corporate investigative units by applying laws and policies to the expert testimony and securing the admissibility of the evidence and analysis. This phase is outside of the scope of this research, but it must be considered in order to create a comprehensive model.

We concentrate on the initial phase of the forensic process, the identification of potential digital evidence (i.e., where the evidence might be found), which is flagged by IDS and, in some sense, by the attack patterns.

3.2 VoIP Evidence Collector

The VoIP Evidence Collector pattern [Pel10] defines a structure and process to collect attack packets on the basis of adaptively setting filtering rules for real-time collection. The collected forensic data is sent to a network forensics analyzer for further analysis. This data is used to discover and reconstruct attacking behaviors.

3.2.1 Context

We are considering a VoIP environment, in which the monitored network should not be aware of the collection process. We assume that evidence is being preserved securely. We also assume a high-speed network with an authentication mechanism and secure transport channel between forensic components.

3.2.2 Problem

How to efficiently collect digital attack evidence in real-time from a variety of VoIP components and networks?

The solution to this problem is affected by the following *forces:*

- General security mechanisms, such as firewalls and Intrusion Detection Systems (IDS), cannot detect or prevent all attacks. They are unable to stop/detect unknown attacks, internal attacks, and attacks that come in the body of the messages (at a higher level). We need to analyze how an attack happened so we can try to stop it in the future, but we first need to collect the attack information.
- A real-time application, like VoIP, requires an automated collection of forensic data in order to provide data reduction and correlation. Current techniques dealing with evidence collection in converged networks are based on post-mortem (dead forensic) analysis. A potential source of valuable evidence (instant evidence) may be lost when using these types of forensics approaches.
- Even though there are a number of best practices in forensic science, there are no universal processes used to collect or analyze digital information. We need some systematic structure.
- The amount of effort required to collect information from different data sources is considerable. In a VoIP environment we need automated methods to filter huge volumes of collected data and extract and identify data of particular interest.

- The large amount of redundancy in raw alerts makes it difficult to analyze the underlying attacks efficiently [Wan05]
- A forensic investigator needs forensic methods with shorter response times because the large volume of irrelevant information and increasingly complex attack strategies make manual analysis impossible in a timely manner [Wan05].

3.2.3 Solution

Collect details about the attacker's activities against VoIP components (e.g., gatekeeper) and the voice packets on the VoIP network and send them to a forensic server. A forensic server is a mechanism that combines, analyzes, and stores the collected evidence data in its database for real-time response.

A common way of collecting data is to use sensors with examination capabilities for evidence collection. In VoIP forensic investigations, these devices will be deployed in the converged environment, thus reducing human intervention. These hardware devices are attached in front of the target servers (e.g., gatekeeper) or sensitive VoIP components, in order to capture all voice packets entering or leaving the system. These sensors are also used by the Intrusion Detection System (IDS) to monitor the VoIP network. Examiners can also use packet sniffers and Network Forensic Analysis Tools (NFAT) to capture and decode VoIP network traffic.

When the IDS detects any attempt to illegally use the gatekeeper or a known attack against VoIP components, it gives alarms to the forensic server, which in turn makes the evidence collector start collecting forensic data.

The evidence collector then collects and combines the forensic information from several information sources in the network under investigation. It will also filter out certain types of evidence to reduce redundancy.

3.2.4 Structure

Figure 2 shows a UML class diagram describing how a VoIP evidence collector [Pel10] and an IDS system integrate. The evidence collector is attached to hosts or network components (e.g. call server) at the node where we need to collect evidence in a VoIP network. Forensic data is collected using embedded sensors attached to key VoIP components or Network Forensic Analysis Tools (NFAT). VoIP components that are monitored can provide forensics information once an attack occurs. The Evidence Collector is designed to extract forensic data and securely transport it (i.e., hash and encrypt) to a forensic server using a VoIP secure channel [Fer07]. The forensic server combines the logs collected from the target servers and the VoIP network and stores them in its database to allow queries via command user interfaces. The network forensics server also controls the Evidence Collectors.

The evidence data collected from VoIP key components includes the IDS log files, system log files, and other forensic files. Other sensitive files may include the system configuration files and temp files. When attached to a terminal device, the Evidence Collector captures the network traffic to record the whole procedure of the intrusion and can be used to reconstruct the intrusion behavior [Ren05]. The evidence collector is also able to filter out certain types of evidence to reduce redundancy.

3.2.5 Implementation

After collecting the desired forensic data, the evidence collectors will send two types of data to the network forensics server, depending on the function performed. If the sensor is attached to a key VoIP component, it will collect logging system and audit data; otherwise (i.e., attached to a terminal device) it will act as packet sniffers do (with the Network Interface Card (NIC) set to promiscuous mode) or NFAT tools extracting raw network traffic data (e.g., entire frames, including the payloads, are captured with tcpdump). These data are used to discover and reconstruct attacking behaviors.

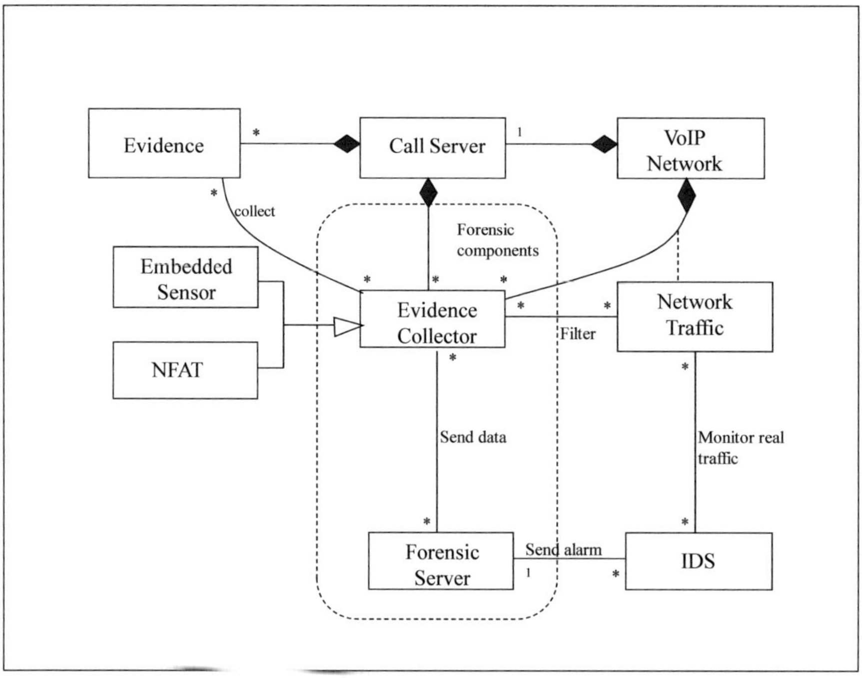

Fig. 2. Evidence Collector Class Diagram

As mentioned before, after each attack against the VoIP network, the forensic data collected from key components and attacking sources may include logging data. The following data may also be useful to discriminate calls and call types:

- Terminal device information
  - Numbers called
  - Source and destination IP addresses
  - IP geographical localization
  - Incoming calls
  - Start/end times and duration
  - Voice mail access numbers
  - Call forwarding numbers
  - Incoming/outgoing messages
  - Access codes for voice mail systems
  - Contact lists
- VoIP data
  - Protocol type
  - Configuration data
  - Raw packets

- Inter-arrival times
- Variance of inter-arrival times
- Payload size
- Port numbers
- Codecs

In order to maintain efficiency when capturing network traffic, we select the data to save, such as source and destination addresses and ports, and protocol type. The evidence collector can then extract all or selective voice packets (i.e., incoming or outgoing) over the VoIP network by applying a filter. The database on the forensics server will store the data sent by evidence collectors in order to perform the corresponding forensics analysis. We can use network segmentation techniques [Fer07] to monitor the voice VLAN traffic independently from data VLAN traffic although the two share the same converged network.

3.2.6 Dynamics

The sequence diagram of Figure 3 shows the sequence of steps necessary to perform evidence collection in VoIP. In this scenario, as soon as an attack is detected against the gatekeeper by the IDS, the evidence collector starts capturing all activities of the possible attackers. The evidence collector will then send the collected data to the forensic server using a secure VoIP channel. Additionally, the collected forensic data is filtered and stored in the system database.

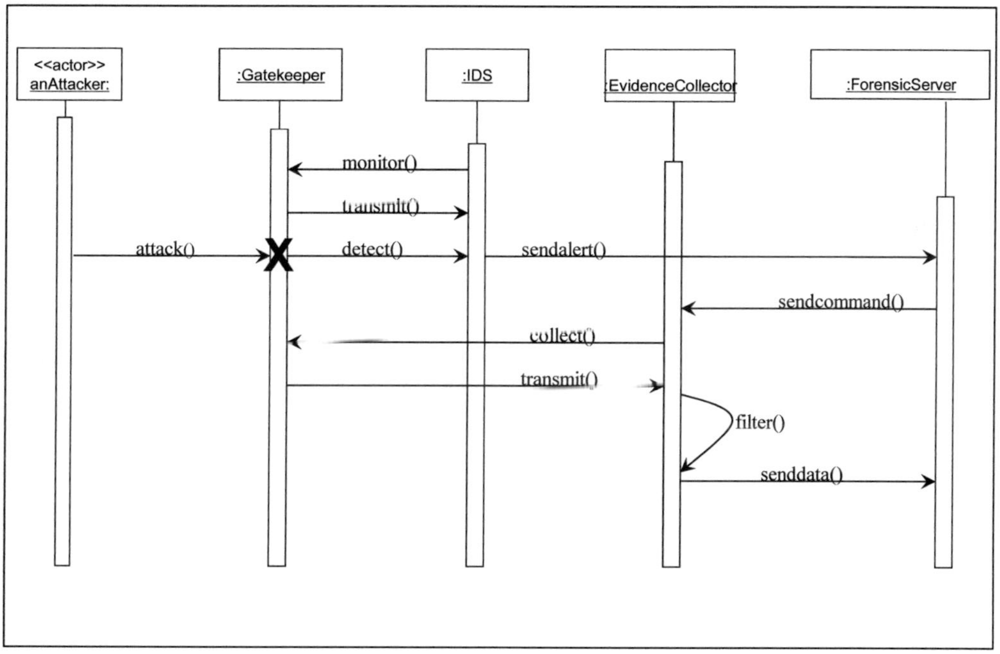

Fig. 3. Evidence Collector Sequence Diagram

3.2.7 Consequences

The *advantages* of this pattern include:

- The use of automated forensic tools as prescribed by this pattern allows effective real-time collection of forensic information which will reduce the investigation time in VoIP incidents.
- Significant logging information can be collected using this approach.
- The approach should be helpful to network investigators in identifying and understanding the mechanisms needed to collect real-time evidence in converged systems, because it provides a systematic way to collect the required information.
- The VoIP Evidence Collector pattern will also enable the rapid development and documentation of methods for preventing future attacks against VoIP networks.
- It is possible to investigate alleged voice calls using the evidence collector since voice travels in packets over the data network.
- For efficiency, the evidence collector can be set up for capturing selectively network packet streams over particular servers such as call, database, and web servers. The network forensics server can control the filter rules on the collector.
- On the other hand, based on the source/destination information, the evidence collector can filter the packets of a particular phone conversation.
- When encryption is present, the evidence collector can capture the headers and contents of packets separately.

The *disadvantages* of this approach are the limited scalability and relative inefficiency of the traffic's monitoring and recording. In large-volume traffic environments, there is a tradeoff between the monitored traffic and the available disk space [Ren05].

4. Protocol anomaly detection

Protocol anomaly detection is based on models characterizing proper use of protocols, and any behavior that departs from the model will be regarded as intrusive or suspicious. In this approach, protocols are well defined, and a normal use model can be created with greater accuracy [Aln08]. The creation of a complete profile of normal network traffic that implements a particular protocol is the core of this protocol behavior detection method. The SIP protocol has specific features that show a sequence of finite states that specify the correct behavior in a VoIP network.

A protocol-based IDS method is able to detect attacks against the converged network using information collected from both signaling and media packets. This method focuses on detecting misuse of the protocol's vulnerabilities. In this technique, the system detects attacks using information that is collected from the protocol headers.

4.1 Technical approach

The protocol-based detection technique defines a structure and demonstrates a process for collecting VoIP attack packets on the basis of adaptively setting filtering rules for real-time collection. The collected data is sent to a network forensics analyzer for further analysis. This data is used to discover and reconstruct attacking behaviors.

In our approach, we used an IDS infrastructure to collect details about attacker activities against VoIP components (e.g., gatekeeper) and the voice packets on the network. The IDS framework is a distributed attack sensing and warning system that uses a series of network-based collection sensors to acquire relevant forensic information so that intrusion analysts can perform effective analysis. This system has been designed to enable high

interoperability between tools used for performing network traffic analysis. It achieves this by storing all collected traffic in a central repository and allowing the analysis tools to run on the collected data. This eases the burden on the sensors (machines used for collecting traffic) by making them simple collection agents.
In VoIP forensic investigations, these devices will be deployed in a converged environment, thus reducing human intervention. These hardware devices will be attached in front of the target servers (e.g., call server) or sensitive VoIP components in order to capture all voice packets entering or leaving the system. These sensors will also be used by the IDS to monitor the VoIP network.
In order to maintain efficiency when capturing network traffic, we select the data to save, such as source and destination addresses and ports, and protocol type. The evidence collector can then extract all or selected voice packets (i.e., request or response) over the VoIP network by applying a filter. The data collected by the evidence collectors is stored in a storage area network cluster and will be used to perform the corresponding forensics analysis. We can also use network segmentation techniques [Fer07] to monitor the voice virtual local area network (VLAN) traffic independently from data VLAN traffic, although the two share the same converged network.

4.2 Structure

Figure 4 shows the UML class diagram of the specification-based IDS approach. This diagram generalizes the intrusion detection process in a VoIP call and shows the caller and callee roles. The model shows how it becomes possible to intercept an access request for a VoIP service. The IDS system uses an attack detector to match the sequence of message requests to the profiles in the user profile set and decides whether the request is an intrusion or not. If an attack is detected, some countermeasures that guarantee to maintain the confidentiality, authenticity, integrity and nonrepudiation of the entire VoIP infrastructure are performed.

4.3 Dynamics

The sequence diagram in figure 5 shows the necessary steps for profile matching when an attack access request has been made using VoIP technology. When the IDS detects any attempt to use the VoIP service without authorization or a known attack against VoIP components, it gives alarms to the system, which in turn blocks the call request through a firewall.

5. Dimensionality reduction and statistical methods for intrusion detection

Dimensionality reduction methods allow detection and estimation in a manifold of smaller dimension than the data stream. This improves the speed of detection and greatly reduces the complexity of the algorithms without compromising performance.
Dimensionality reduction methods have been applied in various domains, such as face recognition and information retrieval systems, to drastically reduce computational costs of processing high-dimensional data via the generation of a low-dimensional feature space that preserves relevant aspects of the data. Dimensionality reduction-based alternative methods use statistical signal processing methods in VoIP networks.
Our method for dimensionality reduction is based on linear random projections. Based on the isometry properties of random matrices and the Johnson-Lindenstrauss lemma, it can be

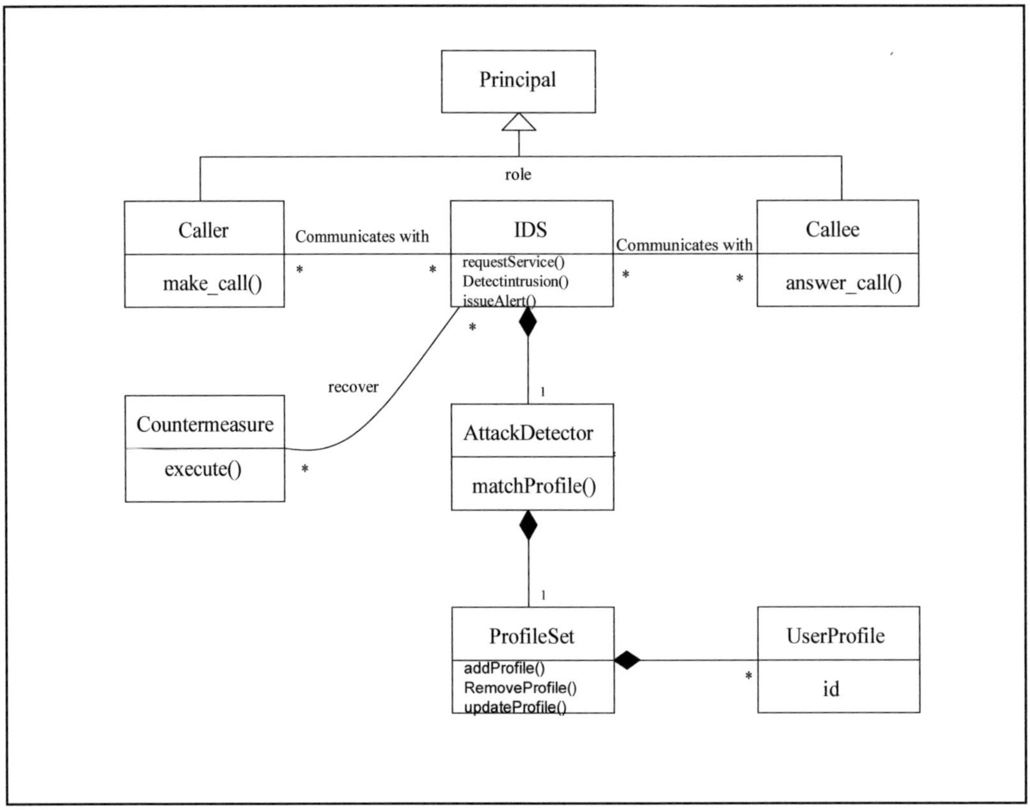

Fig. 4. Class diagram for a specification-based IDS

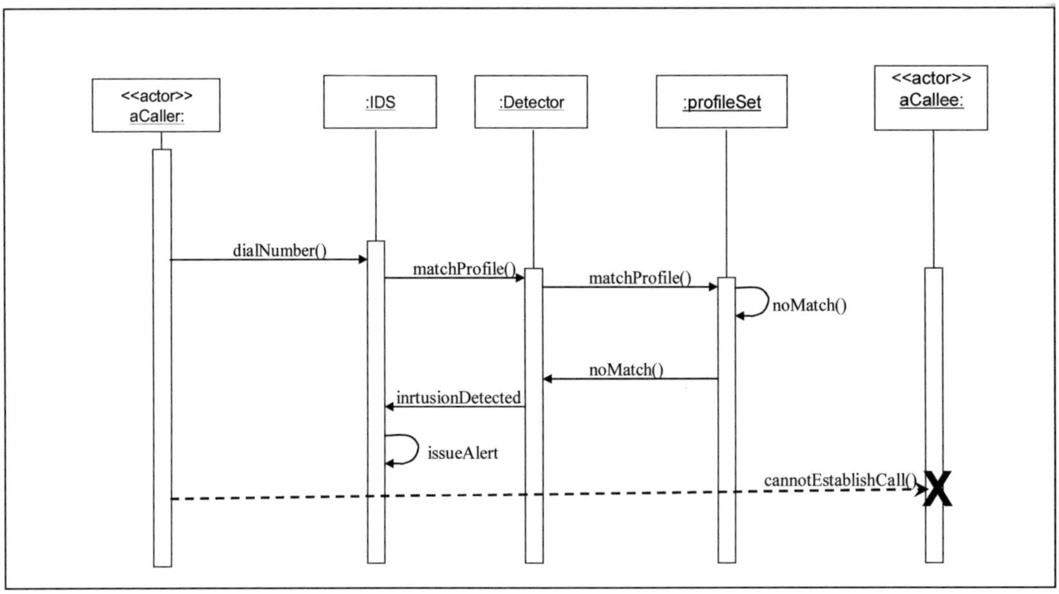

Fig. 5. Sequence diagram for detecting VoIP attacks

demonstrated that dimensionality reduction by random projections preserves the local topology of sparse signal spaces [Don06]. Moreover, if prior information about the normal signal space is known, subspace random projections can be used to further improve the accuracy of detection and separation of the different classes of anomalies [Par09, Wan10]. The incorporation of readily used techniques like Self Organizing Maps and Support Vector machines over projected data samples showing very good results over *randomly* projected data [Arr06, Cal09] are evaluated as well.
The main goal is to develop algorithms to detect and classify anomalies using compressed versions of the original traffic data and possibly learn the different classes of anomalies from live traffic. We expect that this approach will improve the speed of detection and greatly reduce the complexity of the algorithms without compromising performance.

5.1 Technical approach

Dimensionality reduction and statistical methods are used to identify threats in VoIP networks. The proposed intrusion detection system approach provides real-time network intrusion detection by projecting the high dimensional dataset to a lower dimensional space using the random projection technique, then performing intrusion detection in the lower dimensional space using statistical detection methods.
To that end, processing data is separated in two stages. The first stage consists of mapping packets to vectors in a Euclidean space and the subsequent dimensionality reduction. The second stage consists of learning different classes of anomalies and classifying incoming data. A key assumption for the success of the proposed system is the possibility to isolate the anomalies from the underlying normal traffic structure. The algorithms used in this approach model the normal traffic data as part of a manifold or subspace. If this assumption holds for the kind of traffic involved in VoIP communications, then the base of the subspace or the parameterization of the manifold can be used to isolate and filter the normal traffic contributions to the observed traffic prior to compression.
After performing the mapping, subspace random projections are used to jointly reduce and filter the observed vector. The vector corresponding to the payloads and the vector corresponding to the headers are analyzed separately, and a decision is made about the nature of the block of packets using the information extracted from both vectors.

5.1.1 Classification through compressive measurements

If we consider the stream of bits from the RTP, SIP, or RTCP packets as an N-dimensional vector of great dimension, we can solve the problem of anomaly detection from the projections of the data vector in a proper random basis. The idea is to classify all the normal patterns in the compressed domain and then detect the presence of anomalies by contrasting with the typical set elements. In general many problems of classification or detection can be solved directly in the compressed domain as explained in [Dav09]. A particular capability that will be sought is that of reconstructing the original packets from dimensionally reduced samples if traffic is presumed malicious. Part of our research will be to adapt this method to the framework of stream detection and classification of data streams. Detecting intrusions in the projected lower dimension reduces the complexity of the underlying algorithms, which makes it more suitable for real time detection. Moreover, lower dimensional data can be stored and transmitted more efficiently than its higher dimensional data, thereby saving system resources.

Classification algorithm demands repeated computation of similarity between pairs of vectors and the computational overhead increases with the increase in the dimensionality of the vectors. We consider that dimensionality reduction of these vectors will help in classification, reduce the processing time, and improve the efficiency of the IDS. However, the choice of dimensionality reduction method critically depends on preservation of similarity for efficient classification. In our approach we use the compress sensing theory, which states that with high probability, every K-sparse signal $x \in RN$ can be recovered from just $M=O(K.log(N/K))$ linear measurements $y=\Phi.x$, where Φ represents an M×N measurement matrix drawn randomly from an acceptable distribution [Don06]. Therefore, to classify input vectors we use machine learning algorithms such as support vector machines (SVM) and self- organizing maps (SOM).

5.1.2 Stream entropy estimation

A characterization in terms of stream entropy and sequence typicality of the different sections of the RTP, SIP, and RTCP flows is performed to identify and classify normal and potentially malicious traffic flows. Our approach is to use information theoretic measurements of the protocol headers to reveal the presence of higher-than-normal, sustained variation indicative of a covert channel. The entropy estimation is carried out through sparse sampling of the data stream. By the bounds given in [Lal06] for sparse sampling, one can assure that the estimation of the entropy will be within a fixed error margin of the actual value obtaining good levels of accuracy and with a reduced number of measurements and memory space required.

Dimensionality reduction methods based on spectral properties of a data matrix are attractive for application to entropy detection; spectral dimensionality reduction methods include principle components analysis, linear discriminant analysis, and singular value decomposition [Ski07]. These methods have strong statistical foundations, and are provably optimal for preserving variance of a dataset. Therefore, it is expected that they will likewise be optimal for preserving entropy. Application of these methods to entropy computation for network intrusion detection is not completely straightforward, because one must either choose a static feature subspace in which to compute entropy or continually generate new feature subspaces.

6. Converged experimentation testbed

The objective of this testbed is to evaluate developed algorithms in a systematic manner, and to evaluate the state of the art open source, COTS, and GOTS tools to determine holes for focusing future research initiatives. Technically, this task involves the development of simulation components for different signaling protocols, audio and video transports, and codecs. The testbed supports both the generation of normal (real and simulated) VoIP traffic.

This testbed is also used to verify the performance of the stream entropy-based intrusion detection scheme with network attack experiments. The converged testbed supports the generation of normal (real and simulated) VoIP traffic to compute the distribution of baseline stream under normal conditions. The performance of the IP telephony IDS is evaluated with two metrics: detection rate and false-positive alarms.

7. Conclusions and future work

For the purpose of intrusion detection in VoIP, our approach is based on stream entropy estimation, second order statistics, and dimensionality reduction. Entropy-based feature spaces have been shown to be successful for detecting network anomalies. Unfortunately, entropy detection is computationally expensive; indeed, parallel methods have been proposed to allow for more scalable entropy computation. A very scalable alternative to distributed entropy computation is computation of entropy in a compressed domain via dimensionality reduction.

We have run the proposed algorithm against both data transmitted and stored in our IDS database where the tool was successful at detecting attack packets with very high accuracy. Upon integration into IDS infrastructures, we expect this forensic tool will enable a faster response and more structured investigations of VoIP-based network attacks.

The use of dimensionality reduction methods for intrusion detection is a promising direction. The exploration of dimensionality reduction and related statistical approaches will allow network analysts to better understand more complex aspects of intrusion detection in converged environments. These technologies will primarily be targeted toward applications and techniques that capitalize on a distributed attack sensing and warning system.

The approach should be helpful to network analysts for identifying and understanding the mechanisms needed to efficiently detect attacks in converged systems. When encryption is present, the detection tool can capture the headers and contents of packets separately.

Future work will include the design of a structure and process to analyze the collected VoIP forensic data packets. This will allow the detection of attacks against the converged network using information collected from VoIP protocol headers. Future work will also include the creation of a misuse pattern catalog containing a set of all attack patterns we want to capture.

8. References

[Aln08] Al-Nashif, Y.; Hariri, S.; Luo, Y.; Szidarovsky F. Autonomic Intrusion Protection System (AIPS). *IEEE Transactions on Computers* 2008, *6*.

[Arr06] R. Arriaga, and S. Vempala. "An algorithmic theory of learning: Robust concepts and random projection" Machine Learning, Number 2, Volume 63, pages 161-182, 2006

[Bre99] C. Brenton. "Mastering Network Security," Network Press, San Francisco, 1999

[Cal09] R. Calderbank, S. Jafarpour, and R. Schapire. "Compressed learning: Universal sparse dimensionality reduction and learning in the measurement domain", http://dsp. rice.edu/files/cs/cl.pdf, 2009

[Col04] M. Collier. "The Value of VoIP Security", July 2004. http://www.voipsecurityblog.typepad.com/

[Dav09] M. Davenport, M. Wakin, and R. Baraniuk, "Detection and estimation with compressive measurements," *Dept. of ECE, Rice University, Tech. Rep*, 2006.

[DFRWS01] Digital Forensics Research Workshop. A Road Map for Digital Forensics Research 2001. *Digital Forensics Research Workshop 6 November* (2001): http://www.dfrws.org.

[Don06] D. L. Donoho ," Compressed sensing" IEEE Transactions on Information Theory, Number 4,Volume 52, pages 1289—1306 , 2006

[Fer05] Fernandez, E. B.; Kumar, A. A Security Pattern for Rule-Based Intrusion Detection, *Proceedings of the Nordic Pattern Languages of Programs Conference*, Otaniemi, Finland, September 23–25, 2005; Viking PLoP, 2005.

[Fer06] E. B. Fernandez, M.M. Larrondo-Petrie, T. Sorgente, and M. Van-Hilst, "A methodology to develop secure systems using patterns", Chapter 5 in "Integrating security and software engineering: Advances and future vision", H. Mouratidis and P. Giorgini (Eds.), IDEA Press, 2006, 107-126.

[Fer07] Fernandez, E. B; Pelaez, J. C.; Larrondo-Petrie; M. M. Security Patterns for Voice Over IP Networks. *Proceedings of the 2nd IEEE International Multiconference on Computing in the Global Information Technology* (ICCGI 2007), March 4–9, 2007, Guadeloupe, French Caribbean.

[Gra05] Grance, T.; Chevalier, S. "Guide to Computer and Network Data Analysis: Applying Forensic Techniques to Incident Response (Draft)." *Recommendations of the National Institute of Standards and Technology*, August 2005.

[Gree04] D. Greenfield, "Securing The IP Telephony Perimeter", April 5,2004. http://www.networkmagazine.com/shared/article/showArticle.jhtml?articleId=18900070

[Ken06] Kent, K.; Chevalier, S.; Grance, T.; Dang, H. Guide to Integrating Forensic Techniques into Incident Response. National Institute of Standards and Technology, *NIST Special Publication 800-86*, August 2006.

[Lal06] A. Lall, V. Sekar, M. Ogihara, J. Xu, H. Zhang. "*Data Streaming Algorithms for Estimating Entropy of Network Traffic.*" IN ACM SIGMETRICS, p 145-156, 2006.

[Mar01] M. Marjalaakso. "Security requirements and Constraints of VoIP." September 17 2001. http://www.hut.fi/~mmarjala/voip

[Par09] J. Paredes, Z. Wang, G. Arce, and B. Sadler. "Compressive Matched Subspace Detection" European Signal Processing Conf. 2009.

[Pel09] J C. Pelaez. "Using Misuse Patterns for VoIP Steganalysis." *Proceedings of the Third International Conference on Secure Systems Methodologies Using Patterns (SPattern'09).* Linz, Austria, August 31- September 04, 2009.

[Pel10] J.C. Pelaez and E.B. Fernandez. "VoIP Network Forensic Patterns." International Journal on Advances in Security. http://www.iariajournals.org/security/index.html.

[Pog03] J. Pogar. "Data Security in a Converged Network" July 23, 2003 http://www.computerworld.com/securitytopics/security/story/0,10801,83107,00.html

[Ren05] W. Ren, H. Jin. "Distributed Agent-based Real Time Network Intrusion Forensics System Architecture Design." *Proceedings of the 19th International Conference on Advanced Information Networking and Applications* (AINA'05). March, 2005.

[Ski07] D. Skillicorn. "Understanding Complex Data Sets: Data Mining with Matrix Decompositions." Chapman and Hall, Boca Raton, FL, USA, 2007.

[Sta02] W. Stallings. "Network Security Essentials: Applications and standards." Prentice Hall, Upper Saddle River, 2002, 5 - 21

[Wan05] W. Wang and T. Daniels. "Building Evidence Graphs for Network Forensics Analysis." *Proceedings of the 21st Annual Computer Security Applications Conference* (ACSAC 2005). September 2005.

[Wan10] Z. Wang, J.L Paredes and G. R. Arce "Adaptive Subspace Compressed Detection of Sparse Signals" submitted for publication , 2010.